CENTRAL ASIA
AT THE END
OF THE
TRANSITION

Edited by
Boris Rumer

M.E. Sharpe
Armonk, New York
London, England

The EuroSlavic fonts used to create this work are © 1986–2002 Payne Loving Trust.
EuroSlavic is available from Linguist's Software, Inc.,
www.linguistsoftware.com, P.O. Box 580, Edmonds, WA 98020-0580 USA
tel (425) 775-1130.

Library of Congress Cataloging-in-Publication Data

Central Asia at the end of the transition / edited by Boris Rumer.
    p. cm.
Includes bibliographical references and index.
ISBN 0-7656-1575-4 (hardcover : alk. paper) ISBN 0-7656-1576-2 (pbk. : alk. paper)
1. Asia, Central—Politics and government—1991–2. Geopolitics—Asia, Central. 3. Asia,
Central—Foreign relations—1991–4. Asia, Central—Economic policy—1991–5. Asia,
Central—Social policy. I. Rumer, Boris Z.

JQ1080.C44 2005
958'.043—dc22   2004028503

Printed in the United States of America

The paper used in this publication meets the minimum requirements of
American National Standard for Information Sciences
Permanence of Paper for Printed Library Materials,
ANSI Z 39.48-1984.

∞

| BM (c) | 10 | 9 | 8 | 7 | 6 | 5 | 4 | 3 | 2 | 1 |
| BM (p) | 10 | 9 | 8 | 7 | 6 | 5 | 4 | 3 | 2 | 1 |

Contents

Part III: The Internal Social and Political Context

Part IV: The Prospects for Economic Development

List of Tables

Preface

The present volume is the fifth in a series devoted to contemporary Central Asia that M.E. Sharpe began to publish in 1996. The series embodies the results of a broad project supported by the Sasakawa Peace Foundation (SPF) of Japan, the purpose of which has been to promote serious scholarly analysis of the social and economic development of post-Soviet states in the region. It is hardly possible to imagine any aspect of the foreign and domestic condition of these newly sovereign states that has not received appropriate attention in these volumes (which, because of their color, have earned the accolade among participants and readers as the "green series"). The present volume gives considerable attention to the policies of Russia, the United States, and China with respect to Central Asia and to the geopolitical situation that has emerged since the events of 11 September 2001. It also explores a host of other key issues: the influence of the Islamic factor; crisis phenomena in the domestic political situation generated by the character of the ruling regimes; the dynamics and structural asymmetry of economies caused by the hypertrophy of the raw-materials sector; and the deficiencies and failures of institutional reform in the social and economic sphere.

Once neglected by scholars and the mass media, Central Asia has come to receive considerable attention since 11 September 2001. Observers have followed closely the peripeteia in the political struggle among the upper echelons of power, the corruption scandals that involve the top leaders, the court intrigues, the scenarios for the succession of power (increasingly a critical issue, given the ages of the rulers in the countries of the region), the activities of the opposition, the repressive actions of existing authorities to muzzle and control the press, the growing intraregional tensions (e.g., between Kazakhstan and Uzbekistan; Kazakhstan and Kyrgyzstan; and Uzbekistan and Kyrgyzstan), the conflicts over the distribution of water resources, the border clashes that have occurred with growing frequency, and the maneuvering between the two poles of gravity—Russia and the United States. Amidst the rising flood of information, especially on the Internet, it is difficult to distinguish fact from fiction, reliable reports from idle speculation and outright disinformation. Among those aspects of economic life that are quantitatively indeterminate (and based only on the hypothetical estimates of experts), one must note the shadow economy, including the production and transportation of narcotics. There are many publications about the scale of this "business" within the countries of Central Asia that border on Afghanistan, about the complicity and collusion of law-enforcement agencies, and about the destructive impact of this scourge on the general population (and especially the youth) in the countries of this region. One must presume that, if economists were to use reliable data on the turnover of the "narco-business" and other segments of the shadow economy, substantial correctives would result in the assessment of the economic situation in the countries of Central Asia. But such concrete data are not available; nor can one fill this gap simply by relying on information of an anecdotal character. Despite all this, the picture drawn in this volume by independent analysts, in my opinion, does the maximum possible to reproduce reality and give a good sense of the character and dynamics of social and economic development in the countries of Central Asia.

Contributors to this volume are specialists from the academic communities of China, Kazakhstan, Russia, the United States, and Uzbekistan. The reader should therefore not expect that the authors will all hold the same views; indeed, one goal of the "green series" and the attendant conferences and seminars organized within the framework of the SPF program is to stimulate productive discussions. The publications, like the project itself, have no political or ideological agenda. That openness and objective, I should add, correspond to the fundamental principles of the SPF project. As editor of this volume, my task has been to give the authors an unrestricted opportunity to express their views—regardless of whether they correspond to my own opinion. In the current situation, when centuries-old norms of political and economic world order are being destroyed, we need to think long and hard about all the dramatic conditions that permeate the realities of the present day. And this concerns directly the essential questions of politics, economics, and public life of the states examined here and whose term of independent sovereign existence is less than a decade and a half.

The manuscript for this volume was essentially completed in 2004. By the time it appears in print, some months will have passed. There is every reason to assume that this will be a period of dramatic and unpredictable events on the international arena, and that these will inevitably have an impact on the situation in Central Asia. I am well aware that perhaps some (even essential) characteristics of the current reality in the region will fade and possibly be relegated to the dustbin of history. Such is the inevitable fate of books that belong to the genre of contemporary and economic analysis of our incredibly dynamic epoch. Nonetheless, I hope that the basic substance of this volume will retain its significance and continue to shed light on the situation in a region that has so recently emerged from the shadows to attract growing attention.

Boris Rumer
Cambridge, Massachusetts

Acknowledgments

This volume, like the preceding four volumes in this M.E. Sharpe series, is the fruit of a broad project devoted to the study of the political and socioeconomic development of the post-Soviet countries of Central Asia sponsored by the Sasakawa Peace Foundation, the leading Japanese nongovernmental organization in the sphere of international affairs. The editor and contributors would like to express their gratitude to the Foundation and, especially, to Akira Iriyama, Akinori Seki, and Lau Sim Yee, who have devoted considerable attention to the organization of the project and to its conferences and seminars; the latter afforded lively, fruitful discussions that have been of great assistance to the authors of the essays in this volume. This volume owes much to Professor Gregory Freeze, who has been an active participant in the project. The editor would also like to express his gratitude to the Davis Center of Harvard University, which for a quarter of a century has provided a stimulating and supportive environment for his research and writing. Deep gratitude is owed also to the expert staff at M.E. Sharpe and, in particular, to Vice President and Editorial Director Patricia Kolb, with whom it has been my good fortune to collaborate for the last ten years in preparing these five volumes.

Part I

Overview

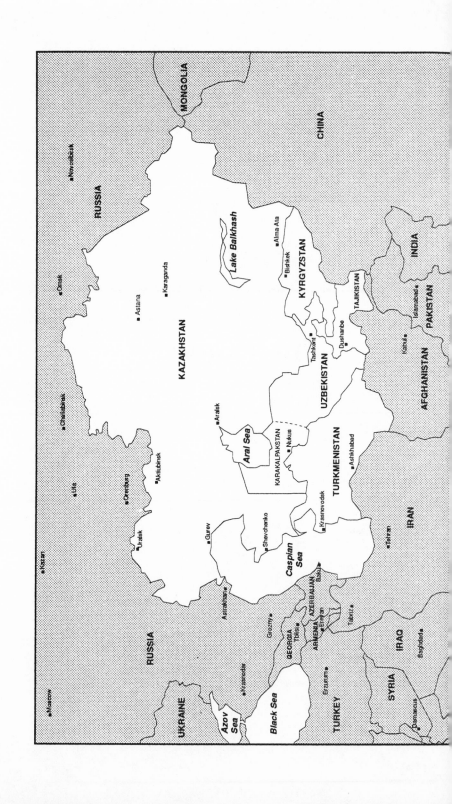

1

Central Asia at the End of
the Transition

Boris Rumer

Whereas the first volume in this series appeared with the title *Central Asia in Transition*, this one appropriately bears a quite different title: *Central Asia at the End of the Transition*, emphasizing that indeed the transition period is now complete. I realize that this title may raise some eyebrows; I admit that I settled on it after some vacillation and after conversations with the coauthors. Of course, I do not intend to suggest that the political, social, and economic development of these countries is complete; on the contrary, one can discern the fiery sparks of future upheavals on their political horizon. But the transition period has come to an end in the sense that the states of Central Asia have largely completed the process of systemic transformation. The social and political structures in the Central Asian countries have acquired a stable and (in terms of basic characteristics) a broadly similar character. The countries have also fixed the shape of their basic features. They have established regimes, with varying degrees of authoritarianism, behind a formal quasi (or pseudo) democratic facade. These regimes range from what is a relatively moderate regime (by regional standards) in Kyrgyzstan to the full-blown despotism that prevails in Turkmenistan.

The foundation of the social and political structure that was created and consolidated in the post-Soviet era will continue to exist for the foreseeable future. Those who created these systems do not have the strength to make fundamental changes even if they wanted to. They themselves have become hostages to the new system. In my judgment, special attention must be given to two issues that are of paramount importance for understanding the situation in Central Asia and surrounding countries, and that became particularly salient in the period since the last volume in this series appeared in 2002: (a) the character and durability of the existing social and political system, and their basic structure in the countries of this region; and (b) the growing competition between Russia and the United States to establish control over the region. This introductory overview will examine in detail these two critical issues. Whereas my introduction to the preceding volume examined the two "regional superpowers" (Kazakhstan and Uzbekistan) but really concentrated mainly on the latter, the reverse is true in the present chapter: it devotes the primary attention to Kazakhstan, which has leaped ahead of the other post-Soviet countries with its impressive economic growth.

Part I. Attributes of the Post-Transition Systems

The Character of Central Asian Regimes

Despite all the differences in the post-Soviet countries of Central Asia (different economies, different geopolitical orientations, different rates of overcoming the Soviet legacy), they share some things in common: an authoritarian character of rule and a corrupting fusion of political power and capital. To begin with, it is important that one does not excessively personalize the ruling regimes. When the current rulers retire or die in power, when these founding fathers (who all came from the same incubator of the upper Communist Party elite, the famous nomenklatura) give way to a new generation that was formed in the post-Soviet era, the fundamental formative elements of the system—quite apart from these personalities—will be preserved. The main goal of the established authorities in these countries is to preserve and reproduce this very power. Like Russian president Vladimir Putin's "managed democracy" (as someone once remarked, no matter what political reforms take place in Russia, these always seem to revert to monocracy), the regimes of Central Asia are virtually nothing other than dictatorships veiled in parliamentary clothing—whether the dictatorship be of a milder form, as in Kazakhstan, or of a harsher variety, as in Uzbekistan. As Dmitrii Furman in his chapter "The Regime in Kazakhstan" in this volume, has observed:

> The omnipotence of presidential authority, of course, is camouflaged. In the twenty-first (indeed, in the twentieth) century an "honest" absolutism is sim-

ply impossible. But our system has placed in its hands an excellent means at once to conceal and to realize this omnipotence. That paradoxical means is law itself. Both an extralegal character and democratic legal patina are inherent in the social and political system that has taken shape here since 1991.

Furman emphasizes this extralegal character is the very essence of the system, declaring that it is "constructed on the contradictions between formal laws and real life, the lifelessness of laws and the lawlessness of life. . . . Use of the law, simultaneously for purposes of arbitrariness and for concealing arbitrariness reinforces the irrational, 'Kafkaesque' fear of the authorities."[1]

In striving to preserve the democratic veneer, the ruling regimes engage in mimicry, and they create quasi-human-rights organizations, various social movements and councils, and political parties, but in fact these are firmly under the government's control. All the efforts by international organizations, the European Union, the U.S. Congress, and the U.S. Department of State to push the authorities here to carry out a real liberalization of public life have, for the present, remained without issue. Any party that seriously calculates on occupying a certain niche in politics must, at a minimum, remain loyal to the regime and leader; it must also establish solid connections with the clan-based structures. If a party does not accept these rules of behavior, it is doomed to remain marginal to political life or to disappear altogether because of repression.

"5:15:80"

The material well-being of the great mass of the populace remains at the same low level as before the collapse of the Soviet Union—notwithstanding the macroeconomic stabilization and growth in the gross domestic product (GDP) during the last few years. For many countries in the "impoverished South," it is typical for the population to be divided into proportions of 5:15:80. Although only a rough approximation, this ratio provides a good representation of the material and social stratification of the population in the countries of this region. Namely, about 5 percent make up the most prosperous stratum, 15 percent are relatively well off, and 80 percent are dispossessed (a significant part of whom have incomes at or below the poverty line). Such a situation will apparently persist for the foreseeable future. There is no question that a mood of discontent and protest is building up in the ranks of that 80 percent. But the majority of the politically and economically active segment of the population (those in the "5" and "15" percent categories) is inclined to preserve the status quo that ensures not only their own prosperity but also stability in the country.

Pervasive Corruption and the Shadow Economy

Another general systemic feature in all the countries of the region is corruption, which has become, in essence, a major factor in the everyday functioning of these societies. All the Central Asian countries have witnessed, during almost one and a half decades of post-Soviet independence, a degradation of the social organization—I would even say its "archaization" to describe the fact that the development of society is determined not only by the level and structure of the economy, but also by the correlation of spheres that are governed by custom, consensus, and law. In the contemporary reality of Central Asia, the relations between actors in social and economic life are predominantly regulated not so much by laws as by customs and norms. The foundation for all this is massive corruption, which is all-encompassing, pervasive, and legitimized in everyday life. Much has been written about this general phenomenon in post-Soviet states,[2] and it has also been a central feature of the regimes in Central Asia.

Corruption—in one form or another, to a greater or lesser degree—is inherent in any social system, including the Western democracies. Thus, corruption scandals are a regular feature of life in France, the United States, and England. But these societies have developed authentic political opposition, free press, and independent courts that conduct a constant, effective struggle to combat and contain this evil. As a result of investigations by the government and parliament, even the heads of large corporations have lost their positions (as was, for example, the case with the chairman of the Boeing Corporation), and high-ranking public officials are convicted and sent to prison (as happened with the foreign minister of France). Corruption of course existed in the Soviet system as well. However, most successor states of the post-Soviet era—whether Russia, Azerbaijan, or the countries of Central Asia—have in effect institutionalized corruption. In Central Asia, as in Russia, venality has become a fundamental trait of the new social and political system; it regulates the functioning of the state apparatus, economic activity, and the day-to-day lives of the population. Indeed, the societies here have come to perceive corruption as a norm of life; it has lost its criminal connotation in public consciousness.

The words of an analyst in Kazakhstan, Sergei Duvanov, can unqualifiedly be applied to all the countries of Central Asia:

> Corruption, which has been elevated to the rank of a state principle, signifies that everything is up for sale, including all the services in the system of state relations. Formally, there is a constitution, laws. . . . In fact, however, all this is a sham. The laws can simply be evaded and ignored if one pays

the officials responsible for the functioning of this or that part of the state mechanism. Bribes and payoffs have turned into an obligatory attribute of social relations. Law-enforcement organs, which are obliged to combat corruption, zealously defend this systematic corruption. As a rule, both the courts and the police are on the side of those who act in accordance with the "understandings" of corruption and punish those who strive to live in compliance with the existing laws.[3]

The very fact that colloquial speech has fully incorporated criminal jargon like "cover" (*krysha*) and "kickback" (*otkat*) is very revealing. Racketeering at the state level has become a fundamental element in the life of society, and official racketeers permeate the state apparatus from top to bottom.

One should also note the unreliability and distortions in the contemporary picture of social and economic life that has been drawn on the basis of the accessible sources. In fact, what can one infer about the true dynamics of the GDP, if approximately 30 percent of the economic activity of the population exists outside the parameters of official statistics and is hidden from taxation? What is the structure and dynamics of this shadow sphere, which envelops practically all sectors of the economy and drug trade, exerts an enormous influence on public morality, and promotes the criminalization of society? To be sure, the shadow economy is not a phenomenon unique to post-Soviet countries; it has always existed, and it still exists in every society. However, during the period of the exploding economic catastrophe of the 1990s, the shadow economy did not in fact play a negative role; on the contrary, it actually made a positive contribution to the efforts by the mass of the population simply to survive. And it has preserved that function to the present time. It also has helped to stimulate initiative and entrepreneurial activity. The shadow economy, moreover, has a number of obvious advantages over the legal economy. It is incomparably more efficient, requires much less overhead, and remains closer to the individual person. And a substantial part of the profits from the shadow economy remains within the country and is spent on production and consumption. To repeat, this is an economy aimed at ensuring survival; it makes an extremely tangible contribution to the national income (though unrecorded in the official statistics) and helps the mass of the population to keep their heads above water. In general, the post-Soviet era has witnessed the process whereby *homo sovieticus* is being transformed into *homo economicus*.

The shadow economy is a complex and qualitatively diverse phenomenon. It has been the subject of considerable attention not only in scholarly studies on the creation of a market economy in post-Soviet countries, but also in the mass media (primarily with respect to various kinds of criminal mafia activities). But there has been virtually no study of segments like the economics of households and the so-called "social economy," which is manifested in the form of support of relatives, friends, and neighbors. It is precisely this aspect of the shadow economy that is so characteristic of the economic life of the population of Central Asia (especially in the countryside and small towns) and that has flourished in the post-Soviet era. Households, small enterprises, the exponential growth of the so-called "shuttle trade"—all this helped to absorb the shock of economic catastrophe in the post-Soviet years and made it possible for thousands and thousands of families to survive. This sphere that operates outside official statistics includes the mass of the people, not only the unskilled underclass, but also many well-educated specialists who, simply to survive, had to abandon their professions and become active in this shadow economy.

Growth Without Development

Another feature common to all the countries of this region has been the positive dynamic of growth in the GDP since the start of the new millennium. That growth is evident not only in official statistics produced by the local regimes, but also from the analyses conducted by independent organizations and experts. In any case, since 1999 economic growth has occurred in the majority of post-Soviet countries regardless of their resource potential and the strategy employed for making the transition to a market economy. The most cogent explanation for this phenomenon rests in the fact that, after the shock of the first years following the breakup of the USSR and the frenetic plundering of national wealth, these countries have entered a phase of picking up the pieces and putting things back together. The lands of Central Asia have begun to modify the structure of the economy, to rebuild its productive sector, and to adjust to domestic and foreign market trends. And although fixed capital was already largely obsolescent at the beginning of the 1990s, the level of physical depreciation (which enterprises in the Soviet time, in the course of compiling inventories for the replacement costs of machinery and equipment, greatly exaggerated) was considerably lower than what official statistics would indicate. The level of utilization of productive capacity was also heavily inflated. The real resources of industrial capacity (including the reserve capacities for mobilization purposes found in many enterprises) predetermined the opportunities for resuming economic growth in these republics. Of course, those countries that, in addition, possessed and utilized export potential had greater opportunities for growth because of the extremely favorable price dynamics for raw material and metal exports. That explains the growth of the GDP in Kazakhstan, Uzbekistan, and Turkmenistan.

But the presence of underutilized capacities, given a government policy aimed at import substitution (despite all its negative aspects), was a very important factor in generating a positive economic dynamic in all these republics. Another factor of great importance was the intellectual, professional capital bequeathed from the Soviet era.

However, one should not repose all hopes on any kind of long-term effect from these factors. The reserves of productive capacity are close to being exhausted. Neither the expansion nor even the simple replacement of physical and human capital has received support. The expenditures for maintenance—to compensate for the depletion of equipment, physical plants, and installations—have been utterly insufficient throughout the post-Soviet era. State enterprises simply lacked the means to replace and upgrade during the crisis years of the 1990s. On the contrary, the strategy of the most significant enterprises in the extractive sector and metallurgy (which had been privatized by foreign, frequently offshore, companies) amounted to nothing more than the maximum exploitation of existing capacities, with no concern for their maintenance, not to mention their modernization. As for human capital, the post-Soviet rate of reproduction (especially in the technical spheres and natural sciences) cannot compensate for its exhaustion and thereby ensure any kind of sustained growth of industrial production, especially in the R&D-intensive branches. In short, the economic growth in this region has been based on reserves that were created in the Soviet era and that are now close to being exhausted. Economic growth has an exceptionally extensive, resource-intensive character. The countries of Central Asia have not laid the requisite preconditions for stable growth; any optimism about the likelihood of encouraging dynamics in the macroeconomic indicators is unwarranted.

To sustain the recent growth it is essential to have greater injections of capital investment. But more than that: if there is not a fundamental restructuring of the economy, if the extractive sector preserves its absolute dominance, if the earnings from that sector are not rechanneled into other spheres of the economy and social life, there is no prospect for social and economic progress—even in those countries of the region that are richly endowed with natural resources. As the economist Arystan Esentugelov has persuasively demonstrated with respect to the economy of Kazakhstan (but his analysis applies no less to the economies of the other countries of the region that rely principally on the exploitation of raw materials): redistribution of earnings from the export of raw materials (natural gas, oil, metals, cotton, and so forth) to the manufacturing and other sectors is practically nonexistent or at an extremely low level. [4] And that, in effect, blocks any substantial structural improvements in the productive sector of the economies. As a result, these countries retain the raw-material orientation of their economy and, in turn, their complete dependence on the prices for raw materials on the world market.

Both corruption and income inequality are closely related, systemic characteristics of development in Central Asia, but they are also found in other countries that rank low on the development scale. As Seymour Lipset and Gabriel Lenz have observed:

> Cross-national studies have found a strong relationship among corruption, income inequality, and poverty. The lower a country's score on the corruption index [indicating a high level of corruption], the more likely it is to have a high Gini coefficient, meaning greater income inequality. A 0.78 increase in the growth rate of corruption is linked to a drastic decline in the rate of income growth among the poor—7.8 percentage points per year.[5]

The positive dynamics in the GDP and some of the other macroeconomic indicators in recent years in the Central Asian countries are justly deemed to be "growth without development," if one understands the ultimate goal of an economy to be that of ensuring social progress. One must also take into account the qualitative characteristics of the growth and its social consequences. In this respect, it is instructive to take note of Yabloko Party chairman and economist Grigorii Yavlinskii's perceptive observation about the significant growth of the Russian economy in recent years:

> There is such an idea of growth without development. That is when your legs, arms, and stomach all grow, but your head remains as before. Growth without development makes it possible to double the GDP. In the Soviet Union the growth rates were still higher—and so what? The Soviet rates of growth were 10–12 percent, and 15 percent per annum. These rates were based on the growth of the production of oil, natural gas, other raw materials. . . . We [in Russia] now have high rates of growth and large opportunities to obtain additional resources from the prices on energy resources. But see what are the results from the perspective of the modernization of society? To what degree does it have an impact on the system of education, public health . . . and all that is vitally important?[6]

Yavlinskii's comments apply just as much to the economies of the Central Asian countries.

The Misuse of "Stabilization Funds"

Under conditions marked by hypertrophic development of the raw-material sector and the consequent dependence on the world prices for the export of these commodities, the governments of Kazakhstan and Uzbekistan (following the example of Russia) have established so-called "stabilization funds." These are essentially financial reserves; their express purpose is to absorb fluctuations in the world prices for the raw material exports from these countries and to finance budget deficits (in the event of a price drop). They, therefore, serve the political purpose of calming domestic public opinion; they appear to show that the wise leaders of their countries are carefully saving for a rainy day. The funds in such schemes are placed in the most reliable (and therefore low-yield) securities and treasury bonds of foreign countries. Although on the one hand this seems reasonable and justified, on the other hand it diverts considerable funds from use within the country. At the same time, these Central Asian governments (again, following the example of Russia) have to secure foreign credits at higher interest rates. This logic seems misguided because it deprives the governments of the opportunity to utilize effectively the capital of the stabilization funds for investment within the country. In effect, this attests to the fact that the diversification of the economy and its restructuring (which would mandate large-scale targeted investments) has not been a priority and essential task in the economic policy of these governments. It is precisely a period of high prices for oil, natural gas, metals, and cotton that make it easier to conduct a policy aimed at structural change in the economy. The accumulation of money in stabilization funds only diverts resources and reinforces the raw-material orientation of the economy.

One must not overlook yet another important issue here: disposition of the resources in these funds is, as became clear in the case of Kazakhstan, in the hands of the president. For all practical purposes, no one else controls or regulates how they are actually used.[7] The very idea of stabilization funds was borrowed from the practice of many oil-rich countries. But such an institution can perform its function effectively only if authority over the control of the funds belongs not only to the president, but also to the parliament and public organizations, making unnecessary expenditures and abuses less likely. Such a system of control and transparency has been created, for example, in Norway and Canada. But Kazakhstan did not emulate that model. Instead, it has classified all of the most important information as top secret: the incomes received from the export of oil, the contractual conditions that government officials concluded with foreign corporations, and the scale and expenditure of money in the stabilization funds. As a result, the opportunities for abuse, peculation, and bribes in various forms are virtually unlimited. There is no reason to assume that the accumulation and expenditure of financial revenues from exports in other Central Asian countries are any more transparent than in Kazakhstan. As for Turkmenistan, there can hardly be any doubt that Saparmurad

Niiazov—the "Turkmenbashi" or "Leader of All Ethnic Turkmen"—personally controls all funds and remains answerable to none.

The Absence of Real Guarantees on Property Rights

A systemic characteristic of the post-Soviet states in Central Asia is the lack of a guarantee—a real guarantee, not merely declarations on paper—about the rights to property. In fact, property is only conditionally held; it is liable to confiscation in the event that the "proprietors" violate this or that agreement with one or another state agency. With respect to Uzbekistan, and still more so Turkmenistan, there is no doubt that the dictator or a regional prefect, under virtually any pretext, can issue an order to requisition the property of anyone they choose. The fact that the right to property is only conditional in Kazakhstan as well is apparent from the case of one of the top financial magnates of the country, Mukhtar Abliazov, who, at the end of the 1990s, was the minister of industry, but who dared to voice open criticism of Nazarbaev. The president thereupon ordered that Abliazov be arrested and imprisoned. Nazarbaev thereby created a precedent for Putin, who has conducted the case of Mikhail Khodorkovskii essentially according to the same scenario. The question is whether any more or less large-scale private property exists in the post-Soviet countries that can be defended through public juridical means? Is there a legal method to draw a distinction between "honest" and "dishonest" property? Does property exist that is protected against seizure and redistribution by the state for whatever reason? Experience shows that such unqualified property rights do not exist. The results of privatization are not being reexamined, but the idea is under reconsideration. The state can either recognize, or not recognize, the right of private property. In this respect the effect of the cases of Abliazov in Kazakhstan and Khodorkovskii in Russia are highly revealing.

A Pernicious Seduction: The Abundance of Natural Resources

To paraphrase the well-known maxim of Leo Tolstoy that all happy families are alike, it is perhaps tempting to declare that all the failed countries rich in natural resources are basically similar. All of them are dependent on natural resources and a cheap labor force. The "comparative advantage" paradigm dominates the thinking of their economists and government bureaucrats. They share the belief that their countries have fundamental advantages based on geography and natural resources.[8] With respect to the economies of Kazakhstan, Turkmenistan, and Uzbekistan, which are based on cheap labor and on primitive exports that are subject to price fluctuations, and which account for more than 90 percent of the GDP in the Central Asia region, it is entirely appropriate to invoke the metaphors like the "curse of oil," "Dutch disease," and "economic indigestion." These terms are used to describe the paradox that has been widely noted and no longer comes as a surprise to economists: over the course of decades, countries rich in natural resources significantly lag behind countries poor in such resources when measured by virtually all economic indicators and quality of life. This is evident, for example, in the results from the analysis of economic indicators of various countries conducted by Jeffrey Sachs and Andrew Warner, who found that the shortage of natural resources stimulates economic activity to a greater degree than does their abundance. Michael Fairbanks came to the conclusion that "the more a nation exports in natural resources, the less prosperity it creates for its average citizens."[9]

Kazakhstan, Turkmenistan, and Uzbekistan (Kyrgyzstan and Tajikistan, less richly endowed with natural resources, may be omitted here) have every reason to think that they can become members of the club that includes oil-rich countries like Sudan, Nigeria, and Venezuela. In the latter countries, thanks to the peculiarities of the socioeconomic system and the authoritarian "kleptocratic" character of the ruling regimes, the flows of petrodollars are not directed toward the development of the non-fuel, non-raw material sectors, the improvement of the social infrastructure, and the expansion of social programs in education and public health. Instead, these revenues are simply used to bring about the boundless enrichment of the ruling elites. However, one extremely important advantage separates the countries of Central Asia from the other members of this club: namely, the high intellectual capital inherited from the Soviet Union, the high level of general education and professional training of the populace. This factor has created conditions that should permit these countries to occupy a higher, more prestigious niche in the international division of labor. Suffice it to say that, in 1991, the year of the breakup of the Soviet Union, approximately 90 percent of the working-age population of Kazakhstan had a secondary, or higher, education. Moreover, these countries inherited from the Soviet Union a network of research centers, universities, and laboratories; they also had at their disposal well-trained staffs of mathematicians, physicists, and specialists in various fields of science and technology. However, given the existing priorities and the characteristic narrow-mindedness of the upper bureaucracy and leaders in these countries, there is no chance that these intellectual resources will be used effectively and as intended.

"Our Misfortune Is That We Live Too Well"

Among the countries of this region, Kazakhstan unquestionably enjoys the most favorable economic conditions. This republic has constantly occupied the top place in Central Asia with respect to the level and dynamics of the GDP (up approximately 8 percent in 2003) and direct foreign investment per capita. What, however, is the qualitative dimension behind this growth? How has it affected the well being of the population? According to data compiled by leading Kazakh experts (sociologist Sabit Zhusupov and economist Bulat Khusainov), the consequences of economic growth "have impacted a small part of the population of the country." One can assume that this "small part of the population" in effect refers to the "5-percent" elite and some in the "15-percent" stratum described above. According to Zhusupov and Khusainov, at the beginning of 2004 "in general the country surpassed the 'second threshold' of poverty, which, according to the standards of the United Nations, corresponds to an income at the level of 2 dollars per day." In 2004 the share of expenditures in the state budget for social needs was reduced from 31.4 to 24.8 percent. The level of the well being of the population was characterized by a per capita monthly income of 30 to 40 dollars, and an opinion poll showed that only 15 percent of the respondents declared themselves to be satisfied with their current material condition.[10] Such is the picture in the richest country of the region.

But Kazakhstan also has its wealthy class. According to an estimate by G. Mataev of Kazakhstan, 5 percent of the population possesses up to 80 percent of the national wealth.[11] The wealthy elite obtained its property in the following ways:

- by plundering and selling the assets that had been created and accumulated during the Soviet era;
- by pocketing foreign credits that had been backed by guarantees from the state;
- by diverting the bulk of the profits of enterprises to personal use rather than reinvesting them to maintain and upgrade the fixed capital and productive capacities.

One must assume that these sources of personal enrichment have been largely exhausted, and that these adept plunderers have turned to the capitalization of substantial means they possess.

Reports about new oil and gas fields give rise to confidence about even higher rates of growth in the economy in Kazakhstan. This admission by one high-ranking bureaucrat in Kazakhstan is characteristic: "Our misfortune is that we live too well."[12] Those who belong to the "5+15 percent" part of the population, apparently, would agree with this cheerful assessment of their living standards. However, such a view would hardly elicit support from the vast majority of the population in Kazakhstan, that is, those who reside in the countryside, who (in the words of a well-known Kazakh journalist with deep rural roots) live in a condition of "poverty and embitterment."[13] The abundance of natural resources has a perverse impact on the government; it gives rise to excessive, inflated hopes and diminishes the pressure on state authorities to conduct a responsible economic policy.

There are many barriers blocking the road to sustained growth, and these should elicit intense concern among economic strategists. Among these the most important is the low level of productivity in the economy. Kazakhstan's GDP growth inspires optimism, but that should not distract one from the fact that the lion's share of the income in the country comes from "rents" (income from the sale of raw materials), with far less coming from capital and a quite insignificant share coming from labor. The state budget is formed on the basis of the rent income and hence is little connected with the economic activity of the population. The share of wages in the price of goods produced in Kazakhstan amounts to roughly 15 percent; that is significantly below the level in developed countries. The cheapness of labor impedes improvement in the quality of labor resources and development of advanced lines of production; it therefore functions to preserve the existing structure of the economy. Under these circumstances, it hardly seems possible to stimulate demand based on purchasing power, and hence increase activity on the domestic market. The result, in short, is a vicious circle.

These systemic features of the economy of Kazakhstan are, to no less (if not greater) extent, characteristic of the economies in the other countries of the region. One can try to forecast the economic policies of Kazakhstan, Uzbekistan, and Kyrgyzstan for the foreseeable future; such predictions are not possible in the case of Tajikistan (where the economy has yet to be rebuilt) and Turkmenistan (where, given the political system, any rational predictions are simply impossible). In the case of the first three countries, however, it appears that a small number of huge corporations will dominate the economy and subordinate state policy to their interests. On the political horizon, one should expect an intensification of the power struggle between the clan structures, and a confrontation between the nouveau riche elite and the "old guard," which holds onto power and is linked to the current leadership through patron-client relationships.

Problems in Restructuring the Economy

Let us return to the systemic problems that bedevil the most successful economy in the region—that of Kazakhstan. And let us imagine that the decision makers in this country (who include, without a doubt, people who are fully cognizant of the consequences of the glaring asymmetry in the economic structure) resolve to undertake decisive structural reforms. Can they realize such well-intended policies? An objective complication that they inevitably must face is the clear need to give up the impressive high rates of growth that, as already shown, have been achieved primarily by prioritizing investment in the energy complex (which devours the lion's share of investment in the productive sphere). But there are good reasons to expect that, in the foreseeable future, export revenues will decline. In that event, even if the stabilization funds and accumulated hard currency reserves are preserved in full, it will inevitably become difficult to maintain the macroeconomic indicators at their previous level. Indeed, if the regime were even to spend all that it had saved for a "rainy day," these resources will not suffice for any extended period of time. In that event, it will then be necessary for the government either to cut budget expenditures (including allocations for social needs), or to increase the budget deficit (which would have to be covered by foreign loans at high interest rates, given the fact that the possibilities for domestic loans are minimal).

To embark consciously on a policy that aims to restructure risk, a leader needs to have not only strategic thinking and a sincere concern about the future of his country, but also the political will to carry out his policies. But even if Nazarbaev realizes the contingency of the current prosperity, his first priority is to hold onto power, and the present, turbulent situation leaves him little room to make any kind of decisive changes in the country's economic policy. Quite simply, Nazarbaev must surmount the chief barrier that makes it virtually impossible to rechannel substantial resources into the non-raw material sectors of the economy. That barrier—which is insuperable under the existing conditions—is the vested interest of the ruling strata of the bureaucracy, which rakes in the lion's share of income from raw material exports and has fused with the elite of business. And the overriding objective of each is to maintain the status quo, to ensure that the existing system—which ensures that the enrichment of each—be preserved. In the first instance, this pertains to the president's family and closest associates, who have become mired in corruption and the battle over the distribution of income from the export of raw materials. The logic and consequences of this struggle pervade all levels of political and economic power in the country. Those organs of the press and internet that have retained their independence publish revelations about the machinations of corporations in oil and other sectors that operate with the protection of the highest authorities. But these revelations do not surprise anyone in a society mired in corruption, and they have no impact on the basic foundations of this system.[14]

In conversations with thoughtful people in the region, one often hears that, to replace the "old guard" that now holds power, eventually there will come forward a new generation of enlightened leaders of the upper and middling ranks, with a different mentality, often with an education received in the

West and therefore westernized, with an open-minded perspective on the world, and a consciousness of their duty to serve their home country. One would like to believe such optimistic expectations. Indeed, many young Kazakhs, Uzbeks, and Kyrgyz have studied in Western universities and business schools in the post-Soviet era. The problem, however, is that many of those who returned (and by no means did all return) have become mired in the corrupt, clan-mafia milieu; seduced by the temptation of easy riches, they now live according to its rules. It is an old story of what happens when new wine is poured into old wineskins.

To sum up, it is necessary to conclude that the economy of Kazakhstan clearly reflects the typical features of economies in countries that lie on the backward periphery of the world. Above all, the profile is clear: an export-oriented model that has a minimum of social redistribution as well as non–raw material sectors that are inefficient and noncompetitive. There is no reason to assume that the oil bonanza will last for long: "The Stone Age did not end for lack of stone, and the Oil Age will end long before the world runs out of oil. . . . Hydrogen fuel cells and other ways of storing and distributing energy are no longer a distant dream, but a foreseeable reality."[15] One must also take into account the strong vested interest of the United States and the other oil consumers in holding down energy prices. The re-establishment of Iraqi oil production (which will presumably occur in the near future) is also certain to have a substantial impact on world oil markets. It is therefore incumbent on Kazakhstan, if it is to ensure sustained economic growth, to adopt a realistic strategy aimed at the diversification of its economy. The comment by Andrei Zuev and Liudmila Miasnikova are entirely applicable to the countries of Central Asia: "Perhaps what is most important in the space of global geo-economics is a dangerous psychological and conceptual shift. Within the framework of the state economy, it is constantly necessary to solve questions of purchasing-power demand, savings, and accumulation. An open, global model of the economy creates the illusion that these problems are resolvable by means of external sources. Accordingly, business and the state redirect their efforts to the struggle for foreign markets and the securement of foreign investments. The problems of preserving and developing their own resources and markets, as well as making the population more active, seemingly lose their urgency and recede into the background."[16]

In assessing the fundamental characteristics of the economies of Central Asia (as is true of all the other post-Soviet states with Russia at the forefront), it is appropriate to ask whether these features (or at least some of them) are attributes of a market economy. One might apply the criteria of the European Union, as reported in *Financial Times* (28 June 2004): "the degree of government influence on the economy; the existence and implementation of transparent and nondiscriminatory company law that ensures adequate corporate governance; the existence and implementation of a coherent, effective and transparent set of laws to ensure property rights and the operation of a bankruptcy regime; and the existence of a genuine financial sector which operates independently from the state." In this case, one can boldly assert that not one of the countries in the CIS, including Russia and the more advanced states of Central Asia in terms of market reforms (viz., Kazakhstan and Kyrgyzstan) meets this definition. All are too susceptible to state interference, weak rule of law, and poor corporate governance.

The Problem of Political Succession

The countries of Central Asia also share another systemic characteristic: the lack of a legitimate, reliable mechanism for the transfer of supreme power. And that is fraught with threats to political stability and all the associated uncertainties that this entails. The current leadership, to be sure, is well aware of the problem. As one analyst has observed: "Indeed, succession appears to be the main preoccupation of these leaders, who have put the well-being of their personal regimes above all else and who have done everything within their (considerable) means to keep succession from happening. . . . As incumbents accumulated power and shaped institutional and constitutional arrangements to secure the authority to match their aspirations for political longevity, they eliminated both potential apparent successors and mechanisms that would make succession a predictable and transparent process."[17]

In today's political praxis, the Central Asian countries have three possible scenarios for the transfer of power: the Yeltsin, Azerbaijani, and Georgian models. It is not so simple to take the Yeltsin route and to hand over power to a loyal successor; it is first necessary to find one's own "Putin." And one also has to be a Yeltsin. But the leaders of the Central Asian republics do not have that Yeltsin quality—a willingness to take political risks, to carry through decisive changes, to act in unconventional ways. On the contrary, they are afraid to change anything, and they trust no one outside their inner circle, which is composed mainly of family members. Therefore, it is highly unlikely that the transfer of power in Central Asia will follow the Yeltsin scenario. The bloodless "revolution of roses" in Georgia, which overthrew President Eduard Shevardnadze (the former head of the Communist Party of Georgia) and brought to power a young, charismatic graduate of Georgetown University (Washington, DC), Mikhail Saakashvili, cannot fail to have an alarming impact on the presidents of Central Asia. According to the authoritative Moscow newspaper *Kommersant*: "When one of the new leaders of Georgia, parliamentary speaker Nino Budzhanadze, was on a visit to Moscow, Vladimir Putin candidly told her that, after the events in Tbilisi, many

The Autocratic Impulse

The Russian president cannot fail to evoke the envy of the rulers in Central Asia. Putin's level of popularity is simply beyond their reach. They cannot dream about such a high rating as his—which has become part of the national identity of Russia (just as, in Voltaire's words, the virginity of Joan of Arc became the property of France among her contemporaries). The Central Asian leaders see that the liberal experiment in Russia has failed, that the moderately authoritarian and modernizing regime that Putin initially tried to create has turned essentially into the monarchy that is so customary for the Russian mentality. To legitimize this institution in Russia, it is necessary to change the constitution, and there is no doubt that the majority of the current parliament would enthusiastically comply— indeed, its own deputies will provide the initiative for this. It is difficult to say how the population will view this evolution of the Putin regime but, so far as the political class of Russia is concerned, the majority—obedient to the Kremlin—is openly inclined to make the leader irreplaceable. Take Zhirinovskii: despite all his buffoonery, he is a calculating, sober politician, who sensitively captures the mood of the masses and the boss, and is publicly sounding out the idea of an unlimited term for Putin. The mass media (above all, television), which is controlled by the Kremlin, intensively inculcate the image of the nation's leader into popular consciousness. It is entirely possible to allow that a significant part of the people would respond positively to the restoration of autocracy. It is interesting to know what Putin himself thinks about this question. In an interview given to journalists Natalia Gevorkian and Andrei Kolesnikov, he said: "I think that this is very unlikely. But, in general, . . . in certain periods of time, . . . in a certain place, . . . under certain conditions, . . . monarchy played (and to this very time plays) a positive role. Monarchy was evidently a stabilizing factor. It is not necessary for the monarch to think whether they will elect him or not, to constantly cater to the immediate situation, somehow have an influence over the electorate. He can think about the fate of his people and not be distracted by petty things." The interviewers note that restoration of the monarchy in Russia is nonetheless impossible, but Putin thinks differently: "You know that much seems impossible and unrealizable, and then—boom! As was the case with the Soviet Union. Who could have imagined that it would go and collapse all on its own?"* Well, it is not difficult to imagine what a "managed democracy" will turn into: if not a traditional monarchy, then, say, a "democratic dictatorship," and Western commentators who explain the meaning of this new oxymoron will call the new model of political organization "the special Russian path." I would note, incidentally, that ideas of this sort hark back to the traditions of Russian political thought. One of its prominent representatives, Konstantin Kavelin, wrote in 1875: "There is no doubt that by all its mass Russia can only be in favor of an autocratic (that is, free) tsar, who depends not on the aristocrats (boyars), not on a plutocracy. History itself forces us to create a new, unprecedented, and unique political system, for which one can find no other name than 'autocratic republic.'"† It is remarkable how Kavelin's idea corresponds to the attitudes of today's Russian supporters of autocracy that the authorities have recruited!

*N. Gevorkian, A. Kolesnikov, and N. Timakova, *Ot pervogo litsa. Razgovory s Vladimirom Putinym* (Moscow, 2000), p. 168.

†K. Kavelin, *Nash umstvennyi stroi* (Moscow, 1989).

leaders of the Commonwealth of Independent States (CIS) 'shit in their pants' (*nalozhili v shtany*)."[18]

As the case of Eduard Shevardnadze in Georgia demonstrated clearly, the epoch when the heads of the former communist parties of the union republics ruled the newly independent states is coming to a close. That applies to Nazarbaev of Kazakhstan, Karimov of Uzbekistan, and Turkmenbashi Niiazov of Turkmenistan; Askar Akaev of Kyrgyzstan, though not the head of the Kyrgyz communist party, nonetheless occupied an important post in its Central Committee. But the Central Asian leaders are not sitting on their hands waiting for the "rose contagion" to strike them too. They are trying various tactics and stratagems to cling to power in their own countries, and they are simultaneously seeking support from without—in Washington and Moscow. It is widely thought in political circles in post-Soviet space that Shevardnadze was overthrown with the blessing of Washington and, indeed, with the active involvement of the U.S. ambassador. The leader of Uzbekistan shares that view. In a seminar at the Davis Center of Harvard University on 7 June 2004, the Japanese ambassador to Uzbekistan, Akio Kawato, recounted how President Karimov, with complete conviction, told him that Washington stood behind the events in Georgia that led to the overthrow of Shevardnadze. Similarly, many analysts also think that the decisive factor in making the dynastic scenario in Azerbaijan a success was the fact that it suited Washington. All this leads to the conclusion that the fate of the leaders of the Central Asian states, to a large degree, depends more on the favorable disposition of the U.S. administration than on any other factor. Moreover, it is also necessary to secure the support of Moscow, if only by demonstrating one's loyalty more in words than in deeds. Does Washington really play the decisive role in the scenarios of regime change in the southern post-Soviet republics, or is this to be attributed to the overactive imagination of Russian and Central Asian analysts? In my view, there is certainly an element of exaggeration here.

Nevertheless, I also think that the strongmen of Kazakhstan, Uzbekistan, and Turkmenistan have good reason to be worried about how Washington regards them (especially following the events in Ukraine). Nazarbaev adheres to the "multi-vector" strategy as a basic principle in his foreign policy. However, it is in the interest of the United States to deal with a leader who is more predictable; who does not take turns playing the Russian, then the American, card; and who adheres to a single—namely, pro-American—position in his foreign policy. Washington, it seems, would also prefer to have as the president of Kazakhstan a client who is more tolerant of dissidents, who is not stained by such a scandalous reputation, who is less concerned about serving the interests of his own clan and kin. For similar reasons, the same pragmatic representatives of the American political elite find President Karimov of Uzbekistan an irritant. The line of defense chosen by the Uzbek leader—"if I go, then my place will be filled by Islamic terrorists" (which corresponds to his credo: "It is better to have hundreds of people arrested than thousands killed")—seems less and less persuasive. As for the Turkmenbashi Niiazov of Turkmenistan, his replacement by a less odious figure is extremely desirable for both Washington and Moscow, not to mention the population that must endure the yoke of this petty tyrant.

There is no doubt that, in theory, the Azerbaijani variant—that is, the Aliev dynastic scenario—is the most acceptable from the perspective of the Central Asian rulers. The latter were probably impressed by the determination and decisiveness with which the late Gaidar Aliev overcame resistance from the opposition (which, incidentally, was more energetic than that which the Central Asian rulers face) and how he ensured the transfer of power to his son Ilham (who had the reputation of being a playboy). Moreover, the leaders of Central Asia must be impressed by the fact that, despite all the excesses of the Aliev regime perpetrated in ensuring that the young Aliev succeed to the presidency (repression of opposition, the arrest and imprisonment of dissidents, etc.), he was recognized as the legitimate president by Moscow, Washington, and others. The goal of the Central Asian autocrats is to find a successor who can be relied upon to ensure their personal security and to safeguard the family's property interests, and who simultaneously would be in a position to hold onto power in spite of the opposition from competing clans and groups.

The problem of succession is becoming ever more urgent and acute. It is fueling the struggle among the regional clans in Uzbekistan and Kyrgyzstan; it generates rumors of discord within the Nazarbaev family; it triggers attempts to overthrow the "Turkmenbashi." The struggle for the "throne" is conducted covertly, behind the scenes. Of course, every stratum in society wishes to avoid turmoil and wants instead to have a peaceful transfer of power. Expectations are low: hardly anyone believes that, as a result of this or that political perturbation, any of these countries will suddenly embark on a radiant future. A great many people are fully apprised of what happens in Russia, for they actually watch Moscow television. And that Russian experience only reinforces their skepticism toward the promises of the democratic opposition to carry out a real liberalization and to bring material improvement in their lives.

With the approach or onset of old age, the choice of the scenario for the transfer of power by the rulers in post-Soviet space, the opportunities to realize this scenario, and the mechanism for succession are determined by the ability of the leader to manipulate interclan contradictions and to keep potential competitors under control. A change of ruler does not at all lead to a change in the character of the regime; in the view of many, it only carries the threat that the situation in the country can become destabilized. The prospects of such an upheaval cannot fail to alarm the majority of the active population, especially those who belong to the upper strata (those in the "5+15 percent"). Apparently, this factor is especially significant in Kazakhstan, which is set apart from the other countries in the region by its relative economic prosperity and relatively moderate political climate. For a realistic assessment of the prospects for a change of leaders in the countries of this region, it is useful to sketch out the main characteristics of the political portraits of three of these leaders: the presidents of Kazakhstan, Kyrgyzstan, and Uzbekistan.

President Nursultan Nazarbaev of Kazakhstan

Nursultan Nazarbaev has had no great difficulty in getting rid of those who have sought to encroach on his virtually unlimited power. To judge from what is known, the Kazakh leader prefers the dynastic scenario for succession. Much has been written in the press and on the internet about this. But his situation has become complicated by a couple of factors. First, he has had difficulty finding a suitable successor, someone who could satisfy all the conflicting factions in his entourage (and even within his family), and in his clientele. In the words of local observers, the Nazarbaev family is "an archipelago of several islands that look with suspicion at one another."[19] Second, an extremely complicated circumstance is the high level of activity not so much on the part of a domestic opposition, as an opposition located abroad and led by former Prime Minister Akezhan Kazhegel'din. The latter has undermined the image of a "wise father of the nation," so carefully cultivated by the court and the regime-controlled press; instead, the opposition has drawn the portrait of a money-grubber, avaricious "godfather" who simply presides over an enormous mafia.

This negative image of the Kazakh president has become widespread in the Western press and in Western public opinion. To a considerable degree this was abetted by hearings in the U.S. Congress and European Parliament (which condemned the Nazarbaev regime for the repression of dissidents), by the declarations of Western human rights organizations (who have spoken in defense of the Kazakhstani journalists persecuted by the regime), and by the reports in the press and internet about the so-called "Kazakhgate" (the corruption scandal that involved Nazarbaev and his entourage). Such a reputation must have had a traumatizing impact on Nazarbaev—given his ambitions, his pretensions to play a salient role in the international political beau monde, and his efforts to appear as a respectable national and even regional leader, reformist, and liberal, and even to occupy the position of chairman of the Organization of Security and Cooperation in Europe (OSCE). All this also has had a substantial impact on public opinion about Nazarbaev in Kazakhstan itself. Access to the internet is unrestricted; day after day the constant flow of compromising material about Nazarbaev inexorably undermines the image of the Kazakh ruler.

Nor does Nazarbaev have security of person and property once he leaves office. To be sure, the Kazakh parliament did pass a law on the preservation of the president's rights in the event he leaves office. But that statute is hardly a reliable guarantee for Nazarbaev's security and protection from confiscation of his property; a new, post-Nazarbaev parliament can just as easily annul this law as it adopted it. The instinct of self-preservation must tell Nazarbaev that he is his own best successor. Hence, in January 2004 the court image maker, Ermukhamed Ertysbaev, sounded out Nazarbaev's intention to seek re-election in the presidential elections of 2006 and thereby extend his rule to 2013—that is, for another ten years. Such is the intent despite the fact that the constitution of Kazakhstan provides for a presidential term of seven years. As Ertysbaev declared, "The question of the president is closed until 2013."[20] Being (it seems to me) a person who is not cruel by nature but who is politically experienced, Nazarbaev apparently realizes that weakness toward those who oppose his power and government could undermine the very foundations of his regime; one can assume that Nazarbaev and his colleagues in the region have all read and mastered the teachings of Machiavelli's *The Prince*. The dramatic experience of Shevardnadze must have made all this painfully clear to Nazarbaev and all his fellow autocrats in post-Soviet space. If oil prices remain high, if the hopes for an expected increase in oil production prove to be justified, if Nazarbaev manages to walk the balancing wire between Moscow and Washington, if the interest of the West (above all, the United States) and the oil companies in preserving the status quo prevails over dissatisfaction with the authoritarian, corrupt regime, then Nazarbaev has a chance to cling to power in the foreseeable future. But that is a lot of "ifs." Finally, of all the post-Soviet rulers, Nazarbaev is by no means the worst.[21] If Nazarbaev fails to hold onto power, there is no reason to assume that he will be replaced by someone who is better in terms of political and moral qualities. That, at least, is the view shared by many living in Kazakhstan.

President Askar Akaev of Kyrgyzstan

Askar Akaev, with good reason, has the reputation of being the most liberal of the Central Asian rulers. To be sure, in recent years that reputation—which became firmly entrenched in the mass media and political circles—has become somewhat sullied. In an interview that I gave to the Kyrgyz journal *AKIpress* in September 2002, I said that "if one makes preserving stability and avoiding chaos the key objective, then under the existing reality (including the concrete alignment of political forces and regional competition) you will find no one better than Akaev. The system formed in post-Soviet years has become too firmly ensconced, it has become too corrupted, it has sunk its roots too deeply and these have become too broadly branched out. Well, let's suppose that someone comes to take Akaev's place. . . . Do you think that anything will substantially change for the better? I think not. Do you think that, if Akaev really wanted to improve the situation, he would succeed? I very much doubt that he would. He himself is a hostage to this system."[22]

Akaev has repeatedly stated that he does not intend to retain power beyond the end of the current presidential term. There have been reports about his attempts to have the presidency transferred to his son. But it is hardly possible to lend much credibility to these reports: the interclan confrontation is too intense, and the opposition to Akaev is too aggressive to allow such a scenario. Akaev himself is holding onto a fragile balance of clan interests; he is relying on a capacity, developed during his years of rule, to maintain a relative equilibrium and to avert a conflict or, at least, not to allow conflicts to increase and completely destabilize the situation in the country. There is no reason to think that the young Akaev (or anyone else from the immediate family or entourage) is in a position to perform the function of stabilizer so successfully. Given the fear of destabilization and the incontrovertible achievements of Akaev in protecting the country from chaos, the majority of the Kyrgyz electorate might be persuaded that it would be better to keep the current president for an indefinite term. One important argument in favor of retaining Akaev in office would be the fact that he enjoys the support of Moscow; he is rightly deemed to be the leader in Central Asia who is most loyal to Russia. But he is also on good terms with the International Monetary Fund (IMF) and the World Bank, which are ready to continue their failed experiment in this country. Indeed, Kyrgyzstan has already received from these and other donors (especially Japan) financial injections that have left its economy dependent on— "addicted to"—outside assistance.

President Islam Karimov of Uzbekistan

The problem of finding an heir who is appropriate in terms of the required parameters is no less acute for President of Uzbekistan Islam Karimov. Indeed, if one is to believe rumors (perhaps deliberately circulated at his own order) about his poor state of health, the situation is even more urgent than in Nazarbaev's case. I personally have an ambivalent sense of the character of the Uzbek leader. But it could hardly be otherwise: the personality of Islam Karimov is itself highly contradictory. I do not at all belong to the ranks of his apologists and am not inclined to compare him with former French president Charles de Gaulle, as have some of his admirers outside Uzbekistan (e.g., A. Migranian and N. Gul'binskii) have done.

Having observed, in the course of many years, the zigzags in the domestic and foreign policies (including economic policies) of the Uzbek leader, I appreciate the complexities of internal and external problems that he must face. Given all that, he is clearly the strongest leader among the presidents of post-Soviet countries with respect to his knowledge of the country's economy, his ability to manipulate interclan contradictions, and his decisiveness and determination to achieve the goals he has set for himself. Nevertheless, he is a despot with all the attendant characteristics: intolerant of different viewpoints, cunning, and ruthless in suppressing those who stand in his way.

Karimov did not dash headlong to demolish the old command economy. It seems that he clearly understood what would happen if the prescriptions of the Bretton Woods institutions were superimposed on the actual conditions of Uzbekistan. Foreseeing the consequences of "shock therapy" (and, given the situation in Uzbekistan, for a number of reasons these would have been

---

The Uzbek de Gaulle

The encomia lavished on Karimov are truly amazing. Thus, Andranik Migranian, a well-known Moscow political writer, after discussions in Tashkent with "representatives of the political elite," came to the conclusion that "Islam Karimov is very popular among the people." From my own personal experience it is perfectly clear that, if Migranian had had any contact with ordinary people, and not merely with "representatives of the political elite," and if these representatives had been even remotely candid with their guest from Moscow and had not feared the consequences of their frankness, then he would have come away with an entirely different opinion as to how popular this "Uzbek de Gaulle" is with the people. Nor is that all: Migranian was impressed not only with the popularity of the president, but also with the richness and diversity of life in the capital of Uzbekistan. He finds Tashkent similar to a "Mediterranean culture," and he exalts everything—its broad avenues, restaurants, and especially "the young girls in miniskirts, the likes of which you do not see in Europe," as well as the "soft striptease" and "belly-dancing" (which, in his opinion, "are more interesting than, say, in Cairo").* I fear that, having been overwhelmed with such impressions and having become acquainted with the opinions of the Uzbek elite, this devotee of erotic dancing in the East has conjured up an image of Tashkent that has little to do with reality.

*"Uzbekistan: Islam Karimov vedet stranu po puti effektivnoi modernizatsii," *Sotsialisticheskaia Rossiia*, 7 February 2002.

---

even more onerous than in Kazakhstan), Karimov declined to liberalize the economy and chose to preserve, in principle, the command system. Thanks to that decision, the economic downturn in Uzbekistan was less severe than in any of the other post-Soviet states (with the exception of the Baltic countries). A positive effect of the economic policy of Karimov was apparent in the fact that he maintained relative stability in the economic and, consequently, the social spheres. However, that stability has now degenerated into economic stagnation and a morally depressed condition of society.

The policies chosen by Karimov and his economic program have, from time to time, borne fruit. However, from the mid-1990s, when it was already time to change directions, abandon the command model of the economy, and embark on a course of liberalization, Karimov proved unable to break free from the previous trajectory. An experienced economist of the old Soviet school, he understood the social consequences of a simultaneous deregulation of prices, large-scale privatization, and a radical weakening of state control over the economy during the first years of independence. He realized the danger that such an experiment would pose for his regime, which still had to consolidate its power. And Karimov chose the right course—especially considering that Uzbekistan had far fewer opportunities for export than did Kazakhstan, that it depended on grain imports, that the price of global cotton markets was low, and so forth. In my judgment, however, Karimov was overly impressed by the favorable results of his policy in the first half of the 1990s—especially when compared with what transpired in Russia and the other post-Soviet republics; he failed to recognize its negative consequences over the long term and failed to see the critical point when it was necessary to make a fundamental change in direction. It is, to be sure, possible that he realized all this and either wanted to avoid the risk of social turmoil, or did not dare to confront the existing mafia-clan Uzbek elite, which had an extremely strong interest in preserving the status quo and which enjoys his protection. It is possible that both of these factors deterred Karimov from adopting new policies. But Karimov cannot fail to see the deterioration that has beset the social program of his rule, which sought to stabilize living standards and to avert impoverishment.

The retraditionalization of social life, the deprofessionalization of entire strata of the population, the exodus of highly qualified personnel from the country, the degradation of literature and art, the suffocating atmosphere of total control over intellectual life—all these are clear signs of the antimodernization overtaking Uzbekistan. And this is the dominant tendency in post-Soviet Uzbekistan. Karimov is seeking to modernize the economy but to block the modernization of society. The antimodernization is manifested in the primitivization of the economy. The enormous social problems that now beset Uzbekistan—unemployment and poverty in the villages and much of the urban population—are being aggravated by rapid demographic growth. Karimov's regime has not given the people a single safety valve to express discontent, nor any real participation in governing the country. When one is in Tashkent, it feels as though one is in a hermetically sealed space.

Outside Uzbekistan, the attitude toward the Karimov regime is black-and-white: either outrage over the violation of human rights and the repression (an outrage that is well-grounded and completely justified), or apologetics for the regime. Such a simplistic dichotomy prevents a realistic understanding of the situation in the country. For the sake of objectivity, it is worthwhile to examine the sources of stability that underpin the Karimov regime. Among the factors that contribute to this conservation, I would point to the following:

(1) *Historical tradition*: the power of a strong ruler is deeply embedded in the social consciousness of Uzbeks. Karimov apparently takes into account the values and expectations of society. Indeed, the complaints of the majority of ordinary citizens do not refer to the authoritarianism and harsh repressiveness, but rather concern the high prices and shortages of goods, the rampant corruption, the arbitrariness of officials and the police, and the poor system of public health. All the public speeches by the president are permeated with populist statements, accusations against the bureaucracy, condemnations of corruption, and promises of an improvement in life and social justice. Such statements amount to a constant flow of promissory notes to the population, but Karimov forever procrastinates in paying them off. People do not believe what he says; they are simply used to having him rule.

(2) *The "Tajik syndrome"* dominates public consciousness and paralyzes the will and capacity to mount resistance to the regime and its policies. After all, before the eyes of all are the horrors that were wrought by civil war in a neighboring country. Many fear that the collapse of the Karimov regime would only lead to bloody chaos in Uzbekistan and to destabilization in the region as a whole. The masses of people place a high value on preserving stability in society.

(3) People are also gripped by the *fear that the Islamists will come to power*—with all the disastrous consequences that this would entail. Generally speaking, a significant part of the population is quite secular. And they have already seen what life in an Islamic republic—under a theocratic dictatorship, as in Iran and in Afghanistan under Taliban rule—can be like. Not surprisingly, the vast majority prefers life under the existing dictatorship of a secular ruler. One should not exaggerate the degree of Islamization in Uzbekistan. By no means is the majority of the population favorably disposed toward an Islamic resolution of problems. The orthodox Islamic component of the population, even in rural areas, is relatively small.

(4) Karimov has formulated a *program of national independence* that is appealing and comprehensible to the population. He was able to link his own person with the process whereby a national elite emerged and consolidated its position; in exchange for the opportunity to make money, that elite has given Karimov the right to absolute power.

(5) In private conversations, people who are involved in Uzbek politics, but who do not belong to Karimov's admirers and who have personally experienced the negative effects of his rule, nonetheless concede that the Uzbek political establishment has *no real alternative to Karimov*: it simply lacks anyone else of equal caliber—in terms of his political experience and his

ability to manage so complex a society as that represented by the regional and clan structure of Uzbekistan.

During the period when Karimov gained ascendancy and bolstered his power, he manifested considerable ability at social maneuvering and resorted to compromises with his opponents (if only temporarily). For some time, however, he has not shown the ability to maneuver and compromise, and has made his regime excessively rigid and inflexible. It is perfectly obvious that Karimov needs to allow some liberalization of public life, to seek ways to collaborate with moderate circles of the Islamic clergy, to moderate the repressive policies, to manifest greater compassion and humanity, and to abandon the quintessentially Soviet style of official propaganda and lies.

As for economic policy, the state continues to control most economic activity, but one does discern some movement in the direction of liberalization. That reverses a tendency evident from 1996–1999, when prices dropped for almost all the goods exported from Uzbekistan and the government froze its market reforms. But since 2000 (under pressure from international financial organizations) the Uzbek leadership has gradually been resuming its efforts to carry out economic reform. Thus, it has introduced the convertibility of the national currency, which has been sharply devalued. The president has also issued decrees aimed at improving the business climate and reforming the banking system. The year 2003 was the most "reformist" in the entire history of independent Uzbekistan: the government substantially simplified the system for registering small business, reduced the bureaucratic apparatus, and accelerated the development of private agriculture (bringing about a significant increase in the number of private farms). It also reduced the taxes on the incomes of enterprises and the population (although, it must be said, these remain at one of the highest levels in the CIS). As a result, there was a major increase in the number of small-and medium-sized enterprises in the private sector. The production of consumer goods expanded, and the output of agricultural goods has also risen. In 2003 Uzbekistan (with the active assistance of foreign organizations) increased the network of credit unions, thereby giving broad strata of the population greater access to credit. That same year the government issued a decree designed to accelerate the privatization of enterprises that were marginally profitable or even operated at a loss. The sharp increase in the world prices on Uzbek commodity exports (cotton, gold, nonferrous metals, and so forth) ensured a favorable balance of trade, which was further enhanced by a complex of tariff and nontariff barriers to imports. As a result, the government succeeded in obtaining a favorable trade balance that amounted to 760.8 million dollars (approximately 9 percent of GDP). In the year 2004 the world commodity prices were also kept at a high level, and that in turn continued to ensure high earnings from exports and a favorable trade balance.[23]

In 2003–2004 the government conducted a policy aimed at macroeconomic stabilization, as it sharply limited direct credits and restricted the supply of cash and credits for the state budget. As a result, it was able to reduce inflation from 27.6 percent in 2002 to 10 percent in 2003 and to 3.7 percent in 2004. In essence, Uzbekistan is now carrying out that phase of reform which a number of other CIS countries underwent in 1994–1996. If the government designs and actually carries out liberal reforms (above all, in the agrarian sector), if it reduces import duties, taxes, and a host of nontariff barriers to trade, and if it implements significant reforms in the banking system, Uzbekistan could embark on a new phase of rapid economic development. The question is whether Islam Karimov has the political will to move in this direction.

At the same time, one should also take note of the negative sides of the economic reality of Uzbekistan, for these significantly diminish the effect of the successes noted above. In particular, the reforms conducted thus far have had a contradictory, halfhearted character. In March 2003, the president issued a decree on reforms in agriculture that provided for many needed changes; as part of the policy of dismantling the command-administrative methods of economic management, the government gave peasants permission to sow crops that they found to be most profitable, to sell their harvests on their own, and to take out a fifty-year lease on arable land. Notwithstanding all these changes, in reality the government retained many fundamental components of the command-administrative system. These include, in particular, the state plan for the production of the most important agricultural commodities (cotton and grain) and the policy of setting low procurement prices for the purchase of agricultural goods. The agricultural market, in effect, is only semi-liberalized: private farmers can sell their harvests at free-market prices, but only after they have fulfilled a procurement plan of sales to the state. And these plans are set at such a high rate that it is almost impossible to fulfill them. This system of disincentives is one of the reasons why the production of cotton dropped by 6 percent in 2003–2004, and the government's response was not concession but coercion; it is not uncommon for local authorities to seize the land leased to peasants who have failed to fulfill the procurement plans prescribed by the state. These persisting elements of the command-administrative system, in many respects, reduce the positive impact of reform in the chief—that is, the agrarian—sector of the economy.

Similarly, the benefits from introducing convertibility in the national currency (the *sum*) were largely undercut by the imposition of strict protectionism and oligopolies in wholesale trade, and also by a further increase in the excise duties on imported consumer goods in May 2004. The sharp rise in prices on consumer goods in 2002, which followed the rise in import duties and excise taxes, led to a significant jump in prices and added hundreds of thousands of people to the rolls of those living beneath the poverty line. The prices of consumer goods in Uzbekistan are now 1.5 to 2.0 times greater than on the borders of neighboring states. The protectionist policies of the Uzbek authorities during the past four to five years have had a negative net effect on the standard of living of the general population—in a word, the life of the common person has grown worse. Such is the contradictory picture of the economic policy of the Uzbek leadership, with its cycle of "on again" and "off again" reform.

Not Everything Is Negative

One should not focus excessively on the shortcomings and thereby ignore the obvious achievements attained during the post-Soviet years. In general, it is an obvious truism that there are serious limitations on the ability of even the most perspicacious expert to draw unqualified conclusions about a given situation at critical junctures of history. As Charles Dickens wrote in *A Tale of Two Cities* about a tumultuous epoch in the last quarter of the eighteenth century: "It was the best of times, it was the worst of times, it was the age of wisdom, it was the age of foolishness, it was the epoch of belief, it was the epoch of incredulity, it was the season of light, it was the season of darkness, it was the spring of hope, it was the winter of despair, we had everything before us, we had nothing before us. . . ."

With respect to Kazakhstan and Kyrgyzstan, one must bear in mind not only the problems described above, but also some clear achievements. Namely, these two countries carried out radical economic reforms, created the foundations of a market, conducted large-scale privatization, made the national currency virtually convertible and its exchange rate quite stable, sharply increased the share of service and consumer sectors in the economy, eliminated the idea of "shortages" of goods from everyday language, and awakened the entrepreneurial spirit that had been systematically repressed under the Soviet rule. In the case of Uzbekistan and Tajikistan, however, it is too early to speak of any substantial socioeconomic progress; and in Turkmenistan, there has been an absolute socioeconomic degradation. One should also keep in mind that the processes associated with rebuilding the economy and the liberalization of public life (even if only in relative terms) have been initiated essentially *ab novo*, without experience and without historical memory, since so much had been effaced from mass consciousness during the seven decades of Soviet rule. The population on the southern periphery of the former empire (as, also, was the case of those living in the central regions) was utterly unprepared for the adaptation of market reforms. The brilliant Russian historian V. O. Kliuchevskii once made the following sagacious observation: "The law of life of backward states among the more advanced is this: the need for reform comes before the people are ready for it."[24] It is easy to imagine the condition of the leaders of the new states, who, at the moment when their countries unexpectedly gained independence, lacked the requisite knowledge appropriate to the scale of the tasks faced, who had no understanding of the fundamentals of a market economy, and who had no experience on the international arena. One can well appreciate the inevitable perplexity and confusion in the face of the unexpected, extraordinarily onerous challenges that they faced. Notwithstanding the fact that for many years they had been in the melting pot of the highly placed party bureaucracy, each of them had preserved his individual character and traits, and these could not fail to have an impact on political policy, on economic strategy, and on the harshness of the repression. Despite all this, the new post-Soviet leadership has succeeded in completely demolishing the former political and economic system, and indeed they did so in historically short periods of time. It would therefore be neither fair nor accurate to come away with a one-sided, purely negative assessment of the post-Soviet development of the countries in this region.

On the Compatibility of Economic Progress and Authoritarian Rule

As suggested by the foregoing, the transition from the Soviet sociopolitical order and the command economy has largely run its course in Central Asia, for the countries here have laid the foundations for a new system and basic structures that are quite solid and well established. But all this only raises a host of critical questions: what kind of formation is this, what is the dominant vector of their development, has capitalism taken root in lieu of the command economies, and can democracy of a Western model be organically woven into the social texture of this region? In the opinion of some American political scientists who specialize on the countries of Central Asia, even to raise the question whether the Western model is compatible with these local cultures is almost tantamount to a kind of racism. If, however, I may be so bold as to violate the norms of "political correctness" that dominate the United States, I would like to challenge the assumptions that Central Asia is fated to follow the standard Western line of development.

The Nobel laureate in economics Douglass C. North has studied the economies of many countries that gained their independence in the second half of the twentieth century. He came to the conclusion that the adoption of a market economic system by itself, without the simultaneous reform of political institutions, was incapable of creating an effective market economy. North examined the experience of countries in Africa and concluded that, although these had been the object of systematic market reforms, the majority of them are now poorer than they were in 1980. Of some three dozen countries on that continent, only two—Botswana and Uganda—showed an annual rate of growth in the GDP that exceeded 3 percent during the period of 1980–2003; two thirds of these countries either experienced stagnation or now find themselves in a worse position than they were when they gained independence in the 1960s. North concludes that the main cause of the failure of reform lies in the fact that the market-oriented policy (the so-called "Washington consensus" that constituted the foundation of the African experiment) contained a fatal flaw: it presupposed that economic reforms by themselves—without a corresponding transformation in political institutions—were sufficient to create an effective economic system. If limits are not placed on the government's domination, if guarantees to the right of property and individual liberty are not provided, argues North, then effective market systems simply cannot exist. He insists that, absent the corresponding political foundations, market reforms will not yield the expected results. And this is true not only for African states but for all developing countries. In his view, history has not seen a single case of an effective market system that was not based on a well-developed political order. North further points out that the African countries have similar political systems, which are distinguished by corrupt authoritarian or dictatorial regimes.[25] Nor can any kind of natural resources ensure economic prosperity, even with a market economy, if such political regimes remain intact—as the examples of Nigeria and Sudan abundantly demonstrate.

In that respect, how does Nigeria differ from oil-rich Kazakhstan—a country where, as one expert estimates, 5 percent of the population owns 80 percent of the national wealth and where the system of income distribution from the oil revenues is close to that in Nigeria? The question applies no less to Azerbaijan. And what about the natural gas giant Turkmenistan, which leaves its population in abject poverty, and which is ruled by a tyrant whose brutality can compete with the most barbaric African dictators like Idi Amin? I would note that this situation also applies to many rulers of African countries whose power is completely legitimate and based on plebiscites and nominal (procedural) democracy. A perfect example here is Robert Mugabe, who has utterly devastated Zimbabwe—formerly the rich state of Rhodesia. It bears noting that the presidents of Kazakhstan, Uzbekistan, Azerbaijan, and even Turkmenistan were, after all, also confirmed in office by popular elections. The real point, however, is what stands behind these "elections" and "referenda."

Does it not follow from North's analysis that the "political foundation" for successful market reforms must be only a liberal-democratic system based on the Western prototype? To be sure, democracies have also had corruption of those in power, patron-client relations, clannishness, and nepotism. At present, indeed, when democracy (or at least a formal procedural democracy) prevails in the majority of countries around the world, many political scientists focus their attention on its darker sides. Farid Zakaria's book, *The Future of Freedom: Illiberal Democracy at Home and Abroad*, cites the example of pseudo-democratic systems where, under the cover of externally democratic attributes (the election of presidents and parliaments), the population is virtually deprived of all fundamental civil rights. Among such countries Zakaria includes Russia and the new republics of Central Asia, in particular Kazakhstan, which he terms a "near tyranny." In Zakaria's view, many countries have not matured to the point where democratic rule can be adopted and function; they would be better off having an authoritarian regime of the "softer" or "liberal" autocratic variety. Singapore, Indonesia, Taiwan, Thailand, Chili, and South Korea achieved economic success under regimes that were politically authoritarian, but offered economic freedom.[26]

The authoritarian rulers of Central Asia profess a commitment to democracy in principle, but simultaneously declare that their peoples are not yet ready for democratic government—because they must undergo a long and difficult path of reform, a transformation in public consciousness, and the burden of historical experience and tradition, all compounded by the recent experience during the Soviet era. Nevertheless, they aver, in the end democracy will prevail; it is only necessary to give enough time for this process to unfold. In the interim, they (and all those who have a vested interest in preserving the status quo) offer reassurances that only the existing form of rule—for all its shortcomings—can ensure stability in their countries and, for better or worse, sustain the current standard of living. Of course, that rationalization is exceedingly convenient and self-serving for those in power. Nevertheless, however much apologists might labor to justify the preservation of the existing regimes, there is simply no way to justify their harsh, repressive character, their attempt to assert total control over society. It is, of course, necessary not only to recognize the hypocrisy of the self-justifying rationalizations offered by the existing regimes but also to take into account domestic realities: the weakness of the state framework, the interethnic conflicts and tensions, the traditional mentality of the general populace, and the political inertia typical of the recent *homo soveticus*. Given all this, there are good reasons to doubt whether a democratic political system in the Western sense is realistically possible and is the most acceptable system for the countries of Central Asia. Rather than casually assume the superiority and inevitable triumph of the Western model, I suggest that we hold a full, open, and objective discussion about the advantages of an authoritarian system of rule (with the proviso that it provide for the liberalization of public life and economic freedom). The scale and character of the liberalization, along with the degree of state *dirigisme* in the economy, should be adapted to the concrete conditions of a country—that is, to its social and economic problems and also to its ethnic and cultural profile. It is precisely on these latter two dimensions that I shall focus here.

The examples offered by Zakaria are persuasive. Japan of course is an exception: it had already launched its industrialization during the Meiji period (i.e., in the last third of the nineteenth century) and, in Lucien Pye's judgment, by the 1930s had become the third or fourth largest economy in the world. But the other "four little dragons" along with the new superpower, China, have demonstrated striking economic success under conditions of authoritarian political regimes. The question, however, is whether one can draw on the experience of these countries of East and Southeast Asia to affirm that an authoritarian regime is also optimal to maintain social order in Central Asia and can have a favorable influence on economic growth. The growth in the GDP and some other macroeconomic indices is possible in the Central Asian states, especially if the market for their export goods remains as favorable as it now is. Nevertheless, this system will bring only minimal improvements in the pattern of social returns (that is, the redistribution of wealth), but only those kinds of change can raise the material standard of living for the broad masses of the population, pay for development of the social sphere (public health, education, pensions, and housing), and finance a general enhancement of the social safety nets. In essence, the existing regimes here are organically and functionally incapable of ensuring social progress: they are too beholden to the "have-alls" to do more than offer palliatives and promises for the "have-nothings."

One must be no less critical toward facile assumptions that capitalism can be established easily and quickly (by historical standards) in these countries. One must concur with the view (expressed by such people as Eduard Batalov) that capitalism is not simply an economic mechanism, but actually represents a certain type of civilization. The classic work by Joseph Schumpeter long ago made this point clearly: "Leaving the precincts of purely economic considerations, we now turn to the cultural component of the capitalist economy—to its socio-psychological *superstructure*, if we wish to speak the Marxian language—and to the mentality that is characteristic of capitalist society and in particular of the bourgeois class."[27] The success achieved by Confucian countries of East Asia, in no small (if not decisive) degree, was

The Cultural Factor

One of the important developments in social sciences during recent years has been to rediscover the role of the cultural factor in social and economic development. In this regard, there has been a renewed interest in the legacy of a political philosopher from the first half of the nineteenth century, Joseph de Maistre, who was anathematized by Marxists and many others as an obscurantist and reactionary. Some of de Maistre's apothegms are still pertinent in today's world: as Sir Isaiah Berlin wrote in the mid-1950s, "Maistre may have spoken with the language of the past, but the content of what he had to say presaged the future."* Particularly resonant with modern thinking are his ideas about the role of culture in social progress; his view that the best political institutions are those that have adapted to the mentality of a given people, their traditions and history; and his opinion that a metamorphosis in the psychology and worldview of a person come not through some revolutionary restructuring of consciousness, but through a process of historical evolution.

Given the mentality of the overwhelming majority of people in Central Asia (who have only a vague notion of the autonomy of the individual), one must recognize that a democratic structure of society based on the Western paradigm has little or no chance of succeeding in this region. It is, after all, dubious whether the vast majority of the population in Uzbekistan or Tajikistan has any clear understanding of what democratic citizenship really means. Even in Russia, where the population has been Europeanized to a far greater degree, recent opinion polls (conducted by the authoritative Public Opinion Foundation) show that a minority of respondents assign top priority to individual liberty; whereas 26 percent find the main precondition for the well-being of a country to lie in the existence of good laws, the majority—62 percent—believe that the presence of a strong leader is the decisive factor.†

The idea that social progress and material prosperity are highly dependent on culture (spiritual values, beliefs, traditions) has become a significant element in scholarship in recent years. Among these, particularly important is the collection of essays edited by Lawrence Harrison and Samuel Huntington, *Culture Matters*. This volume directly challenges the belief of many economists that the effectiveness of economic policy depends entirely on how it is formulated and implemented, not on the culture of a given society. In the editors' words: "For many economists, it is axiomatic that appro-priate economic policy effectively implemented will produce the same results without reference to culture. The problem here is the case of multicultural countries in which some ethnic groups do better than others, although all operate with the same economic signals. Ex-amples are the Chinese minorities in Thailand, Malaysia, Indonesia, the Philippines, and the United States; the Basques in Spain and Latin America; and the Jews wherever they have migrated."[‡] In his chap-ter in *Culture Matters*, Ronald Inglehart observes that "democracy is not something that can be easily attained by simply adopting the right laws. It is most likely to flourish in some social and cultural contexts than in others, and the current cultural conditions for de-mocracy seem relatively unfavorable in Russia, Belarus, Ukraine, Armenia, and Moldova."[§] And to that list I would add the countries of Central Asia.

[*]Isaiah Berlin, "Joseph de Maistre and the Origins of Fascism," in *The Crooked Timber of Humanity: Chapters in the History of Ideas* (New York, 1991), p. 96.

[†]L. Blekher and G. Liubarskii, *Glavnyi russkii vopros* (Moscow, 2003), pp. 125–26, 158.

[‡]Lawrence Harrison and Samuel Huntington, eds., *Culture Matters* (New York, 2000), p. xxiv.

[§]Ronald Inglehart, "Culture and Democracy," in *Culture Matters*, p. 94.

due to so-called "Asian values"—a mental code and world view that is fun-damentally different from that found in Central Asia.

The experience of other countries is not automatically applicable to the newly independent republics of the former Soviet Union. This has been graphi-cally demonstrated in the case of Russia: all the strenuous efforts of Western experts, including the leading specialists on transition and development (economists, sociologists, and political scientists), to transform Russia into a truly democratic society with a capitalist economy have ended in failure. Instead, as we now see, there has arisen something unforeseen and unpredicted, something that does not fit into the familiar, standard model of the Western type. And to a still lesser degree can this Western experience be superimposed on the countries of Central Asia. The unique combination of Islamic traditions and the results of Russification and sovietization over a century and a half have produced the specific traits in the peoples living in the countries of the post-Soviet south; one can scarcely hope to understand this special fusion (and the capacity of the indigenous peoples to resist external influences) simply by invoking the experience of other countries and peoples. A system of free entrepreneurship and market relations can be created in the countries of Central Asia (as has happened in Kazakhstan, for example), but that is still not full-fledged capitalism, with all the inherent economic, social, political, and cultural components of what Max Weber termed "the spirit of capitalism." Capitalism is the product of the historic evolution of a given society; it would be naive to think that it can be easily built and implanted simply by having a well-designed policy and resorting to fast-paced "express" methods of implementation.

Of course, one should treat with caution aggregates such as the "peoples of Central Asia," as if these constituted a more or less homogenous ethnocultural entity. In fact, there is little in common between the children and grandchildren of the formerly nomadic pastoral peoples (Kazakhs, Kyrgyz, and Turkmen) and the sedentary farming peoples (Uzbeks and Tajiks). These differences are also apparent in their everyday behavior, in the degree of their devotion to Islam (the Uzbeks and Tajiks being much more observant Muslims), in the role of women at home and in society (with Kazakh and Kyrgyz women traditionally exhibiting far greater independence), in their work habits, and in a host of other special traits that distinguish each people's character and behavior. It is also possible to discern different degrees of harshness in the authoritarian regimes in these five countries and to identify a significant (if not absolute) correlation between the political cultures and ethnicity in Central Asia. However, to confirm, qualify, or refute this proposition, it would be necessary first to conduct a specialized, interdisciplinary study that would draw heavily on the findings of anthropologists in the region.

Compared with the tyranny that reigns in Turkmenistan, the Nazarbaev regime in Kazakhstan is of course considerably more liberal. To be sure, it has committed its own excesses, including crude threats and intimidation, such as the case where a beheaded dog was left on the doorstep of an oppositionist journalist. Nevertheless, critical assessments of the situation in Kazakhstan periodically cut through the restrictions and barriers imposed by the authorities. Almaty has become not only the financial but also the intellectual capital of Central Asia; it has in effect displaced Tashkent, which in Soviet times had loomed the center of economic and cultural life in the region. This shift in position also is due to the cultural degradation in Uzbekistan, where Karimov has been successful in achieving the deintellectualization of Uzbek society. He has, without doubt, achieved extraordinary control over any manifestation of critical thinking in society, and to a far greater degree than was even true in the Brezhnev era. One need only compare the Kazakh press, which is not under the control of authorities, with its counterpart in Uzbekistan, where such a press cannot exist any more than there can be a real, even constructive, opposition.

Of the five countries of Central Asia, only Kazakhstan is likely to achieve some liberal social-political transformations in the foreseeable future. The challenge that the intellectual community of Kazakhstan faces is that of devising a political ideology, which at once corresponds to the requirements of the modern era and to the country's special past, traditions, and national culture. It seems that the basis of this conception of modernization should be not the antithesis of Western democracy, but a synthesis of various components and values that are embedded in the mentality of the ethos formed in this country. As the Russian political philosopher Aleksei Zubov has observed:

> Different cultural preconditions, different civilizational foundations lead to different methods in the use of innovations—in the social, not economic, sphere, of course—in a non-Western society. Economic, informational, and educational development (which is ineluctable and desirable in any country) serves not to make these countries similar to the West, but to ensure that, while remaining true to themselves (that is, within the framework of their own type of civilization), these can more adequately react to the universal economic and social processes and thereby remain competitive in the new world.[28]

In other words, the conception of the modernization of society should have, as its ultimate goal, not to borrow wholesale the institutions of Western democracy, but to create political and social institutions that ensure social progress, economic growth, the supremacy of law, and guarantees of private property, and in a way that takes into account the mentality, traditions, and historic experience of a given people (including both that of earlier times as well as that acquired during the Soviet era).

Part II. Washington and Moscow in Central Asia: "Colliding Trajectories"

The space of Central Asia, like that of the South Caucasus, has become an arena for a collision of interests between the United States and Russia, but it is also of interest to China, the third participant in the "Great Game." To be sure, for the time being Beijing has characteristically demonstrated a guarded caution and does not actively participate in the emerging confrontation. Beijing's primary interest is to maintain stability in Xinjiang, that is, to repress the separatist movement of Muslim Uigurs; that is why its first priority is to secure the cooperation of the Central Asian regimes in achieving this aim. It is also worth emphasizing the strategic and economic importance that Xinjiang holds for China, with its mineral resources (including oil) as well as its geographic and cultural links with Central Asia, Pakistan, and Afghanistan. Beijing has adopted an extremely ambitious ten-year plan (2000–2010) for the economic development of this northwestern periphery and, with all the means at its disposal, is seeking to integrate Xinjiang into the general development of the country as a whole. And, to realize this plan, China is counting heavily on tapping into the energy and other resources of Central Asia, primarily Kazakhstan. To ensure the delivery of hydrocarbon raw materials from Central Asia, Beijing obviously wants the governments in this region to be stable—and, at least for the present, that is precisely what the current regimes can provide.

It is arguable, however, that the main reason for Beijing's vested interest in maintaining stability in Central Asia lies in something other than economics: Central Asia is very important in terms of strategic geography. In the west and northwest China abuts the Islamic world—Pakistan, Afghanistan, Tajikistan, Kyrgyzstan, and Kazakhstan. The millions of Muslims living in Xinjiang constitute a focus of constant concern for Beijing. In a sense, China thus has its own "Chechnia" in the western region of the country, and indeed not in the form of an enclave (as in Russia), but as a single expanse bordering on the Muslim world, where the separatist ambitions of their Uigur coreligionists enjoy broad moral and material support. These ambitions, and support of them beyond China's borders, poses a real threat to China and only compounds the problems associated with Tibet. In short, the Muslim countries of Central Asia, Afghanistan, and Pakistan represent the southern flank for Russia and the western flank for China. And here the interests of Moscow and Beijing overlap, with both seeking to contain the threats presented by radical Islam. For the present, at least, Beijing is satisfied to cooperate with Moscow on the basis of a power-sharing model in terms of relations to Central Asia. Moscow, as we shall see, takes a different view; it is simply not willing to tolerate parity with anyone else and insists on exercising hegemony over the region.

Such ambitions notwithstanding, in the post-Soviet 1990s three outside powers—the United States, Russia, and China—reached a kind of provisional equilibrium in Central Asia. That equilibrium has now been shattered: 11 September 2001 precipitated a radical change in the existing power structure, leading to a situation in which the United States became the region's principal economic donor and security manager. Although China cannot fail to be concerned about this development, Russia finds this American dominance totally unacceptable.

The American Perspective

Prior to 11 September

The United States, despite its preoccupation with other regions bearing greater significance for its strategic interests, had maintained a vigilant eye on Central Asia even before the events of 11 September 2001. In practice, however, it chose not to become directly involved in the region and instead opted for an attentive, wait-and-see policy. This cautious approach reflected Washington's view that, despite a professed interest in Caspian problems, the region was not a significant priority in terms of fundamental American interests. Instead, the United States saw itself as better positioned to provide tangible economic assistance, whether directly or through international financial organizations. Above all, however, American policymakers sought to preserve the status quo and stability in this region. In particular, this meant that Washington was determined to ensure that none of its geopolitical competitors enhanced their influence over the states of Central Asia. It is useful to see the conjuncture of American and Russian policy in the region prior to 11 September in terms of "colliding trajectories":

> American presence has been expanding throughout these lands since the day the Soviet Union collapsed. . . . American engagement focused on . . . helping the new states consolidate their independence and sovereignty by linking humanitarian relief assistance with economic and political reforms. As the former Soviet states cleared the first hurdles of independence, the United States added a new dimension to its ties with them through security. This has meant first and foremost integration into the transatlantic security framework through participation since the early 1990s in regular security dialogues with countries in the North Atlantic Treaty Organization (NATO), as well as practical military and political-military cooperation in the context of the NATO Partnership for Peace program. Yet, despite their apparent consistency and complementarity, American efforts in the former Soviet lands have been marked by one major internal contradiction: the duality of the U.S. relationship with Russia. On the one hand, American policies on the Russian periphery were not intended to encircle the country or undermine security. To the contrary, these efforts aimed to include Russia in cooperative activities that the United States undertook bilaterally and multilaterally with its neighbors. On the other hand, Russia has never abandoned its great power aspirations in these lands. Soon after the dissolution of the Soviet Union, Moscow sought explicit recognition of its special status in former Soviet states from the international community. But, as a result, U.S. support for the independence and sovereignty of these states became U.S. support for their independence from Russia. The result was

an ambiguity in U.S.-Russian relations, in American policy toward the former Soviet states, and in Russia's role as a partner or an obstacle to American efforts to provide for the security and stability of these states. The United States was pursuing its policies not quite against Russia, but certainly not with Russia's support and endorsement.[29]

After 11 September

The tragedy of 11 September forced the United States to make a radical shift in its policy toward Central Asia, and this has been fraught with far-reaching consequences for the balance of power in the region. The foundation of the new American policy in this region, which marked the onset of a new geopolitical era, consisted of the following triad of objectives (listed in order of importance):

(1) Create military centers that could deploy rapid-response forces in the war against Islamic terrorism or be used in various military operations in Afghanistan and the Middle East. Washington's interest in the countries of Central Asia is explained, first and foremost, by the so-called "Rumsfeld doctrine," which envisions the establishment of strategic centers to base these mobile forces. Rather than concentrate a large mass of troops in Germany and South Korea, the Pentagon plans to disperse them across an enormous territory running from South Africa to China. Hence the deployment of American forces at bases in Uzbekistan, Kyrgyzstan, and other countries in this region constitutes a core component in these plans, and the United States has been entirely successful in realizing this strategy.

(2) Maintain stability in the region and the independence of the countries of Central Asia (the latter denoting independence from the "big brother" in Moscow). Under conditions of the war on international terrorism and Islamic extremism, the Bush administration has embraced a strategy of national security based on pre-emptive action to prevent, not merely answer, terrorist attacks. The zone of national security interests of the United States now stretches around the entire globe; the choice of countries for the location of military air bases and small contingents of mobile military forces determines the patronage—in both material and military-political terms—that Washington is willing to promise. All this assistance helps to bolster the stability of the secular regimes that rule these countries: for Washington, given its definition of interests and strategy, stability bears the highest priority. This American support for repressive authoritarian regimes in Central Asia has of course elicited sharply differing assessments in American political circles and in the mass media. From the perspective of political pragmatism, America is perforce interested in the preservation of these regimes; hence it provides material support and thereby acquires their loyalty as well as the opportunity to use their territories in the war

Editorial Opinion

The contrast between American ideals and the pragmatism of U.S. foreign policy toward authoritarian regimes is often pointed out by the press, as in these *Washington Post* editorials:

"Our Man in Baku": It's clearly expedient for Mr. Bush to back Mr. Aliyev, just as for decades U.S. governments found their interest in propping up dictators in the Persian Gulf. But Mr. Bush himself has said—in one of his several major speeches about democracy—that such policies were mistaken. "Sixty years of Western nations excusing and accommodating the lack of freedom in the Middle East did nothing to make us safe," the president said two months ago. "In the long run stability cannot be purchased at the expense of liberty." It may take the United States decades to overcome the legacy of embracing corrupt dictators in the Arab world. The least Mr. Bush can do is to avoid repeating the mistake in the new oil states of the Caucasus and Central Asia—beginning in Azerbaijan. (25 January 2004)

"Our Man in Tashkent": The Bush administration has often vowed not to repeat the Cold War mistake of embracing useful dictators while ignoring their domestic policies, especially in the Muslim states such as Uzbekistan. To keep the administration honest, Congress passed legislation last year requiring that all aid to Uzbekistan—$57.5 million, including $11.6 million this year in military funds—be contingent on State Department certification that Uzbekistan is making "substantial and continuing progress" in implementing its commitments under the strategic partnership. So far there's been no certification. On the contrary, the State Department's annual human rights report, issued last week, concluded that "Uzbekistan is an authoritarian state with limited civil rights" that continues to repress "freedom of religion and the press as well as opposition political parties." Some in the administration argue that should be enough, that it would be worse to cut off Mr. Karimov than to continue "engagement" with him. The Pentagon would like to keep 1,000 American servicemen at the Karshi Khanabad airbase, at least for the time being. That's why the administration's decision will be important: If it swallows Mr. Karimov's ploys, it will signal to his neighbors, and the world, that the spread of freedom still matters less to the United States than the "wonderful cooperation" of a dictator. (4 March 2004) on terrorism—the end of which is nowhere in sight. But in this case a policy dictated by political expediency plainly contradicts the moral principles proclaimed in American foreign policy (e.g., democratization, the defense of human rights, etc.), and this contradiction has provoked a corresponding reaction in American public opinion.

(3) Pursuit of U.S. interests in making use of the Caspian oil reservoir and the transportation of oil and natural gas resources along routes that are politically and economically advantageous for Washington. To diversify the sources of oil and gas deliveries (especially given the situation in the Middle East), the United States has an interest in ensuring that "the Caspian region be integrated into the global energy system as an independent component, with the export infrastructure being independent of other suppliers of raw materials."[30] That is why the United States is doing everything possible to see that the oil and natural gas of Central Asia be exported through routes that circumvent Russia—even in those cases when this means greater distances and, correspondingly, greater construction costs for the pipelines. From Washington's perspective, it is unacceptable to allow the reliability and uninterrupted flow of oil to depend on the change in the situation in Russia.

Some analysts argue that one goal behind establishing an American presence in Central Asia is to acquire military bases in the very backyard of China. Even if that is a factor, it must be far less important than the three other objectives cited above.

Above all, Washington's policy toward Central Asia is based on the strategy that the American leadership adopted after 11 September. There are three fundamental components that underpin this "Grand Design" in American foreign policy: pre-emption, unilateralism, and hegemony. And it would be a mistake to attribute the organization of this strategy to George W. Bush, for it actually dates back to the sixth U.S. president, John Quincy Adams (1825–1829), who in the estimate of Yale historian John Gaddis was "the most influential American grand strategist of the nineteenth century." After reviewing American foreign policy against this broader historical canvas, Gaddis observes "it's hardly surprising that these preferences for preemption, unilateralism, and hegemony resurfaced in the aftermath of September 11th as American leaders scrambled to regain the security the nation seemed to have lost: deep roots do not easily disappear." The end of the Cold War secured the third of Adams's great principles "the most important one, which was hegemony: a preponderance of power—not a balance of power—and this time on a global scale." The idea that American power should be extended globally belongs not to Bush but to one of his predecessors in the White House: Woodrow Wilson (1913–1921). As Gaddis notes: "And in Wilson's mind, at least, the issue of how far the

American sphere of responsibility must extend to ensure American security had now been settled: it would extend everywhere." Hence the fundamental principles of the so-called "Bush doctrine" correspond to the traditional foreign policy of the United States, and in Gaddis's phrase, it "sounds new only because it's old."[31]

It is perfectly obvious that since 11 September the United States has gained dominance in the region (in both the military-political and economic spheres), notwithstanding the disagreements within the American foreign policy establishment regarding America's role and the duration of the U.S. military presence in the region. Hardly anyone doubts that American military forces will remain in the region for a long time to come. Reuters, for example, reported from Bishkek that "U.S. forces based at an airport in Kyrgyzstan are replacing their tent accommodations with more permanent buildings and said there was no end in sight to their mission in the Central Asian state. . . . The new buildings at Manas [the Bishkek airport] are being put up at a cost of $60 million."[32] The U.S. ambassador to Russia, Alexander Vershbow, made this candid statement about Central Asia in April 2004: "Russia has its own interests (something we recognize), but it is not alone. We also have an interest in this region and would like to discuss this question with Russia so as to avoid competition."[33] During a visit to Moscow in January 2004, the U.S. Secretary of State Colin Powell made a statement that, for him, was uncharacteristically sharply worded: "We recognize the territorial inviolability of Russia, and also its natural interest in the lands it borders. However, to no lesser degree, we recognize the sovereignty and inviolability of Russia's neighbors and their right to peace and respect in their relations with those with whom they share common borders."[34]

The Neoimperial Aspirations of Moscow Revanchists

At the beginning of this decade (and especially after 11 September 2001), it was possible to conceive of a partnership of Moscow, Beijing, and Washington to support stability in Central Asia and to reinforce the region's capacity to serve as a bulwark against the assaults of an aggressive Islamic radicalism. That, however, is no longer the case. As became clear in 2003, and still more so subsequently, Russian policy and the Russian political class have exhibited a transparent irredentism toward Central Asia, thereby all but eliminating any hope for collaboration by the three powers. In the words of Konstantin Kosachev (chairman of the foreign affairs committee of the lower house of the Russian parliament): "Russia is still infected with an imperial hysteria and its unwarranted greatness."[35]

The Neoimperial Rhetoric

Simultaneous with the initial improvement in the economic position of Russia, ideas of a neoimperial revanchism claimed a powerful new hold on the minds of the Russian political class. From the mouths of the leading politicians on the left and the right flanks of the Russian political spectrum, Westernizers and national patriots, communists and liberals comes the pronouncement that Russia's mission in the twenty-first century is to assume responsibility for the territory of the CIS (with the exception of the Baltic states) and, still more bluntly, to assert sole control over this expanse. Thus, the program of the parliamentary bloc of national-patriotic forces of Rodina ("Motherland," which is playing an increasingly significant role on the Russian political scene and gaining ever greater influence over the general populace) declares that Russia "should become the basis for a new union state. This is historically, economically, culturally justified; it corresponds to the interests of the peoples of Russia; it answers the aspirations of the majority of residents in the CIS."[36]

Even according to the convictions of Moscow politicians who are relatively sober-minded (and who do not seemingly suffer from a "great power complex"), "the territory of the former USSR remains the only vitally important space for Russia." The threat that this territory may be lost in a confrontation with the United States or the European Union compels Russian politicians to refocus their main efforts on regaining dominance over this former imperial space. Here is an example of the irredentist clamor that is now characteristic of the political gurus in Moscow. A political commentator Stanislav Belkovskii (rumored to be close to the Kremlin) believes that the only variant of the Russian national project that Putin should realize is that of establishing "Russia's dominance over the historical-geographical field described as the post-Soviet space," with top priority assigned to Central Asia and the South Caucasus.[37] It is impossible, however, to find in these or other programmatic documents or in discussions by influential representatives of the political elite any cogent arguments to explain why control over these regions is so "vitally important" for the well-being and security of Russia. How does one account for so radical a change in the policy of the Putin regime toward its former colonies, including Central Asia? Strictly speaking, during the Yeltsin era the Russian elite in general had no coherent, clearly articulated policy toward Central Asia. Nor could one discern among Yeltsin's circle any inclination toward restoration—the establishment of a new state with the spatial parameters of the former Soviet Union (certainly there were some communists and nationalists who espoused a Moscow-dominated space that encompassed the entire former USSR). In the Putin era, this sudden outburst of ambitious activity has appeared out of the blue! Has Putin awakened a "basic instinct" still found in the mentality of the Russian political class? Apparently the expansionist rhetoric has reinvigorated and recharged the Moscow politicians. As Moscow political analyst Egor Kholmogorov has observed: "'Empire' is the main category of any strategic political analysis in the Russian language. As soon as we start to ponder a full-scale, long-term construction of the Russian state, we begin to think of empire and in terms of empire. Russians are inherently imperialists."[38] It seems as though every Russian politician is an imperialist at heart.

In fact, why indeed should Moscow obsess about its former Muslim provinces? It makes no sense given the fact that Russia has every imaginable natural resource, an impoverished populace characterized by demographic decline, an unstable economy, enormous unpopulated territories in the northeast, the ongoing conflict in Chechnia, and so forth. Russia would seem to have plenty of problems, including difficulties with its own internal Muslims (who comprise 12 to 15 percent of the population in the Russian Federation), making unrealistic its return as the patron for Uzbekistan, Tajikistan, or Kyrgyzstan to deal with all their problems. As Aleksandr Solzhenitsyn pointed out: "We don't have the strength for an empire!—and we don't need it, it has fallen from our shoulders; it is crushing us, it drains us, it hastens our ruin. I am alarmed to see that the re-emerging Russian national consciousness, to a large degree, simply cannot liberate itself from the spatial-power thinking, from the imperial intoxication."[39] I would argue that Solzhenitsyn is no less patriotic than Dmitrii Rogozin, Stanislav Belkovskii, and other political opportunists and ideologists of the so-called "national-patriotic front." But let us examine two archetypical exponents of the neoimperialism.

Anatolii Chubais's "Empire of Liberty"

In October 2003 Anatolii Chubais presented a program that provided a decorative justification for Russia's mission in assuming responsibility over the expanse that was once the Soviet realm. The program unleashed a storm in Russian political circles. According to Chubais, "Russia's mission in the twenty-first century" consists in the construction of an "empire of liberty." It is worth pointing out that Chubais borrowed, without attribution, the term "empire of liberty" from the third president of the United States, Thomas Jefferson. In any case, the "main figure in Russian privatization" and Westernizer (who is known for his pragmatism, which indeed at times borders on cynicism) emerges before us as an unalloyed Slavophile idealist: "For Russia and the Russian people, the search for truth, enduring verities, and justice always come before the primary material impulses of man."[40]

Chubais enumerates all the markers of misery that blight Russian society, including poverty, unemployment, decline in fertility rates, and rapid contraction in the size of the population. In contrast to Solzhenitsyn, however, he finds salvation to lie in economic, cultural, and political expansion across the expanse of the CIS:

> Russia is the sole, unique natural leader across the entire area of the CIS both in terms of the volume of its economy and the standard of living of its citizens. . . . Russia is not simply a leader; it can, and must, do everything possible to expand, strengthen, and consolidate its leading position in this part of the planet during the next fifty years. The ideology of Russia . . . for the entire foreseeable historical perspective must be that of a "liberal imperialism," and Russia's mission is that of constructing a liberal empire. It is precisely this . . . that is inherent, natural, and organic for Russia—historically, geopolitically, and morally. Finally, this task is of such a magnitude that it can help our people, once and for all, to overcome the spiritual crisis and to become truly united and mobilized.[41]

Note that this declaration is not coming from a politician with a reputation of being an uninhibited great-power chauvinist such as Zhirinovskii or Rogozin, for example. Nonetheless, the "spatial-power thinking, the imperial intoxication" has clearly infected Chubais—a leader of the liberal camp in the Russian political elite.

The construction of a "liberal empire" has several components. These include "assistance in the development of Russian culture and defense of Russians and Russian-speaking people in neighboring countries," "expansion of Russian business in neighboring countries both in terms of trade and in the acquisition and development of assets," but also the "support, development, and (if need be) defense of fundamental democratic institutions, and the rights and liberties of citizens in neighboring countries." Chubais's ideas are shared by other intellectuals, who are infused by "a latent understanding" of the need for "an expansion of a tolerant and vivacious Russian culture in the external world."[42]

In the case of the idealist-pragmatist Chubais, the deeds correspond to the words. One after the other, the electric power systems of post-Soviet states have become parts of the gigantic Russian electric power-holding company headed by Chubais himself; at this point the new subunits include Armenia, Georgia, and Kyrgyzstan, but other countries are being targeted for inclusion as well.[43] As for Russia's *Kulturträger* function, it is highly doubtful that the contemporary Russian mass culture (which is mired in vulgarity and which has borrowed the worst from America's trashy show business) can spiritually and aesthetically enrich the peoples of the "near abroad." As for contemporary Russian literature, the prophecy of Evgenii Zamiatin has come to pass: "The future of Russian literature will be its past."

Andrei Kokoshin: The Demonstration of Military Muscle

Chubais objects to the negative connotations associated with the idea of "empire." In his view, "empire" is associated with such words as "civilization," "democracy," "market," and "liberty." Hence, in Chubais's view, the return of Moscow to the post-Soviet space brings only benefits to peoples and does not pursue any imperial interests in a negative, "pre-Chubais" sense.

But another prominent Moscow politician, Andrei Kokoshin, represents a less altruistic perspective. Kokoshin, a deputy minister of defense in the Yeltsin era, is as influential in the military-political sphere as Chubais is in the economic-political sphere. He is, I would say, the number one intellectual of the Russian military-political establishment, serving simultaneously as chairman of the Committee on the Affairs of the CIS in the State Duma and as vice-president of the Russian Academy of Sciences. In Kokoshin's view, Russia's return to the former provinces of the Soviet Union will guarantee the country's "military security and economic security." Taking Kyrgyzstan as an example, Kokoshin explains that "a return, for instance, to Kirgizia is determined by the strategic interests of Russia," avers that "Putin has clearly indicated that the countries of the CIS constitute a zone of our strategic interests," and declares that Russia's return here will include the creation of "an airbase with a rather significant fighting potential." With references to Putin for support, Kokoshin says that "very many questions of economics are decided under the cover of military force," and hence "it is necessary to demonstrate one's own military muscles." As a result, he argues that "in a whole number of areas of the post-Soviet space we must really have either military bases or such agreements that would permit us to deploy our own military contingents there quickly and to take the requisite measures in the strictest military way."

A member of the Kremlin party "United Russia" (which dominates the State Duma), Kokoshin asserts in the name of his party that "in regions which directly border on the territory of Russia and have very great significance for ensuring the security of Russia, we must have military bases (even if small and compact)."[44] There is no doubt that Central Asia belongs to the list of regions that Kokoshin has in mind.

Thus, some enthusiasts for a return to Central Asia intend to sow on its expanse that which is reasonable, good, and eternal; and to develop democracy there, to defend the rights and liberties of its citizens, and to enrich them spiritually—in other words, to bring what the former "little brothers" need and what the population of contemporary Russia has already succeeded in acquiring. In addition, the "new Russians," "new Kazakhs," and "new Kyrgyz" can share valuable experience, although here the influence is more likely to be mutual. By contrast, others—like Kokoshin—urge the use of "military muscle." The demonstration of these muscles in Chechnia somehow does not make much of an impression; it is therefore necessary to also demonstrate them on the expanse of Central Asia.

Of the swarm of Moscow neoimperialists who are ready to charge off to the expanses of Central Asia, I have chosen to summarize the views of Chubais and Kokoshin, two politicians-intellectuals of a very high caliber. Having examined a number of their (and others') publications and statements, I have not found an intelligible, coherent, concrete explanation of the reasons why Russia should seek this economic and military "return" to Central Asia. To be sure, it is understandable in terms of preserving cultural ties with the countries in the region: the umbilical cord linking them to the former imperial center has not yet been cut, nor is that likely to occur any time soon. After all, the Russian language continues to be used by the majority of the urban population in these countries, especially in their capitals, and apparently that will continue to be the case for a long time to come. And in terms of economics and civilization, Russia casts a long shadow over Central Asia. As for the "military return," the creation of military bases in Central Asia requires enormous resources from Russia that, I dare say, could find better use at home. One might also understand that the creation of Russian military bases in Central Asia serves as a counterweight to those of the United States (as, for example, in Kyrgyzstan). However, the United States has established bases in Uzbekistan and Kyrgyzstan as strategic centers for waging war against terrorism and Islamic radicals. These bases were used to destroy the regime of the Taliban, which only the United States was capable of doing. It would have been unthinkable, of course, for Moscow to launch a new assault on Afghanistan. And it is not difficult to imagine what kind of potential threat the aggressive Taliban regime posed for Central Asia and stability throughout this region, and indeed for Russia itself. Both Putin and members of his foreign policy team (although not all) were perfectly aware that the American military intervention in Afghanistan played a significant salutary role for the region and, indirectly, was in Russia's own interest.

Aleksei Arbatov, an authoritative Russian expert on defense issues and former deputy chair of the Defense Committee of the State Duma, has written about the threat posed by the American military bases in Central Asia. In contrast to Kokoshin, he is not politically involved and takes a more sanguine view of the issue:

The Americans will remain in Central Asia for several years, at a minimum, and perhaps longer. For the present, this situation does not create a direct military danger for us. There is no need to threaten us from these bases if one remembers that the United States can reach our territory from many other directions (for example, from Turkey, where the flying distance is much less). One should add that contemporary delivery systems have sufficient range so that there is no need to be "directly alongside." . . . But as for the loss of influence, some comments are in order. Earlier, our influence in Central Asia was virtually monopolistic. Now another player has appeared. And what a player! A superpower in the form of the United States, which can provide both security and economic assistance. . . . Compared with where things stood before 11 September, the situation in the region—from the perspective of security—has improved enormously.[45]

S. Babaeva reflects the judgment of a number of Moscow experts when she writes "without the United States, Russia can no longer provide for security in the region [Central Asia]."[46]

Why Is It "Vitally Important" for Russia to Return to Central Asia?

Returning again to the main question, I have been unable to find any kind of cogent arguments to explain why it is so important for Russia to regain its position in Central Asia. One of the popular town criers for renewing Russian imperialism, M. Leont'ev (who is notorious for toadying up to the powers that be), has informed the readers of *Izvesti'ia* that Russia needs a "reanimation of vitally important interests—in the first instance, in the space immediately around Russia. Russia is not self-sufficient as a sovereign state without the nearest areas of the 'post-Soviet space.' Even economically. And it is still more vulnerable in political terms."[47] It seems inconceivable to claim that Russia is "not self-sufficient." Does Russia not have an abundance of natural resources, its own oil and natural gas, its own territory? What, exactly, is entailed in Leont'ev's version of "self-sufficiency"?

Let's put all this into historical perspective. Patriotic Russian historians have claimed that the conquest of Central Asia in the nineteenth century was dictated by lofty geopolitical calculations and realized by the architects of Russian foreign policy (in particular, by Minister of Foreign Affairs Aleksandr Gorchakov) as a counterweight to the aggressive policy of England. Specifically, Gorchakov sought to contest England's attempt to annex Afghanistan as well as the contiguous territories to its colonies in South Asia, all this being portrayed as an early stage in what Rudyard Kipling famously dubbed the "Great Game." But, according to the testimony of Mikhail Skobelev (the legendary "white general" who actually conquered Central Asia), "the acquisition of Turkestan Krai [modern Central Asia] by Russia came as a pure accident and, as our statesmen have repeatedly declared, lay more as a yoke on Russia rather than bring benefits."[48] As for Gorchakov, in the mid-1860s he regarded Russia as "territorially saturated" and was particularly determined to avoid aggravating tensions with England; hence the Russian advance into Central Asia was directly contrary to his own plans. Minister of War Dmitrii Miliutin held similar views. Nevertheless, "bold, enterprising, and adventuresome generals and colonels continued to seize towns and settlements. . . . But, as is well known, the victors are not judged. Gorchakov had no sooner pacified the British cabinet with assurances that 'there will be no further advances,' when General M. Cherniaev, with a detachment of two thousand men, occupied Tashkent in April 1865."[49] Retroactively, the government of Imperial Russia, for which the military adventures came as an utter surprise, invoked fundamental geostrategic arguments to justify the expansion. Such has often been the case in Russian (and not only Russian) history.

An analysis of the publications, interviews, and statements of current Russian politicians leads one to the conclusion that the motivation behind their efforts to reassert control over the former Central Asian colonies no more corresponds to Russia's vital interests than it did during the time of General Skobelev and chancellor Gorchakov. It is therefore necessary to conclude that the policymakers on the Putin team are inclined to engage in risky adventures, to acquiesce to instinct rather than restructure Russia itself (as Solzhenitsyn urged), and to follow the customary course of external expansion. It is mind-boggling to consider what are truly the "vitally important" domestic problems that await resolution in Russia. But even to begin tackling these problems would make it necessary to risk an exacerbation in social tensions and hence a drop in the president's approval rating (his main political capital). To quote an independent Moscow columnist, Leonid Radzikhovskii: "Puffing out the imperial cheeks (which, as is known in advance, is all for show and will come to nothing) drains off all the country's strength—which is needed for something quite different. The power of Russia will increase . . . through the re-emigration of scholars, the construction of roads. . . . The real problems of Russia include the problems of public health, the army, the pension system, etc. . . . So, will the annexation of Tajikistan and Kirgizia resolve these problems?!"[50] There is no political risk, however, in deferring the resolution of essential problems and playing on the threadbare imperial instincts of the people. But for the political opportunists serving the present regime, these neoimperial games are a sure way to elicit domestic support.

One has to assume that the statements of Moscow's "liberal imperialists" cited above do not go unnoticed in Astana and Tashkent. The yearnings of the "elder brother" will hardly be likely to meet with a favorable response. In particular, the Central Asian leaders must take alarm when they hear blustery declarations about the use of "military force" in order to resolve "economic problems." But should one take such statements seriously? One might just think that Kokoshin shot his mouth off and that he need not be taken seriously. That, however, would be a mistake: Kokoshin gave his interview to *Ekho Moskvy*, the most popular radio station throughout the post-Soviet territory, as millions of people in Russia and abroad (and, via the internet, around the world) listen to its programs. It also has the reputation of rebroadcasting messages that emanate from the very apex of the power structure. One should, in short, pay close attention to what is being said in such a forum.

The Great National Project

In October 2003 the Russian government announced corrections and addenda to the country's military doctrine. These included a declaration that Moscow has the right to conduct pre-emptive strikes throughout the realm of the CIS, without regard for the sovereignty of a state that, in the judgment of the Kremlin leadership, poses a threat to the security of Russia. This programmatic document titled "Urgent Tasks in the Development of the Armed Forces of the Russian Federation" ("Aktual'nye Zadachi Razvitiia Vooruzhennykh Sil Rossiiskoi Federatsii") contains a list of "threats, the neutralization of which is . . . the function of the Armed Forces of the Russian Federation." It lists the "threats" that might emanate from countries in the CIS, including Central Asia:

- instability and weakness of state institutions in neighboring countries;
- expansion of military blocs and associations to the detriment of the security of Russia and its allies;
- discrimination and violation of the rights, liberties, and legal interests of Russian citizens residing abroad.

In all these cases, the Russian government declared that it reserves the right to assess the gravity of the threat and, in turn, the right to launch a preventive strike against the territory of the neighboring countries.

These innovations, which were obviously designed to emulate the "Bush doctrine," were all the more authoritative because they came directly from Sergei Ivanov—the minister of defense and Putin's comrade-in-arms. The obvious purpose here was twofold: to issue a stern warning to some and to strike terror in the hearts of others. Specifically, the warning was directed at more distant lands, while the terror clearly had in its sights the "near abroad"—more precisely, Central Asia and the Caucasus. It was like knocking two balls into separate billiard pockets with a single shot. In the previously mentioned interview with *Ekho Moskvy* in January 2004, Kokoshin further elaborated and spelled out the details of Ivanov's statement from the previous October.

As a result, one gains the sense that, sometime after fall 2003, figures close to President Putin had put the final touches on a grandiose national project that envisioned the re-establishment of a Great Russia, and that would assign it the role of serving as the "overseer for Eurasia." The ultimate goal of this political program is to rebuild the empire of bygone days, but with a new exterior that fits with the requirements of the current epoch. The Kremlin leadership felt ready to embark on this ambitious project after it achieved impressive gains in the economic sphere, established firm control over the mass media, subordinated the parliament and courts, openly used coercion to silence dissenters and political opponents, and raised Putin's approval ratings to astronomical heights (in part by playing on the people's "great power" complex). All this left the regime ready to launch an offensive in Central Asia that would first secure a strong position in the economic sphere, but then shift to the political arena. The offensive is already underway and can claim some success. As for the political campaign, the plan is "to invest colossal resources—economic, technological, and military—for the re-establishment and support of pro-Russian elites in contiguous states."[51] But this of course raises an obvious question: Where is Russia to obtain "colossal resources"?

As for the "demonstration of military muscle," the physique of the Russian army has become so debilitated that it is difficult to imagine that the authors of the great national project and the Moscow military elite are giving serious consideration to the use of military force in the countries of Central Asia. That is true even if the situations foreseen in Ivanov's memorandum should arise. One must assume that they are capable of recognizing, from the dismal experience of the war in Chechnia, the real military capability of the Russian army (which, as Leo Tolstoy described the French Army after the battle of Borodino in 1812, "bears all the chemical components for decomposition"). If, however, one considers the purely hypothetical possibility that the Kremlin should embark on a military adventure in any of the Central Asian states, a host of material and other factors would surely doom such an action to failure. Such an adventure would, in political terms, be utterly irrational and even suicidal. It would mobilize Islamic forces within the countries of the region, undermine the regimes there that have been containing the pressure from Islamic radicalism, and inevitably stoke the fires of anti-Russian propaganda throughout the Muslim world. The consequences for Russia could be catastrophic. Moreover, one need have no doubts that, if

Russia starts to "demonstrate its military muscle" in Central Asia, this would have a deleterious impact on its relations with the United States and the European Union—with all sorts of negative consequences (only some of which, at this point, are foreseeable). Although all this suggests that the rhetoric from Moscow is mere bluster, it is bound to arouse anxiety in the capitals of Central Asia. As Iaroslav Shimov rightly observes: "Among those in Moscow who make the most important political decisions or have an influence on their adoption, there are still enough people who dream up utopian projects that have little to do with reality."[52]

Putin's Position

Should one see Putin as the initiator and prime mover of this revanchist agitation that has overtaken the Russian political class? Perhaps not. It is possible to be skeptical of his statement regarding "Fatherland Day" (carried in a radio broadcast from the Kremlin in February 2003), averring that Russia now has "no imperial ambitions." But, regardless of whether the initiative comes from Putin or somewhere else, the expansionist hallucinations have spread to virtually *all* the political parties and currents along the spectrum—from Alexander Dugin's Eurasianists, the communists, and the national patriots to the liberals (Chubais being a case in point). The newspaper *Zavtra* (which is the mouthpiece of the communists and national patriots) reprimands Putin for declining to rebuild the empire and for ignoring the fact that "imperial ambitions have always been the mainspring of development in Russia, the instrument for the expansion and preservation of our living space."[53] Putin, I submit, has heard the call of the times and has realized the political dividends that can be reaped by exploiting the great-power mentality of the masses—which has never been extinguished and which has caught the attention of perspicacious politicians all across the political spectrum. According to the findings of a sociological study conducted in early 2004 by the authoritative Russian foundation "Ekspertiza," the basis has been prepared in Russian society "for national socialism, Stalinism, and 'Russian fascism.'" Of the two and a half thousand people polled, 60 percent believe that "Russia should be feared, because only then will it be respected."[54] In the course of the electoral campaign, in a meeting with voters on 12 February 2004, Putin apparently began to take into account the mood of the electorate and declared outright that the breakup of the Soviet Union was "a national tragedy."

It is appropriate here again to quote Leo Tolstoy: "What is power? Power is the aggregate of wills transferred to a single person. Under what conditions is the will of the masses transferred to a single person? Under the condition that this person expresses the will of all the people."[55] In addressing the broad masses in spring 2003, Putin assumed the posture of someone seeking to resurrect the Stalin tradition: "Maintaining the state over a broad expanse, preserving a unique community of peoples, with strong positions of the country in the world—all this is not only enormous work. It also entails enormous sacrifices and deprivation for our people. This is precisely the historical path over a millennium. Such is the method for its re-creation as a strong country." Thus, according to Putin, to make Russia a strong country (that is, to rise above its current position), the people must once again suffer "enormous sacrifices and deprivation." As one commentator (who reproduced the Putin statements) notes: "Of course, one would like to try something else in life beside sacrifices and deprivation."[56]

The Practical Subtext

For Chubais, however, the "liberal empire" is not merely a PR stunt or a catchy slogan. This idea has completely practical goals at its foundation:

> If we look at what is happening in the real economy across the space of the CIS, we see that some of our neighbors are moving exactly in the same direction [seizing positions claimed by Russian corporations]. I'll cite an example: Kazakhstan. The rates of economic growth are 10 percent; business is measured in the tens of billions of dollars. As a result, Kazakh business is grabbing the economic space around it. It can, consequently, become the center of a liberal empire. Our corporation [Unified Energy System] sees this, because we are now actively supporting the expansion of Russian business in the countries of the CIS.[57]

Thus, Chubais is plainly talking about "the expansion of Russian business in the countries of the CIS," whereas Kokoshin is proposing that "economic questions be resolved under the cover of military force." Obviously, Chubais and Kokoshin are not loudmouth Duma deputies, mindless political clowns like Zhirinovskii. On the contrary, they are extremely influential representatives of the Moscow political and economic elites—Chubais standing up for those in the energy sector, Kokoshin for those in the military-industrial complex. Both men reflect the position of the Kremlin political elite and, simultaneously, contribute to its formation.

Now that Moscow has embarked on an effort to regain its position in Central Asia, what can it realistically expect to give to the region? Is it really in a position to invest the financial and other material resources (including modern technologies) that are needed for economic development? The answer is perfectly obvious. So long as the Soviet Union existed, Moscow actually did carry out a "great project" to modernize the undeveloped southern borderlands of its empire. For all the negative sides of its colonization, for all the dramatic peripeteia, Russia did in fact invest enormous resources to bring about the economic and cultural development of Central Asia. But at this point Moscow has nothing to give. Instead, it seeks to return to Central Asia in order to *take*. This has been particularly apparent with regard to the largest and most successful country of the region—Kazakhstan. To quote Viacheslav Igrunov (the chairman of the Committee on the Affairs of the CIS in the preceding State Duma): "The most important thing that Russia can now achieve in the post-Soviet space is to traverse quickly the process of rapprochement with Kazakhstan, so that petty differences not undermine this alliance."[58]

Can it possibly be that Anatolii Chubais (the energy tsar of Russia, someone endowed with political perspicacity and, in my view, someone best informed about the real economic and military potential of the country, the full truth about its innumerable problems) seriously proposes to superimpose his "liberal empire" into the system of political coordinates of the post-Soviet era? What is impelling this inveterate pragmatist to propose such steps? Is he simply seeking, despite the debacle of the political alliance he promoted previously, the Union of Right Forces, to acquire new political capital and to preserve his influence in the eyes of the ruling class? He is not the kind of person who would give in to the imperial romanticism preached by the Eurasianists, revanchist national-patriots, and communists. The ideas he has generated, I would suggest, are far more likely to have a prosaic business goal: the point man in Russian privatization has become an ideologist and practitioner of Russian neoimperialism in order to serve the interests of Russia's oligarchical business class. In any case, that is the pose that he has assumed. And the reputation of this outstanding administrator and supermanager has helped to solicit support for himself (and the ideas he has propagated) from a very significant segment of the business circles. But what prospects are offered to Russian capital by gaining access to Central Asia, which has an impoverished population of fifty million, an extraordinarily low purchasing power, and in any case shows a strong preference for non-Russian imports? The answer is simple: Russian capital is seeking to gain control over the rich natural resources of this region. Dmitrii Trenin (an expert at the Carnegie Center in Moscow, with a solid reputation both in Russia and in the West) puts it this way: "The slogan of 'liberal empire' formulated by Anatolii Chubais aims to provide an answer to the growing opportunities and demands of the new Russian capitalism and the state that stands above and behind it."[59] The smell of Kazakh oil has, no doubt, whetted the appetite of the Russian oligarchy.

The optimism that has permeated the statements of government economists and some foreign observers about the economic success of recent years has elicited a challenge from the official Russian press. Alarming warnings about the real state of affairs have also come from Evgenii Primakov. A Putin predecessor as prime minister, Primakov has retained his influence in Russian conservative circles and now heads the Russian Chamber of Commerce and Industry—an institution that can hardly be suspected of opposition to the Putin leadership. In Primakov's view:

> The main factor in growth has been the high prices on the Russian export of raw materials—primarily oil and natural gas. The increase in GDP in 2003 in Russia was also due to an increase in extraction; the country produced 420 million tons of crude oil. However, this volume—a record for the post-Soviet period—was obtained mainly from oil fields that had been opened and developed during the Soviet era. In the absence of significant new capital investments, this source of growth is severely limited. . . . An increase in the rates of growth of the economy of Russia through external factors is at its maximum limits. This conclusion is reinforced by a forecast presented by the Institute of World Economics and International Relations. According to this prediction, in 2004 (for the first time since 1998) Russia will encounter a situation where the external factors of growth are weakening, but the internal factors have not yet been strengthened. It will show that there is no basis for the premise that the development of Russian raw materials can provide for the development of the entire economy of the country in the short term. The accumulation of resources in the raw material sector is being invested to an insignificant degree in other branches of the economy. . . . If one extrapolates the existing practice of "devouring" raw material resources, according to the authoritative testimony of academician Kontorovich (director of the Institute of Geology and Gas in the Siberian Section of the Russian Academy of Sciences), after 2010–2013 we will have not growth in GDP, but a decline as a result of the fall in the volume of extraction of oil and natural gas.[60]

If Primakov's alarming assessment of the situation in the raw material sector reflects reality, then one might well surmise that this indeed provides the main motive for the attempts of the Russian leadership to participate in the exploitation of the raw material resources of Central Asia—above all, the oil and natural gas resources of Kazakhstan. And for Russia's ruling elite, this opportunity for further enrichment represents an irresistible temptation.

The integration-oriented projects of the CIS, adopted on the initiative of Moscow, are essentially subordinated to the interests of Russia. Such projects

Are Russia's Businessmen Better?

Expanding and intensifying the economic penetration in Central Asia, the leaders of Russian corporations are apparently convinced of their professional and intellectual superiority over their Central Asian counterparts and potential partners. But here they might fall victim to the old habit of condescension toward the people who reside in this region. The fact is that many representatives of the post-Soviet generation of big business in Central Asia are not a whit inferior to Russian managers—in terms of their IQ, their operational ability, their knowledge of financial and other aspects of the modern world economy, and their capacity to defend their interests. During the post-Soviet era they have learned a lot and accumulated experience in the course of their contacts with Western corporations. These people include, for example, the first wave of business leaders in Kazakhstan who have emerged to challenge President Nazarbaev and have formed the oppositionist movement called Democratic Choice of Kazakhstan. One such leader is Mukhtar Abliazov; a nuclear physicist by education (with a degree from the Moscow Institute of Nuclear Physics), he founded one of the first financial-industrial groups in Kazakhstan. Another example is the former governor of Pavlograd oblast, Galymzhan Zhakiianov, who graduated from Moscow's equivalent of MIT. And one could name many others, who received an education in excellent universities, and some of whom have even studied in elite business schools in the United States and Europe. I would suggest that they are not in the least inferior, either in intellectual ability or in business skills, to their Russian counterparts.

include the "Unified Economic Space" (*Edinoe ekonomicheskoe prostranstvo [EEP]*, involving Russia, Belarus, Kazakhstan, and Ukraine) and the "Eurasian Economic Community" (*Evraziiskoe ekonomicheskoe soobshchestvo, [EVRAZES]*, including Russia, Belarus, Kazakhstan, Kyrgyzstan, and Tajikistan). To be sure, these have a professed goal of ensuring "mutual economic cooperation." But Kazakhstan is of particular interest, given its rate of economic growth. The leaders of the Russian economy look with envy on the successes of business in Kazakhstan; they are eager to devour the better portions of the Kazakhstani pie left over after the sell-off to transnational (often offshore) corporations. Perhaps Sergei Khrushchev was right when he declared (in an interview with the newspaper *Isvestia*) that "to raise its own economy, Russia has to plunder somebody else."[61]

In short, one should not lose sight of the material impulse behind the expansionist ideas of Russian irredentism. The imperial project has become an integral part of the program for national revival; its propagandists have had some success in shaping public opinion. The idea that Russia should expand into the realm of the former Soviet Union, with the vision that Russia should be a "Eurasian" power, finds support among a significant (if not predominant) part of the population. The results of a public opinion survey of the population that was conducted by the All-Russian Center for the Study of Public Opinion (and published in October 2003) showed that "approximately three-quarters of the population of Russia is convinced that Russia is a Eurasian state with its own special historical path of development. The idea of a special path for Russia prevails, without exception, among all social strata."[62]

Here we are entering the realm of the irrational and emotional, perhaps what some would label the sphere of the "collective unconscious." Here one finds nostalgia for the Soviet Union, together with a sense of humiliation over the loss of national power and pride. One also sees a feeling of inferiority, which is accompanied by the upsurge of anti-Americanism and further compounded by the lack of any unifying and saving national idea (to provide a surrogate that the great-power chauvinists instill in the masses and that has fueled the desire of the Russian business elite for the assets of Russia's neighbors). The initiators of the Great National Project could not put their own house in order and now are claiming the right to do so in the houses of their neighbors. But how do these neighbors like the idea that their "elder brother" is coming back? How does the increasing competition between Moscow and Washington to establish control over Central Asia affect the policies of the states in this region?

Maneuvering Between Moscow and Washington

It is certainly no exaggeration to say that the leaders of the countries in Central Asia simply have no policy, that they utterly lack any system of strategic planning. Instead, all they have are impulsive, extemporaneous reactions to a constantly changing situation. The principal problem facing their foreign policy is this: to paraphrase a Russian proverb about an avaricious, but innocent girl, how are they to "get the money from Washington" without "losing their virginity" (in Moscow's eyes). In other words, how are they at the same time to be Washington's client and Moscow's loyal ally? Their position has become increasingly difficult as the confrontation between Moscow and Washington has intensified; the obvious strategy for the leaders of Central Asia has been to maneuver between the two gravitational poles. They demonstrate their loyalty to Washington by arguing that their regimes perform the function of a bulwark against the inroads of an Islamic onslaught, and that simultaneously they serve to contain Russia's expansionist ambitions. Consequently, they argue, material and military-political support for their regimes is in the interest of the United States itself. At the same time, the leaders of Central Asia make a respectful bow in the direction of Moscow, reassuring the Kremlin of their devotion and their readiness to participate in political and economic associations aimed at the integration of the post-Soviet space.

Take, for example, the statements by President Askar Akaev of Kyrgyzstan— a country that has survived exclusively thanks to the direct or indirect assistance of the United States. In an interview with *Izvestia* in November 2003, Akaev declared that "the Russian factor" represented the principal focus of his policy, and added that "Russia is turning into the locomotive for the economies of Central Asia." That is why, he argued, "without close cooperation [with Russia], Central Asia simply has no future," and he then warned that "a policy of driving Russia out of [this region], if such does exist in the United States, would be shortsighted and not take into account the existing realities."[63] However, during a visit to Washington, the Kyrgyz president sang an entirely different tune. Perhaps the best example of his policy of maneuvering was the decision to allow *both* the United States and Russia to establish military air bases on the territory of Kyrgyzstan.

This "weathervane policy" is also characteristic for the other leaders of Central Asia. For example, at the very end of 2003, President Nursultan Nazarbaev of Kazakhstan gave an interview in *Isvestia* that was permeated with panegyrics of Russia, lauded its "authority on the international arena," spoke sardonically of the West for "celebrating a victory in the Cold War," offered some disparaging remarks about NATO, voiced indignation over America's desire "to put Russia in its place," and so forth. Nazarbaev also expressed his devotion to Russia and Russian interests on the Eurasian continent and spoke critically of American policy in the region. But in March 2004, in an article in the *Washington Times* that bore an unmistakably ingratiating tone, Nazarbaev pronounced himself a client of America, called his country a "key ally of the United States in Central Asia," and glowed with pride over the fact that President George W. Bush and Secretary of Defense Donald Rumsfeld expressed praise for Kazakhstan.[64] In more practical terms, Kazakhstan demonstrated its loyalty to Washington by agreeing to support the Baku-Ceyhan oil pipeline and hence bypass Russia in the transportation of its oil exports.

Notwithstanding the official presidential visits and meetings (which include the inevitable professions of eternal friendship with Russia), the ruling circles in the Central Asian lands show (and periodically voice) growing concern and indignation over the imperial plans, tactlessness, and arrogance of high-ranking representatives of Moscow's political elite. Symptomatic in this regard was the statement by former Minister of Foreign Affairs Abdulaziz Kamilov of Uzbekistan (currently the Uzbek ambassador to Washington):

> It is not entirely clear to me, for example, why the head of the [Russian] border service made bold to judge whether there should be American military bases in Uzbekistan. . . . Apparently, this general forgot that ten years have already elapsed since independent states, with their own governments, came into existence in Central Asia. We understand perfectly well that Russia has, and will have, its own interests in Uzbekistan, as more generally in Central Asia. We understand all this and take it into account. But some people, by force of old habit, still think that it is necessary to make decisions for us.

Having put the representative of the highest Russian military hierarchy in his place, Kamilov proceeded to scold Dmitrii Rogozin, one of the leaders of the Russian national patriots. While still chairman of the Committee on International Affairs of the third Duma, Rogozin had declared that "Russia will make every effort to see that the Americans leave territories that are contiguous with Russia and never appear there again." In response, Kamilov pointed out that only America had defended Uzbekistan from an invasion by the Taliban, which "represented a real threat for us. . . . Therefore we made an absolutely conscious decision to cooperate with America in the struggle with this evil." He added that "Russia, incidentally, acted in the same way."[65]

One has to admit that the "multi-vector orientation" adopted by the leaders of Central Asia has been totally justified. At the present time, the most important thing for Washington is the opportunity extended by Central Asians to use their territories to base mobile military units in the war against terrorism. Important too is the sober recognition of the fact that the ruling regimes really ensure stability in the region. For that purpose, the pragmatists who determine American foreign policy are following the "Saudi model": they have been forced to reconcile themselves with the character of these regimes (which is unacceptable in terms of Western democracy) in the name of America's geostrategic interests. Moscow, for its part, is in no position to be competitive, but it is nonetheless seeking to compete with Washington for control over the regimes and to strengthen its influence in the political, economic, and military spheres. Moscow's activities to advance integration with the "near abroad" are, in general, quite costly: in particular, Moscow supplies the countries of Central Asia with military hardware which, while significantly inferior to its American counterpart, is made available at preferential prices (indeed, for all practical purposes, virtually gratis). But Washington also is supplying Central Asian regimes with arms. Moreover, military colleges and officers' schools in the capitals of both countries are providing training and education to Kazakhs, Kyrgyz, and Uzbeks. As the Russian proverb has it, "an affectionate calf nurses from two mothers."

Russia Is in No Position to Be the "Security Manager" of Central Asia

Thus the Russian-American competition in Central Asia goes on. Igor' Ivanov (formerly minister of foreign affairs and currently secretary of the Kremlin's Security Council) has declared that the principal goal of Russian foreign policy in 2004 was "the strengthening of integration processes in the CIS." Moreover, Moscow apparently is seeking to adapt Kazakhstan, economically and politically, to suit its own interests. However, the question is how Moscow hopes to keep the upper hand over Washington. All the actions taken by Moscow to promote integration, including the numerous associations of members of the CIS under the aegis of Russia, exist only on paper and do little more than feed an army of officials in the capitals of the post-Soviet countries. According to one Moscow expert, who can hardly be suspected of a pro-American bias, "Russian diplomacy is not 'making events' but merely reacting to them. The Russian Ministry of Foreign Affairs, like the Russian army, remains an archaic structure of bygone days and is incapable of managing political processes not only in distant areas, but even in the near abroad."[66]

The neoimperial project—the attempt to re-establish Moscow's control over Central Asia (as well as over the Caucasus)—is doomed to failure: Russia simply lacks the economic and military-political wherewithal to realize this grand design. Neither Russia on its own, nor the Shanghai Cooperation Organization, nor the Treaty on Collective Security (between Russia and the Central Asian countries) can mount serious opposition to an assault on the region by aggressive Islamic radicalism. It is hardly likely that the realists (who are still present in the Kremlin leadership and in the military-political apparatus) have any illusions about all this. Only the United States and NATO can create an effective system of security and support stability in this region. Of course, it is easier to do this by cooperating with Russia. However, given the interests of Russia (if, to be sure, one makes a sober assessment of its interests and the real potential for realizing them—i.e., in the sense of Realpolitik), then the optimal policy for Moscow would be a partnership, not brash claims for military dominance in the region. It would, however, be wrong to think that an absolute majority of the Russian political elite is widely enamored with the neoimperial project. On the contrary, there are realists in Moscow too: "In assessing the more than two years of American military presence in Central Asia, many experts think that the situation has undergone so much change that, without the United States, Russia can no longer provide security for the region. In addition, despite all the traditional ties, it is more complicated for Moscow to reinforce its presence than, in the period since 11 September, is the case for the United States."[67]

I do not in the least wish to idealize American policy toward Russia and, on the contrary, find it sorely deficient in flexibility and coherence. But its Central Asian orientation appears to have justified itself completely and also to correspond to the interests of Russia and of all the countries at war with Islamic radicalism. America is interested in Russia as a partner to help stabilize the situation in Central Asia. Russia, however, finds such a role unacceptable. It seeks to establish hegemony over the Eurasian continent, notwithstanding the fact that it lacks the requisite economic and military capability. Only the United States possesses this capacity. And America has no need for Eurasian territories. Even with regard to the oil and natural gas resources, which are reputed to be impressive in magnitude, America has a limited interest: there are many other sources, no less promising in their potential and much less expensive and problematic in terms of delivery to market. Strategically, however, this region is very important to America because of its proximity to Afghanistan and the Middle East, where the situation is sure to remain unstable for a long time and to require the military and economic involvement of the United States (and indeed the countries of the European Union and NATO). Were the United States to end its presence in the region, that would hardly be a source of joy in Moscow; it would only unleash a mass of problems that Russia, on its own, is in no position to solve.

Notes

1. *Obshchaia gazeta*, 24–30 January 2002.

2. See, for example, the first-class study by Igor' Kliamkin and Lev Timofeev, *Tenevaia Rossiia* (Moscow, 2000).

3. See the report of 9 October 2002 at www.eurasia.org.ru.

4. A. Esentugelov, "Dualism in the Development of the Economy of Kazakhstan," in *Central Asia and South Caucasus Affairs: 2003* (Almaty, 2003).

5. Seymour Lipset and Gabriel Lenz, "Corruption, Culture, and Markets," in *Culture Matters*, ed. Lawrence Harrison and Samuel Huntington (New York, 2000), p. 115.

6. Quoted in an interview of 4 May 2004 in *Russkii fokus*, www.russianfokus.ru.

7. The Western press was filled with publications about the enormous sums of money that were held by members of the Nazarbaev family and his cronies in ac-

counts at foreign banks. These revelations were followed by an official explanation for the billion-dollar account, allegedly a stabilization fund, which was under the personal and exclusive control of President Nazarbaev. All this provoked a storm of indignation in opposition-minded circles in Kazakhstan. However, after these acknowledgments that so amazed people, there were no parliamentary hearings, prosecutorial investigations, or even protest actions from the opposition. Everything remained as it had before.

8. See Paul Krugman, "Does Third World Growth Hurt First World Prosperity?" *Harvard Business Review*, 72 (1994): 113–21.

9. See Jeffrey Sachs and Andrew Warner, "Natural Resource Abundance and Economic Growth" (National Bureau of Economic Research, Cambridge, Mass., Working Paper 5398); and Michael Fairbanks, "Changing the Mind of a Nation," in *Culture Matters*, ed. Harrison and Huntington, p. 274.

10. S. Zhusupov and B. Khusainov, "Opredelenie orientirov," *Ekspert Kazakhstan*, no. 1 (2004).

11. G. Mataev, "K voprosu o poliarizatsii naseleniia v Kazakhstane," *Kazakhtan-Spektr*, no. 1 (2001): 50–51.

12. *Kontinent* (Almaty), 26 August 2003, p. 47.

13. K. Ezhenova, "Obychnaia istoriia," *Exclusive* (Almaty), no. 5 (2003): 13.

14. According to press reports, there have been recent investments to expand the capacity of the oil refineries and to enable more extensive processing of oil products for export. According to the Moscow newspaper *Kommersant*, "the oil-producing countries of Central Asia are carrying out a large-scale modernization of the oil-processing branches, endeavoring thereby to bolster their position in markets. In October 2003, Uzbekistan began a technological upgrade of the Fergana oil-refining plant. The modernization and reconstruction of refineries in Turkmenistan and Kazakhstan are also moving at rapid rates." S. Gavrichev, "Kaspiiskii priliv," *Kommersant*, no. 203 (5 November 2003), supplement.

15. "The End of the Oil Age," *Economist*, 25 October 2003, p. 11.

16. A. Zuev and L. Miasnikova, "Sostoitsia li kapitalisticheskaia revoliutsiia?" *Svobodnaia mysl'*, no. 7 (2002): 46.

17. Eugene Rumer, "Central Asian Leadership Succession: When, Not If," *Strategic Forum* (National Defense University, no. 203 [Washington DC, December 2003]).

18. G. Sysoev, "Prezidenty aziatskoi chasti SNG," *Kommersant-Vlast'*, 25 May 2004.

19. V. Portnikov, "Prezident—eto nadolgo," *Zhurnal*, no. 21 (2003): 11.

20. See www.gazeta.ru/2004/01/31/.

21. For a fuller explication, see chapter 6, "The Regime in Kazakhstan," by Dmitrii Furman in this volume.

22. *AKIpress* (Bishkek), nos. 13–14 (2002).

23. "Uzbekistan Economy, Analytical Review," *USAID-Euro Aid*, no. 4 (2004): 38, 46, 56, 74.

24. V.O. Kliuchevskii, *Ocherki i rechi. Vtoroi sbornik statei* (Petrograd, 1918), p.18.

25. *The Wall Street Journal*, 30 July 2003.

26. Farid Zakaria, *The Future of Freedom: Illiberal Democracy at Home and Abroad* (New York, 2003).

27. Joseph Schumpeter, *Capitalism, Socialism, and Democracy* (New York: Harper Perennial, 1975), p. 121.

28. See Leonid Blekher and Georgii Liubarskii, *Glavnyi russkii vopros* (Moscow, 2003) p. 306.

29. Eugene Rumer, "Collision Avoidance: U.S.-Russian Bilateral Relations and Former Soviet States," *Strategic Forum* (National Defense University, no. 207 [April 2004]), p. 2.

30. See chapter 11, "Economic Ties Between Russia and Kazakhstan: Dynamics, Tendencies, and Prospects," by Stanislav Zhukov and Oksana Reznikova in this volume.

31. John L. Gaddis, *Surprise, Security, and the American Experience* (Cambridge, MA., 2004), pp. 15, 38, 42, 59.

32. "U.S. Solidifies Its Kyrgyzstan Mission," *San Diego Union-Tribune*, 8 June 2004.

33. For the interview with Vershbow, see: "Missiia Rossii v mirovom soobshchestve," United Press International (UPI), 13 April 2004.

34. Kolin Pauell [Colin Powell], "Partnerskie otnosheniia: rabota prodolzhaetsia," *Izvestiia*, 26 January 2004 (www.izvestia.ru/world/article43464).

35. *Izvestiia*, 1 April 2004 (www.izvestia.ru/).

36. See the issue of 31 December 2003 in www.rodina-nps.ru.

37. O. Khrabryi, "Pokhishchenie Evrazii," *Ekspert*, no. 1 (2004); and S. Belkovskii, "Inogda tsivilizatsii gibnut," *Zavtra*, 23 December 2003.

38. E. Kholmogorov, "Imperializm liberal'nyi i natsional'nyi," *Russkii zhurnal*, 13 October 2003.

39. A. Solzhenitsyn, "Kak nam obustroit' Rossiiu," *Russkaia mysl'*, supplement no. 3846 (21 September 1990), pp. 5–6.

40. A. Chubais, "Missiia Rossii v XXI veke," *Nezavisimaia gazeta*, 1 October 2003.

41. Ibid.

42. "Postkolonial'naia matritsa," *Ekspert*, no. 1 (13 June 2004).

43. A. Gordienko, "Chubais privatiziruet Armeniiu," *Nezavisimaia gazeta*, 22 October 2003; and I. Zaslavskii, "Chto kirgizu khorosho," *Gazeta*, 20 February 2002 (www.gazeta.ru).

44. Interview of A. Kokoshin, 8 January 2002, on the radio station "Ekho Moskvy."

45. Quoted in V. Sokirko, "Sredniaia Aziia: igry patriotov," *Rossiia i Musul'manskii mir*, no. 4 (2002): 59–60.

46. S. Babaeva, "Oni uzhe nikogda ne uidut ottuda," *Izvestiia*, 26 January 2004.

47. M. Leont'ev, "Soiuz mecha i orala," *Izvestiia*, 26 February 2004.

48. "Posmertnye bumagi M.D. Skobeleva. Turkestan i angliiskaia Indiia (1876)," *Istoricheskii vestnik*, 1882, no. 11 (as quoted in D. Zamyatin, "Modelirovanie geopoliticheskikh situatsii," *POLIS*, no. 2 (1998): 70.

49. V. Vinogradov, "Kantsler A.M. Gorchakov," *Novaia i noveishaia istoriia*, no. 3 (2003): 133.

50. L. Radzikhovskii, "Osnovnoi imperskii instinkt," *Izvestiia*, 13 October 2003.

51. S. Belkovskii, "Inogda tsivilizatsii gibnut," *Zavtra*, 23 December 2003.

52. Ia. Shimov, "Rossiia kak neobkhodimost'," *Svobodnaia mysl'*, p. 69.

53. "Belka v kolese," *Zavtra*, 25 February 2004.

54. G. Bovt and G. Il'ichev, "V chem narod raskhoditsia s prezidentom," *Izvestiia* 19 March 2004.

55. L.N. Tolstoi, *Voina i mir*, vol. 7 (Moscow, 1951), p. 119.

56. I. Samakhova, "Vse slyshnee rokochut barabany voiny," *Russkii zhurnal*, 11 March 2004 (www.russ.ru/20040311 3/11/04/).

57. Interview with A. Chubais in Izvestia , 3 December 2003.

58. "Nuzhno ne kazat'sia, a byt' velikoi derzhavoi," *Nezavisimaia gazeta*, 26 December 2003.

59. D. Trenin, "Rossiia vkhodit v 'novyi izoliatsionizm,'" *Nezavisimaia gazeta*, 7 December 2003.

60. "Vystuplenie E. Primakova na zasedanii 'Merkurii-kluba,'" *Novosti torgovo-promyshlennoi palaty RF.* For this and other information about the Russian Chamber of Commerce and Industry, see the Web site at www.tpprf.ru.

61. Quoted in E. Kholmogorov, "Imperializm liberal'nyi i natsional'nyi" (published 13 October 2003 on the Web site at *Russkii zhurnal/:* www.russ.ru).

62. See www.kreml.org/state/355113664.10/19/03.

63. "Interv'iu A. Akaeva," *Izvestiia*, 26 November 2003/.

64. "Interv'iu N. Nazarbaeva," *Izvestiia*, 29 December 2003; and N. Nazarbaev, "Progress in Kazakhstan," *Washington Times*, 4 March 2004.

65. M.P. Voshchanov, "Chem grozit Rossii usilenie voenno-politicheskogo vliianiia SShA v Srednei Azii?" *Tribuna*, 6 February 2002.

66. O. Khrabryi, "Pokhishchenie Evrazii."

67. S. Babaeva, "Oni uzhe nikogda ne uidut ottuda."

Part II

The External Context

2

Russia and Central Asia: Problems of Security

Irina Zviagel'skaia

The policy of Russia in Central Asia, including the Caspian region, has long been the subject of investigation in the leading scholarly centers. There have been detailed studies and analyses of the problem of security, Russia's economic and political interests, and its relations with individual states in the region and with external actors. Given the dynamic development of events here, one can hardly say that the subject has been exhausted. Russian-American relations—which have been subject to constant fluctuations (in part, due to American policy within the spheres of traditional Russian interests), new challenges, and asymmetrical responses—could not fail to have an impact on Russia's approach toward this region and toward the structure of international relations in Central Asia. The present study seeks to show the factors that determine the dynamics of Russian politics in the region, Moscow's perception of the American presence, the mounting distrust, and the unilateral actions. This chapter does not attempt to examine all aspects of Russian cooperation with the states of Central Asia, the activity of regional multilateral organizations, and the realization of bilateral agreements. Rather, the principal goal here is to determine the role of the Russian vector in configuring the structure of international relations in this region.

An Unanswered Question

As a geographic region, Central Asia represents an enormous territory, one that extends to include Mongolia, Xinjiang, and Afghanistan. As a political region, however, it encompasses a far smaller territory—namely, the five former Soviet republics that achieved independence in 1991. Suffice it to say that the term "Central Asia" in this particular sense has appeared relatively recently, replacing the early category of "Central Asia and Kazakhstan." The latter term set Kazakhstan apart from the other states on the basis of the special features of its history and culture, ethnic composition, geographic position with respect to Russia, and so forth. In the judgment of many ethnographers, Central Asia is in fact divided into two, quite distinct parts, but the situation is actually considerably more complicated. G. Iu. Sitnianskii, for example, asserts: "On the one hand, the rather large part of southwestern Kazakhstan (Kzyl-Ordin and Chimkent oblasts) is the size of any of the Central Asian states, but is historically drawn more toward Uzbekistan. On the other hand, at least the northern part of Kirgizia (in terms of its geographic, geopolitical, ethnocultural, and other parameters) inclines more toward Kazakhstan than Central Asia. Therefore, in dividing up the region of Central Asia, it is necessary to distinguish two separate parts: the Eurasian Kazakh-Kyrgyz steppe and the sedentary Muslim Central Asian part."[1]

Nomads are more mobile, easily blend into the landscape (in a cultural sense as well), and have little difficulty accepting external influence and adapting it to their own way of life. Historically, Kazakhstan and Kyrgyzstan have been drawn toward Russia more than the other states of the region; to be sure, that did not prevent a diversification of their external ties and the development of nationalist attitudes and movements during the first stages of independent development (which were hostile toward the Russian state and even to individual ethnic Russians). The southern part of Central Asia was separate from Russia geographically and culturally. At the same time, this zone posed the main risk; it was here, following the breakup of the Soviet Union, that Russia maintained a serious military presence (the 201st motorized infantry division and border troops stationed in Tajikistan).

The policy of Russia in Central Asia, which was formed under the influence of various factors (which were different in terms of content and relative weight), reflects the fact that this region does not represent a single ethnocultural and geopolitical unit. Even at the beginning of the 1990s, when the Russian leadership in effect followed a policy of isolationism toward the states of the region and hurriedly reduced its presence and commitments, it still regarded Kazakhstan as an important partner and, along with Ukraine and Belarus, the nucleus for possible unification. At the present time, Kazakhstan posits itself as a Eurasian state. In the words of Dariga Nazarbaeva (daughter of the president of Kazakhstan and the chairman of the Supervisory Council of the International Institute for Modern Politics in Almaty): "Kazakhstan borders on Central Asia, but it is not a Central Asian country. We are a Eurasian state, where the influence of Europe and Western values in general are exceptionally strong. We are not another '-stan' in the sense [that term is used by] some politicians and journalists. Our historical points of orientation include not Saudi Arabia, but Norway, and countries like South Korea and Singapore."[2]

Despite these internal differences in Central Asia, Russia nonetheless has some general interests in the region as a whole. In particular, under no circumstances can Russia tolerate the following:

- the creation of alliances that would be directed against Russia itself;
- the development of powerful movements that would be capable of destabilizing the situation in the region;
- the transformation of Central Asia into an arena for the production and transportation of narcotics;
- contraband in arms and weapons.

It would be extremely dangerous for Russia if conflicts were to develop in this area that were capable of extending beyond the local framework. In the words of A. Arbatov, "the surrounding post-Soviet space represents too great a value and too great a danger for Russia for it to be indifferent to the events transpiring there. . . . One of the most important national priorities of Russia, given the historically unique form that the dissolution of the empire took, is to preserve enough Russian influence over this enormous zone to secure Russian interests there and to neutralize (or at least keep under control) the threats emanating from there. . . . The zone of instability, the power vacuum, the law and order could be filled by the economic, political, and military influence of other powers and alliances from the 'far abroad,' which by no means is necessarily friendly toward Russia or even neutral with respect to its interests. Russia would then be deprived of important communications and links to natural resources as well as to industrial and military installations."[3]

It may be that the extremely one-sided representation of Central Asia as a zone of instability (which is current in Russia), as well as the discord among state agencies in adopting and implementing decisions (which is characteristic of the Russian regime), have caused Moscow to lack a coherent strategy toward the region—that is, a strategy which envelops the full complex of military, economic, political, and humanitarian spheres. In fact, in the course of the decade that followed the breakup of the USSR, there really was no intelligible answer to the question, "Why does Russia need Central Asia?" The Russian withdrawal from Central Asia continued even while its relations with various Central Asian states continued, at different levels of intensity, to develop.

From the beginning of the 1990s, many observers alluded to a resumption of the "Great Game" in the region. To quote two Russian analysts, I. S. Zonn and S. S. Zhil'tsov:

> It is possible that today we are witnesses of how the foundations of new tendencies are being laid for regional development, which allows one to speak of a beginning of "Great Game-II." The difference consists not only in the number of "players," which has increased significantly, but also in the expenditure of funds, which now runs into hundreds of millions of dollars.[4]

That judgment, however, does not seem very cogent. Modern international relations, in many parameters, are qualitatively different from those of the nineteenth century. The issue is not only the number of players, but also the appearance of fundamentally new ones (transnational corporations, international organizations, nongovernmental organizations), which all make use of entirely different sets of tools. The cooperation of traditional state actors, in addition, represents a much more complicated picture than the old confrontation between Russia and Great Britain. It is also necessary to take into account the active role played by the Central Asian states themselves, which are not objects but active subjects in international relations. Finally, the framework of today's international game (if one may call it that) is different, for it encompasses the political region of Central Asia and the Caspian basin.

In the 1990s a highly chaotic process was under way whereby external forces (which have various potentials and resources at their disposal) sought to gain advantage from penetrating an area of the world that had previously been closed to them. The states located in Central Asia faced the question of choosing a path of development, and in the period of transformation they were open to all sorts of political and ideological winds. Ethnic and confessional components, history, and tradition contributed to the active efforts of Turkey and Iran to penetrate Central Asia, as well as to the steps taken by Saudi Arabia and Pakistan to have an influence on religious life and political processes in the region. In addition, Pakistan exhibited a strong interest in establishing control over the transportation links. A traditional interest in this region, along with questions of security and ethnicity, impelled China to strengthen its own position, while simultaneously Western states intended to implant their own liberal values here.

The local regimes found themselves in a quite complicated situation. Their original orientation toward neighboring states, which was cemented by ethnic affinities, fully justified itself, but it could not always correspond to the demands of modern development. That reflected both a search for national identity as well as the very interest in finding new partners who would be more experienced in world politics (Turkey even being a member of NATO). In short, the states of Central Asia swiftly and easily opened the door to the wide world of international contacts. At the same time, modernization directly linked the countries of Central Asia with the development of relations with Western states, with an influx of investment, and with access to modern technologies. In this sense the closest neighbors, despite all the importance of the development of bilateral relations with them, nevertheless occupied a marginal place and, at times, played a destructive role. Even Turkey could not offer capital investment or a system of education that would meet the expectations of the local elite—the diplomas earned from these Turkish schools could not guarantee prestigious jobs abroad. At the same time, Saudi Arabia and Pakistan were generously financing the construction of mosques and the dissemination of religious literature, but that brought radical ideas which were incompatible with local Islam and posed a threat to the secular regimes.

In this political environment, the decline in Russia's influence evoked differing assessments within the states of Central Asia. For example, in the case of Tajikistan, which had experienced the turmoil of civil war, and which had overcome its military-political crisis with Russia's assistance, the Russian withdrawal was barely noticeable. Kazakhstan, because of the special character of its geopolitical location and its ethnic situation (i.e., the presence of a large population of ethnic Russians), preserved high-priority relations with Moscow. Kyrgyzstan endeavored to pursue a balanced policy: it was regarded in the West as "a story of democratic success" (which ensured an influx of assistance), but was always careful to retain a clear Russian vector in its foreign policy. Uzbekistan increasingly distanced itself politically from Yeltsin and Russia, while Turkmenistan, having declared its neutrality, constantly kept its distance (with the exception of questions concerning the shipment of natural gas). Sovereignty became a goal in itself that demolished old regional ties and undermined opportunities to create new, operational multilateral structures. Russia did not exhibit a desire to play a leading role in this process and could not support it economically. Compared with the international tendencies that are characteristic of the modern world, the transitional post-Soviet period was marked by regression, a step backward.

Despite the various schemes for bilateral and multilateral cooperation, and despite the declarations about integration and mutual contacts, the sphere of Russian influence steadily contracted, not so much because of deliberate actions by Moscow (as was the case immediately after the breakup of the USSR) as because of the absence of attempts on its part to strengthen or at least preserve this influence—even in so important a sphere like security. The Treaty on Collective Security, signed in Tashkent in 1992, proved to be far from satisfactory for its member states. From the very outset, this structure had serious limitations, since the creation of the treaty did not so much seek to take into account the fundamentally new situation in the security sphere (by providing for a range of measures to oppose challenges and threats) as to aim at averting the complete collapse of the security system in post-Soviet space. As a result, the experience of integration in the military sphere proved a failure. First, the treaty included member states that were locked in conflict with each other. Second, given the different hierarchy of threats for individual state members of the agreement, there was also a difference in the level of their interest in a single mechanism to provide security. Third, the efforts of each to reinforce its own sovereignty ran contrary to the goal of coordination in the military sphere, and consequently impeded the subordination of national security policy to supranational structures.

By the second half of the 1990s, the value of the Treaty on Collective Security was being increasingly called into question, and in 1999 Uzbekistan refused to reconfirm its membership in the treaty. The reasons for this lay not only in the fact that Uzbekistan, which represented a powerful state in Central Asia and laid claims to leadership in this region, did not express a desire to preserve such a model of military-political relations with Russia that relegated Tashkent to the status of a junior partner. Much more important was the fact that the regime of Islam Karimov had encountered a threat to its very existence (coming from Islamic radicals), and it had no reason to think that it could count on Russian assistance against this threat. The Russian army, mired in the long and bloody Chechen campaign, does not appear in Uzbekistan's eyes as a force that would have the capability of bringing security to Central Asia, since it has obviously been unable to solve this security problem within its own borders. Moreover, the attacks launched by guerrilla fighters of the Islamic Movement of Uzbekistan (in Kyrgyzstan and Uzbekistan in the fall of 1999; and in Uzbekistan in 2000) further demonstrated to Karimov that his Central Asian neighbors also lacked the power to conduct a policy that could keep the extremists at bay. The Kyrgyz army was in complete disarray, while in Tajikistan the authorities had not established full control over the country. According to the available information, the insurgents of the Islamic Movement of Uzbekistan found opportunities to establish bases on the territory of Tajikistan. They were supported by the same field commanders who made up the backbone of the radical Tajik opposition and who had not been integrated into the structures of Tajikistan after the conclusion of a peace agreement in 1997. These commanders had been comrades in arms of militant Islamic leaders Juma Namangani and Karim Iuldashev during the civil war; and they now provided sanctuary in areas of the country that were difficult to reach. The antiterrorist center, established within the framework of the Treaty on Collective Security (with its headquarters in Bishkek), was not regarded by Uzbekistan as capable of guaranteeing effective resistance to the armed Islamists. Consequently, Tashkent sought other, more reliable opportunities to uphold the existing regime and the territorial integrity of the state in the face of Fergana separatism (which was being exploited by the Islamic Movement of Uzbekistan), the growth of social tensions, and the ever-growing doubts about the loyalty of individual representatives of the elite. In this sense, the participation of Uzbekistan in the bloc "GUUAM" (which included Georgia, Ukraine, Uzbekistan, Azerbaijan, and Moldova) was an interim measure, a temporary solution and perhaps also a signal to the United States, but it did not really constitute a real alternative. That alternative was to become the establishment of an American military base at Khanabad, which not only emphasized Uzbekistan as the leading state in the region, but also bolstered internal political tranquility: Who would dare, under such conditions, to pose a new challenge to President Karimov? However, this last thesis is highly controversial and debatable, for Washington's struggle for democracy could lead it to demand unexpected sacrifices from the regime in Tashkent.

Uzbekistan was not the only state in Central Asia concerned about its security: the problem was no less acute for Kyrgyzstan. The latter, however, did not have the option of resigning from the regional military-political structures that were operating under the aegis of Moscow. That became especially true as the West grew increasingly dissatisfied with the specific characteristics of the democracy being practiced in Kyrgyzstan. As for Tajikistan, the presence of the 201st division and Russian border troops in that country constituted a guarantee of the stability of the regime, restrained the manifestations of extremism inside the country, and provided a protective shield along its problematic border with Afghanistan.

A significant event was the formation of the Shanghai Cooperation Organization (SCO) in 2001. Within the framework of this organization, the Russian Federation—for the first time—shared responsibility for security in the region with a powerful outside player, China. In January 2002, at a meeting of the foreign members of the SCO in Beijing, the member states agreed on measures to improve the group's antiterrorism and security capabilities. The lack of a security component to SCO had caused it to fade from view in the immediate aftermath of the 11 September attacks and the subsequent U.S.-led antiterrorism campaign in Afghanistan. The SCO foreign ministers eventually announced that they would begin work on the formation of a regional antiterrorism organization and a coordinated emergency response mechanism. Such moves would enable the SCO to intervene rapidly in a Central

Asian crisis. Foreign Minister Igor´ Ivanov of Russia suggested that the SCO assume responsibility for guaranteeing regional security.[5] All the organizational questions were not finally resolved until the end of May 2003, when the SCO confirmed the structure of the organization, one in which its military-political thrust became increasingly evident.[6] Hence, the SCO was founded not so much for purposes of economic cooperation as for the struggle against terrorism and separatism, which posed a threat both to the local regimes and to the two outside powers.

Although Russia's position had weakened, it nonetheless continued to play a salient role in Central Asia, but within the framework of an increasingly pluralistic regional system of international relations. This picture was, in general, characteristic of Russia's place and role throughout the Commonwealth of Independent States (CIS). By all measures a leader and creator of the CIS, Russia did not have complete freedom of action. Instead, it was subject to the influence of others, not only the other members of the Commonwealth, but also other international players, who had come to act in a rather unfettered way within the space of the CIS. The CIS, individual states, and regions within the Commonwealth are becoming increasingly autonomous, are differentiating their own foreign policy ties, and even are preserving a certain dependence on the Russian Federation.

Forward to Bipolarity?

The formation of a regional system of international relations in Central Asia attests to the high level of political inertia that is characteristic of this region.

This inertia was manifested in the stability of elites who represented the Soviet nomenklatura. Until now power in Central Asia has remained in the hands of the former first secretaries of the Central Committee of the Communist Party of the Soviet Union; there are two exceptions—Tajikistan (where, in the course of the civil war, there was a change of elites) and Kyrgyzstan. Moreover, whereas in the Caucasus a period of rule by nationalist leaders (Abulfaz Elchibey in Azerbaijan and Zviad Gamsakhurdia in Georgia) preceded the return of the old cadres (Gaidar Aliev and Eduard Shevardnadze, respectively), Central Asia did not have national movements that were fighting for independence from which could come a new pool of leaders. Organized opposition existed only in Tajikistan, but even that pursued less ambitious goals—namely, exclusion of the Leninabad elite from power and the reallocation of power in favor of regions that earlier have had no control over key posts and resources. Accordingly, if recent history and national traditions are taken into account, the countries of Central Asia—following the majority of post-Soviet states—could only offer rather harsh authoritarian regimes. To be sure, the spectrum was significantly broader than in the European part of the former USSR—ranging from a "managed democracy" (a term employed by President Nazarbaev of Kazakhstan)[7] on one end to a feudal despotism on the other.

After Central Asia ceased to be closed to the outside world (as it had been when it was part of the unitary Soviet state), its territory became the arena of activity by various players, and the balance of power that rather quickly emerged would be preserved over the course of a decade. Serious changes occurred in 2001 in connection with the formation of an antiterrorist coalition and the intervention of the United States in the region. The attitude of the Russian elite toward the prospect of an American presence was far from uniform. But the majority in parliament, in the military and political community, in the press, and in the academic world took a wait-and-see or negative position. Critics pointed out that:

- the advance of the United States toward Russian borders bore a deliberate character;
- the United States has adopted a strategy of encircling Russia with military bases and establishing military alliances with its immediate neighbors;
- the necessity of an American presence in Central Asia, where it had previously never been and could not be, is highly dubious; and
- the Americans will never leave this region.

Significantly, this new geopolitical situation compelled even those who had been most consistent in advocating a withdrawal from Central Asia to look on the region in a new way. The appearance of Americans, who changed the regional order, also bore an important demonstrative dimension, which finally impelled the Russian leadership to respond and to answer a question that had been left hanging in midair for so long: "Why does Russia need Central Asia?" In general, the Russian political establishment is divided into two camps: forces that call themselves national patriots and forces favorably disposed toward the development of cooperation with the West (above all, the United States). The decision of President Vladimir Putin to take an active role in the efforts of the international antiterrorist coalition (but without committing the country to direct military action) provided an opportunity to demonstrate once again that Russia's policy of seeking integration and cooperation with the West was irrevocable. The president of the Russian Federation and those who supported him in the ruling elite therefore made a strategic choice, as they sought to take advantage of a "window of opportunity" that had now opened. In supporting the actions of the United States and in choosing a policy aimed at the development of military-political and economic relations with the West, Russia acted on the basis of pragmatic considerations. On the one hand, Russian authorities had finally transcended the post-Soviet super-power syndrome; for the first time in its relations with the United States, the Russian leadership acknowledged that it could not count on a partnership of equals. The United States has utilized the new circumstances to assert its leading role in the world; it was essential that Russia finally come to terms with this reality. Given this conclusion, it would only be counterproductive to continue seeking a return to the "zero-sum game" and to transpose its dissatisfaction with American diplomacy (which seemed so pushy and intrusive) into regional competition. On the other hand, Putin's policy differed from the naive Westernization of his predecessor. The decision to cooperate with the West was combined with a determination to restore Russia's position in its traditional spheres of influence.

The actions of the antiterrorist coalition in Afghanistan corresponded completely with Russia's interests. The threats from the Taliban regime, along with the presence of terrorist bases on Afghan territory (where both the Chechen terrorists and the guerillas of the Islamic Movement of Uzbekistan were being trained), were clearly fraught with negative consequences for Russia. The key issue of course was the situation in Chechnia, but Moscow also was concerned about the incursions that insurgents had made into Uzbekistan and Kyrgyzstan. The Russian leadership noted that, after the defeat of the Taliban in Afghanistan and the appearance of the Americans, the general situation in the region stabilized. The threat to local regimes from radical Islamic organizations within the region decreased, and additional channels for obtaining assistance had become available to the region.

After the war in Afghanistan, the system of international relations in Central Asia reflected more signs of cooperation (often involuntary) than growing competition between Russia and the United States. The situation began to change, however, when it became clear that the United States had no plan to withdraw from Central Asia and when the self-assertive style of Washington began to threaten to relegate Russia to an increasingly marginal role (at both global and regional levels). Some specialists hold that the principle of unilateralism in the actions of the United States has contributed to the competition of the great powers in Central Asia.

Central Asia is now experiencing a parody of bipolarity. Russia's role in the region is not sufficiently large that it can be considered a powerful magnetic pole of attraction, while the function of the United States as the second pole is in a process of formation. Nevertheless, in terms of the level of their influence on the situation, both powers surpass China, a major player, and have imposed a corresponding configuration to the regional structure of international relations. One can say that the appearance of U.S. and Russian military bases in close proximity to each other around the city of Kant in Kyrgyzstan reminds one of the recent past. The Russian base, which opened in October 2003, is only 30 kilometers from Manas Airport, where the multinational forces have based their military aviation.

A bipolar structure in international relations, as is well known, continued to exist until the beginning of the 1990s, but then gave way to a world where one "complex leader"—the United States—survived. By no means were the people in Russia readily able to accept, politically and psychologically, this new reality. For some time, at the official level people continued to talk about a multipolar world. In the opinion of the Russian scholar A. D. Bogaturov, it is appropriate to suggest an intensification of tendencies that serve to expand the potential of other world centers. "It is in this sense that one should understand the official statements of the leading figures of the Russian Federation with respect to the movement of the modern world in the direction of a genuine multipolarity, which will leave no room for the hegemony of any one power. But, for the present, it is necessary to confirm something else: the international structure in the form that has emerged by the middle of the first decade of the twenty-first century is the structure of a pluralistic, but unipolar world."[8]

One scholar has put it this way: the United States "holds a position of power unequaled by any other country by virtue of its economic and technological potential, its military might and the associated political ability to shape the international security system. This made it difficult for it to withstand the temptation to conduct security policy on a hegemonic basis, often called a 'unipolar world' policy."[9] The conception of "the expansion of democracy," which was adopted in the United States, proposes to turn the post-communist space into a strategic reserve. By relying on this, the United States—with good reason—could count on preserving the position that it had acquired after the breakup of the USSR. Central Asia was naturally included in the task of realizing this conception. In 1997, the United States officially declared that the Caspian region was within the zone of its strategic interests. The practical activities of the United States created the impression that these interests were subordinate to the broader geopolitical goals of the United States and bore a secondary character with respect to these. Elements of competition with Moscow, to a greater or lesser degree, were to be seen in all spheres of U.S. policy.

The central thrust of that policy in the Caspian region was the formation of a new network of pipelines and commercial transportation links between the East and West: the Transport-Corridor-Europe-Caucasus-Central Asia or TRACECA. The Americans made no secret of the fact that one of the main reasons for proclaiming such a strategy was the U.S. effort to isolate Iran, but the new configuration of pipelines and transportation dealt a blow to the economic interests not only of Iran, but also of Russia. First, these pipelines (Baku-Ceyhan and the Trans-Caspian) would circumvent not only Iran but also Russia; it is across the territory of the latter that, at present, the majority of Caspian energy is brought to Russian and European markets. Second, Russia is one of the key participants in the North-South corridor and highly interested in the development of this corridor and in bilateral cooperation with Iran.

Moreover, realistic appraisals of the cost of extracting and transporting energy resources from the Caspian raise some doubts as to their significance from the perspective of the energy security of the United States. The commercial attractiveness of the new pipelines, in addition, is more than dubious. Noteworthy too was the decision of the American government to give the National Security Council and the U.S. Department of State (and not the Department of Commerce and the Department of Energy) the function of overseeing the Caspian energy projects. Taken together, all this could not fail to create the impression in Moscow that the slogans about combating monopolies and diversifying the routes for the delivery of energy and transportation served only as a cover for a policy that was actually directed at the economic exclusion of Russia from the region and at blocking cooperation between Moscow and Teheran.

Security and military cooperation has also become a high priority thrust in the relations of the United States with the countries of Central Asia, but that is precisely a sphere that Russia had regarded as most important and promising for itself. The United States has actively begun to involve the countries of the region in the NATO program of "Partnership for Peace" by providing assistance in the training of military personnel and by financing joint exercises. As a result, within the framework of this program, units of the armed forces of the United States and other NATO countries, for the first time, have appeared in close proximity to the southern borders of Russia. It bears noting too that all this has transpired against a background of the expansion of NATO to the east. As American specialists have admitted, the fact that contacts between the United States and countries of the region have developed more quickly with the Pentagon than with the State Department has inevitably evoked predictable concern in Moscow.[10] At the same time, at the beginning of the new millennium, the United States did not deem Central Asia a sufficiently important region such that it felt obliged to claim the role of providing a direct guarantee for its security. Even now Washington does not appear to set such ambitious goals for itself, but the expansion of the American military presence and American assistance (including military aid) can create just such an impression in some of the local regimes.

Under these conditions, the Russian leadership—having again discovered, under the influence of a new geopolitical situation, the significance of Central Asia—had no other choice but to assert its own military presence in the region. To quote one assessment of the situation:

> The Russian military, in particular the General Staff, seems to be especially suspicious of U.S. designs in the post-Soviet geopolitical space. The former Chief of the General Staff, Anatoly Kvashnin, has taken repeated swipes at the United States, accusing it of using the war on terror as a pretext for spreading its influence abroad. The top Russian commander's comments would appear to be directed at those U.S. troops stationed in the former Soviet republics of Central Asia as part of Washington's Afghan campaign. Kvashnin stated to the Interfax-AVN military news agency: "It is one thing when a country is fighting terrorism on its own territory and some other countries assist them. But it is quite another thing when, under the guise of fighting international terror, some countries are in fact trying to get involved in the internal affairs of the nation they are meant to be helping."[11]

Russia's return to the region has occurred along three main axes: (1) the establishment of military bases; (2) active efforts within the framework of multilateral security organizations; and (3) development of bilateral interstate military and security relations.

Defense Minister Sergei Ivanov of the Russian Federation, at a press conference after an informal meeting with the defense ministers of NATO (which included the head of the Russian defense ministry), emphasized the following: "We closed our bases in Cuba and in Vietnam, but we are expanding, and will expand, our presence in the countries of the CIS. . . . The purpose of Russian airbases is to provide reliable cover for the fast-response forces of the Collective Security Treaty Organization and to give assistance to the states of the Central Asian region." Ivanov pointed out that, at an earlier point, Russia agreed to the presence of foreign military bases in Uzbekistan and Kyrgyzstan, but only for the period when antiterrorist operations were being conducted in Afghanistan. In Ivanov's words: "We immediately understood the necessity for these, and we did not object, but agreed on condition that this be done only for the period needed to achieve a final stabilization of the situation in Afghanistan, and only for performing the goals announced by the members of the coalition and for nothing else."[12]

The Collective Security Treaty Organization, created in May 2003 in Dushanbe, marked the appearance of a new military-political organization. Observers saw this step as an attempt to create an analogue to the Warsaw Pact on territories that were close to or bordered on Russia. Obviously, there is an obvious exaggeration in such an assessment. At the same time, in the course of the transformation of the original Treaty on Collective Security, the participants agreed on a list of places where Russian bases would be created, and they also adopted a resolution about the delivery of Russian weapons to members of the organization at preferential prices. In mid-June 2004 the member states held a summit in Astana, Kazakhstan. The top priorities of the organization (which were affirmed in the corresponding agreements) include: joint use of military infrastructures; intensification of collective work in military construction; and training of personnel for the organs of power of the states in the organization (on preferential and gratis terms). Members of the organization adopted a document about the main spheres of cooperation with NATO, thereby raising the organization beyond a narrowly regional framework. A new and promising direction of cooperation is the decision to form a mechanism for collective peacekeeping operations that have been authorized by a mandate from the United Nations. The results of the sessions not only represented a testament to the intentions of Russia to increase its role in the sphere of providing security, but also reflected the attempt of the members of the organization to exploit its potential to the maximum.

Only the future can show whether Russia's individual steps will turn into a long-term policy to create a new military infrastructure in Central Asia. But for the present, the response of Moscow appears to be belated. Even Kazakhstan exhibits a tendency to turn to the West or, more precisely, to play on the interest of the West in the construction and modernization of its military infrastructure. Thus, the United States is opening a program to modernize Kazakhstan's Caspian coastlines, continues to finance state contracts in that country to construct military installations (worth 2.9 billion dollars), and is also increasing its expenditures on the training of Kazakh military personnel.[13] Unresolved questions include the cooperation with NATO in the creation of Kazakhstan's own naval forces in the Caspian. Already in March 2003, Kazakhstan was included in the zone of responsibility of the South European Fleet of NATO.[14] The mass media have repeatedly discussed the possibility that the anti-aircraft defense system of Kazakhstan will be modernized with the assistance of a British firm, BAE Systems.[15]

At the same time, Russia is strengthening its relations with the states of Central Asia on a bilateral basis. Thus, on 16 June 2004 in Tashkent, Presidents Putin and Karimov signed a "Treaty on Strategic Partnership," which determined the fundamental principles of the relations of both countries in the military sphere. In particular, these principles include the creation of joint defense-industry enterprises, with a provision for the transfer of some stock in the Uzbek enterprises to Russia as payment for the delivery of

Russian weapons and military equipment. On the eve of Vladimir Putin's visit to Tashkent, he signed a federal law on the ratification of bilateral agreements on the joint use of military aviation and anti-aircraft defense forces in the interests of providing security for the airspace of both countries.[16] The agreements signed represent serious improvements in relations with Uzbekistan in the military sphere. The regime in Tashkent, which is being increasingly subject to criticism in the United States for the lack of democratic reforms, and which is experiencing serious difficulties inside the country, has made a number of substantial steps to accommodate the pragmatic Russian leadership.

It appears that the current policy of the Russian Federation in Central Asia (along with the corresponding structure of international relations that is emerging) in general reflects Moscow's attempt to pursue a more unilateral approach—in response to the increasing unilateralism of American actions. It is possible to offer differing assessments of this tendency. For example, one can understand the concern of the Kazakh scholar Konstantin Syroezhkin over the declaration of the Russian minister of defense about the possibility of a pre-emptive strike (if this is required by the interests and alliance commitments of Russia) and the attempts by Anatolii Chubais to introduce the term "liberal empire."[17] Another point of view, however, is possible: in contrast to Moscow's "pro-Western" policy that had no alternative, the decision to transform the Treaty on Collective Security into a military-political alliance and to establish military bases may, first and foremost, be an attempt to bolster Russia's position in its dialogue with the West and to compel the latter to take more account of Russian interests. In other words, the Russian policy is dictated not so much by the logic of confrontation with the West as by the logic of political bargaining.

If one examines the Russian strategy of strengthening the Collective Security Treaty Organization and the Shanghai Cooperation Organization in a regional, not an international, context, then under current conditions it pursues not so much offensive as defensive goals. Russia wants to confirm that it has every reason to claim a worthy role in the newly emerging system of international cooperation in this region.

In general, bipolarity in Central Asia at the current stage can be regarded as a kind of perceptual phenomenon for Russia. Many specialists link the American presence (apart from operational tasks in Afghanistan) to a long-term strategy of containing Iran and China, not Russia. In particular, it is from this perspective that they assess the significance of the American base in Manas (Kyrgyzstan), the location of which would give the armed forces of the United States the opportunity to act in various hypothetical situations. Suffice it to say that, as American observers have pointed out, the tactical aircraft of the United States can reach the western part of China, where the country's strategic missiles are positioned.[18] However, considering Russia's traditional influence in the region, it inevitably regarded the American presence with much greater alarm than did either Iran or China, and it cannot fail to regard this as an intrusion into its sphere of interests. The current policy of the United States in the region serves to sustain such a perception, which could lead to a shift from "virtual bipolarity" to structural competition.

Unstable Stability

As has already been pointed out, Central Asia is often portrayed as the source of actual or potential conflicts, as a zone of risk and security threats. To some degree, these assessments reflect the real state of affairs.

First, the potential for instability lies in the complex relations between the states in the region. These tensions derive from a host of unresolved problems, such as border disputes, water supply, the dependence of some states on the delivery of energy resources from other states, and so forth. A considerable role here is also played by the competition between individual states and regimes for the mantle of leadership in the region, and further by the complicated personal relations among the leaders themselves.

Second, there is a profound contradiction between regimes and their opponents, which, in the case of Uzbekistan and Tajikistan, consists mainly of Islamist forces. The regimes established in Central Asia are fundamentally secular. One must keep in mind the growth and radicalization of political Islam in Central Asia, its great mobilization potential, and the strength of its appeal and its special popularity in Muslim societies that are undergoing a period of transformation. The Islamic opposition has quickly and effectively filled the ideological vacuum that formed after the breakup of the Soviet Union, but it has also exploited the weakness and lack of unity in the secular opposition to the ongoing process of politization of Islam. The Islamists might not be riding the tide but radical Islamism will definitely remain an integral part of the political scene.

Third, each of the Central Asian states has its own problems, which can lead to a destabilization of the situation, to conflicts, and to civil strife that could easily spill over national borders into neighboring lands. These include poverty, the marginalization of the general populace, and unemployment; all of which, in turn, promote the growth of organized crime and narco-business, and also bolster the extremist movements.

Notwithstanding these numerous challenges, in general the countries of Central Asia have demonstrated stability in the course of their existence as independent states. This region, in contrast to the Caucasus, has not witnessed armed conflicts between states, or wars driven by separatist or irredentist movements. To be sure, such movements do in fact exist, and interethnic tensions are constantly felt. The exception, as already noted, is Tajikistan, where a civil war unfolded in the early 1990s. However, it was precisely the lessons of Tajikistan that have been learned by the regimes in other states. Nowhere else has a single leader permitted the creation of organized opposition. Although differing in the degree of harshness used to repress political opponents, these former leaders of the Communist Party of the Soviet Union are well versed in political-bureaucratic games and have demonstrated a high level of survivability.

To judge from all that is known, only a special kind of detonation device could ignite the above potential for destabilization of the situation. An unregulated procedure for replacing the present leaders might well be such a mechanism. The states of Central Asia, which are located at different levels in social and political development, have yet to develop a political model that would ensure a normal transfer of power by means of democratic procedures. While one should not deny the importance of the national elections and the manifestations of political pluralism found here, it is nonetheless necessary to recognize that these positive steps have had little impact on the character of these regimes, which have remained essentially authoritarian. The authoritarianism of post-Soviet states has been able to ensure a certain level of stability and control, but it cannot provide for an orderly succession and transfer of power. The departure of any leader could unleash a power struggle based on clan or regional interests, and that in turn could trigger new crises and even precipitate civil war.

As is well known, many leaders of Central Asia are concerned to ensure that they remain in their presidential positions as long as possible. They also hope that the American presence will help to bolster their regime of personal power. In fact, the presence of the United States has contributed to greater stability: extremist organizations have begun to act in a more restrained and cautious manner. To quote one analyst: "As President Karimov has noted, the United States 'managed to do alone what the CSTO [Collective Security Treaty Organization] member states could not do together' by playing the decisive role in subduing tensions in Uzbekistan's southern regions."[19] In addition, the leader of the most militant organization of the Islamic Movement of Uzbekistan, Juma Namangani, was killed during the operations of the coalition forces in Afghanistan, and the United States has added the Islamic Movement of Uzbekistan itself to its list of terrorist organizations. At the same time, the association of the United States with authoritarian regimes, which have been repeatedly subjected to criticism for human rights violations, has not contributed to the willingness of these regimes to democratize political life and to enter into a dialogue with the opposition.

The harshest and most authoritarian leaders of Central Asia, however, have serious fears with respect to possible actions by the United States and their own political future, but they really have no choice but to rely on cooperation with the United States. The American operation in Iraq, which was supported by many of the regimes in Central Asia in an effort to show their loyalty to their partner in Washington, did have a rather strong demonstrative effect. In the final analysis, no matter what the leaders of the United States might say, the war in Iraq was really an operation aimed at the overthrow of Saddam Hussein: the Americans have failed either to find weapons of mass destruction or to establish any credible links between Hussein and Al Qaeda. The possibility that the global "hegemon" was willing to use force in order to overthrow a dictator and to democratize Iraq has compelled the leaders of Central Asia—who likewise control significant hydrocarbon reserves and rule by an iron fist—to have second thoughts

Still more instructive have been the examples of Azerbaijan and Georgia. The former witnessed a quite smooth transition (apart from the case where authorities broke up a demonstration by the opposition in Baku) of power from father to son. The response of the United States and Russia only confirmed that they were primarily interested in maintaining stability in this country. A quite different situation prevailed in Georgia, the site of a "velvet revolution," which resulted in the removal of Shevardnadze from his post and the election of President Mikhail Saakashvili (who won a majority of votes). The Georgian case also gave the leaders of Central Asia grounds for second thoughts. On the one hand, the domestic role of so-called "nongovernmental organizations" (NGOs) was obvious; it is precisely their presence in the country and their opportunities to work freely that have become, by Western standards, a yardstick of democracy. On the other hand, the Georgian case could lead one to the conclusion that outside forces can initiate and control a regime change. It is hardly likely that in Central Asia there would be such a "velvet" revolution (as it was in Georgia), but the foreign players might rationalize that such intervention would succeed in preventing a broader destabilization, especially if they act in a pre-emptive way or, perhaps, combine the two models already worked out in the Caucasus.

Under these conditions, the existing regimes—to provide for their own security—should seek a balanced, middle position between the two "poles." As noted by N. Zlobin, President Askar Akaev of Kyrgyzstan behaved quite cleverly when he gave both the United States and Russia permission to establish military bases in his country: "Akaev succeeded both here and there, and one can only envy that." Zlobin added that the "bases of both countries are in his country, and who now will dare to accuse Akaev of violating human rights?"[20]

The asymmetry of Russian and American interests in the region is coupled with an asymmetry in their potential: Russia cannot perform those functions that the poorest states of Central Asia demand of it. Specifically, they need Russia to provide powerful economic assistance, ensure a flow of investment, and in general spend a lot of resources to preserve its influence. In the final analysis, these states are now turning to other sponsors. Tajikistan, for example, has obtained elsewhere a sum estimated at 108 million dollars—a figure that, by Tajik standards, is simply astronomical. As Viacheslav Igrunov (the former deputy chairman of the Russian Duma Committee on the Affairs of the CIS) has pointed out: "Tajikistan is an extremely poor country. But Russia, in its current condition, not only is unable, but does not want to make financial infusions into the 'black holes' of others' economies. And such countries as Tajikistan, Kyrgyzstan, and Georgia become the 'clients' of the United States."[21]

In general, the United States for the moment holds a clear advantage in the states of Central Asia. There is but one line of cooperation where Russia has no competition: by accepting migrant labor, it provides the states of Central Asia with an estimated one billion dollars a year. Seasonal labor in Russia, for all its negative dimensions (the lack of rights of migrant workers; their onerous labor conditions; their concentration in low-paid, low-prestige occupations), nonetheless affords the citizens of Central Asian states an opportunity to earn money and support their families, and thereby help to maintain social stability. In this respect, there is no alternative to Russia's role in Central Asia as a recipient of migrant labor. Under these conditions, Tajikistan, Kyrgyzstan, and Uzbekistan are being transformed into donors of labor. Although in no ways diminishing the significance of Western assistance in the development of national economies and infrastructures, it must be said that local elites have more access to such assistance (hence their vested interest) than to the resources of migrant laborers, which often flow outside the banking and fiscal system. According to an estimate by the International Crisis Group, which has made a study of public opinion in the region, "significant numbers believe that development assistance has had little positive impact or is getting lost or stolen (30.1 percent, Uzbekistan; 54 percent, Tajikistan; and 27 percent, Kyrgyzstan)."[22]

On the whole, in the states of Central Asia one nonetheless feels a strong public interest not only in obtaining assistance, but also in retaining the attention of the West in order to bolster their ties to higher international standards. They are interested in Western-style modernization, in economic growth, in good education, and in social security. The educated stratum also cares for political liberalization.

Conclusion

The emergence of an active Russian policy in Central Asia is manifested mainly in terms of military-political cooperation and, above all, is a reaction to the unilateral actions of the United States. The latter increasingly has brought changes in the geopolitical situation that are perceived to be detrimental to Russia's interests. As a result, Russia has been forced to redefine its position and sphere of responsibility in regional security. Until recently, Russia's actions to strengthen and demonstrate its own presence could be assessed as an attempt to force the West to take into account its interests at both a regional and global level.

At the same time, the overbearing style of American hegemony forces Moscow to define more precisely its own special role in this region. The result has been the emergence of a pseudo-bipolar structure in Central Asia, something that has a chance of persisting in this region for a rather extended period of time—notwithstanding the unipolarity found on a global scale. Formally, Russia cannot operate as an equal in Central Asia. However, the asymmetrical response it has proposed (namely, the reinforcement of existing military-political organizations; the establishment of its own military presence; the development of bilateral relations with local states) plays a much greater demonstrative role than might appear to be the case at first glance. It is seen in the region and abroad (fairly or not is another question) as the return of the Russian Federation to the zone of its traditional interests. Attempts to marginalize the influence of Russia are unrealistic. However loyal the leaders of the Central Asian states might be toward the United States, however strong might be their interest in enhancing their security through American assistance, they have no intention of conducting a policy that would alienate so powerful a neighboring state as Russia. On the contrary, maintaining a balance between Russia and the West gives them greater freedom to maneuver and the opportunity to exploit the potential of relations with both partners.

Russia's influence in Central Asia is often attributed to the presence there of a generation of "Soviet" leaders and "Soviet" citizens—that is, people with whom the Kremlin finds it easier to deal. In fact, the citizens of Russia do have an easier time understanding their psychological mindset and behavioral models, and also recognizing the capacity of Central Asians to adapt quickly to new situations (by creating "Potemkin villages" out of NGOs that are really under government control; by portraying traditional village [mahallah] councils as models of self-government; by exaggerating the threat of Islamic terrorism). Such devices, which Russian citizens themselves must often employ, are capable of deceiving someone from the

West. To be sure, this is a transitional factor: more and more young people are receiving an education in the West, where they easily internalize an exceptionally negative attitude not only toward the Soviet period (which they personally never experienced), but also toward Russian policy as a whole. The creation of a narrow, closed stratum of political compradors is perhaps a guarantee that a state will choose a particular foreign orientation in the future or at least facilitate this choice. But that is no guarantee for the preservation of security. Among the main mass of the population, who now find themselves outside the framework of modernization processes, there is a tendency toward retraditionalization—the reinforcement of ethnic, clan, and local identities.

The development of liberal and democratic values, without question, will breathe new life into the political climate in the states of Central Asia. In the short term, however, it will not bring a fundamental change in the dominant political culture. A policy aimed at a controlled regime change could be especially perilous. Even in the absence of major upheavals, overly hasty attempts to create a pro-Western elite and to instill Western values and models (which are alien to the majority of the population) could create a substantial, tragic gulf between the new leaders and society. Russian influence—more traditional and comprehensible for the communities of Central Asia—which is based on a better knowledge of Central Asia, could ensure a more protracted, and more tranquil period of transformation. One might criticize Russia for being insufficiently active in this sphere, but it would be irrational and mistaken to prevent it from doing so.

Notes

1. G. Iu. Sitnianskii, "Trinadtsatyi mif o Tsentral'noi Azii: otvet Marte Brill Olkott" (http://profi.gateway.kg/2001/).
2. Dariga Nazarbaeva, "Spetsifika i perspektivy politicheskogo razvitiia Kazakhstana," *Mezhdunarodnyi institut sovremennoi politiki, Biulleten' no. 3 (2004): 1.
3. A. Arbatov, *Bezopasnost': rossiiskii vybor* (Moscow, 1999), pp. 134–35.
4. I.S. Zonn and S.S. Zhil'tsov, *Strategiia SShA v Kaspiiskom regione* (Moscow, 2003), p. 148.
5. "Eurasia Insight," 8 February 2002 (www.eurasia.org).
6. Gazeta.ru, 29 May 2003 (www.gazeta.ru).
7. M. Glinkin, "Prezidentskii marafon snova nachalsia v stepi," *Nezavisimaia gazeta*, 12 January 2004.
8. A. D. Bogaturov, ed., *Sistemnaia istoriia mezhdunarodnykh otnoshenii v chetyrekh tomakh. Sobytiia i dokumenty. 1918–2003*, 4 vols. (Moscow, 2003), 3: 10–11.
9. Adam Daniel Rotfield, "Introduction: Rethinking the Contemporary World System," *SIPRI Yearbook. 1999* (Oxford, 1999), p. 6.
10. Fiona Hill, *The Caucasus and Central Asia: How the United States and Its Allies Can Stave Off a Crisis* (Brookings Institution, Policy Brief, no. 80 [May 2001]),

on the Brookings Institution Web site at www.brookings.edu/comm/policybriefs/ pb80.htm.

11. Igor Torbakov, "Russia and the War on Terror: Not a Trusted U.S. Ally," *Terrorism Monitor* (The Jamestown Foundation), vol. 1, no. 9 (15 January 2004).

12. See the report of 10 October 2003 at www.strana.ru.

13. Vladimir Mukhin, "Voennye vyzovy Kaspiiskogo regiona," *Nezavisimaia gazeta*, 16 January 2004.

14. Viktoriya Panfilova, "Vizit zavershilsia, problemy ostalis'," *Nezavisimaia gazeta*, 12 January 2004.

15. Karim Tanaev, "Politicheskaia igra na voennom pole," *Nezavisimaia gazeta*, 23 June 2004.

16. Vladimir Mukhin, "Uzbekskie samolety stanut rossiiskimi," *Nezavisimaia gazeta*, 18 June 2004.

17. K. Syroezhkin, "Na puti k imperii? Vzgliad iz Kazakhstana na rossiiskie realii," 30 November 2003, www.uyghurinfo.net.

18. *Jamestown Monitor*, 16 January 2002.

19. Anette Bohr, "Regional Cooperation in Central Asia: Mission Impossible?" *Helsinki Monitor,* no. 3 (2003): 267.

20. See Zlobin's report of 10 February 2003 at www.gazeta.kg.

21. See the reference to *Nezavisimaia gazeta*, 15 March 2003, in a report of 8 November 2003 at www.uygurinfo.net.

22. "Is Radical Islam Inevitable in Central Asia? Priorities for Engagement," International Crisis Group Asia Report, no. 72 (22 December 2003): ii.

3

Russia: On the Path to Empire?

Konstantin Syroezhkin

History knows many examples when this or that state, or this or that political actor, has experienced a temptation to show the rest of the world that raw power is the determining factor in world politics, and that the state he heads has been chosen by history to change the course of historical development and to establish the limits within which humanity should exist. During such periods the dominant force has been an imperial ideology, with all the ensuing consequences, not only for the empire itself but also for the emperor.

To be sure, although the Peace of Westphalia (1648) envisioned the absolute sovereignty and legal equality of states, it has been repeatedly violated. Still, the principles embedded in this treaty have, until recently, been regarded as incontrovertible. Even the Bolsheviks, who proclaimed that the proletariat had the right to change an "unjust" world order, did not succeed in overturning its fundamental principles. The "communist" empire, like all its predecessors, sank into oblivion, and at one point it appeared that the world had become wiser, and the opposition to these principles had given way to understanding and cooperation.

That, however, did not last for long. The geopolitical vacuum that was formed after the collapse of the most recent empire did not tolerate emptiness, and sooner or later it had to be filled with something else. I have already written in detail about this process within the context of Central Asia.[1]

Within this regional context, by the mid-1990s the results of the confrontation here amounted to the following: (1) a strengthening of the position of the United States and the inclusion of the states of Central Asia within the zone of responsibility of the Central Command of the U.S. military; (2) China's determination to resolve the most critical questions pertaining to its security—namely, border questions and limiting the level of negative influence of Central Asian processes on its Muslim regions; and (3) the almost complete loss of Russia's position and role in the region.

By the end of the 1990s and at the start of the new millennium, the alignment of geopolitical forces in the region had undergone some further changes. The first thing that catches one's attention is the energetic attempt by Russia to recover its influence—which had been almost wholly lost—in the region. To a large degree, this was abetted by the reconsideration of Russia's foreign policy doctrine and by the accession of Vladimir Putin to power. The Central Asian states ceased to be regarded as an "Asiatic underbelly" of Russia and instead shifted into the category of vital strategic interests, on the grounds that they could assist in establishing not only their own security, but also enhance the security of Russia itself on its southern borders.

One should not, however, become overly abstract and lose sight of the objective circumstances. Above all, threats which had previously been discussed only in academic circles, had "unexpectedly" become a reality. These include:

- the growth of drug use, the drug trade, and narcotrafficking across the territory of the states of Central Asia;
- terrorism and extremism in its various forms, including the prospect of possible intervention of Islamic militants as it had taken place in 2000–2001 and "Islamic extremism";
- the problem of unresolved border disputes;
- the latent interethnic conflict; and
- the conflict over water and natural resources.

The foregoing does not represent an exhaustive list of the threats that constituted a high priority for authorities seeking to reconsider the question of national security. Moreover, these problems were characteristic not only for Central Asia but for Russia itself, which had encountered these earlier than did the states of the Central Asian region.

It is necessary as well to take into account a further circumstance. Namely, the states of Central Asia, as a result of their economic and military potential, were in no position to deal with these problems on their own. For its part, Russia understood that, if it failed to localize these threats in the Central Asian region, it would risk letting the threats extend the belt of instability to its own southern borders.

At the end of the 1990s, one can also discern a turning point in relations between the United States and the countries of Central Asia. Specifically, these relations gradually shifted from the economic sphere into primarily the domain of politics. The logic of such a development is entirely understandable: it shows yet again that, in the judgment of the United States, it had achieved a level of influence in the region whereby it could use all possible economic and political levers (both within the boundaries of a country and on a concrete state in the region) in the event of a threat to America's national interests. [2] And the strengthening of Russia's position in Central Asia was, in Washington's view, contrary to U.S. interests.

As soon as the administration of U.S. President Bill Clinton realized that a decade of efforts to draw the states of the region into the foreign policy orbit of the United States might prove in vain, Washington began to exert massive political pressure on the regimes in Central Asia. And it did so not only because the real threats to security in the region proved weightier than those that could be resolved through financial infusions or by landing forces within the framework of the "Partnership for Peace" program. The insistent attempt by the United States to put political pressure on the states of this region elicited a negative response not only in these states themselves, but also—and more importantly—in the United States itself.

If, however, one approaches the question in its global context, then it is obvious that in the beginning of the 1990s, for fully understandable reasons, the United States advanced to assume the role of a new empire. The justification was quite simple: if the other states could not guarantee the security of their borders, then the United States should offer such guarantees. Influential American political scientists proclaimed triumphantly that "the United States has entered the twenty-first century as the greatest, beneficially acting force in the global system, as a country of incomparable power and prosperity, as the bastion of security. Precisely it should direct the development of the world system in an epoch of enormous changes."[3]

A second fact, which is perfectly obvious and cannot provoke objections from anyone, is that the system of international relations—in the form that has existed since the Peace of Westphalia—has been demolished. The main problem of the twenty-first century consists of the following: from the outset of the new century, a system of international relations has emerged whereby it is possible to undertake actions with which the most important world powers are not in agreement, and to do so without fearing the consequences of reactive measures. The main question today is not so much the absence of a bipolar or multipolar world (which ensured a global balance), but the complete change in the rules of the game. And the latter is due to the fact that, since the end of the 1990s, the world order of bipolarity and multipolarity has shifted to a condition of "Pax Americana."

The Sole Superpower

It is impossible to dispute the fact that there are simply no players that can be geopolitically counterpoised to the United States. It is another question to ask to what degree, from the perspective of creating a future world order and the rules of the game in the contemporary world, the United States makes rational use of its superiority.

It was with impatience and secret hopes for the better that the world awaited the appearance of a new president in the White House in 2001. And to be perfectly candid, the majority of people in Kazakhstan and our fellow citizens in the countries of the former Soviet Union had a clear preference for George W. Bush. They secretly hoped for an end to the nauseating rhetoric about the priority of democratic values and human rights; they were weary of the moralizing sermons by the officials in the Clinton administration (who combined this with assertions about the right of the United States to use its armed forces to avert "humanitarian catastrophes" anywhere in the world). In its place, it was fervently hoped, the Republicans would adopt a realistic policy: realistic in the sense that the United States would cease to behave like the world's teacher of democracy and the world's gendarme, that it would redirect its attention to its own problems at home, and that it would permit the other countries to set their own priorities.

On a practical level (as later became clear), this meant that the United States intended to realize its national interests without taking anyone, or anything, into account. And that included the norms of international law that had been formulated by international institutions—above all, the United Nations and the Organization for Security and Cooperation in Europe (OSCE). It also applied to the corresponding obligations that the United States had assumed.

All this became most evident when, following the events of 11 September 2001, the United States stationed military contingents in a number of states in Central Asia. Contrary to expectations, the new administration retained in its arsenal of foreign-policy instruments an important weapon: the application of pressure through its assessment of the human rights situation and the degree of democratization in this or that country. And it would be rather strange if the United States had renounced so alluring a mechanism for advancing its own national interests. If one takes into account the new conception of action undertaken by the United States on the international arena, utilization of this instrument gave Washington an opportunity to justify political aggression against virtually any state.

This ideology was based, in the words of Zbigniew Brzezinski, on the "paranoid conception of the world" that is characteristic of the Bush administration.[4] But this ideology gained particular currency after the events of 11

September 2001, and the emphasis on its application was shifted to territories outside the borders of the United States. If, in the conditions that emerged after the September terrorist attacks, the United States had summoned all civilized countries to create a new world order (one that was based on democratic values and one that took into account the opinion of all, or at least the main, subjects of international law), it would have occupied the place of leader without any competition whatsoever. As such a leader it could have enlisted the support of the world community. That, however, is not what happened.

Instead, the United States appealed to the requisites of its own national interests and, relying on highly dubious and alleged circumstances (which to this very time have not been substantiated) concerning the events of 11 September, the Bush administration placed the main emphasis on finding the "Islamic tracks" behind all this. Moreover, the United States immediately identified the target for retribution: Afghanistan. To be sure, there was nothing strange in this. First, no one (including the states of Central Asia) doubted that the Taliban regime posed a potential threat to security throughout the world as a whole and the region in particular. Second, the majority of intelligence services around the world had information that Afghanistan was serving as the host for camps to train terrorists. Finally, it was precisely in Afghanistan that "terrorist no. 1"—Osama bin Laden—resided. Insofar as Russia and the states of Central Asia held an analogous (or almost analogous) position, the United States obtained carte blanche to station military contingents on the territory of a number of Central Asian states. That appeared to be entirely logical and did not evoke a serious negative response in public opinion in the states of Central Asia.

The majority of specialists understood of course that, to conduct military operations in Afghanistan (given its location at the center of the continent), it was essential to have the support of states located along the Afghan periphery. This support was guaranteed from the outset: on the one hand, all these states were opposed to terrorism and ready to combat it, and, on the other hand, few were ready to cast down an open challenge to America by refusing to participate in the antiterrorist operation. Finally, specialists recognized that, without the consent of Russia (which must have coordinated its actions with China), it would have been impossible for the states of Central Asia to permit the United States to station military contingents on their territories.

One must assume that both Russia and China were fully cognizant of the seriousness of the decision that they had taken. In obtaining legitimate access for its military contingents in the very heart of Eurasia, the United States simultaneously gained an opportunity to pursue goals that went far beyond the antiterrorist campaign in Afghanistan. These included: control over the Caspian region and containment of China; limitations on the presence and possibly, the complete expulsion of Russia and Iran from this region; pressure on the situation within the states of Central Asia, with the prospect of creating pro-American alliances in the region; exercising an influence on the formation of political elites and counter-elites and, if need be, replacement of unwanted political regimes; and the creation of a pro-American government in Afghanistan. As the ensuing events were to show, it is precisely this strategy that the United States proceeded to implement and realize.

No less important is the fact that the terrorist attacks in New York and Washington DC, served to legitimize the hard-nosed foreign policy of the new administration. Washington obtained carte blanche not only for measures that would ostensibly enhance domestic security, but also the right for unilateral intervention in the internal affairs of other states. The Bush administration divided the world into "ours" and "theirs." In his address to the nation on 20 September 2001, Bush vowed to take action against all countries that gave assistance or sanctuary to terrorists. He warned all countries, all regions, that they must choose to stand with the United States or with the terrorists.[5] That was nothing short of an ultimatum. It was entirely natural that the majority of states, even those that which realized that giving the superpower a blank check meant that they would lose something, nevertheless gave their support to the United States in its struggle against international terrorism.

Here I shall not examine why the Western countries supported the United States and what all this led to. My focus here is the position taken by the countries of Central Asia, and also the geopolitical consequences that the antiterrorist campaign by the United States would have for the region.

Let us first consider the Russian response to the crisis and American policy. In a declaration of 24 September 2001, Putin proposed to:

- cooperate with Washington through the channels of the special services for an exchange of intelligence;
- open Russian airspace for transit flights carrying humanitarian goods;
- increase its support of the Northern Alliance in Afghanistan;
- back the decision of the states of Central Asia to make their airfields and military bases available for use by the military units of the United States; and
- participate in international operations of a search-and-rescue character.[6]

It would have been difficult to expect more from Moscow. First, already burdened with the conflict in Chechnia, Moscow did not want to become even more embroiled in the problems of international terrorism. Second, after the bitter experience of military intervention in Afghanistan two decades earlier, Moscow realized that this war would not have a simple victorious conclusion. Third, Moscow did not wish to become involved in a conflict that bore an unmistakable anti-Islamic tenor. Finally, it was extremely important for Russia to maintain the status quo in Afghanistan: this would provide at least some kind of guarantee that the Afghan conflict would not spill over into Central Asia, and it would also ensure that the hydrocarbon resources from the region (above all, those in Uzbekistan and Turkmenistan) would be shipped across Russian territory.

Apparently, however, Moscow also was engaged in trying to calculate the negative repercussions from its participation in the antiterrorist operation. Otherwise, it is difficult to explain the delay in making its official response. Under the situation that then obtained, whereby the beginning of an antiterrorist operation (with the inclusion of the majority of countries around the world and in the Central Asian region) was inevitable, Russia had no choice but to use the attack, with maximum effectiveness, to serve its national interests. The pluses exceeded the minuses.

Having de facto become one of the leaders of the antiterrorist coalition (which alone raised the level of Russian influence in the world), Moscow succeeded in achieving a significant improvement in its rather complicated relations with the United States. The latter recognized that it needed Russia's participation to solve the Afghan problem; hence its bargaining with Moscow was not only inescapable but also appropriate.

The somewhat delayed reaction of Russia also permitted the United States to conduct the necessary consultations. That, in turn, enabled it to avoid any unnecessary confrontation with the Muslim world and not to ruin its relations with the other main players in the region—China, Iran, India, and Turkey. But the main plus for the Kremlin lay in the fact that the world community (and, what was especially important, the countries of the West) fully legitimized Russia's status as an influential world force.

As for the inevitable military intervention of the United States in this region, Russia recognized that the presence of a few American military bases was not tantamount to a full-scale military presence. History has shown, moreover, that it is ultimately quite a burden for sea powers to maintain continental military bases.

Another question is whether the procrastination in the antiterrorist operation and the prospects for its geographic expansion would have an unfavorable impact on Russia's influence in Central Asia.

First, in the event that the United States planned a long-term antiterrorist operation, and that, especially if it expected to expand its geographic scope, it would have been difficult to assess the impact of Russia's participation in this campaign and the military-political presence of the United States in the region—at least from the perspective of Russia's national interests. This is all the more true since in Russia itself opinions differed sharply over its support for the antiterrorist operation and especially over the prospect of an American military presence in Central Asia. And this fact could not fail to have had ramifications for Putin's approval rating.

Second, the prospect that the antiterrorist operation would be geographically expanded to other Islamic countries posed many problems within Russia, where 20 percent of the population is Muslim.

Third, all this could undermine the positions that Russia had just regained in Central Asia. That could ensue from two factors. The first: when Russia gained a new foothold in the region, it did so against a background of intensifying threats from Islamic extremism and terrorism. However, despite all the seriousness of this threat, it is impossible to ignore the fact that it bore a provisional character, that its real social causes came from within the region, not from without. It is precisely for this reason that Russia's re-engagement in the region appears to be less substantial than if it had had an economic basis, with the participation of the large Russian companies. The second, and most important, factor is this: from the outset of the antiterrorist operation, a number of Central Asia specialists and representatives of the political establishment arrived at the conviction (which had no basis whatsoever) that it was necessary to shift the vector of foreign policy toward seeking the patronage of the West. They also believed that the United States could become the guarantor of security in the region—as an alternative to Russia and China. The swift American victory over the Taliban only reinforced this belief. All this set a very dangerous precedent, especially given that such "thinking aloud" can, yet again, have an impact on the leadership of a particular state.

China, except for general phrases about the need to combat international terrorism and to support the United States in this cause, did not clearly define its position. But that is entirely understandable: the intervention of the United States in the Afghan conflict, whatever the form, served to undermine China's entire geostrategy. Since the late 1980s, that strategy had been encapsulated in the formula: "rely on the north, stabilize the western area, but concentrate the main efforts on the east and the south."

Until recently, as we noted above, this strategy had worked quite well. China succeeded in achieving strategic agreements with its northern neighbors. It also successfully maintained normal relations with Pakistan, India, the Northern Alliance, and even the Taliban regime. With the onset of the antiterrorist campaign, however, this fragile equilibrium could be instantaneously destroyed. Moreover, one cannot exclude the possibility that Pakistan might experience yet another schism in society and a radicalization of Islamists, and that a pro-American puppet government would take power in Afghanistan.

China's grievances and claims with respect to the foreign policy of the

United States were no less well grounded. As Beijing emphasized, there can be no "double standards" in the struggle against international terrorism. And if the United States really wants to declare its readiness to "put an end to this evil," then above all it must re-examine its strategy toward Taiwan, Tibet, and Xinjiang. For Beijing (and not only Beijing), it was perfectly obvious that ethnic separatism—in seeking to achieve its political objectives—has increasingly resorted to the tactics of terror. And in this sense, Beijing regards ethnic separatists and terrorists as inseparable conceptions.

The sole action undertaken immediately by Beijing was the reinforcement of its western borders and an increase in diplomatic activities in the West. As President Jiang Zemin emphasized (in a telephone conversation with President Pervez Musharraf of Pakistan): "Antiterrorist operations must be conducted in the presence of incontrovertible evidence, precisely defined goals, and correspond to the principles and norms of the United Nations Charter. . . . A decision to conduct these [operations] must be undertaken by the international community on the basis of a consensus."[7]

As for the states of Central Asia, one can only speak quite conditionally about their participation in the antiterrorist operations, and that is especially true with respect to any strategic interests. It is undeniable, however, that—one way or another—they were drawn into the antiterrorist coalition.[8] Given that the proposed theater of military action was remote from the territory of the United States and its bases in the Indian Ocean, for the military operations to be successful it was necessary that the antiterrorist coalition have military bases in immediate proximity to Afghanistan. For that purpose it would have been difficult to find a better place than the territory of the states of Central Asia. It is precisely for this reason that American diplomacy, in seeking to lease airports in some Central Asian states, undertook colossal efforts that were ultimately crowned with success. In the beginning of November 2001, President Islam Karimov of Uzbekistan signed a treaty with the United States that provided for the lease of the airbase in Khanabad. In early December authorities in Kyrgyzstan announced that they were prepared to make the airports of their republic available to the antiterrorist coalition led by the United States.

By mid-December 2001, the United States had conclusively defined its policy toward Central Asia. Assistant Secretary of State A. Elizabeth Jones, during an appearance before the Senate Subcommittee on Central Asia and the Caucasus, made the following statement:

> Our policy in Central Asia must include a commitment to deeper, more sustained, and better-coordinated engagement on the full range of issues upon which we agree and disagree. These include security cooperation,

energy, and internal strengthening of these countries through political and economic reform. . . . We have told the leaders of these countries that America will not forget in the future those who stand by us now. After this conflict is over, we will not abandon Central Asia. . . . In all five countries we need to expand our ongoing support for democratic political institutions, local non-governmental organizations, and independent media. We are ready to explore new areas of assistance for all five states, but only in exchange for demonstrated, concrete steps toward reform. . . . In addition to wanting these countries to become stable and prosperous, we have three significant U.S. national interests in the region: preventing the spread of terrorism, providing tools for political and economic reform and institution of the rule of law, and ensuring the security and transparent development of Caspian energy reserves.[9]

All the above sounded quite attractive to the leaders of Central Asia.

That was all the more true when the United States assumed the main task of providing security in the region by eliminating the Taliban movement and hence the threat of armed incursions from the territory of Afghanistan. To be fair, however, the leaders of the Central Asian states apparently at this point already realized that this security could hardly be achieved merely by means of an antiterrorist operation. No one, of course, doubted that the antiterrorist coalition had the power to overthrow the Taliban regime. But questions about the subsequent process of establishing order in Afghanistan (and to what degree this was possible in principle) remained unanswered. Consequently, several other factors impelled the Central Asian states to participate in the antiterrorist operation and to make their territories available for stationing American military forces.

Here, it seems, one must say that the onset of the antiterrorist campaign brought good fortune to the political regimes in the states of Central Asia. That good luck extended to several areas. First, an authoritarian regression unfolded, from the middle of the 1990s, all across post-Soviet space, but the indirect participation of Central Asian states in the antiterrorist operation, conducted under the aegis of the United States, gave them reason to think that Washington would no longer raise the question of democracy and human rights in these countries. That created very broad opportunities to bolster the existing political regimes and power structures, and to conduct a campaign against domestic opposition. Thus, President Karimov's apparatus in Uzbekistan intensified its repression; in the final analysis, that ignited armed resistance in a number of regions of Uzbekistan, including in Tashkent itself.[10] Another example was the pressure that President Rakhmonov put on the Party of Islamic Revival in Tajikistan (which, incidentally, constituted part of the government coalition). A similar process transpired in Kyrgyzstan. Finally, Kazakhstan experienced its own political crisis between the fall of 2001 and the spring of 2002.

Second, the financial assistance promised by the United States (in exchange for granting access to use their territories to launch air strikes land operations) enabled these governments to cover the holes in the state budget. And in some cases that aid helped to overcome some large-scale economic problems. This was particularly true of Uzbekistan and Kyrgyzstan.

Third, the antiterrorist operation—which was essentially anti-Islamic—gave the Central Asian regimes an opportunity to deal, once and for all, with the problem of religious opposition. And they could do so while claiming the support of "the most advanced democracy."

Finally, the new situation fostered illusions that the role of Russia and China in the region had decreased and that it was possible to ignore the national interests of those two powers. That seemed feasible from the perspective of a "political game" that exploited the contradictions in the triangle of great powers—the United States, Russia, and China. The United States itself helped to foster this illusion, for it measured the "weight" of a particular state in the region not in terms of the indicators of its socioeconomic and political development, but rather by the extent of its participation in the antiterrorist operation.

At the same time, some things substantially, if not conclusively, diminished the significance of these main factors. One was a principal element in the strategy announced by the United States in its war on terrorism: it denied the right of inviolability not only to terrorists themselves, but also to countries that are suspected of harboring or cultivating terrorist organizations, or having contact with them. The states of Central Asia would become hostage to this strategy: the war on terrorism promises to be a long one, and the prospects for an intensification of extremism on the territory of the states of Central Asia is quite probable (especially if the situation in Afghanistan is exacerbated and the geographic scope of the battle against "Islamic terrorism" is broadened).

A second factor is the uncertainty about how the situation in Afghanistan will unfold. The main forces of the Taliban movement, unquestionably, have been crushed. However, as events since 2002 have demonstrated, that is no guarantee against a resurgence of terrorism and extremism in Afghanistan. The provisional government of Hamid Karzai controlled, at most, Kabul and surrounding area; the other regions of Afghanistan were under the control of leaders from local clans and ethnic groups. The 2004 election of Hamid Karzai as President did not bring sufficient change to the political power structure in Afghanistan. The prospects for a "tribal autonomization" of Afghanistan cannot be precluded.

A third factor concerns the main thrust of U.S. foreign policy in the future. Already during the stage of the antiterrorist operation, it became quite clear that American aims went well beyond the "struggle against international terrorism." It was already perfectly obvious that the United States sought to exploit the acknowledgment of its moral right to retribution (as a pretext without any time limits) and emphasized the long duration of its large-scale battle against international terrorism through the use of military means. Given all this, the United States is seeking to justify its military-political presence in the states of Central Asia. It has therefore created a bridgehead to solve not only the immediate task of crushing the Taliban movement, but also to achieve strategic objectives—namely, weaken the influence of Russia in Central Asia and to establish its predominance over the Caspian region, the Caucasus, the Near and Middle East, South Asia, and—most important of all—China.

As the first phase of the military operation in Afghanistan was close to completion, the United States openly began to indicate to its allies in the antiterrorist coalition their place in the new alignment of geopolitical forces. It all fit within a larger pattern of unilateral, hegemonic actions:

- intensification of the American military presence in Central Asia;
- plans to expand NATO;
- proclamation of the "axis of evil";
- inclusion of Russia, China, Iraq, Iran, Libya, North Korea, and Syria in a list of potential targets of American nuclear strikes;[11]
- unilateral withdrawal from the 1972 Anti-Ballistic Missile (ABM) Treaty;
- refusal to sign the Kyoto Protocol and an agreement to limit strategic weapons;
- military presence in Georgia and Azerbaijan.

All the foregoing shows that the United States is flaunting its superiority— blatantly, inexcusably, and gleefully. Emboldened by the "success" in testing its power in Kosovo and Afghanistan, the United States no longer deemed it necessary to persuade the world community of anything. It ceased to request; it simply began to issue demands.

This also applied to the states of Central Asia. It was not only the American press that made quite negative assessments of America's contact with the "tyrants and satraps" of Central Asia.[12] Analogous judgments have been expressed in reports from international organizations sponsored by the United States and in documents from the U.S. Congress and the U.S. Department of State.[13]

A curious change in emphasis also occurred at the beginning or middle of December 2001, just as military operations in Afghanistan entered their concluding phase. By that point, the need for Uzbekistan's participation was no

longer so clear. If at the end of November U.S. Secretary of State Colin
Powell was still calling Uzbekistan a key partner in the antiterrorist coalition
and announced a substantial increase in the volume of American aid for
Tashkent,[14] the next month the government placed the emphasis differently.
The *Los Angeles Times* underlined the fact that the five Central Asian states
are not only poor and weak, but are ruled by "extremely authoritarian leaders," and it also argued that the war on terrorism gave them a "contract" for
their political activity.[15] The *New York Times* stressed the same idea. It reported that "family and clan" in many areas of Central Asia have more influence than the state, and warned that the population does not "automatically"
follow the will of their presidents and therefore could oppose cooperation
with the United States.[16]

In a certain sense, there was reason to fear that one of these states might
become the target of American efforts to eliminate a "humanitarian catastrophe." In April 2002 Richard Haass, then the director of the Policy Planning
Staff of the U.S. Department of State, published an article in the influential
magazine *The New Yorker* outlining the essence of a doctrine of "limited
sovereignty." He argued that sovereignty entails obligations, including the
duty to protect one's own population from mass destruction. Another is to
deny any support to terrorism. Accordingly, any state that fails to observe
either of these two criteria ipso facto forfeits its claim to sovereignty. That
therefore gives other governments, above all the U.S. Government, the right
to intervene; in the case of terrorism, that also includes the right of "preventive self-defense."[17] A prominent American analyst, Sebastian Mallaby, was
even more blunt, declaring that the time had come, given America's might
and its status as an empire (even if a "reluctant empire"), for it to play a
leading role.[18]

A logical extension of this ideology was the new "Strategy of the United
States in the Sphere of National Security."[19] Adopted in September 2002,
this document proclaimed America's right to launch a pre-emptive strike,
thereby raising doubts about the principle of absolute sovereignty. There is
no need to make a detailed analysis of this document; it has already been
extensively discussed in the world press. But it is useful to note several important conclusions in this document.

On the one hand, it is perfectly obvious that each state not only has the
right, but the obligation, to recognize threats to its security and to devise a
corresponding strategy that makes use of all the power and means at its disposal. It would be strange if the administration of the junior Bush did not
exploit the "moment of new opportunities that opened up to America." In the
final analysis, force has always been the main argument in world politics.
Even Karl Marx in the *Communist Manifesto*—one of the most humane pro-

grams for achieving world domination—emphasized that, when two equal rights meet, the deciding factor is force. So why should the United States, to judge from a text that regards its new strategy of national security no less humane and that regards itself as the messiah, not resort to the use of force to ensure that the new strategy is realized?

On the other hand, can we agree with the proposition that one state should assume the right to determine the template by which all other countries are to live and to punish the disobedient? That is contrary to the nature of human community; it reminds one of the plans for world dominance that have been heard more than once in the history of mankind.

But the most dangerous implication of the new U.S. national security strategy is that the example of using "the right of force" is infectious. Today we already see that, following the United States, other governments are beginning to invoke this right in international relations. Moreover, since these actors do not have military and economic might anywhere near that of the United States, these emulators use the right in quite unique ways—either in the form of military-political blackmail.

The wave of terror and the escalating arms race during the last two years are a direct consequence of the "right of force" now professed by the Bush administration. Countries that, for whatever reason, are not inclined to surrender the most important components of their sovereignty, see this as an adequate response to the attempts of the United States to superimpose its hegemony. The consequences of such a development are obvious:

- the spread of nuclear and missile technologies throughout the entire world, with a corresponding increase of members in the "nuclear club";
- an orientation in foreign policy toward the "right of force" and the emergence, in an increasing number of states, of the supposition of a need to launch preventive strikes;
- a broadening of the spheres for using armed force to defend national interests; and
- a reinforcement of the tendency to use state terrorism as a preventive strike.

Countries that used the United States policies as a way of rationalizing their previous positions have proven to be numerous. Examples include:

- Japan, which has attempted to abandon the constitutional limitations against the use of armed forces outside the borders of the country;
- Israel, which openly flouts all the resolutions of the Security Council of the United Nations;

- France and Great Britain reviewing their nuclear doctrines;[20] and
- Russia, which has not only reconsidered its nuclear doctrine, but has claimed the right to deal a "preventive strike"—a strategy that extends as well to the Commonwealth of Independent States (CIS).

Another result is that, in light of new challenges and risks to international security, it has become completely obvious that national institutions (armed forces; police; and special services) and international organizations (the United Nations; the Organization for Security and Cooperation in Europe; the North Atlantic Treaty Organization; and so forth), which were established to guarantee security, have demonstrated their total inability to carry out their assigned mission. As for the international institutions, in the wake of NATO's aggression against Yugoslavia, their role in resolving international conflicts can only be regarded as negligible.

But the most striking consequence is the fact that the United States, which had arrogated the function of being the "world's gendarme," of late has shown that it cannot perform this role effectively. As a consequence, the world has therefore lost—in the United States—its guarantor in the sphere of international security, finances, technical progress, democracy, and so forth. Without doubt, the United States remains the only superpower, the most powerful country in the world in economic and military terms. But, all around the world, the attitude toward the United States has changed. The dominance of the United States in the world community elicits hostility not only from the other potential power centers, but even from its own allies. Americans are coming to the same conclusion. As Brzezinski has emphasized, the loss of trust in the United States and its growing isolation are all part of an alarming paradox: American might in the world has reached its apogee, but the political role of the United States has sunk to its lowest nadir.[21]

But that paradox is understandable. When a superpower begins to feel itself exceptional and unique, it gradually shifts its foreign policy priorities toward a single goal: thwart the emergence of a potential competitor. In this context, the return to the notion of "Pax Americana" seems entirely logical. However, the demise of any hegemony, even under conditions that are most favorable for it, has three precursors: (1) other states, or coalitions of states, acquire comparable power; (2) the imperial burden saps the strength of the hegemon itself; or (3) the domestic situation creates conditions for moral degeneration. The reality of today is that all three factors, to a greater or lesser degree, are already at hand. It would therefore hardly be sensible to talk about an unconditional dominance of the United States in the first and, especially, the second half of the twenty-first century. Consequently, the principle that is currently dominant in the pragmatic world of today is "every man for himself."

At the Crossroads

The energetic attempt at the dawn of the twenty-first century by Russia to regain its lost influence in the region was facilitated by a multitude of circumstances, some objective and others subjective—a subject about which I have written elsewhere.[22]

This situation did not change after 11 September 2001. The aftermath of those events only brought one new element to Central Asia: the military presence of the United States in the region.

Evidently, Moscow weighed all the "pros" and "cons" for participating directly in the antiterrorist operation. Otherwise, as noted above, it is difficult to explain why it delayed making its official response to the crisis. Under the situation that had already emerged (the inevitable start of the antiterrorist operation and the inclusion in it of the majority of countries in the world and in Central Asia), Russia had but one option: exploit the situation in such a way as to maximize its usefulness for Russian national interests. The pluses outweighed the minuses, as pointed out earlier.

But there is one other curious aspect to Russian policy during this period: the strategy of the United States in the sphere of national security, which elicited a great response among European politicians and jurists, met with virtually no opposition in Russia. Apparently, this phenomenon is explained not by remnants of a Bolshevik mentality in the Russian political establishment (about the messianic role of Russia), but by the fact that the ideas expressed in this strategy were perfectly suited for Russian interests.

In attempting, after a decade of absence, to recover its influence in Central Asia, Russia found that its economic and political position in that region had, if not entirely disappeared, at least had suffered a major erosion. The former union republics and countries of popular democracy demonstrated their independence as sovereign states. Moreover, in some respects they even surpassed Russia itself. It was impossible to ignore the fact that the geopolitical vacuum created by the collapse of the Soviet Union here had already been filled by the end of the 1990s, and that the vacuum had been filled by Russia's geopolitical adversaries. The independent states of Central Asia (and not all of these) could only expect two things from Russia: a guarantee of security in the event of a serious conflict and the delivery of weapons at preferential domestic Russian prices.

Russia took account of all this and paused. In the interim it began to bolster its own armed forces and the structure of regional security. It was also emphatically opposed to the presence of the United States in the Caucasus and Central Asia, resisted the expansion of NATO, denounced the American withdrawal from the ABM treaty, and deplored the obvious erosion of integrating processes within the framework of the CIS.

There is one other curious aspect to international relations in Central Asia during the period between the antiterrorist operation in Afghanistan and the war in Iraq: the increasingly repetitive attempts of official Russia to justify this or that action by the United States, and the stoic silence of China. It would be too simple to explain all this by the desire to maintain relations of strategic partnership with the United States (in the case of Russia), the reluctance to enter into direct confrontation with Russia or the United States (in the case of China), or by some secret agreement between Washington and Moscow to divide their sphere of influence. Such explanations seem all the more inadequate in view of the events occurring in Central Asia and around it.

In my opinion, neither in Russia nor in China were the policymakers so naive. If they permitted actions that blatantly contradicted the national interests of their own countries, then some goal lay hidden behind these decisions. And that goal was to permit the United States, which possessed limited resources for localizing a serious regional conflict, but passionately wanted to do this, to become embroiled in potential conflicts in geographically alien regions, and therefore assume responsibility for resolving future conflicts there. There is no question that the prospects for such conflicts to erupt (sometimes not without the participation of Russia and/or China) were and are, very real. That volatility derived from the socioeconomic situation in these regions and from the democratic rhetoric, which had already demonstrated its destructive power but which the United States, even if it wanted, could not renounce.

Under these conditions, both Russia and China showed their faithfulness to their duties as allies. They established ties with "old Europe" (which found itself in confrontation with the United States) and thereby resolved their own domestic and foreign policy problems. They raised the level of contacts in all directions and gave "wayward sheep" (above all, among the states of the CIS) yet another chance to determine their priorities and their allies in regional security. In other words, Russia and China demonstrated that they had learned not to set unattainable goals for themselves. They simply laid low and awaited a new phase in geopolitical confrontation, but one where suspicion of "imperial ambitions" would be shifted from them to the United States.

One has to admit that this strategy paid off. From the perspective of geopolitics, the year 2002 in Central Asia was marked by the clear dominance of Moscow and Beijing. As if taking revenge for their involuntary retreat at the end of 2001, both countries pursued a policy aimed at bolstering their position in the region. This was manifested with particular clarity in the "diplomatic games" involving regional security organizations: the Collective Security Treaty Organization, the Conference on Cooperation and Confidence-Building Measures in Asia, and the Shanghai Cooperation Organization (SCO).[23]

For entirely understandable reasons, China held the most active position, especially from early to mid-2002. As the foreign ministers of the SCO countries met in January for an extraordinary meeting in Shanghai, they had already reached agreement on a number of questions. If one sums up this meeting,[24] it represented a test to measure the strength of the SCO and the commitment of its members. At this meeting, China, and to some degree Russia, let their allies in the region understand that they were ready to agree to the military presence of the United States, but with certain reservations and limits. As Igor´ Ivanov, the foreign minister of Russia, emphasized: "It is precisely the SCO, which unites like-minded people and neighbors, who are linked by ties of long cooperation and ancient traditions, that should be the system-shaping element in providing security and development in the region. After all, those states which are located here should determine the political climate and the forms for the development of cooperation in the region."[25]

In March 2002 China took its next step. At a meeting in Beijing, Valerii Nikolaenko, the general secretary of the Collective Security Treaty Organization, and the leaders of the Chinese Ministry of Foreign Affairs announced that China supported the development of contact with the members of the Organization. In addition, Beijing declared itself in favor of borrowing from the experience of the Organization in fashioning the fundamental documents and organs of the SCO.[26]

Soon after, Astana was visited by the deputy head of China's general staff, Col.-Gen. Xun Guangkai. He promised to give, free of charge, three million dollars in assistance to the armed forces of Kazakhstan, and he also expressed China's concern "about the presence of the armed forces of the United States in the region." All this showed that China had no intention of surrendering its position there.

In May 2002, Kazakhstan and China signed a protocol demarcating their state borders, thereby resolving one of the main issues in their bilateral relations. That same month, at a jubilee summit in Moscow for the member states of the Treaty on Collective Security, the parties agreed to add the word "Organization" and thereby give the structure a new status, with the prospect of bringing it into the international arena.

In early June of that year, the Conference on Cooperation and Confidence-Building Measures in Asia successfully convened in Almaty for its first summit. Although it did not succeed in resolving all the issues before it, those attending did lay the foundation for the new organization. On 7 June, SCO held its next summit in St. Petersburg, where it "dotted all the i's" for this organization. With the adoption of the Charter of the SCO, this organization formalized the rights and duties of member states. Given the new geopolitical situation that had emerged in Central Asia, this was hardly a superfluous step. Immediately after the summit, the Russian minister of defense, Sergei Ivanov, completed his first official visit to China, where he signed a new agreement on questions involving military-technical cooperation between Moscow and Beijing.

Finally, in the first half of August 2002, a training exercise was conducted in the northern part of the Caspian Sea (in the area around Mangyshlak Peninsula). It involved the Caspian Flotilla and the tactical operational training of the Kazakhstani navy. It was in fact the first such large-scale military exercise to be held in the Caspian Sea since the breakup of the USSR. The states of the region demonstrated to the "new players" who appeared here that they intend to provide independently for their security and that they have the corresponding forces and means to do so.[27]

From a dead stop, the processes of integration now began to move. The Eurasian Energy System (EvrAzES) started to be formed. And, a bit later, the leaders of the four largest states of the CIS came to an agreement about the formation of a Single Economic Space (*Edinoe ekonomicheskoe prostranstvo*), and laid plans to create a supranational organ called the Organization of Regional Integration (*Organizatsiia regional'noi integratsii*). Moreover, Russia began to succeed in recovering that which had seemed to be irrevocably lost: its position in Uzbekistan and Turkmenistan. During his trip to China, India, and Kyrgyzstan in December 2002, Vladimir Putin brought the notion of the creation of the Moscow-Delhi-Beijing Axle. Both the very route and Putin's statements in Beijing and New Delhi, plus the stationing of Russian troops at the Kyrgyz airport in Kant, left no doubt that Moscow has defined its interests and its strategic allies in the region. The majority of analysts, in assessing this trip, could not ignore the statement by Evgenii Primakov about the inevitability of creating, in the near future, a "strategic triangle" in Asia that would be capable of countering the "hegemonism of the United States."

Although one cannot of course agree entirely with such assessments, the very fact that the strategic partnership of the triangle—China, Russia, and India—had been strengthened said a great deal. That is especially true if one bears in mind the fact that it was an illusion to think that the United States was prepared to become an alternative to the tandem of Russia and China in questions of security. Something else also proved to be an illusion: the hopes of some leaders in the Central Asian states that, in exchange for giving support to the "battle against international terrorism," the United States would "forget" about the problems of democracy and human rights in their countries. These leaders, above all, had to assess these circumstances; as was shown in 2002, some drew the correct conclusions, while others had yet to do so.

Evidently, Iraq was of crucial significance in causing the leaders to rethink this question. After the United States used Saddam Hussein to demonstrate one possible scenario for "regime change," the authoritarian leaders of Central Asia began to extrapolate an analogous scenario to their own situation. Not without reason, they thought that if a leader became stubborn, he might face a fate similar to that of Saddam Hussein. Incidentally, the "democratic" opposition in Central Asia overtly invoked this idea. Thus, the Turkmen oppositionist site "Vatan" urged the Americans, who had brought down the regime of Saddam Hussein, to send forces to their own homeland. The patriarch of opposition in Kazakhstan, Nurbulat Masanov, made the following declaration: "If a peaceful path does not bring results, . . . this means that it is necessary to remove people by force, and indeed to do so mercilessly. I regard as irresponsible the position of those who defend Saddam—these are foolish, inconsequential, and irresponsible people." (Discussion at the meeting of the Discussion Club "Politon" in Almaty.)

No less significant, all these events transpired in the context of the opposition that Russia and China waged in a coalition with "old Europe," with variable success, raised to the diplomatic war that the United States was waging against Iraq. Washington, preoccupied with the failure to control the situation in Afghanistan and with plans to deal with Saddam Hussein, gradually relinquished the position that it had energetically sought in Central Asia.

The result of Russia's strategy surpassed all expectations. However paradoxical it might seem, and notwithstanding all the unsatisfactory results in questions of national security, Russia bolstered its international position and, to the surprise of many, substantially expanded its role and significance in global politics.

To be sure, with the completion of the military phase of the Iraq crisis, relations between Russia and the West deteriorated. The alliance of France, Germany, Russia, and China proved not to be as strong as appeared during the initial period of the Iraq crisis. Today one sees competition between the former allies; the main prize is the opportunity to jump onto the steps of the American train as it is pulling out. The Western powers, with respect to Russia, seek to demonstrate that they still regard it as a junior partner, and that they intend to have dealings with Moscow only when necessary. For Putin, it became obvious that his Western strategy had limitations, and that these were determined by Russia's real geostrategic and economic interests. This explains the harsh rhetoric of Russian officials about the expansion of NATO, about Western assessments of its parliamentary and presidential elections, about the Chechnia problem, and so forth. That rhetoric corresponded not only to the logic of a geostrategic confrontation, but also reflected Russia's desire to defend its national interests. The West had simply driven the "Russian bear" into a corner.

Things were more complicated with neighbors from the "near abroad"—republics of the former Soviet Union. On the eve of the elections to the Duma and the impending vote for the president, people responsible for making state decisions began to conduct themselves, to put it mildly, in ways that were hardly appropriate for the situation. Something "broke" in the Russian political machine: once again, as in the mid-1990s, people began to remember the "imperial nature" of Russia and its historical mission on the vast expanse of Eurasia. In this sense 2003 (more precisely, its second half) must be seen, in terms of Russian influence in the "near abroad," as the worst period in the entire Putin era. Seeking some way to react to the West's growing attempt to expand its zone of influence within the post-Soviet realm, Russia behaved like a bull in a china shop, smashing the fragile equilibrium that it had succeeded in achieving between 2000 and the first half of 2003.

The "Liberal" Empire

In late 2003, when Anatolii Chubais first presented his concept of a "liberal" empire, he was scarcely the first person in the new Russia to talk about the need to re-establish an empire. This idea was rather popular and actively discussed in the mid-1990s, when it had become obvious that the breakup of the USSR and the refusal of the new political establishment accept the Asian "underbelly" of Russia had brought nothing but losses.[28] The CIS looked more like a divorce office; it was patently incapable of solving the tasks of integration. Moreover, without waiting for Russia to become the "locomotive of integration," countries in the CIS began to form groups based on their special interests, with the United States serving as their foreign sponsor.

Within the sphere of its traditional influence, Russia gave up one position after the other. Initially it was Ukraine and Moldova, a bit later the South Caucasus, and then Uzbekistan. But Russia's role throughout Central Asia receded, with the establishment of NATO and U.S. military bases in Uzbekistan and Kyrgyzstan, and also with the onset of active Western pressure on Tajikistan. No less serious a threat to Russia's security was the fact that Russian business, with the exception of a few companies in Kyrgyzstan and Kazakhstan, was virtually unrepresented in the region. Finally, Russian politicians could not ignore the fact that Russian language and culture were being deliberately expunged from the public life of the countries in Central

Asia. That tendency, while less clearly evident in Kyrgyzstan and Kazakhstan, was especially strong in Uzbekistan and Turkmenistan.

There was yet another factor that was bound to have an impact on the mood and thinking of Russian politicians: in 2002, Russia had succeeded in undertaking a number of steps to bolster its influence not only in the CIS, but also on the international arena. Russian politicians, who had not yet learned to stop regarding themselves as representatives of a superpower, wanted to show—basically themselves—that the country still had some dry gunpowder left. Moreover, they underestimated not only the fact that, through its very success within the CIS and on the international arena, Russia—paradoxically enough—was indebted to the neoimperial policy of the United States. But any attempt by Russia to engage in its own neoimperialism within post-Soviet space would elicit a negative response.

Russian politicians underestimated something else: in contrast to the United States, Russia—with the exception of ambitions—lacked a real potential to realize its imperial designs. To be sure, some Russian politicians have periodically reasserted the imperial ambitions of Russia. But it makes little sense to pay attention to such declarations or, especially, claims about the purported imperial consciousness of all ordinary citizens. Absent the latter, there is no point in talking about "empire." The problem does not primarily lie in the fact that a classical empire has "provinces" and "overseas territories," not "colonies." Rather, the key point is that all citizens of the classical empire, regardless of their ethnicity and the color of their skin, are subjects, and in this sense everyone—including ethnic outsiders—have equal opportunities to come to supreme power.

Most important of all, the rise of an empire is only possible when the dominant ethnic group is in what L. Gumilev called "a developmental surge" (*passionarnyi pod"em*).[29] Such can hardly be said about contemporary Russia. Indeed, one main threat to imperial ambitions is the possibility that the populations in surrounding countries are actually on a more upward trajectory. From this follows the conclusion, not in the least reassuring, of the Russian political scientist A. Konovalov: "Russia, with its economic problems, has an undeveloped identity and weak state, and for the first time in early modern and modern history risks coming within the field of poles, the gravitational pull of which exceeds the strength of the connections that hold Russia together as a unity state."[30]

In a fit of electoral exaltation, and possibly for other reasons, Chubais (together with other politicians) did not want to take this reality into account. As Chubais's programmatic statement ("Russia's Mission in the Twenty-First Century") trumpeted: "Russia is the only and unique natural leader across the entire realm of the CIS both in terms of the volume of its economy and in terms of its citizens' standard of living." According to Chubais, Russia is not simply a leader: "It can and must, in every possible way, grow, strengthen, and consolidate its leading position in this part of the planet over the next fifty years. The ideology of Russia . . . for the entire foreseeable historical perspective, must be liberal imperialism, and Russia's mission is to construct a liberal empire."[31]

Chubais is not original in these statements: he cannot claim to have authored the idea of a "liberal empire." Rather, as we have seen, the United States had much earlier adopted this idea and had actively (and one could even say effectively) used it not only in the 1990s, but also in earlier periods of its history.

But there is no doubt that Chubais is an excellent pupil. In precise accordance with the logic of the American idea, Chubais declares that "we, of course, do not intend to renounce the principle of the inviolability of borders and territorial integrity of our neighbors," and further adds that "the liberal empire, in its actions in neighboring countries, cannot violate the generally recognized norms of international law." However, like the American proponents, as has been mentioned above of the imperial ideology, Chubais declares that the Russian liberal empire "can and must":

- contribute to the development of Russian culture and the culture of other peoples of Russia, and defend Russians and Russian-speaking citizens in neighboring countries;
- promote the expansion of Russian businesses in neighboring countries both in terms of trade and in terms of acquiring and developing assets;
- take an interest in supporting, developing, and if need be defending fundamental democratic institutions, rights, and liberties of citizens in neighboring countries.[32]

In other words, Chubais is talking about economic and cultural expansion. In the course of television debates on 10 October 2003, Chubais himself confirmed this, declaring that the basis of Russia foreign policy must be the combination of the economic levers of the market and an aggressive expansion. In his opinion, "without economic and political expansion across the expanse of the CIS and beyond its borders, Russia cannot preserve its own territorial integrity and its resources."[33] But it is precisely here, as argued above, that one finds the principal danger of imperial ambitions. Economic and cultural expansion has nothing to do with "empire" in its classic meaning; on the contrary, they are the harbingers of its collapse. That is probably why Aleksei Kara-Murza (a Chubais comrade-in-arms in the Union of Right Forces and, incidentally, a major specialist in this question) has dismissively commented that "the notion of a 'liberal empire' is nonsense."[34]

However, if one takes into account the content embedded in the idea of a "liberal empire" (whether it is the American prototype or the Chubais version), this does not augur well for the countries of the CIS. After all, the Russians are not talking about just any limitations on sovereignty (which is a sign of integration), but its coercive limitation, including the use of economic and cultural intervention, and that is a sign of expansion. And the fact that this idea has recently begun to reverberate in the heads of Russian politicians (including some who belong to a political spectrum quite different from that of Chubais and his team) is a rather dangerous tendency.[35]

Alarming too is the insistence with which Chubais seeks to inculcate his idea in the consciousness of the ordinary Russian citizen. To give his idea greater weight, Chubais has decided to frighten the average citizen. Thus, in an interview with the newspaper *Izvestiia*, Chubais made the following statement: "If we do not create from Russia a liberal empire, which energetically, but correctly, builds up its relations with the economies and societies of neighboring states, then they will do the same to us. If you do not like a liberal empire that has Russia as its center, then you'll get a liberal empire that has Kazakhstan as its center. And Russia will take a backseat. Do you like that? I don't."[36]

One cannot dispute the fact that "Kazakhstan has already turned into the leader in the Central Asian space." In terms of its economy, it really is the regional leader. Moreover, the businesses of Kazakhstan are not averse to investing capital in neighboring states. But Chubais's attempt to frighten people with claims that "Kazakh business is actively buying up property in Russia from the Russian joint-stock company United Energy Systems" is a blatant propagandist device that does not have the slightest basis in reality. Indeed, precisely the reverse is true: the Russian Joint-Stock Company United Energy Systems is eyeing the energy installations on the territory of Kazakhstan and, in precise accordance with the postulates of Chubais, sometimes acts in a pushy and even coarse manner. Recently, some plans by United Energy Systems to create joint Russian-Kazakhstani enterprises have come to a halt; the parties simply could not come to an agreement. That is apparently the main reason for the Chubais statements that aim to strike terror in the hearts of ordinary Russians.

However, despite the fact that the Chubais program is being partly realized (with respect to energy), the attitude of the majority of politicians and analysts—while showing some concern—is mainly condescending toward his idea of a "liberal empire." It is obvious to the majority that this is mainly a public relations stunt and part of the electoral campaigning of the Union of Right Forces.

But there is a rather different attitude toward the ideas articulated by Russian minister of defense Sergei Ivanov and supported by Putin himself—namely, in their theses about reform of the Russian armed forces and Russia's role in the world in general and post-Soviet space in particular. It must be said that in this case there really is something to ponder.

The Ivanov Doctrine

Formally, both the declaration issued by Ivanov and the document prepared by the Ministry of Defense make certain clarifications in the "military doctrine of the Russian Federation," which had been approved by Boris Yeltsin in April 2000.[37] In reality, however, these "clarifications" are truly revolutionary in character.

As for the assessment of the threats posed by the expansion of NATO, the minister of defense read the tea leaves to see the dangers ahead. The ministry document treated these threats equivocally: "If NATO remains a military alliance with the offensive military doctrine that exists today, this will require a radical change in Russian military planning and in the principles for the structure of Russia's armed forces, including a change in Russian nuclear strategy. Russia counts on a further development of constructive political and economic relations with the countries of the European Union, which will be based on the formation of mutually beneficial, fair, and nondiscriminatory relations, but which will also be based on the unconditional recognition of the territorial integrity of the Russian Federation and respect for its right to combat all manifestations of international terrorism."[38] In other words, the new formulation signifies that NATO is no longer regarded as an adversary, but as yet offered no clarity as to what its relations with the alliance will be. But events from the beginning of 2004 confirmed the worst fears of Sergei Ivanov and Russia is today giving serious thought to the right (which it had reserved for itself) to make corrections in its military planning with respect to the country's western flank.

The second important point here is the thesis that Russia's military doctrine now includes the principle of a preventive strike against an alien state. As Sergei Ivanov declared at the meeting: "We cannot categorically exclude the preventive use of force if this will be demanded by the interests of Russia or its all-union obligations."[39] The document presented by the minister of defense, to be sure, contains no direct reference to the possibility of launching a preventive strike. However, the context of the sections concerning the modernization of the armed forces and their objectives, and also the evaluation of the character of external and transborder threats, leave no doubt that the idea of a preventive attack is implicit.

More curious is something else: namely, how the minister of defense justifies making this change in Russian military doctrine. Apart from the rather detailed exposition of the foreign, domestic, and transborder threats, the section of the document on "Current Goals" contains a notion called "the factor of uncertainty"—something absolutely new for this kind of document. This list of "uncertainties" includes: the development of the domestic situation in the key countries of the world; the situation in the countries of the CIS and in regions contiguous with the CIS; and the possibility of returning to the use of nuclear weapons as a real military instrument.[40]

The first of these "uncertainties" concerns the leadership of states that opt for "a reduction of individual components of democracy and the principle of maximum predictability in foreign policy decisions and their correspondence to the principles of international law." Given the conditions that prevail today (nihilism toward international law, the withering of democratic values, and the total unpredictability of decisions), the freedom to deal a preventive strike is total.

The document is still stranger with respect to the CIS: Russia reserves the right to correct "the principles of military planning" in the event "of the emergence of domestic instability both of an interethnic and political character, and also in the event of actions by this or that political regime to curtail democratic transformations."[41]

No less intriguing in this context are the external threats that are designated. The list includes such things as:

- "instability and the weakness of state institutions in border countries";
- "the introduction of foreign troops (without the consent of the Russian Federation and the sanction of the Security Council of the United Nations) into the territories of states that are contiguous and friendly to the Russian Federation";
- "actions that impede Russia's access to strategically important lines of transportation and communication"; and
- "discrimination and suppression of the rights, liberties, and legal interests of citizens of the Russian Federation in foreign states."[42]

As to the last point, a bit later in the document Sergei Ivanov added a clarification: "As for the preventive application of military force in the countries of the CIS, then we do not intend to renounce this if all other means and methods are exhausted and if we have no other way out, when the lives of our citizens and fellow countrymen are threatened."[43] Thus one is made to understand that Russia regards the territory of the CIS as a sphere of its own preferential influence and is prepared to use military force to assist not only the citizens of Russia, but fellow countrymen in the broadest meaning of that word.

And that raises an extremely important point. Recently, the countries of the CIS have had more than enough precedents for what might be termed a curtailment of "democratic transformations" and "the rise of domestic instability both of an interethnic and political character." But too many parties desire to participate in resolving conflicts; competition for the right to be the "cop" in post-Soviet space promises to be intense. And if Russia offers a method that does not in the least differ from that which the United States and Europe impose on the post-Soviet states (which are far from being democratic), it naturally forfeits its advantage.

The Iraq events (which demonstrated that the system of international security created after World War II was obviously breaking down) understandably served to bolster Russia's influence on the CIS and on the positions of individual states. Washington's attempt to legalize the coercive variants of its global supremacy has forced many political leaders to rethink the security of their states and to seek new allies to provide collective security. The position of Russia proved preferable to leaders in the countries of CIS: Moscow is less fastidious in questions of democracy and human rights and above all has proposed to render support for the existing political regimes, not overthrow them. Even Islam Karimov, who was firmly inclined toward the United States, had to admit during Putin's visit to Tashkent: "We have a certain euphoria when we pay attention to distant countries that allegedly should fulfill the vacuum after the collapse of the USSR. . . . We are convinced that we have committed many mistakes because of this euphoria."[44] In particular, Tashkent's "friendship" with Moscow grew stronger after the bombings and murder of policemen in Tashkent and Bukhara in March 2004 and after the European Bank of Reconstruction and Development refused to grant credits to Uzbekistan. Commenting on the results of a trip by Islam Karimov to Moscow in early April 2004, Uzbek minister of foreign affairs Sadik Safaev emphasized that, in Karimov's judgment, "Russia was always regarded in Uzbekistan as a very important factor supporting peace and stability" in Central Asia. Moreover, he noted, the parties had agreed about the need—already by the beginning of summer—to prepare a document that de jure reinforces the strategic partnership relations between the two countries. The rather abstract notion of a strategic partnership will then be filled with substance, above all in the sphere of maintaining peace and stability. A second dimension is Russia's direct participation in the integrating processes of Central Asia; inter alia, these include opening up Central Asia to Russian capital. A third principle factor was Uzbekistan's declaration that it does not plan to join NATO, although it did affirm that cooperation with the alliance remained an important element in Uzbek foreign policy.[45]

The section of the Ministry of Defense document on policy toward territories contiguous with the CIS does not raise objections. The main issue is Afghanistan, a headache not only for Russia, but for the entire world community. As that section emphasizes:

> At the present day, the situation in the majority of regions that border the territories of the CIS is emerging as a circumstance favorable for the security of Russia. However, in the event that large-scale internal or interstate tensions should arise, they may require a substantial change in the stationing of the groups of troops of the Ministry of Defense and other power organs. The situation in Afghanistan and contiguous regions remains the most problematic. Despite the absence of a direct military threat, Russia continues to regard this area as potentially dangerous. There remains the threat of the drug traffic from Afghanistan across in the territory of the Central Asian countries to Russia. The destabilization of the situation in Afghanistan and the possibility that Islamic terrorism will renew its threat from this direction impose new military-strategic and power objectives before the Armed Forces of the Russian Federation, and require changes in the grouping of forces and means that exist at the present time in the southern strategic direction.[46]

As for the "uncertainties" surrounding nuclear weapons, it is worthwhile to examine this in greater detail. After all, it is associated with a second special characteristic of the clarified "Military Doctrine": the new edition refers all too frequently to nuclear weapons.

One cannot disagree with the statement that "the application of armed force without the sanction of the UN Security Council can stimulate a greater demand for the weapons of mass destruction (including nuclear) among regional powers that are seeking to create an instrument that guarantees constraints against possible hostile actions by developed countries."[47] Nor can one contest the statement that the United States, amid the clamor of all its declarations about a reduction in nuclear weapons, is realizing its newest designs and is seriously examining their use as an active component in military operations. But one cannot fully understand the thesis presented in the ministerial document about "the preservation of the possibility of returning to nuclear weapons the characteristics of a real military instrument," all the more since every page contains references to the priority of international law.

On the one hand, there is no doubt that a state has the right to defend itself with all the means at its disposal, and that includes the use of nuclear weapons. On the other hand, under present conditions, there are no generally accepted criteria that permit one to determine unequivocally whether a preventive strike is a means of necessary defense or military-political blackmail. This is a rather alarming tendency, and not only for the member states of NATO that are being discussed in the ministerial document, but also for those non-nuclear states to which Russia has extended security guarantees.

Incidentally, it is precisely this circumstance that elicited the greatest commotion in the West, which once again began to talk about the "unpredictability of Russia." In an interview with Italian news media, Vladimir Putin found it best to correct the justification of the right of the preventive use of force: "If in international practice, in the practice of international life the principle of the preventive use of power is established, then Russia reserves for itself the right to act in an analogous manner to defend its own national interests."[48] This sounds not only more tactful, but most important it is in full accord with the foreign policy principles to which Russia had already appealed.

Third, the clarifications make the defense of Russian economic interests a separate, secondary task of the Russian army. And one cannot really argue with this. As the ministerial document rightly emphasized: "Economic interests become more important compared with political and military-political; in addition, there emerges a more complex combination of the economic interests of individual states and the interests of large transnational companies. As a result, there is a substantial change in the understanding of the conditions sufficient for the application of military force," which is "more and more often being applied to safeguard the economic interests of this or that country."[49] However, in the context of the economic component of Chubais's "liberal empire" for the countries of the Central Asian region, but also for the other states of the CIS where Russia has economic interests, all this is a source of concern.

And one further innovation merits attention. As the document emphasizes, "Russia supports efforts to combat international terrorism within the framework of antiterrorist coalitions, which are an element of global stability and means for establishing a new world order that is more just."[50] This is said within the context of an assessment of strategic partnership with the United States, which, in the judgment of the majority of politicians and analysts (including those in Russia), has made the struggle against terrorism into yet another method for achieving world domination. Since, further on, the text emphasizes the primacy of international law and the role of the UN Security Council in resolving international conflicts, this syllogism remains incomplete. In the contrary case, the result is that Russia has embraced an entirely new kind of rhetoric and in fact has indirectly confirmed the mission of the powerful in this world to establish order around the globe.

Time will show whether such is really the case. For the present, however, with a high degree of certainty one can say that the return to an imperial rhetoric in Russia does not work in its favor. The same can be said about the United States; its main problem today is that it wields much greater power than is needed for the general well-being of countries around the world, including that of America itself.

Conclusion

One can say that "empire" in the classical sense is harmful for both the United States and Russia, and that any attempt to realize this idea is inevitably doomed to fail. Empires are subject to the laws of history. One of these holds that empires generate their own opposition, which assumes different forms—from the strategic regrouping of surrounding states to the emergence of oppositionist groups among them. According to a second law, the creation of an empire always entails costs, and the level of opposition to a given empire depends on its willingness to pay for pacifying oppositionist forces as well as for the socioeconomic and political transformation of the new territories.

The results of humanitarian interventions of the last and current centuries, at the very least, are contradictory. In the Balkans, interethnic conflict only changed the subjects involved. The situation in Afghanistan is far from normal. As noted above, the government of Hamid Karzai controls, at best, Kabul and the surrounding territory; while the remaining areas of Afghanistan, as before, remain in the hands of local clans and ethnic groups. The United States is distancing itself from the task of building an Afghan state; it has been using, in its own interest, the "effect of a presence" of the peacekeeping forces of its allies in Afghanistan. In short, it is acting in strict accord with the conception adumbrated by Henry Kissinger at the very outset of the anti-terrorist operation.[51] Likewise, the situation in Iraq remains volatile and unpredictable. It is, however, obvious that neither the overthrow of Saddam Hussein's regime nor the attempts by the United States to decree the establishment of a democracy there has been to its advantage.

It is becoming increasingly obvious that assumptions about the all-vanquishing power of liberal democracy are coming unglued. The events of the past decade attest to the fact that the liberal democracies, as well as autocracies, are incapable of providing for the security of their own citizens.

Doubts also must be raised about the widespread thesis regarding the unconditional, inexorable spread of democracy and openness, the integration of the world community, and the growth of "transparency." In fact, we are witnessing the opposite. In the world (including in the "countries with developed democracy") there is already a tendency to deny liberal values, to affirm conservatism, "traditional culture" and "ordered development," and to reduce personal and public liberty. That is all the more the case given conditions of limited resources, the intensification of terrorist attacks, and the possibility of a clash of civilizations. One is coming to understand that integration, in a number of cases, can be a factor not only for an increase in national power, but also for its limitation, for discrimination, and for threats to national interests.

No less dubious is the thesis about the emergence of multipolarity. Indeed, one can even agree with Condoleezza Rice that "multipolarity was never a unifying idea. It represented a necessary evil and supported a condition without war, but it never contributed to the victory of peace. Multipolarity is a theory of competition, a theory of competing interests and—worse still—competing values."[52] To be sure, one has to bear in mind that multipolarity is no worse than "Pax Americana."

There is absolutely no basis for the assertion by some analysts that multipolarity is inevitable. Their attempts to substantiate this thesis with references to a unifying Europe, a growing China, and the rise of an Islamic world are not in the least persuasive.

Moreover, it makes no sense to apply the idea of multipolarity to countries and regions that are at an advanced level of economic development and that have moved to the stage of a postindustrial, informational civilization. It is misleading to situate multipolarity within the context of integration and globalization, and to contrast it to political stereotypes of the nineteenth century, where each state acted exclusively in its own interests and against everyone else.

In addition, if a multipolar world is to function effectively, it must have a special governing superstructure. It is highly questionable whether this can be created, given the obvious inability of international organizations to act in resolving today's problems. But in any case, there can be no doubt that the activity of such a superstructure, in the final analysis, will depend on the will of the more powerful countries. That is why "multipolarity" and "diversity" will inevitably turn into a mere fiction. The example of a "united Europe" in this sense is highly instructive.

And who can guarantee that a "multipolar world" will be safe? Will *sovereign* states, having *their own* national interests, be able to reach an agreement among themselves? No less essential is the question whether transnational structures (or, in the definition of the Russian scholar, A. Bogaturov, "transnational networks")[53] can be incorporated into multipolarity. And these are by no means the least important players in the contemporary world.

Finally, for multipolarity to take root and work, it is necessary that the United States adopts this conception. To judge from statements coming out of the White House, however, there is no evidence that this has transpired. The reality of the contemporary world is such, as has already been pointed out, that there are no players that are geopolitically comparable to the United States. Under these conditions at the global level, no kind of geopolitical game is in principle possible. In the best case, the countries at a level below the United States can, through concerted action, only correct some particular aspect of Washington's policy on certain specific questions.

And here I concur with the viewpoint expressed by A. Konovalov:

> Neither the unipolar America-centric model of the world, nor a multipolar scheme of opposing poles, can give an adequate representation of the real processes unfolding in the contemporary world. Nor can they serve as the basis for the formation of recommendations and decision making in the domains of security and foreign policy. The facts provide increasingly persuasive confirmation of the fact that we are observers of the formation of a new bipolarism. Moreover, each of these poles has its own complicated, composite structure. At one pole are gathering the states that recognize the necessity of following, in their domestic policy and in their relations with each other, agreed-upon rules and norms that recognize some basic values and a civilized diversity in the world. At the other pole are gathering those states and nonstate networks (terrorist, criminal, and transnational) that preach radical ideologies, do not recognize the norms of law and moral-ethical limitations, and make the spread of these ideologies their objective.[54]

Under conditions where the mechanisms for providing international security have demonstrated their ineffectiveness, and are in fact discredited, something else must come to take their place. This substitute must provide effective governance and guarantee what people most cherish—a worthy life and an understanding of the rules that govern their existence. No one empire, under contemporary conditions, can give this, insofar as it is contrary to contemporary consciousness for alien values to be superimposed. Consequently, it is necessary to propose something different. And in this context it is cooperation—*not* competition—between Russia, the United States, Europe, and China in the Central Asian region that is not only desirable, but necessary. However, insofar as in reality this does not seem possible to the majority of states, including those in Central Asia, they all are forced to base their foreign policies on the principle of "each man for himself." What does that mean in practice?

First, one should not expect the pressure on Central Asia to weaken—either from the United States or from the power centers forming at a regional and subregional level (above all, Russia and China). However, this is no cause for pessimism. Indeed, just the opposite. The competition of "great powers" in the region will give these countries an opportunity to play both sides of the fence. That may sound rather crude, but it is the only thing that will give them an opportunity not just to survive, but to extract certain dividends from the geopolitical confrontation in the region.

Because of their economic, military, and political opportunities, the states of this region cannot afford to employ a really independent political tactic. They cannot, indeed must not, take an unambiguous position in favor of one side. The basis of their policies, in my opinion, should be to embrace the principle of equidistance from the interests of this or that side. The main task of their foreign policies should be to avoid becoming directly involved in a confrontation. Moreover, to some degree, they should use this conflict to extract additional resources for their own development and to provide for their own security, thereby gradually achieving the requisite level of self-sufficiency.

Notes

1. See, for example, Konstantin Syroezhkin, "Central Asia Between the Gravitational Poles of Russia and China," in *Central Asia: A Gathering Storm?* ed. Boris Rumer (Armonk, NY, 2002), pp. 169–207.

2. Incidentally, the magnitude of American influence has proven illusory even for American researchers who specialize on this region. As Martha Olcott has emphasized, "We are less and less successful in influencing these countries in such a way that their development moves in a direction that corresponds to American interests." See M. B. Olkott [M. B. Olcott], "Razmyshleniia o politike SSHA v Tsentral'noi Azii," *Pro et Contra* 5 (2000).

3. B. Gutter, J. Spero, and L. Tyson, "New World, New Deal: A Democratic Approach to Globalization," *Foreign Affairs* (March–April 2000), p. 80.

4. See Z. Brzezinski, "Another American Casualty: Credibility," *The Washington Post*, 10 November 2003.

5. For Bush's speech of 20 September 2001, see the official text at www.whitehouse.gov/news/releases/2001/09/20010920–8.html.

6. *NTV*, broadcast of 24 September 2001.

7. See *RIA "Novosti,"* 4 October 2001.

8. It is quite symptomatic that this involvement in the antiterrorist campaign occurred against the will of the populations in Central Asia. According to public opinion surveys conducted by the company "Komkom-2 Evraziia" in the beginning of October 2001, in response to the question whether "the missile strikes of the United States in Afghanistan are justified," 43 percent replied "categorically no," 19 percent said "probably not," and only 12 percent said "probably yes." As to the question of conducting military operations in Afghanistan, 78 percent expressed their opposition on the grounds that "any military actions lead to the death of peaceful people." Others (9 percent) believed that "this can provoke terrorists to commit new, done for effects, terrorist acts," 19 percent warned that "this can unleash the third world war, the consequences are difficult to predict," 13 percent thought that "this will worsen the situation in the countries of the Central Asian region." See *Elektronnaia gazeta Navigator*, 10 October 2001.

9. "A. Elizabeth Jones, Assistant Secretary for European and Eurasian Affairs. Testimony Before the Senate Foreign Relations Committee, Subcommittee on Central Asia and the Caucasus," 13 December 2001 (www.state.gov/p/eur/rls/rm/2001/11299.htm).

10. To be sure, the authorities in Tashkent sought to shift the responsibility for the events of 28–31 March 2004 to Hizb ut-Tahrir al-Islami, the Islamic Movement of Uzbekistan, and international terrorist organizations. There were also versions asserting an attempt for a regime change in Uzbekistan and a conspiratorial variant (claim-

ing that Uzbek authorities inspired the disorders to justify further repression of the opposition). Despite all such claims, it is oobvious that this was nonetheless a reaction (even if well organized) to the repressive measures of the Karimov regime and the outrages being perpetrated by law-enforcement organs in Uzbekistan.

11. At the beginning of March 2002, *The Los Angeles Times* published extracts from the secret plan for the use of the nuclear potential of the United States. The newspaper reported that, according to a secret memorandum compiled at the beginning of 2002, the Bush administration gave the Pentagon the task of preparing plans, in the event of unforeseen circumstances, to use nuclear weapons against seven countries. These included not only Russia and the so-called "axis of evil" (Iraq, Iran, and North Korea), but also China, Libya, and Syria. To quote the memorandum itself: "In the event that American-Russian relations significantly deteriorate in the future, it is possible that the United States will have to make a revision in its nuclear potential." China, given its nuclear potential and "growing strategic goals," is characterized by the memorandum as "a country that can become the source of direct and potential, unforeseen situations." This planning for a nuclear strike includes a statement about the three types of "unforeseen" situations: "direct, potential, and unexpected." The memorandum also characterizes North Korea, Iraq, Iran, Syria, and Libya as countries that might qualify for all three forms of threat. See William M. Arkin, "Secret Plan Outlines the Unthinkable," *The Los Angeles Times*, 10 March 2002.

In the beginning of May 2002, John Bolton, Undersecretary of State for Arms Control and International Security, presented a report called "Beyond the Axis of Evil." In it he emphasized that the administration of the United States has made a decision to include three more countries in the "axis of evil": Libya, Syria, and Cuba. These countries are accused of preparing programs to create weapons of mass destruction. Bolton's paper also referred to Russia. Bolton responded to a question about the possibility that Moscow and Beijing would transfer the technology for the creation of weapons of mass destruction to "ill-intentioned regimes." According to Bolton, Russia and China are "unquestionably the two greatest international sources of the spread of weapons of mass destruction." He added that the administration of the United States is discussing these problems with both countries. The United States, according to Bolton, had also determined its strategy of action with respect to this entire group of states. In Bolston's view, "states that sponsor terror and strive to develop weapons of mass destruction must be stopped. Those that do not must expect that they will become our targets." Quoted in S. Strokan', "SSHA udlinili 'os' zla' i razgliadeli za nei Rossiiu i Kitai," *Kommersant Daily*, 8 May 2002.

12. See, for example, the *New York Times*, 2 October 2001.

13. In Congressional testimony on 27 June 2002, Assistant Secretary of State Lorne Craner emphasized: "There is a firm consensus among all U.S. decision-makers that a broadening of cooperation will only be possible if these same governments [in Central Asia] undergo political reforms that will allow the emergence of democratic institutions, without which there can be no lasting stability in the region." See http:// usembassy-australia.state.gov/hyper/2002/0627/epf46.htm.

14. See *Neue Zuricher Zürcher Zeitung*, 16 November 2001.

15. *Los Angeles Times*, 2 December 2001.

16. *New York Times*, 20 December 2001.

17. The article, which appeared in the *New Yorker* on 1 April 2002, is summarized in A. Utkin, *Edinstvennaia sverkhderzhava* (Moscow, 2003), p. 21.

18. See the discussion of the Mallaby article ("The Reluctant Imperialist: Terror-

ism, Failed States, and the Case for American Empire," *Foreign Affairs*, March–April 2002, pp. 2–7); in Utkin, pp. 21–22.

19. For details, see K. Syroezhkin, "Nash parol'—sila i litsemerie," *Kommunent*, no. 21 (30 October–12 November 2002).

20. At a press conference in March 2002, the foreign minister of France, Dominique de Villepin, discussed the nuclear doctrine of France, emphasizing that containment must also include the right to counter threats that come from regional states armed with weapons of mass destruction. A document from the defense ministry of Great Britain, entitled *Missile Defense* and dated 9 December 2002, contained a section arguing that the collective nuclear forces of Great Britain and France continue to function as a restraint on large nuclear potentials. See Ministere des Affaires etrangeres, Dominique de Villepin, "Declarations du porte-parole du Quai d'Orsay," 12 March 2002 (www.diplomatic.gouv.fr); and *Missile Defense: A Public Discussion Paper* (London, 2002), p. 24.

21. Z. Brzezinski, "Another American Casualty: Credibility," *Washington Post*, 10 November 2003.

22. See K. Syroezhkin, "Central Asia Between the Gravitational Poles of Russia and China," in *Central Asia: A Gathering Storm?* ed. B. Rumer (Armonk, NY, 2002), pp. 169–207.

23. The Collective Security Treaty Organization (*Organizatsiia dogovora po kollektivnoi bezopasnosti*) included Russia, Belarus, Kazakhstan, Kyrgyzstan, Tajikistan, and Armenia. It was established in April 2003 on the basis of the Treaty on Collective Security, which had been signed in Tashkent in May 1992 and included Russia, Kazakhstan, Armenia, Kyrgyzstan, and Uzbekistan. In September–December 1993 this original Treaty was signed by Azerbaijan, Georgia, and Belarus; in April 1999, three states—Azerbaijan, Georgia, and Uzbekistan—withdrew from it. The Conference on Cooperation and Confidence-Building Measures in Asia (*Soveshchanie po vzaimodeistviiu i meram doveriia v Azii*) was established at the initiative of President Nazarbaev of Kazakhstan. The Shanghai Cooperation Organization (*Shankhaiskaia organizatsiia sotrudnichestva*) was formed in 2002 from an earlier group called the "Shanghai Five"; it now includes six countries—Russia, China, Kazakhstan, Kyrgyzstan, Tajikistan, and Uzbekistan.

24. See *Jenmin jibao*, 16 January 2001.

25. *RIA Novosti*, 7 January 2002.

26. See ITAR-TASS, 15 March 2002.

27. For details, see K. Syroezhkin, "More mira—2002," *Kontinent*, no. 17 (4/17 September 2002).

28. A highly popular idea in Russia in the first half of the 1990s, this notion argued that Russia could accelerate the integration with the West if it cut off its "Asiatic underbelly"—that is, Kazakhstan and Central Asia.

29. The idea of a developmental surge (*passionarnyi pod"em*) in an ethnic group is suggested in the works of L. N. Gumilev. According to this theory, each group in its development experiences a stage where it has excess energy and uses this energy in a deliberate effort to alter its environment, including actions to influence neighboring ethnic groups. This is the stage of ethnogenesis, when the ethnic groups have the greatest energy, including the assimilation of other ethnic groups and individuals. As Gumilev wrote in one of his works: "The requisite condition for the emergence and continuance of the process of ethnogenesis (up to its extinction), after which the ethnos turns into a relic, is its *passionarnost'*, that is, capacity for

deliberate super-efforts." See L. N. Gumilev, *Etnosfera: istoriia liudei i istoriia prirody* (Moscow, 1993), p. 129.

30. A. Konovalov, "Mnogopoliarnaia illiuziia i ee opasnost'. Vozmozhen li tsivilizatsionnyi regress?" (www.politcom.ru/2003/prognoz7.php).

31. A. Chubais, "Missiia Rossii v XXI veke," *Nezavisimaia gazeta*, 1 October 2003.

32. Ibid.

33. See the materials from 10 October 2003 on the NTV Web site www.ntv.ru.

34. *Vedomosti*, 11 October 2003.

35. In this sense, the complementary assessments on the economic development of Kazakhstan by Vladimir Putin's economic advisor, Andrei Illarionov, and Minister of Economics German Gref—assessments that do not have the slightest relation to reality—are quite symptomatic.

36. *Izvestiia*, 27 November 2003.

37. The quotations from the ministerial document come from the text that was distributed on the internet as *Aktual'nye zadachi razvitiia Vooruzhennykh sil Rossiiskoi Federatsii.*

38. *Aktual'nye zadachi*, p. 18.

39. See the materials for 21 October 2003 at www.gazeta.ru.

40. *Aktual'nye zadachi*, pp. 23–24.

41. Ibid., p. 23.

42. Ibid., pp. 20–22.

43. T. Stanovaia, "Voennaia doktrina Rossii: novye prioritety" (www.politcom.ru/06.10.03).

44. See the report of 7 August 2003 entitled "Pogovorili po dusham," at www.gazeta.ru.

45. See V. Panfilova, "Sotrudnichestvo nado prizemlit' do urovnia konkretnykh del," *Nezavisimaia gazeta*, 28 April 2004. In the beginning of May, the deputy prime minister of Uzbekistan, Rustam Azimov, somewhat dampened the ardor of his colleagues. In a lengthy article in the Uzbek official publication *Narodnoe slovo*, after acknowledging the significance of relations with Russia ("as the greatest trade partner of Uzbekistan and growing international investor"), Azimov nonetheless designated the United States as "strategic partner and key investor for the economy of Uzbekistan." He also termed the states of the European Union as "high priority economic partners" and described Japan as "a strategic partner and greatest donor." See A. Azimov, "Iskhodia iz interesov strany," *Narodnoe slovo*, 6 May 2004.

46. *Aktual'nye zadachi*, p. 24.

47. Ibid.

48. For Putin's interview of 3 November 2003 with the Italian news agency ANSA, the newspaper *Corriere della Sera*, and the television company RAI, see the official Russian government Web site at www.kremlin.ru.

49. *Aktual'nye zadachi*, p. 15.

50. Ibid., p. 18.

51. As Henry Kissinger emphasized in one of his articles, the United States should confine military operations in Afghanistan to the task of crushing the Taliban movement and liquidating the terrorist organization of Osama bin Laden. If America begins to use its army for "nation building" or pacifying the entire country, it will become mired in the very same swamp that ensnared and weakened the Soviet Union. The generally recognized wisdom of creating a government in Afghanistan based on

a broad coalition is desirable, but not justified by that country's historical experience. In Kissinger's view, the optimal outcome would be a neutral government in Kabul holding limited power, with tribal autonomy prevailing in most parts of the country. See Henry Kissinger, "Where Do We Go From Here?" *Washington Post*, 6 November 2001.

52. See K. Rais [C. Rice], "Mnogopoliarnost' kak teoriia sopernichestva," *Izvestiia*, 21 August 2003.

53. A. Bogaturov defines these in the following way: *drug producing networks*, which generate colossal amounts of "black money"; *banking networks* that launder money, and accumulate, increase, and transfer sums to any point in the world in a matter of seconds; and *terrorist networks*, that can use these funds. See A. Bogaturov, "Samooborona transnatsional'nykh setei," *Nezavisimaia gazeta*, 2 July 2003.

54. Konovalov, "Mnogopoliarnaia illiuziia."

4

China's Central Asia Policy: Making Sense of the Shanghai Cooperation Organization

Richard W. X. Hu

China has enormous interests in Central Asia ranging from geopolitical and trade to energy, and the question of the region's security and relations with Russia and its neighbors are vital for stability and economic prosperity in China's Xinjiang Province. Historically, Central Asia was an arena of the "Great Game,"[1] in which the major powers competed for strategic primacy. Today, China's relations vis-à-vis other major powers in the region have a major impact on its bilateral relations with two of the most important geopolitical players in world politics—Moscow and Washington. Central Asia is also an important source of oil and natural gas for the energy-hungry Chinese economy. To strike a balance in global, regional, geopolitical, and economic interests, Beijing needs to pursue an active but balanced policy toward Central Asia.

In order to pursue such a balanced policy objective, Beijing uses the Shanghai Cooperation Organization (SCO) as a significant policy platform to engage major powers as well as its Central Asian neighbors. Diplomatically, SCO is a sensible policy vehicle in Beijing's regional strategy and a successful case of Beijing's "good-neighbor" strategy. The SCO is a new "baby" in Central Asia. It is part of the region's organizational network link with the major global powers. Although Moscow and Beijing thus far have fully cooperated in Central Asia, the SCO provides a good institutional platform for them to share power in the region. After the military operation against the Taliban regime, the U.S. military appears keen on maintaining a long-term presence in Central Asia.[2] Given this changing strategic backdrop, what role will the SCO play in balancing the interests of major powers in Central Asia if the Americans maintain a long-term presence? How will China use the SCO to achieve its policy objectives in Central Asia? This study seeks to address these questions.

When founded in June 2001, the Shanghai Cooperation Organization was applauded as a "brand new multilateral cooperation organization" built on the "Shanghai spirit" of equality and mutual benefits. Some even believed that it would become a new Eurasian geopolitical organization that would help to form "multipolarity" in world politics.[3] It began with security, confidence-building measures between China and the four former Soviet states, and the SCO transformed what had been called the Shanghai Five summit mechanism into a regional cooperative organization seeking to maintain regional stability and promote economic cooperation. Geostrategically, the members of SCO also have pledged to "strengthen their consultation and coordination in regional and international affairs, to support and cooperate with each other in major international and regional issues, and to promote and consolidate regional and world stability."[4] The SCO covers 60 percent of the Eurasian landmass and has a population of 1.5 billion. The emergence of such an organization is a significant event in world politics and fraught with profound implications for the relations among the major powers. Many Western commentators were concerned that Beijing and Moscow not only formed an organization that would offset growing Western influence in Central Asia but constituted a potential Sino-Russian strategic realignment that would challenge U.S. interests worldwide.[5] However, as is evident from developments after 11 September 2001, Washington has not been excluded from the region; indeed, it has rather quickly established a military foothold in Central Asia. Hence this region is now not a special preserve for China and Russia; rather, it is a place where three major powers—the United States, Russia, and China—coexist. Both Moscow and Beijing rendered support to Washington in its war on terror following the attacks of September 11. The Sino-Russian strategic partnership in Central Asia did not develop in an anti-Western direction; the SCO neither can nor seeks to derail Western interests in the region. Instead, SCO shares a common opposition to separatism and terrorism; it reflects the common geopolitical interests that have brought China and Russia together in this regional platform.

This study first examines China's interests in Central Asia. It then reviews the history of the SCO: how it evolved from a border security regime into a regional organization that as yet is still not quite fully developed. The chapter then attempts to answer two fundamental questions: (1) How has the SCO served China's interests in the region? and (2) How and why has the SCO helped China to maintain relatively stable relations with Russia and Washington in Central Asia?

China's Interests in Central Asia

Chinese interests in Central Asia mainly lie in four areas: (1) maintain stable and peaceful borders with Russia and the Central Asian states, which is pivotal in the economic development of Xinjiang and China's other western provinces; (2) cut off any international link with separatist forces in Xinjiang, a matter of grave national security for Beijing; (3) diversify and secure China's access to the energy sources essential for its economic growth; and (4) extend China's influence beyond this region, as something that would be beneficial for China's geopolitical position in the post-Cold War strategic environment.

The end of the Cold War provided an opportunity for China, Russia, and their Central Asian neighbors to form stable border security regimes on their common boundaries. However, as the danger of interstate military conflict fades, the challenge from Muslim separatism and radicalism rises. China, Russia, and the Central Asian republics are all concerned about radical Muslim movements in their territories and around their borders. Since the 1970s, the Turkic Muslim Uigurs in Xinjiang have been conducting a violent struggle for independence. They have killed police and soldiers, planted bombs, and robbed banks. They have also developed connections to radical Islamic movements, and some were trained in religious schools and camps in Afghanistan and Pakistan. Stability in Xinjiang is important to China. It is a test case to determine whether Beijing can control regions inhabited mainly by minority peoples. It is feared that a loosening of Chinese control might encourage non-Chinese populations in other regions, such as Tibet or Inner Mongolia, to increase their own separatist activities, and might also weaken the credibility of China's commitment to reunification with Taiwan. In the security realm, Xinjiang has historically served as a buffer against potential aggressors from the mountains and steppes northwest of China. The region's vast open spaces and relatively small population provide an area where China's People's Liberation Army can conduct both nuclear tests and large-scale conventional military exercises. Uigur militants have acquired much broader connections to the worldwide radical Islamic movements than ever before, and that has forced Beijing to cast an equally wide net to contain them. China has no choice but to become a major player in Central Asia because of this rising tide of Uigur unrest in Xinjiang, because of the security threats along its long and porous borders with three Central Asian republics, and because of the arms and drug smuggling as well as the Islamic militancy emanating from South Asia.[6]

Russia is in a similar position, since it has security concerns in Chechnia and other parts of the Russian Federation. Radical Muslim penetration of other North Caucasus autonomous republics, such as Dagestan, is increasing, as evidenced by non-Chechen participation in terrorist activities in Russia. Russian leaders fear a chain reaction among the country's twenty million Muslims. In the long term, the threat of Muslim insurrection in Central Asia looms ever larger. Most of the Central Asian ruling regimes suffer from a lack of legitimacy and democracy. With economic reforms in these countries sputtering or stalling, corruption rampant, and living standards low, Islamic radicals have an easier time recruiting and training the next generation of militant warriors. Before the fall of the Taliban regime in 2001, drug and weapons contraband flooded across the Amu Darya River and the Tajik-Afghan border. The Central Asian governments are secular, authoritarian regimes that emerged and transformed from the former Soviet system. They are used to relying on traditional ties to Moscow as a kind of life insurance. Russia, for its part, believes that it must either fight the Islamists in the deserts of Central Asia or face them in Northern Kazakhstan, where many ethnic Russians reside. Russia finds it necessary to draw China in as a partner in order to maintain stability in Central Asia.

Xinjiang's stability is a significant concern for Chinese leaders because of the region's importance to China's continued economic development and to its national security. Xinjiang is becoming a primary source of energy for the Chinese economy. The region's most prominent source of energy is oil: Within Xinjiang's boundaries, there are three oil basins—the Turpan, Junggar, and Tarim. The Tarim Basin is reportedly the largest unexplored oil basin in the world, with some estimates of its potential reserves ranging as high as 147 billion barrels.[7] Xinjiang's oil resources are vital to China's future energy security, particularly when its large eastern oil fields (Daqing, Shengli, and Liaohe) mature and their output begins to decline.[8]

China's trade ties with Russia and Central Asia gained new prominence in recent years. In 1997, China and Russia set a target of twenty billion dollars for bilateral trade by the year 2000. Although still running far behind that target, bilateral trade has picked up rapidly in the last few years. China and Kazakhstan (China's largest trading partner in Central Asia) set an ambitious, but perhaps more feasible, goal of one billion dollars for the same period.

Increasing trade along the Russian and Central Asian borders serves a number of interests for China. First, it broadens the relations of China to Russia and Central Asia beyond the issues of security. Increased trade generally fosters greater economic opportunity and cooperation between the countries involved: China's relations with Russia and Central Asia will become more stable as each country assumes a larger role in the economic development of the other. An expansion of trade with Russia and Central Asia is also viewed as a means to promote economic development in China's interior regions. This is not only consistent with the general economic policy of opening up to the world, but also provides a way to address the growing problem of uneven development among China's diverse regions.

Greater economic development, fueled by increased trade with Central Asia, is a central component of Beijing's approach to combating separatism and maintaining long-term stability in Xinjiang. Chinese leaders hope that increased economic interaction with Central Asia will strengthen the secular governments of the region vis-à-vis the religious or ethnically based groups that might actively support separatist groups in Xinjiang. Conversely, increased trade will enhance stability within the potentially volatile countries of Central Asia. This goal is more relevant to China's policy toward Central Asia than to its policy toward Russia.

As pointed out earlier, unrest in Central Asia holds a much greater potential for affecting China's own internal stability than does unrest in Russia.[9] China is constructing railway networks with Central Asian states. This development of interstate railway networks will increase the volume of trans-Eurasian rail trade. For their part, the governments of Central Asia share many of Beijing's concerns about the dangers that transnational ethnic or religious groups pose to regional stability. The Central Asian secular policies and sensitivity to Chinese concern about separatist groups operating out of their countries have made it easier for China to pursue more open economic policies. Sino-Central Asian joint declarations uniformly stress the need to oppose all forms of ethnic separatism, and prohibit organizations and forces from engaging in separatist activities in the respective countries on the other side.

From the Shanghai Five to the Shanghai Cooperation Organization

After the Soviet Union disintegrated in 1992, China moved quickly to establish diplomatic relations with the newly independent states of Central Asia. However, in addition to continuously consolidating bilateral relations with Kazakhstan, Uzbekistan, Kyrgyzstan, Tajikistan, and Turkmenistan, Beijing also became increasingly interested in developing a multilateral mechanism to engage Central Asian republics as well as Russia. This multilateral mechanism naturally developed through what is now called the Shanghai Five.[10]

The Shanghai Five has its origin in the border negotiation between China and the former Soviet Union that commenced in November 1989. China and the Soviet Union shared a common border of about 11,000 kilometers, much of it disputed. As part of Mikhail Gorbachev's rapprochement with China, the governments in Beijing and Moscow agreed to hold talks solving their border dispute in the eastern section (China's northeastern provinces and the Soviet Far East) and the western section (the borders with Soviet republics of Kazakhstan, Kirgizia, and Tajikistan). Although the border demarcation took more time, it was not long before Beijing and Moscow agreed on a series of confidence-building measures in the border areas. When the Soviet Union collapsed in December 1991, Beijing and Moscow agreed to continue border negotiation with three newly independent Central Asian states—Kazakhstan, Kyrgyzstan, and Tajikistan.

China's border dispute with Russia and the three Central Asian states was an unresolved historical issue. Based on the treaties concerning the present boundary between China and the former Soviet Union and on the recognized norms of international law, China and Russia—after years of negotiation—have delimited 97 percent of the alignment of the boundary line and have signed the Agreement on the Eastern Section of the Boundary Between China and Russia and the Agreement on the Western Section of the Boundary Between China and Russia on 16 May 1991 and 3 September 1994, respectively. On 9 December 1999 China and Russia signed the Protocol on the Delineation of the Eastern Section of the Boundary Line Between China and Russia and the Protocol on the Delineation of the Western Section of the Boundary Line Between China and Russia. The signing of these documents and the successful conclusion of the boundary demarcation work marked a formal confirmation of the boundary agreed upon by China and Russia through consultation. And, for the first time in the history of relations between the two countries, the legally established boundary line has been accurately staked out.[11]

In 1992, China, Russia, Kazakhstan, Kyrgyzstan, and Tajikistan began to negotiate border issues on a bilateral basis. Later, Almaty, Bishkek, and Dushanbe joined Moscow to negotiate border disarmament and confidence-building measures with Beijing. From 1992 to 1995, five parties held twenty-two rounds of negotiations. On 26 April 1996, the presidents of China, Russia, and three Central Asian states held a summit in Shanghai and signed the Agreement on Confidence-Building in the Military Sphere in the Border Areas. On 24 April 1997 the leaders of the five states gathered in Moscow and signed the Agreement on the Mutual Reduction of Military Forces in Border Areas. With these two agreements, the five states pledged to take steps to increase trust along the border in areas controlled by their military forces. According to the Chinese media, these two documents were the first such agreements on border disarmament in the Asian-Pacific region and provided a good example for mutual confidence building in modern international relations.

Although friendly relations between China and Central Asia could be traced back to the Silk Road epoch beginning in the eleventh century BCE, their borders had never been clearly defined and demarcated before the collapse of the Soviet Union in 1991. China has a common border with Kazakhstan, Kyrgyzstan, and Tajikistan that runs more than 3,300 kilometers. Resolution of the border issue between China and the newly independent Central Asian states provided a good foundation for future relations. China was one of the first countries to establish diplomatic relations with the five Central Asian countries. After the establishment of diplomatic relations, Beijing did not waste time starting negotiations with Russia and the three bordering Asian countries. In accord with the principle of friendly consultation, these countries conducted open negotiations to resolve boundary problems. In April 1994 and September 1997, China and Kazakhstan signed two boundary agreements. On 4 July 1998, they signed a third agreement. As a result, the 1,700-kilometer boundary has been fixed between China and Kazakhstan. On 4 July 1996 China and Kyrgyzstan signed the Boundary Agreement Between the People's Republic of China and the Republic of Kyrgyzstan. Through continuous negotiations, the leaders of both countries finally signed a supplementary agreement in August 1999 demarcating the approximately 1,000-kilometer boundary between their respective nations. The boundary problem between China and Tajikistan is more complicated. Even so, both countries are actively working on this matter and striving to negotiate a fixed boundary line, stretching more than 400 kilometers, as soon as possible. During then-President Jiang Zemin's visit to Dushanbe, the two states signed the Joint Statement of the People's Republic of China and the Republic of Tajikistan on the Development of Relations of Good-Neighborliness, Friendship and Cooperation Between the Two Countries in the Twenty-first Century. The relevant departments of the two countries also signed the Boundary Agreement Between the People's Republic of China and the Republic of Tajikistan.[12]

Built on the border agreements, the Shanghai Five after 1997 moved to a phase of institutionalized annual summit arrangements. As a mechanism of annual summits and a regional forum on Central Asian security, these ties were not institutionalized until the third summit of the five states in 1998. On 3 July of that year, the presidents of China, Kyrgyzstan, Tajikistan, Kazakhstan, and a special envoy of the Russian president met again in Almaty, Kazakhstan, to discuss regional peace and stability and ways to strengthen economic cooperation. After the meeting, the five countries issued a joint declaration. Henceforth the meetings of the five countries have changed from bilateral meetings (China on one side, and Russia, Kazakhstan, Kyrgyzstan, and Tajikistan on the other) into multilateral ones.

During the fourth summit (held in 1999 in Bishkek), more substance was added to the annual summit, and the common interests of the five countries began to emerge. The joint statement issued after this meeting of the five presidents expressed the intention to act firmly against activities that threatened regional stability. The Bishkek summit also reached an agreement on combating terrorism; it approved Kyrgyzstan's proposal to establish an "antiterrorist center" in Bishkek.

During preparing for the summit in Dushanbe, Tajikistan, at the end of March 2000, the defense ministers of the participating countries met in Astana, Kazakhstan, where they signed a joint communiqué agreeing to conduct joint military exercises and to discuss improvements to the 1996 and 1997 agreements. On 21 April 2000, the authorities in charge of the security law-enforcement agencies of the five countries (who had met in December 1999 and decided on the foundation of the "Bishkek Group") held a second meeting in Moscow and signed two documents. On 4 July 2000, the foreign ministers of the five countries met in Dushanbe and decided to establish an institutionalized, official meeting for foreign ministers. Afterwards they signed a joint communiqué about establishing a council of coordinators for the Shanghai Five countries. The next day the presidents of the five countries held their fifth meeting in Dushanbe and reached an understanding on how to promote cooperation for the twenty-first century. President Karimov of Uzbekistan attended this meeting as an observer. The 2000 summit found it desirable to convert the multilateral cooperation mechanism into a more formal regional institution. The rationale for a formal regional organization, as Chinese President Jiang Zemin stated on behalf of the Shanghai Five, would be:

1. to expand and perfect the Shanghai Five meetings and institutionalize this mechanism in order to develop gradually a comprehensive, cooperative institution at many levels, covering multiple fields;
2. to bolster security cooperation and support each other against threats to regional security;
3. to promote bilateral and multilateral economic and trade cooperation; and
4. to enhance cooperation in international affairs.

The "Dushanbe Declaration," issued at the summit by the leaders of the five states, stressed that the institutionalized meeting of the Shanghai Five embodied the new style of international relations, which were based on equal cooperation as well as mutual trust and benefit. The cooperation of the five countries does not constitute an alliance: it is not established at the expense of relations with other nations, nor is it directed against any third country.

The 2001 Shanghai summit marked the official transformation of the Shanghai Five into an international organization. After signing two border-area disarmament and confidence-building agreements in 1996 and 1997, the Shanghai Five process first was transformed into a mechanism for summit meetings to monitor the implementation of disarmament on the borders of the five neighboring states. As its functions expanded to include fighting terrorism, separatism, and extremism (the so-called three evil forces) and economic cooperation in the region, the leaders of these states found it necessary to move toward the creation of a formal, multilateral international body.

In Shanghai, the leaders of six states (the original Shanghai Five plus Uzbekistan) signed the Declaration on the Establishment of the Shanghai Cooperation Organization. The goals of the organization are broadly stated to include:

- strengthening mutual confidence, friendship and good-neighborly relations between the participating states;
- encouraging effective cooperation in the political, trade-economic, scientific-technical, cultural, educational, energy, transportation, ecological, and other areas;
- promoting joint efforts to maintain and ensure peace, security, and stability in the region; and
- helping to build a new, democratic, just, and rational political and economic international order.

The new organization, it declared, is not an alliance directed against any other state or region. But member states pledged to consult and coordinate their responses to regional and international problems, to render mutual support, and to establish close cooperation on key international and regional issues to contribute jointly to the enhancement of peace and stability in the region and the world. All this proceeded on the basis that preservation of the global strategic balance and stability is of single importance in the modern international situation.

The organizational structure of the SCO is relatively loose. It is largely built around a mechanism of regular meetings at different levels; these include the head of the state, prime minister, and the heads of competent ministries and agencies of participating states. The Council of National Coordinators is the point of contact and central coordinating body; it is charged with drafting key documents and preparing high-level meetings.

Although the goals of the SCO are very broadly defined as a regional cooperation organization, its foundation is based mainly on potential cooperation in three areas: (a) regional stability and opposition to the "three evil forces"; (b) economic cooperation; and (c) potential strategic cooperation. Maintaining regional stability is the foremost objective of SCO; that is where national interests converge and action is taken. At the 2001 Shanghai summit, one of the most significant results was the Shanghai Convention on the Crackdown on Terrorism, Separatism, and Extremism. Although legislative ratification is still pending, this convention would be the most important achievement of the SCO. To combat the "three evil forces," the heads of state formally agreed to establish the SCO anti-terrorism center in Bishkek (emulating the model of a similar center established by the CIS Treaty on Collective Security).[13] In addition, member states pledged to work out corresponding documents of multinational cooperation in a bid to curb illegal arms smuggling, drug trafficking, illegal migration, and other criminal activities. Implementing the agreement would provide a legal basis for Chinese military forces to intercede in Central Asia for anti-terrorism purposes.

On the economic front, the SCO members pledged to make use of the great potential in trade and economic cooperation among the member states. The first meeting at the prime minister level took place in September 2001 in Kazakhstan, and the second convened in October 2003 in Beijing. A vision for future cooperation and agenda was drawn up in the meetings; some large joint projects in transportation and energy cooperation will take place soon. Other cooperative initiatives, such as the Chinese proposal for the six ministers of culture to meet, were also adopted. Cooperation in various functional areas will be instrumental for the long-term institutionalization of the cooperation, for this involves the political socialization of the next generation. The Central Asian states regard the SCO favorably because of its potential economic benefits. After independence, these countries suffered tremendous economic difficulties. They are rich in resources and hope to gain entry to the world marketplace through regional economic cooperation.

While the potential for strategic cooperation in Eurasia and even on the world stage is a big lure of the SCO, the persisting ambivalence (especially after September 11) raises some doubts. As the name indicates, the Shanghai Cooperation Organization is not just a loose forum like the ASEAN Regional Forum (something like what Moscow used to refer to as the Shanghai Forum). It is a formal regional organization of a new kind: it is not a military bloc or political alliance. Instead, it is a formal international organization for regional cooperation (*Di Qu Hezuo Zuzhi*)—named after its birthplace of Shanghai.[14]

The SCO and Sino-Russian Relations in Central Asia

The main driving force behind the SCO is undoubtedly Sino-Russian strategic cooperation, as Beijing and Moscow have convergent—as well as divergent—interests in the region. This pragmatic partnership in Central Asia creates limits and foreshadows the future of the SCO. After the Cold War, both Beijing and Moscow each have viewed Central Asia, with its weak governments and rich natural resources—especially oil and gas—as its own future natural sphere of influence. When the Soviet Union collapsed, the power vacuum in the region posed the danger of ethnoreligious unrest and regional chaos in the former Soviet republics of Central Asia, and that could have led to an Islamic implosion—a clear threat to regional stability.[15] Although that did not actually transpire (or, at least, has not materialized in a dramatic way), Central Asian security remains fluid and volatile. The regional security structure has been slow to take shape. After the break-up of the Soviet Union, the Central Asian states have made high-profile moves to establish cooperative regional security structures in which outside powers play leading roles. These security systems include the CIS Collective Security Treaty Organization led by Russia, the NATO Partnership for Peace Initiative, the European Cooperation Organization, and the more recent Shanghai Cooperation Organization led by China and Russia. The recent institutionalization of the SCO demonstrates that Moscow and Beijing hope to be the leading players in Central Asia and thereby reduce the influence of Turkey, Iran, and, possibly, the United States in the region.

The SCO not only serves the regional interests of China and Russia, but also advances their strategic interests in global politics. Beijing and Moscow share a common desire to counter the global supremacy of the United States and to resist pressure from the West with respect to the rights of independence-seeking ethnic minorities (and human rights in general). All that has furnished much of the impetus for a friendship treaty between Russia and China as well as the creation of the SCO. Both China and Russia vehemently opposed the policy of NATO-led "humanitarian intervention" in 1999 in Kosovo (which did not have the sanction of the UN Security Council) as well as the unilateralist intervention of the United States in Iraq in 2003. The Chinese leaders have repeatedly declared that "hegemony and power politics" are the "main source of threat to world peace and stability" as well as to China's interests. Chinese and Russian media often refer to "U.S. hegemony" and "U.S. power politics" and call for the "establishment of a new international order" under the tutelage of the United Nations.[16] The reason for Russia's willingness to support China's security interests and vice versa may lie in the fact that each country now views the other as its "strategic rear." Russian leaders have often stated that the threats to Russia are NATO's enlargement eastward and radical Islamic forces active in Chechnia and among Moscow's Central Asian allies. Beijing views U.S. predominance in the post-Cold War world—from its success in the Gulf War to its support of Taiwan security—as important threats to China. Russia has stated that "there is only one China" and that Taiwan is China's "internal affair," while Beijing has expressed unequivocal support for Russia's strong-arm tactics in Chechnia. A world system that is not dominated by one country is attractive to both Moscow and Beijing for similar reasons: Economically, it offers them alternative sources of technology, financing, and markets for their raw materials, goods, and services. Moreover, an overburdened U.S. military would pose less of a risk to Russia and China in the regions where they assert their own power. Alternative poles of power would force the United States to spread its resources thin to deal with evolving crises in different regions simultaneously.

Russia's vested interest in the SCO is a natural extension of the stable order with China and its Central Asian neighbors. Moscow has security headaches in the Transcaucasus region, and the source of separatism, terrorism, and religious extremism is closely linked with Islamic militancy in Afghanistan and Central Asia. Central Asia, during the Soviet era, was considered a backyard as well as the soft underbelly of Russia. Moscow is concerned about Western penetration in the region, and the SCO, in addition to the various institutional arrangements that Moscow has created since 1991, would serve as a shield for such defense.

The behavior of Central Asian states amounts to more than simply jumping on the bandwagon. On one hand, they do not want to go back to the old Soviet system; on the other hand, they would like to establish more equal and stable relations with Russia. They have played a balancing game with Russia, the United States, and China with the goal of maximizing security benefits. They share a common security concern about the Islamic militant forces that pose a menace to their domestic stability and want to use the SCO to fend off this threat.

The debate over the name of the SCO reflected differences over the vision and mission of the organization. The orientation of the SCO was touted in the Chinese media as an organization to promote "multipolarity" in world politics and to establish a "new world order" based on "democratic, fair, and rational" principles. But in the run-up to the Shanghai summit in 2001, the Chinese press began to stress the earlier propaganda against the "three evil forces" of separatism, terrorism, and religious extremism. When targeted at Western media, the rhetoric was couched in terms of "law-enforcement cooperation." But, as in the cases of other regional organizations, economic cooperation and trade is an important pillar for the SCO.[17] On the economic front, China may have a longer shot than Russia.

Developments in Sino-Russian relations in recent years have attracted a lot of attention in the West. The prevailing impression is that Moscow and Beijing have forged an opportunistic partnership driven by shared reactions to Washington. Russia draws closer to China whenever the United States becomes pushy and NATO expands further eastward. Each sign of Taiwan's shift toward formal independence backed by moral support and weapons sales from the United States pushes China into Russia's arms. Given the historically weak economic ties and persistent distrust between Russia and China, it is usually thought that Moscow and Beijing will be unlikely to forge an anti-American coalition if Washington would pay due respect to the two countries' roles in world politics. After all, Washington has a tremendous repertoire of economic means and strategic resources to keep Moscow and Beijing largely oriented toward the West. However, the nationalist intensity in each country and the growing Sino-Russian arms sales signify a stronger and more lasting reaction to American power than is usually acknowledges. This marriage of convenience is being bolstered by the unilateralist world policy of the Bush administration. More than just geostrategic interests, the driving forces for the Sino-Russian partnership in Central Asia include a shared need for stable borders and territorial integrity, a common enemy in Islamic fundamentalism, an interest in maintaining Central Asian order, and even a joint realization on the need to navigate the dangerous transition from traditional socialism in a world dominated by capitalist globalization. To these forces we must also add a mutual feeling of bruised national identity vis-à-vis the United States, something that reaches well beyond the preoccupation with NATO or Taiwan. By taking a closer look at the Russia factor in China's external relations and the China factor in Russian foreign policy, we can see the strength of the bilateral ties is much stronger than might have been expected.

In Central Asia, a stable Russian-Chinese relationship could well lead to a more peaceful and less antagonistic relationship between China and Central Asia. In 1992, then-Russian Foreign Minister Andrei Kozyrev told his Chinese counterpart that "Central Asia should remain a CIS sphere of influence and not a sphere of extremist forces, and, in particular, of Islamic fundamentalism. And in this I think we can count on mutual understanding from our great neighbor [China]." The then-Chinese foreign minister, Qian Qichen, responded that Russia and China "have common interests in preserving stability in the Central Asian region," and added that Chinese policy toward Central Asia would take into account the close ties that had been established over time between Russia and the region.[18]

It is natural, however, that Moscow is concerned about China's growing influence in Central Asia. Some Russian policymakers are worried that the SCO could end up abetting Beijing's efforts to expand its influence in Central Asia. When the Shanghai Five began to take shape in 1996–1997, Russia viewed it as a potentially effective method to manage Central Asian geopolitical developments. Russian policymakers, in effect, hoped that the organization would help them retain a traditional level of influence over developments in Central Asia. From the start, however, Central Asian member states— Kazakhstan, Kyrgyzstan and Tajikistan—were reluctant to rely on Russia's guidance. The three Central Asian states, for example, reached border demarcation agreements with China during the late 1990s without ever consulting Moscow.

At the 2001 Shanghai summit, however, not only Uzbek President Islam Karimov but also Tajik President Emomali Rakhmonov called for improved relations with China. Beijing's growing relationship with the Central Asian states has already created difficulties for Russia. Some Russian scholars have argued that the Chinese stance in bilateral discussion with Russia over the use of water resources has hardened. China is contemplating the diversion of water from up to thirty rivers that originate in northwestern Xinjiang Province but that flow into Kazakhstan and Russia. Russian officials oppose these plans. Comments by President Karimov of Uzbekistan seemed to underscore Russian worries. In a report broadcast on Uzbek television on 16 June 2001, Karimov stated clearly that he would not take orders from Moscow and expressed concerns that Russia might try to manipulate the SCO to mount a campaign against U.S. strategic initiatives, such as NATO expansion and a missile defense shield: "I have put my signature under ideas expressed in the Shanghai Cooperation Organization declaration. . . . It says: cooperation, cooperation, cooperation." He added that "this organization must never turn into a military political bloc. . . . It should not be against any country, should not join certain trends, and should not organize subversive activities against third countries." In another sign of defiance, Karimov stressed a desire for improved Chinese-Uzbek ties: "The sympathies of Chinese leaders and the Chinese people, as a whole, lie with the Uzbek people," Karimov said. "We should be interested in creating long-standing relations with China."[19]

As the Shanghai Five was transformed into the SCO, Moscow increasingly encountered a headache in the region—Uzbekistan. President Karimov attended the 2000 summit in Dushanbe as an observer, and in early 2001 Uzbekistan communicated through diplomatic channels that it was interested in joining the revamped organization. After that request had been favorably received, in May 2001 Uzbekistan announced the intent to join the SCO. During the previous two years Uzbekistan had wavered with respect to cooperating with the

Shanghai group, because Karimov did not want to fall under the influence of a security umbrella extended from Moscow. That is why he sought to establish a special relationship ("strategic partnership") with Washington in the mid- and late 1990s, and further consolidated the partnership after 11 September 2001. For Uzbekistan, its admission to the SCO is a natural development of the consolidation of regional international systems after the end of the transition from the post-Cold War period. It is, however, possible that Uzbekistan's membership will complicate the functioning of the nascent SCO, engaging Russia and China more deeply and more quickly in Central Asia than may otherwise have been expected. This may be the case since the source of instability in Uzbekistan differs from that in the other SCO participants; Uzbekistan's admission to the organization has a potential for creating headaches.[20]

Despite these problems, Russian officials decided to proceed with the formal transformation of the Shanghai Five into the SCO. But the aspirations of the Russian establishment now appear more limited, as some policymakers view the SCO as largely an alliance of convenience with the limited aim of containing Islamic radicalism. When asked about the future direction of the SCO in a news conference following the Shanghai summit in June 2001, President Vladimir Putin said that above all, of course, it is a mechanism for consultations: both high-level consultations and those at the level of specialists. It has already been developed and the use of this mechanism will continue, but the organization is becoming engaged in many fields and will be concerned not only with the problems of regional security, but also with cooperation in the broadest meaning of the word. When asked about the significance of the convention on fighting terrorism and separatism, and whether the document means that this remains the most important question for this organization, Putin responded very diplomatically. He said that "if you noticed, I said about the slogan of the Shanghai Economic Cooperation organization [sic] being newly created—it is security through partnership. I personally and my counterparts would like to move the problem of security precisely into this sphere. We hope that by developing cooperation in the region across the board in the fields of culture, education, science, and interaction in the economic sphere, we will create conditions that will by themselves influence the problem of security beneficially."[21]

China is poised to benefit the most from the SCO. However, Central Asia is not Beijing's foreign policy priority, and Chinese leaders understand well that the old connections between Moscow and the states of Central Asia cannot be broken overnight. Not facing any immediate and serious danger from Central Asia, Chinese leaders formulated their long-term Central Asia strategy with considerable confidence. Driven by a domestic development strategy, Beijing's Central Asia policy is a natural spin-off of the economic development strategy. It emphasizes the long-term stability of the region (to avert threats to Xinjiang) and an increase in Beijing's long-term economic and political influence in the region. While China is sensitive to Moscow's role, it mainly pursues an economic-based approach to the Central Asian states to enhance the prospect of regional stability. As one commentator has pointed out: "There is no uncertainty about China's intention, and ability, to play a major role in Central Asia for the foreseeable future. Even if China's vision of a modern Silk Road is never realized, an economically dynamic and militarily ascendant China seems destined to exert tremendous influence over neighboring Kazakhstan and Kyrgyzstan."[22] Beijing does not look for a head-to-head competition with Russia in the region. Moscow understands that the SCO will increase China's political and economic presence in Central Asia.

But the question is whether all this is conducive to Russia's long-term interest in the region. One Russian official involved in high-level negotiations with China stated that Beijing fully acknowledges Russia's special interest in building a relationship with the countries of Central Asia. China does not make Russia its target when it develops relationships with countries in this region. According to him, both countries cooperate on multilateral bases and do not foresee any challenge.[23]

The SCO and the Role of the United States in Central Asia

Although the United States did not have vital interests in Central Asia before 11 September 2001, Washington acted swiftly and made quick headway into the region following the terrorist attacks on September 11. American interest and penetration in the region not only served to stimulate Sino-Russian cooperation but also drove a wedge between Beijing and Moscow.[24] After the breakup of the Soviet Union, the international politics of Central Asia, to some extent, bore similarities to the "Great Game" of the nineteenth century. The newly independent states lacked any clear sense of national and regional identities beyond the simple need of survival as independent entities. States adjacent to the region tried to exert an influence through ethnic or religious ties to the Central Asian states.[25] Turkey and Iran, with their cultural, linguistic, and religious ties, have the greatest will to become involved in the region. However, the economic realities of the countries do not allow them to become major players. China possesses the capacity to penetrate Central Asia, but does not want to expand its influence at the expense of its new strategic relations with Russia. Instead, China has sought a more moderate economic approach that supplies the region with vital trade while avoiding any security guarantees. That leaves the United States as a major external player in the region.

Before September 11, the major goal of U.S. policy toward the region was to foster stability, democratization, free market economies and trade, denuclearization in the non-Russian states, and adherence to international human rights standards. These objectives were supported by another priority of American policy—to discourage attempts by radical regimes and groups to block or subvert progress toward these goals or otherwise threaten regional and international peace and stability. Although a consensus appears to exist among most U.S. policymakers and others on the general desirability of these goals, some urge different emphases or levels of American involvement. Those who endorse current policy or urge enhanced U.S. aid for Central Asia often support the view that political instability in Central Asia can produce spillover effects in important nearby states, including such Washington allies and friends as Turkey. They also point out that the United States has a major interest in preventing terrorist regimes or organizations from illicitly acquiring nuclear weapons-related materials and technology from the region. They maintain that U.S. interests do not perfectly coincide with those of its allies and friends, that Turkey and other actors possess limited aid resources, and that the United States is in the strongest position as a superpower to influence democratization and respect for human rights in these new states. These same policymakers stress that U.S. leadership in world efforts to provide humanitarian and economic development aid will assist in alleviating the high levels of social distress in the region—distress that is exploited by anti-Western Islamic fundamentalist movements seeking new members. Although many U.S. policymakers recognize that a democratizing Russia has a role in the region, they stress that U.S. and other Western aid and investment must bolster the independence of the states and forestall Russian attempts to resubjugate the region.[26]

Russia and China are also wary about U.S. oil and gas interests in Central Asia and the Caucasus. Moscow fears the U.S. presence will further diminish Russian political and military influence in these former territories of the Soviet Union. Thus, although one cannot altogether rule out Russian approval for coordinated U.S.-Russian military action against terrorism, the convergence of U.S. and Russian views about the Taliban's role in promoting terrorism did not extend to the parties on the U.S. State Department's list of state sponsors of terrorism. Indeed, Cuba, Iran, Libya, North Korea, Sudan, and Syria all maintain good political relations with Moscow. The Caspian holds some of the world's greatest unexplored deposits; many of the world's largest oil companies are exploring, producing, and exporting petroleum from this region. Azerbaijan, which produced half of the world's oil a 100 years ago, is at the forefront of attracting investment to exploit its reserves; so too is Kazakhstan, which probably has more oil than all the others. But these are all landlocked states: transporting oil from here to global markets means the construction of pipelines across other countries. That means influence; and where there is influence, there are big powers trying to gain it. The United States, the world's greatest fuel consumer, has its own preferred route—westward from the Caspian Sea across Azerbaijan, Georgia, and its NATO ally Turkey to the Mediterranean, thereby limiting the current dependence on the Persian Gulf and Russia. China is also in the "Game," seeking pipelines east to feed its burgeoning energy demand. Pakistan and India want to see lines going southward, but that prospect seems remote, since it would mean crossing war-torn Afghanistan.

Although Sino-Russian cooperation in creating the SCO and keeping the West out of the region seemed to be rather successful prior to 11 September, the terrorist attacks on that day completely changed the geopolitical map of Central Asia. A month earlier, it would have seemed absurd to predict that American ground forces would be stationed in Central Asia. The success of the SCO was evidenced by the apparent success in bringing Uzbekistan into the fold. The foreign policy of this key country in Central Asia was heavily pro-American during the entire 1990s. Decreasing American diplomatic activity in the region and Islamic insurgency problems nevertheless drew Tashkent reluctantly closer to Moscow and Beijing in recent years. In this context, recent events provide an opportunity for Uzbekistan, and possibly also for other Central Asian states such as Kazakhstan, to break free from Russia and China and to improve political and military ties with the United States. The increased American presence, which amounts to an opportunity for Central Asian states, runs counter to Chinese interests in the region.

The United States war in Afghanistan has helped it to build a stronghold right on China's very doorstep. Whereas China supports the fight against terrorism and worries about the effect of Islamic radicalism in Afghanistan, it is also wary of an American military presence near its border. Indeed, China had spent considerable energy creating the Shanghai Cooperation Organization, and one of its principal aims is to minimize Western influence in Central Asia. Hence China's attitude toward the war on terrorism will depend on its consequences for the region. Most important, the U.S. relationship with both Pakistan and the Central Asian states has changed substantially, and that is something China cannot overlook. China is concerned about the global and regional political and economic implications of the U.S. war in Afghanistan. China is in favor of capturing Osama bin Laden and establishing a more moderate government in Afghanistan; hence Beijing does seem to share many of Washington's fears and possible goals. However, a military engagement in the hunt for terrorists is limited by economic, political, and domestic considerations, notwithstanding China's support for combating terrorism and separatism. China has been able to find a common interest with Washington in fighting terrorism and separatism in the region. Removing the Taliban regime helped to cut off the external linkage to Uigur separatists in Xinjiang. Many Uigurs have been trained in bin Laden's camps.

By institutionalizing the SCO mechanism to combat terrorism and separatism in the region, China has been able to keep its Muslim separatist movement in check. Chinese leaders have considered whether acting against Islamic radicalism with the support of Russia and the United States is preferable to working through a regional organization like the SCO. It seems that the second option better suits the interests of Beijing's cautious policymakers. Hence Beijing will support the struggle against terrorism insofar as that is compatible with China's internal and regional security. Meanwhile, as the decision to extend military assistance to Tajikistan and joint military exercises with Bishkek and Astana shows, China will remain engaged in Central Asia.

The first and most apparent response to 11 September 2001 was the deep support of the Russian people and across the Russian political spectrum for forceful action to combat terrorism. Less obvious, but perhaps more significant, is the priority that President Putin has attached to economic growth. This goal is intimately tied to his success in gaining Russia's inclusion in what is often referred to as a new international economic and security community. Russian military cooperation with the United States to combat international terrorism is probably perceived by Putin as a golden opportunity to achieve membership in this community. The extent of American-Russian military cooperation is likely to hinge on the willingness of both sides to make key concessions. The United States must treat Russia as an equal and integral partner rather than a short-term, junior associate. The United States also will need to make sincere efforts to forge a truly multilateral coalition and to seek an international legal mandate to employ military force. This latter requirement will be difficult to obtain.

Conclusion: The SCO and China in Central Asia

The SCO serves China's policy toward Central Asia in multiple ways. First and foremost, the SCO has institutionalized border security regimes with Russia and Central Asian states, which is fundamental for China's national security. Second, the SCO has institutionalized the struggle against transitional separatism, terrorism, and radicalism. China supports strong antiterrorism measures due to concerns about its own vulnerability to terrorism in its vast northwestern territories of Tibet and Xinjiang. Since the late 1980s, Muslim separatists in the Xinjiang Uigur Autonomous Region have posed an increasing threat to China's territorial integrity. Xinjiang makes up one-sixth of China's total land area. This vast but thinly populated (16.6 million) region holds potentially large oil deposits (though these are unconfirmed) and

China's nuclear weapons testing site. In recent years, Muslim separatist movements have increasingly resorted to violence, including bomb explosions, assassinations, and street fighting. The central government has responded to the unrest with unrelenting resolve. Islamic fundamentalist elements in Central Asia, Afghanistan, and the Middle East have reportedly trained some of the individuals responsible for these attacks. More worrisome, such attacks may have spread to major cities in China. Through the SCO, China has been able to secure closer cooperation with the Central Asian governments to combat terrorism and separatism—a primary focus of SCO. The antiterrorism center of the SCO is to operate out of Tashkent. The Shanghai Cooperation Organization is a critical part of Chinese efforts to stem and eradicate external links to domestic separatist and terrorist cells. Beijing has also reached out to states in the region suspected of providing havens for terrorist organizations. One Chinese security scholar has argued that "China has made some achievements in cooperating with other countries to combat separatists and terrorists. For instance, the Shanghai Cooperation Organization has been successful in employing political means to clamp down on terrorism in this region. The U.S. can learn from China."[27]

In addition to serving its energy interests, the SCO also has geostrategic values for Beijing. The argument that China worries about the likely expansion of the U.S. military presence in Central Asia is not total nonsense. One legacy of the 1990–1991 Gulf War is an enlarged permanent U.S. military presence in the Persian Gulf and Saudi Arabia. Military operations against Osama bin Laden in Afghanistan could bring U.S. armed forces to South and Central Asia, with which China shares over 5,000 kilometers of borders. Some people believe China is worried that U.S.-led military strikes against Afghanistan may lead to a long-term U.S. military presence in the region. However, I believe that the major powers share some common interests in the region—regional stability, antiterrorism, and rebuilding failed states. Major powers can coexist in the region. The SCO should be used as a bridge to engage with other powers, especially the United States, in terms of maintaining regional stability and antiterrorism. Economically, there is great potential for the member states to strengthen their ties.

Notes

1. See Peter Hopkirk, *The Great Game: The Struggle for Empire in Central Asia* (New York, 1990).
2. *New York Times*, 10 November 2001.
3. See, for example, Zhang Mo, "Shanghai Hezhu Zuzhi de Dansheng" (Birth of Shanghai Cooperation Organization), *Jiefang Ribao* (Jiefang Daily), 15 June 2001.
4. Quoted from the Joint Declaration on the Establishment of the Shanghai Co-

operation Organization, 15 June 2001, Shanghai, China. The text can be found on the website of the Chinese Foreign Ministry at www.prcmfa.gov.cn.

5. See Stephen Blank, "Towards Geostrategic Realignment in Central Asia," *Analyst*, CACI Biweekly Briefing, Wednesday, 10 October 2001; and Russian News Room, "Meetings of Putin in Shanghai and Ljubljana Once Again Demonstrate Ability of Moscow to Protect Its Interests," 22 June 2001 (http://wps.wm.ru:8101/chitalka/military/en/20010622.shtml).

6. See Ethnicity and Religion Research Center, China Institute of Contemporary International Relations, *Shanghai Hezuo Zuzhi in Anquen Guan Yu Xin Jizhi* [Shanghai Cooperation Organization's New Concept of Security and New Mechanism] (Beijing, 2002), pp. 31–36.

7. Kathy Chen, "Foreign Oil Companies Find Risks in Exploring China's Tarim Basin," *Wall Street Journal*, 10 October 1994, p. A1 (as cited in Mamdouh Salameh, "China, Oil and the Risk of Regional Conflict," *Survival*, 37:4 [Winter 1995–1996], p. 139).

8. Ethnicity and Religion Research Center, *Shanghai Hezuo Zuzhi in Anquen Guan Yu Xin Jizhi*, pp. 38–43.

9. Lillian Craig Harris, "Xinjiang, Central Asia and the Implications for China Policy in the Islamic World," *China Quarterly*, no. 133 (March 1993): 123.

10. For the history of the Shanghai Five, see Center of SCO Studies, Shanghai Academy of Social Sciences, *Compilation of Materials and Documents of Shanghai Five-Shanghai Cooperation Organization, April 1996–August 2003* (Shanghai, 2003).

11. At present, the only outstanding problem that the two sides are still working on pertains to the alignment of the boundary in the areas of the Heixiazi Island and the Abagaitu Islet in the eastern section of the Sino-Russian boundary.

12. All information is adapted from the websites of the PRC Ministry of Foreign Affairs at www.fmprc.gov.cn.

13. At the SCO summit in May 2003, the leaders of member states agreed to relocate the antiterrorist center to Tashkent.

14. It was somewhat ironic that Beijing, which now seems poised to benefit most from the organization, initially opposed the transformation of the Shanghai Five into the SCO. Beijing's position changed only after a conservative Republican president came to the White House in January 2001 and Sino-American relations turned sour.

15. See, for example, Shirin Akiner, ed., *Political and Economic Trends in Central Asia* (London, 1993).

16. Peng Shujie and Quian Tong, "President Jiang Zemin and President Putin Hold Talks," Xinhua Domestic Service in Chinese, reported as "Jiang Zemin, Putin Hold Talks, Sign Documents," FBIS-CHI-2000–0718.

17. "Planning a Long-term Cooperation Among the Six Nations: An Interview with Assistant Foreign Minister Liu Guchang," *Xinhua*, 12 June 2001.

18. ITAR-TASS World Service in Russian, 1300 GMT, 25 November 1992, p. 3 (cited in FBIS-SOV, November 27, 1992, p. 9).

19. See "Russia Has Misgivings About Shanghai Cooperation Organization," *Eurasia Insight*, 20 June 2001 (www.eurasianet.org).

20. Ibid.

21. Information taken from the Russian Foreign Ministry website.

22. Ross H. Munro, "Central Asia and China," in Michael Mandelbaum, ed., *Central Asia and the World: Kazakhstan, Uzbekistan, Tajikistan, Kyrgyzstan, Turkmenistan* (New York: Council on Foreign Relations, 1994), p. 236.

23. For Grigoryi Logvinov's interview with Kanwa magazine, see *Kanwa*, 10 May 2001.

24. See Ted Galen Carpenter, "Bush Tries to Drive a Wedge Between Russia and China," Cato Institute, 3 August 2001; and International Crisis Group report, "Central Asia: Fault Lines in the New Security Map" (Brussels), 4 July 2001 (www.crisisweb .org/projects/showreport.cfm).

25. Martha Brill Olcott, *Central Asia's New States: Independence, Foreign Policy, and Regional Security* (Washington, 1996); and John Anderson, *The International Politics of Central Asia* (Manchester, 1997).

26. Jim Nichol, "Central Asia's New States: Political Developments and Implications for U.S. Interests," Congressional Research Service/Foreign Affairs, Defense, and Trade Division, IB93108, (31 March 2000).

27. Yan Xuetong, "Great Changes To Take Place in Global Economic and Political Situation: An Interview with Yan Xuetong, Director of the International Affairs Research Institute at Tsinghua University," Liu Jianfeng, *China Economic Times*, 13 September 2001.

5

Islamic Radicalism in Central Asia: The Influence of Pakistan and Afghanistan

Vyacheslav Belokrenitsky

It is quite clear that Islamic radicalism in Central Asia is part of the broader process that has overtaken the contemporary world. Despite its internal roots, it cannot be understood solely in national terms. External ties and contacts, the influence of international forces (both those rather close to the region and those far removed from it) on the emergence and evolution of Central Asian Islamic radicalism, constitute the principal focus of the present essay. The main attention is given to the impact of radical Islam in Pakistan, an influence that comes to Central Asia primarily through Afghanistan.

Before turning to the local variant of Islamic radicalism, it is important to pose the question in more general terms. As a prominent political phenomenon, it has existed since the late 1970s and early 1980s—that is, from the time of the revolution in Iran, the attempt to stage a coup d'état in Saudi Arabia, the execution of Islamists in Syria, the Islamization of the Sudan and Pakistan, and the rise to power of the Taliban in Afghanistan. Since then people have repeatedly laid Islamic radicalism to rest only to find it reappear.[1]

Islamic radicalism (like many other extremist movements) arises from forces that operate on various levels. At the first (international) level, the secondary literature has already pointed out that, when it first emerged, Islamic radicalism was a byproduct of the Cold War—amid a bitter struggle for the minds and hearts of people in the Muslim countries. The West, to a certain degree, counted on Islamic radicalism to weaken the predisposition of the politically active to be drawn toward the left-wing alternative of Soviet Marxism.[2] The second (regional) level is associated with the competition between the Muslim and non-Muslim countries, such as Israel and its Arab neighbors, or Pakistan and India. Moreover, it appeared in combination with an ethnic-national factor (Palestinian Kashmir); hence it often lacked or sublimated the puritanical, fundamentalist component and, instead, acquired a unifying idea of religious irredentism.[3] The third (domestic) level is within a country itself, where Islamic radicalism has been a means for political and ideological opposition to a regime and a weapon for overthrowing the ruling authorities (as in the case of Iran). The revolutionary pathos of domestic politics is closely associated with messianism and maximalism in foreign policy, which (as in the Iranian variant) has been enthusiastically elevated over narrow state interests. The latter, however, in fact had a most important, critical significance, for it ensured the preservation and security of the new ruling order. The fourth level is a subnational and transnational (crossborder) level, where Islamic radicalism broke down into sects and currents. Examples include the Shia among the Hazaras of Afghanistan and Pakistan, Ismailism in the natural habitat of the Pamir junction (Gorno-Badakhshan oblast, the Afghan province of Badakhshan) and the districts of Gilgit and Baltistan in the part of Kashmir under Pakistani control, or Sufism among the Uigurs of Xinjiang Uigur Autonomous Region in China. Moreover, radicalism at the lower level, and to a large degree at the other levels as well, constitutes an assertive or sometimes a defensive response (in a political and ideological sense) capitalizing on certain characteristic basic elements of religious consciousness.

From the beginning of the 1990s, changes in the structure of Islamism have followed the end of the Cold War. The global level was characterized by a "dualism of the center." The collapse of the socialist camp in the USSR brought a precipitous weakening of left-wing ideology in the world. The West lost the need to support its conservative religious alternative, and Islamic radicalism found itself face-to-face with this. Not only Moscow, but also Beijing ceased to play the role of ideological and strategic adversaries of Washington and the entire Western world. What happened was something quite rare—a decline in the level of ideological confrontation. That has impelled Francis Fukuyama to proclaim an "end" of history—as an epoch of struggle between counterpoised global projects for the construction of a better life.[4]

However, as the Russian proverb puts it, "a sacred place does not stay unoccupied": the conflict of interests at the global level continued, but now as a competition of ideas associated with civil (nation-state) and cultural identities that, in turn, were based on religion and civilization. Moreover, in many cases a civic identity (loyalty to one's state and belief in it) proved to be closely linked to a cultural and religious identity and, in some cases, with their syncretic complex.

Pushed to the side, along with the leftist alternative, was "secularism" of a classic variety (with a separation of church and state), and in its place came a new kind of "secularity." The latter consists of having the regime support confessions in proportion to their presence in society. Such a "democratization of secularism" accompanied a natural increase in the political role of religions and religious ideologies. The defeat of atheistic socialism on a world scale proved at once a defeat for secularism and, possibly, the traditions of classical enlightenment and humanism. By the onset of the twenty-first century, one could see an upsurge of forces that rely on conservative antiliberalism, on cultural and religious nationalism, and all of which is transpiring not only in the natural habitat of Muslim civilization.[5]

The new situation, at the same time, has been reflected at all levels and in the vertical cross-section of forces associated with Islamic radicalism. The main impulse consisted in the fact that, on the global ideological axis a transnational underground level has appeared. A clandestine international network emerged in the sphere it unified and directed the struggle of various national groups of Islamists against ruling authorities at all levels—subnational, national, regional, and global. The earlier vertical links have largely forfeited their significance; now (in a post-bipolar world) the regional states could no longer count on the pragmatic goals of the competing centers of power. A new axis appeared after the end of the Cold War to summon all levels of political cooperation, largely placing all streams of radical Islam on a single plane.

Islamism, moreover, has become increasingly extremist. On the one hand, it is desperately applying the methods of a sabotage and terrorist struggle; it prepares and carries out actions to destroy people for purposes of vengeance and intimidation; it endeavors to create a "terrorist hell," relying on the new phenomenon of self-sacrifice by suicide terrorists (*shaheeds*). On the other hand, Islamic radicals proclaim their goal to be not so much that of transforming the existing national territorial states into Islamic states, as that of creating a universal caliphate that knows none of the existing boundaries. Its basis is to be the Islamic code of law (*sharia*), which is binding for the entire Islamic community (*umma*) and transcends national and religious frameworks.[6] There ensues a process whereby the radicalism becomes still more extreme, with an intensification of its ideological isolation and narrowing of its mass base. All this seemingly permits it to become marginalized and subject to ostracism. Marginalizing it, however, has proven difficult for a whole series of reasons. The most important of these is the unwillingness of certain structures in the government, but also some social circles, in a number of Muslim countries to smash such a tool in the political game that Islamic radicalism has always been and continues to be. An additional factor is the humanitarian situation, which is rather favorable for Islamists—namely, the preservation or increase in the mass of those who are poor and unfortunate, who are illiterate and semiliterate, who suffer from various ills, who have been deceived in their expectations, and who have been neglected by the authorities.

The Birth of Radical Islam in Central Asia and the Role of Pakistan

In the history of contemporary radicalism on the territory of Soviet Central Asia, one can provisionally identify several stages.[7] The preconditions for the initial stage emerged in the late 1960s as a result of changes in Moscow's religious policy. In place of the repression practiced by Khrushchev (and characteristic of a Marxist ideological rigor), authorities in the Brezhnev period practiced a more tolerant policy. Beginning in 1968, as Bennigsen and Broxup have pointed out, Moscow gradually began to raise the "iron curtain" that for decades had isolated Central Asia and the Caucasus from the world of Islam.[8] Since then, Muslim leaders in the Soviet Union have repeatedly visited Muslim states to establish contacts with local religious activists and to participate in various international conferences on the subjects of Islam, its culture and education, and inter-confessional dialogue.[9] Simultaneously, the USSR and, above all, Central Asia received visits by delegations of religious activists from Muslim countries to take part in events organized by the leaders of official Soviet Islam—above all, the great mufti of Tashkent, Z. Babakhanov.[10]

This process of partly opening up Central Asia to the external Islamic world proved to be a double-edged sword. On the one hand, it yielded considerable benefits for Soviet foreign policy: it demonstrated freedom of confession in the Muslim regions of the USSR and thereby served to strengthen Moscow's position in the Islamic world. On the other hand, it forced authorities to take measures to support official Islam, and these inevitably served to erode, in public consciousness, the perception that religion and religious practice were forbidden and anachronistic.

The removal "from above" of the public taboo on Islam coincided, in the 1970s, with signs of a renaissance "from below." The thesis that, during the Soviet period, Islam continued to exist in Central Asia on the periphery of official life has been well documented. A significant number of works explain the causes and special features of this process and characterize it both in terms of individual cases and broader patterns of development.[11] Studies have also closely followed the sources of the politicization of Islam—the emergence of radical Islamic currents that created a conceptual platform to oppose the official ideology and policy of secular authorities.

Among the first to examine the question of an Islamic renaissance was A. Abduvakhitov, who prepared an article on this subject already in the Soviet era.[12] His article asserts that the signs of a politicization of Islam in Uzbekistan were already visible at the end of the 1970s. These were manifested, above all, in the dissemination of a religious education that had not received the sanction of the government and that addressed the youth, especially those coming from traditionally religious families (which were often associated with the official figures from the Spiritual Administration of Muslims in Central Asia).[13] Simultaneously, a network of "parallel" Islam appeared. One of its spiritual leaders was a resident of Margilan, Khakim Kari (Khakimdzhan Kori), who was born in 1896 or 1898.[14]

He has been described as one of the spiritual fathers of the most influential, early groups of reformers-renewers by B. Babadzhanov, an author who is now deeply involved in the study of the history and contemporary status of the religious oppositionist movement in Central Asia.[15] At the same time, Babadzhanov emphasizes the contribution of yet another influential teacher-theologian, Mukhammadzhan Rustamov Hindustani (1894–1989), the imam of a mosque in Dushanbe from 1956 until his death.[16] As his name suggests and the facts of his biography confirm, he studied for several years in colonial India and, after a hajj in 1930, returned to his homeland.[17] In my opinion, his experience in India, to a significant degree, may explain his negative attitude toward "Wahhabism" and why he was one of the first to apply the term "Wahhabi" to the radically minded reformers from the group of the "Mujjaddidiya" (renewer).[18]

In fact, in the 1920s in India, the term "Wahhabi" was applied to adherents of a sect that was most hostile toward Anglo-Indian authorities. In the middle of the nineteenth century the British harshly persecuted the "Wahhabis" and were able to put an end to their antigovernment outbursts and terrorist activities. Aware of the connotation firmly associated with this term, the leaders of orthodox circles of Wahhabism (who, at the same time, renounced violent methods of struggle) repeatedly urged the British authorities to refrain from using the term "Wahhabism" in official documents. The British ultimately agreed and began to employ a term that the adherents of this current themselves used—"people of the book" (*Ahle-e Hadis*). However, the negative connotation of "Wahhabism" remained; it continued to be used by the Wahhabis' competitors among the ranks of Muslims themselves.[19] And it was with the latter that Muhammadzhan Rustamov

Hindustani had associated during his years in India; probably this circumstance, not the hajj that he made later (as Babadzhanov suggests), led him to use the terms "Wahhabism" and "Wahhabis" as a designation for those militants who opposed Soviet (representing unholy, not truly Islamic) authorities. These terms later were applied to the Islamist opposition during the civil war in Tajikistan.

The foregoing example makes it quite clear how contemporary historiography has underestimated the contribution of Muslim currents in South Asia (India and Pakistan) to the genesis and dissemination of radical Islamic ideas on the other side of the Hindu Kush Mountains. Of course, the Arab epicenter of traditionalist rigorism played a relatively bigger role.[20]

A direct and indirect influence on the dissemination of Islamist views and ideas in Central Asia, without doubt, resulted from the deliberate policy of military authorities in Islamabad during the Soviet-Afghan war, especially in the mid-1980s. As is evident from a book by Brigadier M. Yusouf (head of the "Afghan Cell" in Pakistan's Directorate of Inter-Service Intelligence [ISI]), the Pakistani military trained a number of groups to act beyond the Amu Darya on Soviet territory. From 1984 to 1987, Afghan mujahideen (fighters for the faith)—trained by the Pakistanis—conducted a series of successful acts of sabotage in the contiguous river areas in Tajikistan and Uzbekistan. One of their main goals was to disseminate copies of the Koran and other literature in native tongues among the local population and, with the latter's assistance, to send these into the heart of Central Asia. Such literature was capable of provoking hostile attitudes toward the Soviet regime, but also served to heighten the feelings of Muslim solidarity. According to this source, the Central Intelligence Agency of the United States assisted in preparing and delivering the Islamic literature to Pakistan. In 1984 alone, Afghani groups—trained by Pakistani intelligence—sent five thousand copies of the Koran across the border. The backbone of these groups came from people living in the northern Afghanistan, above all Uzbeks, among whom there stood out the field commander Vali Beg, a man of peasant origin.[21] Moreover, the base camps of groups entering Soviet territory were located north of Peshawar—in Chitral district, on the border with Afghanistan.

After a series of diplomatic demarches by Moscow, authorities in Washington and Islamabad decided to terminate this sabotage activity.[22] However, the psychological and propagandistic effect from this subversion undoubtedly had serious, long-term impact.

Reports on the activity of the Pakistan intelligence services and their role in promoting Islamic radicalism in Central Asia also appear in literature "from the other side." A participant in the Afghan war, General A.A. Liakhovskii, writes that the organization "Islamic Union of the Northern Peoples of Afghanistan" (*Islamskii soiuz severnykh narodov Afganistana*), established in 1988, launched subversive activities in areas of Central Asia contiguous with Afghanistan, with the goal of liberating Soviet Muslims and creating a "free Turkestan." According to Liakhovskii, the organization had its headquarters in Peshawar and had a certain Azad Beg as its head. Citing information from Soviet military and intelligence organs, Liakhovskii claims that the field commanders of this organization shipped narcotics, weapons, and subversive (mainly Islamic) literature to the USSR.[23] Hence Pakistan's policy had a definite impact on Central Asia during the Soviet era after the conclusion of the Geneva agreements in April 1988 and the withdrawal of Soviet forces from Afghanistan, and also later (right up to the civil war in Tajikistan). It should be pointed out that, notwithstanding the fact that Benazir Bhutto's secular government came to power in Pakistan in autumn 1988, Islamabad did not make any fundamental changes in its military-political strategy. As under the military rule of Mohammad Zia ul-Haq, Pakistan aimed to create a zone "of strategic depth" north of the country's borders—a zone that would consist of areas of Afghanistan and Kashmir under Islamabad's control, but in the larger perspective all of Muslim Central Asia.[24]

The existence of such plans was very likely known in the capitals of the Central Asian republics. The alarm in official circles probably gave rise to glee in the oppositionist groups, which had experienced a feeling of pride over the Muslim victory in the war against the Russian superpower. These attitudes were reinforced by reports that some of the Soviet soldiers taken prisoner by the mujahideen converted to Islam and refused to return home.[25]

The first stage in the history of radical Islamism in Central Asia ended with the breakup of the Soviet Union. Next followed the "hottest" period—that is, the years of civil war in Tajikistan (1992–1997) and then, after a respite, a surge of subversive actions in 1999–2001 by extremists from the Islamic Movement of Uzbekistan. Both episodes were directly tied to events in Afghanistan and the policy of Islamabad.

Pakistan's Islamic Radicalism and the Afghan Jihad

Scholarly and popular literature about Islamic resistance in Afghanistan (especially the works published in Russian) has downplayed, to some degree, the role played by Pakistan.[26] It is difficult to say why this is so. In the Soviet Union, and later in Russia, there was an aversion to laying emphasis on a struggle with Pakistan that, from the perspective of Moscow, loomed as a lesser opponent. The latter traditionally was in the shadow of India and generally seen only as a counterweight within the framework of the region of South Asia. Of significance was the following: although the military—which conducted a campaign of Islamization—had come to power in Pakistan, Moscow continued to see the country as a modern Muslim regime. Hence the Kremlin maintained normal diplomatic relations with Islamabad and continued to cooperate in the economic sphere. Revealingly, at the very height of the military campaign in Afghanistan, the USSR granted Pakistan a preferential credit for over 400 million dollars and provided assistance in completing the construction of a huge metallurgical complex near Karachi.[27] The leaders of the USSR, in all likelihood, regarded Pakistan as a victim of historical circumstances and subject to the fate of being an opponent of Moscow. The main factors, from Russia's perspective, were those who supported the Afghan jihad from without (the United States, Saudi Arabia, China, and so forth) and who used Pakistani territory to conduct a war by proxy. The Kremlin's approach probably reflected a desire to avoid undermining relations with an important economic partner, as well as an underestimation of Pakistan as a rather independent player on the international arena and capable of playing a major role with a long-term perspective.

Nevertheless, the significance of Pakistan in organizing and inspiring the Afghan jihad requires, in my opinion, a more precise and detailed characterization. This pertains both to its direct role as a state and to the activities of radical Islamic forces and the circles that really govern that country.

The "military-Islamist" synthesis (a term that is entirely appropriate) became evident after the army, headed by Mohammad Zia ul-Haq, came to power in Pakistan in the summer of 1977. But it actually emerged around 1974, that is, under the preceding administration of Zulfiqar Ali Bhutto. It was then that the government showed a taste for Islamic rhetoric and for a domestic and foreign policy oriented toward Islam. Characteristic in this regard was Bhutto's decision to accommodate the demands of religious radicals that he declared the modernist, pro-Western sect Ahmadi (of Ahmadis or Ahmadiya) to be "un-Islamic." And, with great ceremony and enormous propagandistic effect, Bhutto held a conference of leaders from Muslim countries in Lahore (the second largest city in Pakistan), it later came to be known as the second summit of the Organization of the Islamic Conference (OIC).

From 1975 the Pakistan-Afghani Islamist corridor began to take shape. The authorities in Afghanistan exposed a conspiracy of Islamists and an attempt to instigate an uprising (in particular, in Panjir Valley); the leaders of the main opposition organizations and antigovernment forces (Gulbuddin Hekmatyar, Burhanuddin Rabbani, and Ahmad Shah Masood) emigrated to Pakistan. As later became known, they conducted military preparations under the leadership of instructors from the elite special services of Pakistan.[28]

Illegal connections across the borders of Pakistan and Afghanistan intensified after the rebellion of the Baluchi tribes in Pakistan in 1974–1977. After suffering a defeat, some of the leftist groups moved to the territory of Afghanistan and established its base camps on that side of the border. After the execution of Zulfiqar Ali Bhutto in April 1979, illegal Pakistani emigres in Afghanistan came to include groups supporting the former prime minister. In Kabul, under the cover of the new procommunist authorities, the opponents to Zia ul-Haq established an underground organization, Al-Zulfikar. Its leader was Bhutto's son Murtaza (interestingly, both he and his brother Shah Navaz were married to Afghani women). Individual Pakistanis, prominent leaders of the leftist movement, became embroiled in the power struggle in Kabul and were imprisoned under Hafizullah Amin.

The various cross-border links between Pakistan and Afghanistan increased after the coup in April 1978 (the so-called "Saur [spring] Revolution"). They received a further impulse after the intervention of Soviet forces on the eve of Christmas in 1979, as official authorities in Islamabad refused to recognize the Afghan government headed by Babrak Karmal. Beginning in 1980, the main forces of the Afghan opposition openly established themselves in Pakistan. By that time, the ideological and political platforms of the combatants in Afghanistan had become clearly defined. On the Kabul side, people fought under a red flag (given the backwardness of the country from the point of view of being ready for "the construction of socialism," Moscow called these forces in the official parlance "proto-socialist or popular-democratic"); those on the other side fought under the green banner of Islam.

Official Islamabad did not want to intervene directly in the military actions for fear of provoking a harsh response from the Soviet Union. The threat from the north, at the same time, provided a convenient excuse to remain in the background and to extract the maximum advantage from Pakistan's status as a front-line state.

These advantages were threefold. First, they included political and diplomatic benefits: Pakistan became a central element in the struggle of a broad international coalition in the south against the advance of an "aggressive Soviet communism." Second, Pakistan gained in prestige and legitimacy: the actions of the military, which had usurped power in the country, appeared in hindsight to be justified, since Pakistan—against the background of the war in Afghanistan—stood out as relatively calm, orderly, and pro-Western. The devotion of military rulers to Islamic values raised Islamabad's authority in the Muslim world, while the confrontation with India increased Pakistan's importance in the eyes of China. Third, there were also material and financial benefits. From the early 1980s, Pakistan became the main avenue for the delivery of weapons, medicine, and foodstuffs to the Afghan mujahideen and the members of their families who were placed in the numerous camps in the Pakistani areas contiguous to Afghanistan. Some weapons did not reach the Afghans and augmented the reserves of the Pakistani armed forces. The transfer of huge resources (according to some estimates, no less than 3.5 billion dollars had passed through Pakistan to the Afghan jihad by the end of the 1980s)[29] created opportunities to divert huge sums to the pockets of officials at various levels as well as staff of private organizations performing various organizational and middleman functions.

Something must also be said about the activity of Pakistani radical Islamic organizations. Without delving into the question of the emergence and evolution of Islamic radicalism in that country, I would only like to note its deep historic roots. This phenomenon developed in close connection with the Arab epicenter of Islamism and correlated with the phases of its rise and fall in the Arab East and entire Muslim world. The last upward phase began in the 1970s and, from a material point of view, resulted from the sudden leap in the income from oil exports. Without doubt, petrodollars from Saudi Arabia had a substantial impact on the political situation in Pakistan in the first half of 1977, where it bolstered the position of Islamist parties during the domestic political crisis that ensued after parliamentary elections in February and March. The seizure of power by the military in July of that year would have been impossible without the tacit support of certain circles in Riyadh. The program of Islamization pursued by the military under Zia ul-Haq had the full backing of the main centers of Islamism in the Arab world. It was on this wave that the leading organizations of political Islam, above all Jamaat-e-Islami (Islamic Society), reinforced their position.

Jamaat-e-Islami played the main role in the jihad against Soviet troops in Afghanistan in 1980–1989. It was the first to create a fighting organization Al-Badr to act in Afghanistan; named in honor of the victory of the prophet Mohammed, it helped the Pakistani special services (above all, the directorate of Inter-Service Intelligence) to establish contact with the Afghan mujahideen. Pakistani intelligence had its closest ties to Gulbuddin Hekmatyar, leader of the Afghan Hezb-e-Islami (Party of Islam). It also received a significant share of the resources directed to those participating in the struggle against communist Kabul and Soviet forces.[30]

Although the military leadership of Pakistan, above all Zia ul-Haq himself, demonstrated a great trust and emphatic veneration of Muslim clerics and *ulama* (religious scholars), in particular from Jamaat-e-Islami, they did not give Muslim leaders access to real power.[31] The refusal of the military to share power and responsibility with the theologians from Jamaat-e-Islami (as it imposed a program of Islamization from above) had diverse consequences on the Afghan war and regional situation.

Above all, the activities of authorities helped to increase competition and dissension within the ranks of Islamists. In the course of a decade, five main currents gradually emerged within radical Islam and showed signs of growing tension and animus. Moreover, the inconsistent policy of the military toward the ulama from Jamaat-e-Islami evidently led to a cooling in relations between Islamabad and Saudi Arabia in the mid-1980s and to a rapprochement with Iran. The latter development at the end of the 1980s encouraged Pakistan's engagement in Central Asia, to a certain degree together with Iran, but this disappeared after the collapse of the USSR and the growing competition with Iran for control over Afghanistan.

After seizing power and launching a campaign for the Islamization of various spheres of the country's social, political, and economic life, the Pakistani army could not control the differences between the adherents of the various Muslim sects and movements. Above all, the schism between Sunni and Shiites became deeper. The attempt of the authorities to introduce uniform rules for the levy of voluntary Muslim taxes (*zakat* [obligatory alms] and *ushr* [tithe]) encountered energetic resistance from the Shiite community and in 1980 led to the creation of its religious political party, Tehrik-e-Nifaz-e-Fiqahe-Jaffariya (Movement for the establishment of Jaffari [i.e., Shiite] law). The Shiite movement is easily radicalized, for it is based on one of the most esoteric branches of Islam.[32]

The military decided to satisfy the basic demands of the Shiites and, in particular, gave them an opportunity to collect and spend the funds from charitable levies. At the same time, the authorities ignored the formation, in remote areas of the country, of radical Sunni groups that directed their hatred at the Shiites. For the most part, these Sunni belonged to the traditionalist, puritanical stream headed by the large religious party, Jamiat-e Ulama-e Islam (Association of Islamic Theologians). The ideological pillar of this party was the tradition that has its roots in the teaching of ulama who were grouped around the seminar established in 1867 in Deoband in northern India. The puritanism of these Deoband ulama, in particular, was apparent in their very critical attitude toward Shiites, while their traditionalism was manifested in a tolerant view of Sufism. As for dogma, they laid an emphasis not so much on the construction of an Islamic state as the predominance of sharia (Islamic law).[33]

As a party of the parliamentary type, Jamiat-e Ulama-e Islam had a solid position in a number of areas of the country, especially among the Pushtun in the northwest. In the first half of the 1980s, it rapidly expanded the network of mosques and *madrassas* (religious schools) under the control and influence of the Deoband ulama. Simultaneously, it created Deoband armed units—above all, the Sipahi-e-Sahaba Pakistan ("Pakistani soldiers of the Prophet"); it established the Lashkar-e-Jhangvi ("army in honor of Haq. Nawaz. Jhangvi," the slain founder of the Sipahi-e-Sahaba Pakistan). In response to the actions of the Sunni extremists, the Shiites became radicalized. Their ranks came to include armed contingents, above all, Sipahi Muhammad ("Soldiers of Mohammad").

Another current radicalized during the "Islamization from above" relied on the traditions of popular Islam among the lower classes. In dogmatic terms, it was shaped by the ulama of the school of Barelvi (named after the religious teacher Ahmad Reza Khan Barelvi and a seminary in northern India), which, under Zia ul-Haq, found itself under pressure by the ulama from Deoband. The political party of Barelvi, Jamaat-e Ulama-e Pakistan (Jamiat-e Ulama-e Pakistan, "Association of Pakistani Religious Teachers") came to oppose the military regime. Its influence noticeably declined, but the creation of armed units, such as Sunni Tehrik (the Sunni Movement) came later, in the 1990s. Nevertheless, from the mid-1980s the countryside and small towns were witness to bloody clashes between the two groups of ulama— those of the Deoband and those of Barelvi schools, but this was overshadowed by the animosity between the Deoband Sunni and Shiites.

A fifth current, which noticeably reinforced its position during the decade when the military held power, can be called Wahhabi. However, it did not have direct genetic ties with the Saudi Wahhabism. The movement Ahl-e Hadis (People of Tradition) had already appeared in colonial India at the end of the nineteenth century, entirely independent from the Saudi center of the truly pure Islam (Salafism or Wahhabism). The movement underwent a second rebirth in the 1960s when, in Lahore (the main city of the largest Pakistani province of Punjab), there arose the Markaz Jamaat-e Ahl-e–Hadis (Center of Society of People of Tradition). Twenty years later the leading position within the framework of this movement belonged to the organization Dawat-wal-Irshad (Summons and Admonition), which was headed by a professor of the Lahore Technological University, Hafiz Saeed, and his military organization Lashkar-e-Toiba (Army of the Pure).[34]

Radical Islam in Pakistan, which increased in influence in the 1980s, acted on what might be provisionally termed three fronts: the internal, Afghan, and Kashmir. Throughout the period of Soviet military engagement in the affairs of Afghanistan, the Afghan front was the most substantial. Moreover, Islamic radicals did not assume the leading role, but only supported the efforts of the country's military leadership and, concretely, its intelligence organs.

A further consequence of the policies pursued by Zia ul-Haq and his coterie was the cooling in the relations between Pakistan and Saudi Arabia. The underlying reasons for this are not fully clear. In any case, in the second half of the 1980s this led to an improvement in Pakistan's ties with the Khomeini

regime in Iran.[35] On the surface that brought a renewal of regional cooperation between Iran, Pakistan, and Turkey; until 1979, this had been represented in the Regional Cooperation for Development and, from 1985, in the
Economic Cooperation Organization. The rapprochement with Teheran was
highly desirable for Islamabad at the concluding phase of the Soviet-Afghan
war, since the final expulsion of the Soviets from Afghanistan was largely
dependent on close Pakistani-Iranian ties. Iran still had millions of Afghan
refugees and hosted centers of Shiite organizations that were fighting with
Kabul under the flag of a holy war of Muslims.

Pakistan was also supposed to coordinate its strategic plans to penetrate
the area north of Afghanistan—the former republics of Soviet Central Asia.
Islamabad proposed to turn these territories into a zone governed by Islam;
that, in turn, would provide Pakistan with a strategic rear in the event of
conflict with India. The intentions of Zia ul-Haq, in principle, were compatible with the views of Ayatollah Khomeini, the spiritual and political leader
of Iran. However, their deaths (in 1988 and 1989 respectively) impeded coordination of the efforts of these two Muslim states.

At the same time, several factors continued to draw Pakistan and Iran
closer together. Primary among these was the vitality unexpectedly displayed
by the Afghan regime of Mohammed Najibullah. So long as he remained in
power in Kabul (until the spring of 1992), the underlying contradictions between groups of his enemies (who received support, on the one hand, from
Islamabad and, on the other hand, from Teheran) were not fully evident. The
changes in the global balance of power also had an impact. As Washington
and Moscow developed closer ties during the final phase of the Cold War,
one consequence was a divergence of goals pursued in Afghanistan by the
United States and Pakistan. The ruling elite in the last military-Islamist regime of Pakistan hoped to extend its success—namely, by exploiting the
withdrawal of the Soviet Union from Afghanistan in order to move north-
ward, into Central Asia. However, the United States was satisfied with the
outcome in Afghanistan and feared destabilizing the center of Asia and
strengthening the position of Islamists in this region (first and foremost, Islamists from Iran, but also those from Pakistan and Arab countries). The split
between the former allies in the Afghan resistance was clearly evident during
the international political crisis that erupted after Iraq invaded Kuwait and the
ensuing war in the Persian Gulf. The growth of anti-American sentiment in the
polity of Pakistan, especially in influential military circles, intensified when
Washington, in October 1990, suspended military and economic assistance to
Islamabad. The American administration refused to deliver the F-16 jet fighters to Pakistan and demonstrated that the United States was shifting to a more
balanced policy in South Asia—one more favorable toward India.

This break with America made Pakistan's policy more amenable to Iran. It was precisely during this period (which included an unfinished war in Afghanistan, crisis in the Near East, and the breakup of the Soviet Union) that Pakistan exerted its greatest influence on the situation in Central Asia. The main instrument for exerting influence was the Pakistani special services, above all the Inter-Service Intelligence. Its agents still had access to Rabbani and Massoud and, together with them, planned operations to destabilize the regime in Kabul and to support opposition Islamist forces in Soviet Central Asia, above all in Tajikistan.[36]

The peak of this influence came in the spring of 1992, when two events occurred simultaneously. One was in Afghanistan: the Najibullah regime was overthrown, and the mujahideen came to power and formed a provisional administration under the pro-Pakistani S. Mojaddedi. At the same time, in Tajikistan, the old order broke down, and the Islamist oppositionists won the first victories in the struggle for power.[37] The visit by the Russian minister of foreign affairs, Andrei Kozyrev, to Kabul in May 1992 signified the nadir in Moscow's engagement in the south.

By the end of that year, however, the situation in both countries changed, but not in favor of Pakistan. Rabbani, elected as the new provisional president of an Islamic Afghanistan in December 1992, extended his authority—notwithstanding resistance to these plans on the part of Islamabad. At the time, the forces supported by Moscow held a clear predominance in Tajikistan, and that predetermined the outcome of the civil war. Pakistan's attempt to promote an upsurge of Islamism in Central Asia and, with the assistance of Islamic forces, to strengthen its own positions in the region encountered three obstacles.[38] One was the lack of sufficient objective conditions in the political consciousness and culture of the indigenous population. Islamism has been successful among a small part of the population and has only won the support of politically significant forces when combined with nationalism—as an ideology justifying Central Asian separatism and independence from Moscow. A second obstacle was the opposition of Iran, which could not abide Pakistan's dominance in Afghanistan and its intercession as the leading player in the new Central Asia. A third barrier was the semi-isolation that enveloped Pakistan because of the decline in American interest, but also because of the regime's domestic weakness (which, in turn, led to the protracted internal political crisis of 1993).

Afghanistan Under the Taliban and the Situation in Central Asia

The mid-1990s marked a kind of pause in the growth of Pakistan-Afghan influence in Central Asia under the aegis of Islamic radicalism. The new government of Pakistan under Benazir Bhutto (who came into power again after the elections in the fall of 1993) endeavored to bring order to Afghanistan and to bolster Pakistan's presence in the center of Asia. Given the weakness of the army and military intelligence, the Bhutto regime relied mainly on Hekmatyar and his Hezb-e-Islami in Afghanistan. It made Jamaat-e Ulama-e Islami its ally and gave it an opportunity to emerge from the shadow of Jamaat-e-Islami and to mobilize those whom it had trained in the tightly woven web of madrassas and seminaries along the borders of Pakistan and Afghanistan.

In all probability, the Pakistan government did not aim to assist the more radical Islamist forces in Afghanistan. Rather, it sought to promote political stabilization and to clear the way for the repatriation of several million Afghan refugees, who lived in numerous camps and temporary settlements in the zone where the Pushtun population had historically resided. Simultaneously, this would facilitate opening a pathway to the north, to Turkmenistan and Uzbekistan, something that was advantageous in commercial-economic and regional political terms. As is well known, the key role in realizing these plans was played by an alternative group in the military bureaucracy that had been formed during the Zia ul-Haq years and had a retired general and minister of internal affairs, Naseerullah Babar, as its head.[39] The latter is often called the "godfather" of the Taliban, the students from Islamic schools who became the core of the movement that emerged as the leading military-political force in Afghanistan in 1994–1996.

During this period, Central Asia was undergoing the process of building and consolidating new state structures. The position of the Islamic opposition in Uzbekistan and Tajikistan had already been undermined in 1992–1993, but persisted. Moreover, the main foreign support for oppositionist Islamic forces came from the Afghan government of Burhanuddin Rabbani; his forces firmly controlled the northern and northeastern areas of Afghanistan bordering on Tajikistan.[40] Iran also played a role, but was of limited importance; it did not want to sour relations with Moscow, which by then had strengthened its position as the guarantor of stability and order in Tajikistan, and indeed throughout Central Asia.

Furthermore, Iran had long since operated with the sober understanding that it lacked the power to combat, simultaneously, the United States and Russia, and it preferred partnership with the latter in order to oppose its more powerful and dangerous adversary.[41] This overriding objective dictated how Teheran would regard the situation in Afghanistan and its relations with Pakistan. The Bhutto government's solicitation of American support inevitably eroded ties between the Muslim neighbors, and the patronage that Islamabad had given the Taliban created a new watershed dividing these two states on the Afghan question.[42]

At a time when, at the official level, Pakistan's capacity to influence the situation in Central Asia was minimal, it did encounter certain opportunities on a hidden, unofficial front. As the struggle of Islamists in Tajikistan abated in 1993–1994 and had completely ended by 1997, the conflict gave rise to a group of militant Uzbeks under Tahir Yuldashev and Juma Namangani (Khojaev). In the early 1990s, they had been associated with the Islamic party Adolat ("Justice"), which operated for a brief period of time in Uzbekistan but was then outlawed. Although the reconciliation in Tajikistan forced the radical Uzbeks to abandon the struggle against Tajik authorities, they retained their base in Tavildara Valley under Islamist control as well as in the Garm raion. This base, under the field commander Namangani, attracted Uzbeks opposed to the regime of Islam Karimov. The main source of income for this underground Uzbek community was the drug business from Afghanistan. In 1995, Yuldashev relocated to Peshawar. Local Islamists from the Jamiat-e Ulama-e Islam, along with agents from the Pakistani Inter-Service Intelligence, provided assistance in the initial organizational phase of creating the Islamic Movement of Uzbekistan. They also helped the Uzbek Islamists establish contact with the Taliban.[43]

At the end of September 1993 the Taliban took control of the Afghan capital, Kabul, but subsequently suffered a severe defeat at the hands of Ahmad Shah Masood's forces. Only by mobilizing all forces (which entailed closing religious schools and seminaries in Pakistan), relying on the assistance of Pakistan's military, and sending young people (who had not finished their schooling) to the front was the Taliban movement able to correct the situation and preserve control over the capital. The Taliban had to resort to yet another total mobilization in May 1997—in the wake of a crushing defeat in northern Afghanistan (around Mazar-e Sharif).[44]

By this time, Pakistan had undergone changes that would have a direct impact on the Taliban. In February 1997, extraordinary elections gave power to a government headed by Nawaz Sharif (leader of the party called Pakistan Muslim League [PML], which was ideologically close to the Islamists in Jamaat-e-Islami). The departure of the Bhutto administration, which had been close to the Taliban movement, signified that Afghan policy would once again be under the full control of the Inter-Service Intelligence. However, Pakistan's earlier ties with Hekmatyar elicited distrust from the Taliban and limited Islamabad's influence in Kabul.

However, since 1996 the Taliban gained a new benefactor: Osama bin Laden, an Arab Islamist of Saudi origin. Having come to Afghanistan and failing to find support from the Shiite radicals in Teheran,[45] he allied with the Taliban and gained control over bases and camps in the mountains bordering Pakistan. Under the cover of the Taliban, he established the center of what would soon become the infamous Al Qaeda, an Islamic-terrorist organization with an Arab leadership but international in its activities. In February 1998, bin Laden and his supporters proclaimed the formation of an ideologically oriented umbrella organization called "the World Islamic Front for Jihad against Jews and Crusaders."

The penetration of the Arab element into the ranks of the Afghan Taliban weakened Pakistan's influence over them. At the same time, Islamabad, which had hastened to announce diplomatic recognition of the Taliban regime, proved partly responsible for their activities—both at home and in the international arena.[46] The radicalization of the conceptual platform of the Taliban, which occurred under the influence of the "Afghan Arabs," led to a deterioration in relations between the Taliban government and Iran.[47] It also provoked the U.S. missile attack on Al Qaeda camps in the mountains of Afghanistan—as a response to terrorist attacks on American embassies in Dar es Salaam and Nairobi.

Meanwhile, the international terrorist network extended its tentacles from Afghanistan into Central Asia. In 1998, Tahir Yuldashev moved the headquarters of the Islamic Movement of Uzbekistan from Peshawar to Kabul; Namangani moved from Tajikistan to Kabul the following year. The Uzbek Islamists not only created their own network of agents, but also joined the ranks of the Taliban, gaining experience in combat and sabotage.[48] Moreover, the religious schools and seminaries in Pakistan functioned as the ideological and personnel rear base for the Uzbek Islamists. In the period between 1991 and 1999, the Haqqaniyya Seminary (*Dar-ul-Uloom Haqqaniyya*) in the town of Akora Khattak provided schooling for approximately sixty people from Uzbekistan, Tajikistan, and Kazakhstan.[49] One must also keep in mind the fact that the first students of the Islamic schools from Uzbekistan had already appeared in Saudi Arabia and Pakistan in the 1980s, and some participated in the Soviet-Afghan war.[50]

With the assistance of Islamists based in Pakistan and Afghanistan, the Islamic Movement of Uzbekistan began to plan sabotage and subversive activities. It is no accident that the Islamists were accused of carrying out a series of large-scale acts of terror and sabotage, above all, the organization of explosions in the center of Tashkent in February 1999.[51] In August of that year, the spiritual leader of the Islamic Movement of Uzbekistan, Az Zubair Ibn Abdur Raheem, issued an appeal for a jihad against the Karimov regime and condemned the leadership of Kyrgyzstan for supporting it.[52] Namangani, relying on his base in the Tavildara valley, in the summer months of 1999–2001 carried out major sabotage operations in the high mountains and contiguous areas in Uzbekistan and Kyrgyzstan. The first incursion in 1999 elicited enormous international resonance when it seized Kyrgyz territory and took a group of Japanese geologists hostage. Significantly, Islamabad was the site for the successful negotiations to release these hostages. The actions of the Islamic Movement of Uzbekistan rose to an especially serious scale in 2000, after Namangani returned to Tavildara from Afghanistan with large reinforcements. Several hundred armed Islamists took part in the military operations. These three years of battling the Islamic insurgents inflicted heavy losses on the regular units and border forces of Uzbekistan and Kyrgyzstan.[53] As a kind of repayment, units of the Islamic Movement of Uzbekistan supported the Taliban forces in their fierce war against the Northern Alliance. In particular, they helped the Taliban in 2000 to seize the headquarters of Masood, military commander of the Northern Alliance, in the city of Talukan (the center of the northeastern province of Tahar).[54]

The advance of the Taliban and allied brigades of international Islamists to the borders of Central Asia forced authorities there to take steps to bolster security. The main sabotage activities of insurgents in the Islamic Movement of Uzbekistan (which included representatives from various nationalities residing in Central Asia) were aimed at the mountainous borders that separate Uzbekistan, Kyrgyzstan, and Tajikistan in the direction of Fergana Valley (which is divided among these three countries). This compelled the authorities of Central Asia to increase cooperation, but did not eliminate pent-up differences (especially between Uzbekistan and its neighbors).[55] The role of Russia increased—as an external support for the system of regional security—because of its contribution in guarding the porous border between Tajikistan and Afghanistan, and also because of its leading position in the antiterrorist center of the Commonwealth of Independent States (CIS). China has also expanded its role in the region. Most notably, in the summer of 2001 it helped establish the Shanghai Forum (an organization of five states), which was transformed into the Shanghai Cooperation Organization, with the participation of China, Russia, and four of the Central Asian states (the exception being Turkmenistan).[56]

Significantly, in all these regional processes Pakistan was on the opposite side of the majority of Central Asian states and Russia. In the second half of the 1990s and after the turn of the century, this loose coalition against Pakistan came to include Iran, the "eternal antagonist" India, and to some degree the "proven friend" China.[57] At the same time, Islamabad used its influence on the Taliban movement and the entire radical Islamist network to put pressure on the countries of Central Asia; it eagerly assumed the role of mediating disputes and reconciling the various parties. Thus, the Pakistan-Afghan "corridor of influence" (which had formed as a result of the activities of the Islamists) on the processes in Central Asia became most salient during the years of active assaults by the Taliban.

Defeat of the Taliban and Strengthening of Islamist Forces in Pakistan

After the events of 11 September 2001, Pakistan returned to a general regional approach in the struggle against extremism and, indeed, occupied an honored position in this. After renouncing many years of support for the Taliban (who refused to surrender bin Laden, blamed for the terrorist attacks in New York and Washington), Pakistan's military under General Pervez Musharraf (who had seized power in October 1999) reaped clear benefits. In the terminology of chess, they sacrificed some pawns to improve their position. Concretely, these steps removed the threat that Pakistan itself would be consigned to the ranks of states that support terrorism. India insisted on such a step, drawing the attention of the international community to Islamabad's support for the activities of extremists in the Indian state of Jammu and Kashmir.

Despite these obvious advantages, Islamabad did not find it easy to support the military campaign of the United States and Great Britain against the Taliban regime. It had, after all, to take into account the fact that the Pushtun population in northwestern Pakistan and the border areas were sympathetic to the Taliban.

The expectations of a negative reaction to Musharraf's decision, to a certain degree, proved justified. Many among the Pushtun in Pakistan's mountainous areas opposed the government's position. Indeed, approximately 10,000 militiamen assembled there and went to aid the Taliban in the Kabul region of northern Afghanistan.[58]

Some of Musharraf's closest associates also opposed the new strategy. Prior to the onset of the international military operation in Afghanistan, he had to make changes in the upper echelons of the armed forces. In particular, the head of Inter-Service Intelligence (Mehmoud Ahmed) was replaced by the head of Military Intelligence, Ehsan ul-Haq. The new head of Inter-Service Intelligence conducted a purge in the organization's leadership, removing, as later became known, fifteen senior officers.[59]

The rout of the Taliban by combined assault of American and British air forces and the field units of the Northern Alliance largely demolished the Pakistan-Afghanistan "corridor of influence" in Central Asia. The battles that the Taliban fought against far superior forces also brought substantial losses to the Islamic Movement of Uzbekistan that fought alongside them. It is widely believed that the fallen included Namangani.[60] A significant number of the Taliban was captured by the Northern Alliance; the prisoners included not only Afghans, but also Pakistanis, Arabs, and people from Central Asia (primarily Uzbekistan) and China's Xinjiang.[61]

To the enormous displeasure of Pakistan, the leaders of the Northern Alliance remanded some of the prisoners (up to 300 people) to India. Seeking to compensate for the loss of prestige in the eyes of certain forces at home, Islamabad evidently encouraged a new wave of sabotage and terrorist activity against India.[62] As the situation in Kashmir deteriorated, in December 2001 terrorists launched an attack on the building of the Indian parliament itself. New Delhi accused Pakistan of encouraging hostile actions and took harsh reprisals: it recalled its ambassador (High Commissioner, the designation used in between the Commonwealth countries) from Islamabad and began to concentrate forces along its border with Pakistan. In early 2002 mutual reproaches resulted in a reduction in the staffs of the diplomatic representations, and India expelled from New Delhi the High Commissioner of Pakistan.[63] In May 2002, right after a large-scale terrorist act in Jammu and Kashmir, the Indian government announced that it would place its troops on the Pakistani border on heightened alert. Pakistan responded with analogous measures. By the end of May and beginning of June, the confrontation of the two armies (numbering more than one million) heightened the probability of armed conflict. The international community reacted with great alarm, given that the two countries had nuclear weapons and missiles.

Although the United States undoubtedly led the efforts to avert the threat of a new India-Pakistan war,[64] Russia and the countries of Central Asia also played a role here. An opportunity came at the Conference on Cooperation and Confidence Building Measures in Asia, held in Almaty, Kazakhstan, at the beginning of June 2002. This was the first summit of an organization created on the initiative of the president of Kazakhstan (who first proposed the idea in the fall of 1992).[65] The conference provided a convenient place to narrow the differences between India and Pakistan, since both the prime minister of India and the president of Pakistan were present. Russian president Vladimir Putin conducted negotiations with both leaders, Shri Atal Bihari Vajpayee and Pervez Musharraf, and sought to arrange a meeting of the two. Although he did not succeed, the conference led to a reduction in tensions. In the fall of 2002, at the initiative of India, the two sides began a mutual withdrawal of troops from the borders. The acute confrontation, which had lasted for about ten months, came to an end.

Islamabad used these events to bolster its diplomatic ties with Russia and the Central Asian states. In June 2002, President Musharraf of Pakistan visited not only Kazakhstan but also Turkmenistan and Tajikistan. Given the traditional tensions between the countries (which supported opposing ethnic groups in Afghanistan—Pushtun and Tajik), this official visit bore considerable symbolic significance. In February 2003 Musharraf made use of an invitation, extended by Putin earlier in Almaty, to journey to Moscow. His official visit, to a significant degree, marked a shift from the geopolitical balance of power in the center of Asia that had emerged in the previous stage—a basic component of which had been the opposite positions held by Russia and Pakistan.

The defeat of the Taliban and the aggravation of tensions with India had a direct impact on the domestic political situation in Pakistan. The military authorities were forced to take steps to rein in the militant Islamists, the so-called "jihadists." In January 2002, after Musharraf made an appeal to the nation that sharply criticized the extremists, the government banned the activity of leading radical organizations, closed hundreds of their offices, and arrested over two thousand activists. Those detained included the leaders from the main religious parties—Jamaat-e-Islami, Jamiat-e Ulama-e Islam, and the like.

These actions provided a clear signal for a change of tactics and realignment of forces. Six of the main political organizations, including Ahl-e Hadis and the Shiite Tehrik-e Islami, announced their willingness to participate in the Pakistan's parliamentary elections scheduled for October 2002, and for that purpose established the pre-election coalition called Muttahida Majlis-e-Amal ("United Front of Action"). The president of the Front was the oldest representative of the moderate Islamism and a leader of Jamiat-e Ulama-e Islam, Shah Ahmed Noorani; his vice-presidents were the presidents of Jamaat-e-Islami and Jamiat-e Ulama-e Islam, Qazi Hussain Ahmad and Fazlur Rahman, respectively. After the spring of 2002, Islamists who were freed from house arrest and from places of provisional incarceration became actively involved in the pre-election campaign.[66] In elections on 10 October, Muttahida Majlis-e-Amal had considerable success. Although their share of the vote in the country amounted to just 11 percent, they succeeded—on the basis of consolidated voting in a limited number of electoral districts—in obtaining 40 seats in the National Assembly (20 percent). Having become the third largest faction in the lower house of parliament, after the elections the Islamists were able to increase significantly their influence on the domestic political process. This was abetted by the fact that Muttahida Majlis-e-Amal had considerable success in two western provinces (the Northwestern Border Province and Baluchistan Province) that have a relatively small share of the population and that border on Afghanistan. In the Northwestern Border Province, the Islamists have constituted an autonomous provincial government; in Baluchistan Province, they formed an administration with the largest ruling party (in national terms).[67]

The alliance achieved at the provincial level with the presidential party did not prevent the moderate Islamists from opposing, for a long time, the central government headed by Prime Minister Mir Zafarullah Khan Jamali. Their main demand of General Musharraf (whose legitimacy as elected president, after a referendum in April 2002, they agreed to recognize) was that he resigns from his position of the Chief of the Army Staff (official title abbreviated as COAS). On the eve of 2004 a compromise was finally reached: Musharraf promised to take off his military uniform at the end of the year, and Muttahida Majlis-e-Amal agreed to approve amendments to the constitution giving the president substantially broader powers than those foreseen in the fundamental laws (in force since 1973). In effect, this signified the transformation of Pakistan's political system from a democracy of the parliamentary type into a presidential-parliamentary system, indeed one where the laws affirmed the controlling role of the army.[68] The significant strengthening of Islamic political parties in Pakistan fully corresponds to what has been noted in the contemporary historical epoch and described above (in the introduction to this chapter)—a tendency for growth in the cultural-religious factor in the political life of many countries, both Muslim and non-Muslim, including India.[69]

A peculiarity of Pakistan at this point was the gradual weakening of the extremist wing of Islamism. The blow dealt by authorities in January and February 2002 was not sufficiently strong and soon allowed the extremists to regroup. Acting jointly with the remnants of Al Qaeda and the Taliban, they prepared and carried out a series of terrorist acts on the territory of Pakistan, Kashmir, and Afghanistan. One of the most sensational terrorist acts was the murder of American journalist Daniel Pearl. One could also cite the explosion at a Christian church in Islamabad and the killing of several French military experts in Karachi. The Pakistani security agencies, in collaboration with American counterparts, were able to track down and detain those guilty in perpetrating a series of terrorist acts, as well as close associates of bin Laden, such as Abu Zubeidah, Ramzi bin al-Shibh, and Khalid Sheikh Mohammed.[70] However, many other leaders of terrorist and radical organizations, above all bin Laden and Mullah Omar, are still at large, presumably hiding in the mountainous areas on the border between Pakistan and Afghanistan.[71]

In the fall of 2003, Pakistani authorities renewed the attacks on extremist groups. In November they outlawed six organizations, including an offshoot of Hizb ut-Tahrir, which had the strongest position in the republics of Central Asia (as will be shown below). The majority of the banned organizations are "reincarnations" of well-known, older structures dating from the 1980s.[72] The vitality of the Islamic extremists attests, apparently, both to the lack of consistent policy on the part of the authorities (and their reluctance to break with the Islamists) and the strength of the latter's support among influential strata of the political community.

At the same time, two well-planned assassination attempts on the life of President Musharraf—which nearly succeeded—were carried out in December 2003, within a period of just eleven days, and signaled a qualitatively new situation.[73] To judge from what is known, the extremists felt that the leadership of the country posed a real threat to themselves and their plans. They therefore attempted to destabilize the situation, to precipitate a crisis among elites, and to return to the situation where they were instruments in the hands of the authorities and, simultaneously, used state power for their own ends.

It was no accident that the suspicion of the investigatory organs focused on groups associated with Al Qaeda and the terrorist struggle in Kashmir, Afghanistan, and even Chechnia. Apart from possible attempts by the bureaucracy to deflect a blow by extremism against itself, there are perhaps hidden traces of a conspiracy by an international network, which feared new losses from the extensive operations of Pakistani authorities.[74]

Thus there are grounds to suppose that, at the present time, radical Islam (Islamism) in Pakistan has split into two currents. One is a moderate variant in the form of parliamentary parties: these have become a systemic element, either becoming part of the power structure or standing close to it. The other consists of extremist groups that are subjected to bans and persecution; they are forced to fight those who hold supreme authority and to oppose the organs of security and counterintelligence that had earlier given them tangible (if secret) assistance.

The Potential Evolution of Pakistan-Afghan Islamism and Its Likely Influence on Central Asia

At present, Pakistan and Afghanistan find themselves at a historic crossroads. The economic and domestic political situation in Pakistan reached its lowest critical point in 1999. The military officials holding power have been partly able to correct the situation. The rates of economic growth have risen; the hard currency financial reserves of the state have increased noticeably (almost tenfold); and the indicators of activity on the stock market have improved. At the same time, the influx of foreign capital remains small, and Pakistan still needs a substantial volume of official aid for development.[75] The country's recovery from the inertia of the past two decades has been sluggish; that is reflected in a low norm of savings and investment and in insufficient funding for the productive infrastructure, energy, and irrigation.

In assessing the social and economic prospects for Pakistan, one must take into account the host of problems that have piled up since the 1980s, most notably with respect to employment, education, and agriculture. While the origins of these problems predate the military Islamist leadership of Zia ul-Haq, it was during his eleven-year rule that they made themselves fully felt.

Unquestionably, the war in Afghanistan also had a negative influence. While Zia ul-Haq actively exploited the war for his own purposes, this success in Afghanistan was a Pyrrhic victory, fraught with catastrophic consequences for society. It eroded public morality, spawned massive corruption, and fueled the growth of a parallel or black market (with a turnover of 50 to 70 percent of the legal market). All this signified a de facto degradation of the state; during the period of the formal democracy of the 1990s, this led to a decline in its control over society, with a corresponding growth in the role of the army and security organs.[76] This parlous condition of the Pakistani polity, to a large degree, explains the resurgence of Islamic radicalism and the wild outburst of sectarian conflict that had brought death to thousands since the early 1980s. Demographic and ecological factors provided the underlying cause for these chronic ills. The indicators for population growth in Pakistan remain one of the highest in the world; in terms of the number of inhabitants (approximately 150 million), it has surpassed Russia to become the world's sixth largest country. The main ecological problem is associated with the shortage of water for irrigation: the salination and water saturation of cultivated land. Both problems have a negative impact on rural and urban employment, and they also contribute to the growth of poverty and illiteracy. According to a number of assessments, approximately 40 percent of the population lives below the poverty line, and about 66 percent of the adults are illiterate.[77]

Preliminary attempts to imagine the future of Pakistan (which, in large measure, depends on the situation in neighboring Afghanistan and, to a certain degree, in Central Asia) usually distinguish two scenarios—one optimistic, one pessimistic. The optimistic scenario presupposes that the present administration will succeed in carrying out the needed reforms in education, that it will establish control over and transform the system of religious education, and that it will continue the struggle against corruption and the black market. Good policies and good governance will make it possible to increase savings and investment, and that in turn can ameliorate the acute problem of unemployment among the youth. All this can undermine the basis of Islamist extremism and limit its "export" and the opportunities for action by international terrorist networks. The pessimistic scenario assumes an intensification of the contrary tendencies.

A more refined approach to prognostication allows one to distinguish not two, but a larger number of scenarios. A group of Indian experts who are engaged in making predictions more generally (not only about Pakistan) foresee five possible variants for development by 2010. In the first scenario, Pakistan would transform into something similar to Turkey—that is, a contemporary state with an economically sufficient rate of development where jihadists are completely eliminated, and the security and counterintelligence organs (above all, the Inter-Security Intelligence) are placed under effective civilian control.[78] The second forecast envisions an inertia scenario, where the country retains its orientation toward conflict in conducting foreign policy in the region, moderate rates of economic growth, and preservation of the Islamic extremists as a force utilized by the authorities. The third prediction postulates that Pakistan will be turned into a theocratic state similar to Iran under Khomeini. Nationalism, jihad, and all-encompassing distrust of the West and India would be coupled with support for ties with Muslim countries and Islamic forces throughout the world. The fourth scenario envisions regression into theocratic anarchy similar to that in Afghanistan under the Taliban. The fifth possibility is a complete collapse of the state and war with India, which would be unleashed by the Pakistani military and would threaten the use of nuclear weapons.[79]

Afghanistan, notwithstanding the stabilization that followed the rout of the Taliban, is also in a phase of uncertainty. More likely than not, its fate over the next few years, to a significant degree, has already been predetermined. The presence of the armed contingents of the United States and the peacekeeping forces of their allies will make it possible to guarantee that the process of political reconstruction will follow the schedule outlined by the transition administration under President Hamid Karzai and by international organizations like the United Nations and the World Bank.

The new constitution of Afghanistan was approved in the beginning of January 2004 by the Loya Jirga (the "Great Assembly" of 500 representatives from all groups of the population). This constitution establishes a form of rule very similar to that in Pakistan. Like the latter, it establishes a Sunni Islamic republic with a strong presidential power and the predominant role of religious law.[80] As in Pakistan, the moderate Islamists (especially those who participated directly in the jihad against the Soviet Union, the mujahideen, and their political and spiritual heirs) are very strong. Apparently, a certain role will be played by the former Taliban who were moderate supporters of the overthrown regime and who represent the Pushtun national element.

The future development of Afghanistan, after a two- or three-year interval, will largely depend on what scenario unfolds in Pakistan. Under the optimistic variant, this will have a double impact—on Pakistan and Afghanistan. Both countries will have the prospect of a "mutually induced" growth, an expansion of trade, and an exchange of capital and labor. This would be encouraged by the cooperation that has grown over the preceding decades because of the human (i.e., refugee) and commercial contacts; it is well known, for example, that the Afghan-Pushtun traders have a strong position in the main Pakistani port city of

Karachi. The formation of an Afghan-Pakistan corridor of development directed toward the Arabian Sea could permit the countries of Central Asia to become involved as well. A certain positive role here could be played, in the future, by the long-discussed project to construct a natural gas and oil pipeline from Turkmenistan to Pakistan (via Afghanistan).[81] The evolution of Pakistan according to other scenarios (including the preservation of the status quo in the main parameters that currently exist) will not favor a steady upturn in the Afghan economy and the process of political stabilization. This influence will become especially negative in the event that scenarios three and four come to pass. Under that hypothetical perspective, Pakistan-Afghan Islamic radicalism would have a major negative impact on Central Asia.

The prospects for a further transformation of the states that belong to the region of Central Asia can also be described in a relatively more optimistic and pessimistic tone. The Islamist thrust from the south can have its greatest influence on the north if, in time, it coincides with the worst, most negative scenarios for the development in Pakistan, Afghanistan, and Central Asia. Under that variant, one cannot preclude the possibility that the entire area from the Fergana Valley to the Arabian Sea will be transformed into a zone dominated by semi-failed, bankrupt states, that the isolationist Islamist forces will become stronger, and that a new caliphate (neofundamentalist) movement will emerge.[82] At the same time, preservation of the status quo in Central Asia will give Islamists a considerable field of action. The present situation in all the states of the region, with the possible exception of Kazakhstan, is characterized as unfavorable for true economic improvement.[83] The degradation of the remnants of Soviet culture, which was European in its roots and modernist in its form and goals, is accompanied by a contraction in the manifestations of modern civilization in the countries of the region, by a return to traditionalism and all that is archaic. It is precisely in this environment that it is easy to disseminate preaching about the force of religion, sacrifice, and extremism. The rise of religiosity is revealed not only in the enhancement of the position of Islam, but also in the growing influence of Christian churches—Orthodox, Catholic, and various Protestant denominations.[84] However, the spirit of self-sacrifice and armed struggle is being spread only within the framework of the Islamic tradition.

In recent years, in connection with a change in external conditions (namely, the defeat of the Taliban and Al Qaeda in Afghanistan), armed attacks by extremists in the republics of Central Asia have largely ended. At the same time, their chief instigator—the Islamic Movement of Uzbekistan—continues to exist and to maintain its bases in Afghanistan and Pakistan. To avoid sanctions imposed on this organization by an international ban, of late it has been operating under the name "Islamic Movement of Turkestan." It is widely thought that the finances for Central Asian extremists pass through Pakistan, and that a Pakistani political party like Jamiat-e Ulama-e islam (more likely, a faction led by Sami ul-Haq) provides direct patronage. According to information obtained from a member of the Islamic Movement of Uzbekistan (who was arrested in May 2003), the organization's leader, T. Yumashev, is hiding in Pakistan and, together with Arab and Chechen fighters, planning new acts of sabotage.[85] This period of clandestine activity has meant that its place as the principal opponent of the Central Asian regimes has been taken over by another movement, indeed, an international one—Hizb ut-Tahrir (the full name of which is Hizb ut-Tahrir ul-Islami, "the Party of Islamic Restoration"). The latter was established at the beginning of the 1950s by an Arab-Palestinian, Taqiuddin an-Nabhani Filastyni; after his death in 1979, leadership shifted to another Palestinian, Abdul Qadeem Zaloom.[86]

The main goal of this party is to propagate the idea of creating a truly Islamic state, caliphate, composed of the Muslims in different countries and regions. The first cells of Hizb ut-Tahrir in Central Asia appeared in 1992–1994 in the Uzbek cities of Fergana, Andizhan, and Tashkent. A burst of activity came at the end of the 1990s and has continued to the present (despite a downturn in 2001–2002). The downturn concerned above all Uzbekistan, where activity peaked in 1998–2000.[87] According to the views of the ideologists of the organization, not one of the regimes in the Muslim countries (including those in such states as Saudi Arabia, Pakistan, and Iran) is a true Islamic state. That is why Hizb ut-Tahrir has made its appeal to combat them all. The category of basic enemies naturally includes the secular regimes of all the Central Asian states, but the main focus of their struggle is Karimov's regime in Uzbekistan.

Hizb ut-Tahrir, in general, engages in education and propaganda work, and it distributes fliers as well as video and audio cassettes. However, the essence of Islamist propaganda consists of a summons to wage a decisive, uncompromising battle with the existing authorities and to prepare mass consciousness for open disobedience and for social transformation. However, it should be noted that, in the fall of 2001, the Central Asian branches of Hizb ut-Tahrir openly supported the Taliban at a time when the latter were fighting against the forces of the international antiterrorist coalition. Thus, although Hizb ut-Tahrir lays an emphasis on propaganda and peaceful methods of resistance, it combines that with well-organized conspiratorial activity and a much broader perspective. This circumstance has elicited, and continues to elicit, alarm in state organs and impels them to ban the party and incarcerate activists. In 2003, the governments of Kyrgyzstan and Tajikistan conducted the most active struggle against Hizb ut-Tahrir, and they arrested a significant number of party functionaries. The authorities in Uzbekistan, earlier than others, managed to suppress the activities of Islamists. By contrast, the government of Kazakhstan has still not banned the party, despite the fact that its activities have been noted in the southern areas of the republic.[88]

To repeat, although Hizb ut-Tahrir represents an organization that is extremist only in its radical-utopian goal, its channels can be used by terrorists, and the dissemination of its ideas prepares the soil for attacks by a radically minded opposition. Rather massive acts of protest have already been observed recently in a number of places in Uzbekistan, and these have elicited concern among Uzbek authorities and their neighbors in the region.[89] Some argue that the repression of propagandists from Hizb ut-Tahrir only increases popular discontent and broadens the political and social base of oppositionist Islam. The scale of actions in the struggle against extremism is impressive. Some observers believe that the prisons of Uzbekistan hold thousands of activists, many incarcerated on dubious grounds or false accusations. Since 1998 some six hundred activists of Hizb ut-Tahrir have been sentenced in Tajikistan to various terms of imprisonment.[90]

The activity of Hizb ut-Tahrir is not only tied to the Arab projection of radical Islamism, although the latter undoubtedly does predominate. Apart from the organizational and financial ties to the Arab underground, it is facilitated by the Koran and Arab literature that preach about the need for an Islamic state. Of the foreign channels, the Turkish should also be noted. It is well known that a branch of Hizb ut-Tahrir had been established there already in the 1960s.[91] The Turkish role is evident as well in the dissemination of translated literature in Turkic tongues, above all, Uzbek.

In 2000, a branch of Hizb ut-Tahrir, as noted above, appeared in Pakistan and legally operated there until banned by the Government in 2003. At the same time, Pakistan has its own centers for enlightenment and propaganda activities, which are typologically and functionally similar to the network of Hizb ut-Tahrir. These include, above all, the organization Tabligi Jamaat ("Society of Appeal"). Genetically and organizationally, it is associated with the Deoband ulama school and the party of the Jamiat-e Ulama-e Islam. In addition, Jamaat-e-Islami has its own educational organizations and each year conducts mass meetings (*ijtima*). It is similar to Hizb ut-Tahrir in its puritanism and spiritual rigorism; it differs in a less articulated political radicalism and in the absence of appeals to overthrow authorities and create a single Islamic state as the immediate goal of a jihad.[92]

It is well known that the emissaries and propagandists of Tabligi Jamaat (and also the organizations associated with Jamaat-e-Islami and a series of educational-charitable funds and schools, including those of the Suf-is Sufi orders) over the past decade have gained entry to Central Asia and have conducted proselytizing and educational activity there. For this purpose, some have learned Russian and translated religious works into that language in order to make them comprehensible to the local intelligentsia.[93] The language barrier remains a substantial obstacle for Islamic missionaries and political activists from Pakistan. But in the future, as English becomes widespread in the region, that problem may recede. The apparently inevitable spread of various contacts of the population of the Central Asian region with the external Anglophone world will facilitate the internationalization of regional Islamism and the establishment of closer, organic ties with Pakistan-Afghan Islamism.

Conclusion

In closing, it should be emphasized that Islamic radicalism in Central Asia, as a geopolitical phenomenon, has passed through several stages. The first was preliminary and preparatory; it encompassed the 1970s and 1980s and was closely associated with the war in Afghanistan that was being waged right along the Soviet border. The second period commenced after the withdrawal of Soviet forces from Afghanistan in 1989 and continued until 1992—that is, until Islamic rule was established in Afghanistan and to the outbreak of civil war in Tajikistan. Islamism may then have achieved its greatest successes, acting as a political counterforce bearing, in addition, a clearly national-state hue. In the third period (1992–1996) Islamism retreated because of the onset of a fratricidal war within the camp of Afghan Islamists and the defeat of the Islamic opposition in Tajikistan. The fourth period brought a new upsurge of Islamic radicalism, as the struggle for power in Afghanistan intensified. The Taliban movement bolstered its position as the most puritanical and aggressive manifestation of radical Islam and, amid the fighting, stood on the very borders of Central Asia. The Taliban, supported by the international Islamic network of Al Qaeda (which is mainly Arab in terms of the composition of its participants), gave a substantial impulse to the activity of the extreme Islamists in Central Asia who, previously, had been mainly united around the Islamic Movement of Uzbekistan. The fifth phase came after the defeat of the Taliban in 2001; it has been marked by a shift of Islamists to defense, to the dominance of clandestine forms of resistance, and to the conduct of propaganda and recruitment work.

The Afghan factor has obviously had an enormous role in the fate of Islamic radicalism in Central Asia. But that Afghan factor has in turn been largely shaped by policies formulated in Pakistan. For the mujahideen, during the period of the Soviet-Afghan war, Pakistan was the main pillar of support, a rear with a deep echelon, without which it would have been impossible to mount resistance to Kabul and Moscow. Pakistan's role increased still more in the second and third phases, when, it appeared, ideological and political protégés came to power in Afghanistan and, in particular, helped to bolster Pakistani influence in Central Asia. However, neither the mujahideen nor the jihadists (Taliban) proved reliable allies. In the second half of the 1990s, Pakistan's influence on the internal Afghan processes substantially decreased—despite the fact that at the official level Islamabad stubbornly supported the Taliban and unofficially provided assistance to Islamic extremists from Central Asia. The corrections that Islamabad has made in its regional policy since 2001 have had a substantial significance. After the refusal to perform the role of the "backyard" for the Taliban and "Arab Afghans" of bin Laden, Islamabad moved in the direction of a more realistic, sober policy with respect to the extreme Islamists. This was expressed in a reduction not only of overt, but also of covert, ties with them; moreover, this concerned terrorist groups acting in Pakistan, Afghanistan, and India as well as beyond the borders of this area—particularly in Central Asia. Apparently, however, right up to the beginning of 2004, Pakistan did not conclusively and irreversibly abandon its policy of using Islamic radicals for domestic and foreign policy purposes. The litmus test for determining whether Islamabad has indeed made a U-turn will be its policy with respect to Afghanistan and Kashmir.

In this regard it is necessary to point out that, for the Pakistani policy of supporting Islamic radicalism, the regions that lie to the north of the country are undoubtedly the main objects of influence. This northern zone can be subdivided into a nearby semicircle (Kashmir and Afghanistan) and a geographically more distant tier (Central Asia and Xinjiang). I would note, parenthetically, that Islamabad also takes an interest in areas even more geographically remote: the Russian regions of the Caucasus and Volga, and also Nepal (located to the northeast of India). The bulk of the latter, and also Bangladesh and the countries of Southeast Asia, belong to another (southern and southeasterly) direction of activity to encourage local support for political Islam.

Pakistani Islamic radicalism now finds itself at a crossroad. It has become noticeably differentiated into a modern current (in terms of the means for conducting the political struggle) and an extremist wing. The socioeconomic and sociodemographic problems of Pakistan create the mass base for the dissemination of oppositionist protest attitudes, which find a ready form of expression in the shape of an Islamist ideology. The powers that be, above all the army generals (including the leadership of the security and counterintelligence services) can utilize the religious-political parties for purposes of neutralizing extreme forces that are subversive for the political system and, simultaneously, mobilize the Islamists for the struggle with external enemies. Given this circumstance, at any moment radical Islamism has a chance again to become an important factor in Pakistan's influence on external processes, including those at work in Central Asia.

The character of Pakistani actions in the Central Asian region will be determined by the type of mutual relations that develop between Islamabad and the ruling regimes there. It should be noted that, from the moment when the newly independent states were formed in the post-Soviet space in the center of Asia, Pakistan has been in a constant search for ways to establish firm, close ties with them. To a large degree, it was at Pakistan's initiative that the Economic Cooperation Organization (ECO) accepted into its membership all the new republics of the region and endeavored to give a concrete form to cooperation within the framework of the ECO. Indicative in this regard is the plan of action that the ECO adopted in the Pakistani city of Quetta at the beginning of 1993.[94] However, it was precisely from this time that interest in regional cooperation among some of the main members (except Pakistan) significantly decreased; hence for the most part the plan remained a dead letter—as a memorandum on intentions. Efforts to strengthen confidence and cooperation, nevertheless, did not cease, and the ECO also remained active. Bilateral and multilateral political and diplomatic contacts were realized; it is sufficient to recall, for example, the joint meetings at the end of the 1990s with respect to regulating the Afghan question in accordance with the 6 + 2 formula (i.e., the states neighboring on Afghanistan plus the United States and Russia). There were also contacts in the economic, commercial, and humanitarian spheres. A new impulse to these efforts came from the direct participation of both Pakistan and the Central Asian countries (with Turkmenistan constituting a partial exception) in the antiterrorist campaign against the power of the Taliban in Afghanistan.

Since the fall of 2001, Islamabad has been actively searching for ways to expand its ties with the Central Asian states—especially Kazakhstan, Uzbekistan, and Tajikistan. At the same time, Islamabad has difficulty overcoming the cool relationship with Uzbekistan, which took shape during the period when Pakistan supported extremists from the Islamic Movement of Uzbekistan. Evident too are the doubts in Tashkent as to whether Islamabad is continuing to encourage Uzbek Islamists. Another factor is Uzbekistan's claims to play an independent role in the affairs of Afghanistan—by encouraging the separatism of Uzbek field commander Dostum in the northern areas under his control.

The leaders in Pakistan evidently understand that Turkmenistan, the most promising partner in the region from an economic point of view, has lost a significant part of its appeal because of the peculiarities in the domestic policies of President Saparmurad Niiazov ("Turkmenbashi"). The largest and most profitable economic project for shipping Turkmen natural gas and oil through Afghanistan to Pakistan will probably not raise sufficient financial resources—because of the unpopularity of the regime of the Turkmenbashi among representatives of international business circles and banking groups. Other projects to build economic bridges have also proven difficult to realize. These include, for example, a project for the transmission of electricity from Kyrgyzstan to Pakistan through China, with the use of opportunities (presented by the existence of the high-mountain Karakorum Highway) to build power lines.

More modest and entirely realizable plans include the expansion of the airline connections to increase the transportation of passengers, including tourists as well as commercial cargoes. Trade can also make use of roadways, which would require a qualitative improvement in the system of roads in Afghanistan.

Without doubt, the cooperation or coordination of Pakistan and Central Asian states like Tajikistan and Uzbekistan could bring tangible results. Moreover, this would be most effective in a situation free from a struggle in the spheres of political and cultural-ideological influence.

In expressing this desire, it must be admitted that the most realistic outcome is one where regional and global-political competition remains a constant in international relations. Hence Afghanistan cannot fully avoid the fate of being a proving ground for various, conflicting forces. In addition, its very political structure to a large degree depends on how its foreign policy preferences develop.

In the future Afghanistan will most likely remain a buffer zone, as it has been historically. This country, like a sandwich, is squeezed between the Central Asian region (controlled by Russia since the second half of the nineteenth century) and Pakistan (British India). The geographic watershed between areas of foreign control and internal forces are the powerful peaks of the Hindu Kush; the Pushtun constitute the southern orientation, while the non-Pushtuns—above all, Tajiks and Uzbeks—dominate the north. It might be noted that the political and associated ethnodemographic trends (the relocation of ethnic groups; changes in the structure of power dominance at the local level) since the last decades of the nineteenth century have borne the character of alternative waves: first as an assault from the south to the north (until World War I), then the reverse (until the end of the 1920s), then again mainly in a northerly direction, followed (in the late 1970s and early 1990s) by the opposite tendency. The current phase is characterized by a certain equilibrium, with a compromise between the Pushtun and non-Pushtun elites (as in preceding intervals). However, the dominant tendency apparently consists in extending the geopolitical and demographic political influence from the south to the north.

Over a certain span of time, of course, that tendency can be erased. The current structural weakness of Pakistan stemming from the centrifugal tendencies can impart a different character to regional processes. It could, for example, evoke the long-existing project to create Pushtunistan, the realization of which would lead to the breakup of Pakistan.

Islamic radicalism would evidently also acquire a new lease on life by relying primarily on the Pushtun-Afghan enclave. It is not impossible that northern Afghanistan will distance itself from such a line of development, while Sind and Punjab will turn into separate secular Muslim states.

For Central Asia, such a scenario will probably not have grave consequences. At the same time, the region will face growing encroachments from the leading states of western, southern, and eastern Asia: Iran, India, and China. Scenarios that provide for the destabilization and political redrawing of the Pakistan-Afghan area will leave Russia in the position of an outside observer; Moscow can win or lose if this comes to pass. The United States and European countries have the greatest interest in the stability of Pakistan and Afghanistan; they have already invested considerable material and moral-political resources in ensuring order and progress both in Pakistan and in Afghanistan. It is precisely their interest, in particular, that forces one to consider the most likely prognosis to envision a gradual improvement in the general regional situation and a reduction in the level of activity by the forces of Islamic radicalism.

Notes

1. On the defeat of Islamism, see O. Roy, *The Failure of Political Islam* (London, 1994).

2. See A. A. Ignatenko, "Islamskii radikalizm kak pobochnyi effekt 'kholodnoi voiny,'" *Tsentral'naia Aziia i Kavkaz*, 2001, no. 1: 117–22.

3. Examples of this type are afforded not only by regions at the crux of Islamic civilization, but—in addition to those cited here—the Bosnian and Sudanese-Ethiopian variants. Typologically similar is the Tamil-Sinhalese conflict in Sri Lanka, which bears the characteristics of Hindu irredentism.

4. F. Fukuyama, "The End of History?" *The National Interest*, 16 (1989): 3–18.

5. As a characteristic example of the upsurge of conservative antiliberalism outside the Islamic states, one could point to the contemporary phenomenon of neo-Eurasianism in Russia. Its indefatigable systematizer and theoretician is A. Dugin. See his *Filosofiia politiki* (Moscow, 2004).

6. The well-known French scholar of Islamism, O. Roy, has called this new variant "neo-fundamentalism." See O. Roy, "Has Islamism a Future in Afghanistan?" in *Fundamentalism Reborn? Afghanistan and the Taliban*, ed. W. Maley (Lahore, 1998), pp. 202–4.

7. The question of radical Islam in Central Asia has not been examined in these terms—notwithstanding the fact that both its origins and subsequent stages of devel-

opment have been analyzed by a large number of authors, indeed, in great detail and at a high level. Taking these secondary materials as the basis for my study, I seek to resolve specific tasks in analyzing the geopolitical context under which radical Islam has developed both in the past and at the present time.

8. A. Benigzen [A. Bennigsen] and M. Broksap [M. Broxup], "Sovetskie musul'manskie religioznye deiateli i musul'manskaia obshchina za granitsei," in *Islam i politika. Sbornik informatsionnykh materialov, izdannykh v perevode dlia sluzhebnogo pol'zovaniia Institutom obshchestvennykh nauk pri TsK KPSS*, no. 4 (Moscow, 1986), p. 142. The same applies to an article by K. Davish [K. Davisha] and A. K. D'Ankoṣṣ (H. Carrere d'Encausse) in another article in the same volume (pp. 69–70).

9. Benigzen and Broksap, "Sovetskie musul'manskie religioznye deiateli," pp. 144–45.

10. Ibid., pp. 143–44; see also the essay by Davish and D'Ankoss, p. 67.

11. For examples of works that characterize the process as emanating "from above" and "from below," see A. V. Malashenko, "Islam versus Communism," in *Russia's Muslim Frontiers*, ed. D. F. Eickelman (Bloomington, IN 1993), pp. 63–78; and S. Abashin, "Sotsial'nye korni sredneaziatskogo islamizma (na primere odnogo seleniia)," in *Identichnost' i konflikt v postsovetskikh gosudarstvakh* (Moscow, 1997), pp. 447–70.

12. A. Abduvakhitov, "Islamic Revivalism in Uzbekistan," in *Russia's Muslim Frontiers*, ed. Eickelman, pp. 79–97.

13. Ibid., pp. 81–82.

14. Ibid., pp. 79–82

15. B. Babadzhanov, "Religiozno-oppozitsionnye gruppy v Uzbekistane," in *Religioznyi ekstremizm v Tsentral'noi Azii* (Dushanbe, 2002), pp. 43–63; and "Islam in Uzbekistan: From the Struggle for 'Religious Purity' to Political Activism," in *Central Asia: A Gathering Storm?* ed. B. Rumer (Armonk, NY, 2002), pp. 299–300.

16. Babadzhanov, "Religiozno-oppozitsionnye gruppy," p. 44.

17. Babadzhanov, "Islam in Uzbekistan," p. 44.

18. The Pakistani journalist Kh. Ahmed, with reference to the book by O. Roy (*The New Central Asia: The Creation of Nations* [London, 2000]), notes that Rustamov Hindustani studied at a seminary in Deoband (India) and was the teacher of the leader of Tajik Islamists, Abdullo Nuri (Kh. Ahmed, "Fergana: Another Valley in Danger" at www.thefridaytimes.com/30.05.01. According to what is the apparently more accurate information of Tajik scholars, Hindustani studied for eight years in a madrassa Usmaniya in the Indian city of Ajmer. See M. Olimov and S. Shokhumorov, "Islamskie intellektualy v Tsentral'noi Azii XX v. Zhizn' i bor'ba Mavlavi Khindustani (1892–1989)," *Vostok-Orient*, 2003, no. 6: 40.

19. In particular, see: Y. B. Mathur, *The Growth of Muslim Politics in India* (New Delhi, 1979), pp. 15–19, 31–32, 152; S. M. Ikram, *Modern Muslim India and the Birth of Pakistan* (Lahore,1970), pp. 91, 478.

20. The centers of religious education in the Arab East for people coming from Central Asia were mainly Egypt and Saudi Arabia. The channel for the influence of radical Islam was, in the first instance, the underground network of "Muslim brothers" (Ihwan-ul-Muslimin), and, in the second place, the Wahhabi (Salafi) organizations. See, for example, M. Z. Razhbadinov, *Radikal'nyi Islamizm v Egipte* (Moscow, 2003).

21. The first edition of a book of the Pakistani military, written in collaboration with the British, appeared in 1992; the second edition was published almost ten years

later. See M. Yousaf and M. Adkin, *Afghanistan—the Bear Trap. The Defeat of a Superpower* (Barnsley, 2001), pp. 192–94, 202–4.

22. Ibid., p. 205.

23. A. A. Liakhovskii, *Tragediia i doblest' Afgana* (Moscow, 1995), pp. 637–39.

24. For details, see *New Horizon. The Muslim World Review* (London), 356 (February 1989): 3–5; S. Shokhumorov, "Afganskie taliby i Pakistan: ot soiuza k raznoglasiiam?" in *Islam na postsovetskom prostranstve: vzgliad izvnutri* (Moscow, 2001), 242–43.

25. According to a list in Liakhovskii (*Tragediia i doblest'*, appendix 13), there were 333 missing in action. According to Soviet intelligence agencies, approximately forty (for the most part, ethnic Russians) were found to be serving in the ranks of the opposition, and some of them had converted to Islam and changed their names. The phenomenon of "Russian Afghans" adopting Islam found reflection in a feature film, "The Muslim," produced in the mid-1990s by the director V. Khotinenko.

26. An exception to this rule perhaps is the book by Liakhovskii, which cites the statements of Mohammad Zia ul-Haq and which repeatedly notes the actions of the Pakistani intelligence services against the USSR and the regimes of Central Asia that replaced it. However, the author does so without any commentary or generalizations.

27. According to Pakistani data, in the first half of the 1980s Moscow gave Islamabad credits of 423 million dollars, which, in particular, enabled the Pakistani government to complete the construction of the Pakistan Steel Mills and, by 1986, to bring it to its planned capacity. A. D. Iakovlev, "Osobennosti ekonomicheskogo razvitiia i vneshneekonomicheskie sviazi Pakistana" (Ph.D. diss., Moscow, 1999), p. 108.

28. A. Davis, "How the Taliban Became a Military Force," in *Fundamentalism Reborn? Afghanistan and the Taliban*, ed. W. Maley (Lahore, 1998), p. 44.

29. S. S. Harrison, "South Asia and the U.S.: A Chance for a Fresh Start," *Current History*, March 1992, pp. 96–97.

30. Yousaf and Adkin, *Afghanistan*, p. 105.

31. S.V. R. Nasr, "Democracy and Islamic Revivalism," *Political Science Quarterly* 110 (1995): 96–97.

32. *Entsiklopediia Pakistana* (Moscow, 1998), pp. 269–70.

33. See B. D. Metcalf, *Islamic Revival in British India: Deoband, 1860–1900* (Princeton, NJ 1982), pp. 87–263.

34. On Indian Wahhabism, and how it differs from Arabian, and the history of the movement Ahle-e-Hadis in Pakistan, see G. V. Miloslavskii, "Vakhkhabizm v ideologii i politike musul'manskikh stran," in *Islam i politika* (Moscow, 2001), pp. 76–80.

35. The present author has already had occasion to cite this circumstance. See V. Ia. Belokrenitsky, V. N. Moskalenko, and T. L. Shaumian, *Iuzhnaia Aziia v sovremennom politicheskom mire. Vzgliad iz Moskvy* (New York, 2001), pp. 136–37; V. Ia. Belokrenitsky, V. N. Moskalenko, and T. L. Shaumian, *Iuzhnaia Aziia v mirovoi politike* (Moscow, 2003), p. 117.

36. Liakhovskii, *Tragediia*, pp. 637–39.

37. In May 1992, a government of national reconciliation was established; a number of its members, including Deputy Prime Minister D. Usmon, represented the Islamic Party of the Rebirth of Tajikistan. See S. Olimova and M. Olimov, "Islamskaia partiia vozrozhdeniia v mezhtadzhikskom konflikte i ego uregulirovanii," *Tsentral'naia Aziia i Kavkaz*, 2001, no. 1: 135.

38. According to General Liakhovskii (who draws upon intelligence data), one attempt

to intervene in the civil war in Tajikistan was undertaken at the end of January 1993. In Peshawar a conference of representatives of Muslim countries (apparently, including Iran) reviewed the measures to provide assistance to "the Tajik brothers" in their "holy war" and resolved to place, at the head of the Tajik armed units, Afghans who had acquired combat experience in the partisan war against the Soviet army. In addition, substantial material funds were allocated for the Tajik Islamists. Liakhovskii, *Tragediia*, p. 640.

39. The Taliban became a military force after a commercial caravan, organized by N. Babar, departed in October 1994 from the Pakistan city of Quetta to the Afghan city of Kandahar, with the intention of going to Turkmenistan; to ensure the success of this operation, by the end of the year they had taken by force Kandahar and all of southern Afghanistan. See Davis, "How the Taliban Became a Military Force," pp. 45–50.

40. It was to these areas that the forces of the Tajik opposition, formed mainly in the camps near the cities of Mazar-e Sharif and Taloqan, were driven. There, in the summer of 1993, came the announcement about the creation of a Unified Tajik Opposition, which was formed from the Party of the Islamic Rebirth of Tajikistan and the Democratic Party of Tajikistan. Characteristically, already in the spring of 1994— under the aegis of the United Nations—negotiations were initiated to reconcile the Unified Tajik Opposition and the official authorities in Dushanbe. Olimova and Olimov, "Islamskaia partiia," p. 136.

41. However, as later became known thanks to publications in the *New York Times*, Teheran changed its tactics in this sphere. Namely, it renounced the conduct of terrorist acts against the United States and concentrated its subversive activities on assistance to Shiite anti-Israeli organizations. The last anti-American act, according to the documents of U.S. intelligence agencies (published by the same newspaper), was the explosion at Khobar Towers in Dhahran, Saudi Arabia, in June 1996. However, already in the summer of 1996, Osama bin Laden—who was famous for his involvement in actions against the United States and who had recently moved from the Sudan to Afghanistan—appealed to Iranian intelligence services. Moreover, the main link between the two sides was the leader of the Tajik Islamists in the Unified Tajik Opposition, Abdulla Nuri, whom the American intelligence services described as a close ally of bin Laden. The attempts to establish closer ties between bin Laden and the Iranian counterintelligence services were undertaken earlier, but ended in failure— because of Iran's position. See J. Risen, "Bin Laden Sought Iran as an Ally, U.S. Intelligence Documents Say" (www.nytimes.com/2001/12/31). It is for this period that there is information about contacts between the Taliban and Tajik Islamists. As S. Olimova and M. Olimov have noted, after the Taliban bolstered their power at the beginning of 1996, B. Rabbani and A. S. Massoud established closer ties to Moscow, and that brought a corresponding change in their relations with the Tajik opposition. The latter entered into clandestine contact with the Taliban, but soon abandoned this (see Olimova and Olimov, "Islamskaia partiia," p. 139). It is worth noting that this happened, in all likelihood, under advice from Teheran, which decided not to support the various Sunni movements, including those emanating from Pakistan, and encouraged the Tajik opposition to seek a real accommodation with Dushanbe.

42. If, until 1994, Pakistan and Iran primarily supported Hekmatyar and Rabbani-Massoud respectively, thereafter Islamabad banked on the Taliban, and Teheran on their adversaries.

43. A. Rashid, *Jihad: The Rise of Militant Islam in Central Asia* (New Haven, CT 2002), p. 104.

44. Ibid., pp. 58–59.

45. See above, note 41.

46. Pakistan's role in the rise of the Taliban during its initial phases is apparent from the presence of its diplomats and agents of the Inter-Service Intelligence at the highest council (*shura*) in Kandahar in April 1996; it met there, amid total secrecy, for two weeks and ended in the election of Mullahas the leader of the Taliban movement, with the title of *amir-ul-muslimin* ("commander of the faithful"), and with the adoption of a program of radical activities to institute a strict Islamic order in Afghanistan. See A. Rashid, *Taliban: Militant Islam, Oil and Fundamentalism in Central Asia* (New Haven, CT 2000), pp. 42–43.

47. This occurred in August 1998 when Taliban units stormed the city of Mazar-e Sharif and subjected the Hazara Shiites to vicious reprisals. See Rashid, *Taliban*, pp. 202, 204.

48. Some people from Tajikistan were among the extremists who joined various radical groups. Two of them, members of the Wahhabi group of Tafkir, were killed in March 1997 in a clash with Pakistani police in one of the refugee camps in Peshawar. Rashid, *Taliban*, p. 137.

49. Rashid, *Taliban*, p. 91. The significance of this seminary in preparing Taliban cadres and Islamists from various countries was, and remains, exceptionally great; it is headed by Maulana Sami-ul-Haq, the most radical leader in Jamiat-e Ulama-e Islam.

50. Ibid., p. 149.

51. E. Abdullaev, "The Central Asian Nexus: Islam and Politics," in: *Central Asia: A Gathering Storm?* ed. B. Rumer (Armonk, NY, 2002), p. 265; "Islam Karimov zakleimil religioznyi fanatizm," *Vremia MN*, 24 February 1999; and A. Dubnov, "Islam Karimov nazyvaet imena," *Vremia MN*, 16 March 1999.

52. Rashid, *Jihad*, pp. 247–49.

53. Ibid., pp. 162, 172.

54. Ibid., p. 174.

55. Along with measures for joint defense, which for the most part were merely rhetorical, Uzbek authorities undertook entirely real steps to protect their country's territory: they mined the border with Kyrgyzstan and Tajikistan and established a strict system of border control. Rashid, *Jihad*, pp. 160–64.

56. *Sistemnaia istoriia mezhdunarodnykh otnoshenii v chetyrekh tomakh, 1918–2003*, 4 vols. (Moscow, 2003), 3: 605–6.

57. Rashid (*Taliban*, p. 77) has pointed out this geopolitical arrangement. Its practical consequence, for example, entailed giving Russia, Iran, and India access to the airport at the Tajik city of Kuliab for purposes of supplying the anti-Taliban forces of A. S. Massoud with weapons and foodstuffs.

58. A. R. Bhatti, "The Pan-Afghan Defense Council to Announce Million-Man March," *The News*, 9 November 2001; and "TNSM Threatens to Target Non-Pashtun Refugees" (www.jang.com.pk/thenews/nov2001–daily/24–11–2001).

59. "Musharraf's Spies Revere Jinnah not Jihadis" (www.dailytimes.com.pk/7–1–2004).

60. P. P. Sikoev, *Taliby. Religiozno-politicheskii portret* (Moscow, 2004), p. 212.

61. At the same time, by no means were all the Uzbeks and other foreigners captured or killed. There is information that Uzbeks, Chechens, and Uigurs took part in combat activities of Al Qaeda in the spring of 2002 (in the Shahi Kot Valley of Afghanistan). See J. Dao, "Taliban and Al Qaeda Believed Plotting Within Pakistan"

(www.nytimes.com/2002/05/28). According to data for the summer of 2003, Arabs and Uzbeks were actively fighting troops of the Afghan government, the regular units of the U.S. Army, and German peacekeepers in the southeastern areas of Afghanistan. O. Tohid, "Taliban Regroups," *Christian Science Monitor*, 27 July 2003.

62. "After Afghanistan, Pak Militants Headed for Kashmir" (www.afgha.com/2001/12/28).

63. "India-Pakistan Tensions Rise Again," in *Prospects of a Dialogue Between India and Pakistan*, IPRI Factfile, vol. 5, no. 6: 27–29.

64. One must also take into account the real influence of the United States and, more broadly, the block of Western countries, on the policies of India and especially Pakistan. Moreover, among the elites and politicized masses of both countries, one sees an attempt to downplay the strength of this influence and to emphasize the role of other players on the international scene—Russia, China, neighboring states, and also international organizations.

65. See "Vystuplenie N. Nazarbaeva na 47–i sessii General'noi Assamblei OON," *Nezavisimaia gazeta*, 9 October 1992; and V. Ovlev, "Kontinental'naia Aziia. Moskva mogla by podderzhat' initsiativy Kazakhstana," ibid., 12 March 1993.

66. See, in particular, V. Belokrenitsky, "Politicheskii islam v Pakistane skoree zhiv, chem mertv," *Nezavisimaia gazeta*, 23 September 2002.

67. The oldest party, the Pakistan Muslim League (Quaid-i-Azam), has been split into independent political organizations—as often happened in earlier historical periods. The ruling pro-presidential party bears the name of the "father-founder" of the state, Muhammad Ali Jinnah, who is called the Quaidi-Azam ("Great Leader") (Jinnah; Quaid).

68. The term, "under the control of the army," refers to the fact that the formation of the National Security Council (which, ex officio, includes the higher military leaders) is prescribed by law. See A. Hassan, "MMA, Govt Sign Deal" (www.dawn.com/24.02.2003). It is not superfluous here to note the substantial similarity in the political structures of Pakistan and Turkey.

69. For example, see: B. I. Kliuev, *Religiia i konflikt v Indii* (Moscow, 2002); and I. Glushkova, *Iz indiiskoi korziny* (Moscow, 2003).

70. "Khalid Sheikh Mohammed Is Biggest Al Qaeda Catch" (www.news.com/29–03–2003).

71. In particular, see A.D. Borchgrave, "Analysis: Al Qaeda's Privileged Sanctuary" (www.efreedomnews.com/24.01.03). It is thought that the most probable areas of Pakistan where bin Laden, Mullah Omar, and others can hide are Northern and Southern Waziristan—agencies in the Federally Administered Tribal Area.

72. "Islami-Tehreek, Millat-e-Islamia, Khuddam ul-Islam Banned" (www.pakistanlink.com/Nov03/16); and "Prominent Leaders Elude Arrest as Offices Raided and Sealed" (www.dailytimes.com/pk/17–11–2003).

73. M. Asghar and B. S. Syed, "President Escapes Attempt on Life" (www.dawn.com/2003).

74. For instance, see "Musharraf: A Moment of Hope—and Danger" (Stratfor, 27 December 2003); "Kashmiri, Chechen Militants Carried Out Attack on Musharraf" (www.straitstimes.asia1.com); and "Afghan and Kashmiri Groups Targeting Musharraf" (www.dailytimes.com.pk/29–12–2003).

75. In the course of Musharraf's visit to the United States in the summer of 2003, Pakistan was promised 3 billion dollars in aid over a five-year period; that is comparable to the scale of military and economic support that Washington extended to the

Zia ul-Haq regime in the early 1980s. For an analysis of this phenomenon, see "The Golden Egg: Tacit Support for Musharraf" (Stratfor, 27 June 2003).

76. See V. Belokrenitsky, "Islamskii radikalizm Pakistana: evoliutsiia i rol' v regione," *Tsentral'naia Aziia i Kavkaz*, 2000, no. 6: 116–31; and O.V. Pleshov, *Islam, islamizm i nominal'naia demokratiia v Pakistane* (Moscow, 2003).

77. N. Malik, "Human Conditions Not Improving in Pakistan: Report" (www.jang.com.pk/thenews/dec2003–daily/05/12/2003).

78. Strategic Foresight Group, *The Future of Pakistan* (Mumbai, 2002), p. 201.

79. Ibid., pp. 103–6.

80. H. Ghafour, "Afghanistan Gets New Name and a Constitution" (www.afgha.com/06.01.04).

81. At issue here are the proposals to construct natural gas and oil pipelines from Turkmenistan through Afghanistan to Pakistan. In 1996–1998, these projects were under active discussion at the initiative of the American company Unocal and a number of other corporations. The policies of the Taliban, however, forced the Americans to drop out of these talks. After 2001 the greatest interest in the development of a pipeline transport system was manifested by the three states involved; this culminated in a corresponding agreement in Islamabad (in May 2002). The cost of constructing two lines (one each for oil and natural gas) is estimated to be three to five billion dollars, and the main task of the state sponsors is to attract foreign investors. The complexity of this project is rooted both in political factors (the unpopularity throughout the world and the unreliability of the Turkmen regime of S. Niiazov; the volatile situation in Afghanistan) and in economic factors (the image of Central Asia's significance as an energy reserve of the world is greeted with substantial skepticism). Therefore it is no accident that the sponsors of these projects anticipate that they will be realized only in the course of a considerable period (up to twenty years), although there is hope that work will soon begin on part of the project—the natural gas pipeline. See "Work on Pak-Turkmen Gas Pipeline May Execute Next Year" (www.pakistanlink.com/Dec03/10).

82. It bears recalling that the caliphate movement seized the Muslim part of India after the end of World War I amid a threat to the existence of the spiritual and political center of Muslim Sunni in the Ottoman (Turkish) caliphate-sultanate. The mass excitement caused by the political propaganda of the caliphate supporters led to the *hijra* (migration) of thousands of Indian Muslims from the western areas (in what is now Pakistan) to Afghanistan. A revolutionary government of India in exile was formed there; its emissaries went to Central Asia, and some even reached Moscow. See Mathur, *Growth of Muslim Politics*, pp. 137–44.

83. See, in particular, B. Rumer, "The Search for Stability in Central Asia," in *Central Asia: A Gathering Storm?* ed. B Rumer, pp. 3–6; and B. Rumer, "Tsentral'naia Aziia—desiat' let spustia. Obzornyi ocherk," *Tsentral'naia Aziia i Iuzhnyi Kavkaz* (Almaty, 2002), pp. 12–13.

84. Rumer, "Tsentral'naia Aziia," pp. 20–23.

85. J. P. Smith, "The IMU: Alive and Kicking?" (www.cacianalyst.org/24.09.2003); and "Former Uzbek Islamic militant Being Interviewed by Media" (www.cacianalyst.org/04.09.2003).

86. Rashid, *Jihad*, pp. 115–36; "Hizb ut-Tahrir Works to Establish Khalifat" (www.syberwurx.com/nation/15.12.00); and K. Mukhabbatov, "Religiozno-oppozitsionnye gruppy v Tajikistane: Hizb-ut-Takhrir," in *Religioznyi ekstremizm v Tsentral'noi Azii*, p. 64.

87. B. Babadzhanov, "O deiatel'nosti 'Khizb-ut-Takhrir al islami' v Uzbekistane," *Islam na postsovetskom prostranstve: vzgliad izvnutri*, pp. 153–69; and "Religiozno-politicheskie gruppy v Uzbekistane," p. 55. Characteristically, of the other articles in the latter collection of essays, one can see that the majority of members in Hizb ut-Tahrir consist of representatives from the Uzbek nationality. See S. Sagnaeva, "Religiozno-oppozitsionnye gruppy v Kyrgyzstane: Khizb-ut-Takhrir," *Religioznyi ekstremizm v Tsentral'noi Azii*, p. 65; and K. Mukhabbatov, "Religiozno-oppozitsionnye gruppy v Tadzhikistane," p. 85. In the judgment of E. Abdullaev, the main area of activity of Hizb ut-Tahrir in Central Asia is Uzbekistan and the neighboring areas of Tajikistan (Sogd oblast) and Kyrgyzstan (Osh oblast), which are populated by Uzbeks. Abdullaev, "The Central Asian Nexus," pp. 286–87.

88. M. Rehman, "Hizb-ut-Tahrir: Making Inroads into Kazakhstan?" (www.cacianalyst.org [4 June 2003]); "More Hizb-ut-Tahrir Members Arrested in Tajikistan" (ibid., 30 April 2003); and "Hizb-ut-Tahrir Seeks to Strengthen Position in Northern Kyrgyzstan" (ibid., 2 April 2003).

89. "Uzbek Policies Under Attack" (www.iwpr.net/21.02.2003); and J. Machleder, "Alternative Political Voices in Uzbekistan" (www.eurasianet.org/18.02.2003).

90. "More Hizb-ut-Tahrir Members Arrested in Tajikistan" (www.cacianalyst.com [30 April 2003]).

91. V. Emel'ianov, "Strana razdrazhaiushchei veroterpimosti," *Nezavisimaia Gazeta*, supplement: *Religii*, 3 December 2003, p. 7.

92. Some of the activities of Tabligi Jamaat did not go unnoticed in Uzbekistan; see B. Babadzhanov, "Religiozno-oppozitsionnye gruppy v Uzbekistane," p. 57. One further attestation to this is provided by one of the recent papers presented by the International Crisis Group in Brussels. This report cites the successful activity of the propagandists of Tabligi Jamaat who had come mainly from Pakistan. Their followers in the region became known under the name "davatchi" (from another Arab term *dava*, meaning sermon and appeal to convert to Islam). See "Is Radical Islam Inevitable in Central Asia? Priorities for Engagement," International Crisis Group, Report no.72 (Brussels, 23 December 2003), p. 7.

93. S. I. Khan and M. Khan, "Among the Believers," *Newsline* (Karachi, February 1998), pp. 40–41.

94. I. V. Zhmuida, "Organizatsiia Ekonomicheskogo Sotrudnichestva i Pakistan," *Zapadnaia Aziia, Tsentral'naia Aziia i Zakavkaz'e. Integratsiia i konflikty* (Moscow, 1995), pp. 138–44.

Part III

The Internal Social and
Political Context

6

The Regime in Kazakhstan

Dmitrii Furman

From the Editor

The following essay examines the process of establishing and strengthening Nazarbaev's authoritarian regime in Kazakhstan. The analysis here is limited to providing an account of how that regime has evolved. The author draws a parallel between Nazarbaev and Yeltsin, offering a comparison of the respective methods that these two post-Soviet figures used to gain and hold onto power. By the time this article appears, the political reality in Kazakhstan would not have undergone any substantial changes. For now the regime continues to preserve a firm grasp on the country, although some new actors have made their way to the wings of the political stage. The changes overtaking the space of the former Soviet Union are accelerating and are fraught with unpredictable outcomes. The "orange revolution" in Ukraine totally nullified the Kremlin's efforts to construct a "mini-Soviet Union" and imparted a significant new impulse to the political dynamics in the countries of the CIS. There is every reason to expect serious perturbations in the states of Central Asia as well. The mounting tensions and unrest here are accompanied by growing pressure from without. And all this obtains no less in Kazakhstan that the author has so graphically described in this article.

The goal of this chapter is to show the logic behind the development and functioning of the political regime of post-Soviet Kazakhstan. In addition, I endeavor to compare the regime in Kazakhstan with that in Russia.

Only by comparing post-Soviet regimes can one understand what in their evolution was determined by a common genesis (that is, by being inherently "post-Soviet"), by more profound factors (above all, the peculiarities of national cultures, which had been repressed during the coercive Soviet unification), and by circumstances (such as the individual traits of their rulers). But the divergence of some post-Soviet political regimes is so great that they cannot be usefully compared with each other; for example, the regimes in Estonia and Turkmenistan could hardly differ more. But it is interesting to compare regimes that are relatively similar, as in the case of Russia and Kazakhstan.

One can classify all post-Soviet states according to their most important political characteristics: do they allow a possible rotation of power, do they permit an opposition to operate peacefully and legally, and can that opposition, within the framework of the constitution, win elections and take power?

With these criteria in mind, we can identify one group of post-Soviet countries where, within the framework of a democratic system, power has already shifted several times. This group includes Estonia, Latvia, Lithuania, and Moldova. In these countries there are permanent "rules of the game" established by constitutions; and there can be various winners in this game.

A second, transitional category includes several other countries that had a change in power, but it came through an armed coup, not democratic means. Such was the case in Azerbaijan, Georgia before the revolution of 2003, and Tajikistan. To a significant degree, Armenia also belongs to this group, since the transfer of power from Ter-Petrosian to Kocharian actually came through a kind of "mild" military coup. Only later were these coups legitimized by elections. In some cases, the change in power occurred by democratic means, but only once (Ukraine before the "orange revolution" and Belarus). In all of these countries, the rulers are seeking to construct a system that will preclude a further rotation in power. But the success of such attempts varies greatly. Thus, in Belarus Aleksandr Lukashenko was able to create a strict regime blocking a further rotation of power. Ukraine and Georgia, by contrast, appear to have very recently joined the category of countries where the democratic rotation of power will be normal.

Finally, a third group of countries is characterized by the "absence of presidential alternatives." These are countries that, in the course of the entire post-Soviet period, have not in general had any rotation of power, and where the same person has governed from the moment that independence was declared (Kazakhstan, Kyrgyzstan, Uzbekistan, and Turkmenistan), or has been appointed as the successor (Russia). Here, rather than have changes in winners and losers under permanent rules of the game; what changes are the rules, not the rulers. One cannot see Russia—which is governed by a successor appointed by Boris Yeltsin—as fundamentally different in principle from the other countries in this group, which have had no changes in power whatsoever. The Russian change was due to an accidental factor—the health and age of the first Russian president.

The possibility of a democratic rotation is not the only criterion for the classification of regimes, and states in the same category may differ in other important characteristics. Thus, some states have not had a rotation but do have a legal opposition (Russia, Kazakhstan, and Kyrgyzstan), but the system is so structured that it is impossible for them to come to power through peaceful means. Uzbekistan has a pseudo-multiparty system (close to the pseudo-multi-party system in "countries with a popular democracy"); the regime in Turkmenistan is better described as totalitarian than authoritarian. Kazakhstan, in terms of its political structure, is especially close to Russia; hence a comparison of these two regimes is of particular interest.

Nazarbaev's Rise to Power

Kazakhstan, while not unique, is a graphic example of the special processes unleashed by the collapse of the communist system, where colossal socioeconomic and ideological changes coexisted with an extraordinary degree of continuity in the ruling elite. That continuity is hardly commensurate with the scale of the socioeconomic and ideological changes. In Russia, the first president, Boris Yeltsin, was a representative of the Communist Party elite, yet nonetheless a rebel who had been expelled from the leadership and then left the party altogether. In Kazakhstan, the first and thus far only president was the last first secretary of the Central Committee of the Communist Party of Kazakhstan—Nursultan Abishevich Nazarbaev.[1]

Nazarbaev was a professional party functionary who had been promoted by an earlier first secretary of Kazakhstan, Dinmukhammed Kunaev. The latter had held this position in Kazakhstan for a very long time, had colossal influence in Moscow, and enjoyed popularity in Kazakhstan itself. In 1984 Nazarbaev became the chairman of the Council of Ministers; he was regarded by Kunaev as his possible successor. In 1986, however, at the XVI Congress of the Communist Party of Kazakhstan, Nazarbaev—sensing the winds of change blowing from Moscow—unexpectedly delivered a perestroika speech highly critical of his own patron and older friend, Kunaev.

Despite an external similarity (in both cases there was an unexpected critical attack on superiors), Nazarbaev's demarche differed greatly from Yeltsin's attack on Gorbachev at the Central Committee plenum of October 1987. Yeltsin's speech was impulsive, plainly not well thought out, and very risky. At this point, Yeltsin could hardly have been thinking that this would mark the starting point of his rise to power. Nazarbaev's speech, by contrast, was relatively audacious, but designed to advance his career. Nazarbaev undoubtedly understood that Kunaev's days were numbered. The very fact that Kunaev had promoted him and indicated him as a successor could spoil his chances for becoming just such a successor. By contrast, his criticism of Kunaev could play well in Moscow: the new general secretary, Mikhail Gorbachev, was seeking young, energetic, and bold leaders, and could accelerate Nazarbaev's rise to power.[2] However, things did not turn out as he had thought. Having decided to appoint as head of Kazakhstan a "Varangian," someone without ties to the local clans, Gorbachev dispatched Gennadii Kolbin to Kazakhstan. But the appointment of a Slav as first secretary only served to ignite the "December events" of 1986 in Alma-Ata, the first mass national demonstration in the USSR.[3] It was not until June 1989 that Nazarbaev finally succeeded in becoming the first secretary of the Kazakh Central Committee.

The short-lived rule of Kolbin was accompanied by repression of those who participated in the December demonstrations and "Kazakh nationalists" in general. In Kazakhstan people were even talking about a "miniature 1937." People therefore greeted Nazarbaev's accession to power with relief, thus giving the new leader a certain "startup capital" of popular (above all, Kazakh) good will. Nevertheless, his position was very difficult. The crisis of the Soviet system was obvious; figuratively speaking, Nazarbaev had just taken a seat in a chair that was about to break apart. In fact, from the very moment he obtained the highest post in Kazakhstan, he encountered a situation where, to preserve, consolidate, and enhance his power, Nazarbaev needed to find new ideological foundations and a new legitimacy—in a word, to make a "new chair" for himself.

In a record-breaking short period of time, and without letting go of power for a single moment, Nazarbaev transformed himself from an orthodox communist into a defender of capitalism and democracy,[4] a proponent of independence for Kazakhstan, and even an observant Muslim. It is of course impossible to believe that in 1990–1991 he suddenly underwent a radical revolution in his worldview. It is obvious that, both before and after the "revolution in Weltanschauung," the only thing that really mattered to him (as indeed to most of those in the Soviet nomenklatura) was his career. Hence his worldview automatically, instinctively adapted to the situation.[5] While the change in worldview to suit the new situation did not present any difficulty, it was quite difficult to preserve and enhance his own power and to create the requisite institutional form and legitimation. All this would require considerable adroitness. Not every leader in the late Soviet era would prove capable of coping with this task. But Nazarbaev did.

Genesis of the Kazakh and Russian Regimes

The genesis of the Nazarbaev regime in Kazakhstan and the Yelstin-Putin regime in Russia is somewhat different.

With certain reservations, one can say that Russia underwent a revolution in 1991, when a mass anti-Soviet movement (even if a minority) brought their leader, Boris Yelstin, to power. This movement made him victorious in the struggle to become chairman of the Supreme Soviet, elected him president of Russia, and finally backed him during the "August putsch" of 1991.

Kazakhstan knew no such revolution, no triumph of a mass movement. The anti-Soviet and anticommunist movement in Kazakhstan was significantly weaker than in Russia.[6] Nevertheless, by the end of the Soviet period, the society of Kazakhstan was seething with agitation and torn by contradictions and, at any moment, could have exploded into bloody anarchy.

While experiencing the socioeconomic and political crisis that beset the entire USSR, Kazakhstan had some specific conditions that made the situation here especially dangerous. The gradual disintegration of the USSR was driving this country toward independence, but its multinational composition made its existence virtually impossible. The titulary nation (Kazakhs) constituted a minority of the population (39.6 percent according to the census of 1989); it was only slightly larger than the more-developed and urbanized Russian "minority" (37.8 percent). Indeed, the latter formed a majority in the capital and in a number of northern oblasts (contiguous with Russia).

In Kazakhstan (as in other republics), the democratic movement unleashed by the Gorbachev liberalization acquired a national, anti-Soviet, and in some measure anti-Russian character.[7] Although Kazakh nationalism was not aggressively anti-Russian, it did raise demands to increase the status of the titular nation, its language, and its culture, which implicitly meant a certain downgrading in the status of Russians and their culture. Such actions inevitably provoked a negative reaction from Russians, especially the Cossack population, which historically had been the avant-garde of Russian colonization and a defender of the empire's borders. In the northern oblasts, with Russians comprising a majority of the population, such attitudes gave rise to demands for autonomy and separatism.[8] Predictably, this movement elicited the support of Russia, and not only from the "communist-patriotic" groups in the Russian Federation. Voices calling for a re-examination of Russia's borders and for the annexation of Kazakhstan's oblasts with a Russian majority periodically were to be heard from the "democratic movement" in Russia; the latter's amorphous, eclectic ideology also contains some nationalist-imperial components.[9] The situation became especially tense in the period between the August putsch (August 1991, when Mikhail Gorbachev was held captive for three days by leading Soviet military and state officials) and the Belovezh Accords (December 1991, when the presidents of Russia, Ukraine, and Belarus decreed the end of the Soviet Union) that is, at time when Yeltsin had not yet conclusively decided to liquidate the USSR. Indeed, during these months Russian authorities began to threaten the other Soviet republics that it would initiate a review of boundaries should they withdraw from the Soviet Union. In September 1991, this led to open clashes in Ural'sk between the separatist-minded Cossacks and Kazakh nationalists (whom the Azat Party had mobilized and sent from all over Kazakhstan), and over the next three months the same thing nearly occurred in Tselinograd (now called Astana).[10]

Seen ex post facto, what happened always appears to have been natural and logical: what happened *had to* happen. And whatever did not come to pass was simply impossible. But the scenario of a bloody nationalist battle and Russian separatism in Kazakhstan, though unrealized, was no less probable than in Moldova. And the consequences of such separatism would have been significantly more terrifying than in a republic like Moldova, since the latter does not border directly on Russia.

In this situation, the task for Nazarbaev was to preserve power (after creating its institutional and ideological foundations) and to redefine his status—from that of Soviet party leader to head of an independent state. That was inseparable from the need to calm, or at least contain, the agitation that then gripped society. The shift to an open national position (entailing, of course, a struggle against the Soviet Union) could not only have resulted in a catastrophe for the multinational Kazakhstan, but might have enabled the rise of other, more charismatic leaders from outside the old nomenklatura elite—that is, Kazakh counterparts to Abulfaz Elchibey of Azerbaijan and Zviad Gamsakhurdia of Georgia.

The tasks that Nazarbaev and Yeltsin then faced were thus very different. To be sure, both aspired to power in a time of profound social crisis. But Yeltsin, standing at the head of an oppositionist movement, could only come to power by inflaming revolutionary passions both in the USSR at large and in Russia itself—by launching a campaign against the Soviet system and its defenders. By contrast, Nazarbaev had already come to power within the framework of the Soviet system; his task was to moderate, not exacerbate, passions. At the same time, it was impossible to preserve both Soviet power and the strong authority of a Russian leadership. However, the greater internal independence of Kazakhstan, so long as it did not take the final step toward full independence, could well be combined with maintaining a weaker Soviet regime.

This difference in situations and objectives gave rise to significant differences in policy and ideological rhetoric.

Balancing Between Opposing Camps

Nazarbaev displayed a very strong political instinct. The ideological and political game that he played during this period can rightfully be called brilliant.

He was able to strike a balance between opposing ideological positions, something not easily achieved. He juxtaposed his dynamism, his openness to the new, and his "reformism" to the narrow-minded, reactionary mentality of the majority of the Kazakh party elite.[11] The relatively weak democrats in Kazakhstan saw him not as an adversary, but as an ally—and even as protector. Or, in any case, for them he was a "lesser evil." At the same time, Nazarbaev—through and through a member of the party nomenklatura—constantly emphasized his evolution and his striving for stability and order. For members of the nomenklatura elite, he was one of their own—that is, someone who would never let them be torn to pieces by the mob. For them too, he was the "lesser evil."[12]

It was more difficult to strike a balance between nationalist Kazakh rhetoric and a policy to achieve sovereignty on the one hand and the "Soviet internationalism" and support of the Union on the other. Such a balance would allow Nazarbaev to be seen favorably both by nationalists (who would regard him as too cautious, but in the final analysis striving to establish an independent Kazakh state) and by Kazakhstani Russians and all the internationalists (who wanted someone to uphold and defend the Soviet Union) and disarmed the Russians). Here Nazarbaev demonstrated amazing mastery; he never crossed over the subtle line that would have deprived him of the support of both sides.

Indeed, in 1990–1991 Nazarbaev was the most popular politician in the entire Soviet Union.[13] He symbolized the "golden mean" between democrats and separatists (seeking to demolish the USSR) and obtuse reactionaries (determined to preserve it at any cost); he proved relatively acceptable to both sides; and he showed amazing agility in balancing between Gorbachev, his right-wing critics, and Yeltsin. The People found in Nazarbaev reason to hope, simultaneously, for the preservation of the Soviet Union, a policy of liberal reform, and the autonomy of republics. But the cautious Nazarbaev declined to assume any honorific positions in Moscow (which, given the gradual breakdown of the USSR, had no firm basis); to do so he would risk losing the less prestigious, but real power in Kazakhstan.[14] He would, in short, not trade a bird in the hand for one in the bush.

In fact, Nazarbaev successfully reaped benefits from the breakup of the USSR and, to some degree, even contributed (however cautiously) to its demise.[15] He thereby preserved his posture as a defender of the Soviet regime and portrayed all his actions to secure the independence of Kazakhstan as involuntary. Kazakhstan, after all, faced a lethal danger from a Russian movement that opposed Kazakhstan's independence or one that demanded the separation of Russian oblasts from Kazakhstan (in the event Russia itself demolished the Soviet Union, but the leader of Kazakhstan defended it). Although these Russian movements proved confused and powerless, such movements served Nazarbaev's interest: Kazakh nationalism, in the face of this Russian threat, could not act against its "own" leader, who was carefully, but inexorably, leading the country toward independence.

Nazarbaev retained his position as the ostensible "integrator" of post-Soviet space and advanced various initiatives for unification (which then "ran into a wall of incomprehension and unwillingness on Moscow's side") throughout the entire subsequent period.[16] Nazarbaev took measures that consolidated Kazakhstan's independence, repressed Russian separatist encroachments, reinforced the ethnically Kazakh character of the state, and brought a change in the ethnic composition of the population (through the emigration of Russians and "Russian-speaking" elements and the repatriation of Kazakhs from other countries). And all that was done behind a smokescreen of appeals for reintegration of post-Soviet space, with Russia at its head.[17] It is impossible to say to what degree Nazarbaev consciously created this smokescreen, or did so unconsciously, as dictated by his unerring political instinct.[18]

The Rise of Personal Rule

The process of "switching seats" commenced in March 1990, when Nazarbaev, while naturally remaining first secretary of the Kazakh Communist Party, became chairman of the Supreme Soviet that had just been elected on a new basis. In April, following the general wave of declarations of sovereignty, the Supreme Soviet of the Kazakh SSR introduced the office of president and elected Nazarbaev to the new position. It had to overcome resistance from Russian deputies, who "instinctively thought . . . that the institution of the presidency . . . will distance the republic from Moscow."[19]

The August 1991 putsch in Moscow accelerated the breakup of the Soviet Union. There is hardly any question that, during these tense days in August, Nazarbaev waited to see who would prevail. His position was equivocal: depending on how things turned out, he could present himself as a staunch defender of the Soviet Union (having warned Gorbachev that his liberalism would not lead to anything good), but also as virtually Yeltsin's comrade-in-arms.[20] After Yeltsin and the Russian "democrats" won, Nazarbaev (in a report at a session of the Supreme Soviet of Kazakhstan on 26 August 1991) declared that he personally averted a storming of the Russian White House, for he repeatedly phoned Gennadii Ianaev (vice-president) and Dmitrii Iazov (minister of defense) to tell them this would be a crime. "Apparently," he said, "it worked."[21]

The collapse of the putsch greatly increased the power of leaders in all the republics. Nazarbaev, for all practical purposes, could ignore the remnants of the Soviet leadership; its power had become nominal and invisible. He could get rid of the "party fundamentalists"[22] who had impeded him; simultaneously, he could also claim to have rescued those same people from the wrath of "bloodthirsty democrats."[23]

Now that the Soviet Union was clearly doomed, it was essential to rush the process of "making a new seat." And remnants of the "old chair" were being put to the torch. In September 1991, the Communist Party of Kazakhstan held an Extraordinary XVIII Party Congress, which resolved to liquidate itself and to create a new party of a "parliamentary type"—the Socialist Party. Nazarbaev did not join the new party. Like Yeltsin in Russia (who had not striven to create and head a party on the basis of "Democratic Russia" and instead pronounced himself to be the "president of all Russians"), Nazarbaev did not want to become tied to a party, which could somehow restrict his freedom of action. Instead, he assumed the role of "president of all Kazakhstanis."[24] The time for creating presidential parties, which were in the presidents' pockets, was to come later in Russia and Kazakhstan.

The process of "reseating" was nearly complete. But it was urgent that Nazarbaev reinforce the new "chair" through a national election; the earlier election by the Supreme Soviet, under the circumstances, was already insufficient. Nor could Nazarbaev permit his power to be less legitimate than that of Yeltsin, who had been chosen through a national election.

Kazakhstan held its first national election for president on 1 December 1991. The preparations for the election were already symptomatic of the new regime. Like Yeltsin in Russia, Nazarbaev established a regime of personal power, one in which legal institutions and norms were in part instruments, in part a cover. But Nazarbaev's specific style was very different from that of the impulsive Yeltsin; the Kazakh was much more cunning and cautious than Yeltsin, preferring to act indirectly through others and remaining behind the scenes.

The Kazakh dissident and leader of the Zheltoksan Party, Khasen Kozhakhmetov (who later changed his name to Kozh-Akhmet) decided to advance his candidacy. He did so not because he had hopes of winning but because he wanted to give voters an alternative and to make himself better known. However, the Central Elections Commission refused to let him participate in the election, because he failed to collect the requisite 100,000 signatures. That enormous number of signatures was, no doubt, set to make the nomination of alternative candidates impossible. In addition, the Central Elections Commission reported violations in his campaign to collect signatures and threatened him with criminal prosecution. A police raid on his headquarters resulted in the theft of lists with 40,000 signatures. Nazarbaev's press office issued a special announcement denying any association to the police action.[25]

Some 88.2 percent of the electorate voted on 1 December 1991, with Nazarbaev receiving 98.78 percent of the vote and only 1.22 percent voting against him.[26] And although even a formal alternative was missing in these elections, these "Soviet" type figures actually did reflect reality. At the time, Nazarbaev unquestionably occupied the midpoint between the diametrical opposites in forces at work in Kazakhstan: if not "good," he was at least "the lesser evil" for them. On 16 December 2001, Kazakhstan proclaimed its independence, becoming the very last Soviet republic to do so.

December 1991 marked the emergence of a new regime in Kazakhstan. It was a regime based on the personal power of a president unfettered by subordination to Moscow, by adherence to any official ideology or party, or (in fact) by a constitution and laws (which were promulgated and amended as the situation required).

Mutability of Leaders and the Social Context

Yeltsin and Nazarbaev came to power through different paths and in very different societies. Nevertheless, they fashioned the same basic type of regime. That the regimes belong to the same type was undoubtedly due to the similarity in the men themselves and in the societies that they governed.

Both Yeltsin and Nazarbaev are creations of the late Soviet nomenklatura. They had long since ceased to take seriously the ossified dogmas of Marxist-Leninist ideology; in the depths of their souls, they aspired to liberate themselves from party discipline, envied Western elites, and possessed enormous ideological adaptability. It was no problem for them to embrace "democratic" ideology if that permitted them to gain and hold onto power, if it provided the requisite legitimacy. The idea of the market and private property, which evoked images of the "sweet life" of Western millionaires, even aroused sincere enthusiasm.

But the ease of Nazarbaev's and Yeltsin's ideological transformations corresponded to a superficiality of their commitment to legal democratic values and institutions. People who have no spiritual travails making a radical change in ideology and even state had no special piety toward the constitutions and laws that after all they themselves had created. Neither man came to power in order to surrender that power for the sake of principles and norms. And both sought to transform their power into something authoritarian, which admitted no alternatives. In doing so, they inevitably committed a host of crimes; now the only option, should they lose power, was judicial prosecution, personal ruin, and (in all likelihood) destruction.[27]

Both were also dealing with societies that, for all their differences, made it possible to construct a system "with no alternatives." For all the obvious and profound differences, in a number of respects the societies of Russia and Kazakhstan were quite similar.

Above all, that included the complete absence of a consensus regarding fundamental principles—even general ones like independence, democracy, and free markets. (The diametrical opposite was to be found in the Baltic republics.) When the breakdown of the Soviet Union, the repudiation of communist ideology, and painful market reforms came to Kazakhstan and Russia, they engulfed societies that were wholly unprepared for such revolutionary changes. In 1994, only 14.4 percent of the people in Kazakhstan believed the collapse of the USSR to be useful (with a still lower rate, 5.2, among Russians in Kazakhstan); 21.3 percent thought it more useful than harmful (compared to 8.9 percent for Russians in Kazakhstan); 27 percent saw it more harmful than useful (24.4 percent for Russians); and 18.8 percent as harmful (50.6 percent for the Russians).[28] Thus, even for the majority of Kazakhs, not to mention the Russians in Kazakhstan, the very existence of an independent Kazakhstan was not regarded as an incontrovertible, self-evident truth. Four years later, in 1998, only 58 percent of the Kazakhs and 21 percent of the Russians in Kazakhstan had a positive assessment of independence; 22 percent of the Kazakhs and 52 percent of the Russians held a negative opinion. As for the future, 23 percent favored unification with Russia, 29 percent unification within the framework of the Commonwealth of Independent States (CIS), 16 percent the restoration of the USSR, 14 percent an independent state outside the framework of any associations or unions, and 10 percent a union of countries in Central Asia. They gave this response to the question "What kind of regime will exist at the beginning of the third millennium?": 28 percent predicted "chaos," 26 percent—"democracy," 16 percent—"regime under a strong arm," and 5 percent—"Soviet power." In addition, the complete absence of consensus, the intense passion, and the strong agitation were not linked to specific alternatives, to clearly formulated positions on the basic questions and programs of parties. The absence of consensus reflected an atomization of society and eclecticism and labiality in political attitudes. Hence some political positions easily turn into their antithesis (the "communist-patriotic" becomes the "democratic" tomorrow, and then "communist-patriotic" the day after) and fuses with the opposite.

One must add that Russia and Kazakhstan lacked virtually any experience in making a power change through democratic methods. Nor had they the experience of democratic self-government. For its part, Kazakhstan lacked any experience as an independent state of the modern type. It found itself in a situation that was unprecedented and frightening.

Such societies—which are fragmented, atomized, and frightened by the unexpected and radical turn of events—are easily manipulated and complaisant toward authorities. They find it difficult to oppose anything. They fear themselves, their anarchic potential; psychologically, they feel the need for a "strong hand" at the helm. Their most important desire is not to have a specific ruler, but to have "order." As the opinion poll showed, many saw "chaos" as the most likely scenario; it was "chaos" that they feared most of all. As to which system is best suited to resolve the country's problems, 4.4 percent said "communism," 7.3 percent—"socialism," 5.9 percent—"capitalism," 2.3 percent—"Islam," 8.8 percent—"democracy of the Western type," and 56.9—percent "any, so long as there is order."[29] This set of values was ideal for constructing an authoritarian regime that could promise to provide this much-desired "order."[30]

In sum, both Yeltsin and Nazarbaev dealt with convenient, complaisant "human material." To put together a regime that would ensure their irreplaceability was a difficult, but entirely realizable objective.

Presidents and Parliaments

Yeltsin and Nazarbaev, having become presidents, next strove to reinforce their power and to eliminate alternatives. They encountered similar problems.

Above all, they needed to overcome resistance and opposition from their parliaments. Both were indebted to these parliaments for elevating them to their present positions. The Russian parliament elected Yeltsin as its chairman; the parliament of Kazakhstan elected Nazarbaev first as its chairman, then as its president. Nevertheless, conflict between the presidents and their parliaments was inevitable.

Above all, the elections of the people's deputies of the RSFSR and the deputies to the Supreme Soviet of Kazakhstan in March 1990 were conducted under conditions of a democratic upsurge. They were probably the freest and most honest elections in the history of these two states. This had an impact on the psychology of deputies, most of whom had won a fierce battle with competitors and felt themselves to be "chosen by the people."

That made the parliaments "ungovernable." Unrestrained by party discipline, having the same eclectic, unstructured, and agitated consciousness and the same low legal consciousness as the people who elected them, the deputies represented a volatile and emotional mass.

The situation was aggravated by the fact that both Russia and Kazakhstan operated on the basis of the old Soviet constitutions, which were unsuitable for the new conditions and had been gradually supplemented by various, contradictory amendments. It was generally believed that new constitutions were needed. But adoption of new constitutions could not occur without a struggle between the branches of power. This struggle was aggravated by the fact that custom rooted in constitutionalism and separation of powers was completely absent. Indeed, the very idea of these things was lacking. Instead, both the presidents and the parliaments laid claims to total power.

The presidents, moreover, could rely on the old social customs that favored monocracy, the traditions of autocracy, and the power of khans and first secretaries. In discussions about the constitution of Kazakhstan, some proposed to call Nazarbaev a "khan," the head of an oblast "sultan," and the heads of raions "beks."[31] These two presidents could also rely on the feeling of inferiority and backwardness (which were deeply ingrained in public consciousness) as well as the fear of democracy (which, while perhaps good for developed countries, would inevitably give rise to chaos and anarchy in Kazakhstan and Russia, especially under conditions of acute social and economic crisis).[32] Furthermore, in the "democratic" part of society (both in Kazakhstan and Russia), enormously influential was the idea that the most important thing was to create the "basis" of a modern society in the form of a market and private property, and that to do this it is possible to violate the requirements of democracy. The latter could be tacked on later, as a "super-structure" to the basis that had already been created.[33] All these arguments in favor of "strong authority" would be repeated, hundreds of times, in speeches by Nazarbaev and various ideologues of his regime.

The Supreme Soviets, for their part, based their claims on a powerful ideological foundation. Both the Gorbachev reforms and the struggle of the radical democrats invoked the slogan of democratization and returning power from the party apparatus to the people. And not simply to the people, but to the soviets. The idea of returning power to the soviets permitted liberal and democratic forces to establish a symbolic connection with the revolution of 1917 and with sacred Soviet symbolism ("All power to the soviets!"). Therefore both the Russian and the Kazakhstani parliaments were dominated by a very deep conviction about their authority and mission.

The social and economic crisis aggravated this conflict between presidents and parliaments. The crisis unfolded against a background of strikes, spontaneous disturbances (even in the army),[34] and the constant threat of ethnic conflict.

There was yet another aspect of this crisis: in addition to the crisis in the relations of the "branches of power," there was also a crisis within the ruling elite. Both Yeltsin and Nazarbaev had risen quickly above their former comrades-in-arms and fellow functionaries; as often happens in such cases, the latter found it very difficult to change from a relationship of equals to one where they were subordinated to the "boss."

In Russia, this aspect of the crisis became manifest in the relations between Yeltsin and Ruslan Khasbulatov, his closest associate and Yeltsin's successor as chairman of the Supreme Soviet. To this must also be added the relations between Yelstin and his vice-president, Aleksandr Rutskoi.

The development of the situation in Kazakhstan was strictly parallel to that in Russia. When Nazarbaev became the popularly elected president, he chose Erik Asanbaev (chairman of the Supreme Soviet) as his vice-president. It thus became necessary to choose a new chairman. On 11 December 1991, despite opposition from Nazarbaev, the Supreme Soviet elected Serikbolsyn Abdil'din, a high-ranking party functionary in the nomenklatura elite who had, until then, been Kazakhstan's representative in Moscow. The election of Abdil'din was a turning point in the relations between the president and parliament.

However, in January 1992, the Supreme Soviet agreed to a significant expansion in the president's authority. It liquidated the local *ispolkomy* (soviet executive committees) and empowered the president to appoint the heads of local administration; they subsequently became the main instrument for the president's control over society. Nazarbaev nevertheless understood that he would not succeed in gaining complete control over parliament. S.A. Abdil'din, naturally, was proud of his victory. (He beat the candidate actively supported by Nazarbaev and was elected against the will of Nazarbaev.)[35] Abdil'din later became head of the Communist Party of Kazakhstan and a constant, indefatigable adversary of Nazarbaev. How Abdil'din understood his role is evident from the caption under a photograph of the two leaders that appeared in the newspaper *Sovety Kazakhstana* on 9 December 1992: "A year has passed since President Nursultan Nazarbaev and the chairman of the Supreme Soviet . . . Serikbolsyn Abdil'din began to perform their duties, as the embodiment of the *two peaks of a single mountain.*"[36] Obviously, such words made a confrontation between the "two peaks" inevitable.

On 28 January 1993 Kazakhstan's Supreme Soviet adopted a constitution. Although the opposition believed it to endow the president with exceptional power and to be authoritarian,[37] to a significant degree it was actually a compromise—one that Nazarbaev found unsatisfactory. Throughout 1993, the pro-presidential mass media of Kazakhstan waged an unremitting attack on parliament; the assault was analogous to the parallel campaign in the Russian "democratic" mass media. In both cases the media portrayed parliament as an obstacle to reform,[38] as an organ that constantly interfered with the work of the present government and that was seeking to assume power on its own.[39] Abdil'din was also accused of having "presidential ambitions."[40] "Presidential ambitions" were beginning to be perceived in Kazakhstan as the most horrendous accusation, something akin to being accused of state treason.[41]

In the summer of 1993, Nazarbaev asked the Supreme Soviet to grant him additional authority, like that of Boris Yeltsin. The Supreme Soviet, however, did not even take up the question.

The presidential-parliamentary conflict that developed parallel in Russia and Kazakhstan had a similar outcome. But their form reflected the differences in the psychology and behavioral style of the two leaders.

Yeltsin was simpler, more primitive and impulsive, and acted in a straightforward manner. Nazarbaev was inclined to wait, leaving it to Yeltsin to act and to clear the road for him. That is the way it was with the breakup of the Soviet Union, when Yeltsin took the main work on himself and Nazarbaev (seemingly opposed him), took advantage of its results as if he had no other option, and also became the head of an independent state. So too it was on this occasion. Yeltsin acted to aggravate the conflict and, in the end, dispersed the deputies by resorting to force and arranging a "blood bath" in Moscow. It proved a success: the people did not rise up to defend the parliament; and Western countries, above all fearing that the communists would return to power or that Russia would degenerate into complete political chaos, in effect sanctioned Yeltsin's coup d'état. This opened the way for Nazarbaev.[42] It was obvious that, if a coup could succeed in Russia, it would be all the easier to carry out one in Kazakhstan. And if the West sanctioned a bloody dispersion of parliament in a European country, then a disbandment that was bloodless and in an Asian country would meet with still greater understanding. However, here too, as always, Nazarbaev moved cautiously, placing others out in front. He staged things such that the initiative for disbanding parliament appeared not to come from him, but practically from the deputies themselves.

Demands that the "reactionary" Supreme Soviet and the soviets in general (as blocking the reforms that would lead Kazakhstan to a radiant future) disband themselves began to be heard in the mass media and at various meetings of Kazakhstani deputies from 1991.[43] But on 16 November 1993 the Alataus raion soviet in the city of Almaty adopted a resolution to dissolve itself and appealed to deputies in soviets at all levels to follow its example: "The soviets . . . remain a symbol of the old regime and old ideology. The tight framework of the hopelessly outdated laws that regulate the work of the representatives of a system . . . has increased the isolation of the soviets from real life."[44] The timing for this step was well chosen: on 2 November 1993 Kazakhstan announced its withdrawal from the ruble zone. With economic chaos reigning in the country, people clearly would not be worried about the parliament.

A wave of self-disbandments of local soviets followed. On 10 December 1993 a totally demoralized Supreme Soviet adopted a resolution: in violation of the Constitution, it gave the president the authority to issue decrees with the force of law and proclaimed its own disbandment. By this time part of the deputies had managed to become employees of the executive branch, the president had appointed others as heads of local administrations,[45] and others had been intimidated into resigning from office.[46]

The majority of the democrats in Kazakhstan, as in Russia, supported the dispersion of the parliament "for the sake of accelerating reform." Sergei Duvanov (a democratic journalist and politician currently in jail) even published an article on 25 November 1993 in *Kazakhstanskaia pravda* with this title: "I Think That Historical Expediency Will Not Harm Democracy," which declares that if parliament stands in the way of reform, then it has to be replaced. "And this must be done quickly."[47]

New parliamentary elections were set for March 1994—in accordance with the constitution that the Supreme Soviet had adopted in January 1993. The elections, in the total absence of a parliament, were under the complete control of the president and those whom he had appointed as the heads of local administrations.

Thus Nazarbaev achieved victory without any bloodshed and, it would seem, more easily than did Yeltsin. But this had a reverse side: Yeltsin's victory was more complete, because it opened the way for the compilation and adoption, by a referendum in December 1993, of a constitution that conferred almost unlimited rights of the president and few rights for the parliament. That is precisely what Yeltsin wanted. The situation in Kazakhstan was different. The constitution had already been adopted. Therefore if Yeltsin had carried out a bloody coup, but only once, Nazarbaev had a bloodless coup, but had to do it twice.

Opposition: The Peril of Moderates

On 7 March 1994, in accordance with the constitution of 1993, Kazakhstan held elections for the new Supreme Soviet. The elections were conducted according to rules stipulated in a presidential decree. The decree provided for forty candidates to be elected on a so-called "State List," compiled by the president. Those candidates did not need to collect the requisite number of signatures for candidacy. Naturally, all of them were elected. In general, the elections were held under conditions marked by the total arbitrariness of the election commissions, appointed by the oblast governors (*akims*), who, in turn, had been appointed by the president. Frequently, these commissions simply refused to register candidates they deemed undesirable.[48] The election also had a peculiarity: the commissions counted ballots left blank as "yes" votes. As a result, the number of votes exceeded the number of voters.

Nevertheless, the composition of the parliament was not what Nazarbaev expected.[49] Externally, its composition seemed significantly more acceptable than that of its Russian analogue, the Duma, which was elected in December 1993 (i.e., after the October coup) and consisted mainly of communists and Zhirinovskii supporters. The opposition in Kazakhstan was significantly more moderate. But this was actually more dangerous for Nazarbaev than its radical counterpart in Russia, which shouted at meetings "Put Boris Yeltsin on Trial!" and called the Yeltsin government an "occupation" regime.

First, as already pointed out, the Yeltsin constitution came after the old parliament had been disbanded and placed strict limits on the role of the new one. By contrast, the constitution of Kazakhstan had been crafted by the old parliament and assigned significant authority to the legislative branch. In this situation, even an irreconcilable opposition (which held a majority in the Russian parliament) was less dangerous to presidential authority than more moderate opposition (indeed, constituting only a minority) in the parliament of Kazakhstan.

The second factor was, in my view, more complicated and more important. The very extremism of the Russian opposition and the moderation of the Kazakhstani opposition made the former weaker and less dangerous for the authorities.

The "red-brown," communist-patriotic opposition in Russia, to a certain degree, played into Yeltsin's hands, because the alternative that they represented was patently unacceptable. The West regarded this opposition as absolutely unacceptable; it was therefore always ready to react with understanding to any action by Yeltsin that aimed at its suppression and at bolstering his own authority. For the Russian elite, the prospect that the communists and "patriots" would come to power was so terrifying that, despite any shocking outbursts by the president, he unquestionably remained for the elite the "lesser evil." The possibility of unifying the main "communist-patriotic" opposition and the relatively small intellectual democratic opposition (the party Yabloko) was completely out of the question. Nor was the communist-patriotic opposition acceptable for the majority of Russians. Despite the fact that Yeltsin was extremely unpopular, and despite the fact that the majority of voters cast their ballots in the Duma elections for the oppositionist parties, they knew that this was not a vote about real power. The prospect of a communist victory in the presidential elections was more frightening, for they understood that Yeltsin would not simply surrender power; hence such a victory would lead to chaos and civil war. The Yeltsin regime also invoked this specter to frighten them. Therefore, although the majority rejected Yeltsin's policies in the Duma elections of 1993, they nonetheless voted for Yeltsin in 1996 (as in the referendum in the spring of 1993).[50]

The situation in Kazakhstan was different. Here there was no bugaboo in the form of "communist-patriots." In general, the combination of communism and nationalism is a phenomenon specific to people in the Russian Federation. The combination of Kazakh nationalism and communism was in principle impossible: the USSR was not a lost "Kazakh empire" (as it was a lost empire for Russia), and nostalgia for the Soviet past was not combined with a specifically nationalist tone in Kazakhstan. In 1994 the Communist Party in Kazakhstan did not even participate in the elections; it was registered only a week after the elections. Its successor, the Socialist Party of Kazakhstan, did participate, having declared its ideal to be the "Swedish model" and having gone into opposition.[51] But after the communist party was re-established and Serikbolsyn Abdil'din (the speaker in 1991–1993) became its leader in 1996 and a real political force, it was much more moderate and more prepared to cooperate with others, including the rightist oppositionist forces, than was the case of the Communist Party of the Russian Federation.

Apart from the Socialist Party of Kazakhstan (which, despite opposition from authorities, managed to send fourteen deputies to parliament), the opposition included a party called the National Congress of Kazakhstan under Olzhas Suleimenov, with thirteen deputies. The opposition also included a few deputies from the Russian movement Lad and leftist trade-unionists and agrarians.[52] Neither the Socialist Party of Kazakhstan nor the National Congress of Kazakhstan were nationalistic (on the contrary, they accused the authorities of trampling the rights of the Russian population), antidemocratic, or antimarket. This was a quite moderate and "responsible" opposition. But precisely this moderation posed a threat to authorities. Such an opposition could not play the role of a "bugaboo," or "horrible alternative," against which it would be possible to justify the use of any means whatsoever. Nor did this opposition suffer from those enormous internal ideological contradictions that split the Russian opposition into a left (main) and right (lesser). Instead, the opposition in Kazakhstan could easily unify the most diverse elements seeking to contest presidential authoritarianism. The result was a broad oppositionist alliance in parliament called "The Progress" that gradually attracted some deputies from the parliamentary majority and the broad coalition of oppositionist forces called "The Republic" (the head of its Coordinating Committee was S. Abdil'din).

A candidate for president who had the support of the moderate Kazakhstani opposition (and the presidential elections were not far off, being fixed for 1996 by the constitution) thus posed a greater danger for Nazarbaev than Ziuganov did for Yeltsin. From October 1994 the mass media openly began to discuss presidential candidacies for the elections in 1996. The only candidate that the opposition proposed to nominate was Olzhas Suleimenov, a popular poet, publicist, and public activist. The latter had obtained a seat in parliament through the state list, which must have been especially galling for Nazarbaev.

The year 1994 was very difficult for the economy of Kazakhstan. After three years of a steady decline in production, the gross domestic product (GDP) fell by 25.4 percent from the previous year. There was no end to this decline, no light at the end of the tunnel to be seen. In October Nazarbaev reconstituted his government, replacing Sergei Tereshchenko with Akezhan Kazhegel'din as its head. But that did not have a major impact on the situation. Hence the prospects of an oppositionist victory in 1996 became increasingly probable. Moreover, both Nazarbaev and Kazakhstani society could not have overlooked the example of two countries in the CIS where the authorities lost elections and the head of state gave up his position to oppositionist candidates: Ukraine and Belarus.

Nazarbaev did not wait passively for 1996 and idly watch as the belief in the lack of an alternative vanished from public consciousness. He acted with the characteristic style of anticipating blows and resorting to simple, but effective and cunning, tricks. The grounds for dissolving the new parliament, formally, did not come from him.

As noted, the 1994 parliamentary elections were accompanied by numerous violations of an electoral law that the president himself had promulgated (some articles of which were contrary to the constitution and plain common sense). This gave rise to many legal suits by candidates who had lost; such suits, naturally, went nowhere. And suddenly, on 6 March 1995, the Constitutional Court issued a verdict in one such suit (involving the female journalist T. Kviatkovskaia): it declared the election in her district, where she had lost, to be void. And since the court voided the elections not because the rules had been flouted, but because these rules violated the constitution, the verdict in effect meant that the new parliament was illegitimate.

As in 1993, Nazarbaev remained behind the scenes, even feigning a protest against the court's verdict, but declared that he was "forced to bow before the force of law." At the last session of the parliament (11 March 1995), the president made the following statement: "Yesterday the Constitutional Court went beyond my objection and the objection by the chairman of the Supreme Soviet. I will say directly and openly that the decision of 6 March was utterly unexpected by me. You can talk and conjecture; that's your business."[53]

The deputies could do nothing. After all, the elections had really been conducted with numerous and sundry violations, and there had been protests (which had been ignored). And it was not even clear against whom they should lodge protests since formally the president was on their side. So the parliament was dissolved.

Olzhas Suleimenov, who had resisted a bit and made a row at meetings, was sent off as ambassador to Italy and then dropped out of the political game. His National Congress of Kazakhstan sank into anabiosis, lethargy and the majority of the opposition gave up.

Writing a New Constitution

On 1 March 1995 Nazarbaev issued a decree On the Formation of an Assembly of the Peoples of Kazakhstan. The organ had vague functions; the president himself determined its composition. Of course, the Assembly was created before the "unexpected" verdict of the Constitutional Court on 6 March 1995; that was done specifically so that, after the dissolution of the Supreme Soviet, it would be possible to rely on an organ that, quite provisionally, could be portrayed as "representative." At its first session on 24 March, the Assembly proposed a referendum on this question: "Do you agree to extend to 1 December 2000 the authority of the president of the Republic of Kazakhstan, N. A. Nazarbaev, who was popularly elected on 1 December 1991?" The most hilarious thing here is that Nazarbaev claimed that the initiative came as a surprise to him.[54]

Literally the next day the president issued a decree on the referendum. Although there was no law authorizing such a referendum, Nazarbaev still had the right—conferred by the first parliament—to issue decrees with the force of law in the absence of a legislative body. His decree fixed the date of the referendum for 29 April 1995. Nazarbaev obviously was acting in haste so as not to give the opposition time to respond. The West protested, but quite weakly.[55]

Here is an example of the official agitation before the referendum:

Yes—to the political and economic stability of Kazakhstan;

Yes—to future of our children and grandchildren;

Yes—to the politics of peace and concord, to a politics without war, without sacrifices, without blood, without hundreds of thousands of refugees;

Yes—to tranquility in our homes and apartments;

Yes—to these five years that the president requests from us so as to lay the foundations for the future of the republic, to determine precisely the paths out of the economic crisis;

Yes—to the Eurasian Union.[56]

According to official data, 91.3 percent of the eligible voters participated in the referendum, and 95.4 percent of these voted "yes."

Right afterward came the time for the constitution. The 1993 Constitution, which Nazarbaev at that time had praised to the skies, was now declared "not to correspond to the spirit of the time" and to have become mired "halfway between a socialist past and market future." In June 1995 the same Assembly of the Peoples of Kazakhstan approved the initiative of the republic's leadership to adopt a new constitution.[57] It was prepared hastily and without undue clamor. Finally, Nazarbaev had the constitution that he wanted; it was "no worse" than that of the Russian Federation. It calls the president the "symbol and guarantee of the unity of the people and state authority, the durability of the constitution, the rights and liberties of the person and citizen."[58] The text describes the powers of the president in twenty-two articles; it declares that "his honor and dignity are inviolable" and that "the support, service, and protection of the president and his family . . . are provided at the expense of the state."[59] He can only be removed from office because of illness or accusation of state treason; whereas the Russian constitution refers to "other serious crimes," stipulation that is missing here. The new Kazakhstani constitution also abolished (as did the Russian constitution of 1993) the office of vice-president; consistent with the post-Soviet model of "presidents without alternatives" there cannot be a second person who has been "elected by the people." These presidents want to have complete freedom of action in naming their successors. In the Kazakhstan case, former Vice-President Asanbaev was sent off to serve as ambassador to Germany.[60]

The parliament, according to the new constitution, consists of two houses: the Majilis (one elected per district [okrug]), and the Senate (two per oblast, elected at meetings of deputies to represent the organs of oblasts; another seven are appointed directly by the president himself). Whereas the 1990 parliament had 360 deputies, and that of 1994 had 144, the constitution of

1995 provided for 114, with 47 in the Senate and 67 in Majilis. The fewer the deputies, the easier it is to control them—all the more so if they are divided into two houses. A vote of no confidence in the government henceforth required a two-thirds majority in both houses.

There was no Constitutional Court, but only a constitutional council, which had limited power compared with the Constitutional Court. The council consisted of seven members; three (including the chairman, who casts the deciding vote) are appointed by the president; the chairmen of the Senate and Majilis each appoint two members.

A referendum of 30 August 1995 approved the constitution. The vote in favor of the constitution was 90 percent (actually just 34 percent, according to the opposition), with only 10 percent voting against.

Finally, in December 1995 there were elections to the new bicameral parliament. It would seem that this time Nazarbaev obtained what he wanted. For all practical purposes, the opposition did not participate in the elections.

A President Empowered and Glorified

If in 1993 Nazarbaev had mainly been emulating Yeltsin in the construction of his regime, from 1996 Kazakhstan had clearly "overtaken" Russia.[61]

Opposition parties (the Socialist Party of Kazakhstan and the National Congress of Kazakhstan) had been deprived of the opportunity to struggle for power. Indeed, they had even forfeited the illusion of power in the form of a parliamentary representation under an ultra-presidential system. In the end, they sank into hibernation and virtually disappeared. To be sure, 1996 did witness the appearance of a new opposition movement (later a party) called Azamat (Citizen), which drew on the intelligentsia for social support, based itself in Almaty, and strove to unify all the opposition into a "Popular Front." But it did not constitute a real threat for the president.

The authorities increased their control over society. The procuracy (State Prosecutor's office) demanded an end to closed sessions of public organizations, where antigovernment plans might be under discussion.[62] The government banned meetings under every kind of pretext, even the threat of epidemics. It also tightened its control over the mass media, especially television, where tenders for the right to broadcast eliminated all independent companies. The company "Khabar" (controlled by Nazarbaev's daughter Dariga) obtained channels and frequencies.[63] A number of earlier oppositionist publications fell into the hands of reliable people, above all, that same daughter Dariga and her husband. Russia did not take analogous measures to control the mass media until significantly later—under Yeltsin's successor.

Nothing and no one could limit Nazarbaev's authority. His power was greater than that of the former first secretaries in Soviet times; the latter were subject to Moscow and bound by party ideology. And his power was greater than that of the Kazakh khans of earlier times. It was also greater than the power of his Russian colleague, who nonetheless had, in some measure, to deal with parliament and to engage in the tortuous electoral campaign of 1996 (and afterwards ended up in the hospital). Yeltsin did entertain plans to take Kazakhstan's path, replacing the elections by a referendum to extend his term, but in the end did not dare to carry them out. Nor could Yeltsin, in contrast to Nazarbaev, simply appoint the governors of oblasts. (Quite recently, his successor, Vladimir Putin, eliminated the election of governors and began to appoint them.)

A survey conducted at the end of 1997 showed that 77.6 percent of those polled regard the president's power to be unlimited.[64] And that is how it was perceived not only in mass consciousness. An article published in *Kazakhstanskaia pravda* by a prominent jurist expresses the following ideas which, without doubt, correspond to the spontaneously appearing ideology of the president of Kazakhstan and his entourage: "I think that the popularly elected president embodies the unity of the Kazakhstani people as the source of state power, combining in himself the fullness of power, independent of its subsequent division into legislative, executive, and judicial branches."[65]

It was natural for a "personality cult" of the president to take shape. To him are sung dithyrambs:

I believe in today, I love Nursultan,
He has justified the belief of the people,
Who have bound up all their hopes in him.[66]

A key figure,
Generator of the idea of making Kazakhstan,
As a secular and democratic power,
Is the president of the republic,
Nursultan Abishevich Nazarbaev . . .
His intellect, competency,
Enhanced by rationalism
Permits him to be a true leader.[67]

We must be thankful to the Almighty,
That our people have such a son.[68]

The head of the Muslims of Kazakhstan, likewise, has declared that "the high spiritual office of mufti obligates me to provide every possible assistance to the realization of the strategic policy of the president."[69] The head of the Russian Orthodox Church in Kazakhstan, Aleksii (Archbishop of Astana and Almaty), goes even further: "God has blessed the Kazakhstani people with a special grace, when from the depths of the people rose such a son as Nursultan Nazarbaev."[70]

How did the president use this unlimited power?

Privatization and Power

As a main argument to justify his omnipotence, Nazarbaev always has invoked the need for energetic steps to move along the path of market reforms. At the third session of the Assembly of the Peoples of Kazakhstan, he declared that it was good that elections were not being held: "We would await two years of electoral squabbling. We would not be up to economic reform."[71]

In reality, as Kazakhstan advanced significantly further than Russia in creating an authoritarian system, it also moved further along the path of market reform. To a question by a Russian interviewer as to what he thinks are the causes of the delays in reform in Russia, Nazarbaev replied: "Not the least important factor here, it seems to me, . . . was played by the political struggle, the schism in the Russian political elite, . . . but also the permanent election campaigns which, as is well known, siphon off much energy and resources."[72] Evidently, to a significant degree Nazarbaev was right. He felt himself more confident than did Yeltsin. After the dissolution of the second parliament and the extension of his term, Nazarbaev in general did not experience any institutionalized resistance and could virtually ignore public opinion. During this period Nazarbaev signed a mass of decrees from his administration, all bearing the force of law. On 29 January 1996, the day before the first session of the new parliament of Kazakhstan, *Kazakhstanskaia pravda* published nine new decrees.[73]

Kazakhstan was more active than Russia in opening its natural wealth to foreign investors, who gained a firm foothold in the energy and fuel complex. The country privatized its electric power stations; it began to privatize its residential housing management; it undertook a pension reform in 1997. As one Russian journalist (who, very probably, was genuinely enthralled by the successes in Kazakhstan) wrote in 1997: "In Kazakhstan (not without cause) people think that in some spheres it is necessary not for Kazakhstan to overtake Russia, but for Russia to overtake Kazakhstan."[74] Gradually, Kazakhstan looked to Russia for an example of authoritarian modernization (the idea toward which Russians seem generally well disposed), almost pushing aside Pinochet's Chile, which had been so popular in the early 1990s.

Naturally, privatization by an authoritarian regime that answers to no one was bound to permit an enrichment of the ruling elite—above all, the president himself and his immediate entourage. Such enrichment does not even presuppose some kind of special avarice; it happens automatically.[75]

In Kazakhstan, as in Russia, the notion of the "Family" and its capital took root. The Family would later encounter some difficulties because of an investigation into money laundering in the West ("Kazakhgate").[76] But in the mid-1990s that was still in the distant future. Naturally, there is no hard information about the wealth of the president and his wife (just as is true of Yeltsin and his family).[77] But all three of Nazarbaev's daughters are married to men who are unquestionably millionaires and who, simultaneously, hold high positions as officials or politicians. Dariga is herself the head of the Council of Directors of the largest media-holding company in Kazakhstan ("Khabar"); her husband, Rakhat Aliev, was a general, head of the tax police, deputy chair of the Committee of National Security, and a millionaire businessman. Dinara's husband is one of the biggest oil oligarchs, Timur Kulibaev; another oil oligarch in the clan is Nazarbaev's nephew, Kairat Satybaldy. The first husband of Aliia was the son of the Kyrgyz president Askar Akaev, Aidar (who worked in the Kazkommertsbank in Almaty); her second husband is also an influential entrepreneur, Daniiar Sakenov.[78]

The role of family and clan connections is greater in Kazakhstan than in Russia. Obviously, people in Kazakhstan accepted the public role of the ruler's kinsmen more "calmly" than in Russia, as if it were something entirely natural. By contrast, Yeltsin's daughters and sons-in-law remained in the background and did not occupy any especially important positions (before the public role of Tat'iana D'iachenko, which was very brief). By contrast, Dariga and all the sons-in-law of Nazarbaev are prominent, authoritative figures in Kazakhstan.

In addition to family connections in the narrow sense, other connections—based on locale, tribe, or horde (*zhuz*)—play a large role in Kazakhstan. The elite of power and property includes all the president's relatives and kinsmen, even remote ones.[79] And it also includes people who happen to come from his home village, Chemolgan; Kazakhstan has even invented a jocular term, "Chemolganization."[80] These connections enable the president and the Family to control literally every sphere of the economy and public life. Finally, this elite is also dominated by people from Nazarbaev's "Great Horde" (*Starshii zhuz*).

At the same time, in the circle of friends and close associates (the "Family" in the broader sense), people who are not ethnic Kazakhs play a significant role. Examples include Sergei Tereshchenko (a Slav and an old Nazarbaev friend and client) and Aleksandr Mashkevich (a Jewish activist, aluminum king, and one of the most influential people in Kazakhstan).[81] One researcher in Kazakhstan suggests this explanation for these people's close ties to the president: "As a result of their ethnic illegitimacy, they will loyally serve their patron."[82] Their presidential connections and enrichment are typical of an order that placed the most strategically important and profitable raw material branches in the hands of foreign, not Kazakh, capital. The authorities endeavor to ensure that the most lucrative and most important export-oriented branches are directly subject to the Family, under its indirect control (through "ethnically illegitimate" clients, who are totally dependent on the president and his family), or consigned to foreign companies (whose owners have no connection to the politics of Kazakhstan). By contrast, access of domestic capital to the nation's resource wealth (apart from the Family) is limited to a few morsels.[83]

Nevertheless, the wealth of the Family, even in the broader sense (i.e., including the distant relatives, close friends, and clients) constitutes only part of the privatized wealth. Later M. Auezov would say of the early post-Soviet period: "It was such a carefree . . . time, when the rapacious instinct was in power. And everyone was grabbing and stuffing his pockets. It was joyous and blissful."[84] All the top state officials and all those close to the president became rich. Prime Ministers Sergei Tereshchenko (1991–1994)[85] and Akezhan Kazhegel'din (1994–1997)[86] became multi-millionaires and each akim had his own "family," his own clientele; the appointment of a new akim often triggered a redistribution of property.[87] Corruption scandals, as a rule linked to the struggle of clans for property, did come to light, but reaction was muted.[88] Only later did the state make the battle against corruption one of its priorities. But a grotesque aspect of this campaign, specific to Kazakhstan, was the fact that the anticorruption campaign was directed by the president's closest relatives: Rakhat Aliev and Kairat Satybaldy. As a result, the campaign served first and foremost to remove competitors to the Family business and to reinforce its control.

The goals of privatization in Kazakhstan, as in Russia, were not only socioeconomic development and the personal enrichment of those who privatized (and those close to them). It also had political goals. In 1991, at a plenum of the Central Committee of the Communist Party of Kazakhstan, Nazarbaev already made this statement: "The communists themselves must provide an example and more boldly become heads of privatized entities."[89] His appeal was heard.[90] The political elite (nomenklatura) quickly turned into a propertied elite. The elite included not only these individuals themselves, but also their children and close relatives; all this gave rise to the jocose expression "economy of nephews." And insofar as privatization, to a large degree, proceeded under the control of authorities and with a minimal role for laws, that impelled the elite to have a vested interest in political power and its consolidation around the president.[91] The elite is beginning to represent an enormous and complex system; the most influential people, who had their own clients, were clients of the "Nazarbaev clan." And they were all bound together by a kind of "collective security" (*krugovaia poruka*). Moreover, the competition and struggle for power of individual groups took the form of a struggle for the attention and generosity of the president, and schisms within the elite, in some measure, served to reinforce his power at the top.

As in Russia, market reforms not only made the elites wealthy, but also left the masses impoverished. As a result, compared with the Soviet epoch, there was an increase in social stratification. There was also a sharp decline in the GDP. That downturn, however, sooner or later had to come to an end and give way to a post-transformation growth. In Kazakhstan this began in 1996 (0.5 percent growth in GDP) and continued in 1997 (1.7 percent). In 1998 Kazakhstan suffered the consequences of the Asian and Russian crises; the GDP again dropped (1.9 percent). But then it began a period of rapid growth, rising 45 percent from 1999 to 2004.[92]

The general dynamics of the decrease and growth in the GDP in Russia and Kazakhstan were similar. But Kazakhstan has quickly overtaken Russia in the rate of development and now is "the most dynamically developing country with a market economy in the entire post-Soviet space."[93] Indeed, the economy of Kazakhstan is one of the fastest growing among the developing economies of the world. Obviously, there are diverse opinions about the reasons for Kazakhstan's relative success (and still more it's stability). To a significant degree, it is undoubtedly associated with the extremely favorable conjuncture of prices on oil. But it is entirely probable that one factor has been the consistency of reform, which has been ensured by the harshly authoritarian rule of someone who really accepts the market ideology. That is all the more true since, in its late-Soviet and post-Soviet interpretation, this ideology coincided with Nazarbaev's own personal interests.

1998: From Celebration to Concern

Probably the happiest year in Nazarbaev's reign was 1998. That year he realized his great dream when the new capital in Astana was officially opened. It was designed to strengthen the new state. Thus, unlike Almaty (which is located on the southern border area), Astana is in the center; relocation of the capital aimed both to promote "Kazakhization" of the northern regions and to liberate Nazarbaev from the pressure of the Almaty population, which is politically active and disposed toward oppositionist activities.[94] The new capital, Nazarbaev's pet project, is supposed to link his name with the future history of Kazakhstan for centuries to come.

This same year, he married his daughter Aliia (who studied in a private school in Switzerland and then became an art student at an American university) to Aidar Akaev (a student in economics at the University of Maryland and, as noted, the son of President Akaev of Kyrgyzstan). This was the first, and thus far the only, marriage between representatives of the ruling dynasties in the CIS. Although the marriage failed, at the time it was a great source of joy for Nazarbaev.[95]

However, in October 1998, in a speech to both houses of the parliament, Nazarbaev unexpectedly announced a program of democratization: "I shall tell you honestly: personally for me, . . . there are no external reasons to embark on such a democratization, limiting my own power." However, he added, "my people have earned their liberty through their suffering." Democratization would include the introduction of additional deputies elected by party lists to the Majilis, granting parliament the right to change the Constitution (if 80 percent of the deputies in each house voted in favor), and so forth. To be sure, all this did not amount to great changes.[96]

But that was not the main point: Nazarbaev had decided to violate the resolution of a referendum held so recently and to have early presidential elections (simultaneously extending the presidential term from five to seven years). Rumors about such plans were already afoot in the summer of 1998. At that point, however, he issued a categorical denial: "No. If my short 'no' is not enough, I'll repeat myself once more: 'No.' The elections will be held in accordance with the Constitution: in 1999 the parliament will be elected, and in 2000 the president."[97] But it subsequently emerged that the rumors were in fact true. Everything happened in the classic Nazarbaev style, now so familiar; he summoned the deputies and told them: "Let's not develop this subject, that is my firm request." When the deputies "insisted," he acquiesced.[98]

Now, at the very apogee of his power, Nazarbaev felt a serious new threat to his authority.

The New Opposition

This new threat was fundamentally different from all that had come before. It resulted not because social and economic crisis gripped the country: on the contrary, it arose because the crisis was being overcome. The challenge did not come from those social forces that existed at the founding of the regime, but from new forces generated by the regime itself and the post-Soviet transformation of society.

The development of Kazakhstan and Russia was relatively parallel. To be sure, some processes and phenomena, inherent in the Kazakh and Russian systems, manifested themselves in one country more clearly and earlier than in the other. Moreover, people in Kazakhstan and in the other post-Soviet republics had, characteristically, inherited from "imperial" times the notion that Russia is always ahead—in good and in bad senses.[99] In fact, however, that was by no means always the case.

The conflict between presidential authority and the new bourgeoisie did not arise in Russia until Putin became the second president. Its most dramatic manifestation was the arrest of Mikhail Khodorkovskii in 2003. In Kazakhstan, however, all this appeared much earlier.

Evidently, such a conflict is inherent in this type of regime. So long as privatization was underway, the newly rich—who had obtained their wealth largely with the help of presidential authority—coalesced around the regime and supported it. Once they had amassed their wealth, they developed new interests. The new bourgeoisie began to understand that, under the conditions of an authoritarian system, their property was very weakly defended. Riches that had been accumulated, with the assistance of the authorities (by legal and quasi-legal methods), could just as easily be taken away by the authorities.[100] The result was a contradiction between the wealth and economic significance of the new bourgeoisie, on the one hand, and its lack of rights and ability to limit presidential power, on the other. The motives of the wealthy had also changed. Once they achieved a certain level of wealth, they sought to convert this into power and into public recognition and respect. At the same time, the authorities became increasingly concerned about the concentration of material resources in the hands of individuals, even if these were partly still dependent on the regime.[101]

All this transpired after society had presumably taken a form that the new regime found convenient and after the liberal opposition of the intelligentsia had virtually disappeared. Society had acquired a new system, different from the late Soviet times; the protest of the popular masses had somewhat abated as the transformation crisis abated and society adapted to the new conditions. Unexpectedly, a new opposition emerged; coming from the new bourgeoisie, it was backed by enormous material resources and was significantly more dangerous.

It is rather difficult to explain why the new opposition appeared in Kazakhstan before it did in Russia. Here it is possible only to present some hypotheses and conjectures.

Above all, Kazakhstan lacked a powerful communist-patriotic opposition. Its absence, as I have already pointed out, was no accident, but resulted from basic differences in Russian and Kazakh history and culture. In Russia, this opposition forced civil society to unite more firmly around the president; that took its clearest and most grotesque form in 1996. The bourgeois elite in Kazakhstan did not experience such constant pressure and threats.

Furthermore, tribal and horde factors may have played a role. People who feel a tribal and horde loyalty can count on the instinctive solidarity of blood kinsmen; they are not so isolated. Kazakh society, which has preserved tribal and horde connections, is not so "atomized" and defenseless before the authorities (in contrast to Russian society).

The president has sought to rely on the solidarity and loyalty of "his own people"—relatives, people from his home region, fellow tribesmen, and people from the Great Horde. He uses them to fill important positions in the state hierarchy and, through them, to maintain control over key (above all, raw materials) export-oriented branches of the economy as well as the mass media.[102] But this also has had a reverse side. Insofar as the representatives of other tribes and hordes have felt themselves excluded from power and from the more desirable pieces of property that has turned them into potential oppositionists. And they could count on support from "their own people." Authoritarianism thus encountered resistance from hordes and tribal loyalties.[103] In Russia, opposition oligarchs are isolated; they find it extremely difficult to elicit sympathy and support in Russian society. In Kazakhstan, a Kazakh oligarch can count, at the very least, on the support of fellow tribesmen.

To some degree, the opposition of the bourgeoisie gains further intensity from a national patriotic factor: namely, dissatisfaction that the economy has been substantially placed in the hands of foreign companies.

The Kazhegel'din Menace

The genesis of a new type of opposition in Kazakhstan was linked to the personality of Akezhan Kazhegel'din, the multimillionaire who served as prime minister from 1994 to 1997.

Kazhegel'din has no direct analogue in Russia. He is, unquestionably, a dynamic and intelligent man, someone who succeeded in the turbulent epoch of the early 1990s. He combines both the qualities of Russian politicians who pushed reform and privatization (such as Egor Gaidar and Anatolii Chubais) and Russian oligarchs (like Boris Berezovskii and Vladimir Gusinskii).

The origins of Kazhegel'din and his wealth remain quite murky.[104] His past includes service in the KGB and participation in the Russian democratic movement in 1989–1990. He came to power from the business sector, where he was chairman of the Union of Industrialists and Entrepreneurs of

Kazakhstan; in that post he replaced Oleg Soskovets, when the latter moved to Russia.[105] Evidently, however, he amassed most of his wealth after he came to power. Nazarbaev, without question, knew that the prime minister did not forget about himself when he managed the economy, but initially Nazarbaev showed no concern. When Nazarbaev was asked whether he was certain that the money of foreign companies being invested in Kazakhstan on very profitable terms was really foreign, not a front for Kazakh money, the president answered: "The pound Sterling in the hands of Kazhegel'din and Rothschild have the same value."[106]

During his tenure as prime minister, Kazhegel'din was a radical and "merciless" privatizer and monetarist, and he made a significant contribution to the effort to attract foreign capital (and to legalize pseudo-foreign capital). The opposition accused him personally, above all, of deliberately excluding Kazakhstani companies from the most profitable raw materials branches.[107] One sees no kind of democratizing tendencies during his years as prime minister—a period, on the contrary, marked by the second dissolution of parliament and referenda to extend the presidential term and to approve the new constitution. As a result, Kazhegel'din elicited the visceral hatred of liberals in Kazakhstan.[108]

His removal on 10 October 1997 was due to several factors. First and foremost, the periodic change of prime ministers by the president is, in general, a normal mechanism of presidential rule in both Russia and Kazakhstan. It gives the president an opportunity to blame the prime minister for various difficulties and misfortunes that have harmed society; it also enables the president to reduce tensions and arouse hopes for new policies that will better correspond to the aspirations of society. Kazhegel'din himself became prime minister in 1994, when Nazarbaev sensed that the discontent had reached such a level of intensity that he had to sacrifice his old and loyal comrade-in-arms, Sergei Tereshchenko. In 1997 it was Kazhegel'din's turn. Moreover, when replacing Kazhegel'din with a new premier (Nurlan Balgimbaev), Nazarbaev made a speech to the parliament, where he reprimanded Kazhegel'din's government, declaring that it had become so obsessed with reforms and macroeconomic indicators that it had forgotten about the simple, ordinary citizen. "You are not forgotten!" the president reassured the simple citizen. "I sincerely feel for you, understand your difficult plight."[109] But there were clearly other reasons for removing Kazhegel'din.

The energetic and competent Kazhegel'din accumulated too much power in his own hands and sought to assert control over oil—the branch of the economy that was most profitable and claimed by the Family itself. As one Russian journalist observed: "The objective (even if quite conditional) counterweight to unlimited presidential power in recent years has not been parliament (the third and therefore quite loyal), but—however strange it might be—the prime minister, whose economic policy has been quite independent."[110] Kazhegel'din did not display a servile loyalty to Nazarbaev, as had his Russian predecessor, Tereshchenko (who, literally, could say that "I serve one person . . . because he is the greatest blessing for the country and for the people"). As the re-election year 2000 drew nearer, Kazhegel'din began to arouse growing concern in the president.[111]

Naturally, the replacement of Kazhegel'din—like any important political step in regimes like that of Kazakhstan—was similar to the spectacle of "bulldogs fighting under a rug." Kazhegel'din was opposed by Rakhat Aliev and his wife, Dariga Nazarbaeva; Aliev, as head of the tax service and the main "fighter against corruption," began to conjure up various accusations of economic crimes by the prime minister; Dariga, who controlled the mass media, began to disseminate all this.[112] At the beginning of 1997, the president reduced the cabinet of ministers, which simultaneously allowed him to transfer the oil branch from the prime minister's control. In September 1997, Kazhegel'din fell ill, went to Switzerland for treatment, and then submitted his resignation. After leaving his post, he was awarded a medal and became an economic advisor to Nazarbaev. Initially he displayed full loyalty and said: "The road into the opposition is closed for me. . . . We have a dynamic, actively working head of state: Let's help him."[113] But if the road into opposition was really closed for Kazhegel'din, then no one would have raised the issue—as none would have dreamed that Tereshchenko could join the opposition. But rumors gradually began to circulate that Kazhegel'din himself had plans to run for president in 2000, and when journalists asked about this, he only gave evasive answers.[114]

Kazhegel'din soon moved toward an open confrontation with the president. He urged the election of the akims[115] and, more generally, a broad democratization that would instill in the population "the habit of resisting the authorities."[116] Kazhegel'din also ridiculed official assertions that the society of Kazakhstan was not ready for democracy: "This is an attempt to put the candy out of reach when they say that the institutions of democracy are splendid, but we are not ready for them. . . . But if we do not begin, then we never will be ready. If you never sit in the driver's seat of a car, you'll never learn how to drive."[117] He also commented on a statement that Nazarbaev made during his trip to the United States, reiterating that Kazakhstan needs time to build democracy and that the United States required two hundred years to achieve this. (Incidentally, this odd conception of American democracy is very widespread among post-Soviet presidents; Gaidar Aliev of Azerbaijan said the same thing.) In any event, Kazhegel'din commented: "If American presidents permitted themselves to falsify election results and arbitrarily to extend their terms of office, then five hundred years would not have been enough for the United States to create a democratic society."[118] Kazhegel'din attempted to win the support of the Russian population by addressing their oppression.[119] He also appealed to Kazakhs from the Little and Middle Hordes by noting the domination of Nazarbaev's Great Horde.[120]

The conversion of Kazhegel'din to the "democratic faith" (*after* his departure from office) can be treated as ironically as the "conversion" of the nomenklatura elite (including Nazarbaev himself) in 1991. Nevertheless, the statements by Kazhegel'din were so well thought out that they appeared to have been preceded by serious intellectual work.[121] No doubt, similar processes were taking place in the thinking of others; his declarations reflected a general "ferment" in the Kazakhstani elite, which had come to regard the authoritarian framework of the Nazarbaev regime as too inhibiting and narrow.

Kazhegel'din is a Kazakh, wealthy, married to a Russian, and a former prime minister. He is acceptable to all—the West (which deems him a "strong pro-market" figure and a democrat) and Russia (upon which he has lavished compliments). Concretely, he has excellent connections in both the West[122] and Russia.[123] He was no Russian Ziuganov or even a Suleimenov in 1994; he was a really dangerous competitor. The "old" opposition—both on the left and on the right—overcame their animosity toward him (as someone who until recently had been the very incarnation of the regime) and rallied around him. Without doubt, he also had the support of the newly rich; among the akims and people in the Nazarbaev entourage, some were ready to "betray" their boss and go over to Kazhegel'din.[124]

The situation has been very clearly described by Ermukhamet Ertysbaev. A former democrat-oppositionist, he became the director of the Institute of Strategic Research and an advisor to the president; he had the capacity and evidently the permission to speak the "cynical truth." In his words: "In Kazakhstan the situation could arise where two reformers of a right-liberal view could begin a struggle for power, and this . . . could lead to unforeseeable consequences."[125]

Evidently, the emergence of Kazhegel'din as a potential competitor precipitated a profound change in the political situation. It forced Nazarbaev, characteristically, "to play at forestalling" and to opt for earlier elections—that is, before Kazhegel'din had time to start "bellowing about" and before the opposition had time to crystallize around him. An additional factor could be the influence of the Russian and Asian financial crisis: in 1998 the growth of Kazakhstan's GDP, which had just begun, temporarily came to a halt. A final factor may have been alarm over the uncertain situation in Russia: the end was nearing for the era of Yeltsin (someone upon whom Nazarbaev could always count for support), and as yet the question of Yeltsin's successor remained unanswered.

The Elections of 1999

The regime made perfectly clear that it had no intention of tolerating opposition and Kazhegel'din's candidacy. Kazhegel'din's press secretary was beaten by unknown assailants. His advisor, who had flown to Astana to give parliament a brochure (with his proposals for the democratic reform of the constitution) was arrested at the airport for "profanities addressed toward security officers and for resisting them." The publication of a book by Kazhegel'din was banned. A newspaper that supported him was fined 370,000 U.S. dollars. There were even some "semi-assassination" attempts on Kazhegel'din himself: somebody shot at him, but missed.[126] However, the real blow was dealt in the inimitable, familiar Nazarbaev style.

A presidential decree forbade the candidacy of anyone who had been subjected to administrative punishment within one year of the elections. Obviously, Kazhegel'din was careful to avoid committing, even inadvertently, any legal offense, but it never occurred to him that he would invite prosecution by participating in the founding assembly of an organization called "For Honest Elections." However, since this was the founding assembly, the organization was not yet registered. But participation in the activities of an unregistered organization is a legal offense. Once again a farce, similar to what we have already seen several times before, played itself out. Nazarbaev himself appealed to the Supreme Court with a request to overturn the decision of the Central Elections Commission to ban the Kazhegel'din candidacy. But the court does not accede to the "pressure" from the president.[127]

With the elimination of Kazhegel'din, Nazarbaev was left without any real competitors.[128] Besides Nazarbaev, participants in the election included the communist Serikbolsyn Abdil'din (who received 11.7 percent of the vote), General Gani Kasymov (called the "Kazakhstani Zhirinovskii" because of the specific style of his speeches[129] and his unrestrained populism,[130] he garnered 4.61 percent of the vote), and the writer-ecologist Engel's Gabbasov (0.76 percent). Propaganda for Nazarbaev filled the mass media not only in Kazakhstan but also in Russia;[131] an "agitation-train" of Russian pop star Barri Alibasov and the group "Na-Na" were dispatched to the Russian oblasts to mobilize support for the president. All this helped Nazarbaev to receive 79.78 percent of the vote.[132]

Parliamentary elections were set for 10 October 1999. Ten positions were to be allocated per party lists; among the parties laying claim to these positions was the Republican People's Party of Kazakhstan, which Kazhegel'din had created and which naturally put him at the top of its list. But, after his exclusion from the presidential elections, Nazarbaev absolutely could not countenance letting him become a member of the parliament.

Whereas Kazhegel'din had been excluded from presidential elections because of an administrative offense, now the authorities employed a weapon that they would repeatedly invoke (both in Kazakhstan and in Russia): accusations of tax evasion. Privatization and, in general, the entire economic life in the 1990s had been conducted without regard to the laws, which indeed were internally contradictory and liable to different interpretations. That gave authorities the opportunity to raise questions about any case of privatization and to saddle a disloyal businessman with a tax audit and the like.[133] In this case, the government launched a criminal investigation against Kazhegel'din for tax evasion. Once again he was shunted aside (this time from parliament); his party—as a sign of protest—refused to participate in the elections.

Apart from Kazhegel'din's Republican People's Party of Kazakhstan, the Central Elections Commission registered eight parties. Four received the minimum qualifying vote (4 percent). As in Russia, the regime initially did not want to encumber itself with parties, but later began to experiment with the creation of its own "pocket" parties. On the eve of the elections, several small pro-presidential parties were merged to form the party Otan (Fatherland), with the old comrade-in-arms and assistant Sergei Tereshchenko at its head. This party won 30.9 percent of the votes and 4 seats. Other pro-presidential parties were also organized, with the goal being to simulate a multiparty system. They included the Civil Party (*Grazhdanskaia partiia*), founded by another Nazarbaev client, A. Mashkevich (it received 11.6 percent of the vote and two mandates); and the Agrarian Party (*Agrarnaia partiia*), which received 12.6 percent of the vote and two mandates. Otan is considered to be the party of state employees (*biudzhetniki*); the Civil Party represents businessmen and workers in privatized enterprises; and the Agrarian Party of course speaks for the agricultural sector. The only oppositionist party to meet the 4-percent barrier was the communists, who received 17.6 percent of the vote and two mandates.[134]

Russia, at approximately the same time, witnessed efforts to create a pro-presidential party. But there the process was less complicated and subtle. By contrast, in Kazakhstan a pro-presidential, pseudo-multiparty system had some elements of a real multiparty system: behind the three pro-presidential parties stood real "clans" of the elite, each of which had a certain social profile and which had differences among themselves. In Russia, "Unity"

(*Edinstvo*) and then "United Russia" (*Edinaia Rossiia*) were purely official parties and devoid of any social complexion.

It is very difficult to determine the role of the events of late 1998–early 1999 in the evolution of the Nazarbaev regime. It is always easy to find signs of a crisis, the beginning of the end, post factum, when the cycle of a regime is already complete. Nevertheless, one gains the impression that these months marked a watershed, separating the period when the regime was developing "upwards" from the later period of decline.

Nazarbaev held a maximum of power in the period after the referendum to extend his term and before the new presidential elections. The elections of 1999 were nonetheless the first to have an alternative (even if only a formal one). The certain "self-limitation," an involuntary step, had been due to pressure. The battles that the regime now fought had become defensive, not offensive. The regime triumphed, but no longer held the initiative.

Nazarbaev had not freed himself from the Kazhegel'din threat when a new, still more dangerous, crisis erupted. Its emergence was linked to some very murky events in the depths of the Nazarbaev family.

The Son-in-Law: Challenge and Defeat

The clans and court factions in Kazakhstan have waged a constant battle, as is always the case in such political regimes. But some new features gradually began to emerge. The clans were "taking root," expanded their clientele, and concentrated enormous resources in their own hands. As P. Svoik later pointed out: "The regime . . . entered a stage of schisms within itself, [dividing] into competing and conflicting clan groups."[135] The struggle among clans became more vicious; it was being fought not only behind the scenes and for access to the president, but to a certain degree openly and without regard for the president. The struggle against Kazhegel'din had been waged not only behind the scenes, but also by investigations and publication of compromising material; all that was organized without the president's knowledge, thereby confronting him with a *fait accompli* and forcing him to take action. The intensification of this struggle was obviously, to some degree, due to the fact that the parties realized that Nazarbaev is not immortal, and they had in view a more distant target: the legacy after Nazarbaev, their place in a post-Nazarbaev Kazakhstan.

It was purely accidental that neither the Russian nor the Kazakhstani regimes (neither Yeltsin, nor Putin, nor Nazarbaev) have male offspring and hence no obvious successors. That stands in contrast, for example, to the case of Gaidar Aliev in Azerbaijan, with his son Il'ham. However, General Rakhat Aliev—the husband of Nazabaev's daughter Dariga, the head of the tax police, and deputy chairman of the Committee of State Security—proved to be very energetic and arrogant. As in any family, the Family in Kazakhstan is a complicated organism; its internal relations are incomprehensible not only for outsiders, but sometimes even for those who belong to it. It is unknown whether Nazarbaev regarded Rakhat as his successor, but the latter undoubtedly envisioned such a role for himself. Moreover, he did not want to sit quietly and bide his time; rather, he began to play some kind of "game" that is not entirely understood. As head of the tax inspectorate, he had accumulated compromising materials on the entire elite of Kazakhstan. Because his wife is a media-magnate, he had no difficulty making this material public whenever he chose. Rakhat and Dariga played a key role in the fall of Kazhegel'din and, once rid of him, Rakhat began—by blackmailing and intimidating businessmen—to assert dominance over the largest firms, one after the other.[136] All that would be of no consequence had not, for inscrutable reasons, internet sites under his control begun to disseminate compromising materials about the immediate entourage of Nazarbaev and even the president himself.

When, at that point, the United States and Switzerland froze President Nazarbaev's accounts, "Kazakhgate" slowly began to unfold. It even forced the parliament, in July 2000, to adopt a law "On the First President of the Republic of Kazakhstan." The law declared that the first president who is "the leader of the people of Kazakhstan, ensuring its unity, the defense of the Constitution, the rights and liberties of the individual and citizen, . . . [he] cannot bear accountability for actions associated with the realization of this status."[137] Again, similar situations gave rise to similar resolutions: Kazakhstan's law of 2000 practically repeats Vladimir Putin's very first decree on the inviolability of Yeltsin. Even so, Rakhat's revelations appear very similar to Nazarbaev's criticism of Kunaev—as a stab in the back of an aging boss.

Rakhat's aggressive activities united everyone against him, including (evidently) other members of the Family and such Nazarbaev loyalists as M. Tazhin (Rakhat's own immediate superior, as head of the Committee of State Security). The latter forbade Rakhat to report to parliament about corruption in the upper echelons of power.[138] Nazarbaev's eyes were opened to the threat from his son-in-law, who had gone too far (as earlier he was warned of the threat from Kazhegel'din). But this case involved his own son-in-law; Nazarbaev could not simply drive him away. Instead, he transferred Rakhat from his position as the deputy chairman of the Committee of State Security and appointed him deputy head of his own bodyguard. And Rakhat continued to make threats of exposure. After a time he was "exiled" as the ambassador to Austria, and his relations with Dariga become a major topic of speculation in the political and leading circles of Kazakhstan.

The struggle between Rakhat and his enemies was already a struggle for power in a post-Nazarbaev Kazakhstan. But while some of the magnates who united against Rakhat had a purely personal and clan motivation (simply seeking to remove a figure who posed a danger for them), other participants had plans to establish new, more legal relations to protect themselves from the arbitrariness of a ruler and his entourage.

For some magnates and high officials who opposed Rakhat, the struggle now turned into a battle against the "autocracy" of the president.

The New Challenge: The Democratic Choice of Kazakhstan

The most active participants in the struggle against Rakhat were young, educated people: officials, politicians, and businessmen. In Kazakhstan they have come to be called the "Young Turks." Their leader is the akim of Pavlodar, I. Zhakiianov, and former minister M. Abliazov. They have proposed ideas close to those of Kazhegel'din.[139] This movement has adopted the name Democratic Choice of Kazakhstan.

Zhakiianov and Abliazov are unlike Kazhegel'din. The former prime minister was born in 1952, had already served in the Soviet system, became an agent of the KGB, and somehow participated in the Russian democratic movement. Hence he belongs to the late-Soviet era, his shift to the democratic movement coming after his removal from power. By contrast, Abliazov and Zhakiianov are young men without any Soviet past. Born in 1963, both are the product of the current regime.[140] They are the incarnation of the new Kazakhstan, of which Nazarbaev has said: "You are my pride, hope, and support."[141] This force grew up under Nazarbaev, but has found his framework too restrictive.[142] Any political motivation always includes elements of self-interest and idealism. But so far as it is possible to judge human motives, the motivation of Abliazov and Zhakiianov is first and foremost idealistic. M. Auezov has said of them: "For the first time people came to the scene who were defined as personalities, who were filled with a feeling of their own dignity, pride, responsibility for all that happens."[143] Their adversary, Nazarbaev's advisor and ideologist, Ermukhamet Ertysbaev, speaks of them in a similar vein: "Abliazov . . . is an idealist. But an idealist in politics is a social catastrophe."[144]

The scale of the movement they have created is greater than that of Kazhegel'din, and it has quickly acquired the character of a revolt by the new elite. To quote Ertysbaev once more: "In Kazakhstan there have appeared many rich and prosperous people, and many of them henceforth want an honest and free competition, transparent rules of the game."[145]

The Democratic Choice of Kazakhstan has attracted support from high-ranking officials, including former members of the cabinet of ministers (those who had been dismissed by Prime Minister Tokaev (whom Nazarbaev sacked for failing to cope with the fronde).[146] These ex-officials then formed their own party, Ak zhol (Radiant Path), which became part of the Democratic Choice of Kazakhstan; more moderate than its leadership, they formed a "bridge" between the radicals and power elite. One newspaper in Kazakhstan published a photograph from the early 1990s showing Nazarbaev with a large group of young, enraptured politicians and businessmen. The newspaper circled those who had gone into the opposition: they constituted more than half of the people in the photo.[147]

If the "revolt" of Kazhegel'din and his subsequent emigre fate can be partly compared with the activity and fate of Berezovskii and Gusinskii in Russia, the "revolt" of Zhakiianov and Abliazov corresponds to the movement that Khodorkovskii attempted to organize in Russia. But these processes, though analogous to those in Russia, developed earlier and on a larger scale in Kazakhstan.[148] Once again, as in Russia, but earlier and on a significantly larger scale, the new "oligarch" opposition has become a gravitational pull for the entire opposition—Kazhegel'din (living in emigration and engaging in his "intrigues" in Kazakhstan),[149] old liberal oppositionists which until then were in the condition of political "lethargy," and communists under the head of Serikbolsyn Abdil'din who became a member of the Political Council of the Democratic Choice of Kazakhstan. As Zhakiianov has proudly declared: "Just a few months ago the population perceived the Democratic Choice of Kazakhstan as a handful of 'affronted' officials and businessmen. Now representatives of many well-known parties and movements have gathered under our banners."[150]

As usual, Ertysbaev has given the most precise evaluation of the threat that the new oppositionist union posed for the authorities: "Do not forget that in Kazakhstan . . . there arose an unprecedented fact: a union of rich people and radical opposition, including the communists. This poses a serious threat of a destabilization of the entire situation in the country."[151] In another interview, Ertysbaev said the following: "The union of the radical wing of the Democratic Choice of Kazakhstan and the entire opposition, which until then had not had a financial policy, represents an explosive mixture and harbors the threat of the potential destabilization of the entire situation."[152]

In January 2002 an assembly of democratic society met at the circus in Almaty. The meeting was broadcast live by one of local television stations ("Tan," which belongs to M. Abliazov); journalists in Kazakhstan compared its impact to the live transmissions from the first Congress of People's Deputies of the USSR.[153] Approximately 900 people from various regions of

Kazakhstan, with representatives of all opposition movements, attended the session.[154] The presiding chair was Abdil'din, the "elder" and the leader of communists. As Zhakiianov declared at the assembly: "The country is living in a climate of fear, total lies, and disbelief in the future, . . . [and] stands before a dangerous line which, if we cross it, we risk encountering a systemic crisis and putting at risk our statehood. The only real alternative to this can be decisive democratic reforms."[155] Those assembled demanded an expansion of the powers of parliament, even the transition to a parliamentary republic, and the election of akims and judges. The main direct demand was for a referendum on the election of the heads of local authorities, and for this purpose it established an initiative group. As was to be expected, the Central Election Commission found irregularities in the lists of participants and refused to register the movement.[156]

Crushing the New Opposition

Authorities are horrified and have responded immediately and spasmodically on every front.

Sometimes, the authorities' fear has led to the urgent promulgation of laws that can only be explained by the panic and horrendous images in the minds of the rulers. Such, without question, was the decree adopted in 2000 on the first president of Kazakhstan—Nazarbaev's reply to "Kazakhgate" and his fears of future prosecution. Another response to the new attack of the opposition was the 2002 decree on the "state of emergency." Whereas earlier the government could declare a state of emergency in the entire country for three days and in oblasts for six days, the new decree provided for thirty and sixty days, respectively. It was now possible to order a state of emergency if there was a threat to the security of citizens and political stability, including such things as an epidemic. Moreover, the decree provided for preliminary censorship and a ban on meetings and even mass performances.[157]

Naturally, the regime launched a campaign against hasty democratization, as something that threatened to lead to chaos, the breakup of Kazakhstan, and so forth. It also mobilized a plethora of letters to the press, declarations,[158] and even meetings[159] against a parliamentary republic and the election of the akims.[160] There were also serious articles that compared radicals from the Democratic Choice of Kazakhstan with prerevolutionary populists (*narodovol'tsy*), who, in their unbridled haste undermined the slow but successful process of modernization in Tsarist Russia.[161]

At the same time, Nazarbaev sought to show that democratization was also his goal, and that his disagreement with the opposition concerned time frames, not principles, and coherence of measures, not general direction. In his words: "If the normal conditions of life . . . have not been created, there is no point in talking about democracy of the American or French type."[162] The president emphasized that "democracy is our consciously chosen path of development, which I proposed to you, and which you accepted," but he warned that "alien prescriptions can harm us."[163] Nazarbaev reiterated his view that "nothing is more important for carrying out reforms than a stable state."[164] He also warned that "we have not matured to a parliamentary form of rule. . . . We categorically reject advice aimed at the artificial acceleration of democratic processes."[165] However, he did not summarily reject even the election of the akims; he was prepared to introduce this change in several rural areas, with the first elected rural akim appearing in May 1999 in Nazarbaev's home village of Chemolgan. Nazarbaev also established a permanent presidential commission, with representatives from political parties, on the problems of democratization.

Simultaneously, Nazarbaev sought to split the opposition. In an appeal to businessmen, he urged them not to become entangled in politics. In his words: "I want to recommend to all our bankers, businessmen . . . not to engage in politics, but to do what they know how to do. . . ." And he told journalists that the state must defend them from the oligarchs, who use the press for their own dirty games: "The state, he declared, must defend the journalist from the oligarch."[166] That is because, he said, "journalists have fallen under the pressure of bags of money."[167] All this bears a striking resemblance to Putin; similar processes give rise to similar methods.

But his most important objective was to separate "responsible opposition, which strives toward the same things as the president, but only too hastily," from the "irresponsible" opposition, which is linked to Kazhegel'din and the communists. Nazarbaev expressed "amazement how reformers and democrats could find themselves together with the bolsheviks and overt conservatives."[168]

The authorities thus attempted to win over the "responsible" opposition. Two leaders of Ak zhol, U. Dzhandozov and K. Kelimbetov, returned to state service and obtained important posts. And both remained members of Ak zhol. Moreover, there was a reregistration of parties under the new law; it raised the demands on parties and sought to liquidate small opposition parties (which it did). All were convinced that Ak zhol would not be registered.[169] But it was.[170]

Then a wave of terror came crashing down on the "irresponsible opposition." Zhakiianov and Abliazov were accused of economic crimes—just as in the case of Kazhegel'din (and Gusinskii, Berezovskii, and Khodorkovskii in Russia). On 27 March 2002 Abliazov was arrested; on 29 March Zhakiianov faced the same threat, but took refuge in the French embassy. When Zhakiianov's wife drove up to the embassy (which was surrounded by pickets), the authorities confiscated her automobile (allegedly on the grounds it was under investigation). Then, on 4 April, Zhakiianov left the embassy—after the authorities had agreed not to imprison him during preliminary investigation, but to keep him under house arrest.[171] But the regime deceived both the French and Zhakiianov: "house arrest" came to mean detention under guard in the barracks of a private firm in Pavlodar. And Zhakiianov soon found himself in a "normal" prison.

All this was very similar to Russian methods. But some elements were especially characteristic of the Nazarbaev regime—when some persons acted against the opposition, but their identities remained unknown. I have already noted the secret gunshots fired at Kazhegel'din. Now came a whole wave of such acts. Thus on 29 March unidentified sharpshooters knocked out the cable of the television transmitter of the company "Tan," thereby ending its broadcasts. The cable was repaired, but again damaged on 15 May. Unidentified people acted in strict concert with authorities. "Tan" lost its right to broadcast. On 19 May a decapitated dog was hung on the window of an opposition newspaper *Delovoe obozrenie-Respublika*, with the following note: "There will be no next time." The dog's head, with the same note, was cast into the courtyard of the building where the newspaper's editor, I. Patrusheva, lived. Previously, she had received funeral wreaths through the mail. On 22 May a bottle with an explosive mixture was tossed into the office of the newspaper's editors, setting the office afire. There was also an organized assault, again by unidentified assailants, on the newspaper *SolDAT*, which had published materials about Kazakhgate. Journalists were beaten, and their equipment seized. The police, naturally, found nothing, dismissing all this as "hooliganism,"[172] and spokesmen for the regime referred to some mysterious "third force."

The journalist S. Duvanov, targeted by a criminal investigation for insulting the honor and dignity of the president, was also beaten by unidentified assailants. Nazarbaev declared that this was "a provocation specially planned and financed by enemies of our country."[173] Shortly thereafter Duvanov was arrested and sentenced to prison for raping a minor, a charge that was almost certainly false.[174]

The arrests of Abliazov and Zhakiianov (along with the conviction of Duvanov) unleashed a storm around the world. To their defense came the U.S. Senate, the Organization for Security and Cooperation in Europe, the European Parliament, and even Kofi Annan. But nothing helped. On 18 July 2002 Abliazov was sentenced to six years imprisonment; on 2 August 2002 Zhakiianov was sentenced to seven years; both were incarcerated in penal colonies. As always, Ertysbaev gave a very interesting and deliberately cynical commentary: "Mukhtar Abliazov, after the trial, said, and I quote verbatim: 'If suddenly justice were really to be rendered in Kazakhstan, then on the bank of the accused would be all—without any exception—the members of the government, and all the akims during the existence of the national state.' Thus Mukhtar, unfortunately, . . . confessed his guilt."[175] The general prosecutor O. Zhumabekov (the functional equivalent of Russia's Ustinov) issued a press release describing the conviction of Abliazov and Zhakiianov as an enormous success in the battle against corruption and, simultaneously, asserted that those deputies who defended them were also corrupt and associated with them by their own secret dealings.[176]

No doubt, Abliazov and Zhakiianov, like Khodorkovskii in Russia, knew what they were getting into: prison was a conscious choice. But one (Abliazov), while saying in his final statement that he was ready to go to prison if it would move Kazakhstan toward democracy, overestimated his strength. After a short time he filed an appeal for amnesty, which was granted. Upon leaving prison he renounced political activity. Zhakiianov remains in prison; Nazarbaev uses him to demonstrate what happens to those who do not capitulate. The Political Council of the Democratic Choice of Kazakhstan urged Zhakiianov to make a similar request for clemency, and he complied. In contrast to the petition from Abliazov, however, his did not express contrition or acknowledge guilt. The petition was rejected, and several new criminal accusations have been raised against Zhakiianov while he has been in prison.[177]

The wave of the Democratic Choice of Kazakhstan suffered the same fate as the opposition of Kazhegel'din. It was crushed by the firmness of the Nazarbaev regime. The latter withstood the challenge. But a series of ever more powerful blows and domestic processes in fact have been rendering the regime less and less stable.

Rising Opposition, Creeping Democratization

Two processes, parallel and interactive, are at work. On the one hand, oppositionist "waves" are arising from within the elite of Kazakhstan; groups are breaking away to demand a regime change. On the other hand, part of the ruling elite is undergoing a process whereby their loyalty to the president is softening or eroding. The elite is losing, increasingly, its monolithic unity; the president is losing, increasingly, his control over it.

This process is unfolding within the Nazarbaev Family itself, which the president is finding difficult to control. The prime minister can be sacked, an opposition oligarch imprisoned, but what is one to do with one's own daughters and sons-in-law, who have amassed colossal wealth and influence, who have acquired an extensive clientele, and who begun to compete openly for the legacy of the aging head of the family? But since, as a result of a natural biological process, the midnight hour is fast approaching, the struggle for the inheritance has become increasingly intense. Events in other CIS countries force one to consider increasingly the options: the highly successful transfer of power in Russia from Yeltsin to his trusted man, though not a relative; the successful, with some bloodshed, transfer by Gaidar Aliev to his son in Azerbaijan; and the events in Georgia that have frightened all the post-Soviet presidents.

Like any family, that of Nazarbaev is a complicated and closed system. The newspapers of Kazakhstan and internet sites are full of rumors and gossip about its internal life. And this manifests more than a simple fondness for "peeking through the keyhole." As in a medieval monarchy, in Kazakhstan the domestic life of the "royal family," even the most intimate relations within it, have direct political significance. Sometimes, this is of the greatest importance. For example, Dariga and her husband Rakhat have reportedly separated or even secretly divorced; it was then said that this was untrue, that Dariga seeks to get "clemency" for Rakhat and have him returned to his homeland from his "exile" in Vienna. But whatever their relations might be, this can have a profound impact on the political future of Kazakhstan.

After Rakhat Aliev's exile, the leading pretenders to successor for a president with no male offspring include Dariga (although her relationship to Rakhat, in Vienna, remains unclear), and a second son-in-law Timur Kulibaev (the husband of Dinara, a man with a quiet and affable manner—the antithesis of Rakhat—and head of the oil sector). Recently there has been much evidence that Nazarbaev's "official" successor may be his energetic daughter Dariga. In 2003 she established her own party Asar (All Together), which, of course, gives unqualified support for the president and his policies. Its main themes, naturally, are "centrism, realism, pragmatism, toleration, and political moderation," but with a slight liberal ideological tint. It has also announced its intention to unite all pro-presidential parties.[178] It is suspected, however, that all this is being done by Dariga either "without her father's blessing" and on her own initiative, or that the blessing was given but, when other members of the family became upset, Nazarbaev made a half hearted attempt to call it off. In any case, he did not attend the founding congress of Asar; when local officials rushed to organize a campaign to join the new party, they suddenly—and to their complete bewilderment—received an order from Astana not to meddle.[179] If that is true, Asar will not become a unifying force, but simply the fourth presidential party (along with the Otan, Civil, and Agrarian Parties); still, it may signify that the party system that seemingly represents the interests of social strata has been transformed into a party system that represents clans. Kulibaev has an enormous fortune and influence, but (unlike Dariga) does not control the mass media; according to reports in Kazakhstani press, he is now endeavoring to fill this gap by gaining a foothold in television. The competition of these two figures is beginning to acquire a public character, and the Family itself is becoming the source of a certain "pluralism."[180]

Apart from the Family groups under Nazarbaev's closest relatives, the ruling elite has other groups headed by "magnates"—people who do not belong to the Family in the narrow sense of the word. These include N. Abykaev (the closest advisor to the president and the head of his administration), S. Utemuratov (head of the Security Council and an oligarch), A. Mashkevich (the aluminum and chrome king, with his well-organized Civil Party), and others. These people are prominent comrades-in-arms or clients of the president himself, not Family members. They could play a decisive role in the inheritance struggle by allying with a Family candidate or even by supporting someone from outside the Family.[181] They could play a role analogous to that of the Russian magnates in the eighteenth century, when the order for succession to the throne was unfixed, and it depended on whom they chose to invite to rule (for example, Anna Ioannovna in 1730 or Elizaveta Petrovna in 1741). Finally, there is the most cohesive and influential group of Ak zhol party adherents, who simultaneously form an opposition party seeking to establish a more democratic regime and constitute part of the ruling elite.

This division of the ruling strata into clans and "parties" creates a situation with relative pluralism, and it is gradually giving rise to certain "pluralistic" or even democratic "habits." People become accustomed to a situation where there are various "power centers" that need their support and among which they can choose. Moreover, they see that, while a direct attack on the president can land one in prison, simple criticism and defense of one's positions—as the Ak zhol members do—is not so frightening and not even so hopeless.

In this situation, institutions that would seem to have only a decorative function (the pro-presidential parties and parliament) begin, like the tin soldiers of Saltykov-Shchedrin, to come alive. The form begins to acquire content. Thus, already in 1999 (in connection with budget questions) some in parliament launched an attack on Kazhegel'din's successor as prime minister, Nurlan Balgimbaev; the attack was led not by liberal oppositionists, for these are virtually absent from this parliament. Rather, the charge was led by loyalists from the presidential party Otan on the grounds that the budget was ignoring the interests of the southern regions. The prime minister did have the backing of other loyalists, but these came from the Civil Party. When a vote of no confidence was moved, it fell just one short of the number required to allow a vote.[182]

This episode might be considered a special exception or simply something that had been staged (the vote of no confidence, after all, was not held, or Nazarbaev planned to replace Balgimbaev anyway). But we see the same picture in the next parliament, which initially was also seen as completely "problem-free."[183] In 2002, the press was already noting an increase in its activism. One began to hear voices demanding that the parliament's power be expanded and that extra-budgetary funds be included in the state budget (under their purview); the parliament also regularly began returning draft bills to the government for additional work. Once again, it was the deputies from pro-presidential parties who had become active and refractory.[184]

In 2003 Kazakhstan experienced something that had never happened before and that graphically showed how much society had changed. The government of Prime Minister Imangali Tasmagambetov submitted to the Majilis the draft text for a land code. Some deputies resisted the proposed law, arguing that it would lead to the formation of latifundia and leave the peasantry landless. The parliament thereupon inserted some relatively significant amendments (a moratorium on the purchase of land by nongovernmental juridical entities; a limit on the purchase of land by these entities and by foreigners; and so forth). The government opposed these changes and itself suddenly called for a vote of confidence. It was a perfectly obvious case of blackmail. A vote of no confidence required a two-thirds vote in both chambers, which was virtually impossible to achieve. However, if the government lost the vote, the president has the right to dissolve parliament and set new elections. In Russia even opposition parties did not vote for no confidence during the first and second Dumas. And it is impossible to compare the composition of the Majilis with those first two Dumas in Russia; instead, the Majilis is more like the present Duma. Nevertheless, 55 of 77 deputies in the Majilis, and 33 of 37 deputies in the Senate, voted for the no confidence bill. Tasmagambetov was, clearly, totally unprepared for such a turn of events; he even declared that the results of the vote in parliament had been falsified. Nevertheless, the government submitted its resignation, which was accepted.[185] Such had never happened in the history of Kazakhstan (or, for that matter, Russia).

What happened? Why did the deputies become so brave? The liberal press had not predicted such a turn of events. And when Tasmagambetov resigned, the press became utterly bewildered and began to write that the president had consciously withheld an order on how to vote, having decided it was time for Tasmagambetov to go. Simultaneously, it claimed that Nazarbaev wanted to demonstrate to the world that Kazakhstan is a democracy. But even if all this were so, the fact that Nazarbaev could let parliament decide the question of his government's fate, and that deputies voted as they wanted (without fear that the parliament, in accordance with the constitution, would be dissolved) speaks to the new relations within the ruling elite of Kazakhstan. We must try to grasp that the previous or the current parliament has deposed a government in order to understand how these relations have gradually become so different from those in Russia.

On 2 December 2003 the chairman of the Majilis, Zh. Tuiakbai, published an article in *Kazakhstanskaia pravda* called "The Experience of Growing Up." Tuiakbai then was by no means a liberal oppositionist; rather, he was close to Nazarbaev and a relative of former Prime Minister Balgimbaev (toward whom the previous parliament came close to expressing no confidence). But in his article Tuiakbai demanded an expansion of parliament's powers, and talked about the need for a real division of powers, and proposed a new electoral law that would make the use of "administrative resources" impossible.[186]

When Nazarbaev speaks of a gradual transition to democracy, this appears to be a purely "instrumental" (if not demagogic) statement by someone who does not want to surrender or share power. No doubt, to a significant degree, that is indeed the case. But it sometimes happens that a person speaks the truth without realizing that it is the truth. During twelve years of independence, Kazakhstan has undergone changes that have drawn it closer to democracy. The Nazarbaev regime, which in the first half of the 1990s steadily moved in the direction of authoritarian control over society, is increasingly losing this control.

Some Comparisons

Our sketch breaks off in midstream: the life cycles of the regimes in Kazakhstan and Russia are not yet complete. Nevertheless, we can draw certain conclusions. And above all, it is possible to compare development in the two countries.

The regimes in Kazakhstan and Russia are obviously of the same type, and both have followed certain general patterns of development. But there are also very great differences.

From the very outset, the regime in Kazakhstan was more authoritarian than its Russian counterpart. The Russian system allows for the election of governors; in Kazakhstan, that remains an unrealized dream of the opposition. Astana is also much more inclined to combat opponents by resorting to crude terrorist methods, such as beatings and arson by "unknown assailants." The Nazarbaev regime, after a referendum extending the presidential term, more quickly achieved maximum authoritarianism. Hence the people of Kazakhstan were right in 1998 to judge the Russian regime as "more democratic" than their own.[187] Today such evaluations are no longer possible. Significantly, during a recent visit by Putin, Nazarbaev proudly announced: "We are on approximately the same level with respect to reforms in both the economy and politics. . . . I am not afraid to say that Kazakhstan has a managed development of democracy."[188]

It is entirely possible that the greater authoritarianism of the regime in Kazakhstan has been a factor in the more rapid process of economic market reforms. Nazarbaev had more freedom of action than Yeltsin; he did not have to pay as much attention to public opinion as did his counterpart in Moscow. And that meant more consistent reform. And this is evidently bearing fruit: Kazakhstan has overtaken Russia in the rate of its economic development.

But this relatively successful development has an obverse side: the signs of breakdown and crisis have appeared earlier in Kazakhstan than in Russia. The Russian regime under Putin is in its prime. Yeltsin's successor, who was an utter unknown, garnered more votes in 2000 than had Yeltsin in 1996, and indeed triumphed in the first round. The Duma, elected in 1999, is incomparably more controlled by authorities than its predecessor. The Duma of 2003 is almost "ideal": The presidential party "United Russia has a constitutional majority, while the right liberal opposition is altogether unrepresented. Russian political development is not moving to bolster democratic elements and facilitate a rotation of power, but rather toward a further strengthening of the authorities' control over society, thereby excluding a rotation. The development in Kazakhstan has been different. The apogee of presidential authority, with no real alternative, came in 1995–1998. The nearly identical political systems in Kazakhstan and Russia (about which Nazarbaev spoke) is the result of a crossing of different trajectories: one marked by growing authoritarianism and management from above (in Russia), and one by just the obverse (in Kazakhstan). Moreover, it seems that this "point of intersection" has already been passed, and that the society of Kazakhstan is more pluralistic and "open" than that in Russia. To quote Nazarbaev's advisor Ertysbaev with respect to the coming presidential elections in 2006: "We do not need 98 percent, as was the case in 1991. We do not need 80 percent, as in 1999. But we need a controlling bloc of the electorate, say, 51 percent."[189] Russia is heading toward 80 or 90 percent, while Kazakhstan is sliding downhill toward 51 percent.

Both regimes face new challenges. In the beginning, they had to overcome resistance from social forces that already existed when the regimes came into being; this resistance came from workers, peasants, the old nomenklatura elite, the intelligentsia, and nationalist movements. The establishment of the regime indicated that it had overcome such resistance. But later, resistance became increasingly evident from social strata that the regime itself had generated—the new bourgeois elite, which increasingly found the framework of the authoritarian presidential regime too restrictive. The appearance of these new forces has given new life to the old opposition and has changed the general structure of the opposition. This is transpiring in both Russia and Kazakhstan. But it happened earlier in Kazakhstan and in a more dramatic form. Khodorkovskii landed in jail when he had hardly begun his political activities. Abliazov and Zhakiianov succeeded in uniting the entire, highly diverse opposition and in presenting their own program. The scale of their support is incomparably greater than the modest backing given Khodorkovskii.

Kazakhstan moved more quickly toward the market than did Russia, and it encountered earlier, and on a larger scale, the emergence of a bourgeois opposition. It is clear that the vectors in the current development of the two countries are simply different. But one cannot say conclusively whether there is a causal connection between them, whether a bourgeoisie (and its consciousness) is forming more quickly in Kazakhstan because of the more rapid development of the market.

However, one can point to some cultural and situational factors that evidently did contribute to the development of an oppositionist mood in the bourgeoisie of Kazakhstan and to the "liberalization" of the regime. Kazakhstan lacks the Russian tradition of an autocratic, and later Soviet, totalitarian imperial state. This tradition in Russia imparts a specifically antidemocratic character to the protests of the popular masses against the bourgeois reforms; it spawns the "red-brown" synthesis so characteristic of post-Soviet Russia—that is, a union of communist and "fascist-like" nationalism that impedes the union of post-Soviet communists with liberals and democrats. Kazakhstan has no such "red-brown" synthesis. The communists are weaker here than in Russia. Most important, they are different. To a much greater degree than in Russia, the communists of Kazakhstan have accepted democratic values and established strong relations of cooperation with the liberal opposition.[190]

Initially, to some degree the Russian autocratic state tradition worked for the communist opposition, but gradually it has come increasingly to favor an authoritarian presidential regime. Russian consciousness, with relief, "recognizes" in the presidential power an autocratic authority that is "normal" and traditional for Russia. Yeltsin actively used autocratic symbols; Putin actively invokes autocratic and Soviet symbolism by emphasizing the traditionalism and the continuity of power. Nazarbaev does not have such a historical pillar of support in Kazakhstan. Although one need not take the idea of a "nomadic democracy" seriously, it is nonetheless clear that the Kazakh past does not provide the same degree of support for an authoritarian system as it does in Russia.[191]

The surviving tribal and horde connections can play a constructive role in the process of democratic development—not merely the negative role that is superficially visible. Russian society is totally atomized; given the lack of a civil society and a system of voluntary organizations, it proves completely defenseless before the authorities. The disunited, atomized individuals cannot mount solidarity to resist the state. A civil society is not more developed in Kazakhstan than in Russia. But the remnants of "pre-state" solidarities and loyalties, to a certain degree, compensate for this weakness and make the individual somewhat less isolated and defenseless. One gains the impression that in Kazakhstan (in contrast to Russia) every power hierarchy and presidential party structure, after achieving a certain level of control, then begins to break down: the struggle of official and oligarchic clans quickly begins rising beyond a safe level. The deputies who had been strictly selected began to vote in ways that surprised authorities. All this requires extensive, labor-intensive research. But I find very persuasive the hypotheses that authoritarian discipline is breaking down and that, to a certain degree, persisting tribal and horde loyalties have played a role in facilitating democratization.

It is hardly an accident that the majority of the leaders of the democratic opposition come from the Middle Horde. The domination of Nazarbaev's Great Horde naturally leads to discontent among Kazakhs in the Middle and Little hordes, and this discontent takes the form of a liberal, democratic opposition. It would hardly be correct to say that here, behind the liberal phrases, are concealed archaic tribal interests. Rather, these interests promote the adoption of a liberal ideology.

Finally, purely accidental factors have played a significant role in the development of opposition in Kazakhstan. The history of regimes like those in Kazakhstan and Russia show the impact of "biological" factors—the age and health of presidents, the various correlations between their life cycles and the development cycles of the regimes. Aging and ill health of a president in such a regime is always tantamount to crisis. This crisis affects all authoritarian regimes, even a monarchy with a well-defined order of succession. That is all the more true for regimes where succession is uncertain, where the aging ruler can designate his successor from various people, and where there is no 100-percent guarantee that the intended heir will in fact come to power. Naturally, as the transfer of power approaches, this situation exacerbates the struggle of court parties, as various groups push different candidates, since none of the magnates can be certain of their own future. In such a situation there is a certain "oligarchization" of the regime and even a "democratization," for the competing groups appeal to ever larger strata of the elite and even to the population at large. In the USSR such was the case in the period of Lenin's illness and then after his death; the same happened after Stalin's death and in all the successive transfers of power. In the post-Soviet history of Russia, a similar situation arose in 1999 when Yeltsin had not yet identified his successor and the elite began to organize itself and even to act independently in promoting its own candidate—Evgenii Primakov.

Of great importance for the fate of a regime is the stage at which this inevitable crisis of succession sets in. The timing is in no way connected with the cycle of the current regime. If a regime is approaching collapse, if it is weakening, if it has already spawned forces that seek to break out of the existing framework, then the biological decline and death of the ruler—who embodies the regime—can prove fatal. If the regime is far from decline, however, a change in rulers can work in its favor: the new ruler will evoke joyous expectations, and he can rid himself of the most odious characteristics of the rule and personalities associated with his predecessor.

In Russia, the crisis of a power transfer was resolved in an almost ideal fashion. First, it happened at a relatively early stage in the development of the regime—before the appearance of a serious conflict between the authoritarian presidential power and the new bourgeoisie, when forces that could attempt a regime change during a crisis situation had not yet fully formed. Second, Yeltsin demonstrated an amazing sagacity: he himself retired and appointed a successor who was virtually unknown and not overly associated with his own rule. The transfer of power to Putin significantly bolstered the regime, and the first Putin years have marked the heyday of the regime.

The situation in Kazakhstan is quite different. Nazarbaev is not as tired and ailing as was Yeltsin toward the end of his reign (although, to be sure, the years have begun to take their toll on the Kazakh leader too). Quite recently it was announced that Nazarbaev intends to compete in the presidential elections in 2006.[192] The crisis of a transfer of power in Kazakhstan still lies ahead. However, forces seeking to erect a more law-based regime are maturing more quickly in Kazakhstan than in Russia. And there is a chance that the forces that are maturing in Kazakhstani society can take advantage of the impending crisis: either, in general, by not allowing an inheritance of power, or by permitting this but under certain "conditions" (to use the term of Russian magnates who attempted to limit autocracy in the accession of Anna Ioannovna) to make the rule of Nazarbaev's successor less personalized and less authoritarian, and to ensure a greater role for law, the parliament, and self-rule. All this could mark the final transition to a normal system of democratic rotation of power.

Conclusion

I have endeavored to provide an objective description of the regime in Kazakhstan. A great deal that has happened in this regime, as in the similar Russian case, is so obviously unattractive that, however much one tries to avoid bias, the resulting picture is hardly pleasant.

However, my goal was not to deliver a moral judgment on these regimes, but to determine their place in the evolution of the two societies. But for that we must raise the question of possible alternatives. Of course, there were alternatives, especially in 1991—that is, when these regimes first appeared. Obviously, there were both good and bad alternatives, with greater or lesser elements of authoritarianism and greater or lesser elements of democracy. But in our view real democracy did not constitute an alternative either for Russia or for Kazakhstan. Countries with such a history, and such a consciousness, like Kazakhstan and Russia, were not capable in 1991 of embracing democracy, a system with a struggle and rotation of power based on elections that took root in the post-communist countries of Central Europe and the Baltics. Consequently, both Russia and Kazakhstan found regimes that were entirely "normal" for these countries.

The figures of the presidents here have also been "normal." They could be a bit smarter or, conversely, a bit dumber. But this would not fundamentally change things. In any case there would still have been the construction of an extralegal system of personal power, duly masked by legal forms. There would still have been the "family economy" and corruption. Only if the president had been a saint would it have been possible, in the post-Soviet era, for the president not to become corrupt and not try, by every conceivable means (legal and otherwise) to cling to power. But a saint could not have become a post-Soviet president. A completely different type of persons took the path to power and created essentially similar regimes—be it the relatively uncultured and impulsive Yeltsin, the born communist bureaucrat and sly manipulator Nazarbaev, the refined intellectual and "quasi-dissident" Ter-Petrosian in Armenia, or the academician Akaev in Kyrgyzstan. Nazarbaev is no worse, for example, than Yeltsin; whatever sins may be on his conscience, they are less than those of the bloody coup of 1993 and the war in Chechnia. Nazarbaev can show even greater objective successes and achievements than the other presidents. An almost unthinkable Kazakh state has been established; there have been no bloody conflicts; and the growth of the GDP is faster than in any other post-Soviet country and ranks among the highest in the world.

Almost all post-Soviet presidents—whose rule rarely allows alternatives—endlessly and in every possible way have repeated one idea: our peoples have not matured enough for democracy, the latter will lead to anarchy and massive bloodshed. So let's not permit the Europeans and Americans to interfere with their own prescriptions and advice. What may be good for them will be our destruction. Sometime we will come to democracy, but that is a vague "sometime." But for the time being, as Nazarbaev said during a trip to the United States: "If there were not here [in Central Asia] five authoritarian regimes, then there would be ten bin Ladens."[193] The self-interest of such statements, their aim of keeping the president in power and disarming Western criticism—all that is obvious. But the self-interest motive of these statements does not yet mean that they are false and are only, as the American researcher M. Olcott writes, "an unsubstantiated justification for the consolidation of power in the hands of the ruling elite."[194]

Recognition of the justness of these comments runs aground on our moral protest. But it does not signify a denial of the absolute moral significance of democracy, or a racist recognition of the eternal hierarchy of peoples. Democracy is an achievement of mankind, which sooner or later will belong to all. But this does not mean that all peoples can master democracy immediately and that those who cannot do it immediately never will or cannot do so—just as the recognition of norms and rules in literacy or knowledge of arithmetic does not mean that a child can learn to calculate and to read in a day or a week.

Those peoples of the USSR who were more developed and more prepared by their history (above all, the Baltic peoples) could switch directly from a communist order to democracy. For the peoples of Russia and Kazakhstan, who had virtually no experience with democracy (and, in the Kazakh case, even the experience of an independent state), such a jump was simply beyond their powers. For them a transition form that combined authoritarianism and some elements of democracy was more natural.

Both the Kazakhstani and the Russian regimes are transitional. In the course of the existence of these regimes, several things have happened: these societies have mastered some elementary democratic and market norms and customs; generations shaped under totalitarianism and bearing its mark in their consciousness have died off; and a new generation reared, if not under democratic, then under significantly freer conditions, has come to the fore. Under these regimes, forces have emerged that find the framework of the old regime too inhibiting and in the end want to demolish these limitations. Even from our brief overview of the evolution of the regime in Kazakhstan, it is obvious how society there has moved forward during the Nazarbaev years, how fundamental democratic values have become rooted, and how the discontent with Nazarbaev and the system he created has grown.

To characterize the two regimes as transitional, as providing the framework under which society is prepared for democracy, does not mean that the transition to democracy can be conceived as an inexorable, gradual strengthening of democracy. The development of societies and of regimes does not coincide. The way a regime develops does not correspond to the logic of social development, but follows its own internal logic. A president who aspires to have a system devoid of alternatives must constantly, ever more intensively prevent the appearance of alternatives by expanding his control and extending the principle of no alternative to all levels and spheres of society. He must make some concessions to society, introducing elements of democracy, but these are nothing more than concessions made under pressure and limited so as not to infringe on the basic principle: no alternatives to their power. A reverse dependency is entirely possible: society can become increasingly ready for democracy, but the regime—precisely for that reason—becomes ever more repressive.

In any case, there is no smooth transition, but a gap, between these regimes in Kazakhstan and Russia, on the one hand, and democracy on the other. A transition to democracy can only occur if these regimes fall. It is inseparable from the situation where society first chooses not someone who is in power or designated by those in power as the successor. This is still not the triumph of democracy, but an absolutely necessary step toward it. But it is clear that resistance to this step on the part of presidential regimes will be fierce, and a simple vote cannot bring this about (as can be seen from the examples of Azerbaijan, Georgia, and Ukraine).

Presidents may be right when they say that their societies have not matured enough for democracy and need time to make this transition. But they will never say that the time has now come, that now I can let loose of the reins of power, and that I can leave the people free to choose whomever they want. They will learn when this time has come, as did Shevardnadze and Kuchma, when they see crowds in the streets demanding their resignation and honest elections.

Notes

1. For a biography that is an apologia (naturally), but significantly more objective than might be expected, see the account by Nazarbaev's aide, Ermukhamet Ertysbaev, *Kazakhstan i Nazarbaev* (Astana, 2001).

2. D. Kunaev, after his relegation to the status of pensioner, could never forgive Nazarbaev for this "stab in the back." The latter, however, used the name of the popular Kunaev to legitimize his own power: when Kunaev died in 1994, Nazarbaev is-

sued a decree memorializing the former first secretary and even establishing a museum in his name. In 2002 a grandiose assembly was held to commemorate what would have been Kunaev's ninetieth birthday. See R. Shbintaev, "Nash Dimash," *Leninskaia smena-Ekspress*, 12 January 2002, p. 3. Official articles emphasized Nazarbaev's closeness to Kunaev and even asserted and even warned that disliked people who opposed Nazarbaev (e.g., S. Abdil'din) should be treated with caution. See N. Morozov, "D. Kunaev—90 let," *Kazakhstanskaia pravda*, 15 January 2002, pp. 1–4; and S. Tereshchenko, "Ne mogu molchat'," *Leninskaia smena-Ekspress K.*, 24 October 2002.

3. The mechanism behind the December events is poorly known and little understood. Later Kazakh nationalists will grossly exaggerate its significance. See the comments by the Kazakh historian M. Kozybaev in *Kazakhstanskaia pravda*, 20 February 2002, pp. 1–2. Later, Kunaev accused Nazarbaev of secretly organizing the demonstration in order to frighten Moscow and to force it to appoint him in Kolbin's place. By contrast, the Kazakh opposition later accused Nazarbaev of organizing the repression (see Ertysbaev, *Kazakhstan i Nazarbaev*, pp. 139–40). It bears noting that these two opposing claims are not necessarily mutually exclusive.

4. Here is an example of his "transition" lexicon from mid-1991: "I believe that the transition to market relations is fully consistent with the theory of Marxism." N. Nazarbaev, "Doklad na plenume TsK KP Kazakhstana," *Kazakhstanskaia pravda*, 23 July 1991, pp. 1–2. Subsequently, the references to Marxism vanished.

5. However typical were such quick and radical shifts in the worldviews of representatives of the Soviet elite, there is still something mysterious here. The terms to describe such a phenomenon are wanting; neither of the two models for such a description "work." The first model is "conversion," when a person really undergoes a radical change in his worldview and his eyes are opened. Thus, Nazarbaev later explained his ideological "revolution" by the influence that was exerted on him by a book of F. Hayek, *Doroga k rabstvu* (Ertysbaev, *Kazakhstan i Nazarbaev*, p. 191). But the very idea of a mass change of worldviews among adult, intelligent people precisely at a time when such a change is advantageous can only elicit a smile. The second model is that of "Shtirlits" (a soviet spy who was a member of Natzi elite, a hero of a famous Russian movie), i.e., a person whose worldview did not change, but previously had to be concealed. But the picture of the Politburo of the Central Committee of the Communist Party of the Soviet Union as comprised mainly of anticommunists is also ludicrous. Of the leaders of the CIS, only Gaidar Aliev used this model to explain his behavior; in all seriousness he declared that, as first secretary of the Communist Party of Azerbaijan, he foresaw the breakup of the USSR and gradually prepared Azerbaijan for independence.

Obviously, the real mental processes of these people cannot be reduced to the terms of "truth" and "falsehood." These terms are applicable only to a small circle of very concrete situations, in which they really could lie or speak the truth, but not to their ideological thinking. When, prior to 1990–1991, one had to speak communist words for one's career, they said them; this does not mean that they lied, pretended to be communists (as Shtirlits pretended to be a fascist). Unquestionably, they not only said these words, but to some degree also thought them, for a successful career required a certain degree of conformity in words and ideas. But when this ceased to be advantageous and even became dangerous, they began both to speak and think differently. That is not so much a conscious adaptation of words and behavior to the requirements of a career as a purely instinctive adaptation of their very thinking.

6. To a certain degree, the relative strength of anti-Soviet movements in various republics was apparent from the voting on the referendum about the fate of the USSR in March 1991. In Kazakhstan, 89.2 percent of the electorate participated, which was a higher rate than in Russia (75.4 percent), but less than in other Central Asian republics, where the rate everywhere exceeded 90 percent. The vote to preserve the USSR was 94.1 percent in Kazakhstan (only 71.3 percent in Russia); the vote against was 5 percent in Kazakhstan (but 26.4 percent in Russia). In almost all the Central Asian republics the voting against preservation of the USSR ran under 5 percent (the sole exception being Uzbekistan, with 5.2 percent). See *Pravda*, 27 March 1991, p. 1. Hence Kazakhstan, in terms of the negative votes and nonparticipation, was lower than Russia, but somewhat ahead of the other Central Asian states. Moreover, the social support for anti-Soviet movements in this period in Russia and Kazakhstan were similar. In terms of voting against the USSR, in Russia rates were highest in capitals —Moscow and Leningrad, in Kazakhstan—in the capital of republic Almaty (8.4 percent).

7. In 1987 the repressed participants in the December events had already created a committee, and then, in 1990, made this the basis for a party "Zheltoksan ("December"). In 1990 a national-democratic parties Azat (Liberty) and Alash (with an ideology containing strong Islamist and pan-Turkish elements) were created. Along with these national-democratic and nationalist movements were others of a more generally democratic, perestroika orientation. Nevertheless, these were objectively also directed against the all-union center and part of the general national-democratic wave. Thus, in February 1989, the well-known Kazakh poet and publicist O. Suleimenov created the movement "Nevada-Semipalatinsk," which was directed against underground nuclear tests on the territory of Kazakhstan. On the parties in the first half of the 1990s, see A. Kurtov, *Partii Kazakhstana i osobennosti politicheskogo protsessa v respublike* (Moscow, 1995).

8. A public opinion survey conducted in 1994 showed that in the Eastern-Kazakhstan Oblast of those Russians polled 42 percent favored the union of northern Kazakhstan with Russia, and in Severo-Kazakhstan Oblast the figure was 37 percent; 11 and 16 percent respectively were in favor of autonomy. See M. Olkott [M. Olcott], *Kazakhstan. Neproidennyi put'* (Moscow-Washington, 2003), p. 97.

9. These ideas were echoed not only by Solzhenitsyn, but also by "Westernizers" and "democrats" like Leningrad Mayor Anatolii Sobchak. In response to a statement by Sobchak in one interview, Nazarbaev had this to say: "Having known Sobchak for a long time and having respect for him, I never expected from him declarations about the former Russian provinces. . . . This can lead to bloodshed. . . . Who needs this? Sobchak or someone else? Any border claims today inevitably mean bloodshed." Interview published in *Nezavisimaia gazeta*, 6 May 1992, p. 5.

10. See *Kazakhstanskaia pravda*, 4 October 1991, 15 November 1991, and 16 November 1991. Although after the terrible year of 1991 the threat of Russian separatism naturally faded, to some degree it persists to the present day. In 1999 the special services of Kazakhstan arrested, in Ust'-Kamenogorsk, participants of a conspiracy headed by Vladimir Kazimirchuk (nicknamed "Pugachev"), the goal being to proclaim a "Russian Republic." See S. Kozlov, "Russkaia respublika v Vostochnom Kazakhstane," *Nezavisimaia gazeta*, 24 November 1999, p. 1; "Terroristam pred"iavleno obvinenie," *Nezavisimaia gazeta*, 26 November 1999, p. 5; and A. Petrov, "Pugachev XX veka," *Moskovskie novosti*, 30 November 1999. The plans of E. Limonov and his "national Bolsheviks" are generally well known.

11. The role of the "reactionary bogeyman" at the time was played by the second secretary of the Central Committee of the Communist Party of Kazakhstan, V. Anufriev, who had declared at a Central Committee plenum in February 1990: "Somebody, comrades, must answer for the collapse of the unity of the party, for the ideological breakdown; somebody must answer, comrades, for the events in Eastern Europe, about which no one wants to speak." Quoted in Ertysbaev, *Kazakhstan i Nazarbaev*, p. 293.

12. As Nazarbaev said in a speech at a conference in 1993: "I'm told that I saved you, former apparatchiks, but I say that this is not so." *Nezavisimaia gazeta*, 4 March 1993, p. 1.

13. Here are the results of a poll conducted in 1991 by the journal *Dialog* about the "politician of the year": 40 percent named Nazarbaev, 36 percent Yeltsin, 26 percent Zhirinovskii, 19 percent Alksins, 18 percent Gorbachev, 13 percent Kravchuk, 12 percent Sobchak, 11 percent Silaev, and 9 percent Khasbulatov. After these came Akaev, Bakatin, Travkin, Shevardnadze, and Iakovlev. (The respondents could choose more than one person. See Ertysbaev, *Kazakhstan i Nazarbaev*, p. 162. According to data from another poll (conducted by the foundation Public Opinion in April–May 1991 in fifteen Russian cities, as well as Kiev and Almaty, and among 100 "minds," such as Bonner and Prokhanov), respondents were asked to identify the "republic, the leadership of which is conducting policies that are best thought through and that answer the interests of the people." More than half of the "minds" and a third of the general pool identified Kazakhstan, with Russia in second place. *Kazakhstanskaia pravda*, 17 August 1991, p. 1.

14. When, in the autumn of 1990, Gorbachev offered Nazarbaev the position as chairman of the Council of Ministers of the USSR, the latter posed a deliberately unacceptable condition: confirmation by the parliaments of all the union republics. In December 1990, in an interview in *Pravda*, Nazarbaev was asked how he felt about the offer to become the vice-president of the USSR, and responded: "If [the vice-president] is given the role described in the draft amendment to the Constitution, then this is just another aide. I do not see myself in this role." Ertysbaev, *Kazakhstan i Nazarbaev*, pp. 159–60.

15. In precisely this manner Nazarbaev initiated, in autumn 1990, the establishment of ties among the republics, bypassing Moscow. The change that Kazakhstan made in the formulation of the question for the referendum about the fate of the USSR also objectively (and perhaps subjectively) represented a step aimed at undermining its significance. Ertysbaev, *Kazakhstan i Nazarbaev*, pp. 164–65.

16. In this respect, the game that Nazarbaev played with Russia was very similar to that played by Lukashenko of Belarus; in some measure they were even competing with each other. Both advanced various proposals for "close integration," but presupposed a degree of equality that Russia could never allow in its relations with the former Soviet republics. The proposals were either rejected or put on hold, and Nazarbaev and Lukashenko feigned resignation. But in Lukashenko, who is simpler and more naive than Nazarbaev, there was undoubtedly as well a greater element of self-deception.

17. Here is a striking example of the brilliant Nazarbaev playing on Russian great power feelings and leaving Russian politicians discouraged: "From the logic of all previous life, . . . Russia could and had to become the center, the core of the CIS. But—and I say this with great regret—for a number of objective and subjective reasons, that did not come to pass. . . . Russia has the largest territory and richest natural resources in the world; it is inhabited by a talented, hard-working people. . . . It is

necessary to say this so that it becomes the center of gravitational pull for all of Eurasia in the twenty-first century." In other words, Russia could have become the heart of the CIS, but failed to do so. Interview with Nazarbaev published in *Nezavisimaia gazeta*, 16 January 1997, pp. 1–3.

18. Nazarbaev can hardly be reproved for specifically repressing ethnic Russians. But he could not fail to be happy about the gradual emergence of a Kazakh majority, for this contributed to giving Kazakhstan greater stability. And he was not always successful in concealing his joy in this matter. Thus, Murat Auezov, a liberal oppositionist, said this in an interview: "Until recently Russians comprised up to 40 percent of our population; now Nazarbaev, in his statements, *not without a flow of victorious reports* [emphasis mine—D.F.], names . . . figures . . . of 39 percent, then 33 percent, and in a recent speech 29 percent." *Nezavisimaia gazeta*, 8 August 1997, p. 3. According to data from the censuses of 1989 and 1999, the proportion of Kazakhs increased from 40.15 to 53.1 percent, while that of Russians dropped from 37.4 to 30 percent. See A. Kurtov, *Demokratiia vyborov v Kazakhstane: avtoritarnaia transformatsiia* (Moscow, 2001), p. 309.

19. Ertysbaev, *Kazakhstan i Nazarbaev*, p. 335. Ertysbaev cites the argumentation of a Russian worker and member of the Supreme Soviet, B. Barchenko: "I believe . . . that legalizing and putting in the hands of a single person, however good he might be, unlimited power, in the absence of a sufficiently developed political culture and strong democratic traditions in our republic, we have a real possibility of acquiring a new dictator in the near future or in a bit more distant time." Ibid., p. 336. This worker-deputy was clearly more intelligent than the majority of politicians and intellectuals.

20. Even Nazarbaev's statement of 20 August 1991, when the fate of the State Committee for the State of Emergency was already decided, contained an ambiguity that admits completely different interpretations. He said that the country had reached a point "beyond which begins the complete and final collapse of society," and he criticized Gorbachev for this, but the latter had not drawn any conclusions. Immediately, however, Nazarbaev said that the state of emergency could only be proclaimed by "relying on the constitutional, legal foundation." *Kazakhstanskaia pravda*, 21 August 1991, p. 1. Subsequently he displayed the same circumspection and prudence: at the last minute he didn't travel to Belovezh to meet the waiting Boris Yeltsin, Leonid Kravchuk, and Stanislav Shushkevich; he thereby avoided falling into the ranks of the "grave diggers" who had buried the USSR. As Shushkevich recalled, Nazarbaev expressed a desire to come immediately, but then claimed to have had flight delays because of a lengthy fueling. Shushkevich, *Soiuz mozhno bylo sokhranit'. Belaia kniga* (Moscow, 1995), p. 307.

21. *Kazakhstanskaia pravda*, 27 August 1991, p. 1.

22. Nazarbaev used this expression in a report to a plenum of the Central Committee of the Communist Party of Kazakhstan in July 1991. See *Kazakhstanskaia pravda*, 23 July 1991, pp. 1–2.

23. It is quite characteristic that the main "fundamentalist" and supporter of the State Committee for the State of Emergency, V. Anufriev, was made a presidential advisor.

24. "I did not join [the Socialist Party]. I believe that the president should be free from any political passions, but may have the support of this or that movement." Ertysbaev, *Kazakhstan i Nazarbaev*, p. 221.

25. Kurtov, *Partii Kazakhstana i osobennosti*, p. 179.

26. *Kazakhstanskaia pravda*, 7 December 1991, p. 1.

27. On the internal logic of the development of the Russian post-Soviet regime, see D. Furman, "Politicheskii rezhim postsovetskoi Rossii," *Svobodnaia mysl'*, 2003, no. 11.

28. See M. N. Guboglo, *Etnopoliticheskaia situatsiia v Kazakhstane v predstavleniiakh ego grazhdan* (Moscow, 1995), p. 268.

29. See V. Dunaev, "Konfliktuiushchie struktury kazakhstanskoi modeli mezhetnicheskoi integratsii," *Tsentral'naia Aziia i Kavkaz*, 1999, no. 5(6): 14–15.

30. See N. Popov and A. Rubtsov, "Skazhi mne, kto tvoi sosed, i ia skazhu tebe, kto ty . . . ," *Nezavisimaia gazeta-Sodruzhestvo*, no. 5 (27 May 1998): 3.

31. See S. Kozlov, "Nazarbaev sozdaet svoiu partiiu," *Nezavisimaia gazeta*, 26 September 1992, p. 1.

32. Yeltsin was burdened by the accusation of destroying the Soviet Union and initiating reforms that subjected the people to impoverishment; because of that, he had to sketch radiant prospects and promise a rapid improvement in material well-being. By contrast, Nazarbaev could more legitimately describe the situation in which Kazakhstan found itself as not due to something he had done. He even dramatized the situation, drawing a picture that encouraged the reader to think that it is impossible to do "without a strong hand." Already in 1991 Nazarbaev was saying: "We await stratification (based on property), unemployment, and a decline in the standard of living." See Nazarbaev, "Doklad na plenume TsK KP Kazakhstana," *Kazakhstanskaia pravda*, 23 July 1991, pp. 1–2. In 1993 he said: "Our hopes that we will raise the masses and realize privatization and reforms from below have not been borne out. Now it is necessary to conduct this process from above." S. Kozlov, "Oppozitsiia dolzhna imet' pozitsiiu," *Nezavisimaia gazeta*, 20 February 1993, p. 1. Elsewhere Nazarbaev declared that "we did a splendid job . . . of carrying out the first stage of market reforms. . . . Yes, material stratification, . . . unemployment, bankruptcy—we are ready for all that." S. Kozlov, "Nursultan Nazarbaev: Khvatit kritikovat', kritikam ne mesto v nashei komande," *Nezavisimaia gazeta*, 4 March 1993, p. 1.

33. This idea, which gave rise in Russia to such a paradoxical phenomenon as the popularity of Stolypin and Pinochet among Russian democrats unquestionably is a Soviet reception of the ideas of the "Chicago economic school" (in some measure an analogue to the Leninist reception of Marxism); the Chicago school was reworked by a consciousness in which the basic structures of Marxist-Leninist thought had been more deeply rooted than those seeking to deny Marxism-Leninism could have suspected. A. Kazhegel'din also recalled: "It then seemed to me (as a young politician, essentially a technocrat) that everything will come about by itself. . . . I, and my fellow reformers, thought that if there is a market, then there will be democracy." See A. Kazhegel'din, *Oppozitsiia srednevekov'iu* (London-Moscow, 2002), p. 247. One could say the same of E. Gaidar and A. Chubais, who, in contrast to Kazhegel'din, however, have never spoken of their mistakes and blunders (insofar as I know).

34. In February, hungry soldiers of a construction battalion rebelled in Baikonur, ransacking the warehouses with foodstuffs and setting fire to barracks. The uprising had a distinctly national dimension: it was a rebellion of Kazakh soldiers against Russian officers. See *Nezavisimaia gazeta*, 27 February 1992.

35. In his "speech to the throne," Abdil'din said: "I think that the Supreme Soviet, for the first time in its history, has chosen a leader without securing the approval of the center [Moscow], without the recommendation of party and other organs." Ertysbaev, *Kazakhstan i Nazarbaev*, p. 352.

36. Ibid., pp. 353–54.

37. Representatives of the Russian and Kazakh political movements that arose

spontaneously were united in their criticism of this constitution. Thus Iu. Startsev (leader of the organization "Unity") declared: "Today we have the very same dictatorship as before. The president, in essence, is the first secretary of the Central Committee, and they want to legalize this situation by adopting this version of the constitution." The chairman of Azat, K. Ormantaev, declared bluntly that "the draft . . . can turn Kazakhstan into a laughing stock." *Nezavisimaia gazeta*, 23 January 1993, p. 3.

38. Serik Abdrakhmanov, leader of the pro-presidential Union of Popular Unity of Kazakhstan, said the following: "I think that, with this composition of the Supreme Soviet . . . it is possible to change little. . . . Hope is now . . . placed more on the representatives of executive authority." *Nezavisimaia gazeta*, 9 June 1993, p. 3.

39. Z. Fedotova, deputy of Abdil'din, said the following at a press conference following the adoption of the Constitution: "I must categorically reject the assertion that the presidium of the Supreme Soviet holds the government and president on a leash." *Nezavisimaia gazeta*, 2 February 1993, p. 1.

40. See S. Kozlov, "Parlament prinimaet novuiu konstitutsiiu," *Nezavisimaia gazeta*, 27 January 1993, p. 3.

41. As the journalist K. Esenova has written: "Now the most serious accusation for any member of the government, parliament, in a word, for a person having any semblance of power, is to be accused of a secret (as a rule) or overt desire to become president." E. Esenova, "Stremiashchiesia k nei bezumny, a dostigshie ee porazheny toskoiu," *Panorama*, no. 47 (December 1994).

42. Ertysbaev writes of "stubborn rumors" that, after the dispersion of the parliament in Russia, Yeltsin asked Nazarbaev to disband his own parliament so that Yeltsin did not appear too much "alone." Ertysbaev, *Kazakhstan i Nazarbaev*, p. 355.

43. "Ekstremisty promakhnulis'," *Kazakhstanskaia pravda*, 2 November 1991, p. 1.

44. Ertysbaev, *Kazakhstan i Nazarbaev*, p. 354.

45. The combination of a deputy's status with work in the executive branch was forbidden by the Constitution. However, the Supreme Soviet did not object and agreed to this violation of the constitution (which had just been adopted), for this was advantageous to the corps of deputies. But it was later to pay dearly for this. See A. Chebotarev, "Rukovodstvu Kazakhstana osnovnoi zakon ne pisan" (www .eurasia.org.ru/20011/free/08_30_Konstitution.htm).

46. The main organizer here was the *akim* (mayor) of Almaty, Z. Nurkadilov: he invited deputies to his office and forced them to write the declarations. See Ertysbaev, *Kazakhstan i Nazarbaev*, p. 368.

47. S. Duvanov. "Ta dumaiu chto istoricheskaia tzelesoobraznost'ne povredit demokratii." *Khazahstanskaia pravda*, 25 November 1993, p. 2.

48. Of 900 candidates more than 200 (naturally, mainly oppositionists) were not permitted to register. See Kurtov, *Partii Kazakhstana*, p. 169.

49. This had already become clear during the elections for speaker. In contrast to his predecessor (S. Abdil'din, who had simply been elected speaker and was unwanted by Nazarbaev), the new Supreme Soviet elected A. Kekilbaev, who supported the president. But about 40 percent of the deputies voted for his opponent, G. Aldamzharov.

50. The question remains open whether the majority really voted for the constitution in the December 1993 referendum (which was held simultaneously with the elections to the Duma). Without doubt, the manipulation of the results of the referendum was on a large scale; it is no accident that the documents pertaining to this were destroyed immediately after the votes had been counted by the Central Elections Commission.

51. As Ertysbaev conjectures, Nazarbaev initially wanted to make the Socialist

Party of Kazakhstan the successor to the Communist Party of Kazakhstan, and hence a strong pillar of support for him (along the lines of the Popular Democratic Party of Uzbekistan). But what worked in Uzbekistan, with its tradition of medieval despotic statehood, did not work in Kazakhstan. The Socialist Party of Kazakhstan from the very beginning proved itself ungovernable; at its first congress, it rejected Nazarbaev's proposal to adopt the name "Democratic Party of Popular Unity" and instead chose the name "Socialist Party." See Ertysbaev, *Kazakhstan i Nazarbaev*, pp. 220–21. Nazarbaev did not come to its second congress in 1992, saying: "What, am I now supposed to come to the congresses of all the parties?" Ertysbaev, p. 222. After the coup of December 1993, the party quickly turned into an opposition group; in the elections of 1994 its candidates, under various pretexts, were not permitted to register. After the second coup (spring 1995), the Socialist Party of Kazakhstan split: part, under Abdil'din, joined the Communist Party of Kazakhstan, while another part (with E. Ertysbaev) shifted to a pro-presidential position. Nonetheless in 1993 Nazarbaev created his own party, the "Union of Popular Unity of Kazakhstan," which the opposition ironically dubbed "the Union of Nomenklatura Unity." See O. Suleimenov, "Monopartizm privodit k bonapartizmu," *Nezavisimaia gazeta*, 12 February 1993, pp. 1–3. But the construction of a presidential party, both in Kazakhstan and Russia, has proceeded at a slow, lethargic pace. The main reason for this, evidently, is the presidents' unwillingness to bind themselves to a party program and party apparatus, which they would then have to take into account.

52. On the composition of the new parliament, see Kurtov, *Partii Kazakhstana*, p. 86.

53. See Ertysbaev, *Kazakhstan i Nazarbaev*, p. 373. In a volume addressed to the Western reader (*My Life, My Times, and the Future* [Northhamptonshire, 1999]), Nazarbaev wrote: "Some . . . commentators assessed the parliamentary crisis as a consequence of my attempts to bolster my personal power. But that was not so. I only obeyed the decision of the Constitutional Court. Should one really have acted to the contrary—put pressure on the judges? . . . But that would really be a trampling of democracy and in the best traditions of totalitarianism." Quoted in Ertysbaev, *Kazakhstan i Nazarbaev*, pp. 375–76.

54. See Ertysbaev, *Kazakhstan i Nazarbaev*, p. 377.

55. On the protests of the U.S. leadership, see V. Kiianitsa, "Diktat demokratii," *Moskovskie novosti*, 12 April 1995.

56. Ibid.

57. In this context I deem it superfluous to dwell on such questions as the illegal, anticonstitutional character of all these actions, and to discuss the multitude of violations of the law that accompanied the referenda. See Chebotarev, *Rukovodstvo*.

58. *Konstitutsii stran SNG i Baltiki* (Moscow, 1999), p. 212.

59. Ibid., p. 216.

60. Insulted, Asanbaev then began to subject the regime to liberal criticism and in one interview quite accurately explained the reasons for the elimination of the vice-presidency: "The institution . . . was conceived for facilitating . . . the transfer of power and as one of the obstacles to the path of giving birth to a regime of personal rule." Such an institution was not for the countries of the CIS. K. Ezhenova, *Svideteli* (Almaty, 2001), p. 17.

61. In the CIS (where, except in Moldova and, more recently, Georgia and Ukraine, the same type of regimes "without alternatives" predominate) there is constantly a kind of "mutual studying" among the heads of these states. Yeltsin's disbanding of the Russian parliament clearly had an influence on Nazarbaev's decision to dissolve his

parliament. Nor was the use of a referendum to extend his term in office an invention of Nazarbaev. Here he follows Islam Karimov, who had conducted just such a referendum. It is entirely possible that, in turn, Nazarbaev's creation of an upper chamber (partly appointed directly by the president himself) served as a model for Lukashenko.

62. Prosecutor General S. Shustov has said: "It was not uncommon to conduct closed sessions of various social organizations, where they discussed question of an overtly constitutional character." S. Kozlov, "Gosudarstvo ustanavlivaet pravovoi proizvol," *Nezavisimaia gazeta*, 17 April 1997, p. 3.

63. S. Kozlov, "Oppozitsiiu vytesniaiut s efira," *Nezavisimaia gazeta*, 26 February 1997, p. 3.

64. Kurtov, *Demokratiia vyborov*, p. 175.

65. Zh. Baishev, "Nad vlast'iu i s narodom," *Kazakhstanskaia pravda*, 29 August 1998. The speeches of Nazarbaev himself periodically manifest a purely monarchist conception of his power: "If the opposition has a position, that can only make the president happy. My goal is to see that we have strong opposition parties and that, while arguing among themselves, they serve their people." *Nezavisimaia gazeta*, 20 February 1993, p. 1. Obviously, Nazarbaev sees the opposition not as opposed to himself, but as court factions that argue among themselves, not with him, and that provide him with various counsel.

66. These lines, from the poet A. Tazhibaev, are quoted in A. Ospanova, "Nursultan Nazarbaev—vypukloe zerkalo kazakhskoi demokratii," *Segodnia*, 31 August 1998, p. 2.

67. B. Aiaganov, *Posttotalitarizm v Kazakhstane: vozrozhdenie demokraticheskikh tsennostei* (Almaty, 1994), p. 94.

68. K. Turysov, "Nekotorye 'mysli vslukh' po povodu oppozitsii," *Kazakhstanskaia pravda*, 15 June 2002.

69. *Kazakhstanskaia pravda*, 5 November 2002, p. 3.

70. Ibid., 17 October 2002, p. 1.

71. S. Kozlov, "Sensatsionnoe zaiavlenie Nursultana Nazarbaeva," *Nezavisimaia gazeta*, 7 May 1996, p. 3.

72. *Nezavisimaia gazeta*, 16 January 1997, pp. 1–3 (interview with N. Nazarbaev).

73. See B. Aubakirov, "Novyi parlament nachal rabotu," *Segodnia*, 1 February 1996, p. 7.

74. Iu. Konstantinov, "Kazakhstan pervyi preodelel pik reform," *Nezavisimaia gazeta*, 6 May 1997, p. 5.

75. Later, the government of Kazakhstan admitted the presence of a secret billion-dollar fund, created from the income received for the sale of oilfields (all such deals were being surrounded by secrecy). Neither the parliament nor the public knew of the existence of such a fund, which was controlled by the president and expended only for extraordinary needs. It is entirely possible that there could not be a clear line between state and personal presidential money given the fact that the system permitted the creation of such funds.

76. "Kazakhgate" arose in 1999, perhaps being accidentally provoked by Kazakhstan's own special services. Seeking the foreign accounts of former Prime Minister A. Kazhegel'din, they appealed to Swiss authorities for assistance. In carrying out this charge, the Swiss stumbled on the accounts of Nazarbaev himself and his daughters. One account had received transfers amounting to 80 million dollars from accounts belonging to the government of Kazakhstan. As soon as Swiss justice took an interest in these transfers, the money was immediately transferred back to the government accounts. Nevertheless, they were "frozen." See A. Guliaev, "Novyi skandal

so 'shveitsarskimi schetami,'" *Izvestiia*, 26 October 1999, p. 4. The flywheel began to come off. In 2001, a South Korean magnate testified that he gave Nazarbaev 10 million dollars to facilitate his business in Kazakhstan (*Moskovskie novosti*, 13 November 2001). In April 2003, Nazarbaev's American advisor, James Giffen, as he attempted to fly to Kazakhstan, was arrested under charges of bribing high officials in Kazakhstan; Giffen has been accused of serving as the intermediary for the leadership of Kazakhstan in obtaining bribes from American companies. See *Assandi-Times*, 4 April 2003, p. 1. When various rumors about the secret accounts of Nazarbaev (despite all attempts by authorities to interdict them) became widespread, then-Prime Minister Tasmagambetov, made a declaration in parliament that Nazarbaev has neither property nor accounts abroad; someone, in an attempt to besmirch the president's name, had opened accounts in his name. See *Delovaia nedelia*, 5 April 2002, p. 1. According to other reports, this "someone" had been found: then-Prime Minister Balgimbaev was supposed to testify that he alone took the bribes through Giffen; Giffen, however, said that he passed them on to Nazarbaev and that he opened accounts in the name of Nazarbaev and his daughters without their knowledge. See M. Abilov, "Delo Giffena— vnutrennee delo SShA," *Assandi-Times*, 6 June 2003, pp. 1–3.

77. The opponents of Nazarbaev assert that he is among the ten wealthiest men in the world. Olkott, *Kazakhstan*, p. 110.

78. On the Nazarbaev family, see "Kazakhi s kirgizami razvelis'," *Ekho* (Azerbaijan), 2 July 2002, p. 5.

79. The most important posts in the cabinet of ministers and in the administration of the president were held by his relatives: A. Esimov (his function, evidently, being to keep an eye on the prime ministers), N. Abykaev, and S. Tursunov. S. Abishev, a relative of the president's wife, Sara Nazarbaev, was the first minister of economic relations of Kazakhstan. See Olkott, *Kazakhstan*, p. 217.

80. On the role of the hordes (zhuzy), see N. Masanov, "Kazakhskaia politicheskaia i intellektual'naia elita: klanovaia prinadlezhnost' i vnutrietnicheskoe sopernichestvo," and N. Amrekulov, "Zhuzy v sotsial'no-politicheskoi zhizni Kazakhstana," *Tsentral'naia Aziia i Kavkaz*, 2000, no. 3: 141. The question of the role of tribal and horde links is very complicated. The tendency for superiors to surround themselves with "their own people" is a normal feature of any bureaucratic power structure. For example, in Russia Putin is now surrounding himself with people from Petersburg. The question is how does this in principle differ from "Chemolganizatsiia"? Evidently, there is nonetheless some difference. In the careers of the "Peterburgers," the main role is evidently played by their acquaintanceship with the president, who also comes from Petersburg, and their career depends on him, but not on belonging to a "clan," which in itself would create solidarity and loyalty. But all this requires further research.

81. A. Mashkevich played a very important role for Nazarbaev in creating a favorable image in the West. He is a prominent Jewish activist, the head of the Eurasian Jewish Congress. Mashkevich and Nazarbaev organized meetings of the rabbis and Muslim clergy of Kazakhstan, which led to this report in the newspaper *Forverts*: "The prosperous life of Jews in Kazakhstan has elicited a broad resonance among their fellow-tribesmen [*soplemenniki*] abroad. . . . It is far from being the case that in every country of the Islamic world the supreme mufti meets with the chief rabbi of Israel. . . . See "Islam-iudaizm: proryv na glavnom napravlenii," *Leninskaia Smena-ekspress*, 5 November 2002, p. 3.

82. N. Amrekulov, "Zhuzy v sotsial'no-politicheskoi zhizni Kazakhstana,"

Tsentral' naia Aziia i Kavkaz, 2000, no. 3: 141. Amrekulov's idea about "ethnic ille-gitimacy" as a factor contributing to the ties between Nazarbaev and Kazakh busi-nessmen is very interesting. It is possible that similar factors explain Yeltsin's protec-tion of the Jewish oligarchs. Chernomyrdin could provoke in Yeltsin the fear like that which Kazhegel'din aroused in Nazarbaev. Abramovich and Berezovskii, just as Mashkevich, could not provoke such fears. It is impossible for them to be presidents in Kazahstsan or Russia

83. Thus, under various pretexts, the authorities did not permit the well-known Kazakhstani company "Butia" (the name comes from the childhood nickname of its owner, Bulat Abilov) to take over the Karaganda metallurgical combine, which was turned over to a Western company. See V. Kiianitsa, "Bitva gigantov na pole chudes," *MN-biznes. Moskovskie novosti*, 5 July 1995.

84. Murat Auezov, "Za vse pridetsia otvechat'(interv'iu)," *Vremia*, 11 July 2002, pp. 12–13.

85. S. Tereshchenko explains the source of his wealth "as due to connections, as due to friends." He notes that the president had an advisor, Aleksandr Aleksandrovich Moskovich, who provided credits of one million dollars, that was then used to specu-late on grain sales: "Yes, yes, that very thing—buy and sell." *Vremia*, 22 August 2002, pp. 10–11.

86. Petr Svoik, a well-known opposition figure in Kazakhstan, characterized the social pyramid of Kazakhstan as follows. At the apex are 50 families, who control Kazakhstan. Under them are 5,000 clients (deputies, ministers, and so forth); beneath them are another 25,000 clients of these clients. Another 500,000 people have a good salary. And the rest are the poor. See P. Svoik, "We Are the Constructive Opposition," *Vremia*, 31 January 2002, p. 11. If, at the end of the Soviet era, the gap in the income between the top 10 percent and bottom 10 percent was four-fold, in 1998 the top decile received 27 percent of the national income and bottom decile 2.3 percent. See Olkott, *Kazakhstan*, p. 257.

87. See S. Kozlov, "Pereprivatizatsiia v Karagande," *Nezavisimaia gazeta*, 18 November 1997.

88. Here is a striking passage from a speech by Nazarbaev at a joint session of both chambers of parliament in September 1996: "Well, you understand. Everyone has gone through . . . such periods of chaos. You understand that the Kennedy family earned its first capital by speculating on liquor goods, when the dry laws were in effect in the United States." Of course, he affirmed the need to combat economic crimes. He noted that in the West the special services have the right to "detain" people and not release them "in the name of the higher interests of the nation." S. Kozlov, "Nazarbaev predosteregaet deputatov," *Nezavisimaia gazeta*, 3 September 1996.

89. *Kazakhstanskaia pravda*, 23 July 1991, pp. 1–2.

90. A poll in February 1996 of 1,000 respondents in cities in Kazakhstan gave the following results: To the question of whom they regard as "the most typical represen-tative of big business in Kazakhstan," they identified "a highly placed official or party functionary" (47.6 percent), director of an enterprise (15.3 percent), people from the shadow economy (12.5 percent), thieves (7.3 percent), Komsomol functionaries (2.9 percent), and scholars (2.0 percent). To the question of the source of start-up capital, respondents identified bank credits (42.4 percent), money from parents (18.6 per-cent), and personal savings (5.2 percent). *Karavan*, 23 February 1996, p. 2.

91. In this regard, the fate of V. Anufriev (the former second secretary of the Cen-tral Committee of the Communist Party of Kazakhstan and a communist "reaction-

ary" who supported the State Committee for the State of Emergency in August 1991) is very interesting. In theory, such a person should have become an adversary of the new regime. Instead, he became one of the directors of the largest banks (KRAMDS). See V. Ardaev, "Oskolki lopnuvshego banka doleteli iz Alma-Aty do Moskvy i drugikh stolits," *Izvestiia*, 17 October 1996, p. 5.

92. See Stanislav Zhukov, "Tsentral'naia Aziia—razvitie, determinirovannoe globalizatsiei," in *Tsentral'naia Aziia i Iuzhnyi Kavkaz. Nasushchnye problemy*, ed. Boris Rumer (Almaty, 2002), p. 128.

93. A. Esentugelov, "Dualizm v razvitii ekonomiki Kazakhstana: strukturno-investitsionnye aspekty ee modernizatsii," in *Tsentral'naia Aziia i Iuzhnyi Kavkaz: nasushchnye problemy*, ed. Rumer, p. 168.

94. On Nazarbaev's comments about the new capital, as freed from the old worldview, see his interview in *Nezavisimaia gazeta*, 9 June 1998, pp. 1–5.

95. Subsequently, rumors arose that, during her studies in America, Aliia became addicted to drugs—a tragedy of many similar families among the "new aristocrats." See *Ekho* (Azerbaijan), 2 July 2002, p. 5.

96. S. Shermatova, "Tsentral'naia Aziia dopustila brak," *Moskovskie novosti*, 21 July 1998. Although this article has nothing more than a description of events and not even hint at any kind of negative feelings or ideas, a court order shut down for two months the well-known newspaper *Diapazon* in Aktiubinsk—for merely reprinting the article. Evidently, the authorities were alarmed by the mere description of the "khanish bliss," since it could evoke envy among simple people. See S. Uspenskii, "Zapret na dva mesiatsa," *Nezavisimaia gazeta*, 9 June 1999, p. 5.

97. N. Nazarbaev, "Kazakhstan neizbezhno stanet protsvetaiushchei stranoi," *Izvestiia*, 4 June 1998, p. 1.

98. S. Kozlov, "Moi narod vystradal svobodu," *Nezavisimaia gazeta*, 2 October 1998, pp. 1–5.

99. Thus, the well-known Kazakhstani journalist S. Mataev said in an interview: "Everything here repeats Russia, with a delay of one to two years." K. Esenova, *Svideteli*, p. 224. In reality, it is just the opposite: the conflicts in Kazakhstan in the second half of the 1990s are being repeated in Russia a few years later.

100. The mechanism for extracting wealth from the oligarchs by legal means (the violations of law in the process of privatization which went "unnoticed" by the authorities, were now "remembered" and "noticed") would be repeatedly applied in both Kazakhstan and Russia. Sergei Tereshchenko gave this ingenuous description of the situation: "They checked me a thousand times. . . . There is nothing; but if they had wanted to find something, they would have." See N. Suleimenov et al., *Kazakhstan 90-kh*, p. 96.

101. N. Masanov, a well-known oppositionist historian and sociologist in Kazakhstan, wrote in 1998: "The authorities have sincerely changed their attitude toward the emerging national bourgeoisie, having discerned in it a serious power and ambitious pretensions. . . . In the end, the national bourgeoisie . . . perished even before it had managed to be born." N. Masanov, "Politicheskaia i ekonomicheskaia elita Kazakhstana," *Tsentral'naia Aziia i Kavkaz*, 1998, no. 1: 88. The last assertion by Masanov, as further events were to demonstrate, was an exaggeration.

102. It is utterly impossible to say the degree to which this policy is conscious or unconscious. A person can quite sincerely think that he patronizes his kinsmen not because they are relatives, but just because they happen to be very clever and able.

103. N. Masanov recounts a very revealing episode: in 1994 academicians, who

mainly represent the Middle Horde, did not allow Nazarbaev to appoint his candidate from the Great Horde as president of the Academy of Sciences. N. Masanov, "Kazakhskaia politicheskaia i intellektual'naia elita," p. 55.

104. For a full-scale study of Kazhegel'din's activity, see Suleimenov et al., *Kazakhstan 90–kh*. This volume is very informative, although, unquestionably, it was written on the orders of the presidential administration, with the goal of exposing Kazhegel'din as a corrupt figure.

105. In presenting him to the parliament, Nazarbaev said that Kazhegel'din "showed himself to be a market person." Suleimenov et al., *Kazakhstan 90–kh*, p. 48.

106. V. Vyzhtovich, "Saliam, investory," *Izvestiia*, 3 July 1997, p. 4.

107. He curtailed the voucher privatization, which was to have become the "trampoline into the cosmos" for the national bourgeoisie, and redirected privatization toward attracting foreign investment. See Masanov, "Politicheskaia i ekonomicheskaia elita Kazakhstana," *Tsentral'naia Aziia i Kavkaz*, 1998, no. 1: 86.

108. A few days before the prime minister's removal (when it was already obvious that the days of his government were numbered), the cochairmen of the oppositionist movement Azamat (P. Svoik, M. Auezov, and G. Abil'siitov) sent Nazarbaev an open letter that censured Kazhegel'din in the strongest possible terms. For example, the letter declared that "on this high post of leader of the government, Mr. Kazhegel'din fully manifested his inherent traits as a petty shop thief." The letter concluded with "a public appeal for the dismissal of Mr. Kazhegel'din from his duties as prime minister . . . and for an objective investigation of his activities, including possible abuses, personal avarice, and exceeding his authority." Suleimenov et al., *Kazakhstan 90–kh*, pp. 197–98. Very soon those who signed this letter found themselves together in the same political bloc with Kazhegel'din.

109. V. Ardaev, "Kazakhstan mozhet stat' 'tsentral'noaziatskim barsom,'" *Izvestiia*, 16 October 1997, p. 3.

110. Idem, "Nursultan Nazarbaev odnim resheniem dostig dvukh tselei," *Izvestiia*, 11 October 1997. The experience with Kazhegel'din taught Nazarbaev a lesson. After the latter's removal, he began to change prime ministers quickly so that they could not become strong and "sink roots." If, between 1991 and 1997, Kazakhstan had only two prime ministers (Tereshchenko and Kazhegel'din), in the period from 1997 to 2003 it had four (Balgimbaev, Tokaev, Tasmagambetov, and Akhmetov).

111. S. Tereshchenko, "Ne mogu molchat'," *Leninskaia smena-Ekspress K.*, 24 October 2002, pp. 1–3.

112. See V. Ardaev, "Kazakhstanskii prem'ier 'propal,'" *Izvestiia*, 1 October 1997, pp. 1–2.

113. Kazhegel'din, *Oppozitsiia*, pp. 457–58.

114. As Kazhegel'din said: "Only if there arises the threat of a liberal modernization of society, then I will certainly participate. . . . But in general I am a professional economist, and high politics is of little interest to me." Suleimenov et al., *Kazakhstan 90–kh*, p. 191.

115. Kazhegel'din said that "if the mayor is elected, then he will look on the entrepreneur as his favorite beet in his favorite garden." Kazhegel'din, *Oppozitsiia*, p. 103.

116. See Ertysbaev, "Nekotorye aspekty prezidentskoi izbiratel'noi kampanii v Kazakhstane (oktiabr'–dekabr' 1998 goda)," *Tsentral'naia aziia i Kavkaz*, 1999, no. 1(2): 48.

117. Kazhegel'din, *Oppozitsiia*, pp. 104–5.

118. Idem, p. 251.

119. In Kazhegel'din's words: "In betraying the Russians, we betray our fore-bears, their choice and their memory. We betray our own past and the future of our children." Kazhegel'din, *Oppozitsiia*, p. 137.

120. Kazhegel'din speaks half jokingly, half seriously, that "when they settle with the Russians, they will take after the Little and Middle Hordes," and recalls the anec-dote about an old Armenian, who, dying, bequeathed this: 'Take care of the Jews.'" Kazhegel'din, *Oppozitsiia*, pp. 138–40.

121. As Petr Svoik has said: "All this democratic rhetoric, which he now possesses to perfection, I think, comes not only from his mind and pragmatism, but also some-what from his soul." Esenova, *Svideteli*, p. 99. The moral problems that arose for the old "intelligentsia" oppositionist Svoik in the shift of Kazhegel'din to the democratic opposition (which until recently had found him so detestable) was analogous to the problems that faced the Russian democratic opposition when Berezovskii and Khodorkovskii came to oppose the regime. Further, Svoik has declared that Kazhegel'din was "one of those who showed that it is necessary, possible to steal, the faster and the more brazen, the better. . . . But what he is now doing is, without question, positive for Kazakhstan." Ibid., p. 101.

122. Incidentally, the daughter of Kazhegel'din, Diana, is married to an Italian count.

123. Here is what the Russian newspaper *Segodnia* wrote of Kazhegel'din be-fore his departure from office: "Having gone through the Western school of busi-ness and being quite far from a clan mentality, he could entirely become that person upon whom Russia could rely in the future. Kazhegel'din categorically denies the possibility of competing with Nazarbaev . . . in 2000; but many analysts believe that he is the sole candidate who could be put up to oppose Nazarbaev. That is all the more true since not only Russia, but also the Western partners of Kazakhstan could be interested in banking on Kazhegel'din. V. Shpak, "Ostrov stabil'nosti," *Segodnia*, 23 July 1997, p. 3.

124. In an interview with a Russian newspaper, Kazhegel'din said the following: "For understandable reasons, I will not directly name those who support me finan-cially. I can say that part of those who help the current president are in any case prepared to help me as well. In addition, there are also others who stand behind them. Some have a political interest, while for others it is purely economic." Kazhegel'din, *Oppozitsiia*, p. 431.

125. E. Ertysbaev, "Nekotorye aspekty," p. 49.

126. S. Kozlov, "Ischezaiut politicheskie protivniki prezidenta," *Nezavisimaia gazeta*, 23 September 1998; and A. Rubtsov, "Oglushitel'naia pobeda s poterei litsa," *Moskovskie novosti*, 24 November 1998.

127. See "Verkhovnyi sud Kazakhstana ne prislushalsia k prezidentu," *Izvestiia*, 26 November 1998, p. 3; and V. Prigoda, "Nursultan Nazarbaev mozhet ne volnovat'sia," *Izvestiia*, 1 December 1998, p. 2.

128. Another potential candidate of the liberal opposition was the ambassador of Kazakhstan to Turkey, B. Tursambaev; hastily appointed deputy prime minister by Nazarbaev, he forgot about his oppositionist stance. See N. Suleimenov et al., *Kazakhstan 90–kh*, p. 253.

129. During one television appearance, he hurled a vase at a journalist who had insulted him; on another occasion, also on television, to demonstrate his strength and courage, he crushed a glass with his hand and suffered lacerations from the shards.

130. G. Kasymov proposed a seven-year program. In 1999 it aimed to eliminate poverty, illness, and crime; in 2000 to improve agriculture; in 2001 to achieve eco-

nomic stabilization; in 2002 to provide social guarantees; in 2003 to ensure a radical upsurge in the economy; in 2004 to eliminate unemployment; in 2005 to reach world levels; and in 2006 to enter the ranks of developed countries. G. Kasymov, "Vlast' neobkhodimo podchinit' narodu," *Nezavisimaia gazeta*, 26 December 1998.

As political scientists in Kazakhstan have suggested, Kasymov was really "undone" by the Nazarbaev aides who were organizing the elections. The goal was to have him perform the role of Zhirinovskii: to drain off part of the protest vote, which would otherwise have gone to more dangerous adversaries. As one analyst argued: "On the eve . . . of the elections, the political elite of the republic undertook to shift the institution of the clown to the local level by exploiting the pre-election image of G. Kasymov, who criticizes and supports the ruling elite." B. Mailybaev, "Pravo naroda na soprotivlenie ugneteniiu i oppozitsionnuiu deiatel'nost' v svet traditsii russkikh i kazakhov," *Tsentral' naia Aziia i Kavkaz*, 2001, no. 4(16): 46. In contrast to Zhirinovskii, however, Kasymov got out of control and in the future joined the general democratic opposition.

131. For a model of such agitation, see Vitalii Tret'iakov, "Kakoi prezident nuzhen Kazakhstanu i kakoi prezident Kazakhstana nuzhen Rossii," *Nezavisimaia gazeta*, 18 December 1998. The article ends with these words: "It is precisely with a Nazarbaev Kazakhstan that we have real prospects for creating a solid, the most stable and essentially unlimited Union."

132. See M. Grigorian, "Al'ternativnye, no ne demokraticheskie vybory," *Tsentral' naia Aziia i Kavkaz*, 1999, no. 2(3); and R. Abazov, "Prezidentskie vybory v Kazakhstane: do i posle," *Polis*, 1999, no. 3.

133. On of the publicists serving the Nazarbaev regime later gave this generalization both for Kazakhstan and for Russia regarding the experience of a struggle for power with the oligarchs: "The history of privatization is remarkable in that everyone has . . . a 'skeleton in the closet,' and the inalienable right of the state . . . as needed to take these 'skeletons' out" and expose them to public view. See Daniiar Ashimbaev, "Oligarkhiia i demokratiia," *Kazakhstanskaia pravda*, 14 November 2003, p. 3.

134. See O. Vorkunova, "Parlamentskie vybory v Kazakhstane," *Ekonomika i politika Rossii i gosudarstv blizhnego zarubezh'ia*, 1999, no. 11 (November).

135. B. Kuz'menko, "Na kraiu politicheskoi areny," *Vremia MN*, 21 September 2002, p. 4.

136. For a description of his meeting and conversation with Rakhat, who demanded a share in the Turan Alem bank, see the memoirs of M. Abliazov: "Kholodnaia vesna 2000 goda," *Assandi-Times*, 29 November 2002, p. 5.

137. See M. Adilov, "Chto ne uchityvaet amerikanskoe pravosudie," *Ekonomika, Finansy, Rynki. Delovoe obozrenie respubliki*, 27 September 2002, p. 1.

138. It hardly makes sense to attempt, on the basis of rumors, to disentangle the twisted ball of court intrigues in Kazakhstan—the "secrets of the Almaty-Astana court." But to understand the characteristics of politics in Kazakhstan, it is worth noting that Marat Tazhin is regarded as a close friend of another Nazarbaev's son-in-law, Timur Kulibaev. See Olkott, *Kazakhstan*, p. 261.

139. See S. Kozlov, "Mladoturki rvutsia k vlasti," *Nezavisimaia gazeta*, 21 November 2001, p. 5. Various materials in the mass media devoted to the Democratic Choice of Kazakhstan and the crisis that ensued after its emergence are collected in S. Markelov and O. Petrovskii, eds., *Kazakhstan 2001–2002. Politicheskii krizis. Fakty i dokumenty* (Novosibirsk, 2002).

140. "These are intelligent guys with a conscience, but in general they . . . are

indistinguishable from the current authorities and the very same oligarchs." See "Beseda s Tursunbaevym," *Delovaia nedelia*, 25 January 2002, pp. 1–2.

141. Ertysbaev recalls: "I remember a scene at one of the banquets . . . in the middle of the 1990s. The president went up to a table where businessmen (Bulat Abilov, Erkin Kaliev, Mukhtar Abliazov and others) were seated. All rose to their feet. The head of state, in a heartfelt and confidential manner, told them: 'You are my pride, hope, and support.'" See "Priamoi put'—ne vsegda samyi korotkii (interv'iu E. Ertysbaeva)," *Vremia*, 8 August 2002, pp. 12–13.

142. Gari Kasymov characterizes these people thus: "They consoled themselves with the idea that diplomas from prestigious European universities, 'knowledge of perfect English,' and free quotations from the pillars of Western market theory will permit them to achieve success in power, as still recent . . . in business. . . . Very soon they realized: all that is useless if you have not fully mastered the methods of behind-the-scenes fighting of the apparatus." See the interview with Kasymov in *Vremia*, 25 April 2002, pp. 12–13.

143. "Khod peremen uzhe ne ostanovit.' (Interv'iu M. Auezova)," *Ekonomika. Finansy. Rynki. Delovoe obozrenie respubliki*, 19 July 2002, pp. 1, 5. A. Kozhakhmetov, who sought to advance his own candidacy as an alternative to Nazarbaev in 1991, but then left politics for business and then again returned to politics, characterizes Kazhegel'din, Zhakiianov, and Abliazov thus: "I think that, in level of education, in level of competence, . . . Kazhegel'din is stronger. But in the level of morality, in the strength of spirit Mukhtar [Abliazov] and Galymzhan [Zhakiianov] are stronger." See the interview with Kozhakhmetov in *Assandi-Times*, 4 April 2003, p. 5.

144. "Pora meniat' vsiu sistemu (interv'iu E. Ertysbaeva)," *Vremia*, 18 April 2002, pp. 12–13.

145. Ibid.

146. The declaration on the establishment of the Democratic Choice of Kazakhstan was signed, in addition to M. Abliazov and G. Zhakiianov, by U. Dzhandozov (deputy prime minister), N. Subkharberdin (chairman of the board of the largest Kazkommertsbank), A. Ashimov (artist), T. Tokhtasynov (chairman of the board of directors of the mining company ALEL and Majilis deputy), B. Abilov (a young multimillionaire and deputy in the Majilis from the presidential party Otan, who was deprived of his parliamentary mandate after joining Democratic Choice), Zh. Ertlesova (deputy minister of defense), A. Baimenov (minister of labor and social defense of the population), G. Amrin (deputy secretary of the Security Council), K. Kelimbetov (first deputy minister of finance), T. Al'zhanov (chairman of the committee for investments in the Ministry of Foreign Affairs), Z. Battalova (senator), N. Smagulov (president of Kazprodkorporatsii), and E. Tatishchev (chairman of the board of Turan Alem, a public joint-stock company).

Among those who supported Democratic Choice were Z. Kakimzhanov (minister of state revenues and head of the customs service); for details see K. Stepanova, "Astana prodolzhaet 'sviashchennuiu bor'bu s korruptsiei,'" *Nezavisimaia gazeta*, 16 April 2003, p. 6, B. Imashev (former head of the anti-monopoly agency), and A. Sarsenbaev (Kazakhstan's ambassador to Moscow). The latter declared: "I support Ak zhol and do not conceal that it was created by my colleagues, friends, and people with similar views. . . . Moreover, I am restrained from joining this party only by the diplomatic mission. But the guys know that I am with them." A. Sarsenbaev, "Astana-Moskva (interv'iu)," *Vremia*, 7 February 2002, p. 13. He later left his position and became an active figure in Ak zhol.

147. "Kak molody my byli, kak verili v sebia," *Ekonomika. Finansy. Rynok*, 5 July 2002, p. 1.

148. In an interview with *Moskovskie novosti*, Dariga Nazarbaev spoke about analogues: "The situation repeats that which was in Russia three to four years ago. The oligarchs, interest groups—are linked to banks: Kazkommertsbank, Narodnyi Bank, and Turan Alembank. . . . In this political wave, the wild card was our opposition, which they (the oligarchs) are using to blackmail the authorities." See "Vostok i zapad glazami zhenshchiny (interv'iu s D. Nazarbaevoi)," *Moskovskie novosti*, 26 February 2002. But Nazarbaeva has forgotten about Kazhegel'din and could not foresee Khodorkovskii.

149. Kazhegel'din, who became more energetic after the creation of Democratic Choice of Kazakhstan, at the time portrayed optimism completely in the spirit of Berezovskii: "I have to celebrate my fiftieth birthday abroad. But the next birthday will already be celebrated in my homeland." See "On vernetsia?" *Vremia*, 27 March 2002, p. 2.

150. "Zashchita Zhakiianova (interv'iu)," *Vremia*, 14 March 2002, p. 12.

151. E. Ertysbaev, "Priamoi put'—ne vsegda samyi korotkii," *Vremia*, 8 August 2002, pp. 12–13.

152. "Pora meniat' vsiu sistemu (interv'iu E. Ertysbaeva)," *Vremia*, 18 April 2002, pp. 12–13.

153. Gul'zhan Ergalieva, "Skazat'—i umeret'," *Assandi-Times*, 17 January 2003, p. 7.

154. M. Kim, "Demokraticheskii vzryv," *Delovaia nedelia*, 25 January 2002, pp. 1–2; and A. Karnaukhov, "Demokratiia rozhdaetsia pod kupolom tsirka?" *Moskovskie novosti*, 29 January 2002.

155. Karnaukhov, "Demokratiia rozhdaetsia."

156. See L. Erzhanova, "Dvizhenie v storonu," *Leninskaia smena—Ekspress K.*, 14 February 2002, p. 1.

157. "Vrediteli napali na polia, vragi naroda golovu podniali," *Karavan*, 24 April 2002, pp. 4–5.

158. Scholars from the Kazakhstan Humanities-Juridical University even issued a whole scholarly statement, which said that the idea of the election of the akim (governor) encroaches on the constitutional prerogatives of the president and that "democracy is not an end in itself, but a constant, all-encompassing social process, which has its own laws and rules." See "Ne stoit verit' pseudodemokratam," *Kazakhstanskaia pravda*, 5 February 2002, pp. 1–4.

159. Thus, the pro-presidential parties organized a meeting in Almaty under such banners as: "We'll not let the president be offended!" and "Kazakhstan is one and not divisible into separate principalities of akims." See "Kto raskachivaet lodku," *Kazakhstanskaia pravda*, 5 February 2002, pp. 1–4.

160. Some arguments deserve mention. Thus, the leaders of the Kazakhs conducted a press conference against Democratic Choice of Kazakhstan, where they said that the election of the akim in Russia led directly to the war in Chechnia. See *Panorama*, 25 January 2002, p. 4. As the Majilis deputy M. Troshinin said: "Precisely the idea of universal franchise (i.e., collective irresponsibility) became, if you will, one of the main reasons for the collapse of the USSR, which had once been powerful and unshakable." See M. Troshinin, "Oboidemsia bez mitingovshchiny," *Kazakhstanskaia pravda*, 29 January 2002, pp. 1–3.

161. The very names of these articles are revealing, for instance: "Stick to the Evolutionary Path," and "Make Haste, But Don't Rush." See M. Adilov, "Gniet s

golovy, a chistiat s khvosta," *Assandi-Times*, 14 February 2003, pp. 1–3.

162. N. Nazarbaev, "Demokratiia—ne nabor dannykh Bogom zapovedei," *Nezavisimaia gazeta*, 28 December 2001.

163. N. Nazarbaev, "Ob osnovnykh napravleniiakh vnutrennei i vneshnei politiki na 2003 god," *Kazakhstanskaia pravda*, 30 April 2002, pp. 1–2.

164. N. Nazarbaev, "Nasha Konstitutsiia—eto osoznannyi vybor naroda Kazakhstana," *Kazakhstanskaia pravda*, 30 August 2002, pp. 1–2.

165. N. Nazarbaev, "Vlast' bol'she ne odinokaia," *Vremia MN*, 19 December 2002, p. 6.

166. "Moia tsel'—postroit' normal' noe demokraticheskoe obshchestvo (beseda N. A. Nazarbaeva s rukovoditeliami SMI)," *Kazakhstanskaia pravda*, 7 February 2002, pp. 1–3.

167. N. Nazarbaev, "Prislushivat'sia k pul'su peremen, nesti liudiam pravdu," *Kazakhstanskaia pravda*, 13 March 2002, pp. 1–2.

168. N. Nazarbaev, "Nikto ne vprave otmenit' demokratiiu," *Kazakhstanskaia pravda*, 26 January 2002, p. 1.

169. See B. Abilov, "Chem khuzhe varit golova—tem luchshe v nei kasha," *Vremia*, 27 June 2002, pp. 12–13.

170. Seven parties passed the re-registration: Ak zhol, the Civil Party, Otan, the Agrarian Party, the Communist Party, the Party of Patriots (G. Kasymov), and the Social-Democratic Party Auyl. See *Delovaia nedelia*, 14 April 2002, p. 2.

171. "Khronika pikiruiushchei demokratii," *Karavan*, 5 April 2002, pp. 2–3.

172. "Vse, krome politiki," *Leninskaia smena—Ekspress K.*, 24 May 2002, p. 5.

173. *Panorama*, 30 August 2002, p.5.

174. *Assandi-Times*, 8 November 2002, p. 1.

175. "Priamoi put'," pp. 12–13.

176. "Zakon o bor'be s korruptsiei deistvuet," *Leninskaia smena—Ekspress K.*, 23 August 2002, pp. 3–4.

177. Iu. Fomenko, "Khodataistvo o pomilovanii otlozheno," *Kazakhstanskaia pravda*, 27 September 2003, p. 1. Later he was allowed to live in a village near the colony.

178. "Asar, znachit vmeste," *Kazakhstanskaia pravda*, 29 October 2003, p. 2. A certain liberal tenor in the position of Dariga can be seen in the fact that, on the question of the relationship to the opposition, she replied that she had a good attitude toward it, for the opposition constitutes "the sanitation workers of the forest." Dariga attracted into Asar someone who had, until recently, occupied the most consistent liberal oppositionist position: Murat M. Auezov. See "Odolet' sem' khrebtov (interv'ui)," *Kazakhstanskaia pravda*, 25 October 2003, pp. 1–4.

179. See: M. Adilov, "V sem'e ne bez 'Asara'?" *Assandi-Times*, 31 October 2003, p. 1.

180. What is transpiring within the Family is suggested by the following, rather unseemly story. The website kompromat.ru published two articles. One reported that Nazarbaev has a second clandestine family; it also relayed details, which suggested that the author (or whoever ordered the article) is very well informed and that, most likely, the article came from within the Family itself. The second article confirmed this, but simultaneously reported that the source of the first article was Nazarbaev's wife Sara and his daughter Dariga. This issue of *Assandi-Times* was bought up by "people in civilian clothes" and then destroyed. See M. Adilov, "Vse mogut koroli! . . . A koroli?" *Assandi-Times*, 12 December 2003, p. 1.

181. For a discussion of different variants in succession, see M. Adilov, "Kuda ukhodiat prezidenty?" *Assandi-Times*, 17 January 2003, p. 3; and D. Musataev, "Akela eshche ne promakhnulsia," *Assandi-Times*, 7 February 2003, p. 1.

182. See S. Kozlov, "Prem'er ministr stal mishen'iu," *Nezavisimaia gazeta*, 11 June 1999, p. 5; and idem, "Pravitel'stvo uderzhalos' u vlasti," *Nezavisimaia gazeta*, 25 June 1999, p. 5.

183. This is the characterization by a journalist of *Izvestiia* elected to parliament in 1999: "The authorities . . . wanted to have a 'problem-free' parliament—and they got it. The government will not have to wrack its brains to convince those elected by the people to vote for this or that draft law, for the budget, for amendments to the Constitution." See A. Guliaev, "Svoi liudi v mazhilise," *Izvestiia*, 9 November 1999, p. 4.

184. See "Vlast' i oppozitsiia: analiz i prognozy (doklad sluzhby politicheskogo analiza Tsentral'no-Aziatskogo agentstva politicheskikh issledovanii APR)," *Ekonomika. Finansy. Rynki*, 26 July 2002, p. 4.

185. D. Akhmetov became the new prime minister. I cannot refrain from quoting his response to the question of one deputy in the Majilis as to how he will treat dissenters: "We are building a state based on the rule of law, and each person has freedom of speech, freedom of thought, and freedom in all their rights. Therefore I simply remain a convinced supporter of the view that we must work within the framework and within the boundaries of our state based on the rule of law. We must not have dissenters; we must build a constructive dialogue—and only in the atmosphere of mutual understanding, constructive decisions, and in the spirit that we are building a unified state, in the spirit that the state of Kazakhstan should be rich. For this there is the president's program, and we should work for its realization. . . ." See "Novaia metlia: pervye ispytaniia," *Karavan*, 20 June 2003, p. 5.

186. Nevertheless the results of the elections of 2004 were falsified and the new Majilis is controlled by the loyalists

187. A public opinion survey in 1998 showed that 28 percent of the people in Kazakhstan believe that Russia is more democratic than Kazakhstan; only 6 percent believe it to be less democratic. See Popov and Rubtsov, "Skazhi mne, kto tvoi sosed."

188. M. Glikin, "Prezidentskii marafon snova nachalsia v stepi," *Nezavisimaia gazeta*, 12 January 2004, p. 1.

189. E. Ertysbaev, "Pora menia vsiu sistemu," *Vremia*, 18 April 2002, pp. 12–13.

190. Of late Russia has also begun to exhibit a similar tendency, but in a much weaker form and clearly associated with the fact that both—the right and the left—oppositions are "on the verge of taking their last breath."

191. Important is not so much the real political system of the Middle Ages, as its image—how it is perceived by modern consciousness. In Kazakhstan, Kazhegel'din can say that the Kazakhs are a democratic people: "We always elected the khans in our country." See Kazhegel'din, *Oppozitsiia*, p. 165. Such a phrase is impossible in Russia.

192. See K. Tanaev, "Nursultan Nazarbaev na tsarstve," *Nezavisimaia gazeta*, 3 February 2004, p. 5.

193. See V. Kara-Murza, "Kazakhskaia oppozitsiia pozhalovalas' britanskomu parlamentu," *Kommersant*, 12 May 2003, p. 511.

194. Olkott, *Kazakhstan*, p. 23. This book begins with the words of the Nigerian writer Chinua Achebe, who writes that his motherland is a splendid country, in which there is everything and "there is no kind of gap in the character of Nigerians," but the "woe of Nigeria consists only in the bankruptcy of its leadership." Olkott believes that this statement is completely appropriate for Kazakhstan. I deem it superfluous to polemicize with this point of view, which is natural for a Nigerian writer, but which appears naive in the book of the American author. For Russia, such logic, "why are we, such a talented and great people, in such a sorry condition?" is also very characteristic of Russian nature.

7

Uzbekistan: Between Traditionalism and Westernization

Evgeniy Abdullaev

In his introduction to the well-known work *Oriental Despotism: A Comparative Study of Total Power*, Karl Wittfogel made the following statement: "At the end of the era of Western colonialism and despite the introduction of parliamentary governments of various kinds, the political leaders of the Orient are still greatly attracted by a bureaucratic-managerial policy which keeps the state supremely strong and the non-bureaucratic and private sector supremely weak."[1] The author saw the origin of this to lie in the limitations on water resources of the so-called "hydraulic" (i.e., irrigation-based agrarian) societies of the East.

Notwithstanding the fact that Wittfogel's book was written a half a century ago, and many of its theses are obsolete, the above proposition remains relevant today. Political processes in the post-Soviet states of Central Asia graphically demonstrate that, regardless of the character of the earlier "colonialism" and regardless of the degree to which democratic procedures have been introduced, the traditional "bureaucratic-administrative politics" of super-powerful state authority have been preserved in all the countries of this region. In terming this policy "traditional," we thereby propose (following Wittfogel) that it is grounded in political traditions that go back to the distant past, and that it does not merely depend on one or another contemporary political leader.

One other Wittfogel thesis on "hydraulic" agrarian societies is also applicable to the states of Central Asia. Insofar as they appear as "the outstanding case of societal stagnation,"[2] then "when such a transformation occurs [in such societies], it occurred only through the direct or indirect influence of external forces."[3] Playing the role of these "external forces" in Central Asia (as in many other regions of the Third World) are the industrially developed countries of the West (and Japan)—both directly and through various international organizations. In other words, this concerns certain changes in post-Soviet Central Asian states that result from Westernization and modernization.[4]

This study will examine how these two, diametrically opposed vectors—traditionalism and Westernization—have determined the contemporary social and political situation in one state of this region, Uzbekistan. In a recent work, I examined the influence of these factors on the process of forming and on the functioning of administrative elites in Uzbekistan.[5] However, the main attention there was given to precisely the factor of Westernization, with far less given to traditionalism. At the time, I wrote that questions associated with traditionalism in personnel policies "must await further study."[6] In this chapter I shall try to examine the impact of Westernization and traditionalism on the broader spectrum of Uzbek society (not just elites), and analyze events that have transpired in that country in the two years since that earlier essay appeared.

Moreover, to consider the degree to which the Wittfogel thesis applies to contemporary Uzbekistan, I shall also try to examine another pessimistic statement about the processes of "traditionalization" and modernization in Uzbekistan. Thus, Boris Rumer has written that "anti-modernization is appearing in all spheres of culture and economics. The retraditionalization of social life, the deprofessionalization of entire strata of the population, the anti-intellectualism emanating from above, the exodus of skilled personnel from the country—all these are clear signs of the anti-modernization that characterizes the reality in post-Soviet Uzbekistan."[7] My study will seek to show that the "reality of post-Soviet Uzbekistan" is characterized by a much more complex interrelationship between the processes of modernization (Westernization) and antimodernization (retraditionalization).

From a methodological perspective, I shall (as in my preceding studies of social and political processes in Central Asia) base this work on a hermeneutic approach, which is grounded in a close reading and reinterpretation of political texts[8] that aims to reveal the various political interests and goals embedded in these sources. At the same time, I shall seek to do this in the maximum possible objective way, free from the emotional component inherent in an "involved observer." Therefore, such ideas as "conservatism," "traditionalism," "stability," "modernization," and the like will be used in a purely descriptive fashion. In particular, following the compilers of the *Penguin Dictionary of International Relations*, I shall use the term "modernization" to denote "a multifaceted process involving . . . the weakening of the extended family in favor of the nuclear, . . . an increase in secular as opposed to sacred values, the replacement of cottage industries with large-scale mass production," and so forth.[9]

As for other conceptual and methodological matters, I fully agree with Noam Chomsky that one does not need any kind of conceptual abstractions, that it suffices to have objectivity, common sense, and a healthy skepticism.[10]

Changes in the Conditions of "Political Stability"

"Political stability" constitutes one of the main values of the "symbolic capital" of the ruling elites in Uzbekistan. As R. Hanks has noted: "The theme of stability has figured prominently in the rhetoric of the Uzbek regime since independence, representing a goal which transcends pluralization of the political environment."[11] At the beginning of the 1990s, the appeal of such a value seemed obvious when compared with the instability of recent years and the breakup of the Soviet Union, but also against the background of the ensuing "shock therapy" applied in a number of post-Soviet states. And by the mid-1990s stability seemed far preferable to the political instability that engulfed neighboring Tajikistan. By the end of the 1990s, the value of political stability was further enhanced by the threat of an "Islamist coup." A more sober reflection after 2000 showed that "shock therapy" in a long-term perspective was not so much of a shock; it proved possible to overcome the civil conflict in Tajikistan; and the threats of Islamism were, at least in part, exaggerated.

In this context, it is evident that "political stability" (like any other ideological value) has its own negative aspect, which Wittfogel has identified as "the outstanding case of societal stagnation." To what degree does contemporary Uzbekistan come under Wittfogel's category? To answer this question, it is necessary to examine both the domestic and foreign policy dimensions within which the policy of "political stability" has been upheld, and to determine the differences in the context after 2000 from that in the second half of the 1990s.

The Domestic Context

With the exception of abortive attempts by the forces of the Islamic Movement of Uzbekistan (IMU) to penetrate the territory of Uzbekistan in 1999 and 2000 and a series of terrorist suicide bombings in Tashkent in 2004, there have not been any substantial changes in the political life of Uzbekistan in the last five years.

Nevertheless, certain new tendencies have emerged in the administrative-political system. The first tendency is clearly evident in all the southern post-Soviet states: the attempt of the ruling presidents to transfer power under the conditions that they retain certain levers of influence over the political process and receive special guarantees for themselves and their family. However, the latter (as the experience of Azerbaijan shows) can be combined with an inheritance of power; that example is attractive for the extreme authoritarian regime in Turkmenistan and for the moderately liberal regime in Kazakhstan. In 2002, Uzbekistan made changes in its constitution that extended the term of the president from four to seven years, renounced the combination of the offices of president and chairman of the Cabinet of Ministers, and transformed the unicameral parliament (Oliy Majlis) into a bicameral institution. This legitimized the extension of the presidential term to 2007 and, simultaneously, reinforced the parliamentary system—as a possible reserve of authority for the ex-president after 2007. It is highly symbolic that, in this regard, the new Senate building in Tashkent was constructed close to the presidential apparatus and his residence. According to the law of 25 April 2003 On the Fundamental Guarantees of the Activity of the President of the Republic of Uzbekistan, the former president of the country will become "a lifelong member of the Senate of the Oliy Majlis of the Republic of Uzbekistan."[12] Previously, according to Article 97 of the Constitution, the former president could become a member of the Constitutional Court. Moreover, it is possible that the ex-president could be elected chairman of the Senate; neither the aforementioned law On the Fundamental Guarantees of the Activity of the President of the Republic of Uzbekistan nor the law On the Regulations of the Senate contained such restrictions for the former president.

However, one cannot preclude other scenarios for "the transformation of power"—that is, other than the relocation of the president to the parliament. Since 2001 observers have increasingly noted the possibility of an "inheritance of power" (which, however, does not necessarily obviate a parliamentary scenario). Lastly, one cannot entirely discount the possibility that the term of presidential power will be extended beyond 2007.

A second tendency has affected the development of the administrative-political system of Uzbekistan over the last five years: the "hermeticization" of the upper stratum of the administrative elites. In other words, the elites have ceased to admit new cadres from the middle echelons and have ceased to renew themselves with younger personnel. I shall say more about this below.

Finally, a third tendency evident in the evolution of the administrative-political system is its growing symbiosis with business—a process that has yielded additional profit for the administrative apparatus. This is confirmed by the results even in those sociological surveys carried out by "Ijtimoiy Fikr" (the government center for the study of public opinion). For example, in a survey of public opinion among young people conducted in 2001, with respect to the problems that obstruct the development of transboundary business, 100 percent of the respondents cited "extortion on the part of customs officials."[13] In another sociological survey, conducted at the end of 2002 among female entrepreneurs all across Uzbekistan, nearly one-fifth (19.3 percent) identified official bribery as an obstacle to their entrepreneurial activity; moreover, about one-quarter of the respondents from Bukhara and Surkhan-dar'ia oblasts and from Tashkent admitted that they personally had encountered extortion and other illegal actions on the part of functionaries.[14]

It is possible to say that, from the onset of this decade, a corruption pyramid has taken on its final form. The lower part is occupied by small- and medium-size business owners, who make numerous payoffs to representatives of government organs and then cover these costs by raising the price of their goods and services. The political leadership of the country is well aware of this situation; the problem of corruption is increasingly cited in declarations by the head of the state—something that would have been unthinkable at the beginning of the 1990s.[15] Nevertheless, Uzbekistan has yet to witness a single, large-scale prosecution for corruption.

Thus, during the past five years, the administrative apparatus has remained stable:

- at the level of the presidential authority—by securing auxiliary levers of power in the event that the presidential term expires;
- at the level of the upper echelon of the administrative elites—by reducing the circle of people who make up this echelon and by reducing the influx of cadres from the middle levels; and
- at the level of the entire apparatus—by preserving the privileged position of the organizations of control (law-enforcement and economic agencies) and by fusing these structures with private business.

All this allows one to draw the following conclusion: the domestic political situation in the last few years, despite the difficulties that the country has experienced, has generally remained stable. This same stability can also be seen in foreign policy.

The Foreign Policy Context

The balancing of the foreign policy of Uzbekistan between the United States and Russia, which lasted throughout the 1990s, had finally run its course by

2002. The position that Uzbekistan assumed with respect to American actions in Afghanistan, together with permitting the United States to establish a military base on its territory, demonstrated the fragility of Uzbek-Russian relations. The optimistic declaration by the Russian ambassador in Uzbekistan, F.M. Mukhametshin, that "Russian-Uzbek relations are today on the upswing" (February 2004)[16] was more an expression of diplomatic rhetoric than a reflection of political realities.

Nevertheless, Uzbekistan did not receive the expected dividends from the United States or (through American mediation) international financial organizations—at least, on the scale that it had anticipated. Notwithstanding the fact that Uzbekistan had complied with many recommendations of the United States (abolition of prior censorship; the invitation to T. Van Boven, the UN special rapporteur on torture, in November 2002; the introduction of freely convertible currency in October 2003; and so forth), the United States did not reduce its pressure with respect to human rights and legalization of political opposition. The reaction of official Tashkent to two political events in 2002 is quite revealing: the collapse of the regime of Saddam Hussein and the resignation of President Eduard Shevardnadze of Georgia in the wake of mass demonstrations. The mass media disseminated a declaration from the Uzbekistan's Oliy Majlis welcoming the liberation of the Iraqi people from the "despotism and arbitrariness of the dictatorial regime of S. Hussein."[17] By contrast, the removal of Shevardnadze—where, to be sure, American interests played a far less significant role—elicited a quite different response from Tashkent. I shall return to that whole episode below.

In general, resolution of the "Afghan problem" (even if still incomplete) has significantly diminished the earlier strategic interest of the United States and Russia in Uzbekistan. For its part, Uzbekistan has also come to believe that the "Islamic threat" from Afghanistan has abated; it has therefore become less disposed to make concessions either to Moscow or to Washington.

The regional policy of Uzbekistan has also undergone a change. After a decade of aspiring to regional economic and political leadership (the last outburst being the attempt to construct an "antiterrorist coalition" in 1999–2000), by the end of 2004. Uzbekistan had shown a relative apathy and growing inclination toward isolation. Relations with Turkmenistan (which were already problematic) ruptured completely in December 2002; relations with Kazakhstan sank to a critical level of breakdown when the latter continued to draw significant financial and labor resources from Uzbekistan. The idea of "Central Asian integration," which had circulated in the 1990s, proved an empty myth. The Central Asian Cooperation Organization (CACO) was established on 28 February 2002; despite a declaration about "the realization of coordinated efforts for the incremental formation of a single economic space"[18] as a goal, CACO inherited the purely decorative functions of its anemic predecessor, the Central Asian Economic Community. In general, at present it is only with considerable reservation that one can speak of Uzbekistan participating in regional cooperation. It has only a purely nominal membership in the transregional blocs of OSCE (the Organization for Security and Cooperation in Europe), GUUAM (Georgia-Ukraine-Uzbekistan-Armenia-Moldova), and SCO (Shanghai Cooperation Organization).

Thus the foreign policy impulse in 1999–2001 (rapprochement with Putin's Russia; dynamic cooperation with Kyrgyzstan, Kazakhstan, and Russia to combat the IMU) and in 2002–2004 (closer ties with the United States after the destruction of the Taliban regime) has come to naught. The conservatism in the domestic policy is systematically reflected in the country's foreign policy conservatism and its growing isolation.

Is There a Traditionalist Alternative to Westernization?

All this raises important questions: To what degree can the situation in Uzbekistan change, and in what direction might this change go—toward modernization (Westernization), or a further intensification of conservatism and traditionalism? To answer these questions, let us examine the basic social institutions that, in my view, are the fundamental (noneconomic) sources of traditionalist and conservative opposition to the processes of modernization:

1. official ideology;
2. personnel policy; and
3. educational system.

The choice of these three factors is based, first, on my empirical observations over many years of the processes of modernization in Uzbekistan, and, second, on the insufficient attention that research has given to the impact of these factors on the political processes in Uzbekistan.

The above list, naturally, cannot pretend to be exhaustive. It does not include, for instance, the *family*, which is such an important institution for preserving traditional and conservative models. This omission, however, was dictated by several considerations. First, the institution of the Uzbek family does not have a direct influence on the political processes in Uzbekistan; its influence is indirect, although that does not make it any less significant. Second, the conservatism and traditionalism of family relations (as is shown, for example, in the experience of Japan and the other Asian countries actively undergoing modernization) are by no means always an impediment to the processes of modernization. Moreover, a study of the family as an institution requires substantial sociological research, but that simply goes beyond the framework of the present analysis. The same can also be said about the no less important institution of economic relations that conserve and reproduce traditional social models.

I shall not examine the influence of the *mahalla* (community) on the retraditionalization of political life, for that question has been recently, and in a rather detailed fashion, treated in a lengthy report by Human Rights Watch in September, 2003.[19] Moreover, I suggest that the role of the mahalla is exaggerated both in the official propaganda and in the critical literature, such as in B. Rumer's paper cited above. Rumer holds that the mahalla plays "an enormous role in the public life of post-Soviet Uzbekistan," and that it "regulates and directs the life of people . . . in all the villages and cities of the country."[20] According to sociological studies conducted in 2001 by the research center "Ijtimoiy Fikr," only a little more than half of respondents (58.8 percent) said that the mahallas play a substantial role in their lives. The proportion of those who replied that the mahallas play no role whatsoever in their lives was highest in Tashkent (39.6 percent), Tashkent oblast (32.1 percent), and Karakalpakistan (24.2 percent). Only 17 percent of those polled believe that the mahalla committees can help them find work.

We therefore have limited ourselves to the three institutions cited above: official ideology, personnel policy, and the educational system. The objective is to reveal those mechanisms that are resistant to modernization (Westernization) and that, in other words, represent a certain alternative to these processes.

The Ideological Alternative

The formation and dissemination of the official state ideology constitute one of the significant differences between the situation after 2000 and that prevailing in the early 1990s. Article 12 of the 1992 Constitution contained the following declaration: "The Republic of Uzbekistan develops on the basis of the diversity of political institutions, ideologies, and opinions. No ideology can be established as a state ideology." To be sure, within a year the president of Uzbekistan noted the need to create "an ideology of national independence," which "should embody the opinion of all forces, movements, social organizations, various strata of the population of our society, their hopes and dreams."[21] Simultaneously, the traditionalist character of the "ideology of national independence" was revealed; the ideology was said to "be based on the centuries-old traditions, customs, language, and spirit of our people."[22] However, until the end of the 1990s, questions that were associated with economic regulation, institutional construction, and legislation diverted the attention of the political leadership of Uzbekistan from the creation of "an ideology of independence."

The situation changed after 2000, when the study of the works of the country's president became obligatory at all levels of education, and when the *hokimiats* (organs of local governance) had a deputy *hokim* specifically responsible for questions of ideology. What became especially evident was the traditionalism of "the ideology of national independence," as well as its tendency not only to combine but to replace other ideologies. In 2001 President Karimov designated, as one of the main goals of "an ideology of independence," that of forming "ideological immunity . . . among our people,"[23] to fill "the vacuum that appeared after the repudiation of the old ideology"[24] with a "new ideology of national independence in order to oppose actively the penetration of an alien ideology and destructive ideas" in Uzbekistan.[25] President Karimov assigned "personnel in the spiritual-educational sphere" the task of "improving and implanting the principles of an ideology of national independence in the consciousness of people."[26] To achieve this objective, a number of innovations were undertaken—in particular, each week personnel in the organs of internal affairs must conduct "an hour of spirituality" (*ma'naviat soati*). Moreover, questions associated with the "ideology of state independence" became a formal part of the state examinations and certification.

It should be noted that the formation of moderately conservative ideologies (which copied the rhetorical figures and methods of the earlier Soviet propaganda) was a process in all the countries of Central Asia, which I have described elsewhere as "post-Soviet proto-monarchies."[27] As in the Soviet period, the main ideologist is the head of state, who emerges as the author of numerous books and articles. In 2000–2001, almost all the presidents issued their own ideological programs: "a national ideology" in Kazakhstan, "an ideology of national independence" in Uzbekistan, and "the book of the spirit" (*Rukhnama*) in Turkmenistan. Apparently, only a shortage of power has prevented the presidents of Kyrgyzstan and Tajikistan from advancing similar ideological proposals; nonetheless, in recent years, they too have presented their own ideological interpretation of the history of their peoples.[28]

In general, the focus of the new Central Asian "national ideologies" on the past, together with the attempt to interpret and mythologize ancient events, constitutes one of the characteristic features of the traditionalism and conservatism in these ideologies. As S. N. Petrova has correctly noted with respect to Uzbekistan, "the turn to history pursues . . . important domestic political goals: create ideological legitimacy for the existing political regime, and consolidate the ruling elites and the entire population of the republic."[29]

Without question, all contemporary political regimes—both in the East and in the West—actively exploit "the resource of history" to this end. However, in the contemporary states of Central Asia (and in this respect Uzbekistan does not lag behind), "the resource of history" has almost completely overshadowed another, no less substantial, component of political discourse—the national strategy for development in the future. Although the states of Central Asia have no shortage of political promises, as a rule these are consigned to an indefinite, remote future.[30] In contrast to these, even the distant and mythologized past invoked by the Central Asian presidents appears concrete and lifelike.

It is no accident, apparently, that the monumental murals which have recently adorned public buildings have replaced the earlier Soviet "heroes" (workers, engineers, and the like—all dressed in the modern clothing and occupied with their work) with personages of ancient and medieval history, or the "masses" garbed in the traditional national dress and expressing sublime, timeless rapture.

A no less significant feature of the "monumental propaganda" of recent years has been the frequent depiction of elderly men (naturally, in a state of relaxation). In our view, this is not merely reflecting the veneration traditionally given to the elderly in Central Asia. The aged are shown on numerous posters (including advertisements) as the bearers and preservers of traditional, conservative views; they wear the traditional dress and drink the traditional beverage (tea) from a traditional tea service. Evidently, the twenty- to forty-year-old "hero" on Soviet posters has been replaced by a sixty- to seventy–year-old elderly man (*aksakal*),[31] and this all fully corresponds to the spirit of the ideology now being propagated. It is no accident that Islam Karimov, when speaking about the formation and dissemination of an "ideology of national independence," has emphasized that "it is essential to carry out this work in a sensible, careful way—like an experienced aksakal gardener who, with tender care, grows young plants."[32]

Thus, the conservatism and traditionalism in the ideology of contemporary Uzbekistan consist of the following components:

• It has inherited the conservative elements of the earlier Soviet ideology: a monopoly against other (as a rule, "alien and destructive") ideas and political programs; the role of the head of state as the main ideologist; methods of conducting propaganda, and so forth.
• It appeals to the past (to the ancient, and artificially constructed, history) of Uzbekistan and invokes national traditions; the new ideology

gives extremely little attention (compared with the values of an ideal-ized antiquity and "great ancestors") to the values of modernity—the growth of production, technological progress, personal initiative, and so forth.

Finally, from the perspective of modernity, the very fact that some kind of "national" (i.e., state) ideology is being propagated is a kind of anachro-nism. Indeed, not only many Central Asians, but also some leading Russian political analysts continue to think that "social relations without an ideol-ogy are an illusion,"[33] and that today we are witnessing "a powerful and comprehensive ideologization of all aspects of contemporary life, both within a country and in international affairs."[34] But in none of the developed or actively developing countries is this "ideologization" (even if it exists at all) expressed as an officially proclaimed ideology. The collapse of the Soviet system has clearly demonstrated the vulnerability of an official ideology, its rigidity, conservatism, and in the final analysis its weakness compared with doctrines that are less formalized and less official.

The foregoing does not mean that the new ideology in Uzbekistan and in the other Central Asian states is only a slightly updated version of a semitraditional, semiliberal rhetoric, or an adapted variant of Soviet ideol-ogy. The reproduction of the former Soviet ideological system is impos-sible in Uzbekistan and other states of the region if only because these lack the financial, organizational, and personnel resources that the Com-munist Party of the Soviet Union had at its disposal. Even the works of President Karimov are published in rather modest press runs (given the country's population of 25 million) and remain inaccessible to a broad readership because of their high price.

Moreover, with the example of Turkmenistan (where Soviet ideological methods, especially those associated with the "cult of the Leader," have been taken to their total realization) before them, the leadership of Uzbekistan exhibits a certain restraint in its ideological policy. Thus, there is only a limited display of portraits of the head of state on the streets—which also indicates a difference between the new propaganda and that of the Soviet era. Finally, liberal dissent—while not welcomed and far from being toler-ated—is nonetheless not repressed as methodically as was the case earlier, even in the relatively unrepressive years of the 1960s and 1970s.

Nevertheless, in a situation where the upper echelon of authority consists of those who began their career in the Soviet period, the temptation to rely on the "ideological experience" acquired then remains rather strong.

Let us now turn to a second alternative to the modernization processes in Uzbekistan: personnel policy.

Personnel Policy

By the start of the new millennium, Uzbekistan was gradually completing the period of intensive state-building, which consisted of the following:

- growth of the administrative apparatus and its renewal through the recruitment of a fresh generation of administrators; and
- redistribution of forces within the ruling elite, with a shift of power from the party-industrial elites to the economic and law-enforcement elites, and from ethnically mixed elites (predominantly Russian) to indigenous elites.

Most important, after 2000 the growth of the state apparatus slowed. New ministries and agencies ceased to appear; given the conditions of budgetary difficulties, several efforts were made to reduce the inflated apparatus. In spite of the annual reductions in the administrative structures, the total number of personnel nonetheless increased because of the addition of technical and service personnel. In particular, it has been revealed that, in the state joint-stock company "Uzbekengilsanoat" (light industry) the maximum staffing prescribed—58 people—has been in fact exceeded by a factor of 2.4 times. An analogous situation existed in the companies "Uzkishlo-qho'jalikkim" (agricultural chemicals), "Uzbekturizm" (tourism), the association "Uzmashprom" (machine-building), the state firm "Uzfarmprom" (pharmaceuticals), where the norms were double what had been prescribed. Significantly, these are the agencies with the greatest resources, for they control the profitable branches of the economy.

According to the two directives adopted by the Cabinet of Ministers in January 2004,[35] the following reductions have been prescribed:

- 26 percent of the deputy heads of ministries and agencies;[36]
- 15 percent of the administrative staffs in ministries and agencies that are financed from the state budget,[37] and 25 percent of the personnel in ministries and agencies that are financed through their own economic activities;[38] and
- 26 percent of the administrative apparatus in the local organs of state administration and in enterprises subjected to local control.[39]

Revealingly, these directives do not even mention law-enforcement organs (which underwent incredible expansion in the 1990s). The tax collection organs (another "sacred cow" in the administration) and their personnel are subject to minimal reduction—a mere 3 percent.[40]

Table 7.1

Age Composition of Leading Cadres: First Half of the 1990s (percent)

Age group	Uzbekistan	Georgia	Russia	Moldova
Up to 49	18	53	65	25
50–59	42	27	22	60
60 and over	40	20	13	15

Source: Iu.V. Artiunian, *Transformatsiia postsovetskikh natsii: po materialam etnosotsiologicheskikh issledovanii* (Moscow, 2003), p. 42.

As for the law-enforcement organs, the lack of the former "Soviet" counterweights in the form of the party apparatus and "red directors" has enabled this asymmetrical expansion and indeed transformed these into autonomous branches of power. One must also take into account the fact that in any society these law-enforcement organs—given the specific sphere of their activity—are the most conservative part of the administrative system. Hence, the disproportionate concentration of power and influence in these organs leads to stagnation in the entire administrative apparatus and in general retards social development. In other words, by itself an expanded administrative apparatus is not necessarily a brake on the processes of administration; however, the asymmetrical growth of those parts that control economic resources (and hence are most vulnerable to corruption) can, without question, be just such an impediment.

As for the rejuvenation of elites and the recruitment of more youthful members (with the accession of a new generation of administrators to the upper echelon), this process had already begun to decline by the end of the 1990s (parallel with the slower rates of growth in the state apparatus). However, even in the first half of the 1990s, the rejuvenation of leading cadres as a way to "modernize the norms of administration"[41] in Uzbekistan, if compared with other post-Soviet states, was proceeding at a rather slow pace (see Table 7.1).

Nevertheless, as already noted above, in the first half of the current decade there has been a full "hermeticization" of the upper echelon of administrative elites, as the influx of new cadres—and hence rejuvenation—has come to an end. This is best illustrated by the phenomenon of "repeat appointments": highly placed administrators, who were demoted several years ago, have returned to their former positions. In 2002–2003 alone, these included S. S. Safaev (formerly the Uzbek ambassador to the United States, now the minister of foreign affairs), A. A. Azizkhodzhaev (formerly the rec-

Table 7.2

Leading Cadres of State of Officials in Uzbekistan: Proportion from Nonindigenous Nations (percent)

Institution	1996	2003
Oliy Majlis[a]	5.3	3.8
Cabinet of ministers	12.3	3.4
Ministries	8.4	5.1
Committees and departments[b]	9.9	4.4
Associations, banks, concerns, corporations, agencies	16.4	7.7
Khokimiiatii (organs of local government)	5.6	0.0

Source: Calculated by the author from the reference works *O'zbekiston Respublikasining Oliy Majlisi, Vazirlar, Mahkamasi, Korakolpog'iston Respublika Vazirlar Kengashi, Viloyatlar va Toshkent Shahar Hokimlari, Respublika Vazirliklari, Davlat K'umitalari, Markaziy Muassaslari, Kompaniyalari, Korporatsiyalari, Banklari, Kontsernlari, Uyushmalari va Boshqa Davlat Hamda Jamoat Tashkilotlari Rahbarlari Telefonlarining Ro'ihati* for 1996 and 2003. Given the nature of the sources, these calculations may contain insignificant inaccuracies.

[a]This includes the presidium, chairmen and secretaries of committees, and heads of sections and their deputies.

[b]Including the general procuracy, higher courts, and academies.

tor of the Academy of State and Public Construction, now a deputy prime minister), and M. Kh. Rakhmankulov (formerly the deputy secretary of the Security Council, now the secretary of the same body).

At the same time, in the course of 2003 alone four long-term political "survivors" suffered a demotion: Minister of Foreign Affairs A. A. Kamilov (initially appointed as the State Councilor for Foreign Policy, a position previously occupied by a deputy minister of foreign affairs; later dispatched as the ambassador to the United States); T. A. Alimov (appointed director of the Republic Integrated Cultural Center); Prime Minister U. T. Sultanov (demoted to deputy prime minister); and V. A. Golyshev (formerly the state councilor on economic questions, now a deputy state councilor). Almost immediately afterward, on 13 February 2004, I. Dzhurabekov, the most influential political figure of the 1990s, was dismissed from his post as state councilor. However, although these men belong to the "older generation" of administrators (all are over 50 years of age), they were replaced by people from the very same generation. Hence the proportion of top functionaries who are in their forties and, especially, the percent who are in their thirties, remains negligible.

Another, no less important, indicator of the traditionalization of administrative elites has been the maximum reduction of people from non-Central

Asian ethnic groups—that is, mainly Russians, Ukrainians, and Jews (collectively termed "Europeans").[42] Table 7.2 shows the scale of the contraction.

Thus, from the mid-1990s, there has been a contraction in the number of administrators in the upper ranks who come from nonindigenous ethnic groups. The reduction has been 73 percent in the Cabinet of Ministers, 40 percent in the ministries, and 56 percent in other state offices and departments. Especially significant, the nonindigenous people have fully disappeared from local government bodies (*hokims* and their deputies in oblasts and in the raions of Tashkent). As for the parliament, Oliy Majlis, the number of nonindigenous was never significant; even in the Soviet era, in 1990, these amounted to just 23 percent.

A caveat is in order here: by itself a reduction in the proportion of nonindigenous elites does not cause the growing conservatism in the state apparatus. First, many of the Europeans who worked in the administrative apparatus from the 1960s and 1970s and who have left their positions were as conservative as people from the indigenous nation. Moreover, the Europeans—in contrast to the majority of their colleagues from the indigenous nation—did not have family-kinship or local support; as a result, they often manifested still greater conservatism and caution in their administrative activities.

Nevertheless, the reduction in the number of European leaders in state structures indirectly (if not directly) served to reinforce the conservatism and traditionalism in these structures. No matter how much they adapted to the strict, hierarchical system of the administrative authorities, they were more Westernized than the majority of indigenous leaders.[43] The very fact that nonindigenous ethnic groups prefer other forms of activity or employment to working in the state structures attests to the fact that certain conservative-discriminatory mechanisms have developed within the state system.

In addition, it should be emphasized that these mechanisms are not driven by any kind of explicit policy with respect to administrators of the nonindigenous population. I therefore do not concur with Boris Rumer's statement that Uzbekistan has a "harsh, discriminatory policy on personnel" and that the regime seeks to force the nonindigenous population to emigrate.[44] In reality, in the mid-1990s one could even observe countervailing processes. The growth of the administrative apparatus gave rise to a demand for qualified administrative personnel. Insofar as a significant part of the Uzbek administrators in the early 1990s switched to entrepreneurial activities, for a certain period the "Europeans" had to play the role of "mobilized diaspora" (in the words of J. A. Armstrong).[45] By 2000 and the following years, the growth of the administrative apparatus and the resources to sustain it (salaries and other perquisites) had come to an end; indeed, in part a kind of reverse process was underway. As a result, this system itself—not the policy—began to drive out the least integrated elements, and inter alia that included functionaries of nonindigenous nationalities. Here I do agree with Rumer that, "with the departure of Russians the cultural atmosphere of a Westernized, most socially active part of society in the cities of Uzbekistan (which had been fashioned in the course of nearly a century and a half) is being destroyed."[46]

Still, in recent years the lower echelon of the administrative system has begun to recruit young functionaries who graduated in the 1990s. In other words, their education came after the breakup of the Soviet Union and, correspondingly, its educational system. Insofar as the number of cadres who have received a post-Soviet education will increase (despite the slowdown in the rejuvenation of administrative elites), it is worthwhile to examine the transformation that has overtaken the system of education, together with the attendant social and political consequences.

The Educational Alternative

Thus, how will the future administrative and political elites of Uzbekistan obtain an education?

On the one hand, the educational system of Uzbekistan in 2004 showed relatively positive indicators if one takes into account the country's economic and administrative stagnation. It has been possible for the contemporary educational system to retain such important parameters as universal access to free education at the primary and secondary level (altogether twelve years). The literacy rate of the adult population in 2003 stood at 99.2 percent. The government's expenditures per pupil for preschool, professional, and higher education were significantly above the average world indicators.[47]

On the other hand, there are less positive signs. The United Nations *Common Country Assessment* for Uzbekistan in 2003 noted that, "as in other social sectors, education has been affected by the difficulties of the transition period. . . . The contents, as well as the processes and organization of education, have not efficiently served the needs of the changing economic, social and political environments in Uzbekistan."[48] I shall try to indicate those problems that are associated either with the retraditionalization of the social and political context in Uzbekistan, or with the quality in the formation of future elites.

One problem, evidently, is *a decline in the quality of education* at all levels—preschool, primary, secondary, and higher. The underlying cause (apart from the low salary of teachers and the consequent egress of qualified personnel) is the sharp drop in the social prestige of a "diploma-holding specialist" in contemporary Uzbek society.[49] A good education is no longer regarded as a guarantee (or, at least, as a precondition) for a prestigious or, at a minimum, a well-paying job. Moreover, to obtain a really quality education (even there, where it is nominally free), one increasingly encounters rising expenses—to buy textbooks, to pay for supplementary lessons, and so forth. A good education is increasingly expensive, but this investment shows a diminishing recoupment. Hence only the wealthy, or those who hope to recover the investment with careers outside Uzbekistan, can allow themselves such an education. Moreover, apart from the growing indirect inflation of a "free education," the system is doing less to educate than just to control students.

There has also been a change in the hierarchy of priorities within the educational system: a massive shift toward the humanities and social sciences. The prestige of science and technology disciplines (with the exception of computers and information technology) has declined significantly; these in no ways compete with the humanities and social sciences, especially economics and law. Significantly, if in the 1960s and 1970s the elites of Uzbekistan deemed it prestigious to have their children study the natural sciences (physics, chemistry, mathematics), the contemporary elites prefer that their children study the social sciences and the humanities. Western foundations have played a significant role in this process, for they have given grants for Uzbeks to study specifically these non-science disciplines in universities and colleges in the United States and Europe. Without denigrating the role of the humanities and social sciences, one should note that the "humanitarization" (more precisely, descientization) impedes the creation and application of new technologies and retards the development of industry as an element in the modernization of society.

Another problem since 2000 has been the contraction in the system of higher education. Thus, whereas 15 percent of the youth of Uzbekistan studied in its institutions of higher education in the 1990s, that quotient had plunged to just 5 percent by 1998. By contrast, in other post-Soviet states this indicator increased—for example, to 28 percent in Russia and Ukraine, and 25 percent in Kyrgyzstan.[50] Since 1998 there has been a further decrease in the number of students enrolled in institutions of higher learning, with a particularly sharp contraction in postgraduate programs for candidate and doctoral degrees (see Table 7.3).

Apart from the obvious economic factors (lack of financial resources; and the low rate of return, in the short term perspective, on resources invested in the educational system), the tendency for the system of higher education to contract has obvious social and political causes. Already in Soviet times study in the capital or oblast institutions of higher education

Table 7.3

Number Enrolled in Post-Graduate Programs for Master's and Doctoral Degrees

Degree program	1998	2000	2002
Doctorate	61	43	49
Master's	599	396	365

Source: The data here are from 33 institutions of higher education subordinate to the Ministry of Higher and Specialized Education; these represent more than half of all such institutions in Uzbekistan.

was one of the main channels for the urbanization of rural youth and their influx into the cities. These rural youths were given certain privileges when they matriculated in such institutions; as a rule, a large number of them remained in the city after they had completed their studies. In the 1990s the government retained and even tightened the Soviet system of residency registration (*propiska*), for it wanted to limit the influx of rural youths to large cities (above all, Tashkent). In part, this policy was due to fears of a repetition of the student disorders of 1988–1989 in the university city of Tashkent, where rural students had played the most active role.

Nevertheless, there remained (and even significantly expanded) another channel for the urbanization of rural youth that had already existed in the Soviet era: employment in urban police forces. However, if the "student channel" of urbanization brought a rise in the educational level of youth and hence its modernization, the "police channel" apparently increased just the antithesis—a conservative, traditionalist orientation.

Paradoxically, although the number of students in institutions of higher learning has decreased, the number of institutions themselves has steadily grown (see Table 7.4). As a rule, however, that growth has come either by breaking up universities or by raising the level (and status) of vocational training programs that existed in the Soviet era. In both instances, the system of higher education replicates the same process of expansion characteristic of the administration in general. Endemic in this system of higher education were the same conservative characteristics that pervaded the administration as a whole: the same bribery that became so notorious, and the transformation of instructors into functionaries who filled out endless "assessment forms" and wrote detailed outlines of their lectures. Although abrogation of the ban on private universities could hardly bring a radical improvement in the situation, it would—at least to some degree—overcome

Table 7.4

Number of Institutions of Higher Learning

Number of institutions	1992	1996	1999	2002
Tashkent only	25	27	29	31
Total in Uzbekistan	54	58	61	63

Source: State Statistical Committee of the Republic of Uzbekistan.

the stagnation in the system of higher education and transform it into a place where the youth fulfills its "educational obligation."

Finally, a third problem associated with the retraditionalization of the system of education is its steady derussification. The dynamics of derussification in elementary and secondary education are show in Table 7.5. Over an eleven-year period (1992–2003), the number of schools giving instruction in Russian in Uzbekistan has decreased by one-quarter, and the percent of pupils in these schools has dropped by nearly half (from 11.5 to 5.9 percent of all pupils). Moreover, that proportion has dropped by two-thirds in Andizhan, Samarkand, and Khorezm oblasts, by three-quarters in Surkhan dar'ia (the latter having the country's lowest proportion of pupils in Russian schools—0.8 percent). In general, the table provides some insight into another tendency: the closer a territory to the capital, Tashkent (where Russian continues to retain a certain place in the administrative and business elites), the more the parents strive to have their children learn Russian. This pertains to Syrdar'ia, Dzhizak, and Tashkent oblasts, as well as Tashkent itself. An exception is Navoi oblast, where a significant Russian-speaking diaspora still resides. Particularly surprising are the data on Fergana oblast; according to these figures, the number of Russian schools (and students enrolled in them) has increased in recent years. However, the general tendency has been for the study of Russian language to decrease.

Nonetheless, as recent research has shown, the number of those seeking to study Russian in the republic remains rather high—over 90 percent.[51] Apart from the fact that Russian (through the Russian mass media, old library collections, higher quality of education in "Russian" schools) continues to remain attractive, there are other, more pragmatic, reasons. Thus, as a result of the mass labor exodus of the Uzbek population to Russia and Kazakhstan after 2000, the demand for a good knowledge of Russian has sharply increased. Moreover, within the republic itself, Russian remains the second language (after English) for those who work for international organizations

Table 7.5

Schools Offering Instruction in Russian, 1992 and 2003

	1992				2003			
	Schools		Pupils		Schools		Pupils	
Territory	Number	Percent	Number	Percent	Number	Percent	Number	Percent
Karakalpak Republic	53	15.9	16,813	13.0	44	11.9	10,211	6.4
Andizhan oblast	62	9.0	26,792	6.8	40	5.6	13,292	2.4
Bukhara oblast	29	6.7	17,103	4.8	30	5.5	8,749	2.5
Dzhizak oblast	45	10	12,070	6.9	23	4.5	10,648	4.3
Kashkadaria oblast	43	4.6	15,079	3.5	22	2.1	6,152	1.0
Navoi oblast	37	14	23,156	19.0	27	9.3	14,561	8.0
Namangan oblast	35	5.9	16,859	5.0	31	4.5	14,830	3.0
Samarkand oblast	100	8.3	42,915	8.8	52	4.6	23,728	3.3
Surkhan dar'ia oblast	37	5.3	11,529	3.7	19	2.5	4,293	0.8
Syrdar'ia oblast	90	25.8	16,548	13.0	51	14.6	8,889	5.8
Tashkent oblast	237	27.0	95,329	25.4	183	19.6	53,578	11.4
Fergana oblast	63	8.2	30,632	6.4	49	5.7	46,229	6.8
Khorezm oblast	23	4.8	10,815	3.6	16	3.0	8,015	2.3
Tashkent (city)	197	45.8	150,452	46.8	164	38.6	118,646	32.3
Total	1,055	12.5	487,048	11.5	751	8.2	341,821	5.9

Source: Calculated by the author from data provided by the Ministry of Public Education.

and donors and the main language in nongovernmental organizations (NGOs) and grant recipients. However, as in the case of setting quotas on positions in institutions of higher learning, the study of Russian and in Russian continues to be strictly regulated by the system of education. Moreover, the restriction on the place of Russian language in the educational system has not been offset by a modernization of Uzbek; on the contrary, the latter—under the banner of a struggle with "Russianisms"—has resurrected an archaic Arab and Persian lexicon, or by an expansion of instruction in English.

Already in 1996 Michael Rywkin drew attention to this tendency in his presentation at a regional conference on security in Central Asia (organized by the Marshall Center). He noted that, over the past century, Russian language had been the channel that enabled the peoples of Central Asia to use (even if in a distorted form) the achievements of modern culture and technology, since the majority of the peoples of Central Asia were (and are) fluent in Russian. "Now," he pointed out, "there has been a turn toward English. However, will English become accessible for even half of the population in the region?"[52] Eight years later, in an article published in 2004 by the well-known Uzbek writer and journalist Sabit Madaliev, we find a negative answer to this question: "I cannot imagine that tomorrow we shall all speak English the way we speak Russian."[53] In fact, it would be more accurate to say *spoke* Russian, since under conditions of a mass exodus of those who speak a literate Russian, the standard of Russian language has gradually been debased and vulgarized.

In this respect, we cannot fully endorse the view of Oliver Roy, who asserts, with respect to the new elites in the states of Central Asia: "Their place of education tends increasingly to be foreign and private schools that have been set up in the republics, the most gifted going to Western universities." Therefore, writes Roy, "within ten or twenty years Russian will no longer be the preferred foreign language of the elites; it will give way to English."[54] Given the current situation (viz., the retraditionalization of the administrative system, the slowdown in the rejuvenation of elites, the reduction in the social prestige of higher education, and, finally, the minimal presence of English in administrative paperwork), the "gifted" graduates of Western schools and universities will be in little demand among either the administrative or the business elites. It may be that English, within four to five years, will be "the preferred foreign language," but only because Russian—from the moment that Uzbek acquired the status of the official state language fifteen years ago—is not yet perceived as "a foreign language," nor is it likely to be so perceived in the near future.[55]

Therefore, despite all the positive tendencies in the contemporary system of education in Uzbekistan, despite the decline in the quality of education, despite its derussification (which, as a rule, is tantamount to its de-Europe-anization), a one-sided "humanitarianization" and the contraction in the system of higher education allow one to speak of a growing traditionalism and conservatism in the educational system.

To summarize, I have examined three spheres where, in my judgment, the past few years have witnessed obvious conservative, anti-Western tendencies: ideology, cadres, and education. All three spheres bear the imprint of strict centralization in the political and administrative system. Given this situation, many liberal attempts in recent years to decentralize administrative power, to transfer part of its authority to local organs of self-rule and to NGOs, have had an extremely insignificant impact on the real alignment of political forces in the state. The administrative apparatus has retained its own strictly controlled and regulated function with respect to the economy; amid the mounting economic difficulties, in fact, it was even forced to increase its pressure on the economic sphere through various instruments of non-economic coercion. The radio journalist B. Abdullaev has graphically portrayed the situation with respect to the economic and investment climate in Uzbekistan: "The doors are open to the West, but the West is not coming, because it is very difficult to work there."[56]

At the same time, the policy adopted after 2000—an orientation toward the West—has undergone a certain transformation. Although in rhetorical terms the policy remains unaltered, there have in fact been changes with respect to the activity of Western organizations in Uzbekistan. What have these been?

A Western Alternative to Traditionalism?

The intensification of contacts with the West after 11 September 2001 and Western influence in Uzbekistan are qualitatively new, although not entirely unprecedented. Since the collapse of the Soviet Union, this has been, at the very least, the third "wave" of a Western presence in Uzbekistan.

The first wave (1991–1995) was characterized not only by the intensive establishment of diplomatic relations with Western countries, but also by the opening of numerous branches and offices of Western companies and by the influx of a large number of Christian missions from the West.

The second wave (1996–2000) brought a significant change in this flow. Namely, because of the lack of freely convertible currency, there was a contraction in the number of Western countries engaged in Uzbekistan. Also, as a result of the ban on missionary activities, there was a no less intensive drop in the number of foreign Christian missions. During this same period, there was an increase in the activity of Western organizations and foundations in Uzbekistan, and projects were launched in the spheres of liberalization, human rights, and so forth. There was also a growth in military cooperation with the United States and NATO.

The appearance of Western military personnel on the territory of Uzbekistan since 2001, it would seem, opened a new stage in the Western presence. It has been characterized by an intensification in military cooperation and by assistance to liberalize the economic and political climate. However, since 2000, that presence has become especially ambivalent, even contradictory, with regard to the Westernization and modernization of Uzbekistan.

On the one hand, it is difficult to underestimate the positive influence of international and Western organizations (which, frequently, are the same thing) on Uzbekistan. The leading position here has been held by the U.S. embassy and organizations that operate under the aegis of the American government. For example, in 2003 alone the U.S. government dispatched to America more than 340 Uzbek citizens under a program for scientific and professional exchange in various spheres (from the administration and delivery of social services to the development of nongovernmental organizations). Within the framework of such programs, since 1993 the U.S. Government has financed the trips of more than 2,700 citizens of Uzbekistan.[57] Not least in importance, thanks to lobbying by Western states and organizations, Uzbekistan has undertaken many significant steps to liberalize political and social life:

- acknowledgment of problems in the sphere of human rights in Uzbekistan and creation of national institutions to protect human rights, including registration of the first human-rights organizations (1996);
- recognition of the role of NGOs and adoption of the law On Nongovernmental Noncommercial Organizations (1999); and
- abolition of prior censorship for mass media; attempts to liberalize the criminal justice and penitentiary systems; and invitation to the U.N. special rapporteur on torture, T. Van Boven, to visit Uzbekistan (2001–2002).

Finally, the local staffs of Western embassies and organizations (together with the institutions that collaborate with them), and also various state and nongovernmental organs that receive Western grants remain the most pro-Western, liberally inclined part of the population of Uzbekistan. The expansion in the network of NGOs that function, as a rule, on the basis of grants from Western and international organizations has been especially significant. Thus, in 2002–2003, the number of registered NGOs in Uzbekistan increased by 66 percent and has approached a total of 3,500 organizations (see Table 7.6).

Table 7.6

Growth of Registered NGOs in Uzbekistan, 1999–2003

Year	1999	2000	2001	2002	2003 (first half)
Number of new NGOs	162	240	340	349	199

Source: Ministry of Justice of the Republic of Uzbekistan.

Nevertheless, the Western presence in Uzbekistan has, to some degree, indirectly retarded the process of modernization.

In the 1990s, Western embassies and organizations (especially those of the United States) endeavored to reduce the influence of Russia in every sphere. Such a position, among other things, led to a significant decrease in the impulses of those democratic processes that continued to operate in Russia in the 1990s after the breakup of the Soviet Union. The United States and West European countries, taken together, were simply in no position to replace Moscow as an equivalent engine of democratization; that is because of their remoteness and the lack of direct levers of influence, but also because of indirect factors (like Russia's "fifth column" in Central Asia—in the form of the Russian and Russian-speaking population of Uzbekistan). Even Putin's Russia of 2000 and later, despite its apparent shift from liberalism to conservatism, remains a much more Westernized and liberal country than Uzbekistan and the majority of other Central Asian states.

Moreover, when seeking out and incrementally building up a "democratic opposition" in Uzbekistan, Western organizations have tacitly encouraged the continuing exodus abroad of the intelligentsia (both the "European" and indigenous). But it is precisely this exodus that is eroding the social basis on which a serious political opposition might be built. For example, through its "green card" system, the United States has made a significant contribution to the process of emigration of young people who were not indoctrinated by the former Soviet ideology and who are quite liberal in their thinking. That is, the United States has facilitated the egress of those who, in real terms, could make a contribution to the process of democratization.

Nevertheless, on the whole, the Western influence in Uzbekistan in the course of the entire 1990s remained a significant stimulus to the processes of Westernization and liberalization. That situation changed somewhat at the end of 2003 and in early 2004.

In 2003, Uzbekistan failed to receive the anticipated amount of financial assistance from the United States and from the European Bank for Reconstruction and Development. Moreover, in both cases, the denial was motivated by the situation with respect to human rights. Furthermore, as noted above, the events in Tbilisi, culminating in the resignation of President Eduard Shevardnadze, also made an extremely negative impression on the Uzbek leadership. Fears of a regime change in Tashkent per the "Georgian scenario" (i.e., with the support of American organizations) proved so serious that the Uzbek government announced a re-registration of international organizations, which were to submit applications by 1 March 2004. The goal was to limit the influence of certain of these organizations, above all, that of the Soros Foundation, whose Georgian branch had allegedly supported political opponents of Shevardnadze.[58] Still earlier, before 1 January 2004, all the mass media in Uzbekistan were also to undergo re-registration, and this included the bulletins published by NGOs.

In addition to this re-registration, the government undertook to increase its control over the grants conferred by international organizations. On 4 February 2004 the Cabinet of Ministers issued resolution no. 56, On Measures to Increase the Efficacy of Accounting for Financial Resources of Technical Assistance, Grants, and Humanitarian Assistance from International, Foreign, Governmental and Nongovernmental Organizations. According to this decree, from the first quarter of 2004 these organizations are to compile an accounting on the "solicitation, use, and monitoring of financial resources" and to submit these reports to the Cabinet of Ministers. Implementation of this resolution will apparently allow the administrative apparatus to tighten its control over the grants (that is, in the final analysis, over the activity of Uzbek grant recipients). At the same time, apparently, this will drive NGO recipients of grants to "share" these resources with the staff of the organs empowered to oversee them.

Finally, in February, the government published an addendum and changes to the Criminal Code of the Republic of Uzbekistan, including Article 175 on "state treason." Apart from espionage and revelation of state secrets, the definition of "state treason" added "any kind of assistance . . . to conducting activities hostile to the Republic of Uzbekistan." Moreover, the object of such assistance was not only "a foreign government" (as in the previous version of the article from 29 August 2001), but "a foreign organization or their representatives."[59] One should not exclude the possibility that, in the absence of a definition of what constitutes "assistance," this could be understood to include the monitoring of human rights by states and organizations if such are judged to be "hostile activities."

Thus, on the eve of the elections to the Oliy Majlis, the leadership of the republic has adopted a rather consistent policy aimed at limiting Western influence on the social and political situation within the country. The organs of the justice are intensifying control over the number of Western organizations; state banking structures are overseeing grants allocated by these organizations; and law-enforcement agencies are monitoring those who collaborate with these organizations. For the present, it is too early to say how thoroughly these measures will be implemented and what the results will be. However, it is obvious that these changes are fully consistent with those processes that we observed in the ideological, personnel, and educational spheres; in combination with the latter, they attest to the fact that the social and political context in the country has become more closed and conservative over the past five years. It lies beyond the limits of this paper to determine whether this closed, conservative context is inevitable, whether it has positive aspects, or to the contrary, will prove purely negative.

Notes

1. K. A. Wittfogel, *Oriental Despotism: A Comparative Study of Total Power* (New Haven, 1955), p. 9.

2. Ibid., p. 420.

3. Ibid., p. 423.

4. Within the framework of this research, I shall use these terms as more or less equivalently; I concur that "the term modernization is used to identify certain processes of social change that historically first occurred in Western Europe and which subsequently became global." G. Evans and J. Newnham, *The Penguin Dictionary of International Relations* (London, 1998), p. 335.

5. E. Abdullaev, "The Administrative Elite of Uzbekistan: After 11 September 2001," in *Central Asia and South Caucasus Affairs*, ed. Boris Rumer and Lau Sim Yee (Tokyo, 2002), pp. 213–35.

6. Ibid., p. 233.

7. Boris Rumer, "Tsentral'naia Aziia—desiat'let spustia. Obzornyi ocherk," in *Tsentral'naia Aziia i Iuzhnyi Kavkaz. Nasushchnye problemy*, ed. B. Rumer (Almaty, 2002).

8. This includes both official (decrees, laws, declarations of the head of state, and statistical data) as well as other published sources (such as the results of sociological studies, interviews, and the like).

9. Evans and Newnham, p. 336.

10. N. Chomsky, *Language and Responsibility. Based on Conversations with Mitsou Ronat*, translated from the French by J. Viertel (New York, 1979), p. 3.

11. R. Hanks, "Civil Society and Identity in Uzbekistan: The Emergent Role of Islam," in *Civil Society in Central Asia*, ed. M. Holt Ruffin and D. Waugh (Seattle, 1999), p. 172.

12. *Vedomosti Olii Mazhilisa Respubliki Uzbekistan*, nos. 3/4 (1323–1324), March–April 2003, p. 107.

13. *Integration Process in the Central Asian Countries and Youth* (Tashkent, 2001), p. 20.

14. "Women-entrepreneurs and Local Authorities. Analysis Based on a Sociological Study Focused on Women in Private Business," *Public Opinion. Human Rights*, 2003, no. 4 (24), pp. 61, 63.

15. In particular, in a report at a meeting of the Cabinet of Ministers on 18 July 2003, President Islam Karimov referred to "a serious danger—corruption, which like rust can devour the system of rule and inflict serious harm to the economic and social-

political stability of any country." I. A. Karimov, *Izbrannyi nami put'—eto put' demokraticheskogo razvitiia i sotrudnichestva s progressivnym mirom*, vol. 2 (Tashkent, 2003), p. 287.

16. "Rossiia-Uzbekistan: s veroi v budushchee," *Trud-7*, 2004, no. 35, p. 6.

17. "Zaiavlenie Olii Mazhlisa Respubliki Uzbekistan po resheniiu irakskoi problemy (priniato 24 aprelia 2003 goda na odinnadtsatoi sessii Olii Mazhlisa Respubliki vtorogo sozyva)," *Vedomosti Olii Mazhilisa Respubliki Uzbekistan*, nos. 3–4 (1323–1324), March–April 2003, p. 103.

18. Paragraph 4, Article 2 in the Treaty Between the Republic of Kazakhstan, Kyrgyz Republic, the Republic of Tajikistan, and the Republic of Uzbekistan on the Establishment of the "Central Asian Cooperation" Organization, Almaty, 28 February 2002.

19. "Uzbekistan. Ot doma k domu: proizvol makhallinskikh komitetov" (www.hrw.org/russian/reports/uzbek/2003/220903_mahal.html). The original English text is also available at www.hrw.org/reports/2003/uzbekistan0903/.

20. Rumer, "Tsentral'naia Aziia," p. 41. In general, however, in his brief statement Rumer perceptively pointed out that the mahallas are subject to the organs of the executive authority, and that the mahallas pose a potential danger (as an institution traditionally associated with religion) for the secular regime in Uzbekistan.

21. I. A. Karimov, *Pravovaia garantiia nashego velikogo budushchego* (Tashkent, 1993), p. 13.

22. Ibid.

23. I. A. Karimov, "Predislovie k rabote, 'Ideia natsional'noi nezavisimosti: osnovnye poniatiia i printsipy,'" *Za protsvetanie Rodiny—kazhdyi iz nas v otvete*, vol. 9 (Tashkent, 2001), p. 204.

24. Reference here is Marxist-Leninist ideology.

25. Karimov, "Predislovie," p. 204.

26. Ibid., p. 205.

27. E. Abdullaev, "Zakon sokhraneniia," in *Malyi shelkovyi put'*, vol. 4 (Tashkent, 2003), p. 149.

28. See E. Rakhmonov, "Tadzhiki: ot ariitsev do Samanidov" (www.tajnet.com/-samanid/book/chapter4.htm); and A. Akaev, "Diplomacy of the Silk Road (a Foreign Policy Doctrine)" (www.sais-jhu.edu/caci/Publications/Akaev.html).

29. S. N. Petrova, "Kul'turno-istoricheskoe nasledie kak resurs vneshnei politiki Respubliki Uzbekistan," *Vostok. Afro-aziatskie obshchestva: istoriia i sovremennost'*, 1998, no. 3, p. 79.

30. Examples include "great future (*buyuk kelajak*)" in Uzbekistan, and "Kazakhstan in the Year 2030" in Kazakhstan.

31. An *aksakal* (from *oq soqol*, "white-bearded") is an elder and, more broadly, a respectful term for an elderly man.

32. Karimov, "Predislovie," p. 204.

33. N. A. Kosolapov, "Ideologiia i mezhdunarodnye otnosheniia na rubezhe tysiacheletii," in *Ocherki teorii i metodologii politicheskogo analiza mezhdunarodnykh otnoshenii*, ed. A. D. Bogaturov, N. A. Kosolapov, and M. A. Khrustalev (Moscow, 2002), p. 236.

34. Ibid.

35. Directives of 5 January 2004: No. 1 (On the Optimization and Reduction of the Number of Administrative Personnel of Republic Organs of State and Economic Administration) and No. 2 (On the Improvement of the Structure of the Territorial Organs of Administration).

36. See Appendix No. 1 to Directive No. 1 of 5 January 2004.

37. See Appendix No. 2 to Directive No. 1 of 5 January 2004.

38. See Appendix No. 3 to Directive No. 1 of 5 January 2004.

39. See Appendix No. 7 to Directive No. 2 of 5 January 2004.

40. See Appendix No. 3 to Directive No. 1 of 5 January 2004.

41. Iu. V. Arutiunian, *Transformatsiia postsovetskikh natsii: po materialam etnosotsiologicheskikh issledovanii* (Moscow, 2003), p. 42.

42. By "Europeans" (within the context of Uzbekistan) one usually understands the Russian-speaking representatives of nonindigenous ethnic groups, who studied in "Russian schools," and enrolled in the "European tracks" in institutions of higher education. This category also includes non-Europeans like Koreans and Tatars.

43. On the basis of sociological studies in a number of post-Soviet cities, Iu. V. Arutiunian came to conclude that the "Westernization" of the Russian population in the "near abroad" (former Soviet republics) was an "inevitability." See Arutiunian, *Transformatsiia*, p. 97.

44. Rumer, "Tsentral'naia Aziia," p. 42.

45. J. A. Armstrong, "The Ethnic Scene in the Soviet Union: The View of the Dictatorship," in *Ethnic Minorities in the Soviet Union*, ed. E. Goldhagen (London, 1968), p. 7.

46. Rumer, "Tsentral'naia Aziia," p. 43.

47. N. Burnett and R. Knobloch, *Public Spending on Education in the CIS—Seven Countries: The Hidden Crisis* (Washington, DC, 2003).

48. United Nations, *Uzbekistan. Common Country Assessment* (New York, 2003), pp. 20, 22–23.

49. According to a sociological survey conducted in April 2002, only 6.8 percent of the respondents declared "education" to be a priority in social values. See *A Social Portrait of Uzbekistan* (Tashkent, 2002), p. 91.

50. United Nations, *Uzbekistan. Common Country Assessment*, p. 22.

51. See "Rossiia–Uzbekistan: s veroi v budushchee," p. 6.

52. See E. V. Abdullaev, "Russkie Uzbekistana—gorodskoi subetnos (opyt sotsiokul'turnogo analiza)," *Tsentral'naia Aziia i Kavkaz*, 2000, no. 5 (11).

53. See http://news.ferghana.ru/detail.php?id=461066187019162.

54. O. Roy, *The New Central Asia: The Creation of Nations* (London, New York, 2000), p. 180.

55. In this respect, I must reconsider views that I myself expressed two years ago. At that time, I thought that "although the influence of the Russian language will be significant in the administrative sphere for a rather extended time to come, it will be actively displaced not only by Uzbek, but also by English." See E. Abdullaev, "The Administrative Elite of Uzbekistan: After 11 September 2001," in *Central Asia and South Caucasus Affairs*, ed. B. Rumer and Lau Sim Yee (Tokyo, 2002), p. 233.

56. Radio Svoboda, 24 May 2001 (www.uzland.uz/2001/may/27.htm).

57. See www.centasia.ru/newsA.php4?st=1077402120.

58. Simultaneously, the official Uzbek press began to publish articles critical of the various initiatives undertaken by the Soros Foundation in Uzbekistan—in particular, a volume published with a subvention by the foundation: *Etnicheskii atlas Uzbekistana* (Moscow, 2002), especially the part written by the executive director of the branch, A. Il'khamov.

59. "Zakon Respubliki Uzbekistan 'O vnesenii izmenenii i dopolnenii v nekotorye zakonodatel'nye akty Respubliki Uzbekistan," *Pravda Vostoka*, 18 February 2004, p. 3.

Part IV

The Prospects for Economic Development

8

Kyrgyzstan and Uzbekistan: Landlocked Agrarian Economies with an Unlimited Supply of Labor

Stanislav Zhukov

More than a decade ago, the five newly formed states of Central Asia joined the ranks of the so-called "transition economies," that is, those making the transition from a planned to a market-driven economy. The interim results of transition among the different countries have varied. A comparison of the experience of Kyrgyzstan and Uzbekistan is of special interest for a number of reasons. At the beginning of the transition process, in terms of level and type of development, these two former Soviet republics were (or seemed to be) very similar to each other. Both countries, in contrast to the other less-developed republics of the former USSR, have been developing under peaceful conditions. However, because of different domestic and foreign factors, Kyrgyzstan and Uzbekistan adopted transformation strategies that were polar opposites to each other. Although the standard clichés become particularly vacuous in post-Soviet reality, one can say (while greatly simplifying) that Kyrgyzstan chose (or was forced to choose) the shock variant of reform consistent with neoliberal orthodoxy, while Uzbekistan, by contrast, chose gradualist reform, with the state playing a central role in this process.

    This study consists of three parts. The first analyzes the main economic and social results of the development of the two countries in the first decade following independence. The second part presents a comparative analysis of these results. The concluding section examines the main lessons that Kyrgyzstan and Uzbekistan can draw from the experience of each other.

The Main Results of the First Decade of Independent Development

The Dynamics of Economic Growth

During the first ten years of independent development, both countries witnessed a decline in per capita gross domestic product (GDP). In 1991–2003, the per capita GDP in Kyrgyzstan dropped at an average annual rate of 3.95 percent (see Table 8.1). In Uzbekistan, this indicator showed a slower rate of decline.

The available assessments allow one to construct a more or less adequate picture of the tendencies in the economic development of the two countries since 1970. It turns out that, in the course of two decades prior to independence, Kyrgyzstan developed at a faster pace than did Uzbekistan. Much of the rather slow rate of growth in the per capita GDP of Uzbekistan can be explained by the heavy demographic burden (caused by the high rates of population growth) on the economic growth of the country. Despite substantial contraction during the last decade, the rate of population growth in Uzbekistan is, as before, still higher than in Kyrgyzstan.

The production decline, which was triggered by the shocks of independence and the transition to a market economy, proved so profound that it erased the efforts of the several previous decades. Thus, in Kyrgyzstan in 1971–2003, the rate of growth of the GDP was negative; in Uzbekistan, this indicator was slightly positive, but very close to zero. As a result, Uzbekistan, which originally lagged behind its neighbor in the level of economic development, has now moved closer to Kyrgyzstan. This is confirmed by a comparison of the per capita GDP (whether measured in terms of the current exchange rate or in terms of the purchasing power parity of national currencies).

Both Kyrgyzstan and Uzbekistan resumed positive GDP growth rates in 1996. In Kyrgyzstan's case, these rates were naturally high (as a result of the relatively greater intensity of the preceding decline). In 2003, the per capita GDP in Uzbekistan was 84 to 89 percent of the 1990 level; in Kyrgyzstan this indicator was just 65 percent. Kyrgyzstan has been developing within the framework of lower inflation, but its economic growth remains unstable. In 2002, Kyrgyzstan proved to be the only country in the Commonwealth of Independent States (CIS) to report negative growth rates for its GDP. The per capita GDP of Uzbekistan has steadily grown on

Table 8.1

Dynamics of Economic Growth in Kyrgyzstan and Uzbekistan, 1970–2003

Indicators	Years	Kyrgyzstan	Uzbekistan
Per capita rate of growth of GDP[a]			
	1971–1990	1.25	1.00
	1991–2000	–5.00	–2.15
	2001–2003	2.90	–0.95/–1.35
	1991–2003	–3.20	–0.095/–1.35
	1971–2003	–0.55	0.25/0.10
Per capita GDP (Kyrgyzstan = 100; Uzbekistan = percent of Kyrgyzstan)			
Soviet rubles (1973 prices)	1970	100	85
	1990	100	82
Current dollars (per official exchange rate)[b]	1995	100	120
	2000	100	128
	2002	100	97
	2003	100	96
Purchasing power parity of national currency	1980	100	67
	1990	100	68
	2000	100	91
	2001	100	89
	2002	100	88
	2003	100	88

Sources: International Monetary Fund, *World Economic Outlook,* September 2003 (database); World Bank, *World Economic Indicators* (for various years); database of the Statistical Committee of the Commonwealth of Independent States; the database of W. Easterly and S. Fischer, updated by M. De Broeck and S. Cohen; data provided by the National Statistics Bureau.

[a]The per capita rate of growth of Uzbekistan is calculated in two variants: one uses the official data, the other uses estimates of the International Monetary Fund.

[b]The per capita GDP of Uzbekistan is calculated as a simple average of the indicators for the official exchange rate and the indicator for the black market exchange rate.

a per annum rate slightly above 3 percent; that corresponds to its modest potential.

One might doubt the veracity of these conclusions given that the statistics on Uzbekistan's national accounts are particularly low in quality and transparency.[1] This author has already, in an earlier publication, pointed out the obvious absurdities and contradictions in the statistics of Uzbekistan.[2]

At the same time, serious shortcomings can also be found in a careful examination of the statistics of Kyrgyzstan. For example, there are reasons to think that Kyrgyzstan's statistics somewhat exaggerate the rates of growth of the GDP by inflating the indicators for output in the agrarian sector and, recently, in the service sphere. Apparently, the quality of Kyrgyz and Uzbek statistics on national accounts are generally comparable; in any case, for a more substantive discussion of this matter, further research is needed.

What were the causes of such a massive decrease in production in Kyrgyzstan and Uzbekistan in the first half of the 1990s? The initial conditions for development in the two countries were similar. In terms of the level of subsidies from the all-union budget during the waning years of the Soviet era, Uzbekistan was even more dependent than Kyrgyzstan.[3] According to the calculations of D. Tarr for 1990, Kyrgyzstan even benefited however, insignificantly, from changes in terms of foreign trade that ensued after the collapse of a united Soviet economy. Uzbekistan, for its part, suffered a slight loss.[4]

Migration also had a sharply negative influence on the dynamics of production in Kyrgyzstan. In 1989–1996 net migration from Kyrgyzstan (the balance of immigrating and emigrating) was 8.6 percent of the 1989 population. In Uzbekistan the analogous indicator amounted to just 3.6 percent.[5] However, so significant a migration was itself driven by the collapse of production.

It also seems clear (although the issue requires further analysis) that the "excessive" decrease in production in Kyrgyzstan was, to a significant degree, due to an inadequate macroeconomic policy. Two factors played an especially negative role. One was the shock-like contraction of demand (see the section on state intervention in the economy, below). The second was the excessively hasty liberalization of key prices, which sharply increased the costs of domestic producers and left them unable to compete with cheaper imports.

It is revealing that the resumption of positive growth rates in Kyrgyzstan came against a background of relatively low prices for primary energy sources (and hence production costs). After 1998, the price of oil and natural gas (which, incidentally, are imported by Kyrgyzstan) in real terms (expressed in dollars) was significantly lower than in the first half of the 1990s, when the country made every possible effort to "get the prices right."

Another factor in the economic growth in Kyrgyzstan was the start-up of gold mining at Kumtor, where much of the country's construction and development was concentrated. The problems that have periodically appeared at this site are a cause of the extremely uneven economic growth in Kyrgyzstan.

Efficiency of Growth

Let us assess the quality of the economic growth of Kyrgyzstan and Uzbekistan in terms of three criteria: (a) labor productivity; (b) energy intensity of production; and (c) efficiency of the agrarian sector. The latter is especially important given that agriculture is the basis of the national economy in both countries.

There are different methods for making a quantitative measurement of labor productivity. As the indicator of labor productivity here we shall use the ratio of the volume of output to employment. Of course, a short period with a positive growth rate is too brief for a serious analysis of broader dynamics in labor productivity. And, until very recently, the growth in the Kyrgyz and Uzbek economies was limited to recovering earlier levels. At the same time, given the goals of this study, it is important to identify several general factors.

In the first half of the 1990s, labor productivity dropped in both countries, but the decline was especially evident in Kyrgyzstan (see Table 8.2). In the second half of the decade, productivity rose in both countries and, until 2000, at approximately the same rate. Only in the last two years has labor productivity risen at a higher rate in Kyrgyzstan; indeed, in 2003 it was a third higher than in 1990. The very rapidity of this increase in labor productivity, however, raises serious questions about the accuracy of national accounts statistics in Kyrgyzstan. Whatever the case, during the years of independence Uzbekistan has moved noticeably closer to its neighbor in terms of labor productivity.

The indicator for the energy consumption coefficient (the consumption of energy per unit of output) is one of the most important indicators of the efficiency of an economic system. A reduction in the energy consumption of production represents one of the general tendencies of world development. As is well known, however, the Soviet economy completely deviated from this world trend and, compared with market economies, had very high energy consumption.

During the past decade, Kyrgyzstan and Uzbekistan have narrowed the difference in their energy consumption coefficient. Whereas, in 1990, Uzbekistan consumed 7.5 times more energy than Kyrgyzstan to produce one dollar of GDP, this difference shrank to 4.5 by 2000. Moreover, if the calculations are based on dollars in 2000, the energy consumption in the Uzbek GDP has changed insignificantly. The tendency for the two countries to converge was due to the more than 1.5-fold growth in the energy consumption coefficient of the Kyrgyz GDP.

Labor productivity in the agrarian sector of Kyrgyzstan, after a sharp

Table 8.2

Indicators of Efficiency in the Economies of Kyrgyzstan and Uzbekistan

Indicator	1990	1991	1992	1995	1996	1997	1998	1999	2000	2001	2002	2003[a]
Labor productivity for the economy as a whole (1990 = 100)												
Kyrgyzstan	100	92	76	54	57	62	63	68	87	98	118	132
Uzbekistan	100	96	85	77	77	78	80	83	85	87	92	101
Relative labor productivity for the economy as a whole (Uzbekistan as percent of Kyrgyzstan)												
Kyrgyzstan	100	100	100	100	100	100	100	100	100	100	100	100
Uzbekistan	70	73	78	100	94	88	90	92	90	89	91	84
Labor productivity in the agricultural sector (1990 = 100)												
Kyrgyzstan	100	83	70	46	52	56	56	55	56	69	61	
Uzbekistan	100	89	81	80	75	78	83	95	102	108	109	

Relative labor productivity in the agricultural sector (Uzbekistan as percent of Kyrgyzstan)											
Kyrgyzstan	100	100	100	100	100	100	100	100	100	100	100
Uzbekistan	67	73	78	118	96	95	100	117	123	123	121
Energy intensity in GDP (1990 = 100; GDP in purchasing power parity)											
Kyrgyzstan		376	323	247	259	212	161	178	159		
Uzbekistan		102	110	101	101	97	100	101	97		
Energy intensity in GDP (1990 = 100; GDP in prices at official exchange rates of 2000)											
Kyrgyzstan		389	341	279	299	249	191	214	196		
Uzbekistan		230	253	115	116	114	119	122	119		

Sources: "Republic of Uzbekistan: Recent Economic Developments," IMF Country Reports, No. 00/36 (March 2000), pp. 49, 52; "Kyrgyz Republic: Selected Issues and Statistical Appendix," IMF Country Reports, No. 03/53 (February 2003), p. 79; Vsemirnyi Bank, *Gosudarstva byvshego Sovetskogo Soiuza. Statisticheskii sbornik.* 1993, pp. 354, 738; IMF, Databank for *World Economic Outlook*; databanks of the Statistical Committee of the CIS; data of national statistics.

[a]Data for 2003 are provisional.

Table 8.3

Yield Rates of Grain and Cotton Crops in Kyrgyzstan and Uzbekistan
(centners per hectare)

	Grain		Cotton	
Year(s)	Uzbekistan	Kyrgyzstan	Uzbekistan	Kyrgyzstan
1913	6.7	6.8	12.2	12.7
1940	4.1	7.6	15.0	14.8
1950	3.9	6.2	15.0	14.8
1956–1960	6.4	9.1	20.3[a]	17.7[a]
1961–1965	7.2	11.2	23.2[b]	22.9[b]
1966–1970	7.4	15.6	25.0	23.4
1971–1975	9.5	18.7	24.5	27.5
1976–1980	19.4	23.6	29.4	28.3
1981–1985	20.8	25.1	26.7	19.1
1986–1990	20.2	24.0	25.7	25.3
1991–1995	17.6	22.1	25.8	23.1
1996–2000	22.2	25.1	22.7	24.8
2001–2003	35.2	27.8	22.8[c]	27.3

Sources: Uzbekistan Economy: Statistical and Analytical Review 2002, p. 53; "V Uzbekistane vysokii urozhai zernovykh" (posting of 16 July 2003 on www.caspian.ru); database of the Statistical Committee of Kyrgyzstan (http://nsc.bishkek.su/Rus/Database/ Tab6.xls); *Narodnoe khoziaistvo SSSR* (various years); database of the Statistical Committee of the CIS; data provided by the National Statistics Bureau.
[a]Data for 1960 only.
[b]Data for 1965 only.
[c]Data for 2001–2002 only.

decline in the first half of the 1990s, rose slightly and then stabilized at approximately 60 percent of the 1990 level. In Uzbekistan an analogous indicator has grown since 1997 and by 2000 had already surpassed the 1990 level. Whereas labor productivity in the agrarian sector was 30 percent lower in Uzbekistan than Kyrgyzstan at the outset of transition, by 2002 the two countries had exchanged places with respect to this indicator.

With respect to the yield of grain crops, another indicator of efficiency in the agrarian sector, throughout the entire twentieth century Uzbekistan lagged somewhat behind Kyrgyzstan (see Table 8.3). That changed in the first years of the new century; Uzbekistan has surged noticeably ahead in grain yields. True, it has lagged in the yield for cotton; to a significant degree, that is due to the discrimination against the "white gold" sector (which is used as a donor for the rest of the Uzbek economy).

As is well known, in recent years Uzbekistan has deliberately pursued a policy of reducing the role of cotton in the national economy and replacing it with the cultivation of grain. Achieving self-sufficiency in grain production is a major goal of state policy. It is thought (and calculations support this view) that the shift from cotton to grain, in strictly economic terms, is inefficient; these calculations show that one hectare of cotton yields 1.2 to 4.5 more in added value than does a hectare of grain.[6] However, by increasing its grain output, Uzbekistan no longer needs to import several million tons of grain to satisfy the demand for bread, thereby enabling the country to conserve the hard currency that is in short supply. Given all this, it is fair to say that the advantage of the cotton strategy over grain still needs careful, detailed study.

Exports, Foreign Direct Investment, and the Foreign Debt

Demand for its exports is at the center of the model for economic growth that Kyrgyzstan seeks to realize. If the Kyrgyz economy fails to make a breakthrough in exports, output is doomed to remain substantially below its potential. However, the dynamics of national exports do not provide grounds for optimism: in spite of all the country's efforts, Kyrgyz exports have not risen in recent years above 500 million dollars. Moreover, in 1998–2002 export incomes were lower than in 1997 (see Table 8.4). In 2003 Kyrgyzstan was unable to exploit the unprecedentedly favorable conditions on world markets. Excluding nonmonetary gold, its exports even declined slightly from the previous year.

Beginning in 2005, the gold mine at Kumtor is expected to cease operating, and that of course will entail a substantial drop in export earnings. Simply to compensate for the lost income from the sale of gold, Kyrgyzstan must increase exports in other sectors by approximately 200 million dollars. That will be difficult to achieve.

Kyrgyzstan had counted on large direct foreign investments, but as it should have been expected, this did not transpire. The domestic market is extremely small; the country lacks the mineral reserves that could attract investors; given its geographic location, Kyrgyzstan has no chance of becoming an "export platform" and integrating itself into the international industrial division of labor. The lack of direct investment from abroad, incidentally, also explains the failure to increase exports.

The only relatively large project to attract foreign capital was the gold mine at Kumtor. With the completion of mass privatization, the influx of foreign investment (which was already modest) practically dried up. Indeed, a significant part of the "foreign investment" was actually Kyrgyz capital that had returned from the Western financial system and offshore zones.

As the example of a successful joint-venture enterprise to mine gold

Table 8.4.

Goods Exports and Direct Foreign Investment in Kyrgyzstan and Uzbekistan

Indicator/country	1995	1997	1999	2001	2002	2003	1995–1999 average	2000–2003 average	1995–2003 average
Export (millions of U.S. dollars)									
Kyrgyzstan	409	604	454	476	485	582	502	512	506
Uzbekistan	3,359	4,387	3,236	3,170	2,988	3,725	3,800	3,287	3,572
Export (percent of GDP)									
Kyrgyzstan	27.4	34.2	36.4	31.2	30.3	29.9	31.7	32.1	31.9
Uzbekistan-1[a]	32.1	29.8	18.9	27.6	30.7	37.5	27.5	29.9	28.6
Uzbekistan-2[b]	41.6	67.2	78.0	73.9	53.0	40.5	58.7	61.7	60.0
Uzbekistan-3[c]	36.2	41.3	30.5	40.2	38.9	38.9	37.5	39.7	38.5
Net flow of direct foreign investment (millions of U.S. dollars)									
Kyrgyzstan	96	83	44	5	5	20	76	7	45
Uzbekistan	-24	167	121	83	65	70	45	73	41
Net flow of direct foreign investment (percent of GDP)									
Kyrgyzstan	6.5	4.7	3.6	0.3	0.3	0.8	4.8	0.3	2.8
Uzbekistan-1[a]	-0.2	1.1	0.7	0.7	0.7	0.7	0.6	0.6	0.6
Uzbekistan-2[b]	-0.3	2.6	2.9	1.9	1.1	0.8	1.7	1.4	1.6
Uzbekistan-3[c]	-0.25	1.6	1.1	1.1	0.8	0.8	0.9	0.9	0.9

Sources: United Nations, Economic Commission for Europe, *Economic Survey of Europe*, NI, 2003, NI 2004.

[a]Uzbekistan-1: GDP is calculated on the basis of the official exchange rate.
[b]Uzbekistan-2: GDP is calculated on the basis of the black market exchange rate.
[c]Uzbekistan-3: Arithmetic mean for GDP per the official exchange rate and the black market exchange rate.

from the Uzbek deposits at Muruntau graphically shows, Kumtor could have been developed by foreigners without a general liberalization of the Kyrgyz economy. Raw material investors, especially in the sphere of gold mining, are little concerned about the general investment and economic climate in the host country. On the one hand, so precious a commodity as gold ensures a level of political and personal contacts in the upper echelons of local authorities that insulates their projects from shifts in the national investment climate. On the other hand, given the specific character of a good like gold, such projects are normally based on individual, not standardized, agreements.

Having suffered a fiasco in moving its goods to world markets and attracting direct foreign investment, Kyrgyzstan was very successful in one sphere: amassing foreign debt. In a record span of time, by 1999 this country—which in the first few years of the post-Soviet period had no foreign debt obligations—raised these to 134 percent of the GDP (see Table 8.5). In 2002, after recognizing Bishkek's inability to service its debt, the Paris Club of investors agreed to restructure the foreign debt of Kyrgyzstan.

A rather tense situation with respect to foreign indebtedness is also emerging in Uzbekistan. That became especially apparent after the sharp devaluation of the national currency (*sum*) in 1999–2002. The growing problem of foreign indebtedness indeed was one of the main factors driving Uzbekistan to renew its dialogue with international financial agencies in 2001.

Standard of Living, Poverty, and Inequality

The massive fall in production led to a sharp fall of living standards in post-Soviet space. At the same time, all the post-Soviet countries (in this regard Kyrgyzstan and Uzbekistan were no exception) witnessed the formation of an extremely tiny stratum with a high level of income. The privatization of the few effective assets demolished the former, quasi-egalitarian system of income distribution and gave rise to a sharply polarized society. The great majority of people sank into absolute poverty; no more than 3 to 4 percent of the population accrued fabulous gains from the process of market transition. Not surprisingly, the winners consisted mainly of those holding political power and their relatives.

The rapidity with which Central Asian societies became mired in poverty and deprivation cannot fail to leave a deep impression. However, the lack of reliable data makes it difficult to analyze this human catastrophe. The large number of specialized studies (almost exclusively devoted to Kyrgyzstan) relies on flawed and contradictory data; nor are these studies entirely comparable or consistent. Still, they do provide a rather accurate and consistent

Table 8.5

Foreign Indebtedness of Kyrgyzstan and Uzbekistan

Indicator/country	1994	1995	1996	1997	1998	1999	2000	2001	2002	2003[a]
Foreign Debt (millions of U.S. dollars)										
Kyrgyzstan	1,244		1,151	1,356	1,480	1,674	1,704	1,678	1,785	1,980
Uzbekistan		1,787	2,357	2,864	3,473	4,685	4,340	4,533	4,886	4,875
Foreign debt (percent of GDP)										
Kyrgyzstan			64	77	91	134	125	110	111	104
Uzbekistan-1[b]		18	17	19	23	25	32	39	50	49
Uzbekistan-2[c]		23	37	43	53	104	106	106	87	53
Uzbekistan-3[d]		20	22	31	38	41	50	57	63	51
Servicing the foreign debt (percent of exported goods and services)										
Kyrgyzstan	5		10	12	20	21	27	31	18	
Uzbekistan		7	9	13	11	20	31	38	36	
Servicing the foreign debt (percent of revenues of state budget)										
Kyrgyzstan	3		23	36	51	72	60	66	38	
Uzbekistan		7	9	13	8	12	24			

Sources: World Bank, *Republic of Uzbekistan: Country Economic Memorandum,* Report No. 25625-UZ (30 April 2003), p. 7; World Bank, *Uzbekistan Social and Structural Policy Review,* Report No. 19626 (25 August 1999), p. 6; *Biulleten' Natsional'nogo banka Kyrgyzskoi Respubliki,* no. 1 (Bishkek 2003), pp. 72–73; database of the Statistical Committee of the CIS; sources cited in table 8.8.

[a]Data for 2003 represent the rough estimates of the author.

[b]Uzbekistan-1: GDP is calculated on the basis of the official exchange rate.

[c]Uzbekistan-2: GDP is calculated on the basis of the black market exchange rate.

[d]Uzbekistan-3: Arithmetic mean for GDP per the official exchange rate and the black market exchange rate.

picture of the dynamics of immiseration in these countries.

If one examines the pauperization process in terms of criteria set by the countries themselves, it turns out that by the mid-1990s between 52 and 57 percent of the population of Kyrgyzstan lived below the official poverty line.[7] Throughout the second half of the 1990s, poverty remained on this high level and, according to some data, even increased. As a rule, the failure to reduce poverty in Kyrgyzstan in the second half of the 1990s is usually attributed to the negative influence of the Russian financial-economic crisis of 1998.[8] Not until 2000 do the statistics show even minimal improvements. However, specialists have concluded that the renewed growth of the GDP in the second half of the 1990s did contribute to a reduction in the absolute and relative scale of poverty, especially in rural areas.[9] According to sample studies based on official data, the proportion of poor households fell from 52.0 percent in 2000 to 47.6 percent in 2001, and to 44.4 percent in 2002.[10]

Nevertheless, there are good reasons to suspect that this official decrease in poverty levels in Kyrgyzstan was probably a mere statistical phenomenon. That is because the government, heeding recommendations from the World Bank, altered the composition of its minimal consumer basket, increasing the share of foodstuffs and excluding more expensive goods and services. The cost of a minimal consumer basket, which is used to determine the level of poverty, dropped from 40 dollars in 1997 to 30 dollars in 2002.[11]

The dynamics of expenditures of the population also suggest a lack of tangible progress in reducing poverty in Kyrgyzstan (see Table 8.6). In 1998–2001, the median expenditures of the urban population remained virtually unchanged. Significantly, both the city and the countryside reported a growth of expenditures among the poorest and poor strata of the population. The expenditures of the upper quintile in the city in 2001 remained on the level of 1998, but dropped by 5 percentage points in the countryside.

Uzbekistan does not conduct national research on poverty. However, drawing on the comparative study by B. Milanovich, one can surmise that Uzbekistan lagged behind Kyrgyzstan in the growth of poverty, especially in the first half of the 1990s. In 1993, only 39 to 66 percent of the population of Uzbekistan had incomes under 120 dollars per month (in the purchasing power of the national currency), compared to the analogous indicator of 86–88 percent for Kyrgyzstan.[12] Significantly, at the end of the Soviet period, poverty in Uzbekistan had actually been far more widespread than in Kyrgyzstan.

The lack of information makes it very difficult to compare Uzbekistan and Kyrgyzstan since the mid-1990s. The most recent studies of the World Bank indicate that, according to the criteria "foodstuff poverty," Uzbekistan's

Table 8.6

Dynamics of Expenditures of the Population of Kyrgyzstan (by Socioeconomic Quintiles, 1998 = 100)

Year	Urban population						Rural population					
	All	I	II	III	IV	V	All	I	II	III	IV	V
1998	100	100	100	100	100	100	100	100	100	100	100	100
1999	80	115	94	97	89	87	99	100	99	99	95	88
2000	98	119	104	105	102	99	102	104	102	106	103	95
2001	100	124	139	110	107	101	107	109	108	109	110	95

Sources: L. Cord, R. Lopez, M. Huppi, and O. Melo, "Growth and Rural Poverty in the CIS-7. Case Studies of Georgia, the Kyrgyz Republic, and Moldava" (paper presented to the Lucerne Conference of the CIS-7 Initiative, 20–22 January 2003), Annex C.

average is better than Kyrgyzstan's.[13] In other words, a smaller percent of the population in Uzbekistan is unable to acquire the foodstuffs needed to ensure the consumption of the minimal quantity of calories.

The data of the Statistical Committee of the CIS support the conclusion that, in terms of per capita consumption, during the last decade Uzbek indicators drew even with those in Kyrgyzstan, and in some respects surpassed them. In terms of basic food consumption and essential social services, Uzbekistan has surpassed or lags only slightly behind Kyrgyzstan.[14]

Kyrgyzstan differs from Uzbekistan in another respect: it has a much less equitable distribution of incomes. The Gini coefficient in Kyrgyzstan approaches 0.5; according to some data, it is even in the range of 0.55 to 0.68. Kyrgyzstan therefore ranks, along with several Latin American and the most backward African countries, in the category of countries having the most unequal distribution of incomes. The initial explosion of inequality first appeared in 1992–1993; it was closely associated with the shock liberalization of the economy. The ratio of the incomes of the top decile of the richest to the bottom decile of the poorest leaped from 4.65 in 1988 to 56.7 in 1993.[15] Thereafter the Gini coefficient somewhat stabilized and even decreased. The renewal of economic growth in the second half of the 1990s brought a new regressive redistribution of incomes. In principle, this corresponds to Simon Kuznets's hypothesis that contemporary economic growth in countries with a low level of per capita income must, in the first stages, be accompanied by an intensification of inequality. It is quite another matter that world experience is laden with sad examples of the fact that the least developed states remain—for decades—in the trap of the most profound inequality.

Real Wages

For the overwhelming majority of people in post-Soviet states, the main source of income is still wages. Accordingly, the dynamic of personal incomes is critically dependent on the dynamics of wages. Quantitative data are available for the dynamics of the nominal, real, and dollar-equivalent wages in Kyrgyzstan and Uzbekistan during the period from 1989 to 2002 (see Table 8.7). To obtain a comprehensive picture, I have used the assessments of consumer inflation that are regularly published by the International Monetary Fund (IMF) and the Economic Commission of the United Nations for Europe.

The existing assessments of the dynamics of real wages in Uzbekistan are highly contradictory, and in my judgment, those of the IMF are closer to the truth. If one relies on the latter assessments, it is possible to conclude that: (a) real wages in Uzbekistan have fallen noticeably less sub-

Table 8.7

Wages in Kyrgyzstan and Uzbekistan

Indicator/country	1990	1991	1992	1993	1994	1995	1996	1997	1998	1999	2000	2001	2002	2003
Average nominal wage (national currency)														
Kyrgyzstan				85	233	368	491	681	841	1,050	1,227	1,455	1,616	
Uzbekistan					265	1,066	2,155	3,215	4,482	7,134	12,492	18,424	27,511	
Consumer inflation (percent)														
Kyrgyzstan (IMF)[a]	4.2	85	853.8	772.4	190.1	43.5	32.0	19.6	10.5	35.9	18.7	6.9	2.0	3.3
Kyrgyzstan (ECE)[b]	5.5	113.9	854.6	1,208.7	278.1	42.9	31.3	23.4	10.3	35.7	18.7	7.0	2.1	3.0
Uzbekistan (IMF)[a]	4.0	109.7	645.2	534.2	1,568.3	204.6	54.0	70.9	16.7	44.6	50.7	48.9	38.7	21.9
Uzbekistan (ECE)[b]	5.8	97.3	414.5	1,231.8	1,550.0	76.5	54.0	58.8	17.7	29.0	24.9			
Real wages (1989 = 100)														
Kyrgyzstan (IMF)[a]	104.5	82.1	59.5	27.8	20.0	22.1	22.4	25.2	28.2	26.0	25.6	28.4	31.0	
Kyrgyzstan (ECE)[b]	106.1	96.4	69.9	48.9	45.8	50.3	50.8	58.9	65.9	60.6	59.7	66.2	72.1	
Uzbekistan (IMF)[a]	106.6	86.5	81.9	136.8	79.0	78.5	103.0	89.9	107.4	118.2	137.2	135.9	146.2	
Uzbekistan (ECE)[b]	104.7	90.3	123.8	99.1	57.9	131.9	173.1	162.6	192.6	237.6				
Average monthly wage in dollars (per current exchange rate)														
Kyrgyzstan				17	22	34	38	39	40	27	26	30	35	43
Uzbekistan[c]				30	27	36	54	48	57	71	41	39	36	42
Uzbekistan[d]					14	28	34	22	25	17	13	15	20	39
Uzbekistan[e]					18	31	42	30	41	44	27	27	28	40

Sources: Uzbekistan Economy: Statistical and Analytical Review, pp. 23, 67; *Economic Survey of Europe*, 2004, no. 1; *World Economic Outlook*, September 2003, database; databases of the Statistical Committee of the CIS.

[a]Database of the International Monetary Fund.

[b]Database of the Economic Commission of Europe.

[c]Wages per the official exchange rate.

[d]Wages per the black market exchange rate.

[e]Wages as the arithmetic mean between the official and blackmarket exchange rates.

stantially than in Kyrgyzstan; and (b) the renewal of economic growth in Uzbekistan brought an accelerated growth of wages. The latter circumstance is the decisive argument in support of the proposition that, with respect to poverty levels, Uzbekistan is in a better position than neighboring Kyrgyzstan.

However, if one uses dollar estimates of wages, the situation is far more complicated. In 2002 the average monthly wage in Kyrgyzstan was thirty-five U.S. dollars; that corresponds to the level there in 1995 and is lower than the indicators for 1996–1998. According to the official exchange rage, the wages in Uzbekistan in 2002 were a bit higher than in Kyrgyzstan. However, if one takes into account the official and parallel black-market exchange rates, the wages in Uzbekistan in 2002 were lower than in 1995–1998, and one-quarter lower than the analogous indicator in Kyrgyzstan.

State Intervention in the Economy

Reducing the state's role (direct and indirect) in the economy to a minimum has been the heart of stabilization programs that international donors have advocated in Kyrgyzstan. It is thought that state intervention in economic life causes numerous, sometimes insuperable distortions that prevent the release of the creative forces of a free, unfettered market.

One of the main methods of de-statification is the privatization of state enterprises. By 1997, the majority of enterprises in Kyrgyzstan had already been put in private hands. Parallel with privatization, the state budget was deprived of its most important source of revenue. Privatization also contributed to the "collapse of the state," which—as a result of the breakup of the USSR and the unified Soviet economy—had already lost most of its capacity to perform the most important social-economic functions. Tax revenues in Kyrgyzstan dropped from 27.1 percent of GDP in 1990 to an average of 16.1 percent in the period 1991–1995, and sank to just 13.5 percent in 1996–2000 (see Table 8.8).

Due to social and political factors, state expenditures were not as sharply reduced. They decreased from 32 percent of GDP in 1992 to an average of 20 percent for the period 1996–2000. In 1994–1997 the budget deficit in Kyrgyzstan declined from 7.7 to 5.2 percent of the GDP.

The struggle to reduce the budget deficit, as the main generator of inflation, lay at the heart of stabilization programs implemented in Kyrgyzstan under the counsel of international financial organizations. The main thrust of these programs was usually aimed at suppressing demand. However, one of the main causes of the extremely acute budgetary imbalance in Kyrgyzstan

Table 8.8

The State Sector in Kyrgyzstan and Uzbekistan (percent of GDP)

Country/Item	1990	1991	1992	1993	1994	1995	1996	1997	1998	1999	2000	2001	2002
Kyrgyzstan: state budget													
Revenues													
Total	38.3	35.1	34.0	24.1	16.7	17.0	16.8	16.6	18.3	16.6	15.3	17.0	19.2
Taxes and fees only	27.1	22.6	14.6	14.8	13.6	15	13.2	12.5	14.2	12.3	15.3	15.9	17.9
Expenditures	39.1	30.6	32.0	23.4	24.4	28.6	22.2	21.8	21.4	19.1	17.3	16.6	20.2
Deficit	-0.8	4.5	1.4	0.7	-7.7	-11.6	-5.4	-5.2	-3.1	-2.5	-2.0	0.4	-1.0
Kyrgyzstan: fiscal deficit (current transactions of the state)													
Revenues						16.7	15.9	16.2	18.0	17.7	15.9		
Expenditures						33.2	25.2	25.3	28.8	30.4	24.9	22.2	23.7
Deficit						-17.3	-9.5	-9.2	-9.5	-11.9	-9.2	-5.0	-5.6
Uzbekistan: state budget													
Revenues													
Total	45.0	45.5	32.8	36.0	29.1	29.6	32.3	30.1	32.4	30.5	28.5	26.0	25.2
Tax and fees only	25.6	26.0	26.4	28.4	23.3	27.7	32.3	27.7	30.7	28.9	26.6	23.4	23.0
Expenditures	45.9	50.4	43.7	39.0	33.3	32.4	35.6	40.4	34.5	32.2	29.5	27.0	26.0
Deficit	-0.9	-4.9	-10.9	-3.0	-4.2	-2.8	-3.3	-1.7	-2.1	-1.7	-1.0	-1.0	-0.8

Uzbekistan: unified state
budget[a]

Deficit

-11.3 -19.6 -4.1 -3.5 -6.3 -2.2 -2.4 -2.5 -2.3 -2.0 -2.2

Uzbekistan: real balance
of state sector

Deficit

-12.4 -2.5 -10.1 -9.9 -2.7 -3.9 -3.5

Sources: Sodruzhestvo nezavisimykh gosudarstv v 2001 g., pp. 407, 411, 652, 655; 10 let Sodruzhestva nezavisimykh gosudarstv (1991-2001), pp. 38-39, 399, 403, 647, 650; Gosudarstva byvshego Sovetskogo Soiuza. Statisticheskii sbornik. 1993 god. (September 1993), pp. 343, 345, 727, 729; The UN System in the Kyrgyz Republic: Common Country Assessment, 2003, p. 46; Republic of Uzbekistan: Country Economic Memorandum, World Bank Memorandum (30 April 2003), p. 7; IMF, Kyrgyz Republic: Financial System Stability Assessment, Including Reports on the Observance of Standards and Codes (February 2003); IMF, Kyrgyz Republic: Statistical Appendix, IMF Country Report No. 01/224 (December 2001), p. 29; V. Summers and K. Baer, "Revenue Policy and Administration in the CIS-7: Recent Trends and Future Challenges" (paper presented to the Lucerne Conference on the CIS-7 Initiative, 20–22 January 203), p. 4; V. Tanzi and G. Tsibouris, "Fiscal Reform over Ten Years of Transition," IMF Working Paper 00/113 (June 2000), pp. 18–19, 24; data provided by the National Statistics Bureau.

[a]Including extrabudgetary funds and expenditures.

[b]Including foreign loans (state and state-guaranteed) outside the state budget, but also the overvalued and deflated profit of the Central Bank.

was the practical application of the ideas of the "Old Washington Consensus." The collapse of a unified Soviet economy meant an end to Kyrgyzstan's subsidies from the centralized all-union budget; it also deprived local enterprises of traditional markets. Privatization of the profitable spheres (for example, alcoholic and tobacco production, which for decades had been the most important sources of budgetary revenues) drove aggregate demand down to still lower levels.

Foreign assistance (which was significant relative to the modest scale of the GDP) helped to avoid a complete economic collapse and enabled the government to maintain a level of expenditures that would avert a social and political explosion. Relative to its GDP, Kyrgyzstan received the largest infusion of foreign resources among all the poorest post-Soviet economies.[16] Moreover, international donors in effect closed their eyes to the fact that the fiscal deficit in 1995–2000 was approximately 10 percent of GDP (dropping to 5 percent in 2001–2002). Once the plug is pulled on foreign assistance, Kyrgyzstan will experience a substantial decrease in state revenues and a new shock of demand compression.

Uzbekistan not only rejected mass privatization, but chose another tactic to offset the collapse of demand caused by the disintegration of a single Soviet economy. At the peak of the breakdown (in 1991–1992), in an effort to compensate for enterprises for losing traditional markets and for the contraction of subsidies from the all-union budget, the government propped up demand through inflationary financing. Thereafter the government began gradually cutting back on expenditures, but most importantly increased tax collections. To a large degree, this was possible because the regime had refused to carry out an ill-considered mass privatization. Simultaneously, the government ensured a compulsory redistribution of financial and investment resources for the state sector (its volume being roughly equal to 10 percent of GDP). As the state later began to liberalize its economy, it substantially reduced the scale of inflationary financing by reducing the budget deficit and especially by cutting back on the redistribution of resources to state enterprises. It also made a parallel reduction in the level of tax collection.

Nonetheless, in the scale of its redistribution of resources through the state budget, Uzbekistan has actually been close to the East European transition economies. Significantly, in the East European economies undergoing market transition, tax revenues decreased relative to GDP, but with rare exceptions did not drop below one third of GDP. De-statification on a scale comparable to that in Kyrgyzstan appeared only in the utterly criminalized war economy of Albania and, for a brief period, in Croatia. The latter, however, in just three years raised tax collections from 14.3 percent of GDP

(1991) to 26.9 percent (1994). By 1998, tax revenues in that country had risen to 31 percent of GDP.[17]

As Jeffrey Sachs pointed out in 1996, preservation of a very high level of state revenues in the three economic leaders of the post-socialist world— Hungary, Poland, and the Czech Republic—was one of the surprises of the process of transition from a planned to a market economy.[18] Having reduced indirect subsidies, the successful transition economies simultaneously preserved (or even increased!) the level of tax collection, thereby enabling them to support social expenditures and ensure mass support for reform. The level of state expenditures in the leading transition economies of Eastern and Central Europe noticeably exceeded the analogous indicators of the fast-growing, developing countries with a similar per capita GDP.

Paradoxically, the massive contraction of state participation in the economy of Kyrgyzstan was accompanied by a simultaneous expansion of the state apparatus. In 1991–2001, the number of people employed in its administrative organs grew by 2.1 times (from 36,600 to 75,800); whereas, at the outset of transition, Kyrgyzstan had 8 officials per 1,000 inhabitants, by 2001 that indicator had risen to 15. During this same period, Uzbekistan increased the number of administrative personnel by 1.32 times, but maintained a ratio of 5 officials per 1,000 inhabitants.[19]

Balance of Gains and Losses

If one assesses the interim results of development in Kyrgyzstan and Uzbekistan, the following (even if hypothetical) questions are entirely appropriate. What results could Uzbekistan have expected in the event it adopted the ideology and practice of the Washington Consensus? And what would have been the results if Kyrgyzstan had opted for a more active state intervention in economic life? The answers are quite obvious. The social and economic situation in Kyrgyzstan would hardly have been substantially worse than it is now. Moreover, it is entirely probable that the real state of affairs would have been somewhat better than a latent socioeconomic catastrophe. Uzbekistan, had it followed the old Washington Consensus, would almost certainly have repeated the drama of what transpired in Kyrgyzstan.

Is it not possible that Kyrgyzstan won in the long-term framework, having laid the preconditions for a future market—at the expense of the inevitable sacrifices and deprivation in the first decade of independence? Is it not possible that Uzbekistan, by contrast, squandered its deficit resources and time in sustaining a clearly nonviable social and economic structure and only delayed its inevitable collapse? To give an adequate answer to these crucial questions, it is essential to make a nuanced assessment of development in both countries during the first decade of independence.

Dynamics and Sustainability of Economic Growth

Over the last decade Kyrgyzstan has devoured what it inherited from the USSR. The profound productive decline in the first half of the 1990s erased the achievements of several preceding generations. The per capita GDP of Kyrgyzstan was lower in 2003 than in 1970. After three years of relatively explosive growth in 1996–1998, the rates drifted downwards and were even in negative territory in 2002. If Kyrgyzstan maintains a per capita GDP growth rate of 3 to 4 percent, it will require almost two decades just to restore the level achieved in 1990. However, domestic investments in 2001–2003 amounted to only half of the 1991 level, while direct foreign investment has averaged about seven million dollars during the same period (see Table 8.4). Given all this, it is not entirely clear whether Kyrgyzstan can sustain a steady rate of growth. As noted above, the production of gold at the Kumtor mines will fall off sharply in 2005, making the midterm prospects of growth still more uncertain.

Uzbekistan survived the first shocks of independence and market transition with fewer losses. Although the average per capita growth in GDP in 1971–2003 was 0.25 percent per annum and, given the unreliability of Uzbek statistics, perhaps even lower, Uzbekistan did not squander but somewhat increased its Soviet legacy. The country is developing at an average annual rate that, in my judgment, corresponds to its modest potential.

Standard of Living

The standard of living and, especially, the quality of life declined sharply in both countries. Moreover, the Uzbek indicators approached and even equaled Kyrgyz levels. That became possible because of the massive decline in incomes and consumption in Kyrgyzstan.

In both countries, personal consumption continues to be restructured toward basic necessities, above all, foodstuffs. Apparently because poverty is more widespread in Kyrgyzstan, the average consumption of food products is lower there than in Uzbekistan.

During the restorative upsurge from the mid-1990s, real wages grew at a faster rate in Uzbekistan than in Kyrgyzstan. However, that conclusion is not sustained if wages are expressed in nominal dollars. Whatever the case may be, economic growth in Kyrgyzstan has not been accompanied by a faster growth in wages (and, therefore, in the personal incomes of the great majority of the populace) than in Uzbekistan.

Efficiency of Growth

In important criteria of efficiency like labor productivity and energy consumption per unit of output, Uzbekistan has drawn noticeably closer to Kyrgyzstan. In grain yields in 2001–2003, Uzbekistan surged ahead of Kyrgyzstan for the first time. The next two to three years will show whether Uzbekistan can maintain this higher rate of growth in labor productivity in the agrarian sector.

Dynamics of the Foreign Sector

In no other sphere did the failure of neoclassical dogmas become so manifest as in the dynamic of indicators for Kyrgyzstan's foreign trade and direct investment. The country has consistently liberalized transactions on current accounts, and later on capital accounts in the balance of payments. It has submitted to the harsh requirements of the World Trade Organization, which requires that Kyrgyzstan maintain a single economic and legal regime for both domestic and foreign companies. Transactions on the hard currency market are freely conducted; investors have no problem repatriating profits; exporters suffer no discrimination vis-à-vis producers operating on the domestic market.

Nonetheless, despite this relatively favorable economic and investment climate (in the neoclassical sense), Kyrgyzstan has not succeeded in attracting significant direct foreign investment. The success in the export sector has also been quite modest. Because of the unusually high product and geographic concentration of Kyrgyz exports, these dynamics are wholly determined by the demand on foreign markets, and also the world price of gold.

In terms of indebtedness and capacity to service foreign obligations, Kyrgyzstan (along with Georgia) proved the most problematic of all the seven poorest countries in the CIS.

Uzbekistan has also failed to have much success either in gaining a niche on world markets, or in attracting direct foreign investment. Yet one should bear in mind that: (a) the export breakthrough, along with direct foreign investments, until recently were not high-priority goals of Uzbek economic policy; and (b) in terms of the trade and monetary balance, and in terms of the capacity to service foreign debts and to support critical exports, Uzbekistan appears to be in a substantially better position than Kyrgyzstan.

Quality of State Intervention

Various international ratings that assess the local institutional environment and the quality of governance have, until recently, given a clear preference to Kyrgyzstan over Uzbekistan. However, these formal indicators have little relevance to economic growth. Although for many years Kyrgyzstan was a leader in market reforms, this did not enable a take off onto a trajectory of stable development based on foreign trade and investment. And it was not for want of sufficient attempts to do so. On the contrary, in this regard the country spent much more than enough energy.

It is another matter that, under the prevailing conditions in Kyrgyzstan, the opportunities for sustained development on the basis of direct foreign investment and export demand have objective limitations. It is hardly a sign of effective governance if a regime chooses and tries to realize goals that are manifestly difficult (if not impossible) to achieve. Still worse, the decade of transition, which was facilitated by foreign assistance, gave rise to a special type of bureaucracy. The tug-of-war within the government, together with the endless reorganizations and purges of personnel, created the deceptive illusion of a chaotic Brownian movement. In reality, behind this mirage of bureaucratic chaos was the drive of local governing groups to divert foreign credits and assistance to their own benefit. International assistance to Kyrgyzstan in the first half of the 1990s reached 15 to 20 percent of GDP, but that was all used in the most inefficient ways–and not only because of shortcomings in the economic policy imposed by foreign donors. A major contribution to the plundering of foreign resources came from the local bureaucracy—to be sure, in collaboration with the numerous foreign advisors and consultants.

In the mid-1970s A. Krueger formulated the thesis about rent-oriented behavior as an obstacle to healthy economic growth.[20] It is ironic that the moving force of rent-oriented behavior of the post-Soviet Kyrgyz nomenklatura (political elite) was assistance from international financial organizations. Worse is the fact that "participation in the assimilation of this aid" became the organizing principle and raison d'être of this elite for many years ahead. As demonstrated in the model of J. A. Tirole (who analyzes the dynamics of the so-called "collective reputation capital"), new members of the organization (or firms) can replicate the behavior of their predecessors for a very long period of time.[21]

But one should not nourish any illusions about the magnitude of corruption in Uzbekistan. If, however, one disregards the upper echelons of local bureaucracy, corruption in that country is largely tied to the physical volume of production. Hence the opportunities for personal enrichment of the locally ruling groups are closely linked to the dynamics of production. Without in the least seeking to justify corruption, one must admit that corruption, under Uzbek conditions, has a "productive character" (figuratively speaking). In our non-ideal world, this is a lesser evil than the parasitic diversion of external resources: "productive corruption" is less of an impediment to economic growth.

Another characteristic distinguishing the Uzbek bureaucracy from the Kyrgyz is its acceptance of discipline. During the past decade, Uzbekistan has had three regimes of economic policy: (a) laying the foundations of a national economy by the elimination of structural distortions inherited from the Soviet era (1992–1995); (b) import substitution by means of a centralized redistribution of resources confiscated from the agrarian sector (1995–2000); and (c) a relative liberalization of the economy (2000 to the present). In all cases the authorities found it rather easy to shift the executive apparatus from one policy to the next. In general terms, the capacity to reformulate goals and objectives of economic policy attests to the flexibility and mobility of the Uzbek bureaucracy and to a higher level of discipline in the state bureaucracy.

The foregoing is not intended to endorse the myth of an "economic miracle" in Uzbekistan. The development of that country after gaining independence is rife with examples of the most primitive mistakes and miscalculations. Thus, in 1995–1999, authorities in charge of the economy blundered in their choice of sectoral priorities for investment, for they concentrated on projects—in motor vehicle production, consumer electronics, petrochemicals, and so forth—that were plainly inefficient.[22] The most substantial mistake was the failure to appreciate the high-priority importance of the agrarian sector (if one excludes the policy to ensure self-sufficiency in grain production); the result was discrimination in favor of industry and urban services. Moreover, the potential for development in Uzbekistan, to a large degree, was not realized because authorities underestimated the destructive consequences of a well-developed hard-currency black market. Indeed, the gap between the official and black market exchange rates was steadily widening. The most serious miscalculation was to underestimate the importance of the export sector.

Lessons for Each Other

What important lessons might Kyrgyzstan and Uzbekistan draw from each other's experience? This question is relevant for both economies. On the one hand, in 1999–2000 Uzbekistan began a gradual liberalization of its entire economic system. Despite the unification of the exchange rate (at present, the difference between the official and black market rates amounts to approximately 1–2 percent) and the liberalization of the current accounts balance (in compliance with Article VIII of the IMF), Uzbekistan is still at an embryonic stage in the liberalization process. The experience of the Kyrgyz economy (which is structurally similar to Uzbekistan and has the greatest openness among post-Soviet countries) is particularly important for Uzbekistan. On the other hand, the Kyrgyz economy is in difficult straits; to escape from the vicious circle of underdevelopment and poverty, it obviously needs new ideas and approaches.

Let us begin with Kyrgyzstan. Hypothetically, it could draw the following lessons from the experience of Uzbekistan:

* Active involvement of the state does not impede economic growth. Under the concrete conditions of Kyrgyzstan, an unfettered market proves to be just as unproductive as totally centralized interference in the economic process.
* The government should shift its main focus from the financial to the productive sphere of the economy.
* Support for economic development requires a high level of centralized expenditures—first and foremost, for education and public health, but also for infrastructure development. Accordingly, it is imperative to increase the income base; that includes having the state participate directly in productive activities.
* State (or state-guaranteed) investment does not exclude but rather stimulates investment activity in the private sector.
* Moderate inflation is not an obstacle to economic growth. Under the conditions in Uzbekistan and Kyrgyzstan, a controlled inflation that stimulates demand is an efficacious lever for lifting the economy from a stagnant equilibrium at a very low level of production and consumption.

This list of general and particular lessons could be extended. The key question, however, is whether Kyrgyzstan is capable of using the experience of its neighbor. To pose the question so baldly suggests the "path dependency" paradigm, which holds that the current actions of economic and political actors were predetermined by all previous development. This paradigm, which has become popular in various subfields of economics and sociology, is a mild euphemism for the old Marxist thesis that historical development is the inexorable result of myriad, contradictory interests (which are manifested in specific social-class and social-cultural contexts).

If one takes into account path dependency, the choice of different models of development in Kyrgyzstan and Uzbekistan was not a simple subjective choice of the ruling groups. This choice was predetermined by the preceding history of the two republics. The point where the trajectories of Uzbekistan and Kyrgyzstan fundamentally diverged was Gorbachev's perestroika. As the Gorbachev team established its authority, on the one hand it endeavored to crush the resistance of the conservative part of the Soviet nomenklatura, and on the other hand sought to broaden its circles of allies. Because the Uzbek cotton complex was so closely intertwined with the nomenklatura-clan networks in the late Soviet period, Uzbekistan found itself in the camp of conservatives. By contrast, the current leadership in Kyrgyzstan has its roots in the more liberal scientific and literary circles; hence it was organically positioned in the group of communist reformists.

The Kremlin's efforts to crush "cotton socialism" helped to consolidate the Uzbek nomenklatura against the external threat emanating from Moscow. To oppose Moscow, it could only rely on local forces and resources; it was therefore forced to defend—through every means possible—the inherited socioeconomic structure against any restructuring. At the moment when the USSR was dissolved, the Uzbek nomenklatura was united around a platform of building a national state. Committed to the process of national construction, the Uzbek establishment was (to put it mildly) suspicious of the ideas of economic and political liberalization that had overtaken much of what was to become the "former USSR" in the late 1980s and early 1990s. By this time, the Uzbek nomenklatura had replaced the former communist ideology with the idea of national state-building and had already established itself as the group holding power and property in Uzbekistan.

In contrast to the elites in other Soviet republics, which were feverishly seeking an ideological platform to retain power and property, and which found that platform in the magic of the "market and democracy," the Uzbek elite did not need to make a new ideological metamorphosis. Moreover, the idea of creating an independent Uzbekistan in the early 1990s was so deeply embedded in the fabric of Uzbek society that it would have been politically dangerous to repudiate a policy aimed at national uniqueness and renewal in favor of shock-therapy liberalization.

In the initial phase Uzbekistan, like all post-Soviet countries, cooperated with the IMF and the World Bank. However, the Uzbek elite quickly understood that the standard programs of stabilization proposed by these financial donors sought to liquidate the existing social and economic structure, but in exchange did not guarantee the creation of an efficient economy (in an abstract market sense). Recognition of this basic fact predetermined the break with international financial organizations that would last until the end of the 1990s.

The social groups that came to power in Kyrgyzstan were less closely integrated into the local structure of power and property, and they were therefore relatively independent of the local power structure and interests. The reformist team therefore acted more readily in imitating the politics of Moscow. Without firm ties to the social order (as in Uzbekistan), the new political superstructure in Kyrgyzstan established its power on the crest of economic liberalization and political democratization in the first half of the 1990s. Large-scale international assistance provided both the resources to conduct reform and the individual well-being of the elite itself.

The contemporary social matrix of independent Kyrgyzstan is fundamentally different from that in Uzbekistan. Hence it cannot simply switch to a more active centralized intervention in the process of social and economic development without stimulation from international donors. Without reconstruction (more precisely, without construction *ab ovo*) of an efficacious government, in principle one cannot count on stable economic and social development in Kyrgyzstan. Moreover, it must not be a "minimalist state," but rather one that is based on a developmental paradigm. As to what a developmentalist state in post-Soviet, post-socialist conditions should possess, some useful ideas have been suggested by scholars working in the economics field of development and structuralism.[23] With respect to Kyrgyzstan specifically, R. Agarwala has formulated general proposals for a new agenda for the government and international donors.[24]

Formally, at least, international financial organizations involved in the post-Soviet transition have admitted the failure of their aid strategies of the 1990s, but that has not led to make any substantive changes in their practical policies.[25] Moreover, they continue to act as though everything was done correctly in Kyrgyzstan, and that the country only needs a further intensification and even radicalization of market transformation. For example, to summarize the practical proposals of a consultant to international organizations, A. Åslund, the Kyrgyz government and donors should concentrate on stimulating exports and should adopt more intensive reforms in the social sphere.[26]

His first proposal, unquestionably, is reasonable, albeit difficult to realize. There are always certain negative foreign factors to explain the failures of the first decade of transition in Kyrgyzstan. In the second half of the 1990s, people sought to blame these on the onerous legacy of the USSR and on the shocks associated with the acquisition of independence. Then the blame was shifted to the Russian crisis of 1998. At present, the main barrier to the development of the Kyrgyz economy has been moved once more— this time, to its neighbors. Of course, from the perspective of an abstract market, both Kazakhstan and Uzbekistan "impede" Kyrgyz exports. To be sure, that will continue in the future; after all, history shows an unending competition of national, group, corporate, and personal interests. In strategic terms, Kyrgyzstan is hardly likely to increase significantly its deliveries to the markets of its neighbors and Russia. Moreover, given that the latter are poor, they will—for decades to come—produce essentially the same assortment of products. In addition, the sheer distance between Kyrgyzstan and Russia, and hence the high transportation costs, mean that Kyrgyzstan can only compete on Russian markets with the most simple agricultural products—and only if a very low level of wages is maintained in the country. And that of course contradicts the goal of overcoming poverty.

In the social sphere, the recommendations propose to reduce expenditures on education, social privileges, and pension payments, and simultaneously to increase the retirement age and to liberalize the labor market.[27] It hardly needs to be said that these proposals will only lead to more poverty and deprivation.

A careful analysis by experts from the IMF and World Bank showed that the economic development of Kyrgyzstan was, to a significant degree, blocked by the institutional environment that arose during the years of transition. As a first step toward healthy growth, it is essential to recognize that this institutional matrix was the product not only of internal forces, but also (if not primarily) foreign donors. Unless all this is reformed, there is no reason to expect positive gains. A second, still more difficult, step consists in jettisoning counterproductive ideas about reducing government to a bare minimum. The issue is not the scale of state involvement in economic life, but the quality of its intervention. A deliberate reinvolvement of the state represents the main challenge for Kyrgyzstan and its donors in the immediate historical perspective.

For its part, Uzbekistan can also learn from the experience of its neighbor —not so much concrete techniques for successful development, but mainly the negative lessons of a conceptual character. The development of Kyrgyzstan after independence shows the following:

- Under post-Soviet conditions, it is essential to be creative in the practical implementation of the IMF slogan about "getting prices right." During the entire course of transition, Kyrgyzstan continued to support relatively low prices on the main productive resource—electric power. After the price insanity in the first half of the 1990s, the prices on electricity also dropped; that was the basis for the renewal of positive growth rates there, as indeed throughout the CIS.
- Parallel to domestic and foreign liberalization, the entire power of state support must be directed at stimulating national exporters. The flow of hard currency is critically important both for supporting macroeconomic stability and for financing the imports of machinery and equipment. The East Asian miracle as a positive example and Kyrgyzstan as a nega-

tive model explicitly demonstrate that exports constitute the key dynamic in an open, small developing economy.

- Probably the main lesson to be learned from Kyrgyzstan is that privatization in combination with liberalization does not automatically generate economic agents with a strategic horizon for decision making. During a period of post-privatization, institutional chaos, short-term maximizers flourish and dominate in the form of financial and trade intermediaries; in industry the "red director" is replaced by highly specialized managers, who are concerned about utilizing the economic assets (often acquired through secret deals on the basis of insider information) for their own personal aggrandizement. The state is "captured" by financial-economic groups; the latter are interested in a quick maximalization of profit at any price, with a subsequent diversion of resources from the national economy. To avoid this post-privatization trap, political authorities must not only keep a functioning economic bureaucracy in good condition, but do everything possible to promote the maturation of the private sector and integrate it into the long-term development of the country.
- Perhaps the sole important positive lesson that Uzbekistan can take from the experience of Kyrgyzstan is that a greater degree of freedom for economic agents does not prevent the realization of strategic national interests. A powerful, independent private sector can and must be a long-term partner of a functional economic bureaucracy.

Conclusion

Thus, more than a decade after the beginning of independent development, Kyrgyzstan and Uzbekistan once again find themselves close to each other with respect to the majority of key economic and social characteristics. Kyrgyzstan fully (though not with absolute consistency) followed the recommendations of the IMF and World Bank, which were formulated in the spirit of the neoclassical mainstream. Uzbekistan, by contrast, demonstratively rejected the advice of the Bretton Woods tandem and chose "its own path," which, in practice, meant weaving together Soviet economic management, import substitution, and active developmentalism.

The paradoxically similar results of such different models of development suggest that, in the long term, the dynamics and level of economic development depend not so much on the instruments of economic policy as on other factors—geographic location, level of internal savings, the character of state authority, the maturity of the private sector, and so forth. In spite of many differences, Kyrgyzstan and Uzbekistan remain primarily agrarian economies with a virtually unlimited supply of labor. The functioning and long-term dynamics of such economic systems are determined by patterns described long ago in a pioneering study by W. A. Lewis.[28] As before, the prospects of Kyrgyzstan and Uzbekistan, to a decisive degree, depend on their capacity to raise the norm of domestic savings and investment, to ensure stable and efficient development in the agrarian sector, and to find optimal proportions between agriculture and industry as well as between export promotion and import substitution.

Notes

1. J. Zettelmeyer, "The Uzbek Growth Puzzle," IMF Working Paper no. 98/133 (1 September 1998).

2. S. V. Zhukov and O. B. Reznikova, *Tsentral'naia Aziia v sotsial'no-ekonomicheskikh strukturakh sovremennogo mira* (Moscow, 2001), pp. 57–58.

3. In 1990–1991, the outright grants (requiring no repayment) from the all-union budget reached 11.2 to 12.5 percent of GDP in Kyrgyzstan and 19.4 to 19.5 percent of GDP in Uzbekistan. See Zhukov and Reznikova, *Tsentral'naia Aziia*, p. 55.

4. See D. Tarr, "How Moving to World Prices Affects the Terms of Trade in Fifteen Countries of the Former Soviet Union," *Journal of Comparative Economics* 18 (1994).

5. See Zhukov and Reznikova, *Tsentral'naia Aziia*, p. 54.

6. Eskender Trushin, "Problems of Development and Reform in the Agrarian Sector," in *Central Asia: The Challenges of Independence*, ed. B. Rumer and S. Zhukov (Armonk, NY, 1998), p. 273.

7. World Bank, *World Development Indicators 2002* (Washington, DC, 2003), pp. 69–70; Kyrgyzstan, "National Human Development Report 2002" at www.undp.kg/publications; World Bank, *Making Transition Work for Everyone: Poverty and Equality in Europe and Central Asia* (Washington, DC, 2001), pp. 35, 37, 73; World Bank, "Poverty in the 1990s in the Kyrgyz Republic," World Bank Report No. 21721–KG (June 2002), p. 5; *Expanding the Country's Capacities: Comprehensive Development Framework of the Kyrgyz Republic to 2010 National Poverty Reduction Strategy, 2003–2005* (Bishkek, 2002), p. 27; and UNICEF, Innocenti Research Centre, *Poverty and Welfare Trends in Kyrgyzstan over the 1990s*, Country Report 2001.

8. J. Falkingham, "Inequality and Poverty in the CIS-7, 1989–2002" (paper presented to the Lucerne Conference on the CIS-7 Initiative, 20–22 January 2003).

9. L. Cord, R. Lopez, M. Huppi, and O. Melo, "Growth and Rural Poverty in the CIS-7. Case Studies of Georgia, the Kyrgyz Republic, and Moldova" (paper prepared for the Lucerne Conference of the CIS-7 Initiative," 20–22 January 2003).

10. "The UN System in Kyrgyz Republic: Common Country Assessment, 2003" (mimeo), p. 46.

11. Calculated on the basis of *Biulleten' Natsional'nogo Banka Kyrgyzskoi Respubliki*, no. 2(86) (Bishkek, 2003), pp. 8, 14.

12. B. Milanovic, *Inequality and Poverty during the Transition from a Planned to a Market Economy* (Washington, DC, 1998), pp. 75, 189.

13. World Bank, *Uzbekistan Living Standards Assessment: Policies to Improve Living Standards.* Vol. 2, Full Report of World Bank Report No. 25923–UZ (May 2003), pp. 10–11.

14. See *Sodruzhestvo nezavisimykh gosudarstv v 2001 godu: Statisticheskii ezhegodnik* (Moscow, 2002), pp. 140–43, 443–44, 448, 679–80, 684.

15. See the World Bank databases: www.worldbank.org/research/povmonitor/coutrydetails/Kyrgyz%20Republic.htm and www.worldbank.org/research/povmonitor/coutrydetails/Uzbekistan.htm.

16. P. R. Lane, "The International Community and the CIS-7" (paper presented to the Lucerne Conference of the CIS-7 Initiative, 20–22 January 2003), table 7.

17. V. Tanzi and G. Tsibouris, "Fiscal Reform over Ten Years of Transition," IMF Working Paper 00/113 (June 2000), p. 18.

18. J. Sachs, "The Transition at Mid-Decade," *American Economic Review* 86:2 (1996): 131–32.

19. Calculated on the basis of data in *Sodruzhestvo nezavisimykh gosudarstv v 2001 g.*, pp. 399, 404, 646, 649.

20. A. Krueger, "The Political Economy of the Rent-Seeking Society," *American Economic Review* 44 (1974): 291–303.

21. J. A. Tirole, "A Theory of Collective Reputations with Applications to the Persistence of Corruption and Firm Quality," *Review of Economic Studies* 63:1 (1996): 1–22.

22. For particulars, see Zhukov and Reznikova, *Tsentral'naia Aziia*, pp. 141–54; and S. Zhukov, "Adapting to Globalization," in *Central Asia and the New Global Economy*, ed. B. Rumer (Armonk, NY, 2000), pp. 161–69.

23. See A. Amsden, J. Kochanowicz, and L. Taylor, *The Market Meets Its Match: Restructuring the Economies of Eastern Europe* (Cambridge, MA, 1994).

24. R. Agarwala, "The Development Debacle of Kyrgyzstan and the Need for a Switch from the Washington Consensus to a Eurasian Consensus" (mimeographed paper; June 2003).

25. For details, see O. Reznikova, "Mogut li vneshnie resursy vystupit' motorom ekonomicheskogo razvitiia gosudarstva Tsentral'noi Azii i Kavkaza?" in *Tsentral'naia Aziia i Iuzhnyi Kavkaz. Nasushchnye problemy*, ed. B. Rumer (Almaty, 2002).

26. A. Oslund [A. Åslund], *Kyrgyzskaia Respublika: k ekonomicheskomu rostu cherez rasshirenie eksporta*, March 2002.

27. Ibid., pp. 38–44.

28. W. A. Lewis, "Economic Development with Unlimited Supplies of Labor," *Manchester School of Economic and Social Studies* 22 (1954): 139–91.

9

Institutional Barriers to the Economic Development of Uzbekistan

Eshref Trushin and Eskender Trushin

The experience of many countries has demonstrated that the poor ones are such because of an uninformed and corrupt economic policy, that is, one that is not based on the construction of efficient institutions of a market economy. The foundation for sustainable economic growth in any country is not the existence of natural resources, but the presence of efficient institutions.[1]

Scholarly literature has come increasingly to recognize that it is precisely institutions that determine the development of a country. Econometric studies show that differences in capital accumulation and output per worker are basically explained by differences in institutions among countries, which are associated with property rights, law and order, and so forth.[2] Aggregate indicators of institutions of governance can explain about three-fourths of the variation in the per capita income of different countries.[3]

Unfortunately, quantitative theory of institutions is still in an embryonic stage. Thus, to assess institutions, one must rely on indirect (often subjective) indicators,[4] thereby opening the door to unwarranted speculation. The attempts to assess institutions with the aid of various ratings, at this point, have an eclectic and subjective character, although such ratings do enable some quantitative assessments. In addition, there is a problem of endogeneity with respect to institutions and economic policies. Simple cross-country linear instrumental variable regressions cannot, because of the problems of endogeneity, provide definitive answers to questions as complex as the interaction of institutions and trade in promoting growth.[5]

For any society, institutions represent the rules of the game (formal or informal), which can simultaneously be regarded as restrictions and stimuli in shaping the political, economic, and social behavior and interaction of people.[6] Obviously, people work in response to incentives, which are either generated or stifled by government policy, but in many respects the policy itself is also determined by the institutions.

The stable development of Uzbekistan depends entirely on the country's capacity to overcome vested interests and to establish developmental institutions. In the transition period to a market, the institutions in Uzbekistan represent a weird admixture of traditional Islamic, Soviet command, and Western institutions. At present, the government can have a significant impact on the formation of the institutions that will determine the future development of the country.

This study seeks to present a critical analysis of the institutions in Uzbekistan from a political-economic perspective. The focus on problems in institutional development should not give the impression that there have been no areas of success in this sphere. The main goal of this analysis is to reveal key problems and to make recommendations, sometimes unorthodox ones, to promote the development of institutions that could help place Uzbekistan on the road to stable economic growth.

The Institutional Context in the Commonwealth of Independent States (CIS)

As part of the process of transition to a capitalist market, liberalization of the economy means a weakening and abolition of limitations, and the government simultaneously renounces economic rents[7] that it had previously received. However, the process of liberalization in Uzbekistan is not taking place instantaneously, because the rents that the state is renouncing have not immediately vanished and indeed remain a focus of conflict. For example, at the time when Uzbekistan started to liberalize foreign trade in 1992, the world prices on many raw materials were several times higher than domestic prices. The government and some private firms obtained rents in the form of the difference between domestic and world prices. After the deregulation of domestic prices, these began to approach those on world markets, but that did not happen instantaneously, and in fact domestic prices have not yet fully come to the level of world prices.

Unfortunately, the main dynamic of the transition period in the CIS countries was the fight for rents and the redistribution of rents—not the creation of a more efficient economy and a just distribution of national income. The CIS countries still possess powerful (albeit degrading) production infrastructures and systems of education; they also suffer from ineffective governance and the lack of political will to improve it.

Throughout the CIS, inadequate institutions have also contributed to the efflorescence of a shadow economy, "state capture," and administrative corruption. Those governments have sometimes conducted ill-advised policies that have dealt harm to economic development and that have evoked apathy and pessimism among investors and the general population. Thus far the CIS countries have not established a system of clear incentives and restrictions that could promote the development of the most effective and innovative enterprises and that could bring the most literate political leaders to power. Economic policy in these countries is often subordinate to the interests of a minuscule clique of oligarchs and corrupt bureaucrats who receive enormous incomes at the expense of the rest of society. As a result, the mass of people suffers discrimination with respect to their economic rights—to establish a private business in whatever sector they desire, to receive a fair share of the product of their labor, and to have their private property securely protected.

Institutionalized changes in the CIS countries have been systematically slow, for they have been restrained by a shortage of external incentives (the so-called "anchors"). The latter, by contrast, did exist in the countries of Central and Eastern Europe in the form of admission to the European Union.[8] From the 1950s to the 1980s, an external incentive in the form of the communist threat was evidently a main factor in inducing powerful institutional improvements in the countries of East Asia, and those improvements in turn led to extraordinary economic growth. The elites in East Asia recognized the threat to their existence from the communist movement and embarked on the requisite economic reforms to enable stable development in their countries. Moreover, the most important institutionalized reforms (in particular, the farmer and land reforms; the transformation of industrial corporations into joint-stock companies; the adoption of laws to protect capitalist private property) had already been initiated by the American military administration as a key part of the postwar effort of the United States to prevent communism from spreading to all of Asia.

Unfortunately, for the elites of Uzbekistan and many other CIS countries, at present there are no such clear external incentives to precipitate fundamental institutional reform. The defeat of the Taliban regime in Afghanistan and the large-scale war on Islamist terrorism has effectively eliminated most foreign threats that could have reinforced the need to develop more effective governance. The financial assistance of the United States (the payments to use military bases) and the presence of raw material resources also diminish the need for reforms that could liberate the creative energy of the population. One study has concluded that the availability of resources, such as unconditional foreign aid and natural resources, can discourage the adoption of good policies and eventually hamper investment and growth.[9]

At the same time, the CIS countries have not yet formed a civil society and established public control over economic policy. A study by the World Bank notes that the CIS countries still have not applied the principle of competition to the spheres of politics and economics. This has permitted influential groups to create for themselves sources of concentrated advantages (that is, economic rents), and this has dealt serious harm to the rest of society—which is concretely expressed in the growth of poverty and inequality. These same privileged groups, which have concentrated economic and political power in their own hands, are currently the principal obstacle to economic reform.[10]

This antireform bloc includes not only the bureaucracy, but also business. It quickly became clear to entrepreneurs in partially reformed countries with transition economies that they could obtain much larger profits by securing privileges than by opening new enterprises or upgrading existing ones. Corruption and payments on the side were a natural result of this system of rent-seeking.[11]

Hellman and Kaufmann see the main problem with corruption to be its influence on the adoption of the rules of the game in the economy and in the inadequately protected rights of private property. [12] Their research is based on an opinion survey of managers in private enterprises in a majority of countries with a transition economy. Their work has shown that firms that participate in corrupt activities, as a rule, enhance the protection of their private property five times more than firms that did not participate in the corrupt dealings. At the same time, a corrupted economy rewards the connections and influence of economic agents, not their competence and innovation.

The majority of economic and political activities in the CIS involves the fight for rents. These rents are created by means of a privileged position of some economic actors, while others are then subjected to discrimination. To obtain economic rents, bureaucrats create artificial barriers to hamper natural economic flows. Therefore bureaucrats often think in terms of a roadblock: if someone wants to pass (that is, open a business, begin new production, receive a license, or receive permission to do something), then that person must pay up. The result is a change in the structure of stimuli: rent-seeking is more profitable than increasing production. This brings colossal losses for the well-being of the rest of society. Moreover, the rent-seeking often acquires an institutional form: powerful, illegal organizations ("pyramids") are constructed within state governance, with each official obtaining his share of a particular rent.

Today economic rents have the following main characteristics:

- Significant expenses are required in order to receive these rents; these outlays differ for various economic agents, depending on how close they are to the needed official.
- The majority of rents are associated with access to the market and securing the right to engage in some kind of activity. This creates high entry barriers; as a result, economic agents often do not start a new business, thereby reducing general economic activity in the country.
- The intensive struggle between clans and other groups encourage people to send rents abroad (capital flight) in order to protect them from political competitors.
- The struggle between dominant groups and clans leads to an attempt to extract the maximum rents now, thereby reducing the potential for collecting rents in the future, not to mention the potential for long-term development in a country. Insofar as various clans control different sectors of the economy, the competition between clans has this effect: some sectors, often ones that are less useful for economic growth, develop at the expense of other, more vital sectors.

The single most important precondition for institutional reform in the CIS countries is political will, pure and simple. That political will, however, must recognize the institutional problems and must have a clear vision of how to solve them. The goal of any responsible government in the transition period is to accelerate the development of those market institutions that promote economic growth.

Although economic theory has clearly resolved some issues (the reforms that are needed to protect the rights of private property, to ensure stable economic growth, and to combat corruption), it has not determined who is to initiate and continue these progressive reforms, and according to what principles. It is not entirely clear to what degree the interests of the ruling circles in the CIS countries would be served by constructing high-quality social institutions that could eliminate opportunities to extract many forms of economic rent—which, indeed, are also received by these same circles. One comes to understand that, in the transition to a market, it becomes necessary to resolve the fundamental political and economic questions that are associated with the transformation of the basic institutions of society. Above all, this includes a guarantee of the private property rights and the development of incentives to encourage productive labor, innovation, and investment.

The Development of Institutions in Uzbekistan

The Pre-Soviet and Soviet Eras

In the pre-Soviet period the territory of Uzbekistan formed parts of three khanates: Kokand, Bukhara, and Khiva. The country was almost entirely agrarian, with a farming system based on crop cultivation (irrigated and unirrigated) and cattle raising (nomadic and semi-nomadic). Hence the political institutions there essentially regulated property in agriculture and ownership of land, harvests, and livestock.

Historically, Central Asia developed three main forms of land ownership: state (*amlak*), religious (*wakf*),[13] and private (*mulk*). In all three khanates the predominant form of land ownership was state land; it accounted for 55 to 70 percent of all land.[14] State property was gradually created in accordance with a precept in Islamic law that the land belongs to whomever irrigates it. Irrigation was organized and performed on the order of the khans; they therefore became the sole proprietors of most of the land. The khan embodied the state; thus "state" land was essentially the khan's private property.[15] Apart from land irrigated on the order of the khan, state land also included idle and confiscated land. State land was allocated for the permanent, hereditary use of *dekhkonlar* (peasants), who had the right to conclude mortgage transactions and to sell their right to use the land. The construction of irrigation canals was carried out by collectives of people; newly developed land was divided among the participating peasants (to possess and use) in proportion to the labor and capital that they had invested in preparing the land for cultivation.[16]

In exchange for the use of this land, the peasant paid a tax that varied between one-eighth and three-fifths of the harvest (in-kind or cash), depending on the type of agreement. The tax rents were divided into two parts: one for the khan, the other for local feudal lords. The latter were the khan's local representatives, that is, the rulers of provinces (*khokimlar, beklar*), and the heads of districts (as well as *amlak-dars*, tax collectors) who were appointed by the khokimlar or beklar.

Thus, the state was the supreme owner of land and did not recognize private land ownership, only the right to hold and use land (individually and collectively).[17] However, state land ownership was subject to a constant process of breakdown, with the formation of private feudal property as grants from the khan for service (as conditional possession). Such a service estate could be reclaimed by the khan at any time; its holder had no right to sell, give away, or bequeath this land. More often the khan granted his ruling feudal lords only the rent from land (in whole or in part), not the right to dispose of the land and peasants. The peasants were juridically free; they were not the property of the khokimlar and khans.

For many years, the main form of land usage on state lands was the commune (*paikal*), which performed the work together—as mutual assistance on land that had been divided into family allotments. Each family had its own allotment (*pai*) of the land held in common; this family land share could be inherited, bought, and sold. Each year, the commune land users redistributed the land among families by lot, for the parcels in a commune differed in fertility, water supply, and degree of salination. Since land parcels were transferred each year to someone else, the users were not particularly concerned about improving the fertility of the soil, or about the condition of the irrigation network on their pai. Rich families engaged in the practice of buying up land allotments; as communal lands became concentrated in the hands of a few, the commune disintegrated. By the mid-nineteenth century communal land utilization (on irrigated and mostly dry farming land) had given way to family land use. Only part of the grasslands and pastures remained in communal use.[18]

The most widespread form of agricultural organization in Central Asia was the sharecropping lease agreement, which was called *chorikorlar* and was known in Islamic law as *Muzara'a*. The leasing agreement was concluded between the owner of the land and its user; it prescribed the proportion of the harvest that belonged to each of the two parties in the agreement. The agreement was based on the principle that the owner of the seeds had possession of the harvest; that corresponded to a precept in Islamic law which regarded the harvest as a return of the seed. The other party received only a share of this harvest. If the seeds belonged to the cultivator (i.e., the peasant), then he had possession of the harvest and paid a leasing fee to use someone else's land and other means of production. If the seeds belonged to the landowner, then he had possession of the harvest, with the cultivator being his hired worker.[19]

In Central Asia, three basic forms of sharecropping were most frequently found.

1. The lessee (*chorikor*) provided only his labor, but the land, water, implements, monetary loan, seeds, and forage were given to him to use. This was an agreement of personal hiring, with piecework payment for the work being part of the harvest. For such use of the land and other resources of production, the lessee paid the lessor three-fifths (60 percent), plus repayment of any inventory and monetary loans.

2. The lessee had everything except the land and water. This was a leasing agreement for land and water; payment for the use of these

means of production ranged between one-eighth and one-quarter of the harvest.

3. The lessee provided the labor, seeds, forage, and monetary means, and he used someone else's land, water, and implements. This agreement was a partnership, whereby the lessee had control over the harvest and usually paid two-fifths of the harvest.

Significantly, according to Islamic law, the harvest had to be divided between the two sides only as proportions, as shares; the division of harvst could not be expressed in absolute figures. Incidental expenditures and poor harvests had a proportionate impact on the shares of both parties. The peasant had an interest in increasing his harvest; he controlled his own work and conducted the farming as he saw fit.

After Russian authorities conquered and colonized the region, they did not make any fundamental changes in the forms of landholding, land utilization, water usage, and the tax system. The only difference was that the land became the property of Russia, and that the taxes went to the tsarist treasury. In 1886, state land in settled areas was transferred by tax commissions to the local population—to those who cultivated it—for permanent hereditary possession and control (along with an official deed to the land). This was only a formal confirmation of the de facto situation; it permitted creditors to buy up the land of peasants if they failed to pay off their debts. Unirrigated and uncultivated lands were not taxed (as was the case before the Russian colonization). Nomadic areas were designated for Russian colonization; this was mainly land in the modern republics of Kazakhstan and Kyrgyzstan.

Russia was interested in the development of cotton cultivation. Its initial attempt to establish cotton cultivation in Central Asia by establishing plantations, like those in the United States, and by ignoring peasant agriculture, ended in failure. Small-scale landholding was dominant; 60 to 75 percent of all agricultural producers had fewer than 2 dessiatinas[20] of land. There was large-scale land possession, but the areas of cultivation were small; hence big landholders practiced the same kind of agriculture as the small landholders, relying on sharecropping leases with repayment in labor. The cheapness of the labor of lessees and hired laborers made it unprofitable to use machinery.[21]

The land rents went mainly to large landholders, many of whom resided in the towns. These big landowners rarely reinvested in agriculture, because their capital could be directed, with less risk and higher profits, into trade, the purchase of raw materials, usury, and the acquisition of land. This buying up of land, which became possible after Russian authorities granted permission in 1886, usually took the form of issuing credits, with the land serving as security and being forfeited in the event of default. In 1914, approximately 265,000 agreements were signed with the land as security; of that number approximately 40,000 (15 percent) ended in the transfer of land to the creditor.[22] Private ownership of land thus became entrenched in the everyday life of the population, and these land transactions continued after the revolution and even after the Soviet government nationalized land in 1925.

After Moscow began to create republics in Central Asia (on the basis of national criteria) in 1924, it also started preliminary work on land reform. To provide legal regulation for sharecropping, the government of Uzbekistan issued a decree in 1924 that treated sharecropping agreements as a written contract for the three main forms of agricultural leases: (a) on land; (b) on land and inventory; and (c) on land, inventory, seeds, and loans. Lease payments for using these means of production were determined as maximum shares of the harvest; anything beyond that, even if the lessee accepted, was declared null and void. In essence, the land reform of 1925 in Uzbekistan preserved the traditional Islamic institution of sharecropping.

In 1925–1928 the government of Uzbekistan not only adopted laws on land reform but also on the nationalization of land and water. These decrees proclaimed the equal right of all toilers to use land, without regard to sex or nationality; they also prohibited transactions on land and declared void any that had already taken place. However, the new decrees did permit the lease of land and hiring of labor, but on condition that the employer himself hold the status of a toiling peasant. The reform allocated land, inventory, and livestock to sharecroppers. Hence they were transformed into private owners of their own agricultural production and also became lessees using state land.[23]

If, before the reform, the majority of households had less than 0.5 dessiatinas of land, that average rose after the reform to 2 to 3.2 dessiatinas of irrigated land. On lands of old and new irrigation, some 79,500 agricultural production units were formed; 97 percent of these were family farms, with just 3 percent in the form of collective farms. In the course of the two years after the reform, family farmers—cultivating this same land of the large landowners—began to receive harvests that were 1.5 to 2 times greater and to pay off their bank loans in advance.[24] Peasant family households became actively involved in cooperatives—agricultural, credit, specialized (cotton, animal husbandry, fruit growing), consumer, and land melioration. Many households were members of several cooperatives.

During the reform period, nearly all the collective farms were small work cooperatives (*arteli*), but some of these had broken up by the fall of 1926. For example, in Samarkand oblast, only 27 of 62 collective farms (43 percent) remained; the average size of a collective farm in 1926 was 26 dessiatinas. In 1928, for all of Uzbekistan, there were only 678 collective farms; 80 percent of these were work cooperatives, but 20 percent were associations that collectively cultivated the land. The average collective farm had 15 families and 53 hectares of land. In 1929, however, the government of Uzbekistan received an order from Communist Party General Secretary Joseph Stalin to liquidate all private farms and forcibly merge them into collective farms. In 1935 the land of a collective farm was fixed permanently, and in 1940 Uzbekistan banned the sharecropping lease of land.[25]

Thus, for the period from the 1930s to the 1980s, a mistaken strategy was applied to agriculture: liquidation of family farms and the massive, coercive organization of state farms and collective farms, which based agriculture on the collective principle. Peasants were deprived of the right to possess the land and the harvest; they were initially turned into serfs without the right to leave agriculture, and later (after Stalin's death) became hired laborers. In essence, the regime established a system of corvee labor (*barshchina*) on the fields of state and collective farms; this labor was in exchange for small individual plots (up to 0.12 hectares) to support subsistence agriculture. A supplementary, minuscule payment for the work performed on state and collective farms (to complement the allotment of a private plot) is essentially the only difference between the Stalinist system of wages and Russian serfdom in the mid-nineteenth century. The Russian and Stalinist system of serfdom—previously unknown to the peasants of Uzbekistan—was a superimposed, inefficient institution.

The peasants ceased to be the masters of their agricultural work. But the heads of the collective and state farms were also not the masters: they all acted in accordance with instructions from above. This system suppressed the entrepreneurial abilities and creative labor of those working at all levels. The regime began to apply industrial methods to the organization of agricultural labor: large brigades that were paid for individual tasks. The Soviet "reforms" of the 1960s–1980s changed only the form of the organization and the payment for hired labor; there was no question of allowing independent peasant households that would own all the agricultural output. It was incessantly said that mechanization, more chemicals, melioration, and the application of technical innovations were needed. But no attention was given to the main thing—making the peasant take an interest in all this. The reform also ignored the principles of independence, self-financing, and economic incentives of agricultural enterprises in the results of production. Unfortunately, many of these characteristics have remained in contemporary Uzbekistan.

Institutional Development During the Years of Independence

Real movement in the direction of market reforms only began after the breakup of the former Soviet Union. The majority of institutional problems characteristic of the CIS also apply to Uzbekistan, albeit with their own special features. In response to the external shocks in the second half of the 1990s, the government of Uzbekistan reacted by closing the economy and reinforcing the closed character of institutions (through an increase in the system of secrecy, lack of transparency, and absence of mechanisms for participatory decision making).

Among countries with transition economies, Uzbekistan has one of the lowest ratings for its development of market reforms.[26] To this point, Uzbekistan still has an economy of the "closed type,"[27] with a very low level of economic freedom.[28] Until 2002, the main instrument in Uzbekistan for keeping a closed economy was the lack of convertibility of the national currency (that is, the government's control over the foreign currency exchange). After the introduction of convertibility in October 2003, the main instrument for maintaining a closed economy shifted to the sphere of higher import duties and excise taxes on imports. In 2002 the government introduced prohibitive import tariffs on "shuttle traders" (*chelnoki*), who often supply raw materials and parts for small- and medium-sized enterprises. The closed economy is also retained by state control over the main raw-material goods for export (cotton fiber, energy, nonferrous metals) and over imports. It has been able to do this through preliminary registration of import contracts and the oligopolization of the wholesale trade.

One should note several of the most important conditions that have contributed to the development of a closed economy in Uzbekistan since it gained independence:

- *The low level of political activity of the population during the first years of independence.* The transition to a market economy and the liberalization of political activity in Uzbekistan at the end of the 1980s was, to a large degree, brought from the outside and inspired by an external political factor—namely, the breakup of the Soviet Union.
- *Significant reserves of mineral and energy resources.* These created favorable conditions for reducing their import and for supporting export and generating income for the state budget (regardless of the trade policies). The rise in gold and cotton prices in 2001–2004 increased the role and impact of this factor.
- *The well-developed system of irrigation inherited from the Soviet era.* This made it possible to obtain stable harvests from 4 million hectares of irrigated land (regardless of the trade regimen).
- *State monopoly on the export of key goods.* These include gold and other nonferrous metals, cotton, and energy. This monopoly was inherited from the former Soviet Union; control over the export of such goods, in technical terms, was relatively simple.

- *Very low level of price elasticity on production.* Such was the case despite the low procurement prices that the state paid for the main goods of centralized exports. With the assistance of administrative measures, the government succeeded in achieving stable volumes of output from gold mining and cotton growing—which are the main sources of exports from Uzbekistan. However, this system based on state marketing boards brought enormous losses—shortfalls in cotton harvests and exports due to the lack of adequate incentives for peasants to increase output and improve efficiency. An analogous policy has led to a crisis in many countries of Africa and Asia.
- *Unfavorable external factors.* These include the greater remoteness from the world's oceans and from world markets, and hence the higher cost of international shipping (which, objectively, reinforces the proclivity to follow a policy of import substitution). A further factor was the negative shock to the terms of trade—that is, a much greater fall in the world prices on Uzbekistan's principal export goods (in the period 1991–1993 and 1996–1999) compared to the prices of imports. One response of the Uzbek government to these shocks, although not a very efficacious one, was the decision to seal off the economy through administrative devises (that is, to control the foreign currency exchange and restrict imports).

After Uzbekistan gained independence in 1991, it experienced the least contraction in its gross domestic product (GDP) among all the countries of the former Soviet Union. The factors behind such a small decrease included not only the closed economy (which made it possible to sustain production even in enterprises that were not competitive), but also institutional stability. Many Soviet institutions were preserved; they only changed their names or underwent superficial modifications. The slogan of President Islam Karimov "do not destroy the old house before the new one is built" counteracted the contraction of production and sustained discipline. This created a more stable business environment and infrastructure for production.

However, by the mid-1990s, once the downturn phase of transition had been overcome, the earlier institutions that had stabilized production became, under the new conditions, a brake on further development. In order to make the transition to a market economy of the capitalist, not feudal, type, it was necessary to create new institutions. Failure to do so would doom the country to stagnation and political instability. At a time when most countries with transition economies had already completed a significant part of the requisite transformation, Uzbekistan was procrastinating (see Table 9.1).

As a result, Uzbekistan finds itself at the "tail-end" of the CIS countries

Table 9.1

Assessments of Structural and Institutional Reforms: South Caucasus, Central Asia, and Russia (based on EBRD numerical indicators)[a]

Country	Privatization and restructuring of enterprises	liberalization of markets and competition	Reform of financial markets	Reform of the infrastructure	General assessment[b]
Azerbaijan	53	63	33	23	43
Armenia	70	67	40	43	55
Georgia	70	73	33	43	55
Kazakhstan	67	60	50	33	53
Kyrgyzstan	67	57	40	11	44
Tajikistan	53	57	13	11	34
Turkmenistan	11	11	0	0	6
Uzbekistan	50	30	30	23	33
Russia	73	60	40	43	54

Source: European Bank for Reconstruction and Development, *Transition Report 2002* (London, 2002).

[a]The assessment for the beginning of 2002 is based on the numerical evaluation of the EBRD (*Transition Report 2002*). The scale of these EBRD quantitative evaluations was mechanically linearized by taking the one-third plus or minus and adding this figure to the whole numbers of grades from 1 to 4. Average of indicators for countries in the Organization for Economic Cooperation and Development is 100.

[b]This general assessment is simply an average of the other four indicators.

with respect to the indicators of economic growth once the low point in the transformatory decline in GDP had been passed. At a time when most of the CIS countries have economic growth that exceeds 5 percent, Uzbekistan continues to show a sluggish rate of growth. Although the official data claim that growth rates exceeded 4 percent in 1997–2003 and jumped to 7.7 percent in 2004, international financial organizations repeatedly report lower rates of real growth and an inflation rate substantially above the official figure.[29]

In terms of per capita GDP, the classification of the World Bank shows that Uzbekistan has dropped from the rank of "low-middle-income countries" to "low-income countries." Economic growth in 1996–2004 did not bring major qualitative changes in the institutional structure of the economy and society. The thinking of state officials, as before, continues to be dominated by the notion that economic development means an increase in production, not the creation of market incentives to promote work, innovation, and investment for the majority of the population. As before, the economy is dominated by administrative methods; clans are dominant in business and the government, with virtually no control on the part of society. The right of private property as an institution is not adequately protected; pessimism permeates the small business environment; and the level of corruption in state governance is high.

In terms of freedom of the press, Uzbekistan ranks 120 out of 139 countries.[30] Individual political websites and articles with politically sensitive information are blocked from the internet. According to the index on per capita access to the internet (Digital Access Index 2002),[31] Uzbekistan ranks 121 out of 178 countries. Although censorship has been formally abolished, neither the press nor television offers any seriously critical materials. The situation with respect to institutional reforms reflects the level of governance (see Table 9.2).

According to some assessments, Uzbekistan has made progress in its level of governance and in general corresponds to the average for the other countries of the former Soviet Union (see Table 9.3). However, in Uzbekistan the situation is significantly worse with respect to the accountability of authorities. In reality, even such an imperfect check on authorities as elections does not function, for neither oblast governors nor district heads are elected. Uzbekistan also lacks a legal political opposition; parliament almost always approves documents that have been drafted by the organs of the executive branch. However, Uzbekistan has improved control over corruption. This probably means that corruption is regulated by the internal mechanisms in the elite; in other words, the elite is attempting to impose some limitations on itself.

In all likelihood, the mass of the population would be satisfied by a rapidly growing liberal economy even if there was a strict restriction on politi-

Table 9.2

Assessment of the Quality of Institutions: Central Asia, South Caucasus, Russia, and China[a]

Country	Freedom of speech and accountability of authorities	Political stability and freedom from the use of arbitrary force	Efficiency of governance	Quality of regulation of the economy and freedom from interference	Legality (guarantee of property rights and fulfillment of contracts)	Control over corruption	Average assessment All indicators	Average assessment All indicators except stability
Azerbaijan	41	39	38	43	43	35	40	40
Armenia	55	56	51	67	52	44	54	54
Georgia	58	17	43	43	33	36	38	43
Kazakhstan	38	86	42	45	40	36	48	40
Kyrgyzstan	41	37	42	52	42	41	43	44
Tajikistan	41	37	31	31	31	35	34	34
Turkmenistan	17	67	25	14	34	32	32	24
Uzbekistan	22	44	35	27	34	36	33	31
Russia	52	60	52	56	43	39	50	48
China	30	78	66	53	57	51	56	51

Source: D. Kaufmann, A. Kraay, and M. Mastruzzi, "Governance Matters III: Governance Indicators for 1996–2002," 8 May 2003, pp. 89–106 (www.worldbank.org/wbi/governance/govdata2002), using B. Weder, "Institutional Reform in Transition Economies: How Far Have They Come?" (Unpublished IMF study; Washington, DC, 2000); IMF, *World Economic Outlook, October 2000: Focus on Transition Economics* (Washington, DC, 2000), p. 136.

[a]Calculated by the authors on the basis of World Bank assessments for 2002. Average of indicators for countries in the Organization for Economic Cooperation and Development is 100.

Table 9.3

Quality of Governance: Comparison of Uzbekistan with the Countries of the Former Soviet Union in 1997–1998 and 2000–2001

| | Percent of countries with worse indicators | | | |
| | Worse than Uzbekistan | | Worse than countries of the former Soviet Union (average) | |
Indicator	1997–1998	2000–2001	1997–1998	2000–2001
Control of Corruption[a]	N/A	29.2	N/A	21.7
Political Instability	37.0	N/A	36.3	N/A
Rule of Law	18.8	27.8	28.5	26.5
Regularity	6.7	11.3	16.2	14.9
Government Effectiveness	6.5	21.1	18.6	21.0
Voice and Accountability	8.7	13.3	32.7	31.8

Source: D.A. Kaufmann, A. Kraay, and P. Zoido-Lobaton, "Governance Matters II: Updated Governance Indicators for 2000/2001" (World Bank Research Working Paper 2772), quoted in: The World Bank, *Uzbekistan Living Standard Assessment. Full Report (May 2001)*, Report No. 25923-UZ (Washington, DC, 2001).
[a]This is a new category, appearing in 2000–2001.

cal liberties. The stagnant economy in Uzbekistan, where about 20 percent of the population consists of youths between sixteen and twenty-five years of age, and where only a small minority is prospering, represents a threat. The growth of social conflicts could, under certain conditions, develop into an uprising much more quickly than many expect.

Economic Policy of Uzbekistan: Main Recent Changes

Beginning on 15 October 2003, Uzbekistan introduced the convertibility of the national currency (sum) in current accounts. In November 2003, the International Monetary Fund (IMF) officially recognized the convertibility of the national currency of Uzbekistan.[32] In the course of 2002–2003, the government conducted a more stringent credit and monetary policy, as it sought to reduce inflation and to stabilize the exchange rate of the sum. Its objective was to reduce the burden of servicing the foreign debt. In addition, the government simplified the registration of small enterprises and reduced the number of inspections of small businesses performed by state organs.[33] In 2003 it reduced the tax on profits from 24 to 20 percent. From February 2004 enterprises obtained the right to sell certain types of goods (energy, metals, mineral fertilizers, and some foodstuffs) freely—through a commodity-raw material exchange—on the domestic market; previously all this had been redistributed through a system of centralized planning.[34] In 2004, it is expected that the government will make a further cut in tax rates (by several percentage points) on the incomes of enterprises and citizens as well as contributions to social funds and will simplify the Tax Code in 2006. These are signs of a long-awaited beginning of a real transition to a market economy in Uzbekistan.

For the present, it is too early to talk about a change in the import substitution strategy for the development of Uzbekistan. The earlier economic policy spawned a growth of economic and social problems in a closed economy; it also undermined the confidence of foreign investors and donors. Prior to the introduction of convertibility, the government offered various arguments against the rapid introduction of convertibility, many of which were unconvincing.[35] Simultaneous with the liberalization of the currency exchange regime, the government raised trade barriers. A resolution of the Cabinet of Ministers (no. 154 from 6 May 2002) imposed, as of June 2002, prohibitive duties on shuttle traders: 50 percent on foodstuffs and 90 percent on other consumer goods. Although it later slightly reduced these tariffs, it increased the duties on sugar and various groats to 30 percent.

For several months in 2002, the government closed the majority of bazaars dealing in consumer goods. As a result, many small enterprises were closed, and several thousand people lost their jobs. In 2002–2003 the Uzbek press published statements about "economic aggression" on the part of neighboring countries, which were allegedly inundating Uzbekistan with cheap, low-quality imports.

Uzbek authorities tightened the movement of people to neighboring countries in an effort to limit the purchase of consumer goods there and to reduce the diversion of domestic consumer demand abroad. It reached the point where Uzbek border guards even dismantled part of a bridge on the border with Kyrgyzstan.

The oligopolization of wholesale trade intensified. According to a resolution of the Cabinet of Ministers (no. 407 from 26 November 2002), wholesale trade was open only to organizations that had a warehouse and charter capital equal to at least 6,000 times the minimum wage. According to data compiled by the International Crisis Group, this resolution effectively allowed only three wholesale trading companies to operate on the market for consumer goods in Uzbekistan. All three companies, moreover, seem to be under the control of members of the government.[36] In the fall of 2003, however, a new resolution from the Cabinet of Ministers reduced the oligopolization of wholesale trade.

For the present, problems remain regarding the convertibility of the national currency. In the provinces, the conversion of national currency for imports is often delayed for several weeks. The very mechanism of conversion is still being realized within the framework of the so-called "currency exchange balance"—an anachronism of centralized planning. A decree of the Cabinet of Ministers still affirms the "optimization of the import of goods as the most important priority of the goal of a structural policy." [37]

It is difficult to agree that closing borders, oligopolizing wholesale trade, and raising trade barriers correspond to the philosophy of a new liberal strategy for the development of Uzbekistan. Moreover, it is very important to see liberalization of the currency exchange not as a goal in itself, but as a necessary stage in opening the economy of Uzbekistan for the formation of new institutions that can promote stable economic growth.

Rather, the introduction of prohibitive tariff duties on shuttle traders in 2002 and the oligopolization of the wholesale trade in consumer goods can be seen as creating new rents, which is not something that will stimulate the economic development of Uzbekistan. The main problems created by rents consist of the following:

- *The rents cause a substantial increase in the price on consumer goods.* And that in turn brings an increase in poverty, aggravates social tensions, and undermines trust in the government. All this has a negative impact on further economic reforms.
- *The rents do not stimulate the expansion of consumer goods production.* First, the high import duties cannot compensate for the institutional factors unfavorable for the development of production. These factors include: (a) the shortage of incentives and skills in effectively managing and marketing goods, along with administrative barriers to opening and running businesses; (b) limited access to the necessary raw materials and semifinished goods because the distribution system for some key raw material resources is centralized; (c) the lack of incentives for the development of enterprises under state control; and (d) the high taxes and mandatory contributions to the state social funds. Higher import tariffs and excise duties on imports that have no precise time frame, and concrete conditionality for development of a particular industry often induce stagnation, for the simple reason that they subvert a healthy competitive environment. Second, a substantial share of the market is filled by goods produced or imported illegally; hence higher import duties do more to stimulate contraband than to encourage domestic production. For example, according to the authors' estimates, about three-fourths of the consumer apparel is smuggled. Third, the volume of the domestic market for some consumer goods is insufficient to enable the development of competitive domestic production.

• *Greater rents are concentrated in the companies that engage in wholesale trade.* This is a clear disincentive for producers of domestic goods because substantial rents derived from protectionism go to the wholesalers.
• *Oligopolization of wholesale trade and consumer goods production creates a powerful lobby.* That lobby has its own vested interest in the status quo.

Liberalization of the currency exchange exposed many structural problems of the economy—namely, the presence of a mass of old and new uncompetitive enterprises and their inefficient corporate management. The bane of nonpayment quickly escalated; a mass of uncompetitive enterprises found themselves in a more competitive environment at a time when their restructuring and privatization were proceeding at a slow pace. In 2003, the backlog of goods increased and wage payments encountered significant delays.

In 2003–2004 the government conducted a policy aimed at macroeconomic stabilization, as it sharply limited direct credits and restricted the supply of cash and credits for the state budget. As a result, it is able to reduce inflation from 27.6 percent in 2002 to 3.7 percent in 2003–2004.

In 2003 Uzbekistan witnessed a new phenomenon: employees went on strike in several enterprises that had failed to pay wages for several months. The foreign press published assessments estimating that unpaid back wages amounted to 1.5 percent of the GDP.[38] These wage arrears were partly due to a Central Bank policy of limiting cash in circulation, making cash withdraw from accounts of enterprises more difficult than ever, the goal being to curtail the demand for foreign currency on the black market. Moreover, there was a strong rush to buy hard currency, for few believed that convertibility, particularly at such "strong" Uzbek sum exchange rate, would last for long. As a result, a large amount of national currency was exchanged into dollars. One should note that the government kept the situation under control and in general maintained political stability.

According to a survey conducted by the International Finance Corporation, in 2002 small- and medium-sized enterprises cut their investment by 15 percent from the previous year.[39] The number of enterprises which believed that the next year would improve the business environment fell by 22 percent; the proportion which believed that conditions would worsen rose by 7 percent.[40] Investment pessimism is going to be exceptionally high among small businesses in some years ahead in spite of official reporting of growing SMEs contribution to the GDP.

Basic Institutional Characteristics in the Economic Sectors of Uzbekistan

Public Sector

Uzbekistan has a large state sector, which creates about one half of the GDP and employs the same proportion of the labor force. The immediate managers in this sector are bureaucrats, with their characteristic lack of incentives to make changes for the better. There is also a problem of asset siphoning that occurs when public enterprises fall into the private hands of managers. The government's domination of the economy crowds out private businesses and private savings.

The bulk of national income is distributed through the government. It distributes the national income both through high taxation and through various centralized redistributions of raw materials (by means of state plans, which are called "prognoses"). According to the authors' approximate calculation, state revenues in various forms (including the incomes from marketing boards) amounted to about half of the GDP in 2001. In addition, the state imposed enormous mandatory social contributions; in 2003, these amounted to 37.2 percent of the payroll bill. For each sum of official wages, small- and medium-sized enterprises must pay the government 1.1 sum (in the form of taxes and various social payments). In 2004 the situation improved somewhat: the ratio of wages and taxation dropped to 1:1.

The high taxes and highly regulated structure of the economy force entrepreneurs to resort to corruption or to operate in the shadow sector. Entrepreneurs cannot pay all the taxes; otherwise, they would not be able to compete on foreign markets or would lose business to entrepreneurs who do not pay all the taxes. The presence and growth of the shadow economy are often advantageous to narrow circles of the bureaucracy, which receives its own corrupt incomes from the shadow sector.

For the period 1998–2004, the tax rates have been reduced, but not enough to dissuade entrepreneurs from operating in the shadow sector. For example, the maximum personal income tax rate was reduced from 45 percent in 1998 to a (planned) rate of 30 percent in 2004. If, however, one considers that the maximum rate applies to a wage of approximately sixty dollars per month (in a situation where the physical subsistence minimum is twenty dollars per capita in the city), the rate reduction provides little incentive to report all of one's wages. Moreover, even those with a wage at the subsistence minimum of twenty dollars per month must pay approximately 16 percent in income taxes (compared to about 5 percent in Kazakhstan).

Cooperation among the government, private businesses, and economists is virtually nonexistent. The government often changes the rules of the game without any broad consultations with business, people, or economists. As a result, the government's economic policy remains highly unpredictable for private businesses. The government forfeits not only much information essential for decision-making, but also lacks moral legitimacy for its policies. Moreover, it often ignores—without cause—the recommendations of international financial organizations and also state economic institutes. Without such cooperation, however, the government's reforms—in the long-term perspective— are foreordained to be ineffective.

The budget process lacks transparency. The details of state budget of Uzbekistan are not published; there is no treasury system to ensure better control and management of the funds in the state budget. Incomes received on the difference between world and domestic prices (in transactions handled by state marketing boards) flow into special funds that remain virtually unknown to the general public.

Information about business regulation is fragmented across hundreds of resolutions, decrees, and laws. Since the government has not codified its rules on business regulation, small- and medium-sized businesses find it difficult to understand the economic regimen and to operate correspondingly. And that leaves entrepreneurs easy prey for corrupt officials. The International Finance Corporation's *Business Environment in Uzbekistan. Report, 2002* notes that the more often small- and medium-sized enterprises have dealings with state organs in their work, the more negative is their judgment.[41]

Uzbekistan has also initiated administrative reform.[42] It has liquidated several associations at the republic level. It has reduced the volume of reports demanded of enterprises. In 2004 it planned to reduce the number of administrative personnel by more than 40,000 (22 percent) and to eliminate superfluous, redundant functions in state agencies.[43] However, this reform was not fully implemented. Whereas the number of administrative personnel was reduced, some state agencies still perform functions that should be assigned to healthy market forces. For example, the state prosecutors were ordered to expand their mission in monitoring agricultural production. The theory and practice advise that one of the main goals of administrative reform must be to separate the functions of organs that establish the rules of the game from those of organs that implement them and oversee the economy. Unfortunately, the majority of administrative organs not only writes the rules of the game but also implements and enforces them—to its considerable private advantage. For the present, the reform has not eliminated this basic source for corruption. We hope that the planned administrative reform will not merely mean a reduction in the number of officials.

A high official feels like a feudal lord-businessman who runs the "estate" assigned to him—be that "estate" an enterprise, corporation, district, oblast, or economic sector. However, this "estate" is not his private property; at any time he can be replaced and transferred to some other sector or sphere. He therefore has no incentive for long-term planning and development of his "estate," a situation that only reinforces the feudal character of institutions.

Nor does Uzbekistan have codified regulations on officials and state service. An official of the middle or lower level is totally unprotected and vulnerable. The constant, pervasive fear of doing something wrong, of provoking the dissatisfaction of superiors and ruining one's career, blocks innovation "from below," from within the bureaucratic machine. Often, the important criterion in the selection of personnel is not ability, but kinship, geographic ties, or loyalty to the leadership.

The salaries of mid- and low-ranking officials stand at the subsistence minimum. For example, a department head in a ministry has an official salary of just fifty dollars per month. This has given rise to the following popular apothegm: "The authorities pretend to pay us a wage for our work for the country, and we pretend to work." Indifference, passivity, fear of displaying initiative, and greed flourish in the bureaucratic machine. As one study has shown, if corruption is widespread, individuals have no incentive to fight back—even if everybody would be better off without it.[44]

Given the conditions of the transition period, much depends on a country's leadership. Interestingly, the government in neighboring Kazakhstan has undertaken a rather advanced administrative reform: it has significantly increased the salaries of officials, adopted a new law on the status of officials, and instituted active, regular competition for various positions. The average age of state officials in Kazakhstan is 30–35 years; many high posts of ministers and their deputies are held by people who are young (under 35 years of age) and who have a Western education. This contrasts sharply with Uzbekistan, where the great majority of high official positions are held by people who are over 45 years of age.

The bulk of information and statistical data that are openly published in most countries (for example, detailed parameters of the state budget, monetary aggregates, deflators, and so forth) are treated as a state secret in Uzbekistan. This secrecy makes it impossible to make full, detailed quantitative analysis of the government's economic policies.

There is also reason to doubt the reliability of official data. For example, according to official data, the level of inflation in 2003 was 3.8 percent (compared to 21.6 percent in 2002). However, can the population of Uzbekistan believe that consumer prices in 2003 rose at such a small rate given the much higher rate of growth in the cost of utilities (from 15 to 63 percent), including gasoline, public transport, and many other important goods and services? It is still more difficult to convince many international experts, especially since the content of the "consumer basket" (its volume, composition, and cost) remains secret.

Moreover, the 3.8 percent inflation rate is below that planned in the state budget for 2003. Therefore, the unexpected reduction of inflation could have a painful impact on those who borrow capital, since they have to repay loans at a much higher real interest rate than they originally planned. Thus the "over-fulfillment" of the plan to reduce inflation cannot be given a one-sided positive evaluation.

One gains the impression that the official statistics, scholarly economic institutions, and public opinion surveys serve only to justify decisions that the government has already made. The state apparatus has not properly developed the function of identifying problems, analyzing them, and compiling the reliable information needed for decision-making. For example, the public opinion center "Ijtimoiy Fikr" published a study called *Uzbekistan: Public Opinion in 2003*. An absolute majority of citizens polled (97.7 percent) gave a positive assessment of the political situation; a majority expressed confidence that Uzbekistan has created all the necessary legal (66.9 percent), social (62.4 percent), and economic (59.7 percent) conditions for the normal work of entrepreneurs and farmers, and the private sector in general. Compared with previous opinion surveys of this center, this one showed an increase in the number of respondents who believe that the state has given everything needed, that no one has the right to demand anything more.[45]

Industry

In 2003 industry employed approximately 9 percent of the labor force and accounted for 15 percent of the GDP. Two main groups have been formed in industry: one represents the "old Soviet" enterprises (which are controlled by the government); the other consists of enterprises with foreign capital and management and more modern equipment. Each branch of industry, as a rule, is dominated by several large enterprises with a state share in the ownership; hence the government holds powerful levers of influence in most industrial branches.

The former ministries, which have been renamed associations and concerns, have continued to intervene actively in the management and marketing of enterprises under their control. The internal informal rules of such associations sometimes remind one of guild rules in medieval Europe. Associations constitute a powerful instrument to lobby for the interests of an entire sector; these institutions often form a cartel, organizations with coordinated plans for production and pricing, and have a rather negative impact on domestic consumers and production efficiency.

The weakness of this corporate governance has been assessed by the European Bank for Reconstruction and Development (EBRD), which situates Uzbekistan at a "2-minus" level on a scale of 1 (worst) to 4-plus (best).[46] In many large corporations there is no division between the government, on the one hand, and the regulation of the functions of the government and business, on the other.[47]

Often, joint-stock companies do not publish in full the indicators of their financial reports. It is typical of joint-stock companies in Uzbekistan to try to avoid paying dividends or allowing their stock to be sold on the free market (for fear of losing control over the enterprises).[48]

Managers of enterprises, who are not adequately controlled by shareholders, often run enterprises to suit their own personal interests. They often channel investments not toward projects that would be most profitable for the enterprise, but ones that give managers the largest possible advantage.

Agriculture

In 2003 agriculture employed approximately 40 percent of the labor force and produced 29 percent of the GDP. It is impossible for Uzbekistan to achieve stable economic growth and to reduce poverty without agricultural reform.

Agricultural land belongs to the state: it cannot be bought and sold on the market, and it can only be granted to agricultural producers to use, not own. At the present time, agricultural production is concentrated in three main forms of enterprises: (a) collective *shirkaty*; (b) individual farms; and (c) peasant household plots.

The "shirkaty" are collective agricultural enterprises; they were formerly state and collective farms (*sovkhozy* and *kolkhozy*); they consist of multifamily production links, which have been allocated land allotments (for a minimum of a three-year period) and property shares. The accounting of material and labor expenditures in the shirkat is performed by the same "check system" employed in earlier collective farms. The shirkaty occupied most of the arable land (until 2004 when they were surpassed by individual farmers) and produced approximately 90 percent of the cotton and 70 percent of the grain.

Many shirkaty, however, operate at a loss. One reason for their unprofitability is the state's low procurement price, which does not cover the costs of producing raw cotton. Moreover, apart from the low procurement price, part of the payment to cotton growers is not made until four to six months after the state buys the cotton. That makes it extremely difficult to settle accounts, in a timely fashion, with the industries that service the cotton industry. [49] Thus, the bulk of added value from cotton production (the difference between procurement and world prices, minus transportation costs), as in the Soviet period, goes to the state, not the peasants. The fact that the peasant does not own the cotton harvest, nor the land itself, is the fundamental problem for agriculture in Uzbekistan. About 80–85 percent of all cultivated land is used for grain and cotton with the government set procurement prices.

The institution of collective farms was forcibly superimposed in Uzbekistan in the Soviet era, but has been retained since the collapse of the USSR. The state and collective farms were renamed shirkaty, but the very essence of the Soviet agrarian system still exists, with minor modifications. The main reason, apparently, lies in the fact that the collective farms are a convenient mechanism for extracting rent from agriculture. The collective farm turns private property (the harvest) into collective property, which is then controlled by the elite in the collective farm—that is, officials are subordinate to higher-ranking officials, not the collective farm workers. There is also one further instrument to alienate the peasant producer from his product: the processing of raw cotton into a final export product—cotton fiber—is concentrated in a few large cotton plants, which are completely owned and controlled by the state. The end result is that rents are extracted from agriculture and used to finance industrialization.

Therefore, a reduction in rents from agriculture and an increase in added value (and incentives) for peasant producers can be promoted not only by replacing collective farms with independent family farms, but also by privatizing the main share of charter capital in cotton processing plants. If officials resist, an alternative is to assist peasants to construct dozens of new mini-cotton plants to process the cotton from several farmers. Each mini-cotton plant would be the private property of these farmers; it would give them physical control over the final export product.

A record-low harvest of cotton in 2003 (2.86 million tons, compared to a planned output of 3.6 million tons) was mainly due to the weak incentives for peasants in shirkaty to grow cotton. After all, current state procurement prices only bring a loss. There are numerous reports of shirkat members smuggling cotton as contraband into neighboring Kyrgyzstan and Kazakhstan, where raw cotton prices are 2 to 2.5 times higher than in Uzbekistan. This shows that the existing shirkat system and marketing boards have run their course and have a negative impact on production.

As in the Soviet era, the centralized planning for the delivery of resources for agriculture has remained inefficient. Some materials are supplied at inflated prices and without regard to demand on the part of the farmers. Moreover, the full volume of these centralized resources does not reach the farmers.

At the same time, during the thirteen years of independence, the independent farmer has gradually emerged as a more efficient form of large scale agricultural producer. According to official statistics, the share of farmers in agricultural output remains very low, but rose to 20.4 percent in 2004. A presidential decree of 2003 gave farmers the right to lease land for up to fifty years, with the possibility of bequeathing this right. In reality, however, it did not give an ironclad guarantee to this right; it is liable to violation by state organs, as indeed has already happened in a number of oblasts. As a result, most farmers engage in animal husbandry, although they do account for 20 percent of the grain and 10 percent of the cotton.

Dekhkonlar—peasants with household plots—produce about 70 percent of the vegetables, potatoes, fruits, and grapes. It is the most efficient form of agricultural business that produced about 60 percent of all agricultural output in 2004, but covers less than 20 percent of the cultivated land. Recently, the subsistence and noncommercial character of such households have intensified; that is, they have increased the share of personal consumption of what is produced, rather than sell the products on the market. The administrative barriers to markets for those who have farms and household plots (in order to sell agricultural products in the cities of Uzbekistan or for export) provide no incentive to increase the production of fruits and vegetables. In addition, the dekhkonlar, who are forced to work on shirkaty, spend significant time performing corvée labor on the collective farms; there they toil in cotton and grain fields, with the harvest going to the state. Local administration is often a decisive factor hampering the development of private farming.

Financial Sector

For liberalization of the currency exchange and trade to succeed, it is necessary to undertake complementary reforms, above all in the financial sector of Uzbekistan. The Central Bank of Uzbekistan was de facto not an independent institution; over the course of many years it has permitted chronic inflation, targeted credits, and the absence of convertibility for the national currency. However, there are signs of growing independence for the Central Bank: the sharp contraction and formal abolition of directed credits at the end of 2002, the more austere money supply (especially the limits on sum in the form of cash), and the introduction of convertibility on current account transactions in 2003.

Unfortunately, market mechanisms for managing the monetary policy of Uzbekistan are still at an early stage of gestation. The main mechanism consists of cash plans for the sum, which bears an administrative character. Although these were de jure abolished in December 2002, they de facto continue to exist. According to these plans, a business has to place all cash in banks and must withdraw funds from its account according to a previously established plan and only within the framework of permissible goals and amounts.

Indirect instruments of monetary regulation through transactions on the open market are also in an embryonic state, for the financial market itself is very narrow and undeveloped. The stock market has little liquidity: its capitalization was approximately 25 percent to GDP in 2004, the volume of trade on the stock market did not exceed 1.3 percent of GDP in 2000–2004. On the stock market, a significant level of insider trading and cross holdings exists. In 2002, for example, the volume of sales in the secondary market (through direct contracts between sellers and buyers) accounted for over 80 percent of the total stock exchange turnover. In July 2003, however, the government issued a new decree that limited trading outside the stock market exchange, and the share of such transactions was still greater than 40 percent in 2004.

Market sources of liquidity are limited. The interbank market is lethargic; in 2000–2001, this market (on the basis of bilateral bank agreements) had few transactions.[50] Although the situation improved somewhat in 2003, as of late 2004 there had been no fundamental changes. Nor is there a universal money market. The real interest rates for state treasury bills were negative until 2003—that is, unattractive. There is almost no secondary market for treasury bills, and this hampers liquidity management of financial institutions.

One goal of financial institutions is to mobilize savings for investment. However, the level of national savings is low—less than 14 percent of GDP. The main cause is the high taxation, which crowds out private savings. The diversion of the farmers' income by various marketing boards and the monopolization of industry (which has intensified in a closed economy) reduces the savings opportunities of the rural populace.

The main and largest segment of the financial sector in Uzbekistan consists of commercial banks. The insufficiently strict distinction between clients and owners of banks, the excessive secrecy of financial data, and the low salaries of managers in state banks—all had impeded an improvement in bank management. The salaries of managers at the higher level in banks under state control are on the order of 100 to 150 dollars per month. Not surprisingly, a major reason for denying credits to small- and medium-sized businesses is the latters' refusal to pay kickbacks that the bank management[51] sometimes extorts (on the level of 5 percent of the credit amount).[52] These "informal payments" (bribes) induce banks to choose not the best projects, but borrowers who pay kickbacks; the borrowers, in turn, think that the bribes obviate the duty to repay the loan on time, thereby creating higher risks for the entire banking system. However, banks often have to refuse to provide loans because of high systemic risks in the given distorted business environment with high volatility of regulations, particularly in tax sphere, and unsecured property rights. These factors partly explain that share of commercial banks' credits in investment financing is less than 2.5 percent.

More than 85 percent of the banking system is concentrated in six large banks, which are under state control or influence. Approximately three-quarters of all banking assets and 70 percent of all foreign trade transactions are in the Central Bank of Uzbekistan, which belongs wholly to the state. This bank is a shareholder in five other commercial banks. Although there do exist small private banks, the large state and semi-state banks enable the government to exert considerable control over credit policy and to force banks to perform other functions of state policy. For the present, the privatization of the large banks is proceeding at a slow pace.

Approximately three-quarters of all credits are guaranteed by the government, with the great majority of these credits passing through the large state-controlled banks. For banks this means that, in the case of credits backed by the government (i.e., taxpayers), there is no special need to make a detailed study of business plans of credit applicants or to worry about repayment in general. Therefore, the banking system exhibits the typical problems described in the scholarly literature:[53] (a) state banks are vehicles for patronage; as long as state banks play a prominent role, lending tends to be scarce and costly for many enterprises; and (b) the continued presence of state banks has severely limited the financial sector and economic development in transition economies.

The banks in Uzbekistan are obliged to perform functions inappropriate for commercial banks, leading to higher costs of bank transactions. Banks are obliged to analyze wholesale and retail trade to ensure that trade regulations are observed, to track organizations that provide paid services to consumers (to ensure that the volume of services provided are in line with the revenues received), to organize the inspection of cash transactions, and to submit data on transactions to tax authorities.[54] As a result, banks are burdened with a surfeit of paperwork.

In Uzbekistan, state inspection functions undermine confidence in banks. According to a survey conducted by the International Finance Corporation,[55] small- and medium-sized enterprises do not view banks as effective financial intermediaries—because of legal restrictions on cash withdrawals, bank bureaucracy, lack of cash in banks, high commission fees, unofficial payments to banks employees, and the slow processing of bank transactions.

Non-banking and contractual savings institutions have only begun to develop. Since 2002, with the support of foreign organizations, there has been an active development of credit unions, the number of which has reached fourteen. However, the total capital of these unions is incomparably less than the capital in the banking system.

Trading on the currency exchange is not developed. The only banks operating on official currency exchanges are obliged to purchase and sell hard currency through the Central Bank alone. An interbank currency exchange is almost absent. This leads to a great bureaucratization of the currency exchanges and exchange rates. The exchange rate is set by the Central Bank for one week. There are also delays in carrying out the conversion of declarations from banks, since conversion is done within the framework of the currency exchange balance set by the government.

External Sector

The existence of marketing boards (trading organs that enable the government to control the export of cotton, nonferrous metals, and energy resources—which constitute about two-thirds of exports) and the policy on domestic prices of goods subject to centralized export undermine incentives to produce these goods. For example, in 2002–2003, the ratio of state procurement prices to the prices on analogous goods in neighboring countries was about 40 to 45 percent for cotton and 75 to 85 percent for grain (a calculation based on official currency exchange rates at that time).[56]

The prohibitive import tariffs on shuttle traders and the closing of borders to the free movement of people since 2002 demonstrates an intention to maintain a closed economy in Uzbekistan.

The limited diversification of exports (more than 60 percent of the export income comes from cotton and gold) makes the economy excessively dependent on the permanent fluctuations in the world prices of these two goods.

Fortunately for Uzbekistan, in 2002–2004 the country experienced a rapid growth in the world prices for main export commodities: cotton, gold, natural gas, and nonferrous metals. For the period 2002–2004, world prices rose 32 percent for gold, 33 percent for cotton, 83 percent for copper, and 40 percent for natural gas. However, this price rise can have dangerous consequences: an increase in hard-currency earnings from state trade will reduce the government's dependence on foreign donors and the domestic private sector, and that in turn enables it to slow the pace of market reforms and development of the private sector. Under these conditions, the government can finance itself by relying on centralized exports, that is, without relying on the private sector, small businesses, and the support of the general population. Moreover, the permanent external price shocks for the main goods exported and imported create the need for a constant adjustment of the budget, the banking system, and the currency exchange rate.[57] Unfortunately, the adaptation of the government to external shocks has often come through the isolation of the economy.

Regional Disintegration

The main cause of Uzbekistan's isolation from neighboring states and its policy of promoting regional disintegration is the policy of import substitution, with an emphasis on administrative methods of regulating the economy. For example, according to one internet source, the Cabinet of Ministers of Uzbekistan adopted a secret decision to limit trade with Kazakhstan and Kyrgyzstan.[58] This triggers economic and political disputes with neighboring states. For example, some Tajik specialists even assert that "Uzbekistan, in a unilateral fashion, is conducting an undeclared economic blockade with respect to Tajikistan."[59]

Despite the reduction in trade flows between countries of this region, problems concerning the use of water, energy resources, communications, and transportation are of vital, mutual interest. But most of the signed agreements in this sphere do not function, for they lack a mutually acceptable mechanism for implementation and enforcement. The key problem is that no fundamental resolution has been devised to resolve contradictions in the interests of countries with respect to the distribution of water and energy in the region. It is necessary to establish optimal regimens and fair prices for the use of both these resources—that is, one based on the conception of opportunity costs.

One major reason for poor cooperation and integration in the region is the lack of a clear understanding of the gains and losses that integration—and its absence—entail for each country. The situation reminds one of the old anecdote about how two economists are walking down a street, and one suddenly exclaims: "Look—there is a $100 bill on the street!" To which the other replies: "You're mistaken. According to economic theory, if that were a $100 bill, someone would have picked it up long ago!" Apparently, the governments in this region do not have an adequate grasp of the scale of economic losses in their countries caused by the lack of sufficient regional integration. Hence a good quantitative analysis of opportunity costs and benefits from regional integration for key sectors in every country in Central Asia would be a very useful step toward closer cooperation. So far as the authors are aware, such a serious analysis has not been undertaken.

Moreover, the governments in Central Asia are not ready to accept the fact that the gains from regional integration would be distributed asymmetrically. Namely, industry in Kazakhstan and Uzbekistan would benefit from enlarging their markets, whereas Kyrgyzstan and Tajikistan would derive greater advantages of access to large markets of Kazakhstan and Uzbekistan. Gains from regional integration with cross-border exchange of resources would be largely enjoyed by regular consumers (because of the inflow of cheaper goods), labor-intensive industries (due to labor migration from

Uzbekistan and Tajikistan), transportation sectors, and competitive domestic producers of consumer goods. Major short-term losers may include domestic monopolies that produce goods for countries in the region (since their power would be undermined by foreign competitors). Hence valid institutions for compensating the losers and for resolving conflicts should be established to promote integration.

Kyrgyzstan and Tajikistan have an interest in establishing a fair price on the use of water by countries in the region. This water lies on the lower reaches of the Syr Darya and Amu Darya rivers. In the future, Kyrgyzstan and Tajikistan (and probably Afghanistan) will make more active use of these rivers to produce electric power and irrigate crops. The latter, however, could receive a fair, scientifically based, not just ad hoc bargained compensation, for observing an adequate regimen in the utilization of water from the rivers in this region. But that would upset the customary irrigation regimen for water usage in other countries and lead to smaller harvests for them. At the present time, attempts to cooperate on energy and water usage in the region have only led to ineffective half-measures. The present equilibrium will be upset as soon as Kyrgyzstan and Tajikistan embark on stable economic growth, for that will entail an increase in the demand for electric power and an infusion of domestic investments to expand the hydroelectric power system. The current balance also can be upset if foreign investors (for example, China, Pakistan, India, other foreign creditors, or international financial organizations) are prepared to build hydroelectric power stations in Kyrgyzstan and Tajikistan to export cheap electricity.

Efficient water usage in the region, which is dictated by the growing deficit of water resources (because of the increase in population and production), above all means that it is essential to introduce an efficient mechanism to pay for water consumption in Kazakhstan, Turkmenistan, and Uzbekistan. In southern Kazakhstan, that will lead to a change in the structure of plantings and to the bankruptcy of inefficient farms. In Uzbekistan and Turkmenistan, it will provoke serious additional social tension in rural areas (where most of the population lives): farmers there are in no position to pay for water to compensate for opportunity costs, given the states' low procurement prices on cotton and grain. In short, greater stability and efficiency in regional cooperation depend directly on the development of market mechanisms for economic management in all these countries, but above all in Uzbekistan.

Among recent negative developments in regional integration, it should be noted that the Central Asian Bank for Cooperation and Development, which was established in 1994, has been closed in all the countries of the region. This was due partly to shortcomings in its administration, but also to the lack of real interest in seeing that the bank succeeds.

On the whole, unfortunately, one must admit that hitherto Central Asia has not created any stable institution for regional economic cooperation, one that could provide for a sharing of risks and mechanisms to resolve conflicts.

Indeed, one can see no signs in Central Asia of a common foreign trade policy, coordination of economic policies, free trade, and high level of mobility for capital and labor. Artificially high trade barriers, which some countries of the region have created in an effort to protect and develop domestic industry, have not been useful. That is because, under such conditions, many sectors lack the incentives to develop, generate innovation, and become more competitive. However, cooperation and integration with more liberalized countries (Kazakhstan and Kyrgyzstan) would undoubtedly advance the economic and political liberalization of the entire region. Regional institutions of cooperation could contribute to the development of more efficient institutions in each of the countries in Central Asia.

Clans as an Economic Institution

Clans are a multifunctional economic institution. On the level of "elites," they can be seen as organizations that engage in competitive struggles and seek economic rents. Clans also provide insurance for members in "bad times," whereas an undeveloped market offers no protection in a situation fraught with large and diverse risks. As in ancient times, when people could not survive without their tribes, a businessman in an underdeveloped market cannot succeed without the support of his clan. On the level of common people (i.e., those who are neither in the government nor in big business), clans help individuals to endure conditions of uncertainty and defenselessness—that is, conditions of the transition period where one person often cannot survive alone.

Clans are also inclined to engage in state capture and to distort state policy in order to create rents. These therefore constitute important antireform forces.

However, the role of clans is quite complex. For microeconomic modeling, the domination of clans indicates the need to take into account not only economic behavior at the level of households and firms (as is usually done in economics courses), but also the behavior of clans. The latter, notably, are capable of an intraclan division of labor and strategic decisions. For example, many clans at the elite level specialize members on different goals, such as high posts in local organs of administration, law enforcement, and the judiciary, or in private business, and so forth. Clans repulse competition from other clans by relying on the assistance of relatives in the organs of state power.

Moreover, the clan can effectively defend the rights of private property of its members. An important advantage of the clan system is the possibility of building contractual relations based on trust, thereby reducing transaction costs. Clans, so to speak, provide a guarantee for the performance of contractual obligations among members of a clan (i.e., among "their own"). This is especially valued within the context of a shadow economy, where relations are not juridically fixed.

Clans dominate in the government and economy, given the patriarchal traditions of the majority of the local population. Uzbekistan is quite a large country, with several historically developed regional and ethnic groups, and these constitute the basis for the corresponding clans. The competition among clans, which is not limited by strict formal rules, obviously determines the political and economic agenda of the country. This competition has caused the orientation of government attention on a short-term, temporary horizon. And the decline of influence of a strong clan entails enormous costs for its members, since it enables another clan to appropriate the majority of rents in the country, oblast, district, or industry. Such a situation is characteristic of a country with a pyramidal structure of power and attests to substantial domestic political instability. The rules of the game for clan members are determined, above all, by the interests of the clan, not the country. Such a system, with the domination of several competing clans, makes it difficult to have an effective division of power between the executive, legislative, and judicial branches.

The Main Characteristics of the Economic Institutions of Uzbekistan

The following constitute the basic characteristics of institutions pertinent to the economy of Uzbekistan.

- Strong state control, a large role and share of state property in the economy, weak public accountability and transparency—all this imparts a feudal character to the institutions of governance. These have the pyramidal structure typical of many poor countries. Moreover, officials are essentially given "estates" in the economy, from which they collect various rents. The seeking and collecting of rents, as a rule, are realized by clans.
- The instrument used to counteract the objective tendency for a single economy to segment and disintegrate into different feudal "estates" and "principalities" is a strong, coercive centralization of economic, political, and social institutions that relies on top-down administrative mechanisms. Moreover, local initiatives "from below" are almost al-

ways suppressed, thereby inducing apathy toward innovation at all levels of state administration.

- Rent-seeking is the moving force in the political economy of reform. Any program of economic reform that ignores this fact is doomed to fail.
- The main type of rent-seeking in a country involves the creation of entry barriers to markets. This is the worst form of rent-seeking, since officials and their clients—in order to extract rents—have to suppress (by refusing permits and licenses, or threatening to shut down a business) a large number of useful economic transactions. The potential losses from blocked transactions exceed these rents by a factor of ten.
- The country has an acute shortage of balancing and shock-absorbing institutions, as well as institutions to resolve the conflict of interests between different groups of society.
- While cooperation between government and business is weak, there is often a perverse form of fusion between business and bureaucracy. Frequently, officials (or their relatives) assume the role of businessmen, actively conducting their own business "on the side" through front people, thereby gaining unequal opportunities to engage in business. This leads to the practice of granting various economic advantages to individual enterprises, associations, and concerns—not to branches and sectors of the economy as a whole. This causes enormous distortions in market signals and incentives; it also creates unequal operating conditions for all entrepreneurs.
- There is an orientation toward short-term goals. The competition between clans, uncertainty regarding the rights to rule their "estate," and the unfixed time that one remains in a given post—all this undermines any confidence in what might happen tomorrow. As a result, officials and clans seek to squeeze the maximum rents at the present time and to ignore the interests of long-term, steady development.
- The economy suffers from the asymmetry of information, secrecy and distortions of statistics, lack of clarity about functions, weak public accountability, and inadequate transparency. The main institutional constraints often come from foreign and international organizations, but also the natural limitations of the available natural and financial resources.
- The bureaucracy lacks a system of merit-based promotion; that undermines the criteria of competence and hard work and reinforces clan influence.

Among the general populace and foreign investors, the foregoing erodes confidence in the economic policy of the government. It also promotes apathy and a corrupt bureaucracy.

The main forms of illegitimate economic rents in Uzbekistan are:

- monopolization and restrictions on competition from imports because of tariff and nontariff barriers to trade;
- exemption of individual enterprises, associations, and concerns from taxes and import duties (which is done within the framework of some kinds of state programs, and without any official determination and enforcement of concrete conditions for the further development of production);
- low procurement prices on raw materials, followed by their resale at higher prices through marketing boards;
- corrupt management of state resources, including budgetary expenditures.

According to our estimates, which are based on the difference between actual consumption and registered production and imports, the shadow economy accounts for about half of the GDP and employs approximately 40 percent of the labor force. However, the institutions of the shadow sector require a separate study. The existence of the large shadow economy reduces the efficiency of any measures of economic policy, since the policy is based on indicators known to be false. In any case, the institutions of the shadow economy require a close study of their own.

Recommendations

Creation of Systems to Give the Government Qualified Advice

The high level of uncertainty and the lack of solid analysis of the consequences of economic decisions serve to impede a change in policy. The government is not always capable itself of calculating the impact of decisions it has taken, or to make a comprehensive assessment of possible alternatives for the political, political economic, and economic situation in the country. The government cannot always see certain alternatives and corresponding net gains or losses in the resolution of economic problems if these have not been adequately examined by professional analysts. If an objective, full analysis of specific decisions was undertaken at the outset, it would be possible to avoid many mistakes.

For example, the consequences of introducing high import duties on shuttle traders were not well considered. According to the World Bank's survey of poverty, a 1-percent increase in the cost of the consumer basket leads to about 0.73 percent rise in the level of poverty. [60] As a result of the introduction of high import duties on shuttle traders and the monopolization of wholesale trade in 2002, the cost of the consumer basket (according to some estimates) rose by 20 percent. At the same time, the incomes of the majority of the population did not rise—as a result of the increased protectionism, whereas enterprises faced institutional barriers to expansion. The rise in the cost of the consumer basket implies an increase in poverty (other conditions remaining unchanged) of 14.6 percent (0.73 x 20 percent); that is, poverty affected approximately an additional one million people, with all the ensuing social consequences and high price for a society.

Another example is the fact that a full thirteen years after gaining independence, Uzbekistan finally simplified the system for registering a business, and today it is at a level that is not the best, even by the CIS standards. This is very strange if one considers that the new small enterprises not only produce goods, but also create jobs, reduce monopolization, improve innovation activities, and lower social tensions. Most paradoxical of all is the fact that small businesses also produce revenues for the state budget and feeds a host of various officials (who receive bribes from small businesses).

It is interesting to note that, after the simplification of registration and, as a consequence of the increase in the number of firms, the volume of bribes from small businesses probably increased. According to the International Finance Corporation, the number of respondents from the small- and medium-sized enterprises who admitted giving bribes to officials rose from 5 percent in 2001 to 25 percent in 2002.[61] Among the transition countries, Uzbekistan ranks third in the frequency of informal payments, and in May 2003 43 percent of the small- and medium-sized enterprises reported that they recently had to dole out bribes.[62]

So far as society is concerned, corruption is always an evil. But it is better to have "corruption and economic growth" (from an increase in the number of firms) than "corruption and economic stagnation" (due to the fact that new firms find it difficult to start up). This shows that rents from artificial entry barriers (i.e., rents assessed by a small group of bureaucrats) not only stifle the development of the market and economy, but also prevent a still larger group of bureaucrats from obtaining larger rents. There is a plethora of examples of reforms that can be advantageous both for bureaucrats and for society as a whole, but that for the time being are not being realized because of the lack of corresponding analysis.[63]

Another example is provided by a document from the Cabinet of Ministers (on the results of economic reforms in 2003). It stated: "The Cabinet of Ministers notes that in 2003 the policy on the liberalization and reform of the economy was consistently carried out, and as a result . . . the average annual money in circulation contracted to 10.9 percent to the volume of the GDP."[64] The paradox of this passage lies in the fact that the ratio of broad money to GDP, which is implied here and known as the coefficient of monetization, is an indicator of development in the financial sector. The *higher* it is, the better. Therefore the *decrease* in the coefficient of monetization cannot be a positive event for the economy and still less can it possibly be interpreted as an achievement of economic policy in 2003. On the contrary, it is a serious problem, although characteristic in an initial period of macroeconomic stabilization. Whereas the average monetization among CIS countries increased in 2001–2003, in Uzbekistan it fell. Unfortunately, such confusions abound in the development programs, official statements by members of the government, and in various resolutions.

A group of qualified economists, who know how to conduct prompt and thorough research, and how to present an analysis in the terms comprehensible to decision makers and the public, could avert many mistakes in economic policy. A simple beginning—regular, candid, professional discussions of economic problems among the country's leading economists—would make a substantial contribution to understanding these problems and the ways to resolve them.

De Soto's Idea

In the contemporary, fast-changing economy it is vitally important to conduct quick and competent economic analysis in order to avoid crises and take advantage of opportunities. New ideas, which often appear in economic development, must be carefully analyzed and applied to a country. One interesting idea that has attracted the attention of governments in the region of Central Asia is presented in *The Mystery of Capital: Why Capitalism Triumphs in the West and Fails Everywhere Else* by Hernando de Soto.

The main idea of the book can be expressed as follows: It is necessary to have a legal, standard, and universal registration of the rights of private property. especially for assets that had no previous legal owners. This makes these assets more liquid and renders capitalism more capable of functioning. This change will be especially helpful to the poor strata of the population, which possesses a mass of illegal assets (for example, in the form of unregistered housing, for which economic transactions are very limited). As a result, this capital, which is enormous, does not participate in economic growth. Capitalism is based on legal private property, which must be effectively protected.[65]

As de Soto justly notes, the existence of a zone of prosperity in a "sea of poverty" masks the horrendous inability of a state to create, maintain, and respect the legal property rights of the majority of its citizens.[66] He adds that many problems result from the fact that legal rights are at odds with how a country actually lives and works.[67]

There are many similarities between the situation in Uzbekistan and what de Soto writes about some poor countries of the world. The peasants of

Uzbekistan often lack valid documents on their harvest, and a plethora of regulations cut off rural inhabitants from legal residence and employment in the cities. Villagers who lack the subsistence minimum are often forced to work in the cities for just any ancillary work in order to feed themselves and their families back home. They stand and wait for any work on the so-called "mardiker-bazary," the informal labor markets in cities; they must constantly pay bribes to the police for working illegally in the city, and so forth. The mass of excessive administrative barriers drives people into the illegal economy, which is an enormous source of bribery income for officials.

But there are also substantial differences between Uzbekistan and the de Soto model. The majority of people in Uzbekistan live in houses or apartments, which have a legal status. Almost all the assets in Uzbekistan are registered and belong to someone, although, to be sure, many assets belong to the anonymous state, with no real owner. For example, the majority of agricultural land belongs to the state, with officials acting in its name; it is difficult to find land that is not registered, even formally, to some kind of owner.

The countries of the former Soviet Union have begun the transition to a market from a position where the national income was distributed rather equitably, and where the level of education, law observance, and development of the infrastructure was significantly higher than is the case now. However, most transition economies in the CIS almost entirely lacked market institutions, especially the right of private property. In the former totalitarian system, the overwhelming majority of material assets were registered, although the formal private property rights did not come until privatization. Thus the majority of "huts" of the poor were registered; their inhabitants received the titles of ownership during privatization (if they did not already have these). While there are bureaucratic problems of obtaining permission to build or expand urban housing, these are not so onerous as in the cases described by de Soto. Illegal construction of housing and the search for work, along with the complex of associated problems that are characteristic of Latin American countries, are restricted in the CIS countries by the institution of residency registration (*propiska*), which severely limits the mobility of the labor force and contradicts human rights.

De Soto correctly notes that, to bestow legitimacy on the rights of private property, it is necessary to link law with the existing social contracts, which determine the really operating rights of property.[68] In fact, however, granting a title of ownership does not guarantee protection for private property. The problem of CIS countries lies in the fact that such social contracts have not yet been created, for the simple reason that private property rights were not historically developed in the former Soviet Union.

The main problem is the presence of powerful vested interests that strive to block the granting of real, formal rights to the majority of the population. Formal laws and private property rights have still not transformed assets into capital; that requires a whole array of institutions, as de Soto understands. Given the absence of effective market institutions and given the lack of powerful political lobbying for such institutions, property cannot give secure advantages. For example, de Soto suggests that the poor can use their "huts" as collateral in banks and for other transactions; in fact, however, the prospects for this in Uzbekistan are not promising. In particular, the banks in Uzbekistan reject such collateral, for the law makes it very difficult for them to seize the house and evict a family in the event it defaults on its loan.

Imagine that, per the advice of de Soto, the mass of poor were to come to banks and offer their huts as collateral for credits. First, the value of these huts would fall sharply. Second, if the banks try to seize these huts in the event of default (and this could be widespread), that could ignite a social explosion. Aware that the government would not allow this to happen, the banks would simply refuse to accept the deeds to huts as collateral. Third, it is not advantageous to banks to have nonliquid property on their balance sheets, since they have to pay taxes on property that, in the end, may not even yield a profit. Fourth, a mass of speculators would spring up, seeking to exploit the legalized capital of the poor to construct financial pyramids, as has already happened in many countries of the former Soviet Union. This raises the question whether financial institutions would be effective in opposing speculators and making use of the new, legalized capital. Fifth, who would carry out these reforms for the poor, why, and for what purpose, if even simpler, obvious reforms for the benefit of the majority of the population have not been undertaken?

There is a danger that one de Soto's theses will be taken too literally— namely, his suggestion that the main goal of politicians should be the creation of conditions to legalize the shadow economy.[69] It is interesting to note that de Soto's ideas about legalizing capital are gaining popularity in Russia and in Kazakhstan, where the elites have been especially active in supporting and applying them, but more likely out of their own self-serving goals for the private legalization of the capital of corrupt people.

In general, de Soto's ideas (on the condition that they are correctly realized and that the requisite political is present) can be applied and adapted to the conditions of Uzbekistan.

Liberation from the Yoke of an Import-Substitution Policy

Until the blockage created by the previous policy of a closed economy has been cleared away, Uzbekistan will find it very difficult to achieve success in liberalizing its economy. Frequently, the policy of a closed economy did not resolve existing problems and only gave rise to new ones. The main problem is that a closed economy has created powerful vested interests, which—over the course of many years—have become accustomed to receiving large rents. However, the earlier policy also spawned a number of other problems.

The import-substitution strategy of development in a closed economy actively used the banking system for investment (with direct targeted credits) in industrial sectors and service spheres that the government itself had chosen. After economic liberalization and under the conditions of an open economy, by no means will all these targeted credits yield a return; indeed, a mass of enterprises may go bankrupt. One can cite the obvious examples of plants constructed with foreign credits that are virtually at a standstill. Many government investment projects in the mid-1990s relied on an unrealistic currency exchange rate, but that false premise went out the window when the sum was sharply devalued in 1999–2000. Nor could loans to agricultural producers be repaid in sustainable way, given the price and institutionalized policy of past years. The difficulties in repaying government-backed credits have intensified, and the banking sector already finds itself in a quite vulnerable position, because the government in fact does not rush to repay the guaranteed credits.

Banks are already encountering the negative consequences of the former practice of issuing directed credits. According to an EBRD assessment in 2000, approximately two-thirds of all credits in the country were targeted, which in turn means a government guarantee of one type or another. These guarantees gave the banks no incentive to monitor the loans closely. This raised politically sensitive questions: What should be done with the assets of such unprofitable enterprises? And how are the foreign credits (which were used, or are being used, to construct such enterprises) to be repaid?

According to data published by the IMF in 2000, Uzbekistan has a very small share of nonperforming loans and a high ratio of weighted average capital of banks to liabilities (over 5 percent). However, this can be a sign of inadequate classification of bad credits, and may also treat government-backed loans as 100 percent reliable. According to our estimates, the real share of defaulted loans in the country is in the range of 7 to 12 percent, which is a heavy burden on the banking system.[70]

It is essential to accelerate the privatization and consolidation of the large banks that earlier served as "pockets" for the government. The restructuring of indebted enterprises should be conducted in a way that gives a leading role to commercial banks. This will contribute to decentralization and to less bureaucratization of the restructuring process; bank managers will be better motivated and prepared to make a proper assessment of the financial potential of enterprises. This will permit banks to understand the position in which their clients find themselves. Naturally, banks should receive greater rights to the property of debtor-enterprises and the opportunity to change management of such enterprises.

The most important macroeconomic indicator for banks is the currency exchange rate for the sum. A stable currency exchange rate permits the government and commercial banks more easily to settle accounts regarding foreign credits. Therefore the stabilization of the nominal currency exchange rate for the sum in 2003 and its appreciation by approximately 1 percent deserve special attention.

The government is seeking to stabilize the currency exchange rate by reducing the demand on foreign currency in the shadow sector, and to do this it has reduced the supply of Uzbek sum in the form of cash. This goal also impelled the government to increase protectionism in 2002, especially against imports by shuttle traders, although the latter were often used by enterprises to import components and parts for production. The government did succeed in lowering inflation, mainly by reducing the supply of cash. However, the predictable consequence of austerity in the monetary and trade policy was a slower rate of economic growth, which depends on credits and imported component parts. In September 2003, the IMF forecast that economic growth in Uzbekistan in 2003 would not exceed the 1-percent level, and that in turn means a drop in tax revenues and the financial stability of those economically active.

In our opinion, support for a competitive exchange rate of the sum would permit the government to create a more favorable environment for the development of business, and that would help commercial banks establish a stable client base. One of the fundamental incentives for exports and import substitution is a competitive exchange rate for the sum, which would permit products of nontraditional export to become price-competitive. However, support for a competitive exchange rate, which requires the devaluation of the sum in real terms, poses a serious challenge to the banking system.

Given the danger of a systemic banking crisis because of nonperforming loans, it is essential to eliminate unprofitable enterprises quickly (through restructuring), change the law on bankruptcy in favor of creditors, allow debt for equity swaps of enterprises, and adopt other large-scale measures. Otherwise, a lethargic banking reform can cause a long delay in the transition to stable economic growth.

Another problem in the previous policy was the common practice of over-invoicing imported equipment—that is, declaring elevated prices on imported equipment and component parts in order to obtain a larger volume of official currency conversion. As a result, the property value of enterprises with imported machines and equipment was substantially inflated, and this artificial initial price makes it difficult to privatize them. Repricing the value of imported goods on the basis of a fair price is a politically sensitive question. An alternative could be the holding of open privatization tenders.

Constructing Political Support for Reforms

The lack of sufficient incentives for productive labor and business activity leads to stagnation, a decline in production, and a contraction in the base from which to extract rents. In recent years, in fact, the volume of rents available for redistribution has shrunk. For example, the black-market exchange rate premium had dropped to zero as of October 2003, and in 2003 the country had a record-low harvest of cotton (meaning smaller rents from cotton exports). At the same time, given that the general population is willing to endure a lot and remains politically inactive, the natural process of reducing rents has proceeded very slowly.

In our judgment, the resistance of circles with a vested interest in the status quo and a closed economy will gradually recede—at the same rate as the available rents decrease. The decline in rents will naturally ensue from the lack of incentives to expand production and upgrade its efficiency. Moreover, the resistance of vested interests can be reduced by providing compensation and replacing old rents with new ones—to be sure, not so much that they will create an impediment to economic development.

An analysis of the interests of different groups shows that economic liberalization in Uzbekistan will not be a simple, easy process (see Table 9.4): it is heavily dependent on the posture of vested interests. It is possible that a new political conflict in the country will develop in Uzbekistan—between the new businesses (which would like to have more equal, clear conditions for their activity) and old businesses (which is closely associated with the bureaucratic machine).

The economic interests of small businesses, farmers, and manufacturing exporters favor economic development in the country as a whole. Therefore the development of these groups is a decisive factor in reform, for they determine the level of incomes and employment, the business climate, and the stability of the economy. Accordingly, the government could easily ascertain if its decisions are promoting economic development by examining whether its policies contradict the interests of these key groups. To obtain the opinion of the latter, it would be very desirable to create a presidential economic council with representatives elected from the above business groups.

If the question of the liberalization of trade were put to a national referendum, what would be the likely result? To extrapolate from the findings of sociological studies in several other countries, it seems probable that a referendum in Uzbekistan would endorse a liberalization of trade.[71] After all, the level of human capital in Uzbekistan is relatively high; the majority of the adult population works in the service sphere; and approximately 40 percent are employed in agriculture (where Uzbekistan has strong competitive advantages). All these sectors would benefit from liberalization. At the same time, only about 9 percent of the adult population is employed in industry; moreover, about one quarter of these adults work in enterprises that, in all likelihood, would find themselves in difficult straits after liberalization.

There is now a search in Uzbekistan for new rents—in the form of more stringent protectionism, including a program to localize industrial production. However, unrestricted rent-seeking can run the economy into the ground; vested interests themselves need to limit the rent-seeking to a level that maximizes the volume of rents at the current point in time. This is possible only by stabilizing the basic groups that receive rents, by redistributing rents within the groups, and by having a clear vision of the future situation.

However, if the government launches a full-scale liberalization that sharply reduces the rents of its political supporters, it could be quickly replaced by competing influential groups. Hence the government must compensate, in an acceptable way, the rents lost by vested interests and co-opt them as allies of reform. To achieve this, it must adopt a new policy of shifting rents.

It is also essential to stimulate the self-organization of private businesses "from below," especially by uniting farmers and small business enterprises in strong voluntary associations. The inclusion of these associations in decision making should be a process based on transparent, regular meetings. There are already examples of the successful effort of such associations to fight vested interests. For instance, the association of businesswomen in Uzbekistan became a lobbyist and obtained an amendment to the resolution of the Cabinet of Ministries from 27 October 2003. As a result, Uzbek enterprises received a legal channel to sell their goods through registered individual entrepreneurs on the retail markets.[72] This means a substantial reduction of oligopolization on the wholesale market.

The existing financial structures, including the chamber of entrepreneurs and goods producers, are not effective in defending the rights of private businesses. That is why entrepreneurs have no adequate confidence in these organizations. For example, according to a report of the International Finance Corporation, in 2001–2002 only 56 to 62 percent of the entrepreneurs polled knew about the Department for the Support and Protection of Small and Medium Entrepreneurship (a division of the Ministry of Justice). Of those who knew about its existence, less than 7 percent had appealed to this office for protection from possibly unfair actions on the part of state organs.[73]

Table 9.4

Analysis of the Possibility for Economic Liberalization in Uzbekistan

Group	Goals	Views	Resources
"Vested interests"	Preserve their own influence and opportunities to obtain rents	Liberalization is not necessary for successful development	Very large
	Reduce external influence	Economic liberalization can be dangerous for domestic stability	
		Liberalization is possible in exchange, and on condition of, large foreign assistance to offset the negative effects it will generate	
Exporters	Increase their profits and influence through liberalization	Uncertainty as to whether they can find a "place in the sun" on foreign markets	Weak lobbying (due to the lack of means in view of the heavy tax pressure)
Import-substitution producers	Support their profitability and production through various measures of protectionism	See a serious threat in liberalization; lobbying is their main hope for survival	Employ relatively few, but have a large volume of sales
			Well organized and concentrated in the cities

Service sector	Increase profits through privileged access to imports	There is no clear set of opinion Some branches (transportation, tourism) will definitely win; others (financial sector) can suffer from liberalization in the short term	Employ a third of the labor force and account for a third of the GDP
Small business	Improve living standards	Support liberalization, which will give greater opportunities for business	More than 170,000 small businesses, but their political weight is small and they are greatly dependent on officials
Majority of the rural population	Obtain the means to exist	Support liberalization because it will bring larger incomes from the sale of agricultural goods and lower prices on consumer goods	Represent 60 percent of the population and 40 percent of the labor force; economic mobility is low, and they are not politically active
Majority of the urban population	Improve living standards	Generally favor liberalization, which will bring more opportunities to earn money; however, there is the threat of losing some of their customary work	More mobile and active than the rural population but not organized

Economic reforms must be directed toward the development of medium-sized business, for the latter is the bastion of political stability and democratic institutions. Very large and huge enterprises are themselves capable of defending their own private property rights. Such protection often occurs in the form of oligarchical rule, with a discrimination against the economic liberties of the majority of the population—as happened in Russia during the rule of Boris Yeltsin.

Easterly, who bases his analysis on data from cross-country data, drew the following conclusions: (a) the initial share of the middle class in the national income predetermines future economic development, and that is a positive tendency; and (b) a high degree of inequality poses a large and statistically significant barrier to the development of mechanisms to promote economic growth. Therefore, income disparities determine the long-term development of a country: the less the inequality, the faster the development.[74]

Strengthening the self-government of citizens and establishing the election of regional and district heads will substantially improve the situation. It is necessary to develop a healthy competition between different clans, regions, and political groups.

It is also essential to conduct an informational campaign to promote the new institutional reforms and, above all, to organize the majority of the population (which will benefit from the reforms). It is also important to disavow the opposition of powerful vested interests. A limitation on the worst forms of rent-seeking can be achieved by demonstrating to the public the most negative consequences of such actions.

In the transition period, amid the colossal restructuring of institutions, it is impossible to construct only a system of economic incentives that could unambiguously direct any economic agent toward the development of the country. All countries with successful development had an ideology or a vision of development that would augment economic incentives and would give concrete, clear orientations for all. Needed too is a comprehensible ideology of economic development for the mobilization of entrepreneurs to make productive investments, to limit elites in their rent-seeking, to supply a more equitable distribution of the national income, and to defend property rights. It is also necessary to have an ideology that favors openness, the creation and intensification of competition, and the assimilation and adaptation of the best foreign experience. This would receive the trust of the broad strata of the population and provide control over the progress of the reforms.

Liberalization of the economy will mean substantially different conditions for business. It would make sense to consider financial amnesties for certain financial and tax abuses in the past, with the goal being to bring this productive business out of the shadows. The return of healthy production, which had fled into the shadows (because of excess and confused regulation, corruption, and enormous taxes), to the legal sphere of the economy would by itself ensure rapid economic growth.

Political support of the reforms would also emerge from the capacity of the government to support the poorest strata of the population. The very poor can lean toward extremist political forms that aim at a redistribution of the national wealth. The sharp inequalities in income, which emerged during the first years of independence, can predetermine a negative development for the entire following economic policy. Social conflict can intensify, and reforms can be scuttled, if the voice of the mass of the poor population is ignored.

The experience of many countries shows that the initial conditions of strong income disparities give rise to influential groups with vested interests, and the latter are capable of subordinating the state's economic policy to their own needs and appropriating significant amounts of national wealth. For example, a study by Engerman and Sokoloff explains the difference in the evolution of fundamental economic institutions and economic growth between North and South America by the degree of inequality in wealth, human capital, and political influence.[75]

Uzbekistan has its own rather effective system of social protection of the population through the mahallah (local community) committees. However, these committees need to be freed from superfluous functions of political monitoring on behalf of central authorities, for that undermines the popular trust in the mahallah committees.

Rents from privatization can provide compensation to vested interests for their support of liberal reforms. Although privatization in Uzbekistan has been conducted with extreme slowness, this process has accelerated in recent years because of the decline in the profitability of state enterprises. A decree of the Cabinet of Ministers makes it possible to privatize gratis an enterprise that is experiencing financial difficulties, but in exchange for the obligation to preserve its profile after privatization and to invest in the enterprise.[76]

Officials would like to privatize the spheres that they control, with the goal of consolidating these permanently as their private property. The natural outcome of this process would be the transition to large property owners through insider privatization, with the subsequent consolidation of their property rights—such was the model in Russia during Boris Yeltsin's rule. Clans and the state property under their control would, after privatization, constitute the usual oligarchical groups (as in Russia). There is a danger that the main state monopolies would simply reappear as private monopolies, turning the country's political system into a plutocracy. Therefore, if effective levers of influence for small business and farmers over the decision making of the government are not created, during a subsequent stage of development Uzbekistan could fall into the same trap of oligarchical rule as did Russia.

For a stable social contract between the state and farmers in Uzbekistan, the following schema for the organization of production and export may be useful. The state shares the profits and losses of cotton production with the farmers; the state receives up to 25 percent of the cotton harvest in-kind (as a onetime tax, and in exchange for subsidies on water and electricity and for state investments); the remaining 75 percent of the cotton harvest belongs to the farmers as private property. The farmers are free to sell their harvest to whomever they want, including export. This schema corresponds to the principles described in the Islamic laws on the distribution of shares of production between farmers and cultivators, which actually existed on the territory of Uzbekistan under the market economy that preceded the Stalinist collectivization of agriculture. Moreover, such a schema is clear and comprehensible; it provides built-in stabilizers of revenue with respect to any results of production. The state can use its share of 25 percent to support low prices on cotton raw materials for light industry until the latter has completed its restructuring.

Conclusion: Reform Alternatives

In order for Uzbekistan to make the transition from a command economy with feudal traits to a market economy of the capitalist type, it can borrow the formal institutions of more developed countries. Institutional innovations are not patented; they are not encumbered by any property rights.

It is naive, however, to think that the import of effective market institutions means the fastest possible transplantation of advanced foreign institutions, all through the simple promulgation of the corresponding laws. It is thought that, with a reduction in the intervention of the state in the economy, the market itself can put everything in the right place. It has often been recommended as well that the most advanced institutions be borrowed and that the pace of institutional development be maximally accelerated.

However, imported institutions and a market cannot take root in chaos. History knows a multitude of examples to show this. For example, the mindless import of the Western institution of private property to agricultural land in Iran led to massive ruination of the peasants. The latter sought to move to the cities, could not find work, turned into a Lumpenproletariat, and later provided the basis for revolution. Therefore an important criterion in importing the most modern institutions is the degree of their compatibility with the informal institutions in the recipient countries—that is, with its traditions, customs, and mentality. This helps to ensure that new institutions will take root, maximize the existing productive transactions, and enhance the freedom of the typical economic agent.

Another strategy for importing institutions foresees a preliminary experimentation and preparation of conditions for new institutions. For example, researchers of the Chinese economy attribute its success to the systematic use of institutional experiments, whereby various modifications of this or that institution undergo a test in different regions of the country, compete with previous institutions, and adapt to them.[77]

For these purposes, an effective reform strategy must foresee the organization of a constant open dialogue between the government and different groups of society to coordinate decisions and help create a consensus. The state, as the initiator of reform, can use the levers of industrial and social policy to compensate those who suffer losses as a result of the reforms.

For example the change of rulers in China as a result of administrative reforms in 1983 proved possible because of the significant list of privileges granted to retired officials. Namely, they retained access to government information as well as official automobiles and apartments; and many of them became advisors to the new appointees.[78] For society it is more advantageous to obtain reforms that significantly improve the well-being of many, notwithstanding the compensation of officials' privileges.

There exist two main alternatives to obtain support for effective institutional transformation in Uzbekistan.

The first is to direct the maximum effort at the construction of democracy as the main institution of society; within that framework it would be possible to achieve maximum mass support for economic development. The main question here is who will suddenly want to construct democracy and combat corruption (and how and why)? Moreover, democratization of society and a serious campaign against corruption (by cutting off the flow of rents) will provoke, at the very least in the short term, political destabilization of the entire pyramid of power. Thus this is a rather unrealistic alternative for Uzbekistan in the immediate future. However, it is necessary right now to resolve the pent-up economic problems.

Of course, it is possible to wait for some kind of economic crisis and use that to initiate the necessary political changes. However, every crisis is dangerous, since political changes can follow some unforeseen scenario. Under conditions where potential social conflict has accumulated, and where it is possible to envision the clash of national minorities and growing influence of fundamentalist groups, the crisis can have long-term, negative repercussions. Moreover, there is no guarantee that the new elites will undertake adequate economic reforms and be capable of continuing them.

A second alternative is to build political support for reform among vested interests through an intelligent policy of switching rents. The essence of this policy is to have those interests renounce rents that bring pure harm to the economy—above all, from barriers that block access to the market. At the same time, however, one could create new rents, which would stimulate the development of the country's economy and would also stimulate vested interests to participate in productive activity. Of course, this alternative is a less desirable, but more realistic choice.

It should be noted that the process of redirecting rents from harmful to less pernicious forms can get out of control and turn into the usual administrative corruption. However, Bhagwati has pointed out the significant difference between corruption aimed at creating rents ("rent-seeking corruption") and corruption aimed at participating in the sharing of rents ("rent-sharing corruption"). According to Bhagwati, rent-seeking corruption results in excess profits on the basis of an artificially created monopolistic power, but as a rule monopolies bring about a substantial decline in efficiency. By contrast, rent-sharing corruption makes it possible for vested interests to obtain a certain share of the profit. This creates incentives for them in the sense that economic growth makes the total "pie" of profits as large as possible.[79]

Rent-sharing corruption must be as clear and equitable as possible for all clients—in contrast to the traditional bribes. The latter not only function as a tax on business, but also discriminate and segment business, since not all businessmen have the same access to the "services" of bureaucrats. Bribes also create more uncertainty for business, since it is unclear on what terms an official will take a bribe and whether he will do what he has promised.

At the same time, whereas the struggle against corruption (the goal being its complete extirpation in Uzbekistan) demands endless efforts in the political arena, the reorientation from rent-seeking corruption to rent-sharing corruption can be much easier and, most important, realistically achievable. For example, the key officials can receive commissions for the expansion of exports; alternatively, they might be given some of the stock of export enterprises. Although such measures might seem unjust and unwarranted, it can help remove superfluous barriers and accelerate privatization.

An absolutely necessary element in redirecting rents is an export orientation, the goal being to "anchor" rents in the competition on the world market. This anchor has proven its effectiveness in the countries of East Asia, where a clear, stable system of rents (with more equitable opportunities to receive them) played an important role in industrialization. Industrial policy there, for example, largely promoted the creation, manipulation, and timely destruction of rents.[80]

Export orientation should be understood as an economic policy that creates conditions whereby the export of most producers is more advantageous than import substitution. This means that large rents should be created in export production—along with a reduction of rents in import substitution. After all, the latter is already protected by large transportation costs on the delivery of goods to Uzbekistan.

An export orientation would push the vested interests and monopolists onto world markets, and that would create incentives to raise the quality of management and production throughout the entire economy. With an export-oriented policy, Uzbekistan would be more interested in friendly ties with foreign states, especially its regional neighbors, in order to secure markets and transit for its exports.

We have already examined in detail the questions of making a transition from a closed economy to export orientation, as well as the paths for doing this. And we have given an assessment for such a transition according to fifteen criteria for the countries of Central Asia.[81] The basic components of such a policy consist of the following:

- support a competitive real effective currency exchange rate as the basic instrument for export orientation;
- intensify marketing in foreign markets and create private marketing systems; and
- establish an effective system of finance and insurance for exports.

For the development and successful switching of rents, and also for an effective import of institutions, it is very important to have a state apparatus that is of high quality. In this regard, it is essential to carry out broad administrative reform; this must be a top priority. Necessary elements of such a reform must include:

- establishing an effective institution for consultations between the government, private business, and professional economists;
- sharp reducing the excessive functions of state agencies and their interference in the economy;
- improving the incentives for the effective work of officials, and increasing their salaries severalfold;
- stimulating competition between different agencies in providing administrative services for business and control over each other; and
- ensuring that each agency is directly accountable to the population.

Restructuring the economy and confidence in the reforms can be achieved only with the assistance of a new technocratic Cabinet of Ministers. And the latter must have its hands untied, but be publicly monitored. This cabinet must act quite quickly and decisively, and it must not be fettered by past mistakes.

The potential for increasing the productivity of labor in Uzbekistan is enormous. Just by improving management and marketing alone, it is possible to double labor productivity in the majority of enterprises over the next three to four years. This figure is completely realistic, as has been demonstrated by the experience of changing management in some enterprises.

Although the policy of switching rents is very dangerous (since it can provoke corruption), this is apparently the only real option for development in Uzbekistan—short of a revolution. The majority of the problems of development of Uzbekistan is quite typical of many developing countries and can be resolved in a relatively short period of time. There are great opportunities for maneuvering if one approaches these problems in a practical way and on the basis of modern economic theory.

Notes

1. Easterly and Levine find no evidence that resource endowments affect country incomes directly other than through institutions, nor do they find any effect of policies on development once controlled for institutions. They conclude that bad policies are only symptoms of long-run institutional factors and that to correct policies without changing the institutions will bring few long-term benefits. See W. Easterly and R. Levine, "Tropics, Germs, and Crops: How Endowments Influence Economic Development," National Bureau of Economic Research (NBER), Working Paper No. 9106, pp. 1, 31.

2. See D. Rodrik, A. Subramanian, and F. Trebbi, "Institutions Rule: The Primacy of Institutions over Geography and Integration in Economic Development," CID Working Paper No. 97 (October 2002), pp. 2, 22 (www.cid.harvard.edu/cidwp/097.htm); R. Hall and C. Jones, "Why Do Some Countries Produce So Much More Output Per Worker than Others?" NBER Working Paper No. 6564 (June 1999). Easterly has demonstrated that variables that are standard in growth regressions such as financial depth and real overvaluation, and initial conditions like health, education, fertility, and infrastructure generally improved from 1960–1979 to 1980–1998. Thus, growth in developing countries should have increased, not decreased, according to the standard regression determinants of growth. However, in fact the average per capita income growth in developing countries in 1980–1998 was 0.0 percent, compared to 2.5 percent in 1960–1979. See W. Easterly, "The Lost Decades: Developing Countries' Stagnation in Spite of Policy Reform, 1980–1998," February 2001, p. 2 (http://are.berkeley.edu/~harrison/globalpoverty/Easterly_01_The_Lost_Decades.pdf).

3. International Monetary Fund (IMF), *World Economic Outlook*, April 2003, p. 105.

4. Rodrik et al., "Institutions Rule," pp. 2–3.

5. D. Dollar and A. Kraay, "Institutions, Trade, and Growth: Revisiting the Evidence," World Bank Policy Working Paper No. 3004 (2003), pp. 19–20.

6. D. North, "The New Institutional Economics and Third World Development," in *The New Institutional Economics and Third World Development*, ed. J. Harriss et al. (London, 1995), p. 23.

7. In this chapter the term "rents" is understood as economic excess profits obtained on the basis of a privileged position.

8. IMF, *World Economic Outlook*, April 2003, p. 102.

9. A. Dalmazzo and G. de Glasio, "Resources and Incentives to Reform," IMF Staff Papers, vol. 50, no. 2 (July 2003), p. 250.

10. Vsemirnyi Bank, *Obratit' reformy na blago vsekh i kazhdogo. Bednost' i neravenstvo v stranakh Evropy i Tsentral' noi Azii* (Washington, D.C., 2001), p. 14.

11. O. Havrylyshyn and J. Odling-Smee, "The Political Economy of Stalled Reforms," *Finance and Development* 37 (2000).

12. J. Hellman and D. Kaufmann, "Confronting the Challenge of State Capture in Transition Economies," *Finance and Development* 38 (2001): 31–35.

13. *Wakf* is a permanent Muslim foundation for religious and charitable purposes (for example, paying the clergy at mosques, endowing schools and hospitals, and so forth).

14. A. M. Davydov, *Agrarnye preobrazovaniia i formirovanie sotsialisticheskogo zemlepol' zovaniia v Uzbekskoi SSR* (Tashkent, 1965), p. 17.

15. L. I. Dembo, *Zemel' nyi stroi Vostoka* (Leningrad, 1927), p. 14.

16. Ibid., p. 58.

17. K. Marks, *Kapital. Kritika politicheskoi ekonomiki*, vol. 3 (2d ed.; Moscow, 1962), p. 354.

18. Davydov, *Agrarnye preobrazovaniia*, p. 23.

19. Dembo, *Zemel' nyi stroi*, pp. 74–75.

20. The prerevolutionary Russian dessiatina (*desiatina*) was equal to 1.0925 hectares, or approximately 2.7 acres.

21. Dzh. Gelbreit, *Novoe industrial' noe soobshchestvo* (Moscow, 1969), p. 106.

22. Davydov, *Agrarnye preobrazovaniia*, p. 74.

23. Dembo, *Zemel' nyi stroi*, pp. 83–84.

24. Ibid., p. 150.

25. Davydov, *Agrarnye preobrazovaniia*, pp. 202–4.

26. European Bank for Reconstruction and Development (EBRD), *Transition Report 2002* (May 2003).

27. The term "closed economy" is used here in the sense proposed by J. Sachs and A. Warner ("Economic Reforms and the Process of Global Integration," *Brookings Papers on Economic Activity*, no. 1: 118 [1995]). They define a closed economy as one which has at least one of the following characteristics: an average import duty in excess of 40 percent; the exchange premium on the black market is over 20 percent; nontariff barriers are applied to more than 40 percent of the country's imports; or the state has a monopoly on the main goods exported. The last two characteristics are still pertinent to the situation in Uzbekistan.

28. See the Heritage Foundation, *Index of Economic Freedom: 2003* (http://new.neritage.org/research/features/index/2003).

29. IMF, *Republic of Uzbekistan: Recent Economic Developments, March 2000*. "IMF Staff Country Report No. 00/36" (Washington, DC, 2000).

30. The rating on the freedom of the press comes from the organization "Reportery bez granits" [Reporters without Borders], an internet site (www.centrasia.ru), posted on 11 September 2003. Interestingly, on this list, the United States held only a rank of 17.

31. See the report at www.itu.int/newsarchive/press_releases/2003/30.html.

32. IMF Press Release No. 03/188 (11 November 2003): "The Republic of Uzbekistan Accepts Article VIII Obligations" (www.imf.org/external/np/sec/pr/2003/pr03188.htm).

33. A presidential decree of 20 August 2003 substantially simplified the registration of enterprises, reducing the term: previously unspecified, the decree limited registration to a period ranging from one to a maximum of four weeks.

34. Resolution of the Cabinet of Ministers from 5 February 2004 ("On the Application of Market Mechanisms to the Realization of Highly Liquid Forms of Products").

35. S. V. Rosenberg, "15 Arguments about Current Account Convertibility Frequently Heard in Uzbekistan" (www.imf.uz/arguments.htm).

36. International Crisis Group, "Asia Report No. 46. Uzbekistan's Reform Program: Illusion or Reality?" (www.crisisweb.org/projects/asia/centralasia/reports/A400894_18022003.pdf), p. 19.

37. Resolution of the Cabinet of Ministers from 14 January 2004: "On Supplementary Measures for the Realization of the Program for the Localization of the Production of Finished Goods, Components, and Materials on the Basis of Local Raw Materials during the period 2004–2005."

38. Shamil' Baigin, "Zhestkaia denezhnaia politika dushit uzbekskuiu ekonomiku—bankiry," Reuters, 9 March 2004 (www.reuters.com/locales/newsArticle.jsp?type=businessNews&locale=ru_RU&storyID=4524514).

39. International Finance Corporation, *The Business Environment in Uzbekistan. Report, 2002* (Washington, DC, 2002), p. 88.

40. Ibid., p. 33.

41. Ibid., p. 24.

42. Decree of the President of Uzbekistan, "On Improvements in the System of Organs of Economic Administration" (22 December 2003).

43. "Administrativnaia reforma—katalizator ekonomicheskogo pod"ema," *Narodnoe slovo*, 11 March 2004, pp. 1–2.

44. P. Mauro, "The Persistence of Corruption and Slow Economic Growth," IMF Working Paper, WP/02/213 (November 2002).

45. "Uzbekistan: obshchestvennoe mnenie—2003" (reported on 27 February 2004 at www.centrasia.ru).

46. European Bank for Reconstruction and Development, *Transition Report 2002: Agriculture and Rural Transition* (London, 2002).

47. However, a presidential decree (22 December 2003) ordered "the power of the organs of economic management do not include the functions of state governance, but also administrative interference in the activity of enterprises."

48. I. Pugach, A. Nazarov, Kh. Kutlieva, and L. Mirsagatova, "Informatsionnaia zakrytost' predpriiatii—bar'er dlia investitsii i rosta," *Ekonomicheskoe obozrenie*, 2003, no. 11 (November): 15–24.

49. "Sanatsiia i bankrotstvo sel'khozpredpriiatii v Uzbekistane," an article based on a report by the Center for Economic Research, 5 December 2003 (www.centrasia.ru).

50. K. Zhuraeva, I. Chen, K. Talipov et al., "Razvitie denezhnogo rynka v Uzbekistane," *Ekonomicheskoe obozrenie*, 2002, no. 5 (May): 4.

51. International Finance Corporation, *Business Environment*, p. 90.

52. International Crisis Group, "The Failure of Reform in Uzbekistan: Ways Forward for the International Community" (report no. 76 [11 March 2004]), p. 18.

53. K. Sherif, M. Borish, and A. Gross, "State-owned Banks in the Transition: Origins, Evolution, and Policy Responses" (http://inweb18.worldbank.org/eca.eca. nsf/), pp. 2, 78.

54. International Finance Corporation, *Business Environment*, p. 42.

55. Ibid., p. 11.

56. A. Abdukadyrov, "Valiutnyi rynok: osobennosti i problemy regulirovaniia," *Novosti Uzbekistana*, 7 May 2004, p. 4.

57. One study has found that, on average, shocks to commodity prices are very long-lasting. If fluctuations in prices continue for a period of time, then the cost of stabilization schemes will likely exceed any associated smoothing benefits, and adjustment to the new long-run levels of national consumption and income is the preferred policy response. This study has found, for instance, that the period of price shocks is one to four years for gasoline and wheat, five to eight years for copper, nine to eighteen years for cotton and sugar, and still longer for gold, natural gas, and crude oil. These commodities comprise key exports and imports of Uzbekistan; hence the price shocks are likely to be long-lived for the Uzbek economy.

58. A. Taksanov, "Uzbekskaia tamozhnia: dat' 'dobro' ili luchshe otdat'?" (Reported 29 November 2003 at www.centrasia.ru).

59. "Narashchivanie potentsiala stran-chlenov ESKATO dlia uregulirovaniia protsessa globalizatsii. Predmetnoe issledovanie po Respublike Tadzhikistan," June–September 2003 (seminar materials), p. 8.

60. World Bank, "Uzbekistan Living Standard Assessment. Full Report" (Report no. 25923–UZ [May 2003]), p. 14.

61. International Finance Corporation, *Business Environment*, p. 76.

62. World Bank, "Uzbekistan Living Standard Assessment," p. 47.

63. The authors are prepared to demonstrate a model based on game theory that there can exist two relatively stable equilibria in the economy amid the same volume of rents as a result of corruption. The first equilibrium is characterized by a small number of transactions and economic stagnation; the second is characterized by economic growth.

64. "Reshenie zasedaniia Kabineta Ministrov Respubliki Uzbekistan 'Ob itogakh sotsia'no-ekonomicheskogo razvitiia, otsenke khoda ekonomicheskikh reform v 2003 godu i osnovnykh napravleniiakh dal'neishei liberalizatsii ekonomiki v 2004 godu," *Narodnoe slovo*, 11 February 2004, p. 1.

65. Hernando de Soto, *The Mystery of Capital: Why Capitalism Triumphs in the West and Fails Everywhere Else* (New York, 2000). [Russian translation: Ernando de Soto, *Zagadka kapitala. Pochemu kapitalizm torzhestvuet na Zapade i terpit porazhenie vo vsem ostal'nom mire* (Moscow, 2001).]

66. Ibid., p. 81.

67. Ibid., p. 97.

68. Ibid., p. 175.

69. Ibid., p. 161.

70. We should note that, if the share of defaulted credits exceeds 10 percent, this is classified as a banking crisis. See A. Demirgue-Kunt and E. Detragiache, "The Determinants of Banking Crisis in Developing and Developed Countries," IMF Staff Papers No. 45 (Washington, DC, 1998).

71. A. M. Mayda and D. Rodrik, "Why Are Some People (and Countries) More Protectionist Than Others?" National Bureau of Economic Research, Working Paper No. 8461 (September 2001).

72. V. Zarudnaia, "Dostuchat'sia do pravitel'stva . . . pytaiutsia uzbekskie tovaroproizvoditeli," Zamon-info, 24 December 2003, reported on 27 December 2002 at (www.centrasia.ru).

73. International Finance Corporation, *Business Environment*, pp. 31, 81.

74. W. Easterly, "Inequality Does Cause Underdevelopment: New Evidence," Center for Global Development, Working Paper No. 1 (January 2002).

75. S. Engerman and K. Sokoloff, "Factor Endowments, Inequality, and Paths of Development among New World Economies," NBER Working Paper No. 9259 (2002).

76. "O dopolnitel'nykh merakh po uskoreniiu privatizatsii gosudarstvennykh nizko rentabel'nykh, ubytochnykh, ekonomicheski nesostoiatel'nykh predpriiatii i ob"ektov" (26 August 2003).

77. G. Roland, *Transition and Economics. Politics, Markets, and Firms* (Cambridge, MA, 2000); and V. M. Polterovich, "Transplantatsiia ekonomicheskikh institutov," *Ekonomicheskaia nauka sovremennoi Rossii*, 2001, no. 3 (www.cemi.rssi.ru/ecr/2001/3/docl.htm).

78. David Li, "Changing Incentives of the Chinese Bureaucracy," *AEA Papers and Proceedings* 88 (1998): 393–403; and Polterovich, "Transplantatsiia."

79. J. Bhagwati, *The Wind of the Hundred Days* (Cambridge MA, 2000).

80. UNCTAD Secretariat Report to the Conference on East Asian Development: *Lessons for a New Global Environment*, Kuala Lumpur, Malaysia, 29 February to March 19, UN, Geneva 1996.

81. E. Trushin and E. Trushin, "Challenges to Economic Policy in Central Asia: Is a Miracle Possible?" in *Central Asia: A Gathering Storm?*, ed. Boris Rumer (Armonk, NY, 2002), pp. 376–428.

10

Kazakhstan: The Development of Small Raw-Material Exporters Under the Constraints of Globalization

Stanislav Zhukov

In recent years the rate of economic growth in Kazakhstan has surpassed that reported in the majority of countries in the Commonwealth of Independent States (CIS). Indeed, international financial organizations have recommended the economic policy of Kazakhstan's government as a model for emulation. For many reasons, however, Kazakhstan has encountered serious obstacles in achieving sustained growth based on markets. The small population and low level of incomes make it impossible to orient mainly toward the domestic market. The lack of access to an ocean and the country's geographic isolation from the leading world centers of production and consumption create additional barriers to establishing efficient production and becoming part of the international division of labor. Given such unfavorable objective conditions, Kazakhstan had to make extraordinary efforts to become a model worth emulating.

This study consists of four sections. The first examines the dynamics, factors, and quality of growth in the economy of Kazakhstan over the last decade. It gives particular attention to the social and ecological aspects of growth—dimensions that have not received much attention in the scholarly literature. The second section investigates the political economic structure of power and property that has emerged in Kazakhstan and that has held firm control over the direction and content of economic policy there. The third section analyzes the macroeconomic and social consequences of the structural reforms that Kazakhstan has implemented (and on a scale greater than in the majority of post-Soviet states). The final section raises the question of possible alternative paths of development under the constraints of globalization.

The Dynamics, Factors, and Quality of Economic Growth

Dynamics of Growth

In 1996–2003, after the precipitous decline of production in the first half of the 1990s, Kazakhstan demonstrated impressive rates of economic growth. The country's gross domestic product (GDP) increased at an annual average rate of 5.5 percent during this period. In 2000–2003 annual GDP growth amounted to nearly 11 percent. Given the decrease in population, the per capita increase in GDP amounted to approximately 7 percent during the whole 1996–2003 period, placing Kazakhstan among the world leaders of economic growth. In the post-Soviet space, Kazakhstan has demonstrated the highest per capita growth rate, being surpassed only by Armenia and (if one accepts official statistics) Turkmenistan (see Table 10.1). Kazakhstan is one of three (perhaps two) countries in the CIS where the per capita GDP in 2003 was actually higher than it was in 1990 (i.e., before independence). The mid-term perspectives appear to be equally favorable: over the next decade, to judge from the dynamics of the GDP, Kazakhstan will continue to have one of the most rapidly developing economies in the world.

Structure and Factors of Growth

These high rates of growth in Kazakhstan were due to an accelerated increase in the production and export of oil. As statistical data clearly show (see Table 10.2), the decline in oil production ended in 1995, with output increasing 2.2 times in 1996–2003. The massive export of oil coincided with a rise in world energy prices; hence during 1998–2003 the physical volume of oil exports increased twofold, but the revenues from these exports rose threefold. Thus, whereas oil revenues amounted to 7.5 percent of the country's GDP in 1998, this indicator had risen to 23.6 percent by 2003.

The GDP moved upwards not only because of the increase in oil exports, but also because of the delivery of metals (including steel, zinc, and copper) to world markets. Despite some noticeable fluctuations, the prices on ferrous and nonferrous metals have also tended to rise in recent years. Given all this, the rapid increase in Kazakhstan's GDP is hardly surprising.

Table 10.1

Countries of the Commonwealth of Independent States: Average per Capita GDP Growth (1990–2003)

Country	1990–2003	2001–2003	2003 as percent of 1990 Per capita GDP	2003 as percent of 1990 Total population
Armenia[a]	−1.15	12.10	86	85
Azerbaijan[a]	−2.55	9.50	72	110
Belarus	0.95	5.75	113	96
Georgia	−1.95	7.20	52	79
Kazakhstan	0.20	10.45	103	91
Kyrgyzstan	−3.20	2.90	65	114
Russia	−1.70	5.65	79	98
Tajikistan	−4.85	8.05	50	124
Turkmenistan[b]	0.55/−1.95	19.55/7.00	108/77	126
Ukraine	−4.20	8.05	57	92
Uzbekistan[b]	−0.95/−1.35	3.30/1.45	89/84	124

Sources: Based on data compiled by the Statistical Committee of the Commonwealth of Independent States and on national statistics.

[a]The population figures are based on the author's assessment.

[b]For Turkmenistan and Uzbekistan, the indicators are calculated on the basis of official and independent sources.

Obviously, the future dynamics of Kazakhstan's economy will be increasingly determined by the production and export of oil. That is analogous to what is happening in Russia, where the dynamics of the GDP have followed the movement of oil production over the last twenty-five years (see Table 10.2). The same holds for Kazakhstan, where the accelerated growth of oil production fully accounts for that country's economic successes in recent years. Russia, Azerbaijan, the oil producing states of the Persian Gulf, and many other states have experienced analogous development and extraordinarily high rates of growth. In Saudi Arabia, for example, the per capita GDP grew at an annual rate of 5.8 percent in 1960–1980, with an even higher per annum rate in 1960–1970 (6.45 percent).[1]

Direct Foreign Investment: The Motor of the Oil Sector

The growth in oil production was enabled by a massive influx of direct foreign investment into the economy of Kazakhstan. During the period from 1991 to 2003, Kazakhstan absorbed a net of approximately 15.5 billion U.S. dollars in direct foreign investment (influx minus outflow). This represented over 60 percent of the all direct foreign investment in the economies of the

Table 10.2

Dynamics of Oil Production and GDP in Kazakhstan, Russia, and Azerbaijan (1979–2003)

Year	Kazakhstan Oil production 1979 = 100	Kazakhstan GDP 1979 = 100	Russia Oil production 1980 = 100	Russia GDP (Ponomarenko) 1980 = 100	Russia GDP (Easterly and Fischer) 1980 = 100	Azerbaijan Oil production 1980 = 100	Azerbaijan GDP 1980 = 100
1980	100	100	100	100	100	100	100
1981	101	99	101	102	101	107	98
1982	102	93	102	103	102	107	91
1983	108	97	103	106	105	109	90
1984	119	95	103	108	107	115	80
1985	119	97	99	110	109	117	77
1986	124	99	103	114	112	120	74
1987	128	100	104	115	114	114	78
1988	134	103	104	117	117	123	77
1989	133	100	101	119	116	113	74
1990	135	102	94	117	114	104	70
1991	139	97	85	112	109	100	66
1992	135	92	73	95	92	78	62
1993	120	84	65	87	83	60	58
1994	106	73	58	76	71	48	54

1995	107	67	56	73	68	42	52
1996	120	68	55	70	67	43	51
1997	135	69	56	71	68	45	51
1998	136	68	55	68	64	50	64
1999	158	70	56	72	68	54	78
2000	185	77	59	79	75	60	79
2001	208	87	64	83	79	65	84
2002	247	95	70	87	82	72	86
2003	269	104	78	93	88	80	87

Sources: W. Easterly and S. Fischer, revised by M. De Broek and V. Cohen; A. N. Ponomarenko, *Retrospektivnye natsional'nye scheta Rossii, 1961–1990* (Moscow, 2002), p. 227; database of the International Monetary Fund; national statistics of Azerbaijan, Kazakhstan, and Russia.

Table 10.3

Economic Significance of Direct Foreign Investment in Post-Soviet Oil and Natural Gas Exporting Countries

Country	Net direct foreign investment as percent of GDP (average unweighted indicators)			Net direct foreign investment as percent of gross investment in fixed capital (average unweighted indicators)		
	1991–1994	1995–1998	1999–2002	1989–1994	1995–1998	1999–2001
Azerbaijan	3.2	21.6	7.9	2.5	75.3	22.2
Kazakhstan	4.6	5.6	9.45	13.3	31.6	50.2
Russia	0.9	0.8	1.1	2.2	4.3	7.6
Turkmenistan	1.8	3.4	3.45			

Sources: United Nations Economic Commission for Europe, *Economic Survey of Europe, 2003*, No. 1; UNCTAD, *World Investment Report, 2002*; UNCTAD, *World Investment Report, 2003*; Sodruzhestvo nezavisimykh gosudarstv, *Statisticheskii ezhegodnik* (for various years); data from national statistics.

post-Soviet "south" during the first decade of independent development, and about one-quarter of all such investments in the economies of the entire CIS. Kazakhstan, with a population one-tenth that of Russia, attracted one-half as much direct foreign investment.

Direct foreign investment became the most important macroeconomic factor in Kazakhstan's economy. In 1991–1998, these investments represented 5 percent of the GDP, but in 1999–2002 rose to 9.5 percent (see Table 10.3). Taking a different measure, direct foreign investment accounted for 13 percent of the gross investment in fixed capital in 1989–1994, rose to about one-third in 1995–1998, and climbed to about one-half in 1999–2001. At least three-quarters of all direct foreign investment in Kazakhstan goes to oil production; it is therefore no exaggeration to say that direct foreign investment in the oil sector directly accounts for the current economic success of the country.

The Social Costs of Growth

Some commentators give a particularly high assessment of Kazakhstan on the grounds that its "economic processes are almost totally free of politics and populism."[2] However, a careful analysis of the social underside of "Kazakhstan's economic miracle" reveals some striking things. The contemporary economic processes in Kazakhstan are not simply free of populism but, figuratively speaking, are "free of the population." During the last five years, a flood of petrodollars has inundated the economy of Kazakhstan. Part of this has inevitably trickled down to the poor and poorest strata, somewhat mitigating the acute social problems. However, the overwhelming mass of the population could hardly imagine that their country ranks among the world-class champions in economic growth.

An examination of official social statistics that report income levels and the scale of poverty shows that, according to the official hard-currency exchange rate, in 2003 the average monthly wage in Kazakhstan was 156 U.S. dollars (see Table 10.4). That is a rather good indicator among post-Soviet economies; only Russia has a higher average wage in dollar-equivalents. Nevertheless, restoration of the pre-reform level of wages has moved at an extremely slow pace; as a result, in 2003 the average wage here was only 48 percent of the 1989 level. Matters are still worse in the agrarian sector, which employs more than a third of the labor force. In 2002 wages in the agricultural sector were only 40 percent of the wage level in the economy as a whole.

The situation with respect to pensions in Kazakhstan has become truly depressing. The key was the introduction of an "accumulative pension system" that commenced operation in 1998; it divided pensioners into two categories—recipients of "labor pensions" and recipients of "social assistance" (welfare). The latter includes the disabled, the aged, and those who lost a family provider. They number approximately 790,000 people (5.3 percent of the population). After a 30 percent reduction in 1999, the average social assistance was essentially frozen at a level of 22 to 24 U.S. dollars; by 2001, that dole was only about 71 percent of the subsistence minimum.

Labor pensions are now received by one and a half million people, or 11.1 percent of the population of Kazakhstan. These pensions were sharply reduced in 1999–2000 and have since been basically frozen at 35 U.S. dollars per month. As a result, even in 2002, the pension (in nominal dollars) was below its level in 1995–1997. Only from mid-2003 did the labor pensions finally begin to grow: on the eve of impending parliamentary and presidential elections, authorities obviously decided to ameliorate the plight of the elderly—the most disciplined and predictable cohort of voters.

According to official data, approximately one-fifth of the population has an income below the subsistence minimum, and approximately 7 to 8 percent have an income less than the minimal food basket and must live in dire poverty. It bears noting that the statistical picture of a reduction in poverty was largely due to the fact that in 1999 the government reduced the subsistence minimum and the cost of the minimal food basket.

Paradoxically, large-scale poverty appears in a country that, over a decade, has steadily demonstrated very high rates of economic growth. If one excludes the upper income groups (viz., people employed in the extractive

Table 10.4

Dynamics of Selected Social Indicators for Kazakhstan, 1995–2003

Indicator	1995	1996	1997	1998	1999	2000	2001	2002	2003[a]
U.S. dollars (per official exchange rate)									
Wages in the economy as a whole	79	101	112	119	91	101	118	133	156
Wages in agrarian sector	45	52	51	48	35	40	47	53	55
Pensions (at year's end)	31	49	47	45	36	31	34	38	24
Social assistance (at year's end)				42	29	24	24	22	
Subsistence minimum			46	47	28	28	31	31	
Cost of minimum food basket	26	26	29	30	20	20	22		
Index of Wages (1989 = 100)			28	29	31	36	40	44	48
Pensions									
As percent of average wage	39	49	42	38	40	31	29	29	35
As percent of subsistence minimum			102	96	129	111	110	123	
Social assistance as percent of subsistence minimum				89	104	86	77	71	
Percent of population with incomes below subsistence minimum		34.6	38.3	39.0	34.5	31.8	28.4	24.2	21.7
Percent of population with incomes below minimum food basket			12.7	16.2	14.5	11.7	11.7	8.9	7.8
Pensioners (thousands)									
Total	2,917	2,940	2,853	2,771	2,681	2,828	2,541	2,482	2,446
Recipients of labor pension				2,027	1,921	1,830	1,749	1,691	1,660
Recipients of social assistance				745	760	798	792	792	786

Sources: Statistika SNG, 2003, no. 6: 199; 2002, no. 5: 113; Sodruzhestvo nezavisimykh gosudarstv, *Statisticheskii ezhegodnik. 2003*, p. 366; idem, *Statisticheskii ezhegodnik. 2002*, p. 56; "Sodruzhestvo nezavisimykh gosudarstv v 2003 godu," *Ekspress-doklad*, pp. 51, 53; *Kazakhstan, 1991–2002*, pp. 105–7; and also the operational data for national statistics.
[a]Data for 2003 represents provisional estimates.

sectors, metallurgy, financial services, officialdom, and the criminal mafia), it turns out that the incomes of the rest of society barely (at best) exceed the subsistence minimum. The capital cities of Astana and Almaty, along with the areas that produce oil, metal ores, and smelted metal represent islands of prosperity in a sea of poverty and destitution.

The official statistics on employment convincingly show that the majority of the population in Kazakhstan has had almost nothing to do with the country's economic growth. A comparison of data from the 1999 census with the annual estimates on employment (as cited in statistical yearbooks) reveals that the census missed approximately two million of the employed (see Table 10.5).[3] Such a striking gap—where the census "lost" nearly a third of the labor force (!)—admits two possible interpretations.

On the one hand, in all likelihood the real population of Kazakhstan is substantially less than officially claimed. One cannot preclude the possibility that the migration from Kazakhstan in the 1990s was much greater than the published estimates. There is indirect evidence to support this suggestion: the Russian census of 2002 reported approximately two million more people than expected from the calculated indicators.[4] Much of this "surplus" may have included previously unregistered migrants from Kazakhstan. In addition, Kazakhstan's census apparently made an incomplete count of those employed in trade and other services, or the jobless and those only sporadically employed.

Both hypotheses are complementary, not mutually exclusive. In any case, the data show that approximately 1.5 to 2.0 million people lack a regular income, or are engaged in the statistically unrecorded informal sector.

Moreover, beginning in 2000 the national statistical service of Kazakhstan made a fundamental change in its method of calculating employment—a change that has only confused, not clarified, the situation. In 2001 the official figure for those employed was 500,000 (almost 10 percent) larger than the previous year (see Table 10.5). It might seem that this surge was due to the rise in the minimum retirement age (an issue treated in more detail below). However, if this hypothesis is correct, that does not explain why practically all the "newly employed" were in agriculture. Moreover, a year earlier, approximately 430,000 who had previously been listed in trade, along with 150,000 from other branches, were shifted to the category of agriculture. Such striking discrepancies and inexplicable corrections make the demographic and social statistics of Kazakhstan as unreliable as those of Turkmenistan.[5]

The social and economic structure of employment shows, however, that the main tendency in the first decade of independence was an explosive

Table 10.5

Sectoral and Socioeconomic Structure of Employment in Kazakhstan, 1989–2002

Indicator	Census data		Data from national periodical publications				
	1989	1999	1998	1999	2000	2001	2002
Entire economy (thousands of people)	7,735	4,177	6,128	6,105	6,201	6,699	6,709
Economic sector (thousands of people)							
Agriculture	1,730	1,115	1,360	1,342	1,948	2,379	2,380
Industry							
Total	1,591	695	903	904	855	830	824
Extractive		175	124	129	137	166	167
Manufacturing		370	627	628	573	514	504
Electric power, gas, water		150	152	148	146	150	153
Construction	824	142	223	211	226	264	268
Trade	612	450	1,405	1,398	971	1,006	1,007
Transportation and communications	802	362	560	576	550	506	504
Other services	2,129	1,463	1,677	1,674	1,651	1,714	1,739
State administration	327	324	346	344	314	281	280
Socioeconomic structure of employment							
Hired employees							
Total (millions)	7,389[a]		3,783	3,354	3,504	3,863	4,030
Percent of labor force	96		62	55	57	58	60
Self-employed							
Total (thousands)	327[a]		2,345	2,751	2,697	2,836	2,679
Percent of labor force	4		38	45	43	42	40

Sources: Itogi vsesoiuznoi perepiski naseleniia 1989 g. Vol. 3: Gosudarstvennyi komitet Respubliki Kazakhstan po statistike i analizu, Respublikanskii informatsionno-izdatel'skii tsentr (Alma-Ata, 1992), p. 4; Sodruzhestvo nezavisimykh gosudarstv. *Statisticheskii ezhegodnik. 2003*, p. 363; Sodruzhestvo nezavisimykh gosudarstv. *Statisticheskii ezhegodnik. 2002*, p. 56; *Zaniatoe naselenie Respubliki Kazakhstan, 2* (Almaty, 2002), pp. 21, 26, 66–67; data from national statistics.
[a]Data for 1991.

increase in the so-called "self-employed." In 2002 their number reached 2.7 million people (40 percent of the total labor force); that compares with 327,000 people (4 percent of the labor force) at the end of the 1980s. Such a massive sector of self-employed, which does not easily lend itself to accurate counts, makes it possible to manipulate the statistics on employment, wages, and other social indicators. As a result, an analysis of employment statistics allows one to conclude that Kazakhstan lacks reliable data on the labor force and sources of income for one to two million people. Inter alia, this makes it impossible to construct an objective picture of the true magnitude of poverty and hardship in the country.

The Environment: "Devastating Growth"

It is well known that economic growth in Kazakhstan during the Soviet era entailed a sharp intensification in the burden on the environment. Gigantic projects in the sphere of hydroelectric power and irrigation, the cultivation of virgin lands, the mining and processing of uranium ores, nuclear explosions to create underground oil and gas depositories—these are only some of the most glaring examples from the history of a "nature-devastating" type of economic growth.

The profound drop in production in the first half of the 1990s eased the burden on the environment, for contraction of productive and personal consumption helped reduce the emission of pollutants. But the resumption of economic growth in the mid-1990s again intensified the burden being placed on the environment. Each year Kazakhstan produces about 10 tons of natural goods per capita—double the rate in European economies.[6] The main sources of ecological pollution are the country's two leading economic branches: oil and metallurgy.

The rapid growth of oil production in the Tengiz oilfields brought a rapid accumulation of a byproduct—sulfur. Approximately 10 million tons of sulfur have already piled up in open deposits; a pyramid of this volume would occupy an area equal to about two hundred soccer fields. Given the characteristics of hydrocarbon deposits on the Caspian shelf near Tengiz, the accumulation of sulfur tailings will increase sharply in coming years. In the initial stages alone, for example, development of Kashagan will produce about one million tons of sulfur byproducts per year.[7]

There are also other ecological problems associated with the oil industry. One is the burn-off of the accompanying gas—up to four billion cubic meters per year.[8] Another, less well known, is the radiation in the oil produced in Kazakhstan. According to data from the Institute of Nuclear Physics, the total volume of accumulated radioactive waste from oil production is nearing 1.3 million cubic meters. During the twenty years that the Uzen oilfield has operated, it alone produced a volume of alpha radionuclides almost equal to that of the plutonium dispersed at the Semipalatinsk testing grounds for nuclear weapons.[9]

The mining and metallurgy complex of Kazakhstan annually processes tens of millions of tons of various ores, with 95 percent as tails. The result has been the buildup of tens of millions of tons of waste,[10] approximately 7 million tons of which is toxic.[11] As the Ministry for Environmental Protection of Kazakhstan has admitted, by the middle of 2003 the largest metallurgical enterprises of the country (including Kazakhmys, with copper enterprises and the Ust'-Kamenogorsk lead and zinc plant; Kaztsink; and Aksuk ferrous alloy plants) have not complied with the norms for environmental protection.[12]

Despite the intensive and growing burden on the environment, Kazakhstan imposes virtually no ecological costs on production. The operating and capital expenditures for environmental protection amounted to 48 million U.S. dollars in 2000 and 153 million in 2001 (with mining and mineral resources companies paying only slightly over 10 percent of that amount).[13] In 2002, all the ecological payments and fines in the budget amounted to just 52 million U.S. dollars, or 0.2 percent of the GDP; the corresponding figures for 2003 were 85 million U.S. dollars and 0.3 percent of the GDP. Expressed in absolute terms, this is a whole order lower than in the other transition economies, and the majority of these have practically no extractive industry. Moreover, from these miserly sums the amount expended on ecological projects amounted to just 10 million U.S. dollars (or 0.04 percent of the GDP) in 2002, and then dropped to just 7 million dollars (0.02 percent of the GDP) in 2003.[14]

A generalizing indicator of the low ecological quality of growth in Kazakhstan (as in the majority of post-Soviet economies) is the proportionate use of energy resources. Reduction in the energy intensity of production is a general pattern in world development. The economies of the former Soviet republics, however, totally deviate from that global trend and, in contrast to market economies, have a very high level of energy intensity. In 2000, if measured in purchasing power parity, Kazakhstan spent 2.23 times more on primary energy resources per unit of GDP than did the developed countries; it expended 2.17 times more than did developing countries that export manufactured goods; it used 1.73 times more than the transitional economies of Central and Eastern Europe and the Baltics (see Table 10.6). Revealingly, the accelerated economic growth in Kazakhstan since 1998 has included an increase in the relative energy intensity of the GDP.

Table 10.6

Relative Consumption of Energy Resources per Unit of GDP[a]

Indicator	Kazakhstan			
	1980	1990	1999	2000
Developed market economies (= 1.0)	3.02	3.84	2.19	2.23
Transition economies of eastern and central Europe and the Baltics (= 1.0)	1.96	2.39	1.64	1.73
Developing countries exporting industrial goods (= 1.0)	3.80	4.01	2.17	2.17

Sources: IMF, *World Economic Outlook. Database,* September 2003; World Bank, *World Development Indicators 2003* (CD-ROM).
[a]GDP in purchasing power parity of national currencies.

Internationalization of Kazakhstan's Economic Assets

For a number of reasons, Kazakhstan encountered serious obstacles to steady, market-based growth. The small size of the population and its low level of income made it impossible to orient production toward the domestic market. As a result of internal and external liberalization, the inherited economic structure has split into two sectors: an export sector consisting of two or three dozen enterprises in oil production and metallurgy, and virtually all other production (which, because of the new configuration of demand and prices, has mostly proved uncompetitive—even on the domestic market). Under these conditions, the use of natural rents has become the main nerve center of economic policy.

R. M. Solow, a Nobel laureate in economics who has made the most significant contribution to the neoclassical interpretation and quantification of the process of economic growth, has formulated a short list of what he regards as the most urgent problems that developing countries face. The resolution of these, he argues, is critically important for understanding development in the peripheral zone of the globalizing world. His analysis raises two questions regarding the use of natural resources. First, what should be the optimal (or at least good) temporal schedule for the development, exploitation, and conservation of renewable and nonrenewable resources in a developing country? Second, what portion of the resource rents should be reinvested, and how should this reinvestment be distributed between the resource branch and other branches of the economy?[15]

From a superficial point of view, these academic questions may appear close to the emotional discussions about the use of natural rents, a "hot-button" issue in recent years in Kazakhstan and in all the raw-material exporters in the post-Soviet space. But that is not the issue here; it is not only (or even not so much) that the participants in these discussions, depending on their position, are concerned almost exclusively about the redivision or protection of rights to rents. Rather, Solow (and, of course, not only Solow) looks at the problem of the utilization of natural rents from the perspective of maximizing healthy economic growth in a long-term perspective. From an economic point of view, the use of nonrenewable natural resources as an intermediate input in the process of production represents a deduction from the national wealth. Through the consumption of these goods, this nonrenewable part of the national wealth must be transformed into physical and human capital that can sustain economic growth once the natural resources have been depleted.

Unfortunately, post-Soviet space lacks economic or political actors who have at least a strategic perspective on growth, not to mention the practical mechanisms to turn this strategic vision into reality. Moreover, contemporary Kazakhstan has largely ignored the question of optimizing the use of natural resources for purposes of sustained development. During the period of the takeoff of the ethnocratic wave in the first half of the 1990s and the feverish privatization in 1995–1997, the ruling and dominating Kazakh groups[16] actively exploited the thesis that Kazakhstan could be quickly transformed into "an oil bonanza." As a result of this frenetic privatization, a significant part (if not the majority) of local oil deposits and dozens of metallurgical enterprises fell into the hands of foreign and offshore capital.

N. Amrekulov, who has conducted research on the political-economic structure of contemporary Kazakhstan, has characterized it as a marionette offshore state that does not control its own economic assets.[17] That is not entirely accurate, for the former nomenklatura (political elite) has been able not only to preserve political power, but to constitute itself as the new proprietor and to rely on a global environment, not the local socioeconomic base. In fact, many offshore companies are controlled (to a significant degree) by people from the post-Soviet Kazakh nomenklatura, which has thereby established its property rights to economic assets and insured itself against systemic risks. Such a practice is widespread in the prolonged historic process in the country of establishing the institution of private property.[18] The genesis of post-Soviet power and property is organically integrated into the global political economic matrix.

At the same time, a significant part of the local economic assets has had to be surrendered to foreign capital, for Kazakhstan lacked its own resources and technologies to develop these. The main form of long-term contracts to develop and exploit the hydrocarbon deposits of Kazakhstan was an agreement on production sharing or analogous contracts. De jure, national governments preserve sovereignty over their natural resources; de facto, however, control over the resources and, especially, the financial flows shifted into the hands of transnational corporations.

Internationalization of Kazakhstan's main economic assets through the de facto transfer of control to nonresidents has consolidated the country's special position in the global system. The direction, rate, and rhythm of growth in the Kazakh economy, along with its structure, are primarily determined by global, not local, factors.

The structure of control over the most important oilfields of Kazakhstan (and, for comparison, Azerbaijan) that emerged by mid-2003 is evident from the data in Table 10.7. Column one of the table reflects the structure of control over the twelve largest surface oil and gas fields of Kazakhstan. The second column adds the oilfield at Kashagan on Kazakhstan's segment of the Caspian shelf; the third column includes both Kashagan and the Azerbaijani oilfields at Azeri-Chirag-Giuneshli. As the data on the shares of various participants show, the development of the Caspian hydrocarbon resources is obviously subordinated to the corporate strategies of American, European, and Japanese corporations. And, in the final analysis, the strategy of development of the Caspian resources will be determined by the situation on the world oil market. Kazakhstan itself will receive a small share of the earnings from its own natural resources.

As to the concrete terms in the agreements on the profit sharing with oil companies and offshore owners of metallurgical enterprises, very little is known. One can, however, draw some conclusions about Kazakhstan's share from several indirect indicators. Thus, in 1999 the budget revenues from the oil sector amounted to just 7.3 percent of the value of oil exports; this indicator rose to 13.6 percent in 2000, and then to 33.6 percent in 2001. In 2002, the budget revenues from the oil sector (together with the growth in the assets of the National Fund) amounted to just over a third of the income from the export of crude oil. To be sure, Kazakh oil is sold on the market at a noticeably lower level than the average world price. The main export market of Kazakhstan since 2002 has been the Bermuda Islands. Oil is sold to firms registered in this offshore zone of the contemporary world, and then resold at higher prices to final users.[19] If one takes all these circumstances into account, Kazakhstan apparently controls about a fifth of the real earnings from oil exports; that roughly corresponds to the share of Kazakh companies in agreements and consortia to develop the largest local oil deposits.

Another revealing indicator is the level of taxation on the largest local exporters. In 2000, the tax payments of metallurgical enterprises amounted to 9.8 percent of their aggregate sales; in 2002 this indicator rose to 11.4 percent.

Table 10.7

Shares of Investors in the Largest Oilfields of Kazakhstan and Azerbaijan

Twelve largest inland oilfields of Kazakhstan		Twelve largest inland oilfields of Kazakhstan plus Kashagan		Twelve largest inland oilfields of Kazakhstan plus Kashagan and Azeri-Chirag-Giuneshli	
Country of shareholder	Share (percent)[a]	Country of shareholder	Share (percent)[a]	Country of shareholder	Share (percent)[a]
United States	35	United States	30	United States	31
Kazakhstan	30	Kazakhstan	18	Kazakhstan	15
Great Britain	4	Great Britain	9	Great Britain	13
Italy	4	Italy	9	Italy	7
Canada	4	Netherlands/Great Britain	7	Netherlands/Great Britain	5
Russia	4	France	7	France	5
China	4	Japan	3	Japan	5
Others	15	Canada	3	Canada	2
		China	3	Norway	2
		Russia	2	China	2
		Others	9	Azerbaijan	2
				Russia	2
				Turkey	1
				Others	8

Source: O. Reznikova, "Perspektivy pritoka priamykh inostrannykh investitsii v ekonomiku gosudarstv Tsentral'noi Azii i Kavkaza," in *Tsentral'naia Aziia i Kavkaz. Nasushchnye problemy*, ed. B. Rumer (Almaty, 2003), p. 120.

[a]Shares are calculated on the base of the country affiliation of the energy companies.

The taxes on oil producing enterprises in 2001 amounted to 18.4 percent of the aggregate sales, but in 2002 that suddenly dropped to 14.4 percent.[20]

Although the terms of the agreements on oil production are closed to detailed analysis, professional economists have come to the firm opinion that Kazakhstan made a huge concession to the world oil industry. Namely, in order to obtain foreign investment, Kazakhstan signed international contracts that substantially reduced its share of the income from oil companies (as compared with the global practice generally accepted at the time).[21] According to data supplied by former Minister of Finance Z. Kakimzhanov, the tax payments of oil companies amount to just 15 to 18 cents on the dollar.[22] Apart from the fact that the tax burden on oil producing and metallurgy companies is not high, raw-material exporters minimalize tax payments by resorting to the practice of transfer pricing. According to data from the International Monetary Fund (IMF) and the Center of Economic Information of the Government of Kazakhstan, the annual budget losses from the use of schemes on transfer pricing in the oil industry amount to a half billion dollars.[23] Transfer pricing is also widespread in the metallurgical industry under the control of nonresidents.[24]

If one takes these and other circumstances into account, it is obvious that Kazakhstan has virtually no control over the utilization of natural rents. Attempts, ex post facto, to improve the terms by renegotiating agreements were doomed from the outset. As one leading Kazakh economist, A. Esentugelov, rightly pointed out: "It only remains for us to hope that Kazakhstan still has a lot of unknown reserves and undeveloped deposits, and that with respect to these the mistakes and miscalculations of past years will not be repeated."[25] The same is true with respect to the metallurgical industry, which has also been transferred to foreign control. In this situation, authorities can only defer the beginning of oil prosperity for another five to seven years, and to schedule the arrival of the "petroleum paradise" for 2020–2035.[26]

Structural and Institutional Reforms

The orthodox neoliberal transformation propounded by international financial organizations makes structural and institutional reform an integral component of change in post-Soviet countries. Kazakhstan, which has been so vigorous in making such reforms, has earned kudos from the IMF; the latter, as already noted, lauds the Kazakhstan model not only for other states in the CIS, but also for developing countries. However, hard information about the results and, above all, about the macroeconomic implications of Kazakhstan's structural reforms is inordinately scanty.

The National (Oil) Fund

In 2000 Kazakhstan created a National (Oil) Fund. The Fund was designed to serve two goals: stabilization and savings. In the event of a fall in world energy and raw material prices, the Fund's resources would compensate for the declining revenues to state and local budgets. In the long term, the Fund is to accumulate the means from enterprises in the raw materials sector and to invest these resources in foreign financial assets with a high degree of reliability, with the objective of obtaining investment income.[27] By the end of 2002, the Fund had 1.9 billion U.S. dollars, or 7.8 percent of GDP. In 2003, the Fund rose to 3.6 billion U.S. dollars (12.1 percent of GDP).[28] Moreover, the annual budgetary expenditures at all levels barely exceed 5.0 billion U.S. dollars; the accumulated resources are quite sufficient to compensate for possible losses due to a worsening in the global price conditions for a number of years.

The macroeconomic implications of diverting such significant resources from an underdeveloped economy with a very poor population will be examined in detail below. Here I would only like to emphasize that both in 2001 and in 2002 the return on the investments of Kazakhstan's National Fund was lower than the level of domestic inflation. Furthermore, that occurred when the return on the assets was approximately 4.0 to 4.5 percent in 2001, and 3.5 to 4.0 percent in 2002.[29] Parallel to all this, Kazakhstan attracted foreign credits and investments at a much higher interest rate. Hence, in financial terms, Kazakhstan—through the National Fund—continues to provide credits for the external economy. It turns out that the resources could be used in a far from optimal fashion, not only through investment in what is manifestly noncompetitive production, but also through theoretically irreproachable financial schemes.

In 2003 the return on the portfolio of the Fund reached 8.69 percent, which is two percentage points above the official level of domestic consumer inflation. At the same time, the general expenditures of the republic's budget to service the National Fund amounted to 400 million U.S. dollars.[30] Consequently, the drain on resources is continuing.

Tariffs on Electric Power

One of the main ideas of all post-Soviet reformers is to make the tariffs on electricity higher for the general population than for enterprises. They think that the redistribution of payments for electricity from the real producer sector to the household, with a parallel crawling increase in energy costs, will lighten the burden of costs for producers and thereby stimulate economic growth. And that in the future will bring about a rise in the standard of living.

Kazakhstan, like leading countries in the Organization for Economic Cooperation and Development (OECD), requires the population to pay 1.5 times more for electricity than industry (see Table 10.8). In that respect, it is a model of neoliberal policy. To be sure, it thereby forgets that the incomes of a significant part of the population are close to the subsistence minimum, and that the structure of national income is distorted to favor profits over wages.

The main paradox, however, is the fact that these relatively low energy tariffs (provided at the expense of the general populace) benefit the oil and metallurgical industries. And the latter channel their profits into accounts in Western banks and offshore world financial centers; in other words, they are diverting resources from the economy of Kazakhstan. This means that there is no need to wait expectantly for the promised rise in the standard of living of the population.

Pension Reform

In 1997, Kazakhstan became the first country in the CIS to establish an accumulative pension system. Beginning the next year, 10 percent of each employee's wages were automatically transferred to a state or nonstate pension fund. Moreover, in a country where the average life expectancy in 1997 was 70.2 years for women and only 59 for men,[31] the government raised the retirement age for both men (from 60 to 63) and women (from 55 to 58). At the same time, the state confirmed its obligation to pay pensions that had been earned earlier within the framework of the former solidary pension system.

The radicalism of Kazakhstan's pension reform astonished even the experts at the IMF.[32] In contrast to many developed and developing countries with a rapidly aging population (which undermines the basis for a solidary pension system), Kazakhstan has a society where young demographic strata are still predominant. In 2001 the group aged 65 and older constituted just 7.5 percent of the population (compared to 12.6 percent in the United States); those under age 14 comprised 26.3 percent of the population (compared to 21.1 percent in the United States).[33] Experts from the World Bank hold that the age structure of the population, in principle, would permit Kazakhstan to maintain a solidary pension system.[34]

To judge from gross indicators, the pension reform has unquestionably been successful. At the beginning of 2004, the pension funds had accumulated 2.56 billion U.S. dollars. Relative to the GDP, the assets of the pension funds rose from 3.2 percent in 1999 to 8.3 percent in 2003.[35] However, what is really inside this "black box" called a pension reform?

Table 10.8

Dynamics of the Price of Electricity: Kazakhstan and Selected Countries of the Organization for Economic Cooperation and Development (OECD) (U.S. dollars)

Indicator/area	1995	1996	1997	1998	1999	2000	2001	2002	2003
Cost of 1 kilowatt/hour for all consumers									
Kazakhstan	0.032	0.03	0.038	0.047	0.032	0.027	0.026	0.027	
Cost of 1 kilowatt/hour for industrial consumers									
Kazakhstan		0.021	0.023	0.033	0.020	0.017	0.018	0.019	
OECD[a]	0.079	0.074	0.068	0.063					
Cost of 1 kilowatt/hour for residential consumers									
Kazakhstan	0.032	0.03	0.038	0.047	0.031				0.028
OECD[a]	0.127	0.121	0.114	0.11					

Source: European Bank for Reconstruction and Development, *Transition Report 2003*, pp. 158, 186; www.eia.doe.gov/emeu/international/eleprii.html.

[a]Average for Selected Countries of OECD.

An interesting feature of Kazakhstan's pension reform is the absence of requisite control over financial flows. Thus, at the end of 2001 (four years after the reform began), *one-fifth* (!) of the pension fund assets were "wandering no one knows where" (in the words of a pension analyst in Kazakhstan).[36] That represented approximately 200 million U.S. dollars in absolute terms; these are resources that had been withheld from the wages of employees, but had not arrived at the account of the pension fund. By the end of 2002 the "lost resources" had decreased, but still amounted to 120 million U.S. dollars.[37] Obviously, the "lost" resources were intensively working for the personal and group interests of those employed in the administrative infrastructure created to service the new pension system.

More fundamental is something else: did the transition to a mixed solidary-accumulative pension system solve a cardinal, two-sided goal: on the one hand, reduce future state expenditures on pension payments and, on the other hand, create a sufficient surplus to support a decent standard of living for the future pensioners?

Today, six years after the new pension system went into effect, the answer is negative. In view of the fact that the state had to index the minimum pension (and, in all probability, will have to do this repeatedly in the future), future budgetary expenditures to sustain the solidary pension system will prove substantially higher than assumed in 1997–1998. In 2002–2003 the government made substantial changes in the new pension system. Most important, it introduced guarantees on pension savings being held in private funds. Earlier such guarantees applied only to the state accumulative pension fund. In the event of bankruptcy, the state is now obligated to compensate for pension contributions, which are indexed for inflation.[38] This commitment, unquestionably, will increase the burden on future budgets and, to a large degree, it makes the very privatization of pension savings pointless. That is true, to be sure, only if one assumes that the goal of the reform was not to support financial intermediaries.

More significant, the 10-percent deductions from current wages will not suffice to guarantee a decent level of pension support in the future. As calculations have shown, even under the most favorable conditions (i.e., a real income, minus inflation, yields 5 percent for the pension fund), a male who retires after thirty years will receive a pension equal to just 33 percent of the (then) current wages; a female will draw just 20 percent. By the time of death (given life expectancy), the pension (as a percent of wages) will drop to 17 percent for men and 8 percent for women.[39]

Apart from the social and political side, this problem also has a gender dimension. By 2001 the average life expectancy of a man in Kazakhstan had fallen to 57.8 years, and that of a woman to 68.3 years.[40] If a woman retires at the legal age of 58, that leaves her (according to statistical averages) approximately ten years to live alone. The former USSR provided women with pensions at a rather high level: they retired at age 55 and drew a pension equal to 55 to 85 percent of their wage.[41] At present, because of the low pay for female labor, the accumulative system allows women to build up—in the course of their working life—extremely small pension savings. That is why specialists from the World Bank have proposed to raise the retirement age and to increase the amount of mandatory deductions for the accumulative pension system.

Revealingly, advocates of the accumulative pension system seek to evade questions about the macroeconomic aspects of its operation. Some studies have shown that in Chile (which served as the model for Kazakhstan's pension reform) the adoption of an accumulative system did not cause national savings to grow, but to contract.[42] This undermines the neoclassic postulate that privatization of the pension system will have a beneficial effect on long-term economic growth. But that is not the only issue here.

The means accumulated by the pension savings system, like the National Fund, constitute part of national savings, and in the case of pension assets, these are compulsory savings by low-income groups. Even if one leaves aside moral and ethical considerations, it is obvious from the clear decline in the condition of human capital in Kazakhstan that such savings come at the cost of under-utilization of educational and medical services; in the case of the low-income strata of the population, the forced pension savings mean a reduction in food consumption. It is not self-evident that savings at the expense of education, medicine, and social services in the long-term perspective will prove an effective mechanism to stimulate stable economic growth. Indeed, under-consumption may have a severely depressing impact on economic growth.

It is possible that the population of Kazakhstan will, on a mass scale, choose other ways to utilize their earnings. In 2002, the fifth year since the accumulative system was introduced, 5.4 million people (of 8 million in the labor force) had registered to participate in the pension plan. Of those who registered, only 2 million actually made regular payments into the pension funds.[43] The majority of the working population is absolutely right to think that investment in their own consumption, health, the education of their children, and perhaps the development of small business—in sheer economic terms—is much more efficient than savings in a highly risky pension system.

Consumption is not a deduction from economic growth, but its most important stimulus. Primitive notions that one should initially concentrate on securing growth and only later think about the social sphere are unwarranted in theoretical terms. More important, such ideas have long since been refuted by the experience of many successfully developing countries.

Given that the absolute and relative costs of pension assets continue to rise quickly, the problem of preserving these assets becomes ever more acute. State securities are the main instruments for holding the pension funds (see Table 10.9). In the private sector, pension funds can only be invested in companies of Kazakhstan that are on the "A" listing at the country's stock market (that is, they have adopted international standards of bookkeeping, undergone an audit based on international standards, and so forth). In the middle of 2003, there were only fourteen such corporations and banks in Kazakhstan.[44]

Notwithstanding the fact that there are so few banks and corporations, the latter have succeeded in attracting nearly a third of all resources in the accumulative pension system. If one takes into consideration the fact that these corporations (like the economy of Kazakhstan as a whole) are critically dependent on the dynamics of world prices on energy sources and raw materials, the relative lack of diversification of the portfolio of the pension funds will not contribute to raising the stability of the accumulative system.

At the beginning of 2003, approximately 65 to 80 percent of the portfolios of nonstate pension funds consisted of dollar instruments, and even in November 2003 the share of such holdings was about 50 percent.[45] Altogether, the pension funds (both state and nonstate) at the beginning of 2003 had parked 57 percent of their total portfolio in hard currency instruments. By 1 October 2003, in response to the global instability of the dollar and its devaluation relative to Kazakhstan's currency (tenge), this share of the portfolio dropped to 38.6 percent. There was a corresponding increase in the portfolio share held in state securities, primarily the short-term notes of the National Bank. Given that the return on short-term notes does not exceed 5 to 7 percent in nominal terms, the growth of the pension assets in real terms (i.e., adjusted for inflation) proves significantly lower than the levels postulated in the actuarial calculations of international experts.

According to the results for 2003, the average weighted real return of nonstate pension funds proved negative (–1.06 percent), with thirteen of sixteen funds showing a negative return.[46] This means that Kazakhstan is hardly likely to fit within the parameters of an increase in pension savings, as discussed above, and the payments to future pensioners will prove even lower than the modest amounts previously expected.

During a short period of operation of the accumulative system, on at least two occasions Kazakhstan's monetary authorities had to throw the pension funds a life preserver. In April 1999, immediately after the devaluation of the tenge, pension funds were permitted to convert short-term state bonds into government Eurobonds at the exchange rate existing prior to the currency devaluation. This artificial swap averted a collapse of pension savings

Table 10.9

Structure of Investment Portfolios of Pension Funds in Kazakhstan (percent)

Portfolio category	1999	2000	2001	2002	2003
Securities of the Ministry of Finance and the National Bank					
Total	93.67	74.39	58.67	47.88	53.12
Hard currency bonds of the Ministry of Finance	51.46	0.71			
Eurobonds	35.65	65.91	42.95	22.56	12.19
Notes of the National Bank	2.40	4.33	4.90	12.24	23.18
Bank deposits	1.64	2.55	8.44	8.78	6.85
Stocks and bonds of foreign emitters, securities of international financial organizations	0.99	6.52	6.55	14.09	9.52
Stocks and bonds of companies in Kazakhstan	1.96	15.89	23.23	27.94	29.73
Domestic municipal bonds	0.29	0.23	0.63	0.45	0.21
Others	1.45	0.42	2.49	0.86	0.56
Total	100	100	100	100	100

Source: Statisticheskii biulleten', no. 10 (January 2004); National Bank website (www.nationalbank.kz).

and simultaneously enabled the government to finance its own expenditures by drawing on pension funds.[47] The second time was in the summer and fall of 2003, when pension funds—on a massive scale—transferred assets from dollar instruments to short-term, low-yield notes of the National Bank. In both cases the government resorted to emergency methods in situations where the real exchange rate of the tenge changed vis-à-vis the dollar. Obviously, this entertaining game of transferring resources from one type of asset to another yields handsome dividends to the few participants in this game, but it cannot go on forever. It is even difficult to imagine the magnitude of upheaval that so fragile a system would undergo in the event of a one-time shock (or multiple shocks over a short period of time) triggered by a drop in oil prices, devaluation of the national currency, and/or a reduction in the exchange rate of the dollar on a global scale.

But it is not only the fact that, at the current levels of return, the accumulative pension assets (like the resources centralized in the National Fund) are subject to the constant threat of depreciation through inflation and global hard currency risks that are completely beyond Kazakhstan's control. To treat the National Fund and the pension savings exclusively as financial assets clearly impedes the use of these resources to invest in physical and human capital. While these factors are not sufficient to cause successful development, all known examples of such development show that it is impossible without activating the investment process and massive investment in people.

Having agreed to support the convertibility of the tenge, monetary authorities in Kazakhstan were forced to support high (relative to the modest size of the national economy) levels of gold and hard currency reserves. These reserves enable the government, to maintain technical convertibility of national currency at the officially supported exchange rate. Under the system that now exists, the resources of the National Fund and, to a certain degree, the resources of pension funds constitute insurance reserves that cannot be used for current and investment expenditures. In 2003 the sum of the net gold and hard currency reserves, the assets of the National Fund, and the funds in the accumulative pension system amounted to 37.4 percent of the GDP. The majority of these resources were placed outside Kazakhstan. In the larger sense, that is the cost for having initially integrated Kazakhstan's economy into the global system through its financial, not its productive, sector.

Amnesty of Capital and Property

In the summer of 2002, Kazakhstan became the first state in the CIS to declare an amnesty on capital. Altogether, it legalized 480 million U.S. dollars; 82 percent was in cash (dollars), 11.4 percent was transferred from accounts in foreign banks, and 6.5 percent was in Kazakhstan's own currency.[48] In other words, considering the absolute scale of capital flight in the first half of the 1990s (one half to one billion U.S. dollars per annum), the results of the amnesty were quite modest.

In the opinion of some commentators (who urge that Kazakhstan's experience be applied to other post-Soviet countries), the authorities who declared the capital amnesty "knew precisely what they wanted (and how to do it): achieve the country's prosperity, economic growth."[49] A rather different view is held by the active participants in this process and by several serious analysts. As noted in one of the rare econometric studies of the impact of amnesty on the dynamics of macroeconomic indicators, the amnesty had the reverse effect of what was expected. Namely, it contributed to "the laundering of shadow money and its subsequent flow abroad. . . . If earlier this shadow money had circulated within the country's economy and had at least some utility, it now began to circulate abroad and exclusively in the interests of the legalized owners."[50]

If, from a macroeconomic perspective, this legalization made little sense for the economy of Kazakhstan, it nonetheless bore a profound social and political meaning. The process of legalizing was accompanied by a parallel destruction of all declarations of personal incomes and property for the period from 1995 to 2000. Hence, according to local legislation, obligatory declarations are filed only by three categories of taxpayers: entrepreneurs, civil servants, and people who acquired expensive property. It is not difficult to surmise that the group most interested in legalization was a corrupt officialdom.[51] The amnesty, in effect, enabled the regime of the dependent offshore quasi-oligarchy to augment its social base.

Kazakhstan is now preparing for a second stage of legalization—this time, it involves the legalization of property. As before, the party most interested in this new campaign consists of officials and the offshore owners of local economic assets. By controlling the mechanisms and instruments of privatization, officialdom—especially its upper echelons—has effectively established control over property and the few efficient economic assets in the country. And they did so by circumventing formal procedures and using the levers of power and insider information.

Experts, both in and close to the government, claim that the legalization of property can have a positive macroeconomic effect, since it purportedly will lead to a growth of tax revenues and stop capital flight abroad.[52] However, because of persistent political and economic risks, the second stage of legalization cannot achieve these goals. The periodic intensification of the power struggle among different groups within

Kazakhstan's elite and the regular purges carried out by the president do not in the least serve to stimulate the repatriation of wealth (i.e., back to national economic space) or the legalization of property rights. It is still less risky to hold personal wealth in Western banks and to control property through complex schemes based on the use of offshore accounts. To judge from all this, the composition of the true proprietors of Kazakhstan's economic assets is hardly a cause for surprise. The revelation of this information, however, does not correspond to the interests of either the authorities or real owners.

In addition, the one-sided raw material specialization of Kazakhstan's economy, together with the extreme fragility of the macroeconomic stabilization thus far achieved (which could be instantaneously destroyed by a fall in world oil prices), greatly increase the risks of conducting work transparently in Kazakhstan. All this, taken together, increases the probability that the government will legalize property, but that the profit and personal wealth of the semi-anonymous officials and offshore bourgeoisie will, as before, accumulate in a world financial system outside national economic space.

Managed Democracy as an Imperative Project for the Global Periphery

An unbiased analysis shows that Kazakhstan can hardly be regarded as a successful economic and political model worthy of replication in other countries. If one assesses Kazakhstan's social and economic model in a highly simplified schematic form, it is possible to argue that a dual economy stabilized under globalization. Globalized oil production and metallurgical sectors, which provide jobs for about 2 to 3 percent of the local labor force, have accelerated their deliveries to export markets. The economic policy of authorities amounts to sharply reducing the tax burden on these sectors and minimizing their expenditures on the labor force, energy resources, and ecology. In recent years the National Fund and the accumulative pension system have begun to finance (and possibly subsidize) the globalized sector, the export and financial flows of which accumulate outside Kazakhstan. In the future authorities in Kazakhstan are preparing for a final privatization of the pension system, with the participation of foreign capital.[53]

The overwhelming mass of the population has little connection to the globalized sectors that are in any way profitable. The ruling and dominant groups remember the general populace only on the eve of elections, when they suddenly make a minimal transfer of resources to the social sphere.

Recently, international financial organizations have taken note of the glaring contradiction between Kazakhstan's explosive economic growth and the continuing social degradation of the country. As a representative of the World Bank, while speaking at a round table in mid-2003 on the use of incomes from oil exports, emphasized: "One of the puzzles of Kazakhstan (both for the World Bank and for the IMF) is the low level of investments in the social sphere."[54] The answer to the riddle is quite simple: a small part of the country's export earnings belongs to Kazakhstan itself, and even these modest revenues are allocated in strict accordance with the imperatives of globalization.

Is there an alternative to this situation? Globalization restricts the opportunities for underdeveloped states to influence economic and social processes within their own national space. Such states are deprived of the opportunity to conduct a policy in the traditional sense. Kazakhstan is an open raw material economy with a liberalized balance of current and capital accounts and internationalized economic assets. Under these conditions, the government of Kazakhstan must make its policies (monetary, fiscal, budgetary, investment, and social) correspond to the harsh demands imposed by globalization. The ruling peripheral regimes are forced to direct their energy toward adapting their countries to these global imperatives. As one researcher on the processes of political development and democratization in the developing world has noted, the regimes—having lost the possibility of controlling social and economic processes—find the solution in the governance of the polity, that is, in the unending directed reconstruction of political space.[55]

The experience of Kazakhstan shows that, for a certain period of time, such governance can exist by creating a virtual picture of successful market transition in a relatively free informational and political environment. However, the possibilities of using mass media technologies to sustain broad illusions about impending market prosperity are not infinite; the regime can find culprits to explain the delay (the onerous Soviet legacy, the global financial crisis of 1997, the financial-economic collapse of 1998 in Russia, and other passing factors), but these will not work forever. The massive poverty and deprivation, along with the awareness by the majority of the population that they have no real prospects to improve their economic and social position, are beginning to exert a growing impact on the political processes. And that has forced the ruling regime to change to a new program of rule.

The new phase is distinguished by the appearance of one or several "state parties," the establishment of executive control over the parliament and "opposition," and purging of the informational and political environment. By an irony of fate, the former Soviet nomenklatura (which is in a process of constant social mimicry) is realizing the goals of all the phases of post-Soviet transition. And the nomenklatura is doing this because there simply is no other active social agent in post-Soviet space.

Competing parties from the same dominant groups that claim the role of opposition have no real alternatives to current policies. Rather, they focus exclusively on seizing the levers of power and controlling the privatized assets. This, incidentally, fully explains the low level of support of such a virtual opposition, and the ease with which the ruling regime periodically takes care of its competitors in the struggle for power and property.

In Kazakhstan, the goal of the regime—a "managed democracy"—is to defend the peripheral offshore quasi-oligarchy. It is revealing that the newly created pro-presidential party "Asar" has positioned itself between two camps:

- the opponents of reform (who "do not want and who cannot prepare for life under the conditions of global competition," i.e., those who do not have a niche in the existing system of offshore capitalism and nontransparent financial flows and property relations); and
- those forces that transferred complete control over the country to transnational corporations, weakened central authority, and turned Kazakhstan into a raw-materials appendage.[56]

Consequently, the key center of internal political life in the foreseeable future promises to be one where the ruling regime spurns the expiring "communist" electorate of critics from the left (which is dying off through the natural process of aging) and defends itself against external challenges precipitated by "Kazakhgate." Simultaneously, competing groups and leaders from the so-called "opposition" will make an ever more intensive effort to take power. However, even in the event of a change in the main political personalities in Kazakhstan, that will mean only a change in the virtual shell of the ruling regime, not its content.

Managed democracy in any of its various post-Soviet forms does not give a country the opportunity to leave the ranks of the global periphery. An alternative to this course of events could be the radicalization of bourgeois-democratic market transformations, with a reliance on national protocapital, with the powerful support of unprotected social strata and groups on the part of the state. An example of the latter could be found in several successful transition countries of Central and Eastern Europe and in the new industrial countries of Asia. Fortunately for them, these countries do not face the "resource curse" of so much oil and natural gas.

Notes

1. Calculated from data in World Bank, *World Development Indicators* (CD-ROM, 2003).

2. "Chto meshaet amnistirovat′ kapital?" *Vedomosti* (Moscow), 2 December 2003, p. A-4.

3. As far as is known to me, the first to draw attention to the striking discrepancy between the data in the census and in current studies of the labor market of Kazakhstan was L. A. Fridman, *Ocherki ekonomicheskogo razvitiia stran Tsentral′noi Azii posle raspada SSSR* (Moscow, 2001), pp. 47–48.

4. For the main results of the Russian 2002 census, see www.perepis2002.ru/content/221/2219–article.asp.

5. On the paradoxes of demographic statistics in independent Turkmenistan, see the detailed analysis in S. V. Zhukov and O. B. Reznikova, *Tsentral′naia Aziia v sotsial′no-ekonomicheskikh strukturakh sovremennogo mira* (Moscow, 2001), chapter 2. It should be noted that the real picture in Turkmenistan can be established with sufficient reliability by recalculating the available statistical series. It is much more complicated to assess the demographic and social situation in contemporary Kazakhstan.

6. O. Tarnetskaia and N. Medvedeva, "Thoughts Regarding Improvement of the Investment Climate," *The Energy of Kazakhstan* (Almaty), 1999, no. 4: 33. Statistical Yearbook of Kazakhstan 2003. Agency on Statistics of the Republic of Kazakhstan, Almaty 2003, p. 233–34.

7. "Vyrastut na shel′fe ostrova," *Kazakhstanskaia pravda*, 7 December 2001 (www.caspian.ru).

8. U. Kozhantaeva, "Kochegary podnebes′ia," *Delovaia nedelia* (Almaty) www.caspian.ru/cgi/article.cgi?id=1018.

9. On the problems of radioactive security of the byproducts from oil and gas production, see www.kazaag.kz/showarticle2.php?articleD=33952.

10. A. M. Shalinskii, "Zagriaznenie okruzhaiushchei sredy i ekologicheskaia politika Kazakhstana," Tsentr regional′nykh i transgranichnykh issledovanii, VolGUB2002 (www.transbound.narod.ru/annual1/shalinsky.html).

11. I. Vorotnoi, "Strana otkhodov," *Izvestiia-Kazakhstan* (Astana), 28 January 2004, p. 7.

12. T. Koroleva, "'Ministr Samakova': Proiskhodiashchie v nastoiashchee vremia avarii i katastrofy pri dobyche i transportirovke nefti govoriat o negotovnosti otechestvennykh i inostrannykh kompanii obespechit′ polnuiu ekologicheskuiu bezopasnost′ provodimykh rabot," *Panorama* (Almaty), no. 22 (June 2003).

13. Agentstvo Respubliki Kazakhstan po statistike, *Kazakhstan: 1991–2002 gody* (Almaty, 2002), p. 39.

14. Calculated on the basis of Zh. Kaksheeva, "Tekhnogennaia katastrofa ne za gorami?" (www.respublika.kaz/index.php?art=2003112124); and I. Vorotno, "Strana otkhodov?" *Kazakhstan: 1991–2002 gody*, p. 39. The data for 2003 are preliminary.

15. See R. M. Solow, "Candidate Issues in Developmental Economics," in *Frontiers of Development Economics: The Future in Perspective*, ed. G. M. Meier and J. E. Stiglitz (New York, 2001), p. 514.

16. The notion of "ruling and dominant groups," which is quite appropriate for analyzing the special features of the social structure in developing countries, was

introduced by M. A. Cheshkov. See his *Kritika predstavlenii o praviashchikh gruppakh razvivaiushchikhsia stran* (Moscow, 1979).

17. N. Amrekulov, *Razmyshleniia o glavnom. Puti k ustoichivomu razvitiiu* (Almaty, 1998), p. 146.

18. For details on this question, with a focus on Kazakhstan, see Zhukov and Reznikova, *Tsentral'naia Aziia*, pp. 134–37.

19. A. Tazhutov, "V bor'be za nash eskport ofshory pereigrali SNG" (www. megapolis.kz/2003/09/25a04–01.shtml).

20. M. Adilov, "Kto moet 'money' v neftianom krane?" (www.respublika.kz/ index.php?art=2003090517).

21. See, for example, the discussion in Tsentr analiza obshchestvennykh problem, *Minotoring formirovaniia i ispol'zovaniia dokhodov ot syr'evykh sektorov Kazakhstan. Obsuzhdenie proekta Biudzhetnogo kodeksa. Materialy dlia kruglogo stola* (Astana, 18 September 2003).

22. Tsentr analiza obshchestvennykh problem, *Monitoring formirovaniia i ispol'zovaniia dokhodov ot syr'evykh sektorov Kazakhstana. Materialy kruglogo stola* (Almaty, 2 June 2003), pp. 25–26.

23. P. Svoik, "Grigorii Marchenko takoi zhe garant stabil'nosti natsional'noi valiuty, kak Zagipa Balieva—chestnykh vyborov" (www.navi.kz/articles/?artid=4173); "Republic of Kazakhstan. Selected Issues and Statistical Appendix," IMF Country Report No. 01/20 (January 2001), p. 12.

24. B. Khusainov, "Ekonomicheskoe razvitie Kazakhstana v usloviiakh globalizatsii," *Tsentral'naia Aziia i Kavkaz*, 2001, no. 4: 156.

25. A. Esentugelov, "Dualizm v razvitii ekonomiki Kazakhstana: strukturno-investitsionnye aspekty ee modernizatsii," in *Tsentral'naia Aziia*, p. 184.

26. Ia. Razumov, "Glava Natsbanka predal ostrakizmu pessimistichno nastorennykh analitikov," *Panorama* (Almaty), no. 13 (April 2003).

27. For details on the mechanism for the operation of the National Fund of Kazakhstan, see M. Ospanov, "K voprosu o Natsional'nom fonde v biudzhete razvitiia Kazakhstana," in *Tsentral'naia Aziia*, pp. 218–230.

28. M. Ospanov, "K voprosu," p. 221; and data of the National Bank of Kazakhstan.

29. See "Otchet o postupleniiakh i ispol'zovaniia Natsional'nogo fonda Respubliki Kazakhstan za 2001 i 2002 gody" (www.nationalfund.kz).

30. P. Svoik, "Natsfond dlia strany ili strana dlia natsfonda?" (www.navi.kz/articles/?artid=6437).

31. World Bank, *World Development Indicators 2003* (CD-ROM).

32. See Marta de Castello Branco, "Pension Reform in the Baltics, Russia, and the Countries of the Former Soviet Union," IMF Working Paper (February 1998).

33. World Bank, *World Development Indicators 2003*.

34. E. S. Andrews, "Kazakhstan: An Ambitious Pension Reform," ECSHD, World Bank (3 January 2001), p. 6.

35. *Statisticheskii biulleten','* No. 10 (January 2004); National Bank of Kazakhstan (www.nationalbank.kz); Agentstvo RK po statistike, "Sotsial'no-ekonomicheskoe razvitie Respubliki Kazakhstan v ianvare 2004 goda (operativnye dannye)" (www.stat.kz); and Agentstvo RK po statistike, *Statisticheskii ezhegodnik Kazakhstana 2003* (Almaty 2003), p. 166.

36. "Gde iskat' pensionnye nakopleniia?" (Material submitted to the electronic journal, *K obshchestvu bez korruptsii*, 2001, no. 1 (www.transparencykazakhstan.org).

37. See www.gazeta.kz/art.asp?aid=36860.

38. I. Polevoi, "Pensionnye fondy: svershilas' 'barkhatnaia revoliutsiia'" (www.gazeta.kz/art.asp?aid=28460).

39. "Republic of Kazakhstan. Selected Issues and Statistical Appendix," IMF Country Report No. 03/211 (July 2003), p. 68.

40. World Bank, *World Development Indicators 2003*.

41. P. Castel and L. Fox, "Gender Dimensions of Pension Reform in the Former Soviet Union," World Bank, p. 1.

42. See C. Mesa-Lago, "Pension System Reforms in Latin America: The Position of the International Organizations," *CEPAL Review*, no. 60 (1996): 73–98.

43. See www.gazeta.kz/art.asp?aid=24420.

44. G. Marchenko, "Nedoverie preodolevat' ochen' tiazhelo," *Izvestiia* (Moscow), 16 June 2003, p. 8.

45. O. Khe, "Po otsenke Natsional'nogo banka effektivnost' investitsionnogo upravleniia pensionnymi fondami neuklonno rastet," *Panorama* (Almaty), no. 42 (October 2003).

46. A. Dzhalilov, *Finvlasti obeshchaiut*.

47. For details, see Andrews, "Kazakhstan," pp. 43–44.

48. "K obshchestvu bez korruptsii," 2002, no. 1 (www.transparencykazakhstan.org).

49. "Chto meshaet amnistirovat' kapital," *Vedomosti* (Moscow), 2 December 2003, p. A4.

50. N. Nurseit, "Issledovanie urovnia dollarizatsii ekonomiki Kazakhstana," *Al'Pari* (Almaty), no. 4–5 (2002).

51. "Amnistiia kapitalov rabotaet na interesy goschinovnikov," *Kontinent* (Almaty), no. 13 (4–17 July 2001); and materials offered in the electronic journal, *K obshchestvu bez korruptsii*, 2001, no. 1 (www.transparencykazakhstan.org).

52. I. Galkina, "Igra v Lego" (www.transparencykazakhstan.org/info/review/2003/0703/lego.htm).

53. A. Dzhalilov, "Sredi pokupatelei GNPF pravitel'stvo i Natsbank khotiat videt' mezhdunarodnye finansovye instituty," *Panorama* (Almaty), no. 4 (30 April 2004).

54. U. Kozhantaeva, "Zolotoi kliuchik poterialsia," *Delovaia nedelia* (Almaty), no. 22 (6 June 2003).

55. P. Cammack, "Globalization and the Death of Liberal Democracy," *European Review* 6 (1998).

56. N. Drozd, "Vozmozhno, partiia 'Asar' sozdaetsia kak struktura, v interesakh i 'pod davleniem' kotoroi budut delat'sia politicheskie ustupki," *Panorama* (Almaty), no. 42 (October 2003).

11

Economic Ties Between Russia and Kazakhstan: Dynamics, Tendencies, and Prospects

Stanislav Zhukov and Oksana Reznikova

It is only in a global context that the economic relations of Russia and Kazakhstan can be adequately understood and assessed. Globalization has penetrated the nonmarket space of Eurasia, initiating the long and painful processes of building a state and market economy. In the last 150 to 200 years, the economy of this part of Eurasia was an integral part of the Russian, and later Soviet, economy. The communication and transportation systems of the Caucasus and Central Asia with the outside world ran almost exclusively across Russian territory. At present, in Kazakhstan (as in post-Soviet space as a whole), Russia no longer holds a monopoly or even the initiative of action. Russia, although still the largest and most developed economy of Eurasia, lacks sufficient economic, military, and political resources to propose a geopolitically and geoeconomically attractive project to Central Asia and the Caucasus. One evidently should concur with Boris Rumer that, in economic, political, and military terms, Russia cannot aspire to be the key "manager of Eurasia," and indeed by no means are all the new Eurasian countries ready to acquiesce in giving it such a role.[1]

Bilateral Relations

The economic relations of Russia and Kazakhstan have developed on two levels: one is bilateral, the other global. Each level has its own inherent logic; each entails certain prerogatives and set of participants. If one speaks of bilateral relations, then after many excesses (triggered by the dissolution of a single Soviet economy and the appearance of state and customs boundaries), cooperation gradually adjusted toward standard market norms. For Russia, cooperation with Kazakhstan is an economic and even geographic imperative. The two countries share a land boundary running approximately six thousand kilometers in length. Twelve Russian regions, with an aggregate population of several million people, border directly on Kazakhstan. The distances between cities and industrial centers in Novosibirsk and Omsk oblasts, the republic of Altai, and other regions of the Russian Federation, on the one hand, and regions of northeastern Kazakhstan, on the other, make economic cooperation imperative. If one takes into account transportation costs, this cooperation is more natural than economic ties of Siberia-European Russia or north-south Kazakhstan.

In 2003 Kazakhstan ranked as the fourteenth largest importer of Russian products, taking in 2.5 percent of total Russian exports.[2] Kazakhstan's share of Russian imports that year was 4.3 percent. Still more significant is Kazakhstan's market for Russian machinery and equipment (see Table 11.1). In 2003 Kazakhstan imported goods worth nearly one billion U.S. dollars; that represented 8.9 percent of all Russian exports from the machine-building branchsector. This is the highest indicator for the past ten years (when Russia first began to compile normal customs statistics). The supply of Russian machine-building instruments, equipment, and means of transportation to Kazakhstan's market (following the profound contraction caused by the crisis in 1998) exhibits an obvious tendency to grow. The diverse bilateral cooperative ties inherited from Soviet times have been preserved in metallurgy, atomic energy, and the chemical industry of the two countries. The energy systems of Kazakhstan and Siberia are also closely intertwined.

Because of Kazakhstan's geographic position, that country is of critical importance for Russia's economic ties with the rest of Central Asia. Russian trade with Kyrgyzstan, Tajikistan, Turkmenistan, and Uzbekistan must, of course, traverse the territory of Kazakhstan.

Economic cooperation with Russia is even more important for Kazakhstan. Russia is the second greatest export market for Kazakhstan's goods (surpassed only by the Bermuda Islands); in 2003 Russia took 15.2 percent of the total exports from Kazakhstan (see Table 11.2). Bermuda ranked as Kazakhstan's largest export market only because this offshore zone buys a

Table 11.1

Structure of Trade: Russia and Kazakhstan (millions of U.S. dollars)

Indicator	1994	1995	1996	1997	1998	1999	2000	2001	2002	2003
Exports										
Fuel and energy goods	828	817	710	555	563	242	450	612	576	676
Machinery, equipment, means of transportation	442	546	600	889	418	386	613	782	648	957
Foodstuffs and agricultural raw materials	97	153	242	167	171	132	232	220	178	274
Metals and metal products	252	300	301	293	270	129	308	379	304	464
Chemicals and petrochemicals	285	319	417	344	263	196	383	497	430	552
Total	2,198	2,555	2,550	2,471	1,893	1,222	2,247	2,778	2,403	3,279
Imports										
Fuel and energy goods	722	920	965	854	651	398	753	698	727	857
Machinery, equipment, means of transportation	131	122	208	197	77	46	78	64	47	73
Foodstuffs and agricultural raw materials	179	329	514	618	292	299	358	171	76	205
Metals and metal products	538	617	426	251	118	83	158	190	182	303
Chemicals and petrochemicals	120	278	491	414	376	319	386	450	454	487
Total	1,996	2,675	3,041	2,743	1,884	1,391	2,200	2,018	1,946	2,475

Sources: Gosudarstvennyi tamozhennyi komitet Rossiiskoi Federatsii, *Tamozhennaia statistika vneshnei torgovli Rossiiskoi Federatsii. 2003g.*, 2: 640–41; ibid., 2002g., 478–79; ibid., 2001g., pp. 472–73; 1999g., pp. 377, 449–51; 1997g., pp. 501–2; 1996g., pp. 484–85; 1995g., pp. 486–88.

Table 11.2

Main Export and Import Markets of Kazahkstan (percent)

Exports		Imports	
Year/country	Percent	Year/country	Percent
1995		1995	
Russia	45.1	Russia	49.0
Netherlands	9.7	Uzbekistan	7.1
China	5.7	Turkmenistan	6.4
Switzerland	3.6	Germany	5.3
Germany	3.3	Turkey	3.3
1998		1998	
Russia	28.9	Russia	39.4
Italy	9.2	Germany	8.6
Great Britain	9.0	United States	6.3
China	7.2	Great Britain	5.0
Switzerland	6.1	Turkey	4.8
2000		2000	
Russia	19.5	Russia	48.7
Bermuda	14.9	Germany	6.6
Virgin Islands	11.6	United States	5.5
Italy	9.8	Great Britain	4.3
China	7.3	Italy	3.1
2001		2001	
Russia	20.3	Russia	45.8
Bermuda	14.8	Germany	7.3
Italy	11.1	United States	5.5
China	7.2	Italy	4.3
Germany	5.9	Great Britain	3.8
2002		2002	
Bermuda	20.7	Russia	39.1
Russia	15.7	Germany	8.7
China	10.5	United States	7.0
Italy	9.5	China	4.7
Switzerland	8.1	Great Britain	3.9
2003		2003	
Bermuda	17.0	Russia	39.1
Russia	15.2	Germany	8.9
China	12.8	China	6.0
Italy	7.9	United States	5.6
Ukraine	3.2	Ukraine	3.9

Source: Customs statistics of the Republic of Kazahkstan.

substantial part of the country's oil. In the next few years, because of the increase in Kazakhstan's deliveries of oil and natural gas to global markets, the share claimed by the Russian market in Kazakhstan's exports may shrink significantly. However, Russia will continue to be the chief market for non-oil exports from Kazakhstan. Similarly, Russia also is the principal source of imports to Kazakhstan; in 2003 it accounted for 39.3 percent of Kazakhstan's purchases abroad.

In a word, whatever the variant for the development of events, neither Russia nor Kazakhstan has a rational alternative to close bilateral trade and economic cooperation.

The Global Perspective

At the same time, post-Soviet Kazakhstan poses serious challenges to the fundamental economic interests of Russia. During the Soviet era, the growing inability of Eurasia to become integrated into the technological, economic, and political megatrends of a rapidly globalizing world led to the disintegration of the USSR, indeed at a rapid rate without historical precedent. The breakup of the Soviet Union, in turn, contributed to the emergence of forces and players in a zone that had previously been closed to the outside world. The initiative for action in the Eurasian space shifted to developed countries, especially the United States and, to some extent, China. That was all the more true because of the extremely strong internal demand for the leading world economic and political powers to take a more active role in Central Asia and the Caucasus. Thus, from the moment these new states acquired independence, they sought to gain access to the world market. Economically, all the post-Soviet states (and Kazakhstan is no exception here) had an extremely strong interest in obtaining assistance from international financial organizations and developed countries. The countries expected to receive an influx of the foreign investments and technologies essential for modernizing their backward economies. Significantly, in 1993–2003 Russia accounted for just 2.3 percent of direct foreign investment in Kazakhstan; it therefore occupied only ninth place on the list of investor countries, surpassed by Turkey and China, not to mention the leading developed countries (see Table 11.3). To be sure, some of the Russian investment in Kazakhstan comes from offshore zones of the modern world economy; many Russian companies are also active in Kazakhstan in the capacity of resident firms. However, this does not fundamentally change the essence of the matter.

If one takes into consideration the imperatives for the mid-term perspective, the following factors will shape the relations of Russia and Kazakhstan.

First, Russia and Kazakhstan are competitors on the world market. Beyond the fact that the economies of both countries have acquired a character that is increasingly raw-material oriented, the competition between them (more precisely, between companies operating on the territories of the two countries) will only intensify. According to some forecasts, by 2005 the

Table 11.3

Gross Influx of Direct Foreign Investments in the Economy of Kazakhstan, 1993–2003

Country	Annual investments (millions of U.S. dollars)					Aggregate direct foreign investments, 1993–2003	
	1999	2000	2001	2002	2003	Millions of U.S. dollars	Percent of total
United States	905.8	951.2	1,460.4	1,011.4	1,086.1	7,719.1	29.90
Great Britain	160.0	481.8	600.6	622.7	592.6	3,517.7	13.62
Italy	126.2	351.0	488.3	469.1	373.8	1,846.7	7.15
Switzerland	23.8	20.6	361.0	520.0	630.5	1,682.5	6.52
Netherlands	250.3	114.4	211.1	401.0	617.3	1,627.5	6.30
China	49.6	90.1	211.9	64.7	248.5	1,076.6	4.17
Canada	9.4	157.3	490.5	165.4	7.8	1,065.9	4.13
Turkey	30.9	30.2	58.1	70.5	104.8	737.3	2.86
Russia	0.0	0.0	211.7	214.4	197.0	623.1	2.41
France	8.0	33.2	64.9	123.6	161.3	499.4	1.93
Japan	4.3	18.1	32.1	59.6	96.1	491.6	1.90
Germany	15.6	69.5	50.6	37.4	63.9	413.1	1.60
Indonesia	0.0	68.1	47.0	0.0	0.0	294.3	1.14
Virgin Islands	0.0	0.0	42.2	148.0	87.7	277.8	1.08
South Korea	0.0	0.0	67.9	45.6	82.4	196.0	0.76
Total	1,852.1	2,781.2	4,556.6	4,105.8	4,595.7	25,820.3	100.0
CIS States only	55.0	173.3	232.3	219.7	209.8	916.4	3.55

Source: Data of the National Bank of Kazakhstan (www.nationalbank.kz).

production of oil in Russia will exceed 485 million tons, rising to 550 million tons by 2008.[3] Kazakhstan plans to produce more than 60 million tons in 2005, raise that to 90 million tons in 2010, and (with the inclusion of production from the Caspian shelf) increase this to more than 150 million tons by 2015.[4] Russia exports more than one half (about three quarters, if petroleum products are included) of its total oil output; Kazakhstan exports four-fifths of its oil production. Moreover, the oil of both countries goes to the same markets, and it is even exported over the same pipelines.

Second, without direct access to the sea, Kazakhstan must export its energy resources across the territories of neighboring states. To this point, most of Kazakhstan's oil exports to the world market pass through the territory of Russia. In principle, however, a relatively small oil exporter is always interested in reducing its dependence on a larger oil-exporting neighbor; it is constantly driven to seek alternative routes to deliver its hydrocarbon raw materials to consumers.

Third, Russia and its oil companies actually are competing not with Kazakhstan, but with transnational corporations. As a result of the frenetic campaigns of liberalization and privatization in the 1990s, Kazakhstan consigned a significant share (if not the majority) of its oilfields in the Caspian region to foreign capital. The main form of long-term contract to develop and exploit oilfields in the region was a production sharing agreement or similar contract. De jure the national government retained sovereignty over its natural resources, but de facto it relinquished control over the resources and financial flows to transnational corporations. By the middle of 2003 Kazakhstan's share in international projects to develop the twelve largest oilfields inland and offshore in the Kashagan field amounted to just 18 percent (see Table 11.4).

Revealingly, Kazakhstan generally does not participate in the consortia to develop the largest new oilfields of Karachaganak and Kashagan—two areas that are to provide a substantial part of the growth of Kazakhstan's oil production in the foreseeable future. American and Western European corporations control, respectively, 30 and over 33 percent of the stock of these international consortia. Russia's Lukoil and Gazprom succeeded in being included in the international projects as partners of the leading world energy companies. However, the share of the Russian participants amounts to just 2 percent.

Little is known about the specific terms of the sharing of profits agreements between Kazakhstan and Western oil companies. According to information leaked to the press, Kazakhstan receives 20 percent of the oil, foreign investors receove the remaining 80 percent. Only after the companies have been compensated for their initial investments are the proportions reversed.

Table 11.4

Shares of Investors in the Largest Oilfields of Kazakhstan

Twelve largest inland oilfields of Kazakhstan		Twelve largest inland oilfields of Kazakhstan plus Kashagan		Twelve largest inland oilfields of Kazakhstan plus Kashagan and Azeri-Chirag-Giuneshli	
Country of shareholder	Share (percent)[a]	Country of shareholder	Share (percent)[a]	Country of shareholder	Share (percent)[a]
United States	35	United States	30	United States	31
Kazakhstan	30	Kazakhstan	18	Kazakhstan	15
Great Britain	4	Great Britain	9	Great Britain	13
Italy	4	Italy	9	Italy	7
Canada	4	Netherlands/Great Britain	7	Netherlands/Great Britain	5
Russia	4	France	7	France	5
China	4	Japan	3	Japan	5
Others	15	Canada	3	Canada	2
		China	3	Norway	2
		Russia	2	China	2
		Others	9	Azerbaijan	2
				Russia	2
				Turkey	1
				Others	8

Source: O. Reznikova, "Perspektivy pritoka priamykh inostrannykh investitsii v ekonomiku gosudarstv Tsentral'noi Azii i Kavkaza," in *Tsentral'naia Aziia i Kavkaz. Nasushchnye problemy*, ed. B. Rumer (Almaty, 2003), p. 120.

[a]Shares are calculated on the base of the country affiliation of the energy companies.

Obviously, given the colossal capital intensity of oil projects in Kazakhstan, by the time the investors have been compensated for their investments the oilfields will be largely or almost entirely depleted. To a significant degree, this situation resulted from the fact that Kazakhstan did not possess (and still does not) the financial resources and technologies needed to develop its complex oil deposits. Nonresidents established a similar control over the country's other attractive asset—its metallurgical enterprises.[5]

The internationalization of Kazakhstan's main economic assets during the first round of the petroleum game in the 1990s reinforced the country's dependence on the world system. The direction, tempo, and rhythm of Kazakhstan's economy, like its structure, are determined primarily by factors of a global, not local, character.

Fourth, the Caspian region, thanks to its hydrocarbon resources, turned into a relatively important focal point of geopolitics. The diversification of energy sources, with the objective of reducing the critical dependence on the import of hydrocarbons from the Middle East and the OPEC member countries, is one of the most important components of the economic and national security of the United States and Europe. Not surprisingly, U.S. energy strategy aims at substantially increasing the delivery of oil and natural gas from the Caspian region to the world market.[6] The expansion of energy imports from the Caspian region is also a high priority of the European Union.[7] Given that, in the midterm perspective, Kazakhstan, Azerbaijan, and Turkmenistan are capable of becoming rather large suppliers of oil and natural gas, the leading importers of hydrocarbons have an interest in seeing that the Caspian region is integrated into the global energy system as an independent entity, and that its export infrastructure is not connected with other suppliers of energy. That is why the United States is extremely suspicious (to put it mildly) of plans to transport the Caspian hydrocarbons across Iran. For the same reason, importers of hydrocarbons want Caspian oil and natural gas to reach world markets without passing through Russia. It is no accident that the largest international projects in Central Asia and the Caucasus have focused on energy and transportation corridors that would give these landlocked countries access to the Mediterranean Sea. The project for an energy corridor (in the American interpretation, an "East-West" energy corridor; in the European variant, the program INOGATE) proposes to ship Caspian oil through Georgia and Turkey. Parallel to the oil and natural gas pipelines, a powerful transport system linking Europe and Asia through the Caucasus and Central Asia is proposed (the TRASECA project [Transport-Corridor-Europe-Caucasus-Central Asia]).

The geopolitical players, not local governments, are choosing the routes to deliver Caspian hydrocarbons to world markets. Here purely economic considerations can even recede to secondary importance. A special advisor to U.S. President Bill Clinton on questions involving Caspian hydrocarbons, Richard Morningstar, candidly admitted that, in the course of the "oil game," the U.S. administration had to overcome a lack of understanding and resistance on the part of the American business community.[8]

In the next five to seven years, several routes to transport oil from the Caspian region to world markets are planned. There are three such routes: (a) the system of pipelines, inherited from the USSR and traversing Russian territory; (b) the Caspian Pipeline Consortium (to the Russian port of Novorossiisk, then through the Bosporus Straits to the Mediterranean Sea); and (c) the route Kazakhstan-Azerbaijan-Georgia-Turkey. The last route, widely known as the Baku-Tbilisi-Ceyhan pipeline, not only permits a diversification of export opportunities for Kazakhstan and Azerbaijan (simultaneously reducing the critical dependence of these two oil exporters on Russia), but will also help to ameliorate the economic situation in Georgia.

The function of defending oil and gas deposits and the pipelines (which are controlled primarily by American and British corporations) is likely to be assigned to the U.S. military. American and NATO military contingents of various sizes are already based in Kyrgyzstan, Tajikistan, Uzbekistan, and Turkey. At the present time, consideration is being given to the question of expanding the military cooperation of the United States and NATO with Kazakhstan, Azerbaijan, and Georgia. The NATO summit in Istanbul (June 2004) devoted special attention to Central Asia and the Caucasus. NATO has appointed special representatives for relations with these regions and also supports the initiative of Georgia, Azerbaijan, and Uzbekistan to devise plans for individual partnership with NATO.[9]

The significance of the Caspian oil region in the global framework, despite the relative modesty of its reserves of hydrocarbon raw materials, is enhanced by mounting instability in the Middle East. Notwithstanding the fact that Kazakhstan and Azerbaijan are burdened with serious social and economic problems, at present both are relatively stable countries. In the event of destabilization in the Middle East, the Caspian Sea region could help to alleviate disruptions in supply from the Middle East.

Stimulating Global Competition

Kazakhstan is directly interested in maintaining tensions and heightening the geopolitical and geoeconomic competition of the largest world and regional powers and the leading energy companies in the region. However paradoxical it might seem, the exacerbation of competition (which in many respects is really a "virtual" competition) contributes to stabilizing the special system of "power and property" that has taken root in Kazakhstan. Reviewing the geopolitical aspects of global competition, Sabit Zhusupov (president of the Kazakhstan Institute of Social and Political Information and Forecasting) candidly observed: "We see that the Shanghai Cooperation Organization is picking up steam and has very ambitious plans, and that in turn activates the United States. Parallel to all this, the interests of Russia are coming unraveled."[10] Decoded, this statement means that for Kazakhstan (and especially for the current leadership): real or virtual global competition is a powerful tool not only for survival, but also for economic growth. If such competition did not exist, Kazakhstan could expect substantially fewer resources from abroad. Moreover, if any of the external powers predominated, the local ruling and dominant groups would inevitably have to carve out a niche for themselves and, in the post-Soviet neologism, "line up" behind a patron. The much-advertised "multi-vector" approach in Kazakhstan's foreign policy is only possible if there is geopolitical competition.

Even more important for the country's accelerated economic development, and even its survival, is the need to stimulate geoeconomic competition for local hydrocarbon resources. Professional economists have come to the firm view that, during the first round of the oil game, Kazakhstan made a critical decision that marked a turnaround in the world's oil industry: it signed international contracts agreeing to substantially smaller payments from the oil companies than what had earlier been customary.[11] Of course, ex post facto attempts to renegotiate the terms of signed agreements were doomed to failure. As a leading economist in Kazakhstan has noted, the country can only hope that more reserves are discovered and that the country would negotiate more successfully in the future.[12]

Recognizing that the "Kazakhstan economic miracle" is based exclusively on the increased production of hydrocarbon raw materials and the extremely high world prices on oil, and that the high rates of GDP growth came amid a depressing situation in the social sphere, Kazakhstan has been seeking to open a second round of the oil game—this time, in the Caspian shelf region. By the middle of 2002 it adopted a program to develop Kazakhstan's sector of the Caspian Sea. According to official estimates, the reserves of hydrocarbons there amount to eight billion tons. Contracts concluded on terms more favorable to Kazakhstan should provide an influx of resources for the state budget and give the government greater freedom in conducting its social and economic policy. New large investments in the oil sector are essential because, during the entire last decade, Kazakhstan has essentially devoured its legacy from the Soviet era. If one excludes Kashagan, all the contracts concluded with foreign oil companies have dealt with existing deposits or areas where preliminary geologic exploration was already conducted in Soviet times. By 2010–2015 the peak production will come from new oilfields, such as Tengiz, Kashagan, and Karachaganak, and output in the old oilfields may begin to decline. To start the second round of the oil game, Kazakhstan is attempting to intensify the competition between companies from different countries.

The attempt to draw China into the oil game might give particular intensity to the competition. In 1997, the People's Republic of China (PRC) and Kazakhstan had already signed a general agreement to construct an oil pipeline along the route Atyrau-Kenkiiak-Kumkol-Atasu-Druzhba and on into China. The pipeline's capacity was set at 20 million tons of oil per year; its initial cost was estimated to be between 2.7 and 3.5 billion U.S. dollars. The Chinese government agreed to assume a significant part of the expense. For an indefinite period of time, however, this project has been put on hold.

In 2001–2003, parallel to the growth of consumption of hydrocarbons in the PRC, China again became more active in Kazakhstan. At present, Chinese companies have invested more than one billion U.S. dollars (primarily in oil production); that represents 4.2 percent of the gross direct foreign investment in Kazakhstan. It bears recalling that Russia's share amounts to 2.3 percent.[13] In 2003 the China National Petroleum Corporation (CNPC), within the framework of its projects in Kazakhstan, extracted 4.65 million tons of oil.[14] At the same time, CNPC controls negligible oil reserves in Kazakhstan. Attempts by Chinese capital in March–May 2003 to join an international consortium to develop the Kashagan deposits came to naught. The European and American oil and gas corporations did not allow Chinese companies to join in the project.[15] The limited volume of resources now controlled by Chinese companies makes it pointless to build a huge oil pipeline from Kazakhstan to China.

Under these conditions, Kazakhstan and China have chosen a tactic of small, incremental steps—an oil pipeline, albeit with less capacity than that originally conceived, will be built in several stages. According to the plan, by 2007 Kazakhstan can deliver 10 million tons of oil to China.[16]

Theoretically, to become a serious independent player in the Caspian, China would need a multibillion-dollar investment to develop a large local oilfield. The requisite financial resources are of such a magnitude that, together with the lack of sufficient experience in developing offshore oil deposits, China is unlikely to make a breakthrough in the oil sector of Kazakhstan. A fundamental change in this situation is only possible if China makes a strategic decision to diversify oil imports by increasing the delivery of hydrocarbons from the Caspian region, and if Chinese corporations can gain control over several of the large oil deposits there.

One cannot dismiss the possibility that American and European consortia will deliver the oil from Caspian oilfields to the PRC. The integration of Central Asia and the Caucasus into the international division of labor and world relations is proceeding under the imperatives of globalization. The processes of globalization are generating a new paradigm for competition and cooperation. Competition over for the Caspian resources can lead to the formation of the most unexpected strategic alliances of transnational corporations and national states.

Within the framework of round two of the oil game, Kazakhstan has been trying to encourage the Russian oil companies Lukoil and Rosneft' to become involved in the Caspian shelf. Moreover, in 2002–2003 Kazakhstan fundamentally changed its tax system from that of the 1990s. Having given the greatest oilfields on land and Kashagan on more than preferential terms, Kazakhstan gained some experience. Whereas Lukoil managed to conclude a contract under the old tax regime, Rosneft' will have to decide whether gaining oil fields under the new tax regime carries too large and heavy a price (in technological and financial senses).[17] Significantly, the agreements with the Russian companies bear a long-term character and in the foreseeable future will lead to geological prospecting work.[18] Some experts think that the Russian companies are hardly in a position to make the requisite multibillion-dollar investment to develop the oilfields on the shelf and that, sooner or later, they will have to resell part of their assets to the world's oil grandees.[19]

Prospects

Parallel with the second round of the oil game in Central Asia and the Caucasus was the beginning of the global "natural gas game." Given the fact that Russia is the largest exporter of natural gas to world markets (accounting for 29.0 percent of the world exports on gas pipelines in 2003), and given that it has 26.7 percent of the proven world reserves of the blue fuel,[20] the stakes for Russia are even higher in the natural gas game than in the oil game. Kazakhstan plans to increase its production of natural gas by 2010 to 30 billion cubic meters, with 25 billion cubic meters going for export; it has become one of the most active players in the natural gas game. To judge from previous experience, the gas game will follow the same scenario as that of the oil game: Western corporations will be the real exporters of natural gas produced in Kazakhstan. In order to ship this gas to world markets, it is necessary to cross through the contiguous states. Natural gas can reach markets in Europe either by going through Russia or through Azerbaijan.

For the Russian economy (with its relatively low domestic prices on natural gas), the appearance of new natural gas exporters promises to bring new problems.

On the one hand, the producers of natural gas from Kazakhstan will hardly be satisfied with the price level that, until recently, Gazprom has used in its dealings with the traditional suppliers from Central Asia. The protracted process of bargaining and reaching agreements has already begun; Kazakhstan has set the price acceptable at the Kazakh-Russian border at 49 to 54 U.S. dollars per 1,000 cubic meters. The minister of energy and natural resources of Kazakhstan has declared bluntly: "Russia must share its profitable markets."[21] The price structure for Kazakhstan's suppliers can trigger a review of the delivery terms for natural gas from Uzbekistan and, what is especially important, Turkmenistan. If the new price terms do not satisfy Kazakhstan's suppliers, they can choose to favor exporting through Azerbaijan. Indeed, Kazakhstan and Azerbaijan have begun discussions about the possibility of exporting natural gas to Europe over the Baku-Tbilisi-Erzrum pipeline, which is supposed to commence operations in 2006.[22] Moreover, in the mid-term perspective Uzbekistan and Turkmenistan could also be included in shipping natural gas on the Azerbaijan route.

On the other hand, regardless of the export route chosen by the natural gas producers, the European Union will necessarily be included in the Eurasian natural gas game. The European Union has an interest both in finding alternatives to the existing suppliers of natural gas and in changing the basis for price setting on the European natural gas market. If so powerful a player as a unified Europe participates in the game, and especially if it acts in tandem with the new and traditional suppliers of natural gas in Central Asia, this could lead to a change in the system of long-term contracts for natural gas deliveries and, in the final analysis, to a drop in prices on the European market. For Russia, this will mean substantial losses in export earnings.

So long as, in terms of the global structure, Russia remains an exporter of hydrocarbons and other raw materials with a low level of processing, it is doomed to remain a secondary player—that is, one that must adapt itself to the plans and strategies of the leading global powers. In principle, the only way to change this long-term scenario is to reallocate resources from the raw materials sector to the manufacturing branches of industry. At present, however, serious preconditions for that are simply not discernible.

Nevertheless, these complex realities should not impede the development of bilateral economic ties with Kazakhstan. Indeed, Kazakhstan (more precisely, transnational corporations operating on its territory) is actively bolstering its positions on the traditional Russian export markets. To judge from what is known, in the coming years the Russian oil and natural gas companies will face growing competition from Kazakhstan.

At the same time, that should not prevent Russian business from taking advantage of opportunities on Kazakhstan's domestic market that are generated by that country's explosive economic growth. As the data in Table 11.5 show, Kazakhstan is one of the few countries with a market where Russia is not simply a supplier of hydrocarbon raw materials and metals with a low level of processing, but also is an exporter of finished industrial goods.

Of course, the macro-balance of possible gains and losses can nonetheless prove to be to Russia's disadvantage. It has, however, no other rational course of action. In addition, the growing competition with Kazakhstan on raw-material markets could drive Russia to raise its domestic prices on energy. For all the painfulness of such a step, in the long term the country really has no alternative to doing this.

For its part, Kazakhstan must not pass up the opportunities on the growing Russian market. Kazakhstan's enterprises that have been able to adapt to market conditions of development will inevitably find that the domestic market is too small and that the internal purchasing power is too limited. Russia, especially contiguous regions, represents a natural market for Kazakhstan's goods. The Russian market also offers some opportunities for Kazakhstan's banks. Because the latter have a relative over-accumulation of capital, their assets are more and more actively being drawn upon to provide credits for Russian enterprises. For example, the leading commercial bank of Kazakhstan (Kazkommertsbank) issued a credit of 30 million U.S. dollars to modernize the West Siberian metallurgical complex.[23] Moreover, of late there has been an increasingly widespread tendency for capital and property of the two countries to become intertwined. Banks in Kazakhstan, for instance, have acquired partial control of two Russian banks—Moskommertsbank[24] and Slavinvestbank.[25]

The objective economic factors and the growing degree of unification in the organization of economic space within the framework of the Eurasian economic community will continue to promote an expansion and intensification of cooperation in the economies of Russia and Kazakhstan.

Table 11.5

Structure of Exports of Russia (percent of aggregate exports)

Export item	World		World without CIS		CIS countries[a]		Kazakhstan		China	
	2000	2003	2000	2003	2000	2003	2000	2003	2000	2003
Fuel and energy goods	53.1	57.8	54.0	59.5	47.3	47.8	20.0	20.6	6.7	19.8
Metals and metal goods	16.9	13.8	18.0	14.3	10.1	8.7	13.7	14.2	28.6	20.1
Machinery, equipment, means of transportation	8.8	8.6	7.5	7.1	17.0	20.0	27.3	29.2	13.7	14.3
Chemicals and petrochemicals	7.2	6.7	6.7	6.3	10.2	10.2	17.0	16.8	15.2	12.5
Foodstuffs and agricultural raw materials	1.6	2.1	1.0	1.5	5.3	5.6	10.3	8.4	1.4	1.3

Sources: Gosudarstvennyi tamozhennyi komitet Rossiiskoi Federatsii, *Tamozhennaia statistika vneshnei torgovli Rossiiskoi Federatsii. 2003g.*, 2: 640–41; ibid., 2002g., 478–79; ibid., 2001g., pp. 472–73; pp. 377, pp. 449–51; 1997g., pp. 501–2; 1996g., pp. 484–85; 1995g., pp. 486–88.

[a]Excluding trade with Belarus.

Notes

1. Boris Rumer, "The Search for Stability in Central Asia," in *Central Asia: A Gathering Storm?* ed. B. Rumer (Armonk, NY, 2002), pp. 47–53.

2. Here (and elsewhere) calculated from: *Tamozhennaia statistika vneshnei torgovli Rossiiskoi Federatsii. 2003 god*, vols. 1–2 (Moscow, 2004).

3. P. Kollison, A. Machanskis, and A. Moshkov, "Eksport nefti: Proizoidet ozhidaniia," *Vedomosti* (Moscow), 4 March 2004.

4. See www.oilcapital.ru/news.asp?IDR=t0&IDNEWS=36917.

5. For details about the privatization of several large exporters of Kazakhstan, see S. V. Zhukov and O. B. Reznikova, *Tsentral'naia Aziia v sotsial'no-ekonomicheskikh strukturakh sovremennogo mira* (Moscow, 2001), pp. 134–37.

6. See *National Energy Policy. Reliable, Affordable, and Environmentally Sound Energy for America's Future. Report of the National Energy Policy Development Group* (Washington, DC, 2002), pp. 12–13.

7. European Commission, *Energy: Let Us Overcome Our Dependence* (Luxembourg, 2002).

8. "From Pipe Dream to Pipeline: The Realization of the Baku-Tbilisi-Ceyhan Pipeline" (http://ksg.harvard.edu/news/news/2003/pipeline_051503htm).

9. "Istanbul Summit Communiqué Issued by the Heads of State and Government Participating in the Meeting of the North Atlantic Council (28 June 2004)" (www.nato.int).

10. *Panorama* (Almaty), no. 10 (March 2004).

11. For example, see Tsentr analiza obshchestvennykh problem (Astana), *Monitoring formirovaniia i ispol'zovaniia dokhodov ot syr'evykh sektorov Kazakhstana: obsuzhdenie proekta Biudzhetnogo kodeksa. Materialy kruglogo stola* (2003).

12. A. Esentugelov, "Dualizm v razvitii ekonomiki Kazakhstana: strukturno-investitsionnye aspekty ee modernizatsii," in *Tsentral'naia Aziia i Kavkaz. Nasushchnye problemy 2003*, ed. Boris Rumer (Almaty, 2003), p. 184.

13. Calculated on the basis of data from the National Bank of the Republic of Kazakhstan.

14. E. Butyrina, "'CNPC-Aktobemunaigaz' v 2003 godu na 6% uvelichila neftedobychu," *Panorama* (Almaty), no. 2 (January 2004).

15. See "CNOOC ne puskaiut v Kashagan," *Vremia novostei* (Moscow), 13 May 2003; "Zapadnye kompanii blokiruiut priobretenie Sinopec doli v Kashagane" (posting of 14 May 2003 at www.rusenergy.com).

16. R. Bakhtigareev, "Kazakhstan ne nameren predostavliat' 'Rosneft'i nalogovye l'goty v ramkakh proekta Kurmangazy," *Panorama* (Almaty), no. 15 (April 2004).

17. E. Butyrina, "Rosneft' ne khochet uchastvovat' v proekte 'Kurmangazy' v sootvetstvii s novymi nalogovymi trebovaniiami v RK," *Panorama* (Almaty), no. 13 (April 2004).

18. "Opredeleny podriadchiki po razvedochnomu bureniiu na strukture Kurmangazy," *Panorama* (Almaty), no. 27 (July 2003); E. Butyrina, "KazMunaiTengiz i Lukoil Oversiz podpisali soglashenie o sovmestnoi deiatel'nosti po kaspiiskomu proektu 'Tiub-Karagan,'" *Panorama* (Almaty), no. 2 (January 2004).

19. M. Yakovleva, "Astana's Balancing Act," *Russian Petroleum Investor* (Concord, MA), January 2004, p. 63.

20. BP, *Statistical Review of World Energy*, June 2004.

21. U. Kozhantaeva, "Gazovoe karate po vsem frontam," *Delovaia nedelia* (Almaty), no. 16 (April 2004).

22. "Kazakhstan pri poiske novykh marshrutov eksporta uglevodorodov iskhodit iz ekonomicheskoi tselesoobraznosti i politicheskoi stabil'nosti" (www.rusenergy.com/ newssystem/opened/37/20040318/408450.htm).

23. *Ekspert* (Moscow), no. 19 (24–30 May 2004), p. 10.

24. "Kazakhstan i Rossiia uvideli drug druga cherez 'odno okno'" (www.moskb.ru/ press60.html).

25. [E. Tatishev], "A Market Economy Is Like Spring—It Is Inevitable," *Diplomat* (Moscow), no. 7 (2004), p. 37.

Index

About the Editor and Contributors

Evgeniy Abdullaev is a political scientist conducting research in Tashkent, Uzbekistan.

Viacheslav Belokrenitsky is the head of the Department of the Near and Middle East at the Institute of Oriental Studies (Russian Academy of Sciences, Moscow).

Dmitrii Furman is a leading research fellow at the Institute of Europe (Russian Academy of Sciences, Moscow).

Richard W. Hu is a professor at the University of Hong Kong.

Oksana Reznikova is a senior research fellow at the Institute of World Economy and International Relations (Russian Academy of Sciences, Moscow).

Boris Rumer is an associate at the Davis Center at Harvard University (Cambridge, Massachusetts).

Konstantin Syroezhkin is the head of the Analytical Center (Almaty, Kazakhstan).

Eshref Trushin and **Eskender Trushin** are economists conducting research in Uzbekistan.

Stanislav Zhukov is a senior research fellow at the Institute of World Economy and International Relations (Russian Academy of Sciences, Moscow).

Irina Zviagel'skaia is a leading research fellow at the Institute of Oriental Studies, the Russian Academy of Sciences, Moscow.